Training Guide: Installing and Configuring Windows Server 2012 R2

Mitch Tulloch

PUBLISHED BY
Microsoft Press
A Division of Microsoft Corporation
One Microsoft Way
Redmond, Washington 98052-6399

Library of Congress Control Number: 2014935078
ISBN: 978-0-7356-8433-1

Printed and bound in the United States of America.

First Printing

Microsoft Press books are available through booksellers and distributors worldwide. If you need support related to this book, email Microsoft Press Book Support at mspinput@microsoft.com. Please tell us what you think of this book at http://www.microsoft.com/learning/booksurvey.

Microsoft and the trademarks listed at http://www.microsoft.com/about/legal/en/us/IntellectualProperty /Trademarks/EN-US.aspx are trademarks of the Microsoft group of companies. All other marks are property of their respective owners.

The example companies, organizations, products, domain names, email addresses, logos, people, places, and events depicted herein are fictitious. No association with any real company, organization, product, domain name, email address, logo, person, place, or event is intended or should be inferred.

This book expresses the author's views and opinions. The information contained in this book is provided without any express, statutory, or implied warranties. Neither the authors, Microsoft Corporation, nor its resellers, or distributors will be held liable for any damages caused or alleged to be caused either directly or indirectly by this book.

Acquisitions Editor: Anne Hamilton
Developmental Editor: Karen Szall
Editorial Production: nSight, Inc.
Technical Reviewer: Michael Toot; Technical Review services provided by Content Master, a member of CM Group, Ltd.
Copyeditor: Ann Weaver
Indexer: Jack Lewis
Cover: Twist Creative • Seattle

Contents at a glance

Contents

What do you think of this book? We want to hear from you!

Microsoft is interested in hearing your feedback so we can continually improve our
books and learning resources for you. To participate in a brief online survey, please visit:

www.microsoft.com/learning/booksurvey/

Chapter 4   Deploying domain controllers   153

Chapter 10 Implementing Group Policy   513

What do you think of this book? We want to hear from you!

Microsoft is interested in hearing your feedback so we can continually improve our books and learning resources for you. To participate in a brief online survey, please visit:

www.microsoft.com/learning/booksurvey/

Introduction

This training guide is intended for information technology (IT) professionals who need to upgrade their skills to support Microsoft Windows Server 2012 and Windows Server 2012 R2 in their workplace. The primary focus of the book is on job-role training for system administrators and IT support staff in midsized to large environments. The book contains detailed technical information and hands-on practice exercises to help you prepare for deploying, managing, and maintaining servers running Windows Server 2012 or Windows Server 2012 R2. The book assumes that you have at least three years of experience administering previous versions of Windows Server, including experience with operating systems deployment, Active Directory administration, server virtualization using Hyper-V, network and storage management, file and print services, and Group Policy.

Because automation is an essential skill for administrators who manage the modern, virtualized data center, much of this book focuses on learning how to administer server roles and features using Windows PowerShell. Although it will be helpful if you have at least rudimentary knowledge of using Windows PowerShell to manage earlier versions of Windows Server, readers who have no prior familiarity with Windows PowerShell should be able to learn and perform most of the exercises in this book.

This book also covers some of the topics and skills that are the subject of the Microsoft certification exam 70-410. If you are using this book to complement your study materials, you might find this information useful. Note however that this book is specifically designed to help you in the job role; it therefore might not cover all exam topics. If you are preparing for the exam, you should use additional study materials to help bolster your real-world experience. For your reference, a mapping of the topics in this book to the exam objectives is included in the back of the book.

By using this training guide, you will learn how to

- Assess the hardware and software in your current environment to plan for a migration to Windows Server 2012 or Windows Server 2012 R2.
- Build customized reference images of Windows Server 2012 and Windows Server 2012 R2 and deploy them using the Microsoft Deployment Toolkit.
- Perform remote server management and role installation using Server Manager and Windows PowerShell.
- Deploy domain controllers using Server Manager and Windows PowerShell.
- Administer Active Directory and enable advanced Active Directory features using the Active Directory Administrative Center and Windows PowerShell.
- Ensure DHCP availability, implement DNSSEC, and perform network administration tasks using Windows PowerShell.

- Deploy, configure, and manage Hyper-V hosts and virtual machines using Hyper-V Manager and Windows PowerShell.

- Deploy Storage Spaces and provision and manage shared storage using Server Manager and Windows PowerShell.

- Deploy and manage print servers using the Print Management console and Windows PowerShell.

- Plan, configure, and manage Group Policy using the Group Policy Management console and Windows PowerShell.

System requirements

The following are the minimum system requirements your computer needs to meet to complete the practice exercises in this book. To minimize the time and expense of configuring physical computers for this training guide, you might want to use a virtualized test environment instead of physical servers. Note, however, that

- The exercises in Chapter 1 *recommend* using a physical server instead of a virtual environment.

- The exercises in Chapters 7 and 8 *require* using a physical server instead of a virtual environment.

Hardware requirements

This section presents the hardware requirements for Hyper-V, the hardware requirements if you are not using virtualization software, and the software requirements.

Virtualization hardware requirements

If you choose to use virtualization software, you need only one physical computer to perform the exercises in this book except for the two chapters noted above. That physical host computer must meet the following minimum hardware requirements:

- x64-based processor that includes both hardware-assisted virtualization (AMD-V or Intel VT) and hardware data execution protection (DEP). On AMD systems, the data execution protection feature is called the No Execute or NX bit. On Intel systems, this feature is called the Execute Disable or XD bit. These features must also be enabled in the BIOS.

- 8 GB or more RAM.

- 500 GB or more available hard disk space.

- Integrated 1 GbE networking.

- Integrated SVGA (800 x 600) or higher video.
- DVD-ROM drive or bootable USB media.
- Internet connectivity.

Physical hardware requirements

If you choose to use physical computers instead of virtualization software, the following lists the minimum hardware requirements for the practice exercises in this book:

- Two servers, each with a 1.4 GHz or faster processor, 2 GB or more RAM, 500 GB or more available hard disk space, integrated 1 GbE networking, integrated SVGA (800 x 600) or higher video, and a DVD-ROM drive. At least one of these servers must
  - Include hardware-assisted virtualization (AMD-V or Intel VT) and hardware data execution protection (DEP). On AMD systems, the data execution protection feature is called the No Execute or NX bit. On Intel systems, this feature is called the Execute Disable or XD bit. These features must also be enabled in the BIOS.
    - Have at least two additional physical disks (either internally or externally connected) of a type supported by the Storage Spaces feature (for example, SAS or SATA disks).
- One workstation with a 1 GHz or faster processor, 2 GB or more RAM, a 250 GB or greater hard disk drive, a network card, a video card, and a DVD-ROM drive.
- All three computers must be physically connected to one another and to the Internet through a Network Address Translation (NAT) router or gateway device.
- The test network that includes these computers should be isolated from your production network. (For example, your test network cannot already include a Dynamic Host Configuration Protocol [DHCP] server that automatically assigns addresses to computers.)

Software requirements

The following software is required to complete the practice exercises:

- Windows Server 2012 R2. You can download an evaluation edition of Windows Server 2012 R2 from the TechNet Evaluation Center at *http://technet.microsoft.com/en-US /evalcenter/dn205286.*
- Windows 8.1 Enterprise. You can download an evaluation edition of Windows 8.1 Enterprise from the TechNet Evaluation Center at *http://technet.microsoft.com/en-US /evalcenter/hh699156.aspx.*
- The Microsoft Assessment and Planning Toolkit 9.0 (MAP 9.0). You can download MAP 9.0 from the Microsoft Download Center *at http://www.microsoft.com/en-ca /download/details.aspx?id=7826.*

- The Windows Assessment and Deployment Kit (ADK) for Windows 8.1. You can download the ADK for Windows 8.1 from the Microsoft Download Center at *http://www .microsoft.com/en-us/download/details.aspx?id=39982*.

- The Microsoft Deployment Toolkit (MDT) 2013. You can download MDT 2013 from the Microsoft Download Center at *http://www.microsoft.com/en-us/download/details .aspx?id=40796*.

- Microsoft Office 2013. You can download an evaluation edition of Office Professional Plus 2013 from the TechNet Evaluation Center at *http://technet.microsoft.com/en-US /evalcenter/jj192782.aspx*.

- If you are not using virtualization software, you need software that allows you to handle .iso files. This software needs to perform either of the following functions:
  - Burn .iso files to CDs or DVDs (requires CD/DVD recording hardware) or copy them to bootable USB media.
  - Mount .iso files as virtual CD or DVD drives on your computer.

Acknowledgments

The author would like to thank the following individuals:

- Karen Szall, Senior Content Development Manager at Microsoft Press
- Sarah Vostok, Associate Project Manager at nSight, Inc.
- Mike Toot, who was Technical Reviewer
- Ann Weaver, Copy Editor at nSight, Inc.

Errata, updates, & book support

We've made every effort to ensure the accuracy of this book and its companion content. You can access updates to this book—in the form of a list of submitted errata and their related corrections—at:

http://aka.ms/TG410R2

If you discover an error that is not already listed, please submit it to us at the same page.

If you need additional support, email Microsoft Press Book Support at *mspinput@microsoft.com*.

Please note that product support for Microsoft software and hardware is not offered through the previous addresses. For help with Microsoft software or hardware, go to *http://support.microsoft.com*.

We want to hear from you

At Microsoft Press, your satisfaction is our top priority, and your feedback is our most valuable asset. Please tell us what you think of this book at

http://aka.ms/tellpress

The survey is short, and we read every one of your comments and ideas. Thanks in advance for your input!

Stay in touch

Let's keep the conversation going! We're on Twitter: *http://twitter.com/MicrosoftPress*.

CHAPTER 1

Preparing for Windows Server 2012 R2

Successful execution of any task always begins with planning. If your job involves the migration of your organization's IT infrastructure to Microsoft Windows Server 2012 R2, you need to prepare both your environment and yourself for this task.

This chapter describes common deployment scenarios and outlines the steps involved in a typical server deployment or migration process. The chapter also examines some approaches and tools you can use for assessing the readiness of your environment for migrating to Windows Server 2012 R2.

Lessons in this chapter:

Before you begin

To complete the practice exercises in this chapter

- You should have some familiarity with the new features and capabilities found in Windows Server 2012 and Windows Server 2012 R2. If you are not, see the sidebar titled "Additional Learning Resources" below.

- You need to download an evaluation version (.iso file) of Windows Server 2012 R2 from the TechNet Evaluation Center at *http://technet.microsoft.com/en-US/evalcenter /dn205286*. The evaluation version provided is Datacenter edition, but you can choose to install it as Standard edition during setup if you prefer. You will need to burn this .iso file to recordable DVD media by using a DVD writer. If your computer's BIOS supports booting from a USB device, you could also copy the downloaded .iso file to a USB flash drive or USB external hard drive and use these media for installation purposes.

- You need to download the Microsoft Assessment and Planning (MAP) Toolkit version 9.0. You can download MAP 9.0 from the TechNet Library at *http://technet.microsoft .com/en-us/library/bb977556.aspx*.

- You need a minimum of one physical server system available for testing purposes. At least one of these servers should meet the minimum hardware requirements for installing Windows Server 2012 R2, as described at *http://technet.microsoft.com/en-us /library/dn303418.aspx*. The system hardware should also meet the minimum requirements for installing MAP 9.0.

- You need a client computer that has Microsoft Excel 2013 or Microsoft Excel 2010 installed for viewing the reports generated by MAP. If you have an Office 365 subscription, you can also use the Excel Web App for this purpose.

Additional learning resources

The starting point for business and technical decision makers to learn about Windows Server 2012 R2 is the high-level overview on the Microsoft Server And Cloud Platform page found at *http://www.microsoft.com/en-us/server-cloud /products/windows-server-2012-r2/*.

The Windows Server 2012 R2 home page on TechNet at *http://technet.microsoft .com/en-us/windowsserver/hh534429* is the starting point for experienced IT pros to learn about the Windows Server 2012 R2 platform. From this page, you can learn how to plan, deploy, manage, and support Windows Server 2012 R2 in your environment. If you're mainly interested in learning about the new capabilities introduced in Windows Server 2012 R2, you should see the topic "What's New in Windows Server 2012 R2" and the subtopics linked from that page in the TechNet Library at *http://technet.microsoft.com/en-us/library/dn250019.aspx*.

IT pros who deploy, maintain, and troubleshoot Windows Server-based environments should also familiarize themselves with the Windows Server home page on TechNet at *http://technet.microsoft.com/en-us/windowsserver*. From this landing page, you can

- Read the latest news about the platform.

- Watch videos on TechNet LIVE, Channel 9, and other sites.

- Read blog posts on TechNet and from IT pros around the world.

- Post your questions to TechNet Forums and have experts answer them.

- Read technical documentation about different server roles and technologies.

- Download evaluation versions of different Windows Server versions.

- Access training materials on the Microsoft Virtual Academy and from other sources.

- Subscribe to the TechNet Flash Newsletter to keep informed of the latest developments in the platform.

- Look up Knowledge Base articles and find other help for troubleshooting problems.

Lesson 1: Planning for Windows Server 2012 R2

The success of a deployment project depends on careful planning combined with meticulous execution. First, you need to define the scope of the project so that you know where you want to end up. Then, you need to lay out a project plan that involves pilot testing to familiarize yourself with the new platform and to identify any potential issues that might arise during the process. You also need to perform a thorough assessment of your existing environment to ensure there are no surprises coming and develop a methodology to migrate existing servers and roles. Finally, once deployment is underway, you need to perform continued testing to ensure everything is happening as planned.

After this lesson, you will be able to:

- Describe six possible deployment scenarios for organizations that want to take advantage of the new features and capabilities found in Windows Server 2012 R2.
- Understand some of the steps involved in a deployment process, including pilot testing, assessment, server migration, and role and feature migration.
- Explain how to install and use the Windows Server Migration Tools to migrate server roles from earlier Windows Server versions to Windows Server 2012 R2.

Estimated lesson time: 30 minutes

Deployment scenarios

Deployment projects involving servers can be categorized in a number of ways, depending on whether you are deploying a new infrastructure, upgrading or consolidating an existing infrastructure, or implementing a new infrastructure model such as cloud computing. In addition, deployment can differ depending on whether you are migrating your existing infrastructure or only a portion of it; whether you plan to reuse existing hardware or move to new hardware; whether your environment is managed or unmanaged; whether your existing infrastructure is large or small, centralized or distributed, heterogeneous or homogeneous; and many other factors.

With so many different ways of envisioning and scoping deployment projects, it's obvious that there is no single approach to planning and executing such projects. However, there are some steps and considerations that are common to all deployment projects, and being aware of such best practices and implementing them can help ensure the project's success.

I'll begin by describing six deployment scenarios for organizations that want to take advantage of the new features and capabilities found in Windows Server 2012 R2:

- Greenfield
- Forest upgrade
- Existing environment
- Server consolidation
- Private cloud
- Hybrid cloud

Greenfield

In terms of infrastructure, a *greenfield* deployment is one in which no infrastructure currently exists. For example, let's say that Contoso, Ltd., is a new company that needs an on-premises infrastructure deployed for its rapidly growing workforce. A greenfield deployment of an infrastructure based on Windows Server 2012 R2 might include steps like these:

- Designing, acquiring, and implementing the underlying network infrastructure of switches, routers, access points, and other networking hardware.
- Designing the Active Directory environment using the guidelines and best practices found in the AD DS Design Guide at *http://technet.microsoft.com/en-us/library /cc754678(v=WS.10).aspx.*
- Purchasing system hardware that has been certified for Windows Server 2012 R2.
- Performing a pilot deployment to determine whether the planned infrastructure will meet your business needs and to anticipate any possible problems that might arise during the rollout.
- Rolling out your production infrastructure using whatever deployment tools you've decided to use. We examine some of these tools in Chapter 2, "Deploying servers."

The main advantage of a greenfield deployment is that it gives you the opportunity to get it right from the start. However, businesses are always evolving and are rarely static, so even if you carefully plan for future growth you might still be faced with challenges in evolving your infrastructure to address events such as mergers, acquisitions, and spinoffs of business units. And in reality, most readers of this Training Guide who are looking to upgrade their job skills are most likely working at companies that have one or more existing Active Directory forests in place and are contemplating migrating them to Windows Server 2012 R2, which is what the next scenario is about.

Forest upgrade

Administrators of Active Directory environments have traditionally been cautious, even paranoid, about performing schema upgrades by using the Adprep.exe command-line utility. With the release of each new version of Windows Server comes a new schema version, and in the past, the task of introducing domain controllers running the new version of Windows Server into your existing Active Directory environment has required that you first prepare your forest by upgrading the schema. The reluctance that administrators have about performing such upgrades is based largely on three concerns:

- The process of upgrading a forest schema by using Adprep was often a cumbersome one on previous versions of Windows Server and involved using a variety of different credentials to log on to specific domain controllers, copy Adprep files, and run Adprep from the command line with various parameters. The more complex the process, the greater the chance of an error occurring.

- There was the possibility that something might go wrong during the schema upgrade process, resulting in a corrupt forest that requires you to perform a forest recovery, which can be a difficult and time-consuming process.

- There was the possibility that the schema upgrade might go well but result in side effects, such as enterprise applications that break and no longer function properly.

The recommended approach to avoiding such problems is to create a test environment that mirrors your production environment in terms of its Active Directory schema, network services, and business applications. By using Adprep to upgrade the schema of your test forest, you can better anticipate any problems that might arise when you upgrade the schema of your production forest. For information on how to mirror your production schema into a test environment so that you can perform such testing, see the article "Export, Compare, and Synchronize Active Directory Schemas" from the April 2009 issue of TechNet Magazine at *http://technet.microsoft.com/en-us/magazine/2009.04.schema.aspx*.

Clearly, these are not trivial concerns when your job as administrator potentially is at stake. So before you perform a forest upgrade, you need to be well prepared. For example:

- You need to understand the schema upgrade process and its possible impact on your environment.
- You need to have a forest recovery plan in place as a backup solution for your worst-case scenario.

Beginning with Windows Server 2012, however, Microsoft has endeavored to alleviate many of the concerns administrators often have about performing forest upgrades. For example:

- Adprep functionality is now integrated into the Active Directory Domain Services (AD DS) installation process. In most cases, this eliminates the need to separately run Adprep prior to introducing domain controllers running the new version of Windows Server into existing AD DS infrastructures running Windows Server 2008 R2.
- The new AD DS installation process includes prerequisite validation to identify potential errors before installation begins. For example, if the installation process determines that **adprep /domainprep** needs to be run to prepare the domain, verification is done first to ensure that the user who initiated the process has sufficient rights to perform the operation.
- The Windows Server 2012 or Windows Server 2012 R2 forest functional level does not add any new features to a forest. It ensures only that any new domain added to the forest will automatically operate at the Windows Server 2012 R2 domain functional level.
- The Windows Server 2012 or Windows Server 2012 R2 domain functional level adds only one new feature to a domain. This new feature relates to Dynamic Access Control (DAC) and therefore is unlikely to affect any existing applications and services in your environment.

Despite these improvements to performing schema upgrades and raising forest and domain functional levels, you should use careful planning and due care when completing these tasks. These issues are addressed further in Chapter 4, "Deploying domain controllers," and in Chapter 5, "Active Directory administration."

IMPORTANT **FOREST UPGRADES AND FUNCTIONAL LEVELS**

After upgrading your schema, you might want to raise your forest and domain functional levels. As a best practice, follow these practices:

- Before changing your forest functional level, take at least one domain controller offline from each domain in your forest.
- Before changing the domain functional level of any domain, take at least one domain controller offline from the domain.

In both cases, you should make sure that the domain controllers you take offline do not hold any operations master roles in the forest or domains.

Keep the domain controllers offline for 48 to 72 hours after changing functional levels; if no issues are found, you can return the offline domain controllers to service. If issues are discovered, you can use your offline domain controllers as the source for rebuilding servers if a rollback to a previous functional level is required.

Existing environment

Existing businesses that currently have Windows Server 2008 R2 or earlier deployed and that want to take advantage of the new capabilities of Windows Server 2012 or Windows Server 2012 R2 can do so without ripping out their infrastructure and replacing it with a new one. All they need to do is introduce servers running Windows Server 2012 or Windows Server 2012 R2 into their environment and promote them as domain controllers. Doing this automatically upgrades the schema, and administrators can raise the forest and domain functional levels to Windows Server 2012 or Windows Server 2012 R2 with minimal fear of it having a negative impact on their existing applications and services. Of course, regardless of this, you should still be sure to first test your schema upgrade and functional level changes in a test environment that mirrors your production environment just to make sure there will be no issues that might impact your business.

Some new features of Windows Server 2012 and Windows Server 2012 R2 can be implemented into existing Active Directory environments without making significant changes to the existing forest, such as upgrading the schema or raising the forest or domain functional levels. A situation in which this might be done is when deploying new DHCP servers to take advantage of the new DHCP failover feature of Windows Server 2012 and Windows Server 2012 R2 that ensures continuous availability of DHCP services to clients. For information on how to implement this new capability, see Chapter 6, "Network administration."

The introduction of member servers running Windows Server 2012 or Windows Server 2012 R2 into an Active Directory forest based on an earlier version of Windows Server results in a mixed environment of servers running different versions of Windows. By not introducing new domain controllers running Windows Server 2012 or Windows Server 2012 R2, administrators can continue to manage their environment by using existing tools and processes. Although this seems like a simpler and less risky approach than upgrading your forest as described previously, there are several disadvantages to following this approach:

- Some new features and capabilities of Windows Server 2012 and Windows Server 2012 R2 can be implemented only when your Active Directory environment includes domain controllers running Windows Server 2012 or Windows Server 2012 R2. These features might have limited functionality or might not work at all when your Active Directory schema hasn't been upgraded to Windows Server 2012 or Windows Server 2012 R2 level. In general, information about such limitations might be buried in the TechNet Library documentation for Windows Server, which means you need to do some research before you try deploying Windows Server 2012 or Windows Server 2012 R2 member servers with roles and features installed in your existing Active Directory environment.

- Some of the server administration tools built into Windows Server 2012 and Windows Server 2012 R2 that are included in the Remote Server Administration Tools (RSAT) for Windows 8 and Windows 8.1 have limited or no functionality when managing servers running earlier versions of Windows Server, such as Windows Server 2008 and Windows Server 2008 R2. You might have to install additional updates on servers running these earlier versions of Windows Server to manage them using the Windows Server 2012 or Windows Server 2012 R2 server administration tools or using RSAT for Windows 8 or RSAT for Windows 8.1. For more information, see KB 2693643 at *http://support.microsoft.com/kb/2693643*.

So although rolling out a few Windows Server 2012 R2 member servers with a few roles and features installed might seem like a good idea and less risky than performing a forest upgrade, the gains you experience from following this approach might not be worth the effort involved.

Server consolidation

Server consolidation involves using virtualization to consolidate multiple server workloads onto a single virtualization host. With the greatly increased scalability of the Hyper-V role in Windows Server 2012 and Windows Server 2012 R2, businesses can often migrate much or even all of their existing Active Directory infrastructure based on a previous version of Windows Server and run it on a cluster of Hyper-V hosts running Windows Server 2012 or Windows Server 2012 R2. In other words, they can migrate their existing physical servers into a virtual environment. For more information, see Chapter 7, "Hyper-V virtualization."

Private cloud

Cloud computing provides organizations with new options to increase efficiencies while reducing costs. The traditional data-center approach, in which the organization deploys and manages its own Active Directory infrastructure on-premises, has known stability and security, but the infrastructure servers involved often run at less than 15 percent utilization. Virtualizing the data center by using server consolidation can increase utilization, reduce cost, and simplify management, but this approach lacks the elasticity to rapidly meet changing demands as your business grows or experiences market changes.

Cloud computing can simplify management and reduce cost even further while providing elasticity and the perception of infinite capacity for the IT services your business uses. Cloud resources are pooled so that they can be allocated on demand as the needs of the business grow or shrink. If additional resources are needed, they can be provisioned without the need for extensive planning and testing beforehand.

Cloud computing can be provisioned according to three possible service models:

- **Software as a Service (SaaS)** The cloud is used to deliver an application to multiple users, regardless of their location or the type of device they are using. Compare this model with the more traditional approach of deploying separate instances of applications to each user's PC. This approach typically is used to deliver cloud-based applications that have minimal need for customization. Examples include email, Customer Relationship Management (CRM), and productivity software. The advantage of this approach is that application activities can be managed from a single central location to reduce cost and management overhead.

  An example of a SaaS offering from Microsoft is Office 365, which provides users with secure access from anywhere to their email, shared calendars, instant messaging (IM), video conferencing, and tools for document collaboration. For more information on Office 365 for business, see *http://office.microsoft.com/en-us/business/*.

- **Platform as a Service (PaaS)** The cloud is used to deliver application execution services, such as application runtime, storage, and integration for applications designed for a prespecified, cloud-based architectural framework. This enables you to develop custom cloud-based applications for your business, which you can then host in the cloud so that your users can access them from anywhere over the Internet. PaaS also enables you to create multitenant applications that multiple users can access simultaneously. With support for application-level customization, PaaS enables integration with your older applications and interoperability with your current on-premises systems, although some applications might need to be recoded to work in the new environment.

  An example of a PaaS offering from Microsoft is Windows Azure Cloud Services, which enables you to deploy highly scalable web applications built with C#, PHP, Python, Node.js, or Java. An instance of Cloud Services represents a logical container for two types of roles: web role instances and worker role instances. The web role provides an ASP.NET programming model you can use for programmatically provisioning node instances of a web farm. The worker role exposes a programming model you can use for implementing batch processing farms with resources. For more information on Windows Azure Cloud Services, see *http://www.windowsazure.com/en-us /documentation/services/cloud-services/*.

- **Infrastructure as a Service (IaaS)** The cloud is used to create pools of computer, storage, and network connectivity resources, which can then be delivered as cloud-based services billed on a per-usage basis. IaaS forms the foundation for the other two cloud service models by providing a standardized, flexible, virtualized environment that presents itself as virtualized server workloads. In this approach, the organization can self-provision these virtualized workloads and fully customize them with the processing, storage, and network resources needed and with the operating system and applications needed. The organization is relieved of the need to purchase and install hardware and can simply spin up new workloads to quickly meet changing demand.

An example of an IaaS offering from Microsoft is Windows Azure Virtual Machines, which enables you to provision, deploy, and manage virtual machine instances in the Windows Azure public cloud. These virtual machine instances can be provisioned from a gallery of stock virtual hard disks (VHDs) that include different versions of Windows Server, SQL Server, and Linux. For more information on Windows Azure Virtual Machines, see *http://www.windowsazure.com/en-us/documentation/services /virtual-machines/*.

In the context of Windows Server 2012 R2 , the cloud service model under consideration here is the IaaS model, which can be implemented by using the Hyper-V role of Windows Server 2012 R2 with Microsoft System Center 2012 R2.

 When IaaS is implemented in such a way that a customer deploys the cloud on-premises in its datacenter, the solution is called a *private cloud*. There are several ways an organization can implement a private cloud solution:

- By having the customer build and host the private cloud in its own datacenter, using Windows Server and the System Center family of products

- By having the customer purchase a dedicated private cloud appliance with Windows Server and System Center preinstalled and configured

- By having a partner company host the customer's private cloud

Migrating an organization's existing Active Directory infrastructure into a private cloud sourcing model can be straightforward or complex, depending on a number of different factors. Because of this, it's often best if you enlist a Microsoft partner to help you design and implement a solution that meets the needs of your organization.

If you want to explore the private cloud approach further, there are several places you can start:

- You can download evaluation versions of Windows Server 2012 R2 and System Center 2012 R2 from the Server And Cloud Platform page at *http://www.microsoft.com/en-us /server-cloud/solutions/virtualization-private-cloud.aspx*. Then you can use these platforms to create a proof of concept private cloud using documentation in the TechNet Library, such as *http://technet.microsoft.com/en-us/library/gg610625.aspx*.

- You can purchase an IaaS private cloud with a prevalidated configuration from server partners in the Microsoft Private Cloud Fast Track program. These offerings combine Microsoft software, consolidated guidance, validated configurations from original equipment manufacturer (OEM) partners, and other value-added software components. For more information, see *http://www.microsoft.com/en-in/server-cloud /fast-track.aspx*.

- You can use the Microsoft Pinpoint site to find a partner in the Microsoft Private Cloud Service Provider Program that can host a dedicated private cloud for your organization. For more information, see *http://www.microsoft.com/en-in/server-cloud/find-a -partner.aspx*.

Hybrid cloud

When IaaS is implemented as a combination of an on-premises private cloud solution and a public cloud service such as Windows Azure Virtual Machines, the solution is called a *hybrid cloud*. The hybrid cloud approach enables organizations to extend their infrastructure into the cloud for greater flexibility and agility so they can scale on demand to meet rapidly changing business requirements.

Microsoft believes that the hybrid cloud approach is the key to helping organizations cloud optimize their business. Beginning with the R2 release of Windows Server 2012, Microsoft uses the term "Cloud OS" to represent its visionary approach to how IT can deliver innovative new hybrid solutions that can address the needs and challenges that businesses are facing today. These needs and challenges include

- The need for new tools to automate datacenter provisioning, management, and monitoring in addition to tasks and workflows both in the datacenter and in the cloud. These tools must be able to manage both physical and virtual workloads on-premises and across public and service-provider clouds. They also need to be scalable, flexible, and secure.

- The challenge of managing diverse mobile devices like tablets and smartphones that are frequently personal devices owned by the users themselves rather than corporate assets. Existing technologies need to be integrated with new platforms that allow device registration and enrollment, policy-based management, and management from the cloud. There is also the challenge of delivering a secure and personalized experience on any device, anywhere and at any time.

- The need to deal with the apps users run on mobile devices. Deploying and managing these apps presents new challenges to accelerate the application life cycle, the handoff from developer to infrastructure specialists.

- The challenge of dealing with greater amounts of data than ever before. Big data needs powerful new tools for business intelligence to unlock the value of data stored both on-premises and in the cloud.

- The challenge of accomplishing all of the above without breaking ever-constrained IT budgets.

Microsoft's Cloud OS vision for hybrid computing consists of three key platforms:

- **Windows Server 2012 R2**   Provides the foundation for building enterprise-class datacenter and hybrid cloud solutions that are simple to deploy, cost-effective, application-focused, and user-centric.

- **System Center 2012 R2** Delivers a unified management experience across on-premises, service provider, and Windows Azure environments in a manner that's simple, cost-effective, application-focused, and enterprise-class.

- **Windows Azure** Provides an open and flexible cloud platform for building, deploying, and managing applications using almost any language, tool, or framework and running them in a secure public cloud hosted in a global network of Microsoft-managed datacenters. Windows Azure also enables you to integrate your public cloud applications with your existing on-premises IT environment to enable hybrid cloud capabilities.

If you want to explore Microsoft's hybrid cloud approach further, you can complete the following steps:

1. Begin by downloading evaluation versions of Windows Server 2012 R2 and System Center 2012 R2 and getting a trial subscription for Windows Azure from the Server And Cloud Platform page at *http://www.microsoft.com/en-us/server-cloud/solutions /hybrid-cloud.aspx*.

2. Next, use these platforms to create a proof of concept private cloud using documentation in the TechNet Library, such as *http://technet.microsoft.com/en-us/library /gg610625.aspx*.

3. After this, you can use Windows Azure Virtual Machines to deploy virtual machine instances running Windows Server 2012 R2 in the Windows Azure public cloud by using the documentation found at *http://www.windowsazure.com/en-us /documentation/services/virtual-machines/*.

4. Finally, learn how to use System Center 2012 R2 App Controller to manage these virtual machine instances across the private cloud and the Windows Azure platform from a single console by downloading the free ebook *Microsoft System Center: Cloud Management with App Controller*, which is available from the Microsoft Press blog at *http://blogs.msdn.com/b/microsoft_press/archive/2013/11/26/free-ebook-microsoft -system-center-cloud-management-with-app-controller.aspx*.

MORE INFO **MICROSOFT HYBRID CLOUD**

For more information on Microsoft hybrid cloud solutions, see *http://www.microsoft.com /en-us/server-cloud/solutions/hybrid-cloud.aspx*.

✔ **Quick check**

- Is Microsoft's cloud-based Office 365 an example of Software as a Service (SaaS), Platform as a Service (PaaS), or Infrastructure as a Service (IaaS)?

Quick check answer

- Office 365 is a SaaS offering in which the cloud is used to deliver an application to multiple users, regardless of their location or the type of device they are using.

Deployment process

As I said earlier, there is no single approach to planning and executing deployment projects. However, there are some best practices that apply in various degrees to the different scenarios discussed earlier, and from these you can identify some of the key steps that should be involved in any deployment or migration process. I'll briefly focus on providing some guidance for the following four steps, which are common to most infrastructure projects:

- Assessment
- Pilot testing
- Deployment/migration
- Role/feature migration

Note that to help you use the information in the upcoming sections, some of it is presented in the form of a series of questions that you can use as the basis for creating worksheets for implementing your project.

Assessment

Assessment involves determining the readiness of your organization's infrastructure, hardware, applications, and personnel for migrating your infrastructure to Windows Server 2012 R2. Although some of this will be examined in more detail in the next lesson, here are some of the key questions that you need to address as part of the assessment process:

- Have you inventoried all the hardware in your environment?
- Do you have any tools for performing an inventory of your infrastructure?
- Is your existing server hardware capable of running Windows Server 2012 R2?
- Is your existing server hardware capable of supporting the various roles and features of Windows Server 2012 R2 that you plan to deploy in your environment?
- Will your existing storage hardware work with Windows Server 2012 R2?
- Is your network infrastructure ready for Windows Server 2012 R2?
- Are your various network appliances (for example, firewalls, VPN gateways, and so on) capable of interoperating with Windows Server 2012 R2?
- If you plan to deploy DirectAccess, do your network infrastructure and appliances fully support Internet Protocol version 6 (IPv6)? Does your Internet Service Provider (ISP) support IPv6?
- Have you inventoried all the operating systems and applications in your environment?
- Are there any operating systems or applications in your environment that have compatibility issues with Windows Server 2012 R2?
- Will you be virtualizing any of your existing operating systems or applications on Hyper-V hosts running Windows Server 2012 R2?
- Have you inventoried the server roles on each of the servers of your infrastructure?

- Is there anything you need to consider with regard to virtualizing any of the server roles currently running on your servers or migrating these roles into the cloud?
- Have you assessed your budget to ensure you have sufficient funding to purchase any hardware or software needed for your project?
- Have you assessed the potential cost savings and return on investment (ROI) your organization can achieve by migrating to Windows Server 2012 R2?
- Are your IT staff members ready for the project? Do they need any additional training?

Pilot testing

Pilot testing involves more than just installing the software and playing around with it. You should start by creating a test plan that defines the scope and objectives of the testing you want to perform. You should also define a testing methodology that describes the architecture of your test environment, your testing tools and techniques, and the type of automation you plan to use for your testing. You then need to identify the resource on which you need to perform your testing and establish a schedule for performing your various tests. Finally, you should have a process for evaluating the results of your testing to see whether the objectives you set have been achieved.

The following are some key questions that you need to address during pilot testing of Windows Server 2012 R2:

- Why are you pilot testing Windows Server 2012 R2?
- Who will be performing the testing?
- What training will the testers need before they can perform their testing?
- What are the specific objectives of your test process?
- What scenarios will you be using as the basis for performing your testing?
- What roles and features do you plan to test?
- How will you test each of these roles and features?
- What hardware will you require to perform your tests?
- What additional software will you require to perform your tests?
- Will you be using any scripts or automation as part of the test process?
- Where will you set up your test environment?
- How will you ensure that your test environment will not affect your production environment?
- What is the schedule for performing your testing?
- How will you record your results for later analysis and evaluation?

Deployment/migration

Deployment or migration of Windows servers can take several different paths, depending on the scenario you decide to implement. The choices you make concerning the deployment or migration process can be dictated by various factors, including cost, timeframe, the topology of your organization, the complexity of your infrastructure, and the server roles you currently have deployed in your environment. Some of the key questions that you need to address concerning the process include the following:

- Do you have a rollback plan in place in case something goes wrong with the deployment or migration?

- Have you performed a full system backup of the servers you'll be migrating?

- Which of the following methods will you be using for deploying or migrating your servers?

    - New computer, in which you either deploy Windows Server 2012 R2 yourself on bare-metal hardware or purchase preconfigured server systems from your vendor and further configure the servers as desired.

    - In-place upgrade, which keeps the current hardware and upgrades the current server operating system to Windows Server 2012 R2. If you follow this approach, make sure you are aware of the supported upgrade paths for your existing server operating systems.

    - Refresh, which keeps the current hardware, saves the state information (operating system and application settings) of the current installation, wipes the hardware to remove the current operating system, performs a clean install of Windows Server 2012 R2, and restores the state.

    - Replace, which saves the state of the current installation to a network location, retires the current hardware, performs a clean install of Windows Server 2012 R2 on new hardware, and restores the state.

- Have you acquired and learned how to use tools such as Microsoft Deployment Toolkit (MDT) and System Center Configuration Manager (SCCM), which you can use to perform server deployments and migrations? Use of these tools is discussed in Chapter 2.

- Will you be migrating any physical servers into virtual environments? If so, you might need System Center Virtual Machine Manager (SCVMM) or other tools for performing the physical-to-virtual (P2V) migrations of your server workloads.

- Will you be migrating any servers running operating systems that are no longer supported, such as Windows 2000 Server, which might require special procedures such as migrating to an intermediate operating system before migrating to Windows Server 2012 R2? For more information, see Chapter 7.

- Will you be migrating any servers across processor architectures? For example, migrating a server running a 32-bit version of Windows Server 2003 to Windows Server 2012 R2, which is only available as 64-bit software?

- Have you developed plans for migrating the roles on each of your servers? Role migration should be planned concurrently with server migration. See the next section for more information on this topic.

- Have you developed plans for migrating any business data stored on any of your servers? Will you be migrating your storage hardware and your servers? Is your business data safely backed up to prevent data loss from occurring during the process?

- Have you developed specific plans for migrating Microsoft server applications, such as Microsoft Exchange, Microsoft SQL Server, and Microsoft SharePoint? The migration of server applications such as these requires special planning and consideration. Search the TechNet Library if you require more information on planning the migration of Microsoft server applications.

- Have you discussed your deployment or migration plans with the vendors of any third-party server applications you have deployed in your environment? Will the new operating system require a new version of these applications?

- Have you developed plans to ensure business applications and services remain available to users during the deployment or migration process?

- Have you informed your user population about any possible service interruptions or problems that might arise during the deployment or migration?

- Have you laid out a schedule for performing your migrations and determined the order in which you'll be deploying or migrating your servers?

- Have you assigned responsibilities to different members of your deployment and migration team?

- Have you thoroughly tested your deployment and migration plans in a test environment that mirrors your current production network?

Role/feature migration

A key aspect of server deployment is the migration of server roles and features together with configuration settings and data. To migrate roles and features from earlier versions of Windows Server to Windows Server 2012 or Windows Server 2012 R2, you can use the Windows Server Migration Tools. These tools include best-practices documentation and are designed to ensure the role and feature migration process goes smoothly and without errors.

Windows Server Migration Tools can be installed on the following operating systems:

- Windows Server 2003 with Service Pack 2
- Windows Server 2003 R2
- Full installation option of Windows Server 2008
- Full installation option of Windows Server 2008 R2
- Server Core installation option of Windows Server 2008 R2
- Server with a GUI installation option of Windows Server 2012
- Server Core installation option of Windows Server 2012

- Server with a GUI installation option of Windows Server 2012 R2
- Server Core installation option of Windows Server 2012 R2

The source server is the server from which you are migrating the role or feature, and the destination server is the server to which you are migrating the role or feature. For example, the source server might be running a Full installation option of Windows Server 2008 R2 and the destination server might be running a Server Core installation option of Windows Server 2012 R2. The Migration Tools must be installed on both the source and destination servers, and you must be a member of the Administrators group on both servers.

The following migration paths are supported:

- Migrating between 32-bit and 64-bit architectures
- Migrating between physical machines and virtual machines
- Cross-subnet migrations

The following migration paths are not supported:

- Migrating between source and destination servers that have different system UI languages.
- Roles on the Server Core installation option of Windows Server 2008 cannot be migrated because the Microsoft .NET Framework is not available on this installation option.

The sections that follow demonstrate how role and feature migration can be performed.

Installing the Migration Tools on the destination server

The following procedure shows how to install and configure the Migration Tools on a destination server running Windows Server 2012 R2. The goal is to be able to migrate a role such as the DHCP Server role or the Windows Server Update Services (WSUS) role from an existing server running Windows Server 2008 R2 to a new server running Windows Server 2012 R2. To install the Migration Tools on the destination server, complete the following steps:

1. Open a Windows PowerShell session with elevated rights on a server running Windows Server 2012 R2 in your environment.

2. Execute the following command to install the Windows Server Migration Tools feature on the remote server running Windows Server 2012 R2 and named SERVER7:

   ```
   Install-WindowsFeature Migration -ComputerName SERVER7
   ```

   If the local server running Windows Server 2012 R2 you are logged on to is a Server Core installation, type **powershell.exe** before executing the Windows PowerShell command just shown.

   If the local server running Windows Server 2012 R2 you are logged on to is a Full installation, you can also install the Migration Tools on the remote server by launching the Add Roles And Features Wizard from Server Manager.

3. Open an elevated command prompt by typing **cmd** in your elevated Windows PowerShell session and change the current directory as follows:

```
Cd %systemroot%\system32\ServerMigrationTools
```

4. Create a deployment folder on the destination server by running the SmigDeploy .exe utility. This utility creates an installation package for performing the migration and places it in a new folder named C:\downloads\<*subfolder*>, where <*subfolder*> depends on the operating system version and architecture of the source server. For example, if the source computer has AMD64 architecture and is running Windows Server 2008 R2, run SmigDeploy.exe using these parameters:

```
SmigDeploy.exe /package /architecture amd64 /os WS08R2 /path C:\windows
```

This creates a new deployment folder named C:\downloads\SMT_ws08R2_amd64 on the destination server and copies the Migration Tool files to the folder.

5. Copy the deployment folder to the local drive of the source computer running Windows Server 2008 R2 by using any appropriate method.

For more information on installing and using the Windows Server Migration Tools on Windows Server 2012 or Windows Server 2012 R2, see *http://technet.microsoft.com/en-us /library/jj134202*. There are also specific role and feature migration guides available on TechNet at *http://technet.microsoft.com/en-us/library/dn486809.aspx* for Windows Server 2012 and at *http://technet.microsoft.com/en-us/library/dn486773.aspx* for Windows Server 2012 R2.

Installing the Migration Tools on the source server

The following procedure shows how to install and run the Migration Tools on a source server running Windows Server 2008 R2 to which you have already copied the deployment folder from the destination computer. Note that additional steps might be required for migrating certain roles, such as the Hyper-V role, the Routing And Remote Access Services role, and others. To install the Migration Tools on the source server, complete the following steps:

1. Open a Windows PowerShell session with elevated rights and execute the following command to load the Server Manager module:

```
Import-Module ServerManager
```

2. Install the Windows Server Migration Tools feature by running this command:

```
Add-WindowsFeature Migration
```

3. Note that if your source server is running an earlier operating system such as Windows Server 2008 or Windows Server 2003, you also need to install the Microsoft .NET Framework and Windows PowerShell on the source computer and then run SmigDeploy.exe on it to register the Windows Server Migration Tools cmdlets into Windows PowerShell.

You can now launch the Migration Tools from either the destination server or the source server. For example, to launch them from a destination server running Windows Server 2012 or Windows Server 2012 R2, right-click the Windows Server Migration Tools tile on the Start screen and click Run As Administrator on the app bar, as shown here:

This opens a custom Windows PowerShell session from which you can run the various Windows Server Migration Tools cmdlets, as shown in Figure 1-1.

FIGURE 1-1 Display the list of available Windows Server Migration Tools cmdlets.

For help with the syntax of these cmdlets, use the Get-Help cmdlet. For more information on installing the Windows Server Migration Tools on Windows Server 2008 R2 and earlier, see *http://technet.microsoft.com/en-us/library/dd379545(v=WS.10).aspx*.

***TIP* GET YOUR MIGRATION QUESTIONS ANSWERED**

A good place to get help with your server migration questions is the Migration forum in the Windows Server forums on TechNet at *http://social.technet.microsoft.com/forums /en-US/winserverMigration/*.

Lesson summary

- Each type of infrastructure migration scenario (greenfield, forest upgrade, mixed environment, server consolidation, private cloud, hybrid cloud) has both benefits and challenges for organizations wanting to take advantage of the new features and capabilities found in Windows Server 2012 and Windows Server 2012 R2.

- Forest upgrades to Windows Server 2012 and Windows Server 2012 R2 are simpler than with previous Windows Server versions because of the integration of Adprep.exe into the AD DS role installation process.

- Four key steps for any infrastructure migration project are pilot testing, assessment, server migration, and role and feature migration.

- The Windows Server Migration Tools ease the process of migrating roles and features from previous Windows Server versions to Windows Server 2012 or Windows Server 2012 R2.

Lesson review

Answer the following questions to test your knowledge of the information in this lesson. You can find the answers to these questions and explanations of why each answer choice is correct or incorrect in the "Answers" section at the end of this chapter.

1. Which of the following are disadvantages of the existing environment deployment scenario? (Choose all that apply.)

   A. It gives you an opportunity to get it right from the start when it comes to implementing an infrastructure based on Windows Server 2012 R2.

   B. Some new features and capabilities of Windows Server 2012 R2 might have limited functionality or might not work at all when this deployment scenario is implemented.

   C. Server management might become more complex because of the need to use separate tools for managing servers running Windows Server 2012 R2 and those running earlier Windows Server operating system versions.

   D. It can help your organization improve server utilization and reduce costs.

2. Which of the following is *not* an enhancement that Microsoft made in Windows Server 2012 and Windows Server 2012 R2 to alleviate some of the concerns administrators often have about performing forest upgrades? (Choose all that apply.)

   A. Adprep functionality is now integrated into the AD DS installation process.

   B. The new AD DS installation process includes prerequisite validation to identify potential errors before installation begins.

   C. The Windows Server 2012 and Windows Server 2012 R2 forest functional levels add several new features to a forest.

   D. The Windows Server 2012 and Windows Server 2012 R2 domain functional levels add only one new feature to a domain.

3. Which of the following migration paths is *not* supported by the Windows Server Migration Tools?

   A. Migrating between x86-based and x64-based architectures

   B. Migrating between source and destination servers that have different system UI languages

   C. Migrating between physical machines and virtual machines

   D. Cross-subnet migrations

4. Which Windows PowerShell cmdlet for the Windows Server Migration Tools can you use to get the set of all Windows features that can be migrated from the local server or from a migration store?

   A. Export-SmigServerSetting

   B. Send-SmigServerData

   C. Get-SmigServerFeature

   D. Import-SmigServerSetting

Lesson 2: Assessing the readiness of your environment

The assessment phase is an important step of any server migration project. During this phase, you assess the readiness of your environment for the deployment of Windows Server 2012 R2. A key aspect of this phase is determining whether your current server hardware and the hardware you plan to purchase will support running Windows Server 2012 R2 and the various server roles and features you need to deploy in your environment. As this lesson demonstrates, performing such an assessment can be done in various ways, using different types of tools.

> **After this lesson, you will be able to:**
>
> - Describe the Windows Server 2012 R2 editions and system requirements.
> - Explain how to perform a manual assessment of a server infrastructure and describe some of the tools you would use to do this.
> - Describe the capabilities of version 9.0 of the Microsoft Assessment and Planning (MAP) Toolkit for performing inventory and assessment and for generating reports.
> - Describe the six phases involved in using MAP to perform an assessment of your environment.
> - Describe some of the wizards that MAP uses to collect data about your environment.
> - Describe the reports that MAP generates.

Manual assessment

If your current server infrastructure is very small (only a handful of servers), you can perform a manual assessment by using the documentation that came with your server hardware, viewing and recording server BIOS information, exporting system configuration information by using msinfo32.exe, inventorying roles and features by using the Get-WindowsFeature cmdlet of Windows PowerShell, and performing similar types of procedures. Once you have compiled information about your servers, you can validate them against the hardware requirements for the different Windows Server 2012 R2 editions.

Windows Server 2012 R2 editions

Microsoft has simplified the licensing model with Windows Server 2012 R2 by eliminating the Enterprise edition of previous versions of Windows Server. In addition, the Standard and Datacenter editions that are designed for midsized and large organizations now have feature parity, and they are both licensed by processor plus Client Access License (CAL). The only difference between the Standard and Datacenter editions is the virtualization rights included with the license:

■ **Standard edition**   This edition provides full Windows Server functionality with two virtual instances.

■ **Datacenter edition**   This edition provides full Windows Server functionality with unlimited virtual instances. The Datacenter edition also includes a new feature called Automatic Virtual Machine Activation (AVMA) that helps ensure Windows products are used in accordance with the Product Use Rights and Microsoft Software License Terms. AVMA enables you to install virtual machines on a properly activated Hyper-V host running Windows Server 2012 R2 without having to manage the product keys for each individual virtual machine. AVMA works even in disconnected environments and provides real-time reporting on usage and historical data on the license state of virtual machines.

> *MORE INFO*   For more information on AVMA, see *http://technet.microsoft.com/en-us /library/dn303421.aspx*.

In addition to the Standard and Datacenter editions, two other editions of Windows Server 2012 R2 are available that are designed for more specialized use:

■ **Essentials edition**   This edition is intended for small business environments and includes a simpler interface, preconfigured connectivity to cloud-based services, a 25-user and 50-device limit, and no virtualization rights.

- **Foundation edition**   This edition is an economical, general-purpose server released through OEM channels only and has a 15-user account limit and no virtualization rights.

Further discussion of these two editions is beyond the scope of this book.

REAL WORLD   **WINDOWS SERVER LICENSING**

In the past, the licensing of Windows Server editions has been a complex and confusing subject that often made it difficult for organizations to determine how much they should budget for licensing costs and whether they were in compliance. With Windows Server 2012 and Windows Server 2012 R2, Microsoft has simplified the licensing model for Windows Server so that you can more easily determine how many licenses you need to purchase to run the number of physical and virtual instances of Windows Server 2012 or Windows Server 2012 R2 you need in your environment. For more information and examples of different licensing scenarios, see the information on the Microsoft Volume Licensing site at *http://www.microsoft.com/licensing/about-licensing/windowsserver2012 -R2.aspx*.

System requirements

The minimum system requirements for installing the Standard and Datacenter editions of Windows Server 2012 R2 are as follows:

- A 1.4-gigahertz (GHz), 64-bit processor
- 512 MB of RAM
- 32 GB of available disk space
- A network adapter card
- A graphics adapter that supports Super VGA (1024 × 768) or higher resolution

Bear in mind that performance depends upon hardware, and your servers will need to exceed these minimum requirements to provide acceptable performance in most scenarios. For example, if you plan to install MAP 9.0 on your server to perform an assessment of your environment, you will need system hardware that meets the following minimum requirements:

- A dual-core, 1.5 GHz processor
- 2.0 GB of RAM
- 1 GB of available disk space
- A network adapter card
- A graphics adapter that supports Super VGA (1024 × 768) or higher resolution

In addition, the inventory, assessment, and reporting performance of MAP are based primarily on the speed of the CPU and the amount of available RAM of the computer on which MAP is installed.

Windows Server Catalog

If you plan to purchase new system hardware and deploy Windows Server 2012 R2 on such hardware, you can assess the readiness of the new hardware before you purchase it by using the Windows Server Catalog website shown in Figure 1-2, which identifies system and peripheral hardware from different vendors that has been certified for Windows Server 2012 R2. For more information, see *http://www.windowsservercatalog.com.*

FIGURE 1-2 Use the Windows Server Catalog website to assess whether hardware has been certified for Windows Server 2012 R2.

Using the MAP Toolkit

The Microsoft Assessment and Planning (MAP) Toolkit is an inventory, assessment, and reporting tool you can use to assess your current IT infrastructure and determine the right Microsoft technologies for your business needs. MAP uses Windows Management Instrumentation (WMI), Active Directory Domain Services (AD DS), SMS Provider, and other technologies to collect data from your environment and inventory hardware, software, and operating systems. MAP does this without installing any agent software on the target devices. MAP then provides you with an analysis of the collected data to help you plan for server migration, desktop refresh, server consolidation through virtualization, or cloud-capacity and migration.

The latest version, MAP 9.0, can help simplify the planning process for migration to the following Microsoft platforms:

- Windows Server 2012 R2
- Windows Server 2012
- Windows 8
- Windows 7
- Microsoft Office 2013
- Microsoft Office 365
- Windows Volume Licensing usage tracking
- Remote Desktop Services Licensing usage tracking
- Microsoft SharePoint 2013 usage tracking
- Microsoft Exchange 2013 usage tracking
- Microsoft Lync 2013 usage tracking
- Microsoft SQL Server 2012 usage tracking
- System Center Configuration Manager 2012 usage tracking
- Windows Azure Virtual Machines
- Server and Cloud Enrollment (SCE)
- Software inventory by means of Software ID tags

As Figure 1-3 shows, there are six phases involved in using MAP to perform an assessment of your environment. The first four phases are steps you need to perform before you run MAP in your environment. The final two phases involve running MAP to perform the assessment and generate a report of the results.

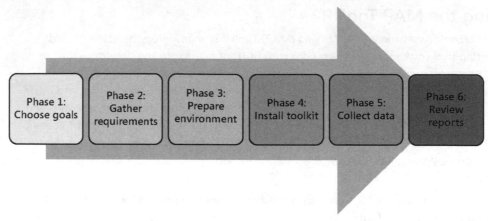

FIGURE 1-3 Six phases are involved in performing an assessment using MAP.

Phase 1: Choose goals

In this phase, you familiarize yourself with the different inventory, assessment, capacity planning, and software-usage tracking scenarios that MAP supports. You decide which wizards to use and what selections to make in these wizards.

Phase 2: Gather requirements

MAP uses various collection protocols to communicate with devices on your network to collect data to use in performing the various assessments. Because the communications performed by these protocols are subject to the administration and security settings of your environment, you must gather the user accounts and passwords needed to connect to and successfully inventory the devices in your environment prior to running MAP. In this phase, you gather this information required to configure MAP.

Phase 3: Prepare environment

MAP uses several different communication protocols based upon your goals and how your environment is configured. These include WMI, Active Directory Domain Services (AD DS), SQL Server commands, VMware Web services, and SSH with remote shell commands. In this phase, you prepare your environment to ensure that MAP can successfully connect to and gather information from the target machines in your environment.

Phase 4: Install the MAP Toolkit

In this phase, you download and install MAP using the options that best suit your environment and goals. The latest version of MAP is available as a free download from the Microsoft Download Center at *http://www.microsoft.com/en-us/download/details.aspx?&id=7826.*

Phase 5: Collect data

In this phase, you use MAP to gather information about your environment. Figure 1-4 shows the new user interface of MAP, which has been redesigned starting with MAP 8.0. On the left is a navigation pane that enables you to choose from a list of scenario groups. A *scenario group* is a set of related scenarios for which you can collect inventory data and perform other kinds of assessment tasks.

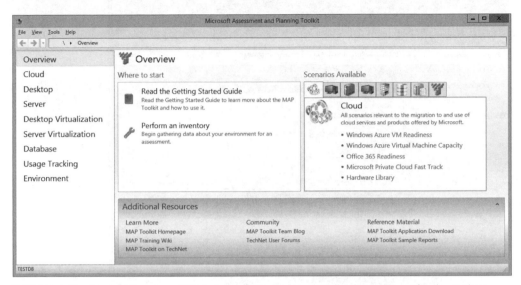

FIGURE 1-4 The Overview screen of MAP shows that no assessment has been run yet for the environment.

The initial item in the navigation pane is called Overview, and it provides a high-level overview of all the data collected in your environment, short descriptions of the different kinds of scenarios for which you can perform assessments, and a list of supporting resources. The Overview screen shown in Figure 1-4 indicates that no assessment has been performed yet. If an assessment had already been performed, an Environment Summary tile would provide a brief summary of the results of the assessment.

To start your first assessment, you can just click the Perform An Inventory item under Where To Start on the Overview page. This launches the Inventory And Assessment Wizard, as shown in Figure 1-5. This wizard walks you through a series of pages on which you can select one or more inventory scenarios, configure discovery methods, specify Active Directory credentials, and perform other actions to configure how the assessment will be performed.

The Inventory And Assessment Wizard is not the only wizard available to you in MAP. There is also the Performance Metrics Wizard, which you can use to collect performance data such as CPU, memory, network, and disk utilization information. MAP enables you to collect such data for Windows servers and clients and for Linux- or UNIX-based servers. MAP then uses the collected performance data to perform capacity planning for scenarios such as server consolidation and desktop virtualization.

To demonstrate the capabilities of MAP, I'm going to use it to try to discover all of the Windows computers currently present in my test lab. Figure 1-5 shows the Inventory Scenarios page of the Inventory And Assessment Wizard with Windows Computers selected for assessment in my environment.

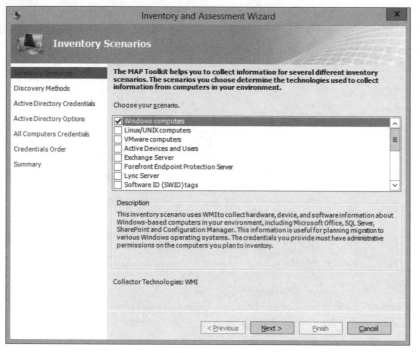

FIGURE 1-5 Select the Windows computers for assessment in the environment.

As the next page called Discovery Methods shows in Figure 1-6, there are a variety of methods MAP can use for discovering Windows computers in an environment. You could import a list of names of computers you want to assess from a text file. You could specify a range of IP addresses on your network and scan these addresses for the presence of Windows computers. Or you could query Active Directory Domain Services (AD DS) for a list of Windows computers in an Active Directory forest. I've chosen this last option for this walkthrough.

The Active Directory Credentials page shown in Figure 1-7 is used to specify credentials that MAP can use to connect to Active Directory to retrieve the names of Windows comput-ers in the forest. The remaining wizard pages may vary depending upon the options selected on previous pages.

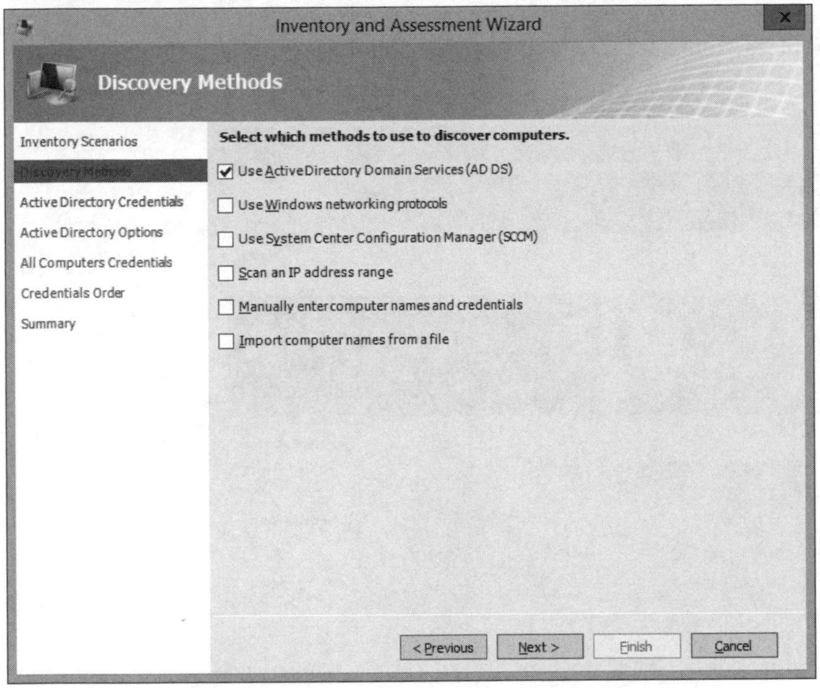

FIGURE 1-6 Query Active Directory for computer names.

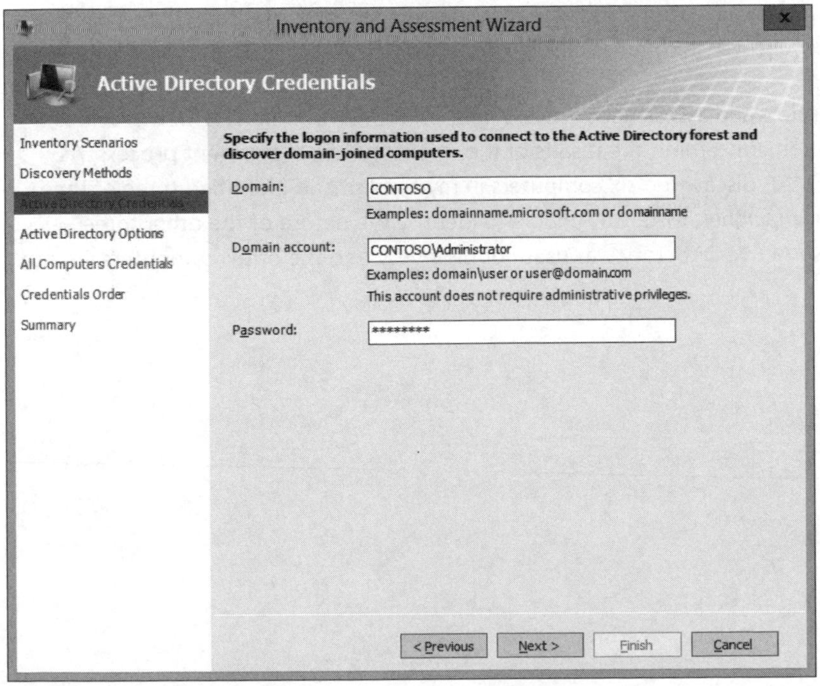

FIGURE 1-7 Specify credentials for connecting to Active Directory.

After you finish the wizard, the process of performing inventory and assessment of the environment takes place. Figure 1-8 shows MAP discovering the Windows computers in my test lab.

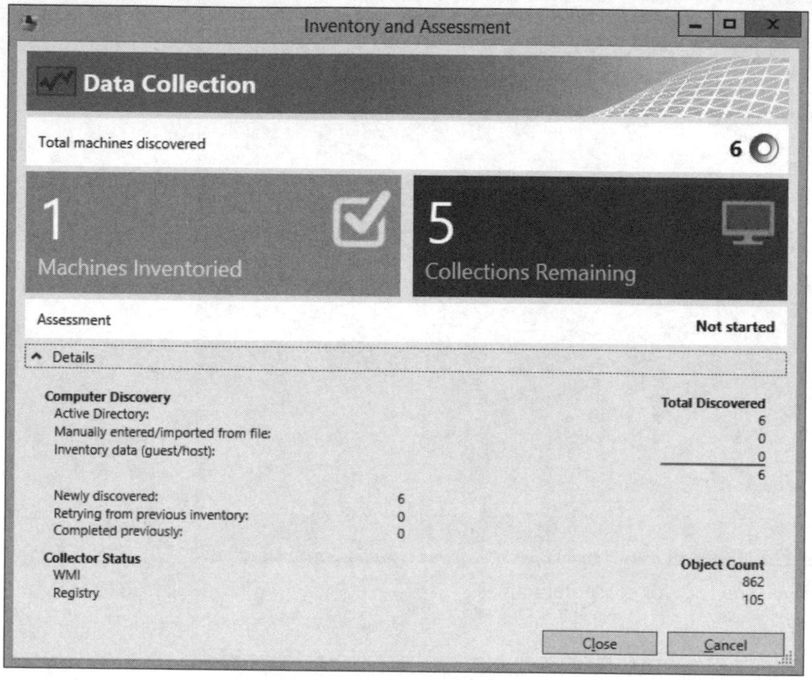

FIGURE 1-8 Computer discovery is currently underway.

When the inventory and assessment process finishes, the Environment screen provides summary information concerning the results of the inventory and assessment process. As Figure 1-9 shows, MAP discovered six computers in my test lab and identified three of these as Windows Server machines. MAP was unable to identify the nature of the other three computers because Active Directory was used for discovery and the other computers are not domain-joined.

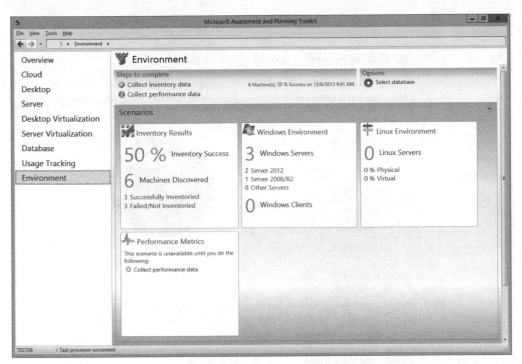

FIGURE 1-9 The Environment screen shows the results of computer discovery.

Clicking the Windows Environment tile, as shown in Figure 1-9, enables you to drill down to view more detail about the Windows computers in my environment. Figure 1-10 shows this as the Windows Environment Summary screen. The pie chart indicates that two of the three Windows servers are physical machines and the third is a virtual machine. However, this screen does not tell which of my servers is running as a virtual machine. I need to generate a report as described next to view that level of detail.

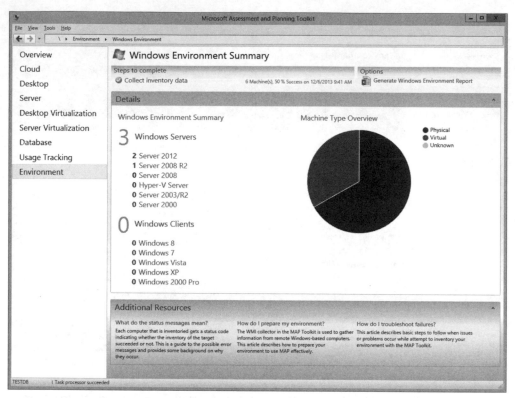

FIGURE 1-10 The environment contains both physical and virtual machines.

Phase 6: Review reports

The final phase of the process is using MAP to generate reports. MAP can generate different kinds of reports depending on the scenario group selected and the way you configure assessment to be performed. For example, clicking the Generate Windows Environment Report option at the top right of Figure 1-10 causes MAP to generate a comma-separated values (.csv) file containing the detailed results of the assessment. This .csv file can then be opened in Microsoft Excel, as shown in Figure 1-11, for review and further analysis. From this figure, I can determine that the server named SRV180 is a virtual machine running Windows Server 2008 R2 Enterprise edition as its guest operating system.

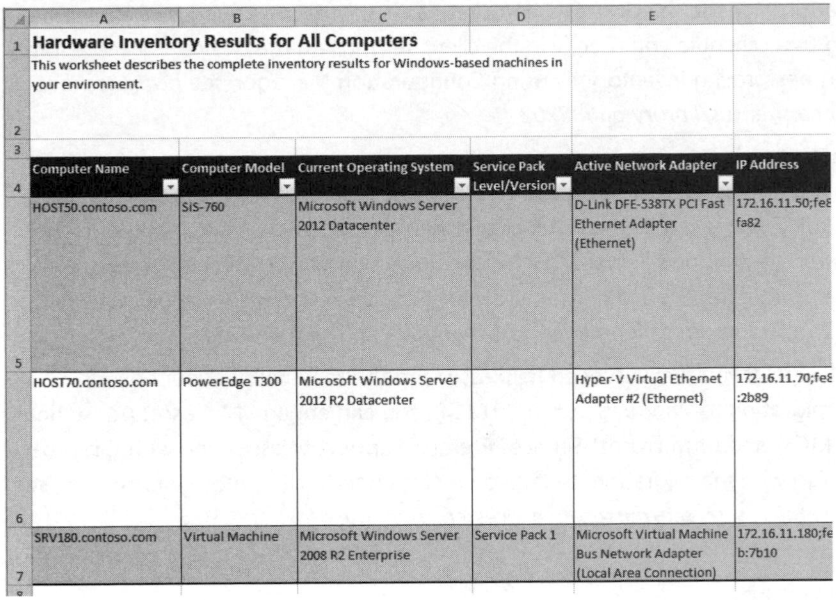

	A	B	C	D	E	
1	**Hardware Inventory Results for All Computers**					
2	This worksheet describes the complete inventory results for Windows-based machines in your environment.					
3						
4	**Computer Name**	**Computer Model**	**Current Operating System**	**Service Pack Level/Version**	**Active Network Adapter**	**IP Address**
5	HOST50.contoso.com	SiS-760	Microsoft Windows Server 2012 Datacenter		D-Link DFE-538TX PCI Fast Ethernet Adapter (Ethernet)	172.16.11.50;fe8 fa82
6	HOST70.contoso.com	PowerEdge T300	Microsoft Windows Server 2012 R2 Datacenter		Hyper-V Virtual Ethernet Adapter #2 (Ethernet)	172.16.11.70;fe8 :2b89
7	SRV180.contoso.com	Virtual Machine	Microsoft Windows Server 2008 R2 Enterprise	Service Pack 1	Microsoft Virtual Machine Bus Network Adapter (Local Area Connection)	172.16.11.180;fe b:7b10

FIGURE 1-11 The highest level of detail is found in the reports MAP generates.

✔ **Quick check**

■ Which MAP wizard can you use to collect performance data for capacity planning for server consolidation?

Quick check answer

■ The Performance Metrics Wizard

Other tools and methodologies

Besides using MAP or performing a manual assessment, there are other tools and methodologies you can use to assess the readiness of your environment for migration to Windows Server 2012 R2. The tools you can use include the following:

■ **System Center Configuration Manager**   System Center 2012 R2 Configuration Manager provides a comprehensive solution for change and configuration management for the Microsoft platform. Configuration Manager enables you to deploy operating systems, software applications, and software updates throughout your organization; monitor hardware and software inventory; monitor and remediate computers for compliance settings; and even remotely administer computers. By using Configuration Manager, you can collect detailed information about the hardware of client devices in your organization, including servers managed by Configuration Manager, and then use this information to determine Windows Server 2012 R2 migration readiness.

Configuration Manager hardware inventory runs on devices managed by SCCM according to a schedule you specify in the client settings on the device. For more information on performing inventory by using Configuration Manager, see *http://technet.microsoft.com/en-us/library/gg682202*.

- **Third-party products**   If you are using a third-party systems-management product for managing the hardware and software infrastructure of your organization, you will likely be able to use the product to assess the readiness of your environment for migration to Windows Server 2012 R2, provided that your systems-management product is up to date. There are also third-party dedicated inventory and assessment products available from different vendors that you can use if desired.

- **Outside help**   If you feel you need help assessing the readiness of your environment for migration to Windows Server 2012 R2, you can engage Microsoft Consulting Services (MCS) and/or Microsoft Services Premier Support to assist you with this process and also with the migration itself if you feel it's needed. For more information, see *http://www.microsoft.com/microsoftservices/en/us/home.aspx*.

Lesson summary

- If your current server infrastructure is very small, you can perform a manual assessment of your Windows Server 2012 R2 migration readiness.

- You can perform a manual assessment by using vendor-supplied documentation, built-in tools, information about Windows Server 2012 R2 editions and system requirements on Microsoft's website, and the Windows Server Catalog.

- For larger environments, version 9.0 of MAP helps you perform inventory, assessment, and reporting so that you can assess the readiness of your environment for migration to Windows Server 2012 R2.

- Assessing your environment using MAP involves six phases: choosing goals, gathering requirements, preparing your environment, installing MAP, collecting data, and reviewing reports.

- You can also use System Center 2012 R2 Configuration Manager, third-party products, and even outside help to assess your Windows Server 2012 R2 migration readiness.

Lesson review

Answer the following questions to test your knowledge of the information in this lesson. You can find the answers to these questions and explanations of why each answer choice is correct or incorrect in the "Answers" section at the end of this chapter.

1.   Which tool can help you ensure that new hardware you purchase will work properly with Windows Server 2012 R2?

   A.   The msinfo32.exe utility

   B.   The Get-WindowsFeature cmdlet

    C. System Center 2012 R2 Configuration Manager

    D. The Windows Server Catalog

2. During which of the six phases of performing an assessment using MAP would you ensure that MAP can successfully connect to and gather information from the target machines in your environment?

    A. Phase 2: Gather requirements

    B. Phase 3: Prepare environment

    C. Phase 4: Install MAP

    D. Phase 5: Collect data

3. When you generate reports after performing a Windows Server 2012 R2 readiness assessment using MAP, where can you find information about the IP address and current operating system installed on each system inventoried?

    A. On the Overview screen of the MAP user interface

    B. On the Environment screen of the MAP user interface

    C. On the Windows Environment Summary screen of the MAP user interface

    D. In the Windows Environment Report .csv file, which you can open to view in Microsoft Excel

Practice exercises

The goal of this section is to provide you with hands-on practice with the following:

- Performing a manual installation of Windows Server 2012 R2 onto a bare-metal server system and familiarizing yourself with the Start screen and desktop

- Using MAP 9.0 to perform a readiness assessment of your server

To perform the following exercises, you need the Windows Server 2012 R2 evaluation .iso file that you downloaded from the TechNet Evaluation Center. You should burn the .iso file to recordable DVD media or copy it to a bootable USB device for installation purposes. You also need a physical server system available for testing purposes that meets the minimum hardware requirements for installing Windows Server 2012 R2, as described earlier in this chapter. The server should also meet the following additional requirements:

- The server should be a bare-metal system; that is, there should be no operating system installed on it. If the server already has an operating system installed, you should remove it by booting using installation media for any version of Microsoft Windows until you reach the Setup Wizard page that allows you to delete all existing partitions on the hard drives of the server.

- The server hardware should meet the minimum requirements for installing MAP 9.0. See the readme.htm file included in the MAP download for more information on these requirements.

You also need a client computer that has Microsoft Excel 2013 or Microsoft Excel 2010 installed for viewing the reports generated by MAP. If you have an Office 365 subscription, you can also use the Excel Web App for this purpose.

Exercise 1: Performing a manual installation

In this exercise, you perform a manual installation of Windows Server 2012 R2 onto a bare-metal system. You then use your Windows Server 2012 R2 installation to familiarize yourself with the Start screen (modern UI) and desktop.

1. Start the server and insert the DVD media onto which you burned the Windows Server 2012 R2 evaluation .iso file that you downloaded from the TechNet Evaluation Center.

2. If necessary, press the appropriate keystroke combination to display the boot menu and enable you to boot the system from its optical drive or from the bootable device containing Windows Server 2012 R2 installation media.

3. When the Windows Setup Wizard appears, select the appropriate language to install, the time and currency format, and the keyboard or input method.

4. Click Next and then click Install Now.

5. On the Select The Operating System You Want To Install page, select Windows Server 2012 R2 Datacenter Evaluation (Server With A GUI) and click Next.

6. On the License Terms page, select I Accept The License Terms and click Next.

7. On the Which Type Of Installation Do You Want page, select Custom: Install Windows Only (Advanced).

8. On the Where Do You Want To Install Windows page, click Drive 0 Unallocated Space and click Next.

9. Once the installation has finished and the Settings screen is displayed, type a password for the default Administrator account and then click Finish.

10. Once settings have been finalized and the logon screen is displayed, press Ctrl+Alt+Del and log on using the built-in Administrator account.

11. When Server Manager opens, click Local Server in the Navigation pane and view the properties of your server. Write down the name of your server because you'll need this information for the next exercise.

12. Move the pointer to the lower-left corner of your screen and click the Start icon to display the modern UI.

13. Click the tile named Desktop to display the Windows desktop.

14. Press the Windows key to display the Start screen.

15. Press the Windows key again to display the desktop.

16. Click the Server Manager icon on the taskbar to maximize Server Manager.

17. Move the pointer to the upper-right corner of the screen until the Search, Start, and Settings charms are displayed and then swipe the pointer downward to display the Charms Bar.

18. Press Esc to make the Charms Bar disappear.

19. Press the Windows key+C to make the Charms Bar appear again.

20. Click the Settings charm to open Settings and then click Server Info. The System Control Panel item opens while the Charms Bar disappears. View the information about your computer and then close it.

21. Press the Windows key+I to open Settings again and then click Help. Take a moment to explore how Help works and then close it.

22. Press the Windows key+Q to open the Search pane with the focus set to Everywhere. Type **paint** and press Enter to open Microsoft Paint. Close the program.

23. Move the pointer to the lower-left corner of your screen, click Start, type **paint**, and press Enter to open Microsoft Paint. Close the program.

24. Press the Windows key+Q, type **background**, press the Down Arrow key until Change Desktop Background is highlighted, then press Enter and change the background of your desktop to the solid color white.

25. Right-click the Start icon and examine the menu options available.

26. Click the Windows PowerShell icon on the taskbar to open a new Windows PowerShell session.

27. Type **shutdown –s –t 0** and press Enter to shut down your server.

Exercise 2: Using MAP

In this exercise, you install MAP 9.0 on the server used in Exercise 1 and run MAP to perform an assessment and generate a report.

1. Start your server and log on using your Administrator credentials.

2. Copy the MAP installation files to the Documents folder on your test server and then double-click the MAPSetup.exe file to launch the Setup Wizard.

3. Follow the prompts of the wizard, accepting all the defaults, until installation of MAP is completed.

4. Right-click the taskbar and select Properties.

5. Select the Navigation tab.

6. Select the check box labeled Show The Apps View Automatically When I Go To Start.

7. Select the check box labeled List Desktop Apps First In The Apps View When It's Sorted By Category.

8. Click OK and then press the Windows key to display the Start screen.

9. Scroll horizontally if needed until you can right-click Microsoft Assessment And Planning Toolkit and then select Pin To Taskbar at the bottom of the screen.

10. Press the Escape key to return to the desktop.

11. Click the MAP icon on the taskbar to launch MAP.

12. In the Microsoft Assessment And Planning Toolkit dialog box, type **TESTDB** in the Name field and click OK to create an inventory database for MAP.

13. After the inventory database is created, you are returned to the Overview page of the MAP user interface.

14. Click Perform An Inventory under Where To Start on the Overview page to launch the Inventory And Assessment Wizard.

15. On the Inventory Scenarios page, select Windows Computers and click Next.

16. On the Discovery Methods page, clear the Use Active Directory Domain Services (AD DS) check box, select the Scan An IP Address Range check box, and click Next.

17. On the Scan An IP Address Range page, in both the Starting Address and Ending Address fields, enter the IP address you previously assigned to your test server and then click Next.

18. On the All Computers credentials page, click Create, type *<servername>* **\Administrator** in the Account Name field, where *<servername>* is the name of your server.

19. Type the password for the Administrator account in the Password and Confirm Password fields and then click Save.

20. Click Next twice and then click Finish.

21. Watch the progress in the Inventory and Assessment dialog box as it occurs and then click Close when the assessment has completed.

22. Select the Server scenario in the left pane and view whether your server has met the system requirements for installing Windows Server 2012 R2.

23. Click Generate Windows Server 2012 Report on the right side of the page. When the report has been generated, click Close.

24. Open My Documents in Windows Explorer and navigate to the TESTDB folder inside the MAP folder.

25. When My Documents opens in Windows Explorer, copy the report (.xlsx file) that MAP generated to a client computer that has Microsoft Excel installed.

26. Open the report in Microsoft Excel and view its contents.

Suggested practice exercises

The following additional practice exercises are designed to give you more opportunities to practice what you've learned and to help you successfully master the lessons presented in this chapter:

- **Exercise 1**   If you have a test environment with Active Directory deployed and with servers and clients running different versions of Windows, install MAP 9.0 on a server or client in the environment and perform some of the other types of assessment and readiness tests in the different scenario groups available.

- **Exercise 2**   Try using the Windows Server Migration Tools to migrate a server role from a server running Windows Server 2008 R2 SP1 to another server that has a clean installation of Windows Server 2012 R2.

Answers

This section contains the answers to the lesson review questions in this chapter.

Lesson 1

1. **Correct answers: B and C**

    A. **Incorrect:** The opportunity to get it right from the start when it comes to implementing an infrastructure based on Windows Server 2012 R2 is an advantage of the greenfield migration scenario, not the mixed environment scenario.

    B. **Correct:** Some new features and capabilities of Windows Server 2012 R2 can be implemented only when your Active Directory environment includes domain controllers running Windows Server 2012 R2. These features might have limited functionality or might not work at all when implementing a mixed environment migration scenario because your Active Directory schema hasn't yet been upgraded to Windows Server 2012 R2.

    C. **Correct:** Some of the server administration tools built into Windows Server 2012 R2 and included in the Remote Server Administration Tools (RSAT) for Windows 8.1 will have limited or no functionality when managing servers running previous versions of Windows Server. You might have to install additional updates on servers running previous versions of Windows Server to manage them using the Windows Server 2012 R2 server administration tools or RSAT for Windows 8.1.

    D. **Incorrect:** Improving server utilization and reducing costs is a benefit of the server consolidation approach to server migration and is not relevant to a mixed environment migration scenario.

2. **Correct answer: C**

    A. **Incorrect:** In Windows Server 2012 and Windows Server 2012 R2, Adprep functionality is integrated into the AD DS installation process, which in most cases eliminates the need to separately run Adprep prior to introducing domain controllers running the new version of Windows Server.

    B. **Incorrect:** The new AD DS installation process includes prerequisite validation to identify potential errors before installation begins. For example, if the installation process determines that **adprep /domainprep** needs to be run to prepare the domain, verification is done first to ensure that the user who initiated the process has sufficient rights to perform the operation.

    C. **Correct:** The Windows Server 2012 and Windows Server 2012 R2 forest functional levels do not add any new features to a forest. They ensure only that any new domain added to the forest automatically operates at the Windows Server 2012 or Windows Server 2012 R2 domain functional level.

D.   Incorrect: The Windows Server 2012 and Windows Server 2012 R2 domain functional levels add only one new feature to a domain. This new feature relates to Dynamic Access Control (DAC) and therefore is unlikely to affect any applications and services in an Active Directory environment based on Windows Server 2008 or Windows Server 2008 R2.

3.   **Correct answer: B**

    A.   Incorrect: The Windows Server Migration Tools supports migrating between x86-based and x64-based architectures.

    B.   Correct: The Windows Server Migration Tools does not support migrating between source servers and destination servers that have different system UI languages.

    C.   Incorrect: The Windows Server Migration Tools supports migrating between physical machines and virtual machines.

    D.   Incorrect: The Windows Server Migration Tools supports cross-subnet migrations.

4.   **Correct answer: C**

    A.   Incorrect: The Export-SmigServerSetting cmdlet exports selected Windows features and operating system settings from the local computer, and it stores them in a migration store.

    B.   Incorrect: The Send-SmigServerData cmdlet migrates folders, files, and associated permissions and share properties from a source server to a destination server through port 7000. The destination server must be in the same subnet as the source server, and the cmdlet Receive-SmigServerData must be run on the destination server at the same time Send-SmigServerData is running on the source server.

    C.   Correct: The Get-SmigServerFeature cmdlet gets the set of all Windows features that can be migrated from the local server or from a migration store.

    D.   Incorrect: The Import-SmigServerSetting cmdlet imports selected Windows features and operating system settings from a migration store and applies them to the local computer.

Lesson 2

1.   **Correct answer: D**

    A.   Incorrect: The msinfo32.exe utility is useful for performing a manual assessment of existing Windows Server installations.

    B.   Incorrect: The Get-WindowsFeature cmdlet is useful for performing a manual assessment of existing Windows Server installations.

    C.   Incorrect: System Center 2012 R2 Configuration Manager enables you to deploy operating systems, software applications, and software updates throughout your organization; monitor hardware and software inventory; monitor and remediate computers for compliance settings; and even remotely administer computers.

D. Correct: The Windows Server Catalog identifies system and peripheral hardware from different vendors that has been certified for Windows Server 2012 R2.

2. **Correct answer: B**

A. Incorrect: During Phase 2: Gather requirements, MAP uses various collection protocols to communicate with devices on your network to collect data to use in performing the various assessments. Because the communications these protocols perform are subject to the administration and security settings of your environment, you must gather the user accounts and passwords needed to connect to and successfully inventory the devices in your environment prior to running MAP.

B. Correct: During Phase 3: Prepare environment, MAP uses several different communication protocols based on your goals and how your environment is configured. These include WMI, Active Directory Domain Services (AD DS), SQL Server commands, VMware Web services, and SSH with remote shell commands. During this phase, you prepare your environment to ensure that MAP can successfully connect to and gather information from the target machines in your environment

C. Incorrect: During Phase 4: Install MAP, you download and install MAP using the options that best suit your environment and goals.

D. Incorrect: During Phase 5: Collect data, you launch MAP and select wizards to begin the data-collection process for your environment.

3. **Correct answer: D**

A. Incorrect: The Overview screen of the MAP user interface provides a high-level overview of all the data collected in your environment, short descriptions of the different kinds of scenarios for which you can perform assessments, and a list of supporting resources. It does not display the IP addresses of discovered computers.

B. Incorrect: The Environment screen of the MAP user interface has four tiles named Inventory Results, Windows Environment, Linux Environment, and Performance Metrics. None of these tiles displays IP addresses of discovered computers.

C. Incorrect: The Windows Environment Summary screen of the MAP user interface enables you to drill down to view more detail about the Windows computers in the environment. However, it does not display the IP addresses of discovered computers.

D. Correct: The Windows Environment Report .csv file, which you can open to view in Microsoft Excel, includes the IP address and current operating system installed on each system inventoried. Examples of column headers in this .csv file include Computer Name, Computer Model, Current Operating System, Service Pack Level /Version, Active Network Adapter, and IP Address.

CHAPTER 2

Deploying servers

Whether you administer a small business with a server room in the back office or a data center for a large enterprise, deploying servers is a key part of your job. Although installing a handful of servers can still be done manually, provisioning hundreds or thousands of server workloads in a virtualized data center is an entirely different affair.

Windows Server 2008 introduced the Server Core installation option with a reduced servicing footprint that made it ideal for enterprise deployment, but smaller organizations often chose the GUI option because it was easier to configure after installation. With Windows Server 2012 and later now supporting post-installation conversion between Server Core and GUI, however, Server Core has become the default installation option for organizations of all sizes.

A key step in the process of planning for server provisioning is setting up a build lab where you can build and maintain the reference images you will be deploying in your production environment. In addition to Windows Server 2012 R2, such images can include applications, software updates, and device drivers needed to ensure a successful install. Microsoft provides tools, some of them free, that organizations can use for implementing deployment strategies that meet their needs.

This chapter provides you with the basic knowledge you will need to perform your job by deploying servers running Windows Server 2012 R2 using the tools and best practices Microsoft recommends.

Lessons in this chapter:

Before you begin

To complete the practice exercises in this chapter

- You need Windows Server 2012 R2 installation media, either in the form of an .iso file (if you will be performing the practice exercises using virtual machines running on a

Hyper-V host) or on bootable media (if you will be performing the practice exercises using physical systems).

- You should have two server systems available for testing purposes that meet the minimum hardware requirements for installing Windows Server 2012 R2. These server systems should have no operating system installed, and they can be either physical systems or virtual machines running on a Hyper-V host. The network where the servers reside should have Internet connectivity.

- You also should have at least rudimentary knowledge of using Windows PowerShell.

Lesson 1: Installation options

Choosing which installation option to deploy is an important consideration when planning the deployment of your servers. Windows Server 2012 and later include capabilities for post-installation conversion between the Server Core and Server With A GUI installation options. They also include a Minimal Server Interface option that can provide additional benefits in some scenarios. In addition, a capability called Features On Demand enables administrators to completely remove the installation binaries for roles and features that won't be needed for their servers. This lesson describes these various capabilities and how to perform the conversion task.

After this lesson, you will be able to:

- Understand the different installation options and their possible benefits.
- Understand the Minimal Server Interface option.
- Use Server Manager or Windows PowerShell to convert between installation options on a running Windows Server 2012 installation.
- Use Windows PowerShell to convert between installation options on an offline virtual hard disk (VHD) of a virtual machine on which Windows Server 2012 has been installed.
- Understand the Features On Demand capability and its possible benefits.

Estimated lesson time: 20 minutes

Understanding installation options

Administrators of smaller Windows Server environments in the past have traditionally relied heavily on GUI-based tools for administering servers because such tools are easy to use. Scripting might occasionally have been used for some repetitive tasks, such as performing a bulk creation of user accounts in Active Directory, but most server management was done through the GUI in one of the following ways:

- By logging on interactively to a server's console
- By logging on remotely to a server using Remote Desktop Connection (Mstsc.exe)
- By using the Remote Server Administration Tools (RSAT) installed on a workstation

With the shift toward centralizing IT infrastructure within data centers and cloud computing, however, most midsized and large organizations now prefer to automate as much Windows Server administration as possible by using scripting. With the enhanced Windows PowerShell support in Windows Server 2012 and later, such automation has become much easier.

Choosing an installation option

The default installation option when you install Windows Server 2012 and later is the Server Core Installation option instead of the Server With A GUI (formerly called Full) option as in previous versions of Windows Server. The reasons for this change are as follows:

- Server Core requires less disk space than Server With A GUI, which can be important in data centers that use virtualization to consolidate multiple virtualized server workloads per physical host machine.
- Server Core has a smaller attack surface, which makes it more secure for data center and cloud computing.
- Server Core requires fewer software updates, which means less servicing overhead.
- Administrators can switch between different installation options after Windows Server 2012 or later has been deployed, which means you can change your Server Core installations to Server With A GUI installations without having to wipe and reinstall.

This means that administrators should always install the Server Core option when deploying Windows Server 2012 or later unless they have a compelling reason to install the Server With A GUI option instead.

Managing servers in small environments

Administrators in small environments that have only a few servers can still take advantage of all the benefits that come from running the Server Core installation even if they don't feel confident working from the command line. They can do this by following these steps:

1. Install Windows Server 2012 or later on the servers using the Server With A GUI installation option.

2. Perform all initial configuration of the server by using the GUI tools available in this installation option.

3. Use Windows PowerShell as described later in this chapter to convert the Server With A GUI installation to a Server Core installation.

4. Install the Remote Server Administration Tools (RSAT) for Windows 8.1 on a client computer running Windows 8.1 and use these convenient GUI tools for managing servers running Windows Server 2012 or later.

This procedure makes it easy for such administrators to configure their servers while still allowing them to take advantage of the smaller attack surface, servicing overhead, and disk space requirements of the Server Core option.

You can obtain RSAT for Windows 8.1 from the Microsoft Download Center at *http://www.microsoft.com/en-us/download/details.aspx?id=39296*. Note that the earlier version, RSAT for Windows 8, can only be used to manage servers running Windows Server 2012, not Windows Server 2012 R2. Both of these versions of RSAT have limited functionality for managing Windows Server 2008 R2, Windows Server 2008, and Windows Server 2003. For a detailed compatibility matrix showing which management features these versions of RSAT support, see Microsoft Support article KB 2693643 at *http://support.microsoft.com/kb/2693643*.

Minimal Server Interface

In addition to the two installation options (Server Core and Server With A GUI) from which you can choose when you deploy Windows Server 2012 and later, there is a third installation option available called the Minimal Server Interface. This installation option can be configured only after deployment by using either Server Manager or Windows PowerShell. It has all the functionality of Server With A GUI except for the following capabilities, which are not included:

- User interface (Start screen and desktop)
- Windows Explorer
- Internet Explorer
- Some of the Control Panel utilities

The Minimal Server Interface installation has a smaller servicing footprint than the Server With A GUI installation, but administrators can still use it to run local GUI management tools for administering a server.

Converting between installation options

You can use either Windows PowerShell or, in some cases, the Server Manager console included in Windows Server 2012 and later to convert between different installation options. For example, to use Server Manager to convert between a Server With A GUI installation and a Minimal Server Interface installation, launch the Remove Roles And Features Wizard and remove the Server Graphical Shell feature, as shown in Figure 2-1.

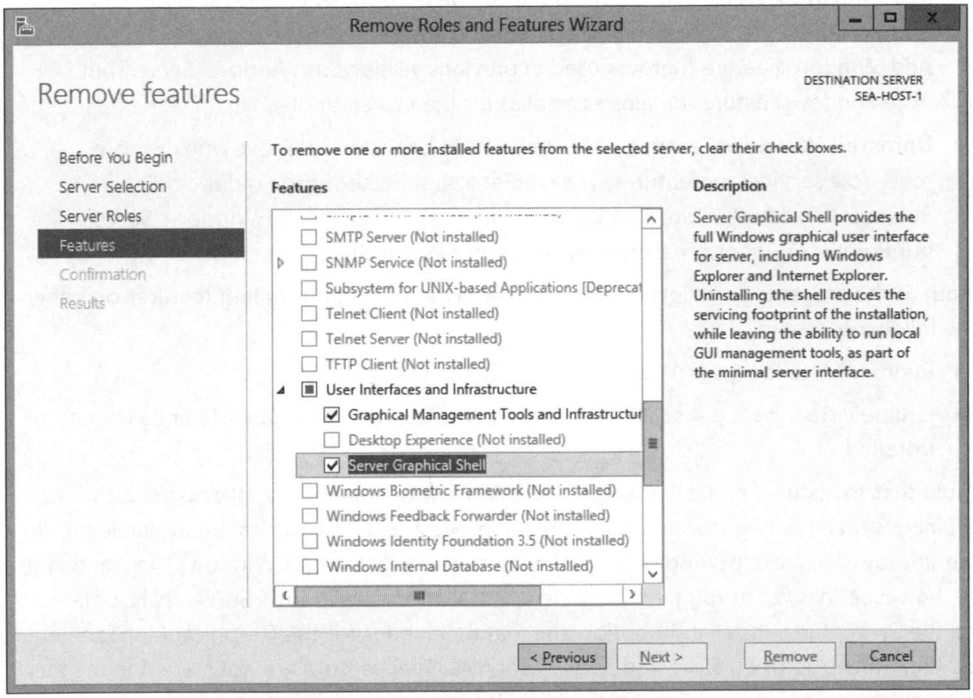

FIGURE 2-1 Convert a Server With A GUI installation to a Minimal Server Interface installation.

As Figure 2-1 shows, Server With A GUI installations of Windows Server 2012 and later have two features installed that are not installed on Server Core installations:

- **Graphical Management Tools And Infrastructure** This feature includes various infrastructure components and components that provide the Minimal Server Interface that supports GUI management tools, such as MMC consoles. It does not include Windows Explorer, Internet Explorer, or the Start screen. The Windows PowerShell name for this feature is Server-Gui-Mgmt-Infra.

- **Server Graphical Shell** This feature includes components that provide the full graphical user interface, such as Windows Explorer, Internet Explorer, and the Start screen. The Windows PowerShell name for this feature is Server-Gui-Shell.

In addition, a feature called Desktop Experience can be installed to provide Windows 8 or later features such as desktop themes, photo management, and Windows Media Player. The Windows PowerShell name for this feature is Desktop-Experience.

Using Windows PowerShell

In most cases, administrators will want to use Windows PowerShell to convert between the different installation options, especially if they are managing remote servers in a data center or Infrastructure as a Service (IaaS) cloud environment. The two Windows PowerShell cmdlets used for converting between different installation options of Windows Server 2012 and later are the following:

- **Install-WindowsFeature** This cmdlet can be used to install one or more roles, role services, or features. The cmdlet also supersedes the older cmdlet Add-WindowsFeature that was used in previous versions of Windows Server, but Add-WindowsFeature remains as an alias for the newer cmdlet.

- **Uninstall-WindowsFeature** This cmdlet can be used to remove one or more roles, role services, or features. The cmdlet also supersedes the older cmdlet Remove-WindowsFeature that was used in previous versions of Windows Server, but Remove-WindowsFeature remains as an alias for the newer cmdlet.

Both of the preceding cmdlets can be used for installing or uninstalling features on either of the following:

- Running installations of Windows Server 2012 or later
- Offline virtual hard disks (VHDs) on which Windows Server 2012 or later has been installed

Note that to install a particular feature on a Windows installation or offline VHD, the feature binaries first must be available for installation. Most feature binaries are available locally in the side-by-side store (%windir%\winsxs folder) on installations of Windows Vista and later. Note, however, that when you perform a clean installation of Windows Server 2012 or later using the Server Core installation option, the feature binaries for the Graphical Management Tools And Infrastructure feature and Server Graphical Shell feature are not staged in the local side-by-side store of a Server Core installation. This means that if you want to install these features on a Server Core installation, you must specify an alternate source for their binaries—for example, a mounted .wim file of a Windows Server 2012 or later installation of the same service pack level. Alternatively, you can allow the feature binaries to be downloaded and installed from Windows Update, although this can take some time with larger feature binaries. These two methods for obtaining feature binaries that are not available in the local side-by-side store are demonstrated in one of the practice exercises in this chapter.

> ***MORE INFO*** **WHAT DOES "STAGED" MEAN?**
>
> When you want to service a Windows installation by adding or removing a feature, the package containing the binaries for installing that feature can be in one of three states:
>
> - **Installed** The package has been installed and is present in the WinSxS folder.
> - **Staged** The package has not been installed but is present in the WinSxS folder.
> - **Absent** The package is not installed and is not present in the WinSxS folder. This state is also sometimes referred to as "disabled with payload removed."

Packages that are not present in the WinSxS folder can still be installed in Windows Server 2012 and later if you use the *–Source* parameter for the Install-WindowsFeature cmdlet to specify a mounted .wim file. As an alternative, you can omit the *–Source* parameter and allow the necessary package to be downloaded from Windows Update. The Features On Demand capability in Windows Server 2012 and later, described later in this lesson, also enables administrators to remove packages from the WinSxS folder, which could not be done on installations of previous versions of Windows.

Converting Server Core to Server With A GUI

To use Windows PowerShell to convert a Server Core installation of Windows Server 2012 or later to a Server With A GUI installation, run the following command:

```
Install-WindowsFeature Server-Gui-Mgmt-Infra,Server-Gui-Shell -Restart
  -Source C:\mountdir\windows\winsxs
```

The path C:\mountdir\windows\winsxs for the *–Source* parameter in the preceding command specifies a mounted Server With A GUI image in the install.wim file in the \sources folder of your Windows Server installation media.

Alternatively, you could allow the necessary feature binaries to be downloaded and installed from Windows Update by omitting the *–Source* parameter as follows:

```
Install-WindowsFeature Server-Gui-Mgmt-Infra,Server-Gui-Shell -Restart
```

Note that if you previously converted a Server With A GUI installation to a Server Core installation and did not remove the binaries for these features, the binaries remain staged in the WinSxS folder and therefore do not need to be downloaded from Windows Update.

Converting Server Core to Minimal Server Interface

To use Windows PowerShell to convert a Server Core installation of Windows Server 2012 or later to a Minimal Server Interface installation, use this command:

```
Install-WindowsFeature Server-Gui-Mgmt-Infra-Restart -Source C:\mountdir\windows\winsxs
```

The explanation of the *–Source* parameter is the same as in the previous section. To download and install the feature binaries from Windows Update instead of a locally mounted .wim image, use this command:

```
Install-WindowsFeature Server-Gui-Mgmt-Infra -Restart
```

Converting Server With A GUI to Server Core

To use Windows PowerShell to convert a Server With A GUI installation of Windows Server 2012 or later to a Server Core installation, run the following command:

```
Uninstall-WindowsFeature Server-Gui-Mgmt-Infra,Server-Gui-Shell -Restart
```

Converting Server With A GUI to Minimal Server Interface

To use Windows PowerShell to convert a Server With A GUI installation of Windows Server 2012 or later to a Minimal Server Interface installation, use this command:

```
Uninstall-WindowsFeature Server-Gui-Mgmt-Infra -Restart
```

> ✔ **Quick check**
>
> - What action does the Windows PowerShell command **Install-WindowsFeature Server-Gui-Mgmt-Infra –Restart** perform when it is run on a Server Core installation of Windows Server 2012 R2?
>
> **Quick check answer**
>
> - It converts the server to a Minimal Server Interface installation by downloading the necessary feature binaries from Windows Update.

Converting between installation options in offline VHDs

To convert an offline VHD on which a Server Core installation of Windows Server 2012 or later has been installed, run Install-WindowsFeature with the *–Source* parameter as shown previously, but also include the *–vhd* parameter to specify the path to the .vhd file. For example, consider a virtual machine named SERVER6 whose system drive is a VHD located in the following folder on the Hyper-V host:

C:\Users\Public\Documents\Hyper-V\Virtual Hard Disks\SERVER6.vhdx

If the virtual machine is offline (stopped), you can convert the Windows Server installation on the VHD from Server Core to Server With A GUI by performing the following steps:

1. Create a new folder named C:\mountdir on your Hyper-V host. You will use this folder to mount the install.wim file on your Windows Server installation media so that the Install-WindowsFeature cmdlet can obtain the necessary feature binaries from the WinSxS folder of a Server With A GUI image in the .wim file.

2. Insert your Windows Server installation media into your Hyper-V host.

3. Open a command prompt on your Hyper-V host and type **dism /get-wiminfo /wimfile:D:\sources\install.wim** to display the index numbers of the Windows Server 2012 or later images in the .wim file. Make a note of the Server With A GUI image that is from the same edition as your Server Core installation. For example, if you installed the SERVERDATACENTERCORE image on your server, note the index number of the SERVERDATACENTER image in the .wim file.

4. Mount the .wim file by typing **dism /mount-wim /wimfile:D:\sources\install.wim /Index:<n> /mountdir:C:\mountdir /readonly** at an elevated command prompt, where *<n>* is the previously noted image number.

5. Open the Windows PowerShell console and run the following command:

```
Install-WindowsFeature Server-Gui-Mgmt-Infra,Server-Gui-Shell
  -vhd " C:\Users\Public\Documents\Hyper-V\Virtual Hard Disks\SERVER6.vhdx"
  -Source c:\mountdir\windows\winsxs
```

6. Restart the server and then start the virtual machine using Hyper-V Manager, open it using Virtual Machine Connection, and confirm that it is now running a Server With A GUI installation of Windows Server.

Features On Demand

Beginning with Windows Server 2012, you can completely remove the installation binaries for features from the side-by-side store (WinSxS folder) of a running Windows installation or an offline VHD on which Windows has been installed. Administrators may consider doing this on some installations for the following reasons:

- To further reduce the disk footprint of the installation
- To enhance the security of the installation by removing binaries for features that will not be needed

To completely remove the binaries of a feature, use the Uninstall-WindowsFeature cmdlet with the *–Remove* parameter. For example, if you convert a Server With A GUI installation to a Server Core installation, the binaries for the Server-Gui-Mgmt-Infra and Server-Gui-Shell features remain staged in the side-by-side store. If you decide that you will not be reinstalling those features, you can remove their binaries by running the following Windows PowerShell command:

```
Uninstall-WindowsFeature Server-Gui-Mgmt-Infra,Server-Gui-Shell -Remove
```

Note that if you remove the binaries for a feature, you can still reinstall the feature later (and stage the binaries in the side-by-side store again) by using the Install-WindowsFeature cmdlet and either using Windows Update for downloading the binaries or specifying a mounted .wim file using the *–Source* parameter, as described previously.

There are many things that you can do with these tools for online and offline installations. For an in-depth discussion of converting between installation options, see *http://technet .microsoft.com/en-us/library/hh831786.aspx*.

Lesson summary

- The Server Core installation is the default installation option for Windows Server 2012 and later.
- You can use Server Manager to convert a Server With A GUI installation to a Server Core installation or a Minimal Server Interface installation.
- You can use the Install-WindowsFeature and Uninstall-WindowsFeature Windows PowerShell cmdlets to convert between different installation options on a running installation of Windows Server 2012 or later.

- You can use the Install-WindowsFeature and Uninstall-WindowsFeature Windows PowerShell cmdlets to convert between different installation options on an offline VHD of a virtual machine that has Windows Server 2012 or later installed.

- You can use the Uninstall-WindowsFeature cmdlet to completely remove the installation binaries from the side-by-side store of a running installation of Windows Server 2012 or later or an offline VHD of a virtual machine that has Windows Server 2012 or later installed.

Lesson review

Answer the following questions to test your knowledge of the information in this lesson. You can find the answers to these questions and explanations of why each answer choice is correct or incorrect in the "Answers" section at the end of this chapter.

1. Which installation option of Windows Server 2012 R2 potentially has the smallest disk footprint?

   A. Server With A GUI

   B. Server Core

   C. Minimal Server Interface

   D. Full

2. What action does the following Windows PowerShell command perform?

   ```
   Uninstall-WindowsFeature Server-Gui-Shell -Restart
   ```

   A. It converts a Server Core installation to a Server With A GUI installation.

   B. It converts a Server With A GUI installation to a Server Core installation.

   C. It converts a Server Core installation to a Minimal Server Interface installation.

   D. It converts a Server With A GUI installation to a Minimal Server Interface installation.

3. You deployed a Server Core installation of Windows Server 2012 R2 in a virtualized environment running on a Hyper-V host. Because of limitations in available storage space for the host, you want to further reduce the disk footprint of your Server Core installation. Which of the following actions could you perform to try to do this? (Choose all that apply.)

   A. Uninstall any roles or features that are not needed on the server.

   B. Use the *–Remove* parameter with the Uninstall-WindowsFeature cmdlet to remove the binaries for unneeded roles and features from the local side-by-side store on the server.

   C. Use the *–Source* parameter with the Install-WindowsFeature cmdlet to specify a mounted Windows Image (.wim) file where binaries you removed from the local side-by-side store on the server can be found.

   D. Use Server Manager to remove the binaries for unneeded roles and features from the local side-by-side store on the server.

Lesson 2: Preparing the build lab

Building images of Windows operating systems involves many considerations. Understanding the life cycle of image management is foundational for successfully building and deploying Windows images. Microsoft Deployment Toolkit (MDT) is the tool of choice for building Windows images, and setting up a build lab with MDT can help simplify the task of deploying Windows operating systems. This lesson explains the image life-cycle management process and how to set up a build lab that uses MDT 2013 to build reference images of Windows Server 2012 and later.

After this lesson, you will be able to:

- Understand the image life-cycle management process.
- Understand how to set up a build lab for creating reference images for deploying customized installations of Windows Server 2012 or later.
- Describe the steps of the reference image build process.
- Explain how to set up a technician computer for deploying Windows Server 2012 or later using MDT 2013.

Estimated lesson time: 15 minutes

Understanding image life-cycle management

The goal of image life-cycle management is to facilitate the process of building and maintaining reference images of Windows operating systems that can be used for deploying Windows to target systems. Depending on the version of Windows being deployed and the needs of your organization, such target systems might be

- Client PCs or tablet devices
- Physical server systems
- Virtual machines on Hyper-V hosts in the data center
- Virtual machines running in an Infrastructure as a Service (IaaS) private cloud

A *reference image* is a standardized Windows operating system image (.wim file) that might include some or all of the following:

- Applications
- Device drivers
- Software updates or hotfixes
- Per-user customizations
- Per-machine customizations

NOTE **PER-USER VS. PER-MACHINE CUSTOMIZATIONS**

Per-user customizations of reference images generally involve changes to the default user profile. These changes will then be applied to each new user who logs on to the system. Per-machine customizations involve modifications that apply to all users who log on to the system. An example of a per-machine customization is configuring the image so that Remote Desktop is enabled on systems on which the image is deployed.

Per-user customizations are commonly implemented only when engineering reference images of Windows client operating systems such as Windows 8.1. Per-user customizations are not commonly implemented when engineering reference images of versions of Windows Server.

Build lab vs. production environment

The process and tools used for building reference images should be kept separate from the process and tools used for deploying images, as illustrated in Figure 2-2. The *build lab* should contain only systems, tools, and other software needed to create and test reference images you will be deploying in your *production environment*.

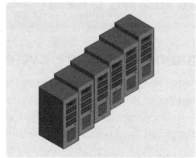

Build Lab   Production Environment

FIGURE 2-2 Keep your build lab and production environments separate from each other.

Setting up your build lab

The build lab is used for building and testing reference images that will later be deployed in your production environment. The components of a build lab can vary, but they should generally include the following:

- **Hyper-V host**   Most of the image engineering process can be performed within a virtual environment. For building reference images of Windows Server 2012 or later, you need a physical host system that supports hardware virtualization and is running Windows Server 2008 R2 or later with the Hyper-V role installed.

- **Technician computer**   The technician computer has the necessary tools installed for building reference images of Windows Server 2012 or later. In the example of a build lab shown in Figure 2-3, the technician computer is a virtual machine running on your Hyper-V host, but it could also be a physical system if Hyper-V is not being used in the build lab.

- **Reference computer**   The reference computer is the system from which the reference image is created by sysprepping and capturing the installation of Windows on the computer. This reference computer must be a bare-metal system—that is, it must have no operating system installed on it. In the build lab shown in Figure 2-3, the reference computer is another virtual machine running on your Hyper-V host, but it could also be a physical system if Hyper-V is not being used in the build lab.

- **Physical systems**   These are samples of the different types of system hardware used in your production environment on which you will later be deploying your reference image. After you build your reference image, you should test it by deploying it on these sample physical systems to make sure no issues will arise when you deploy it in your production environment. These sample systems can be virtual machines if you will be deploying your reference image only onto virtual machines in your production environment—for example, if you will be deploying some type of private-cloud solution.

- **DHCP server**   Network connectivity must be established between the technician and reference computers before the technician computer can be used to deploy Windows onto the reference computer, so a DHCP server can be used to dynamically assign an IP address to the reference computer. However, a static IP address can also be manually assigned to the reference computer at the start of the deployment process. The DHCP server is therefore optional, but it is recommended to simplify the automation of the reference-image build process.

- **Windows Deployment Services**   This is a server running Windows Server 2008 R2 or later that has the Windows Deployment Services role installed. This server can be either physical, as shown in Figure 2-3, or virtual (running as a virtual machine on the Hyper-V host). The Windows Deployment Services server simplifies the task of deploying the reference image onto the sample physical systems by eliminating the need to burn your images onto bootable media to kick-start the reference-image testing process. This server is optional if you will be deploying your reference image only onto virtual machines, because you can easily mount your boot images manually in Hyper-V for deploying your reference image to virtual machines in your build environment.

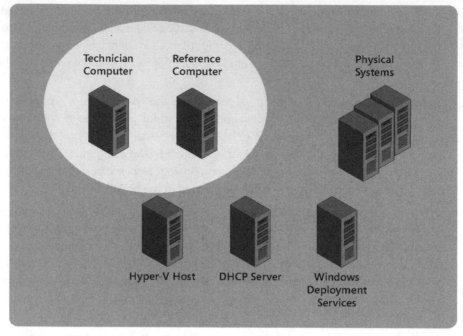

FIGURE 2-3 This is an example of how to set up a build lab.

Windows PowerShell for Windows Deployment Services

The biggest improvement to Windows Deployment Services in Windows Server 2012 R2 is the addition (at last!) of Windows PowerShell support. Previously, in Windows Server 2012 and earlier, if you wanted to automate repetitive tasks by using Windows Deployment Services you needed to use the Wdsutil.exe command-line utility, which enabled you to configure WDS servers, add or remove images, create capture or discover images, export or make copies of images, configure namespaces, configure and manage multicast transmissions, start and stop WDS services, and perform many other kinds of tasks. Unfortunately, the syntax of Wdsutil.exe is difficult and its output is challenging to parse in scripts, so in practice the utility was of limited use for automating complex deployment scenarios.

Beginning with Windows Server 2012 R2, however, there are now almost three dozen new Windows PowerShell cmdlets that can be used to automate almost any task involving Windows Deployment Services. Writing scripts that use these new cmdlets is easy for administrators who are familiar with the basics of Windows PowerShell because these new cmdlets follow the standard syntax for Windows PowerShell cmdlets.

To display a complete list of the available cmdlets in the WDS module, use Server Manager or Windows PowerShell to install the Windows Deployment Services server role, as described in Chapter 3, "Server remote management." Then open a Windows PowerShell prompt on the server and type the following command:

```
Get-Command -Module WDS
```

To get help concerning any cmdlet, use the Get-Help cmdlet in the usual way. For a complete list of the Windows Deployment Services cmdlets and their syntax with examples, see *http://technet.microsoft.com/library/dn283416.aspx*.

Quick check

- Why are per-user customizations not usually performed when building a reference image for server deployment?

Quick check answer

- Administrators generally don't bother customizing the desktop environment of servers because they usually manage them remotely using administrative tools and scripts.

Understanding the reference-image build process

After you set up your build lab, you can begin building and testing the reference images you will be deploying on systems in your production environment. As Figure 2-4 shows, the general steps in the process of building a reference image are as follows:

1. **Customize the deployment process**   Use the technician computer to customize the process of deploying Windows by choosing whether to include applications, software updates, hotfixes, language packs, out-of-box device drivers, and various per-user or per-machine customizations when the operating system is deployed.

2. **Deploy the image to a reference computer**   Next deploy Windows onto your reference computer along with any additional software or customizations you configured.

3. **Sysprep the deployed image**   The System Preparation Tool (Sysprep) then executes on your reference computer to prepare the installation for cloning by removing machine-specific information, such as the computer's security identifier (SID).

4. **Capture the deployed image**   The sysprepped installation is then captured in the form of a Windows Image (.wim) file and copied to the technician computer. The captured and sysprepped image is now referred to as the reference image.

5. **Deploy the reference image to the test systems** Then use the technician computer to deploy the reference image to sample systems in your build lab. These sample systems can be either samples of physical systems taken from your production environment or virtual machines running on the Hyper-V host in your build lab.

6. **Verify the result** Now log on to the sample systems on which you deployed your reference image. Perform any tests needed to ensure that the deployed image works properly and has all the software and customizations your production environment requires.

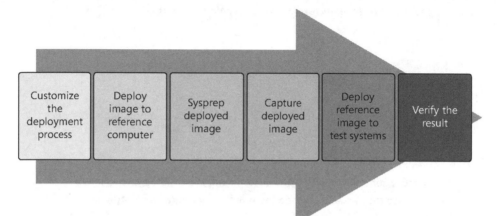

FIGURE 2-4 These are the steps involved in building and testing a reference image.

Setting up the technician computer

To set up a *technician computer* for building reference images to deploy Windows Server 2012 or later, you need the following tools:

- **Microsoft Deployment Toolkit (MDT) 2013**   MDT is a free Solution Accelerator from Microsoft that includes comprehensive tools and guidance for automating and customizing operating system and application deployment. MDT 2013 is available in both x64 and x86 versions, and it can be used to deploy Windows 8.1, Windows 8, Windows 7, Windows Server 2012 R2, Windows Server 2012, and Windows Server 2008 R2. For more information about MDT and to download the latest version, see *http://technet.microsoft.com/en-us/solutionaccelerators/dd407791.aspx.*

- **Windows Assessment and Deployment Kit (ADK) for Windows 8.1**   The ADK is a collection of tools you can use to customize, assess, and deploy Windows operating systems to new computers. The ADK supersedes the Windows Automated Installation Kit (Windows AIK) used by MDT 2012 and earlier, and it includes additional tools that previously had to be downloaded separately. For more information about the ADK and to download the latest version, see *http://technet.microsoft.com/en-us/library /hh824947.aspx.*

In addition to the preceding tools, you also need the following:

- Windows Server 2012 or later installation media (.iso file or DVD)

- Any applications, language packs, software updates, hotfixes, or out-of-box device drivers that you want to include in your reference image

Navigating MDT and ADK versions

Be sure you understand the different versions of MDT and ADK available and how they work together; otherwise, you might face limitations regarding the versions of Windows Server you will be able to build and deploy in your environment. This is especially important if you will also be using MDT to build and deploy client versions of Microsoft Windows.

Here are the salient points you need to keep in mind:

- You cannot use MDT 2012 or earlier to deploy either Windows Server 2012 R2 or Windows Server 2012. You also cannot deploy either Windows 8.1 or Windows 8 using this version of MDT.

- MDT 2012 Update 1 was the first version of MDT to enable you to deploy Windows Server 2012 and Windows 8. However, you cannot use this version of MDT to deploy either Windows Server 2012 R2 or Windows 8.1.

- MDT 2013 is the first version of MDT that enables you to deploy Windows Server 2012 R2 and Windows 8.1. You also can use this version of MDT to deploy Windows Server 2012 and Windows 8.

- MDT 2013 requires that you install the ADK for Windows 8.1; MDT 2012 Update 1 requires that you install the ADK for Windows 8. You cannot use the ADK for Windows 8.1 with MDT 2012 Update 1 or use the ADK for Windows 8 with MDT 2013.

This gets even more confusing if you're using MDT with System Center Configuration Manager because only specific versions of MDT are supported for different versions of System Center Configuration Manager. A full discussion of such matters is beyond the scope of this book (though integration of MDT with System Center Configuration Manager is described in Lesson 4), but you can easily find relevant guidance by searching TechNet.

Upgrading MDT versions

If you are currently using MDT 2010 in your environment for deploying Windows Server 2008 R2 or Windows 7, upgrading to MDT 2012 Update 1 is fairly straightforward:

1. Back up your deployment share.

2. Uninstall the Windows AIK on your technician computer.

3. Install the ADK for Windows 8 and reboot the computer.

4. Open the Deployment Workbench for MDT and upgrade your deployment share.

5. Regenerate the boot images in your deployment share.

6. Use the new boot images for your deployments.

Note that there is no need to uninstall MDT 2010 before installing MDT 2012 Update 1.

If you are currently using MDT 2012 Update 1 in your environment for deploying Windows Server 2012 or Windows 8, upgrading to MDT 2013 is also straightforward:

1. Back up your deployment share.

2. Uninstall the ADK for Windows 8.

3. Install the ADK for Windows 8.1 and reboot.

4. Upgrade your deployment share.

5. Regenerate your boot images.

6. Perform your deployments.

Additional steps might be required in both of these scenarios if you are also using Windows Deployment Services and/or Configuration Manager as part of your deployment infrastructure. Note also that you cannot upgrade directly from MDT 2010 to MDT 2013; you first need to upgrade to MDT 2012 Update 1.

Lesson summary

- A reference image is a standardized Windows operating system image that might also include applications, device drivers, software updates, and customizations.
- You should generally keep your build lab separate from your production environment.
- A build lab that uses MDT and other components can be set up in a virtualized environment running on a Hyper-V host.
- The reference-image build process includes steps such as customization, reference-system deployment, sysprep and capture, test system deployment, and verification.
- To build reference images for deploying Windows Server 2012 or later, you should use MDT 2013 with the ADK for Windows 8.1.

Lesson review

Answer the following questions to test your knowledge of the information in this lesson. You can find the answers to these questions and explanations of why each answer choice is correct or incorrect in the "Answers" section at the end of this chapter.

1. Which of the following is *not* recommended when setting up your build lab? (Choose all that apply.)

    A. Using a Hyper-V host for performing image engineering within a virtual environment

    B. Using virtual machines for testing your reference image when the servers in the production environment in which you will be deploying your reference image are physical systems

    C. Using a DHCP server to dynamically assign an IP address to your reference computer

    D. Installing the necessary tools for building reference images on your reference computer

2. Which component of a build lab helps eliminate the need to burn boot images onto DVD media to kick-start the reference-image testing process?

    A. DHCP server

    B. Technician computer

    C. Reference computer

    D. Windows Deployment Services

3. A Windows installation that has been sysprepped and captured is referred to as what?

    A. A reference computer

    B. A reference installation

    C. A reference image

    D. A test system

Lesson 3: Building images

After you set up your build lab, you're ready to build your reference images. This lesson describes the steps involved in installing and configuring MDT 2013 to build Windows Server 2012 R2 reference images. The lesson also describes how to test your images to ensure they will work properly when deployed in production.

After this lesson, you will be able to:

- Understand the steps involved in building reference images for Windows Server 2012 R2 deployment.
- Install MDT 2013 and the ADK for Windows 8.1.
- Create and configure deployment shares by importing operating-system source files, out-of-box device drivers, applications, and packages.
- Create and customize task sequences for building and deploying images.
- Understand the function of the two MDT configuration files.
- Generate installation boot media by updating a deployment share.
- Deploy and capture a reference image by using MDT 2013.
- Test reference images to ensure they work as intended.

Estimated lesson time: 30 minutes

Building reference images using MDT 2013

To use a technician computer to build reference images for deploying Windows Server 2012 R2 using MDT 2013, you need to perform the following steps:

1. Install the ADK on the technician computer.
2. Install MDT 2013 on the technician computer.
3. Create a deployment share using the Deployment Workbench.
4. Import the Windows Server 2012 R2 operating-system source files.
5. Import any out-of-box drivers needed by the target production systems.
6. Import any applications you want to include in your image.
7. Import any packages—such as hotfixes, software updates, or language packs—that you want to include in your image.
8. Create a task sequence for deploying, sysprepping, and capturing the reference image.
9. Customize the MDT configuration files to automate some or all of the deployment process.

10. Update the deployment share to create boot images for kick-starting the deployment process.

11. Deploy Windows Server 2012 R2 onto the reference computer, run Sysprep, capture a reference image, and copy it to the deployment share.

Step 1. Installing the ADK for Windows 8.1

The ADK for Windows 8.1 can be installed on the following versions of Windows:

- Windows Server 2012 R2

- Windows Server 2012

- Windows Server 2008 R2

- Windows Server 2008 with Service Pack 2 (SP2)

- Windows 8.1

- Windows 8

- Windows 7

- Windows Vista

The ADK also requires the Microsoft .NET Framework 4.5 and installs it automatically if it is not already present on the computer.

To install the ADK, you must perform the following steps:

1. Ensure that the computer on which you will be installing the ADK supports installation of the product and that all the necessary software requirements have been met.

2. Download the installation bootstrap file (adksetup.exe) for the ADK from the Microsoft Download Center at *http://www.microsoft.com/en-us/download/details.aspx?id=39982*.

3. Double-click the installation bootstrap file and follow the prompts to install the ADK components you want to install on the computer. The components from which to choose include the following:

    - Application Compatibility Toolkit (ACT)

    - Deployment Tools

    - Windows Preinstallation Environment (Windows PE)

    - User State Migration Tool (USMT)

    - Volume Activation Management Tool (VAMT)

    - Windows Performance Toolkit

    - Windows Assessment Services

    - Microsoft SQL Server 2012 Express

> **NOTE** **ADK COMPONENTS**
>
> For a basic Windows Server deployment using MDT, the only ADK components you need are the Deployment Tools and the Windows Preinstallation Environment (Windows PE). For the deployment of desktop versions of Windows, you might need other ADK components as well.

Step 2. Installing MDT 2013

MDT 2013 can be installed on the following versions of Windows:

- Windows Server 2012 R2
- Windows Server 2012
- Windows Server 2008 R2
- Windows 8.1
- Windows 8
- Windows 7

The software prerequisites for installing MDT 2013 on Windows 7 or Windows Server 2008 R2 include the following:

- Microsoft Management Console version 3.0
- Microsoft .NET Framework 3.5 with Service Pack 1 (SP1) or later
- Windows PowerShell version 2.0 or later

The software prerequisites for installing MDT 2013 on Windows 8.1, Windows 8, Windows Server 2012 R2, or Windows Server 2012 include the following:

- The ADK for Windows 8.1
- Microsoft .NET Framework 4.0, which is included in the operating system
- Windows PowerShell version 3.0, which is included in the operating system

These software requirements are outlined in the release notes for MDT 2013, which you can download from *http://www.microsoft.com/en-us/download/details.aspx?id=40796*.

> **NOTE** **USMT**
>
> The MDT 2013 Release Notes suggest that the User State Migration Tool (USMT) of the ADK is also a prerequisite. However, USMT is intended for migrating user profiles on client versions of Windows, and it is not needed for these exercises.

To install and configure MDT 2013, you must perform the following steps:

1. Ensure that the computer on which you will be installing MDT 2013 supports the installation of the product and that all the necessary software requirements have been met.

2. Download the appropriate version (x64 or x86) of the MDT 2013 Windows Installer (.msi) file for the platform on which you will be installing it by using the download link on the Microsoft Deployment Toolkit home page at *http://www.microsoft.com/en-us/download/details.aspx?id=40796*.

3. Double-click the .msi file and follow the prompts to install MDT 2013 on the computer.

Step 3. Creating a deployment share

After you install the ADK and MDT on a computer, the next step is to create a deployment share. A *deployment share* is a shared folder on the technician computer that will be used to contain and manage the following items:

- Operating-system source files for building and deploying images
- Out-of-box drivers for target systems that need them
- Applications to be deployed on target systems
- Packages—for example, software updates or language packs
- Task sequences, which are used to control the deployment process
- Advanced configuration features, such as selection profiles, the MDT database, media deployment points, and linked deployment shares
- Hidden items not displayed in the Deployment Workbench, such as Windows PE images for initiating the Lite Touch Installation (LTI) deployment process on target systems

In addition, the deployment share includes a Monitoring node that can be used for monitoring the progress and status of LTI deployments while they happen.

To create a deployment share, you must perform the following steps:

1. Launch the Deployment Workbench, which is used for building, capturing, and deploying Windows images to target systems.

2. Right-click the Deployment Shares node and select New Deployment Share.

3. Follow the prompts of the New Deployment Share Wizard and do the following:

    - Specify the path, the share name, and a description for the deployment share.
    - Configure the deployment share by selecting or clearing the options shown here:

    ☑ Ask if a computer backup should be performed.
    ☐ Ask for a product key.
    ☐ Ask to set the local Administrator password.
    ☑ Ask if an image should be captured.
    ☑ Ask if BitLocker should be enabled.

Figure 2-5 shows the Deployment Workbench after creating a deployment share called MDT Deployment Share.

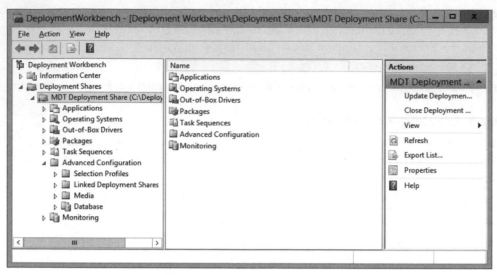

FIGURE 2-5 The Deployment Workbench has MDT Deployment Share selected to show its structure.

Step 4. Importing operating-system source files

After you create a deployment share, the next step is to use the Deployment Workbench to import source files for the operating systems you plan to deploy. Before you can build and capture a reference image of a master installation of a supported version of Windows, you must import a full set of source files for that version of Windows. You can also import previously captured image files or images stored on a Windows Deployment Service server on your network into your deployment share.

To import the source files for a Windows operating system, you must perform the following steps:

1. Launch the Deployment Workbench if it is not already running and expand the node for the deployment share you created earlier.

2. Right-click the Operating Systems node in your deployment share and select Import Operating System as shown here:

3. Follow the prompts of the Import Operating System Wizard to import a full set of source files for the Windows operating system you plan to deploy.

Step 5. Importing out-of-box drivers

If the computer on which you will be deploying your master installation of Windows requires any special device drivers, you should import these drivers into your deployment share. This is especially important when deploying server versions of Windows onto systems that have mass storage devices, such as RAID controllers, that are either very old or very new, because in both cases the drivers for these controllers might not be included with Windows Server 2012 R2. If you don't import boot-critical mass storage drivers into your deployment share, MDT might not be able to find a local storage device on which to install Windows.

To import out-of-box drivers, you must perform the following steps:

1. Obtain the device drivers needed for the hardware on which you will be installing Windows.

2. Launch the Deployment Workbench if it is not already running and expand the node for the deployment share you created earlier.

3. Right-click the Out-of-Box Drivers node in your deployment share and select Import Drivers.

4. Follow the prompts of the Import Drivers Wizard to import the drivers into the deployment share.

Finding and importing device drivers

Device drivers can be one of the most frustrating and problematic aspects of Windows deployment for a number of reasons:

- It can be difficult to find the drivers you need. Some vendors, such as Dell and HP, provide special tools for finding and downloading drivers for their hardware, and you will have to learn how to use their tools.

- Device drivers must be in a certain form before you can import them into the Deployment Workbench. Specifically, you need the driver's INF file. If the vendor makes its drivers available as .cab files, you can easily extract these into a folder and import them into the Deployment Workbench. If the vendor makes them available as Setup programs (.exe files), however, you might need to use a third-party tool like WinRAR to extract the driver files from the .exe file before you can import them.

- Driver incompatibilities can cause problems during deployment. For example, if you use the wrong mass storage driver when deploying Windows to a system, the installation process might fail. This problem often arises when a deployment share is being used to deploy several different versions of Windows and you have imported all the drivers for each of the versions into the Out-of-Box Drivers folder of your deployment share. When you do this, during the deployment process Windows will decide which drivers to use by using Plug and Play. Unfortunately, with this approach a 32-bit driver might end up getting installed on 64-bit hardware or vice versa, resulting in a failed deployment.

You can prevent such problems by creating a hierarchy of subfolders beneath the Out-of-Box Drivers folder, with each subfolder representing a specific Windows version and architecture. You can then further differentiate drivers according to the make and model of the system hardware to which they apply by creating a deeper subfolder hierarchy, such as the following:

```
Out-Of-Box Drivers
--- Operating System 1
------ Make 1
--------- Model 1
--------- Model 2…
------ Make 2…
--- Operating System 2…
```

You then import the specific drivers needed for each Windows version or architecture into the appropriate driver subfolder. You can then use another MDT feature called *selection profiles* to associate each driver subfolder with a different task sequence, which enables each task sequence being used to deploy a different version or architecture of Windows on each make or model of hardware in your environment. The downside of the driver subfolders approach is that it is more work to set up than just dumping all the drivers into the Out-of-Box Drivers folder and letting Plug and Play decide which ones to use during deployment.

Step 6. Importing applications

If you plan on deploying applications when you deploy Windows to target systems, you can import the application source files into the Applications node of your deployment share. Including applications is common when deploying client versions of Windows, but it is less frequent when deploying server versions of Windows because of the complexity of installing and configuring server applications such as Microsoft Exchange, Microsoft SharePoint, and Microsoft SQL Server.

Step 7. Importing packages

If you need to include software updates, language packs, or other packages when you deploy Windows, you can import these as packages into the Packages node of your deployment share. Packages must be in the form of .cab or .msu files if you want to import them into your deployment share.

> *NOTE* **SOFTWARE UPDATES AND DEPLOYMENT**
>
> Software updates can also be installed on your master installation by specifying a Windows Server Update Services (WSUS) server in the CustomSettings.ini file of your deployment share.

Step 8. Creating a task sequence

The next step is to create a task sequence. A *task sequence* defines the series of steps that will be performed during the deployment process and determines whether any additional software or customizations will be included when Windows is installed. For your build lab, you need to create a task sequence of type Standard Server Task Sequences that can be used to deploy Windows, with any additional software or customizations indicated, onto the reference computer. You can also use this task sequence to run Sysprep on the deployed installation of Windows, capture an image of the installation, and copy it to the Captures folder of the deployment share on your technician computer.

You can create task sequences by right-clicking the Task Sequences subfolder of a deployment share and selecting New Task Sequence to launch the New Task Sequence Wizard, shown in Figure 2-6.

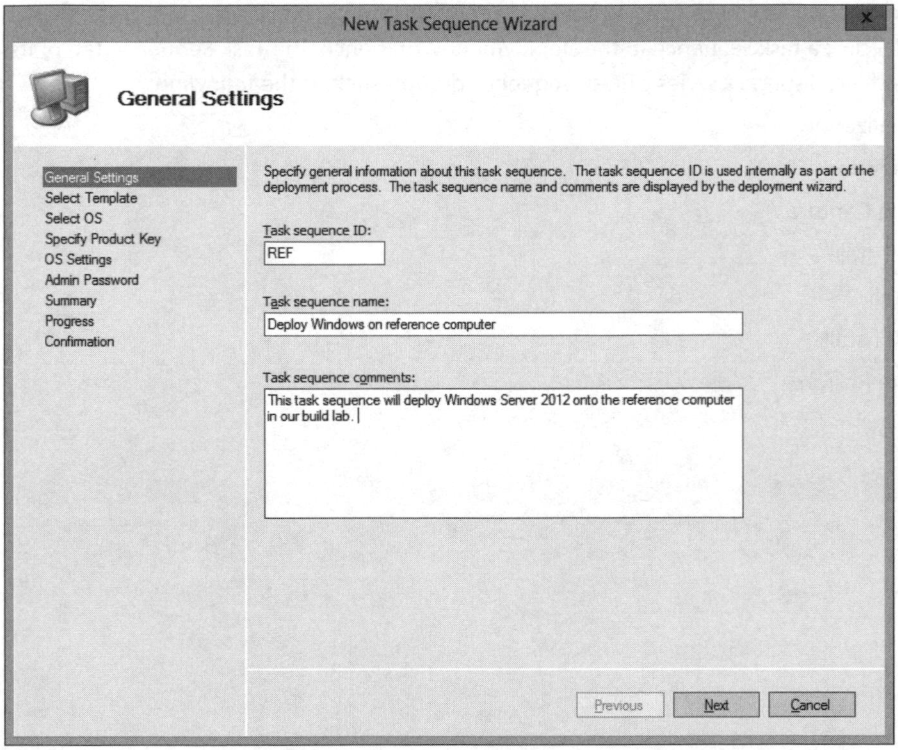

FIGURE 2-6 Create a new task sequence for deploying Windows to the reference computer.

Step 9. Automating the deployment process

At this point, you can choose to automate some or all of the deployment process in your build lab. You can implement automation in two ways. First, you can automate the general flow of the deployment process by modifying the two configuration files associated with the deployment share, located at C:\DeploymentShare$\Control:

- **BootStrap.ini**   This file contains any information needed to successfully establish a connection between the deployment share and the computer on which Windows will be installed.

- **CustomSettings.ini**   This file is used to control the remainder of the deployment process by displaying or hiding various pages of the Windows Deployment Wizard, which runs on the computer on which Windows is being installed.

Second, you can automate various aspects of the deployment process by making modifications to the task sequence used to perform your deployment. As Figure 2-7 shows, when you double-click a task sequence in the Deployment Workbench, the Task Sequence tab of its properties sheet displays a series of task-sequence groups, such as the following:

- Initialization
- Validation
- State Capture
- Preinstall
- Install
- Postinstall
- State Restore

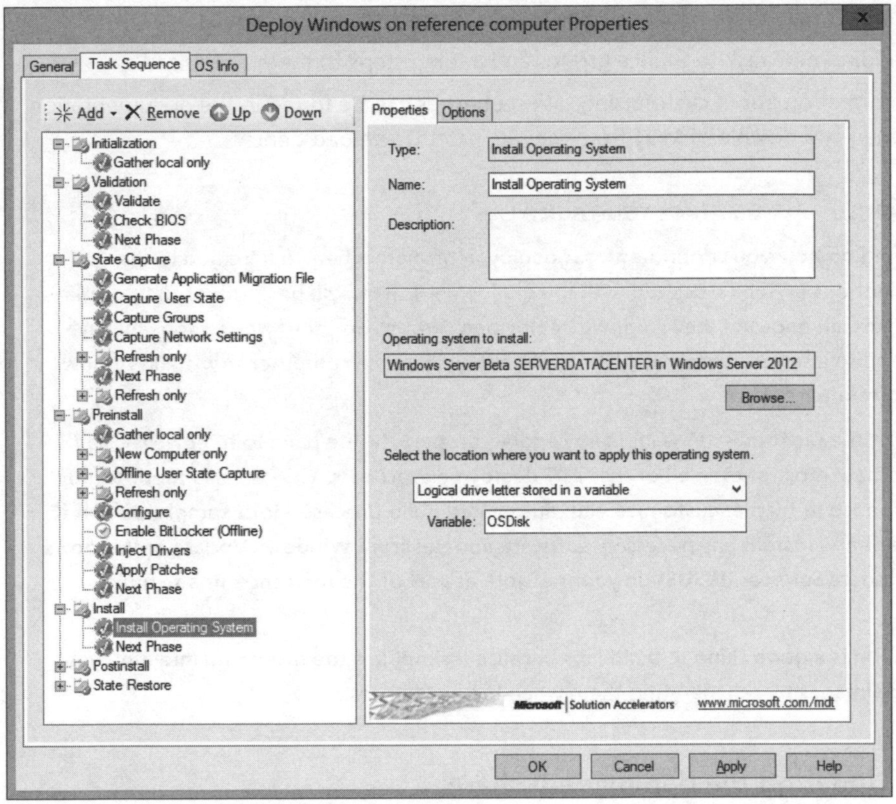

FIGURE 2-7 Customize a task sequence.

Each task-sequence group corresponds to a particular phase of the deployment process and consists of one or more task-sequence steps. For example, the Validation phase, which identifies whether the target computer is capable of running the scripts necessary to complete the deployment process, performs the following three steps in the order shown:

1. **Validate**   Verifies that the target computer meets the specified deployment prerequisite conditions

2. **Check BIOS**   Checks the BIOS of the target computer to ensure that it is compatible with the operating system you are deploying

3. **Next Phase**   Updates the *Phase* property to the next phase in the deployment process

You can customize your task sequences in the following ways:

- By modifying the values and selections of properties on different task-sequence step pages

- By moving selected task-sequence groups or steps up or down to change when they take place during the overall deployment process

- By adding new task-sequence steps to existing task-sequence groups
- By adding new task-sequence groups and adding steps to them as desired

More information about customizing task sequences can be found in the documentation included when you download MDT from the Microsoft Download Center.

REAL WORLD **AUTOMATING YOUR BUILD LAB**

Depending on how you configured your deployment share when you created it, the CustomSettings.ini file associated with the deployment share will be configured to display most (if not all) pages of the Windows Deployment Wizard. In other words, you will have to respond to a series of prompts displayed on the reference computer to install Windows on the computer.

If you edit the CustomSettings.ini file by adding property/value pairs to it, however, you can automate most or even all of the MDT deployment process. You can also modify your task sequence to further customize your automated build process—for example, so that it downloads and installs any necessary software updates from Windows Update or Windows Server Update Services (WSUS) on your network as part of the reference-image build process.

Automation is a good thing in build labs because it simplifies the task of maintaining your reference images by regenerating them when the need arises.

Step 10. Updating the deployment share

Before you can use the technician computer to build a reference image, you must update the deployment share to create or regenerate the boot images that will be used to kick-start the deployment process on the reference computer. To update a deployment share, right-click it, select Update Deployment Share, and follow the wizard prompts. Updating a deployment share might take several minutes. The process creates two types of boot media:

- **LiteTouchPE_*arch*.iso** ISO files can be created for two architectures (x64 and x86) and can be either burned or copied to installation media and used to boot physical computers or attached to virtual machines to boot them into the deployment process.
- **LiteTouchPE_*arch*.wim** WIM files can also be created for two architectures (x64 and x86) and imported into a Windows Deployment Services server (if you have one) to enable target systems (physical or virtual) to PXE-boot into the deployment process.

NOTE **SELECTING BOOT IMAGE FORMAT**

Because Windows Server 2012 and later can be installed only on x64 system hardware, you must use either the LiteTouchPE_x64.wim or LiteTouchPE_x64.wim files as your boot image for kick-starting the deployment process. You cannot use ISO or WIM files for the x86 architecture for deploying Windows Server 2012 or Windows Server 2012 R2.

Step 11. Deploying the master image and capturing the reference image

At this point, you are ready to use your technician computer to deploy Windows Server 2012 or later, along with any additional software or customizations you have specified, to the reference computer in your build lab. To do this, you complete the following steps:

1. Boot the bare-metal reference computer by using the boot image (either ISO or WIM) created in step 10.

2. Proceed through the steps of the Windows Deployment Wizard as they appear on the reference computer, responding to each prompt as appropriate. For example, on the Capture Image page shown in Figure 2-8, you can select the option Capture An Image Of This Reference Computer, which installs Windows, runs Sysprep, captures an image, and copies the image over the network to the Captures folder of your deployment share on your technician computer.

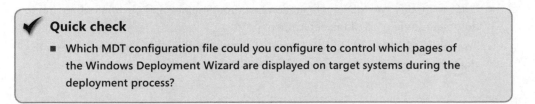

FIGURE 2-8 Specify that an image be captured when the installation is finished.

✔ **Quick check**

- Which MDT configuration file could you configure to control which pages of the Windows Deployment Wizard are displayed on target systems during the deployment process?

Testing reference images

After you build your reference image, you should first deploy it on a test system in your build lab to make sure everything works as intended. Depending on whether your production environment has physical servers or virtual machines, you can choose either physical servers or virtual machines as your test system.

To test your reference image, use your build lab to do the following:

1. Create a new task sequence of type Standard Server Task Sequence that you will use to deploy your reference image to your test system.

2. Prepare your boot media for the deployment process by doing one of the following:

   ■ Burning the LiteTouchPE_64.iso file to DVD media for manually booting a physical test system

   ■ Attaching the LiteTouchPE_64.iso to a virtual machine for manually booting a virtual test system

   ■ Importing the LiteTouchPE_64.wim file into a Windows Deployment Services server for automatically booting a test system (physical or virtual) by using PXE boot

3. Boot the test system and deploy your reference image onto it.

4. When the deployment process has completed, log on to your test system and verify that the software and customizations you specified to be included in the installation have been installed and applied as intended.

When you're satisfied that your reference image works properly, you are ready to deploy it onto systems in your production environment.

Lesson summary

■ The ADK for Windows 8.1 should be installed on the technician computer before installing MDT 2013.

■ A deployment share is a shared folder on the technician computer that can contain operating-system source files, out-of-box drivers, applications, packages such as software updates, task sequences, and other advanced configuration features.

■ You can modify two MDT configuration files (BootStrap.ini and CustomSettings.ini) to automate some or all of the deployment process.

■ You can customize task sequences to modify which actions are performed during the deployment process.

- Updating a deployment share generates boot media that can be used to kick-start the deployment process.
- You can use MDT in your build lab to deploy a reference computer and to sysprep and capture its installation as a reference image.

Lesson review

Answer the following questions to test your knowledge of the information in this lesson. You can find the answers to these questions and explanations of why each answer choice is correct or incorrect in the "Answers" section at the end of this chapter.

1. Which of the following is *not* a software prerequisite for installing MDT 2013 on a technician computer running Windows 7 to deploy Windows Server 2012 R2?

   A. Microsoft Management Console version 3.0

   B. Microsoft .NET Framework 3.5 with Service Pack 1 (SP1) or later

   C. Windows PowerShell version 2.0 or later

   D. The latest version of the Windows Automated Installation Kit (Windows AIK)

2. When building reference images, what step should you always perform after importing your operating-system source files, out-of-box drivers, applications, and packages into your deployment share; creating and customizing any necessary task sequences; and modifying the configuration files for your deployment share?

   A. Deploy and capture the reference image.

   B. Update the deployment share.

   C. Create selection profiles.

   D. Create linked deployment shares.

3. What is the name of the task-sequence group that controls the phase of the deployment process during which the BIOS of the target computer is checked to ensure that it is compatible with the operating system you are deploying?

   A. Validate

   B. Preinstall

   C. Install

   D. Postinstall

Lesson 4: Deploying images

After you build your customized reference image of Windows Server 2012 or later, you can use various tools and approaches for deploying the image in your production environment. In addition to manual installations, which are suitable only for organizations that have a handful of computers to deploy, the two main deployment strategies are *Lite Touch Installation (LTI)* and *Zero Touch Installation (ZTI)*.

After this lesson, you will be able to:

- Make decisions concerning which deployment strategy and tools should be used to set up the deployment infrastructure of your production environment.
- Explain the LTI approach to deploying Windows images and the tools needed for this approach.
- Describe the steps involved in performing an LTI deployment using a reference image created in a build lab.
- Explain the ZTI approach to deploying Windows images and the tools needed for this approach.
- Describe what System Center Configuration Manager provides for deployment that MDT with Windows Deployment Services doesn't provide.
- Describe some of the benefits of integrating MDT with System Center Configuration Manager.

Estimated lesson time: 15 minutes

Preparing the deployment infrastructure

Setting up the deployment infrastructure for your production environment involves making the following decisions:

- Which type of deployment strategy (LTI or ZTI) best meets the needs of your business
- What deployment tools are needed to implement your deployment strategy

Figure 2-9 shows the general setup for a deployment infrastructure in a production environment. For the LTI approach, all components except System Center Configuration Manager are generally required. For the ZTI approach, all the components shown should usually be used.

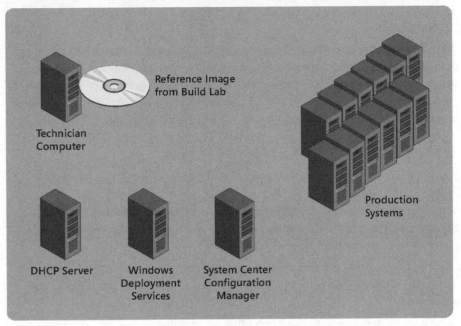

FIGURE 2-9 This is the general setup for a production-environment deployment structure.

Using the LTI approach

LTI is a high-volume deployment strategy for small to midsized organizations that combines MDT with Windows Deployment Services, a server role of Windows Server 2008 and later that enables new computers to be deployed through network-based installation. By including Windows Deployment Services in the deployment infrastructure of your production environment, target systems such as bare-metal servers can PXE-boot using the LiteTouchPE_x64 .wim boot image created when you update the deployment share in the MDT Deployment Workbench.

In a deployment infrastructure based on MDT and Windows Deployment Services, the deployment process works like this:

1. In your build lab, create a reference image of Windows Server 2012 or later with any applications, drivers, software updates, or packages needed for servers in your production environment.

2. The next step depends on whether your build lab is isolated from your production environment:

   - If your build lab is isolated from your production environment, copy the deployment share folder from the MDT technician computer in your build lab to removable media. Then paste the deployment share folder into the file system of the technician computer in your production environment, share the folder, open it in the

Deployment Workbench, and update the network path references in the Bootstrap .ini file as needed.

- If your build lab shares network connectivity with your production environment, you can use the Linked Deployment Shares feature to replicate the deployment share in your build lab to the technician computer in your production environment. The advantage of this is that when you make changes to your build lab, the changes are reflected in your production environment. The disadvantage is that you might have task sequences or other customizations in your production environment that should be used only for your build lab.

3. Next use the Deployment Workbench in your production environment to create a Standard Server Task Sequence for deploying your reference image to target systems. Modify the settings in the CustomSettings.ini file to automate the steps of the deployment process. Then update the deployment share to regenerate the boot images in the \Boot folder of your deployment share folder.

4. Import the LiteTouchPE_x64.wim boot image from your deployment share into the Boot Images folder of the Windows Deployment Services server in your production environment.

5. Turn on each target system in your production environment, press F12, and select the option to PXE-boot the system.

6. The target systems then download the LTI boot image from the Windows Deployment Services server, connect to the deployment share, and install the reference image.

Using the ZTI approach

ZTI is a high-volume deployment strategy for midsized to large organizations that combines MDT with System Center Configuration Manager, which is part of the System Center family of products from Microsoft. System Center Configuration Manager provides a complete systems management platform that organizations can use to do the following:

- Deploy operating systems, applications, and software updates
- Monitor and remediate computers for compliance purposes
- Monitor hardware and perform software inventorying
- Remotely administer computers

Compared to the LTI approach, which uses MDT with Windows Deployment Services, the ZTI approach to deployment, which uses System Center Configuration Manager, provides the following additional benefits:

- Support for replication. (MDT requires using Distributed File System Replication.)
- Support for performing multicast deployment. (MDT requires using Windows Deployment Services.)
- Support for the bandwidth management of image transfers.
- Support for reporting on driver availability for devices across your organization.

- Support for complex repartitioning schemes and for formatting disks. (This can also be done using MDT, but it requires custom scripting using Diskpart.)
- Tolerance of poor or intermittent network connectivity.
- Support for client operating system–initiated deployment.
- Support for fully unattended deployment.
- Support for offline deployment from media and CD/DVD spanning.
- Support for encryption and password protection.

Although System Center Configuration Manager can be used by itself for deploying Windows to target systems, integrating MDT with System Center Configuration Manager provides additional advantages, such as task-sequence templates for different types of deployment scenarios, wizards to create packages and task sequences from MDT templates, wizards to create new boot images, and more.

To deploy Windows Server 2012 R2 using the ZTI approach, you should use the following:

- MDT 2013
- System Center Configuration Manager 2012 R2

> **MORE INFO** **SYSTEM CENTER CONFIGURATION MANAGER 2012 R2**
>
> For more information on System Center Configuration Manager 2012 R2, visit the System Center Technical Resources page on TechNet at *http://technet.microsoft.com/en-us /systemcenter/default*.

Lesson summary

- Key decisions in planning a deployment infrastructure for a production environment are selecting a deployment strategy and choosing tools for implementing your strategy.
- LTI is a high-volume deployment strategy for small to midsized organizations that combines MDT with Windows Deployment Services.
- Windows Deployment Services enables bare-metal target systems to PXE-boot using the LiteTouchPE_x64.wim boot image created when your MDT deployment share is updated.
- ZTI is a high-volume deployment strategy for midsized to large organizations that combines MDT with System Center Configuration Manager.
- The ZTI approach to deployment using System Center Configuration Manager provides many additional benefits over LTI, especially for larger organizations.
- Although System Center Configuration Manager can be used by itself for deploying Windows to target systems, combining System Center Configuration Manager with MDT provides some additional advantages.

Lesson review

Answer the following questions to test your knowledge of the information in this lesson. You can find the answers to these questions and explanations of why each answer choice is correct or incorrect in the "Answers" section at the end of this chapter.

1. Which of the following is *not* true concerning the LTI approach? (Choose all that apply.)

   A. LTI is a high-volume deployment strategy for midsized to large organizations that combines MDT with System Center Configuration Manager.

   B. You use LTI to deploy the reference images created in your build lab onto systems in your production environment.

   C. You can use LTI to deploy Windows Server 2012 R2 onto physical systems only, not virtual machines.

   D. You can start LTI by pressing F12 on each target system and selecting the option to PXE-boot the system.

2. Which of the following are benefits of using the ZTI approach over LTI? (Choose all that apply.)

   A. Support for bandwidth management of image transfer

   B. Support for reporting on driver availability for devices across your organization

   C. Tolerance of poor or intermittent network connectivity

   D. Support for fully unattended deployment

Practice exercises

The goal of this section is to provide you with hands-on practice with the following:

- Converting between installation options
- Building a reference image by using MDT 2013

To perform the following exercises, you need the following:

- A server with a clean installation of Windows Server 2012 R2 using the Server With A GUI installation option. The server should be a stand-alone server belonging to a workgroup, have Internet connectivity, and have no additional roles or features installed. You should be logged on interactively to the server using a user account that is a member of the local Administrators group. For the purposes of these exercises, the name of the server is assumed to be SERVER1.

- A second server that meets the requirements for installing Windows Server 2012 R2 but that currently has no operating system installed. This server should be connected to the same network as the first server. It will be used as the reference computer for Exercise 2.

Both servers can be either physical server systems or virtual machines running on a Hyper-V host. If your Hyper-V host is running Windows Server 2008 R2, you must install the hotfix described in *http://support.microsoft.com/kb/2744129* before virtual machines with Windows Server 2012 R2 installed can run on the host. This is not an issue if your Hyper-V host has Windows Server 2012 or later installed.

If you will be using physical server systems for Exercise 2, you will need a DVD writer drive and recordable DVD media so you can burn the .iso boot image file created by MDT onto DVD media to deploy the image onto your reference computer.

Exercise 1: Converting between installation options

In this exercise, you install and configure a Server Core installation of Windows Server 2012 R2. You then use Windows PowerShell to convert your server first to a Minimal Server Interface installation and then to a Server With A GUI installation, using a locally mounted image rather than over the Internet.

1. Boot your server using Windows Server 2012 R2 installation media. If you are using a bare-metal physical server, insert your installation media and turn on the server. If you are using a new virtual machine, select the Install An Operating System From A Boot CD/DVD-ROM option on the Installation Options page of the New Virtual Machine Wizard, select the .iso image file for your installation media, complete the wizard, and start the virtual machine.

2. When the Windows Setup Wizard appears, verify your language, time/currency, and keyboard/input settings and then click Next.

3. On the next wizard page, click Install Now.

4. On the Select The Operating System You Want To Install page, select Windows Server 2012 R2 (Server Core Installation) and then click Next.

5. On the License Terms page, read and accept the license terms and then click Next.

6. On the Which Type Of Installation Do You Want? page, click Custom: Install Windows Only (Advanced).

7. On the Where Do You Want To Install Windows? page, click Next to begin installing Windows. Your server will reboot several times during the installation process.

8. When the installation is finished and the logon screen appears, click OK, type a password for the built-in Administrator account twice, press Enter, and click OK to log on to your server. Because you installed Windows Server 2012 R2 using the Server Core Installation option, you will see only a command prompt window and no desktop.

9. Type **sconfig** and press Enter to run the Server Configuration command-line utility.

10. Type **2**, press Enter, and then type **SERVER1** as the new name for your server. Press Enter twice, wait for your server to restart, and then log on again as Administrator.

11. Type **sconfig** in the command prompt window to run the Server Configuration command-line utility again. Press Enter whenever needed to select configuration options and run commands.

12. Type **8** to display a list of network adapters on the server. Make a note of the index number of an active network adapter, type this index number, and then press Enter.

13. Type **1** to configure IP address settings for the selected adapter.

14. Type **S** to specify that the adapter will have a static IP address assigned to it. Note that you must choose the IP address, subnet mask, default gateway, and DNS server settings you assign to the adapter to enable your server to have connectivity with the Internet.

15. Type the IP address you want to assign to the adapter.

16. Type the subnet mask you want to assign to the adapter.

17. Type the default gateway you want to assign to the adapter.

18. Type **2** to configure DNS server settings for the adapter.

19. Type the IP address of the preferred DNS server you want to assign to the adapter.

20. Type the IP address of the alternate DNS server you want to assign to the adapter.

21. Type **4** to return to the main menu of the Sconfig.exe utility.

22. Type **6** to verify that your server has Internet connectivity by checking Windows Update for any recommended updates for your server.

23. In the new command prompt window that opens, type **R** to search only for recommended updates for your server.

24. When a list of recommended updates appears, type **A** to download and install all recommended updates on your server.

25. If a Restart Required dialog box appears, click Yes, wait for your server to restart, and then log on again as Administrator.

26. Type **mmc.exe** in the command prompt window and verify that the Microsoft Management Console (MMC) is not available in the Server Core Installation option.

27. Disconnect your server from the network so that it cannot access the Internet.

28. Type **mkdir C:\mountdir** to create a new folder to mount the install.wim file found in the \sources folder of your installation media.

29. Type **dism /get-wiminfo /wimfile:<*drive*>:sources\install.wim**, where <*drive*> is the drive letter for your server's bootable media. Make a note of the index number of a Server With A GUI image in the install.wim file.

30. Type **dism /mount-wim /wimfile:<drive>:\sources\install.wim /index:<index_number> /mountdir:C:\mountdir /readonly** to mount the image that has the index number you noted in the previous step.

31. Type **powershell** and press Enter to change the command prompt window to a Windows PowerShell console.

32. Run the command **Install-WindowsFeature Server-Gui-Mgmt-Infra –Restart –Source C:\mountdir\windows\winsxs** to convert your server from a Server Core

installation to a Minimal Server Interface installation. When the feature is finished installing, wait for your server to restart and then log on again as Administrator.

33. Close the Server Manager console when it opens.

34. Type **mmc.exe** and press Enter in the command prompt window and verify that the Microsoft Management Console (MMC) is available in the Minimal Server Interface option.

35. Close the MMC and reconnect your server to the network so that it can access the Internet again.

36. Type **powershell** and press Enter to change the command prompt window to a Windows PowerShell console.

37. Run the command **Install-WindowsFeature Server-Gui-Shell –Restart** to convert your server from a Minimal Server Interface installation to a Server With A GUI installation. Because the feature you are installing must first be downloaded from Windows Update, the installation might take several minutes to complete. When the feature is finished installing, wait for your server to restart and then log on again as Administrator.

38. Verify that the server now has a standard Windows desktop that includes all administrative tools and utilities.

Exercise 2: Building a reference image by using MDT 2013

In this exercise, you install and configure MDT 2013 and its prerequisites on SERVER1, your stand-alone server running Windows Server 2012 R2 that you used in the previous exercise. You then use MDT to deploy Windows Server 2012 R2 on a reference computer (your other server system), run Sysprep.exe on the installation, capture an image from it, and upload the captured reference image to the deployment share on your technician computer.

1. Log on to the Server With A GUI installation of Windows Server 2012 R2 that you used in Exercise 1 using a user account that is a member of the built-in Administrators group on the server.

2. When Server Manager opens, select Local Server from the navigation pane.

3. Make sure that the Computer Name property displays SERVER1. If it doesn't, click the current server name and change the name of the server to SERVER1. Reboot the server when prompted and return to step 1 above.

4. Make sure that the network interface card (NIC) on the server has TCP/IP configured properly so that the server has connectivity with the Internet. If it doesn't, click the current NIC settings and manually configure an IP address, subnet mask, default gateway, and DNS server address as needed.

5. On the Local Server page, in the Properties tile, change the IE Enhanced Security Configuration setting from On to Off for Administrators.

6. Press **Windows key+R,** type **iexplore**, and press OK to launch Internet Explorer in desktop mode.

7. Open the URL *http://www.microsoft.com/en-us/download/details.aspx?id=39982* in Internet Explorer and use it to download the ADK for Windows 8.1 installation bootstrap file (adksetup.exe) from the Microsoft Download Center.

8. Double-click the bootstrap file to launch the Assessment And Deployment Kit installation wizard and accept the default options on the Specify Location, Join The Customer Experience Improvement Program, and License Agreement pages.

9. On the Select The Features You Want To Install page, make sure only the following options are selected:

   ■ Deployment Tools

   ■ Windows Preinstallation Environment (Windows PE)

10. Click Install to install the selected ADK components on the computer. Note that the installation might take some time because of the size of the download.

11. Download the Windows Installer (.msi) file for the x64 version of MDT 2013 from the Microsoft Download Center by following the link on the Microsoft Deployment Toolkit home page at *http://www.microsoft.com/en-us/download /details.aspx?id=40796&fwLinkID=325278*.

12. Double-click the .msi file to launch the Setup Wizard and follow the prompts to accept the Microsoft Software License Terms and install the default MDT components.

13. Press the Windows key to switch to the modern user interface.

14. Click the Deployment Workbench tile to launch the Deployment Workbench.

15. Right-click the Deployment Shares node in the console tree and select New Deployment Share.

16. Proceed through the New Deployment Share Wizard using the default options on the Path, Share, and Descriptive Name pages.

17. On the Options page, clear all the check boxes except the one labeled Ask If An Image Should Be Captured.

18. Finish the wizard to create the deployment share.

19. Right-click the Operating Systems node of your deployment share and select Import Operating System.

20. Proceed through the Import Operating System Wizard using the default options on all pages except for the Source page, where you must specify the path to a directory where the Windows Server 2012 R2 installation files can be found. For example, you could specify the DVD drive on the computer where your Windows Server 2012 R2 installation media has been inserted.

21. Right-click the Task Sequences node of your deployment share and select New Task Sequence.

22. On the General Settings page of the New Task Sequence Wizard, type **REFIMG** as the task sequence ID and **Capture Reference Image** as the task sequence name.

23. On the Select Template page, leave Standard Server Task Sequence selected.

24. On the Select OS page, select a Windows image that doesn't have CORE as part of its name.

25. On the Specify Product Key page, leave the option Do Not Specify A Product Key selected.

26. On the OS Settings page, type **Contoso Ltd.** in the Organization field.

27. On the Admin Password page, type **Pa$$w0rd** in both fields.

28. Complete the wizard to create your new task sequence.

29. In the Task Sequences node of your deployment share, right-click the new task sequence you created and select Properties.

30. Switch to the Task Sequence tab of the properties sheet.

31. Expand the State Restore task-sequence group to show the task-sequence steps within it.

32. Click the Windows Update (Pre-Application Installation) step to display its properties.

33. Switch to the Options tab for this step and clear the following two check boxes:
    - Disable This Step
    - Continue On Error

34. Click Apply and verify that the Windows Update (Pre-Application Installation) step now has a green check-mark icon beside it.

35. Click the Windows Update (Post-Application Installation) step to display its properties.

36. Switch to the Options tab for this step and clear the following two check boxes:
    - Disable This Step
    - Continue On Error

37. Click Apply and verify that the Windows Update (Post-Application Installation) step now has a green check-mark icon beside it.

38. Click OK to close the properties of your task sequence.

39. Right-click the node representing your deployment share and select Update Deployment Share.

40. Accept the default options of the Update Deployment Share Wizard to update your deployment share and create boot media for kick-starting the deployment process. This might take several minutes to complete.

41. If your build lab is using virtual machines in a Hyper-V environment, copy the LiteTouchPE_x64.iso file from the C:\DeploymentShare\Boot folder on your technician

computer to a shared folder (for example, C:\Boot) on your host machine. Make sure the shared folder has NTFS and shared folder permissions to allow Everyone full access to the contents of the folder. If your build lab is using physical systems instead of virtual machines, burn the preceding ISO file to bootable media.

42. If your build lab is using virtual machines, create a new virtual machine as your reference computer, configure it to connect to the virtual network on which your technician computer virtual machine resides and assign the LiteTouchPE_x64.iso file to the virtual DVD drive of your new virtual machine. Then start the new virtual machine and open the virtual machine in a Virtual Machine Connection window. If your build lab is using physical systems, insert your bootable media into the reference system and turn on the system.

43. When the Welcome screen for Microsoft Deployment Toolkit appears on your reference computer, click Configure With Static IP Address.

44. In the Configure Network screen that appears next, clear the Enable DHCP check box and specify an IP address, subnet mask, default gateway, and DNS server address so that your reference computer can communicate with both your technician computer and the Internet. Then click Finish to return to the Welcome screen and click Run The Deployment Wizard To Install A New Operating System.

45. In the User Credentials dialog box, type **Administrator** for the user name, type **Pa$$w0rd** for the password, and type the host name of your technician computer for the domain. (If your technician computer is domain-joined, you can specify the AD DS domain name instead of the host name.)

46. Click OK to launch the Windows Deployment Wizard.

47. On the Task Sequence page, select the task sequence named Capture Reference Image you created earlier and click Next.

48. On the Computer Details page, type **REFCOMP** as the computer name and click Next.

49. Verify the language and time settings on the Local And Time page and then click Next.

50. On the Capture Image page, select Capture An Image Of This Reference Computer. Make a note of the file name that will be assigned to the captured .wim file and the folder to which the .wim file will be uploaded on the technician computer and then click Next.

51. On the Ready page, click Begin to start the deployment process. Observe the following actions as they are being performed:

   A. Information is gathered about the reference computer.

   B. The operating system is installed on the reference computer.

   C. Software updates are downloaded from Windows Update and installed on the reference computer.

D. The Windows installation on the reference computer is sysprepped to remove machine-specific information.

E. The Windows installation on the reference computer is captured as a .wim file, and this file is then uploaded to your technician computer.

52. When the deployment is finished, verify that a reference image named REFIMG.wim now exists in the Captures subfolder of the deployment share on your technician computer.

Suggested practice exercises

The following additional practice exercises are designed to give you more opportunities to practice what you've learned and to help you successfully master the lessons presented in this chapter:

- **Exercise 1**   Modify the CustomSettings.ini file in Exercise 2 of this lesson to hide all pages of the Windows Deployment Wizard by providing responses to the information for which these pages would prompt you when you deploy Windows Server 2012 R2 onto your reference computer.

- **Exercise 2**   Set up an LTI deployment infrastructure with MDT, Windows Deployment Services, and a DHCP server and use it to deploy the reference image you created in Exercise 2 of this lesson to a physical system that meets the requirements for installing Windows Server 2012 R2.

- **Exercise 3**   Download an evaluation copy of System Center Configuration Manager 2012 R2 from the TechNet Evaluation Center and learn how to perform a ZTI deployment of the reference image you created in Exercise 2 of this lesson.

Answers

This section contains the answers to the lesson review questions in this chapter.

Lesson 1

1. **Correct answer: B**

    A. **Incorrect:** The Server With A GUI installation option has one more installed feature than the Minimal Server Interface option and two more than the Server Core option.

    B. **Correct:** The Server Core installation option requires the least disk space.

    C. **Incorrect:** The Minimal Server Interface installation option has one more installed feature than the Server Core option.

    D. **Incorrect:** Full installation is the name used for the Server With A GUI installation option on previous versions of Windows Server.

2. **Correct answer: D**

    A. **Incorrect:** To convert a Server Core installation to a Server With A GUI installation, you can use the following command:

    ```
    Install-WindowsFeature Server-Gui-Mgmt-Infra,Server-Gui-Shell -Restart
    ```

    B. **Incorrect:** To convert a Server With A GUI installation to a Server Core installation, you can use the following command:

    ```
    Uninstall-WindowsFeature Server-Gui-Mgmt-Infra,Server-Gui-Shell -Restart
    ```

    C. **Incorrect:** To convert a Server Core installation to a Minimal Server Interface installation, you can use the following command:

    ```
    Install-WindowsFeature Server-Gui-Mgmt-Infra -Restart
    ```

    D. **Correct:** This command will convert a Server With A GUI installation to a Minimal Server Interface installation.

3. **Correct answers: A and B**

    A. **Correct:** If you have any roles or features installed on your server that are not needed, you can reduce the server's disk footprint by uninstalling them. When you do this, however, the binaries for these roles and features will remain staged in the local side-by-side store on the server.

    B. **Correct:** You can use the Uninstall-WindowsFeature cmdlet with the *–Remove* parameter to completely remove the binaries of a role or feature from the local side-by-side store on the server. Doing this can further reduce the disk footprint of your server.

C. Incorrect: The *–Source* parameter is used with the Install-WindowsFeature cmdlet to enable roles and features to be installed when their binaries are not present in the local side-by-side store on the server.

D. Incorrect: To remove the binaries for unneeded roles and features from the local side-by-side store on the server, you must use Windows PowerShell. You cannot use Server Manager to do this.

Lesson 2

1. **Correct answers: B and D**

   A. Incorrect: Most of the image engineering process can be performed within a virtual environment running on a Hyper-V host.

   B. Correct: If the servers in the production environment to which you will be deploying your reference image are physical systems, you should use sample physical systems taken from production for testing your reference image.

   C. Incorrect: Automation of the image-building process can be simplified by using a DHCP server to dynamically assign an IP address to your reference computer.

   D. Correct: You must install the necessary tools for building reference images on your technician computer, not your reference computer.

2. **Correct answer: D**

   A. Incorrect: A DHCP server can be used to dynamically assign an IP address to the reference computer.

   B. Incorrect: The technician computer has the necessary tools installed for building reference images.

   C. Incorrect: The reference computer is the system on which the reference image is created.

   D. Correct: The Windows Deployment Services server simplifies the task of deploying the reference image onto the sample physical systems by eliminating the need to burn your boot images onto DVD media to kick-start the reference-image testing process.

3. **Correct answer: C**

   A. Incorrect: The reference computer is the system from which the reference image is created by sysprepping and capturing the installation of Windows on the computer.

   B. Incorrect: The installation of Windows on the reference computer is known as the *reference installation*.

C. Correct: The sysprepped installation of Windows on the reference computer is captured in the form of a Windows Image (.wim) file and copied to the technician computer. The captured, sysprepped image is referred to as the *reference image*.

D. Incorrect: Test computers are systems (virtual or physical) on which the reference image is deployed to verify that the image works as intended.

Lesson 3

1. **Correct answer: D**

   A. Incorrect: Microsoft Management Console version 3.0 is a prerequisite for installing MDT 2013 on a technician computer running Windows 7.

   B. Incorrect: Microsoft .NET Framework 3.5 with Service Pack 1 (SP1) or later is a prerequisite for installing MDT 2013 on a technician computer running Windows 7.

   C. Incorrect: Windows PowerShell version 2.0 or later is a prerequisite for installing MDT 2013 on a technician computer running Windows 7.

   D. Correct: The Windows Assessment and Deployment Kit (ADK) for Windows 8 is a collection of tools you can use to customize, assess, and deploy Windows operating systems to new computers. The ADK supersedes the Windows Automated Installation Kit (Windows AIK) used by earlier versions of MDT, and it includes additional tools that previously had to be downloaded separately.

2. **Correct answer: B**

   A. Incorrect: Before you deploy and capture the reference image, you should update your deployment share to create or regenerate the boot images that will be used to kick-start the deployment process on the reference computer.

   B. Correct: After performing all these steps, you should update your deployment share to create or regenerate the boot images that will be used to kick-start the deployment process on the reference computer.

   C. Incorrect: Selection profiles are an advanced feature of MDT that can optionally be used in a build lab where appropriate.

   D. Incorrect: Linked deployment shares are an advanced feature of MDT that is generally used in the deployment infrastructure of a production environment, not in a build lab.

3. **Correct answer: A**

   A. Correct: The Validate task-sequence group controls the steps in the phase that verifies that the target computer is capable of running the scripts necessary to complete the deployment process. This includes checking that the BIOS of the target computer is compatible with the operating system being deployed.

   B. Incorrect: The Preinstall task-sequence group controls the steps in the phase that completes any tasks that need to be done (such as creating new partitions) before the target operating system is installed on the target computer.

C. **Incorrect:** The Install task-sequence group controls the steps in the phase that installs the target operating system on the target computer.

D. **Incorrect:** The Postinstall task-sequence group controls the steps in the phase that completes any tasks that need to be done before restoring the user-state migration data. These tasks customize the target operating system before starting the target computer the first time (such as installing updates or adding drivers).

Lesson 4

1. **Correct answers: A and C**

    A. **Correct:** ZTI is a high-volume deployment strategy for midsized to large organizations that combines MDT with System Center Configuration Manager. LTI is a high-volume deployment strategy for small to midsized organizations that combines MDT with Windows Deployment Services, a server role of Windows Server 2008 and later that enables new computers to be deployed through network-based installation.

    B. **Incorrect:** To use LTI to deploy Windows Server 2012 R2, begin in your build lab by creating a reference image of Windows Server 2012 R2 with any applications, drivers, software updates, or packages needed for servers in your production environment.

    C. **Correct:** LTI can be used to deploy Windows Server 2012 R2 onto both physical systems and virtual machines.

    D. **Incorrect:** LTI can be started by pressing F12 on each target system and selecting the option to PXE-boot the system using a Windows Deployment Services server.

2. **Correct answers: A, B, C, and D**

    A. **Correct:** System Center Configuration Manager provides support for bandwidth management of an image transfer. MDT alone does not.

    B. **Correct:** System Center Configuration Manager provides support for reporting on driver availability for devices across your organization. MDT alone does not.

    C. **Correct:** System Center Configuration Manager tolerates poor or intermittent network connectivity. MDT alone does not.

    D. **Correct:** System Center Configuration Manager provides support for fully unattended deployment. MDT alone does not.

CHAPTER 3

Server remote management

S erver management deals with the performance of key operational tasks on servers in your environment. These tasks include occasional or one-time tasks like adding new a new role or feature to a server, periodic tasks such as reviewing event logs, and urgent tasks like troubleshooting alert messages. In small and midsized environments, you can perform many of these tasks manually by using the graphical user interface (GUI) server-management tools included in Microsoft Windows Server platforms. In large environments such as data centers and cloud-computing infrastructures, most operational tasks are auto-mated using scripts.

Windows Server 2012 and Windows Server 2012 R2 include two main tools for remote server management: Server Manager and the Windows PowerShell scripting platform. You can use these two tools to manage both the physical and virtual servers within your organi-zation's infrastructure. This chapter introduces the capabilities of these tools and shows how you can use them to manage Windows servers across your environment.

Lessons in this chapter:

Before you begin

To complete the practice exercises in this chapter

- You need to know how to perform a clean install of Windows Server 2012 R2 and perform initial configuration tasks like configuring the server's TCP/IP settings for Internet connectivity.

- You also should have at least rudimentary knowledge of using Windows PowerShell.

Lesson 1: Server Manager

Server Manager was completely redesigned in Windows Server 2012 to make it easier for administrators to simultaneously manage multiple Windows servers remotely. Server Manager is capable of managing large numbers of servers, but it is intended mainly for small and midsized environments that typically have no more than a few dozen servers deployed at a site. This lesson introduces the features of Server Manager in Windows Server 2012 and Windows Server 2012 R2 and demonstrates how to perform some common server management tasks.

> **After this lesson, you will be able to:**
> - Use Server Manager pages to configure the local server.
> - Use Server Manager to manage multiple remote servers.
> - Configure Windows servers for remote management.
> - Deploy the Remote Server Management Tools (RSAT) for Windows 8.1.
>
> **Estimated lesson time: 30 minutes**

Navigating Server Manager

To use Server Manager effectively, you need to be able to navigate through its various controls, menus, and pages. This section summarizes the most important things you need to know in this area.

Menus

At the top of Server Manager (shown in Figure 3-1), you find the following controls and menus:

- Back and forward buttons you can use to navigate through the history of the pages you previously selected
- A breadcrumb you can use to navigate quickly through any hierarchical views
- A refresh button you can use to manually refresh Server Manager when its view becomes out of date
- The Notifications flag, which you can use to view any alerts or information about tasks being performed on the servers you are managing
- The Manage menu, which you can use to add roles and features to (or remove them from) the servers you are managing, add servers to the pool of managed servers, create new server groups, and configure Server Manager properties
- The Tools menu, which you can use to access other management tools such as Microsoft Management Console (MMC) consoles, the System Information and

System Configuration utilities, Windows PowerShell consoles and Integrated Scripting Environments (ISEs), and so on

- The View menu, which you can use to zoom your Server Manager view in or out and show or hide the Welcome To Server Manager information on the Dashboard

- The Help menu, which includes a link to the Server Manager forums on TechNet

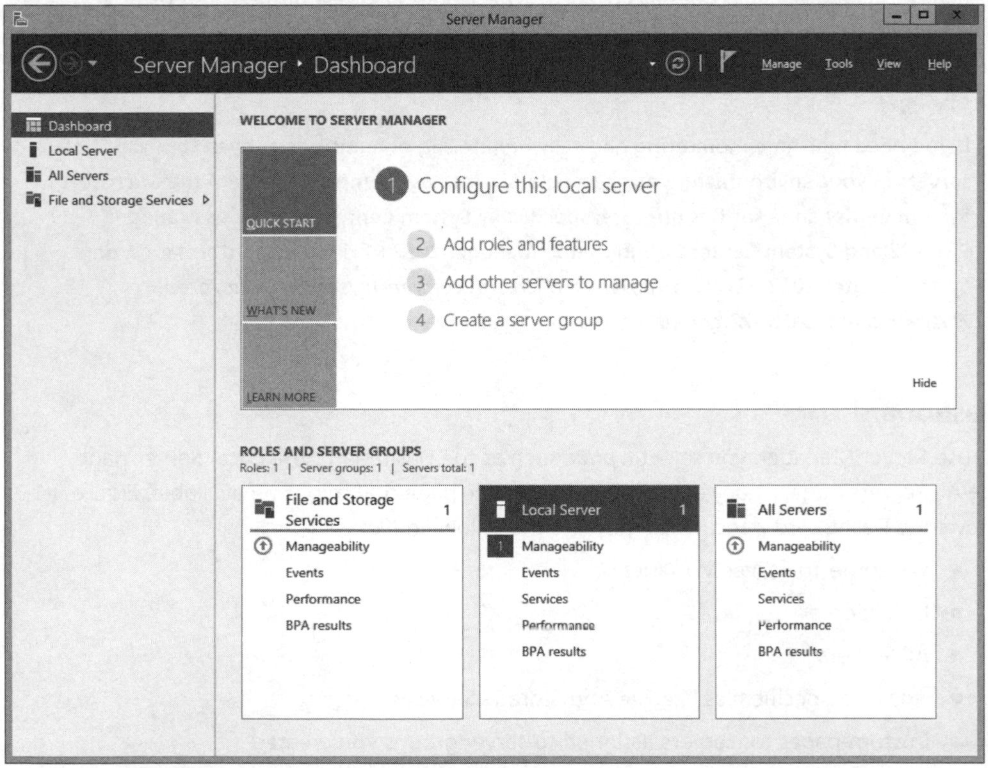

FIGURE 3-1 The Dashboard page of Server Manager includes various controls and menus along the top.

> *NOTE* **KEYBOARD SHORTCUTS FOR SERVER MANAGER**
>
> You can also quickly navigate Server Manager by using keyboard shortcuts. For a list of Server Manager keyboard shortcuts, see *http://technet.microsoft.com/en-us/library /jj134206*.

By default, Server Manager refreshes every 10 minutes by collecting updated information for all servers being managed. You can change the refresh interval by opening the Server Manager properties as follows:

1. Click the Manage menu on any page and select Server Manager Properties.

2. In the Server Manager Properties dialog box, specify the desired data refresh period in minutes.

You can also use this dialog box to configure Server Manager to not start automatically at logon.

Dashboard

To use Server Manager, you select a *page* such as the Dashboard, the Local Server page, the All Servers page, or any additional role-specific page that might be available. Figure 3-1 shows the Dashboard page, which displays the following *tiles*:

- Welcome To Server Manager
- Local Server
- All Servers
- Any role-specific tiles like File And Storage Services
- Custom pages for servers assigned to server groups you created

Tiles consist of a title bar with multiple thumbnails beneath. A *thumbnail* reflects certain data collected about the servers being managed. When something is wrong with a server or server role, an alert is raised on the appropriate thumbnail to enable you to take remedial action to correct the problem. The five types of thumbnails displayed in tiles are as follows:

- **Manageability**   Indicates whether servers are online or offline, whether Server Manager is receiving reporting data from specified servers, and any issues with the ability to manage the servers
- **Events**   Displays alerts whenever an event is logged that matches the severity levels, event sources, or event IDs on specified servers during specified time intervals

- **Services**   Displays alerts whenever problems arise with services on managed servers and enables you to attempt to restart the affected services

- **Performance**   Displays performance alerts for different resource types (CPU or memory) on specified servers during specified time intervals

- **BPA Results**   Displays alerts generated from running the Best Practices Analyzer (BPA) against managed servers

> *MORE INFO*   **BEST PRACTICES ANALYZER**
>
> The Best Practices Analyzer functionality included in Windows Server 2012 and Windows Server 2012 R2 is demonstrated in Chapter 4, "Deploying domain controllers."

If the title bar of any of the tiles on the Dashboard (with the exception of the Welcome To Server Manager tile) is colored red, one or more alerts have been raised. For example, in Figure 3-1 the title bar of the Local Server tile is colored red. A red box with the number 1 is also displayed next to the Manageability thumbnail in this title to indicate that the alert has to do with the manageability of the local server. To view more information concerning this alert, click the Manageability thumbnail in this tile. To go directly to the Local Server page, click the title bar of the Local Server tile.

Local Server

The Local Server page displays the following tiles:

- **Properties**   Enables you to view and configure various settings of the local server, including computer name, domain membership, whether Remote Management or Remote Desktop is enabled, the TCP/IP settings for the server's network cards, whether Windows Update is enabled, and more. (See Figure 3-2.)

- **Events**   Displays events logged on the local server.

- **Services**   Enables you to view the services for the local server, start services that are currently stopped, restart running services, and perform other service-related tasks.

- **Best Practices Analyzer**   Enables you to initiate a BPA scan to determine whether you need to perform any further configuration for the local server to function properly with all its installed roles.

- **Performance**   Enables you to configure performance alerts on the local server so that alerts will be raised when CPU usage exceeds a specified threshold or available memory falls below a specified level.

- **Roles And Features**   Displays all roles and features installed on the local server and also enables you to install additional roles or remove installed roles.

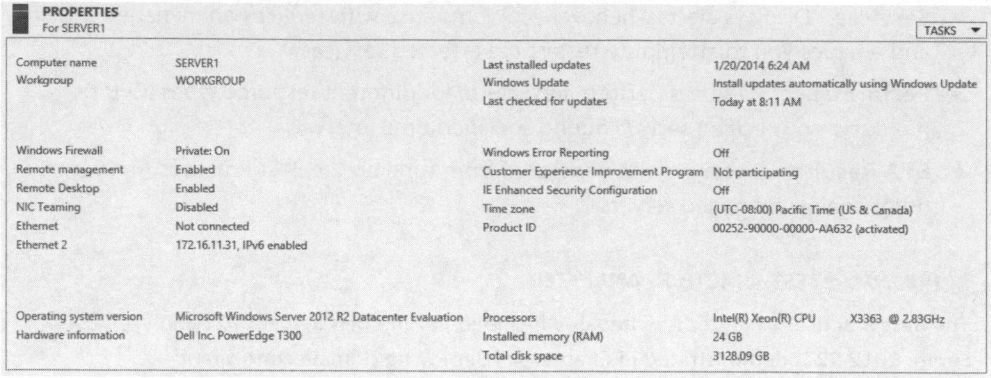

PROPERTIES For SERVER1			TASKS ▼
Computer name	SERVER1	Last installed updates	1/20/2014 6:24 AM
Workgroup	WORKGROUP	Windows Update	Install updates automatically using Windows Update
		Last checked for updates	Today at 8:11 AM
Windows Firewall	Private: On	Windows Error Reporting	Off
Remote management	Enabled	Customer Experience Improvement Program	Not participating
Remote Desktop	Enabled	IE Enhanced Security Configuration	Off
NIC Teaming	Disabled	Time zone	(UTC-08:00) Pacific Time (US & Canada)
Ethernet	Not connected	Product ID	00252-90000-00000-AA632 (activated)
Ethernet 2	172.16.11.31, IPv6 enabled		
Operating system version	Microsoft Windows Server 2012 R2 Datacenter Evaluation	Processors	Intel(R) Xeon(R) CPU X3363 @ 2.83GHz
Hardware information	Dell Inc. PowerEdge T300	Installed memory (RAM)	24 GB
		Total disk space	3128.09 GB

FIGURE 3-2 Use the Properties tile on the Local Server page to view and configure various settings.

> *NOTE* **MORE TO COME**
>
> You'll learn more about working with the tiles just described in the next lesson and also in the practice exercises at the end of this chapter.

All Servers

The All Servers page of Server Manager, shown in Figure 3-3, is where you can simultaneously manage multiple remote servers in your environment. Initially, this page displays only the local server, but you can find other servers in your environment and add them to this page to manage them. How to do this is explained in Lesson 2 of this chapter.

The All Servers page displays the same types of tiles displayed on the Local Server page. The difference is that on the All Servers page, the Events tile (for example) shows events logged on all servers being managed, not just the local server.

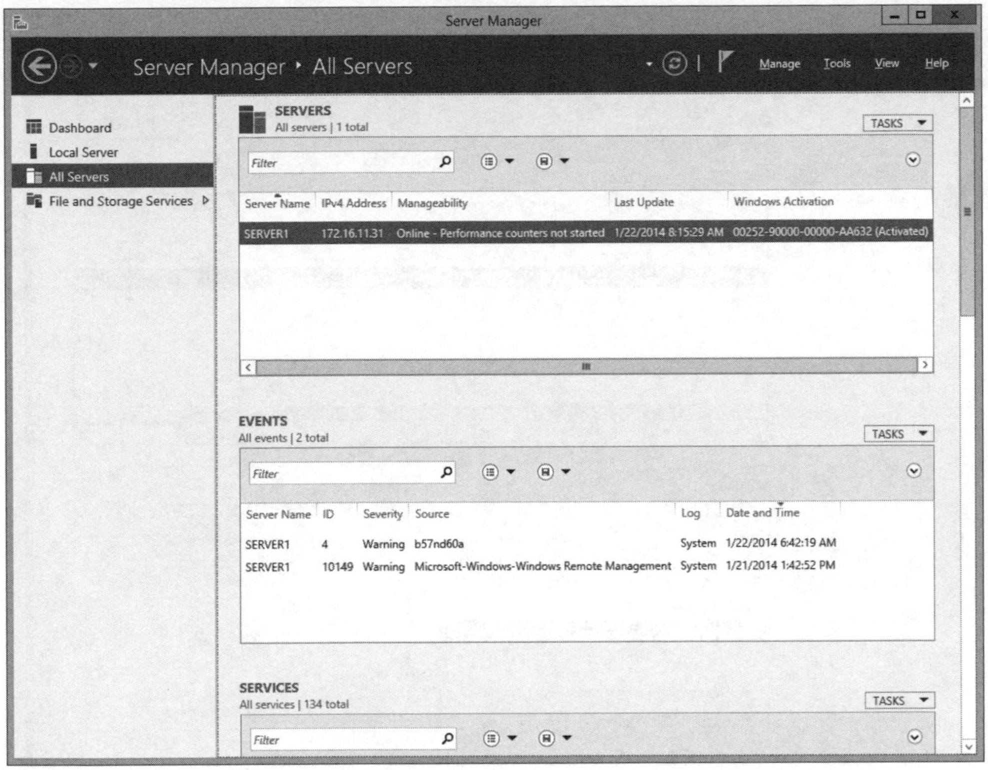

FIGURE 3-3 Use the All Servers page of Server Manager to simultaneously manage multiple remote servers.

Role-specific pages

Depending on what additional roles and features you have installed on your server, other pages might be available on the left side of Server Manager. For example, Figure 3-3 shows one role installed on the server named SERVER1—namely, the File and Storage Services role, which is installed by default on a new installation of Windows Server 2012 or Windows Server 2012 R2. If you select the File And Storage Services page (shown in Figure 3-4), Server Manager provides you with a hierarchy of additional pages for managing other servers and for managing the volumes, disks and storage pools on the selected server. By integrating file-server management tools directly into Server Manager, you can manage file servers without the need to separately open the MMC consoles, as you had to do in Windows Server 2008 R2 and earlier.

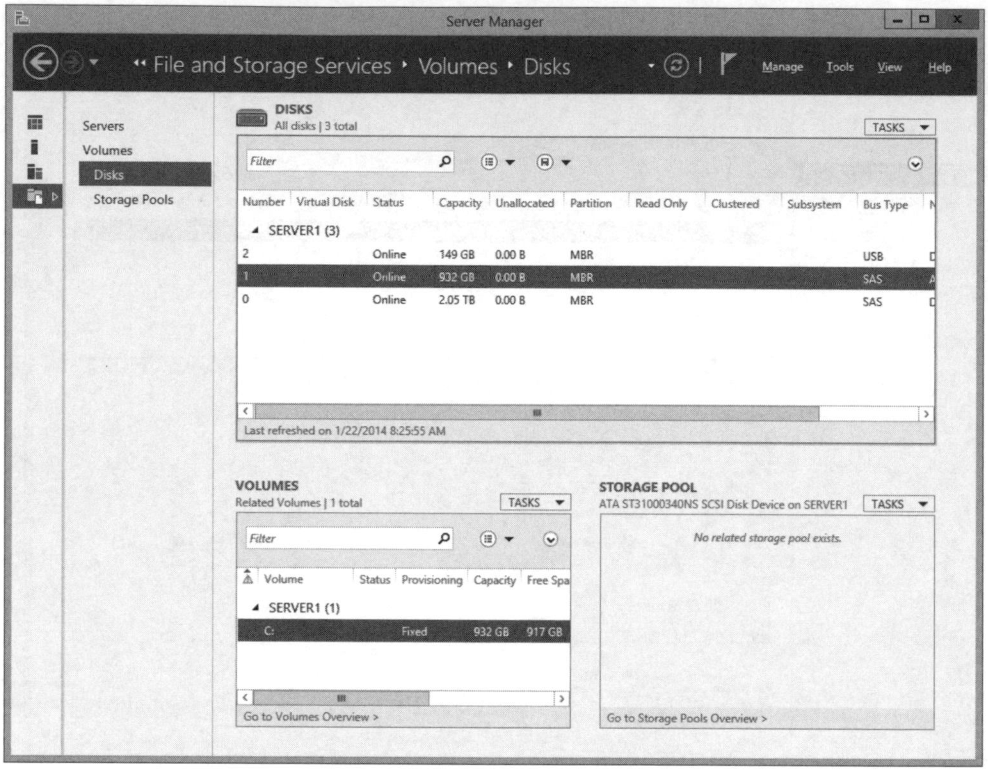

FIGURE 3-4 The File And Storage Services page displays an additional hierarchy of pages for managing Windows Server 2012 and Windows Server 2012 R2 file servers.

REAL WORLD **THE FUTURE OF WINDOWS SERVER MANAGEMENT**

The new Server Manager introduced in Windows Server 2012 probably represents the future of GUI-based management of Windows servers for smaller organizations. In Windows Server 2012 RTM and Windows Server 2012 R2, Microsoft has integrated the management of two roles into Server Manager: File And Storage Services and Remote Desktop Services (RDS). As a result, you don't need to use separate MMC consoles to manage either file servers or servers running various RDS role services. Instead, you can fully manage these roles from within Server Manager. It's likely that future releases of the Windows Server platform will include even more roles and features that have their management functionality integrated into Server Manager, and this should provide motivation for you to become thoroughly familiar with how to use Server Manager.

Configuring remote management

By default, Windows Server 2012 and Windows Server 2012 R2 are configured to enable remote management by Server Manager running on another computer. This makes it easy to start using Server Manager to remotely manage servers running Windows Server 2012 or Windows Server 2012 R2. When certain prerequisites have been met, you also can remotely manage servers running Windows Server 2008 or Windows Server 2008 R2 by using Server Manager on Windows Server 2012 or Windows Server 2012 R2. However, the remote management capability for managing servers running Windows Server 2003 from these platforms is limited.

> **NOTE** **SERVER MANAGER AND WORKGROUP SERVERS**
>
> Server Manager is mainly intended for remotely managing Windows servers in a domain environment in which the Active Directory Domain Services (AD DS) role has been deployed. You can remotely manage workgroup servers by using Server Manager, but doing so requires additional configuration to get that functionality working and it has some limitations with regard to management functionality. For more information, see the topic "Add and manage servers in workgroups" on the TechNet page at *http://technet .microsoft.com/en-us/library/hh831453*.

Configuring remote management on Windows Server 2012 R2

Although remote management is enabled by default in Windows Server 2012 R2, you can choose to disable or re-enable it if desired. To determine whether a server running Windows Server 2012 R2 is enabled for remote management, do one of the following:

- Start Server Manager on the local server, select the Local Server page, and view the state of the Remote Management setting in the Properties tile. This setting should display as either Enabled or Disabled, and you can modify the setting by clicking it.

- Run the %windir%\system32\Configure-SMRemoting.exe command-line tool from an elevated command prompt using the appropriate parameter as follows:

  - **Configure-SMRemoting –get** Displays whether remote management is enabled or disabled

  - **Configure-SMRemoting –enable** Enables remote management if it is currently disabled

  - **Configure-SMRemoting –disable** Disables remote management if it is currently enabled

> *IMPORTANT* **CONSEQUENCES OF DISABLING REMOTE MANAGEMENT ON SERVERS**
>
> Everything you can do by using Server Manager to manage servers running Windows Server 2012 or Windows Server 2012 R2, you can also do by using Windows PowerShell. That's because Server Manager is just a GUI way of running Windows PowerShell commands against remote servers. So if you disable remote management on a server by using either method just described, any applications or commands that require Windows Management Instrumentation (WMI) or Windows PowerShell remote access for remotely managing the server will fail.

If you have confirmed that a remote server running Windows Server 2012 R2 has remote management enabled but you are still unable to remotely manage the server by using Server Manager, try the following:

- If the remote server is on a different subnet, verify that there are no network firewall settings blocking remote management between the two subnets.

- Run Server Manager using the built-in Administrator account instead of a different administrator account to ensure sufficient credentials to perform the operation.

Configuring remote management on Windows Server 2012

Although remote management is enabled by default in Windows Server 2012, you can choose to disable or re-enable it if desired. You configure remote management on servers running the RTM version of Windows Server 2012 in the same way you configure remote management on servers running Windows Server 2012 R2.

Configuring remote management on Windows Server 2008 R2

Remote management is disabled by default in Windows Server 2008 R2. To enable remote management, you can use Group Policy, Server Manager, or Windows PowerShell. For detailed information on how to do this, see *http://technet.microsoft.com/en-us/library /dd759202.aspx*.

Configuring remote management on Windows Server 2008

Remote management is disabled by default in Windows Server 2008. To enable remote management, you must configure the Windows Remote Management (WinRM) service that implements WS-Management on the server. For detailed information on how to do this, see *http://technet.microsoft.com/en-us/magazine/ff700227.aspx*.

Configuring remote management on Windows Server 2003

Remote management is disabled by default in Windows Server 2003. To enable remote management, you must configure Windows Firewall and DCOM on the server. For detailed information on how to do this, see *http://msdn.microsoft.com/library/aa389286.aspx*.

> *NOTE* **REMOTE MANAGEMENT OF WINDOWS SERVER 2003**
>
> Remote management of Windows Server 2003 computers using Server Manager in Windows Server 2012 or Windows Server 2012 R2 is limited to receiving online or offline status information.

Remotely managing Windows Server 2012 from Windows Server 2012 R2

You can use Server Manager on Windows Server 2012 R2 to remotely manage servers running Windows Server 2012, provided you first install the following features and updates on the remote servers:

- Microsoft .NET Framework 4.5, which you can install using the Add Roles And Features Wizard in Server Manager.
- Windows Management Framework 4.0, which is available from *http://www.microsoft .com/en-us/download/details.aspx?id=40855*.

Remotely managing Windows Server 2012 R2 from Windows Server 2012

You cannot use Server Manager on Windows Server 2012 to remotely manage servers running Windows Server 2012 R2. You must use the version of Server Manager in Windows Server 2012 R2 if you want to remotely manage servers running Windows Server 2012 R2.

Remotely managing Windows Server 2008 or Windows Server 2008 R2 from Windows Server 2012 R2

You can use Server Manager on Windows Server 2012 R2 to remotely manage servers running Windows Server 2008 or Windows Server 2008 R2, provided you first install the following features and updates on the remote servers:

- Microsoft .NET Framework 4.0, which is available from *http://www.microsoft.com /en-us/download/details.aspx?id=40855*Windows Management Framework 3.0, which is available from *http://www.microsoft.com/en-us/download/details.aspx?id=34595*

- The performance counter hotfix described in Knowledge Base article KB 2682011, which is available from *http://support.microsoft.com/kb/2682011*

For more information, see the following TechNet Library page: *http://technet.microsoft .com/en-us/library/hh921475*.

Remotely managing Windows Server 2008 or Windows Server 2008 R2 from Windows Server 2012

You can also use Server Manager on Windows Server 2012 to remotely manage servers running Windows Server 2008 or Windows Server 2008 R2, provided you first install the following features and updates on the remote servers:

- Microsoft .NET Framework 4.0, which is available from *http://www.microsoft.com /en-us/download/details.aspx?id=17718*

- Windows Management Framework 3.0, which is available from *http://www.microsoft .com/en-us/download/details.aspx?id=34595*

- The hotfix described in Knowledge Base article KB 2682011, which is available from *http://support.microsoft.com/kb/2682011*

For more information, see the following TechNet Library page: *http://technet.microsoft .com/en-us/library/hh921475*.

✔ **Quick check**

- You are trying to configure a role on a remote server running Windows Server 2012 R2 using Windows PowerShell commands, but they don't seem to be working. What command should you run on the remote server to verify that remote management is enabled on it?

Quick check answer

- Configure-SMRemoting –get

Running Server Manager on client Windows

You also can run Server Manager from a client computer running Windows 8 or Windows 8.1 by deploying the appropriate version of the Remote Server Administration Tools (RSAT). RSAT was first introduced in Windows Vista. Microsoft provided it to enable administrators to remotely manage Windows servers from their workstations instead of having to enable Remote Desktop on the servers and use Remote Desktop Connection to remotely manage them. In the Windows Vista and Windows 7 versions of RSAT, administrators had to use the Turn Windows Features On Or Off item in Control Panel to enable remote tools after installing RSAT before they could use these tools for managing remote servers. Beginning with the Windows 8 version of RSAT, however, the tools included in RSAT are all enabled by default.

Versions of RSAT

There are two versions of RSAT available for managing servers running Windows Server 2012 and Windows Server 2012 R2:

- **RSAT for Windows 8.1**   You can use the tools in this version of RSAT to remotely manage servers running Windows Server 2012 R2 or Windows Server 2012 from a workstation running Windows 8.1. You can obtain this version of RSAT from the Microsoft Download Center at *http://www.microsoft.com/en-us/download/details .aspx?id=39296*.

- **RSAT for Windows 8**   You can use the tools in this version of RSAT to remotely manage servers running Windows Server 2012 from a workstation running Windows 8. You can obtain this version of RSAT from the Microsoft Download Center at *http://www .microsoft.com/en-us/download/details.aspx?id=28972*.

Both of these versions of RSAT include the following tools for remotely administering servers:

- Server Manager
- MMC snap-ins and consoles
- Windows PowerShell cmdlets and providers
- Some additional command-line tools

Benefits of using RSAT

The benefits of using RSAT for Windows 8 or RSAT for Windows 8.1 for managing servers include the following:

- It enables you to remotely manage multiple servers in a data center or in the cloud from a client computer—for example, from an administrator workstation in your office.

- It reduces licensing costs by eliminating the need to install Windows Server 2012 or Windows Server 2012 R2 on the computer you will use for managing your servers.

One scenario in which deploying RSAT for Windows 8.1 can be especially helpful is when your servers running Windows Server 2012 or Windows Server 2012 R2 are deployed as

Server Core installations, because it can simplify the job of configuring and managing servers that don't include GUI management tools like Server Manager.

Deploying RSAT for Windows 8.1

To download RSAT for Windows 8.1, go to *http://www.microsoft.com/en-us/download/details .aspx?id=39296*. After you install RSAT for Windows 8.1 on a client computer running Windows 8.1, Server Manager automatically opens by default on the client computer. If it doesn't, you can start Server Manager as follows:

1. On the Start screen, click the Administrative Tools tile.
2. In the Administrative Tools folder, double-click the Server Manager tile.

If you don't see the Server Manager or Administrative Tools tile on the Start screen, hover the mouse pointer over the upper-right corner of the Start screen and click Settings. If Show Administrative Tools is turned off, turn it on.

> **IMPORTANT   UNINSTALL PREVIOUS VERSIONS OF RSAT**
>
> If you have a previous version of RSAT already installed on your workstation, make sure you remove the earlier RSAT version before you install the latest version. Only one version of RSAT can be installed on a Windows client computer at any time.

Lesson summary

- Server Manager is organized into various pages, many of which have similar functionality using tiles and thumbnails.
- The Dashboard provides basic server-monitoring functionality for displaying various kinds of alerts.
- Remote management is enabled by default on Windows Server 2012 and Windows Server 2012 R2 to make these servers easier to manage.
- Configuring remote management on servers running Windows Server 2008 or Windows Server 2008 R2 requires additional steps.
- By installing the Remote Server Administration Tools (RSAT) for Windows 8.1 on a secure workstation running Windows 8.1, you can remotely manage servers from a single client computer.

Lesson review

Answer the following questions to test your knowledge of the information in this lesson. You can find the answers to these questions and explanations of why each answer choice is correct or incorrect in the "Answers" section at the end of this chapter.

1. You want to use Server Manager to manage all the Windows servers in your environment that are being used as print servers, but there is no Print Services page available in Server Manager. Why? (Choose all that apply.)

   A. All your print servers are currently offline, having been taken down for maintenance.

   B. None of your servers have the Print And Document Services role installed on them.

   C. None of the servers in your server pool have the Print And Document Services role installed on them.

   D. All print servers are running an earlier version of Windows Server and have not been configured for remote management.

2. How can you verify that remote management has been enabled on a server running Windows Server 2012? (Choose all that apply.)

   A. By examining the Dashboard of Server Manager running on that server.

   B. By examining the Local Server page of Server Manager running on that server.

   C. By examining the All Servers page of Server Manager running on that server.

   D. By examining the output of the Configure-SMRemoting –get command.

3. Your organization has a mixed environment of servers running Windows Server 2012 R2 and Windows Server 2008 R2. You want to manage your servers from a secure workstation running Windows 8.1, so you install the Remote Server Administration Tools for Windows 8.1 on this workstation. Which of the following statements best describes the management capabilities of this arrangement?

   A. You can manage all roles and features on servers running Windows Server 2012 R2 and servers running Windows Server 2008 R2.

   B. You can manage all roles and features on servers running Windows Server 2012 R2 and some roles and features on servers running Windows Server 2008 R2.

   C. You can manage all roles and features on servers running Windows Server 2012 R2 but no roles and features on servers running Windows Server 2008 R2.

   D. You can manage all roles and features on servers running Windows Server 2012 R2, but you need to install the Remote Server Administration Tools for Windows 8.1 on a workstation running Windows 7 to manage roles and features on servers running Windows Server 2008 R2.

Lesson 2: Server management tasks

You can use Server Manager to perform many kinds of server management tasks. This lesson demonstrates how you can perform some key management tasks using Server Manager.

Adding servers

To manage remote servers using Server Manager, you first need to add the servers to the *server pool*. You can add both physical and virtual servers to the server pool. As described in the previous lesson, no additional configuration is needed for adding servers running Windows Server 2012 or Windows Server 2012 R2 to the server pool. Servers running Windows Server 2008 or Windows Server 2008 R2, however, must be configured for remote server management before they can be added to the server pool. Servers running Windows Server 2003 cannot be added to the server pool.

To add servers to the server pool, do the following:

1. From any Server Manager page, click the Manage menu and then click Add Servers to open the Add Servers dialog box.

2. Click the Active Directory tab if you want to search Active Directory for servers you can manage. To search Active Directory, you can limit your search to the following:

   ■ Location, which you can use to find servers in the domain or only domain controllers. (See Figure 3-5.)

   ■ Operating System, which you can use to find servers running a specific operating system.

   ■ Name (CN), which lets you type the name or the first part of the name of the server or servers for which you are searching.

3. Alternatively, click the DNS tab to query your DNS servers for servers you want to manage by their computer names or IP addresses.

4. Alternatively, click the Import tab to specify a text file containing a list of computer names of servers you want to manage.

5. Whichever approach you use to find the servers you want to manage, when you find them, click the control to add the servers you selected to the server pool. Note that, as shown in Figure 3-5, you can select multiple servers to add.

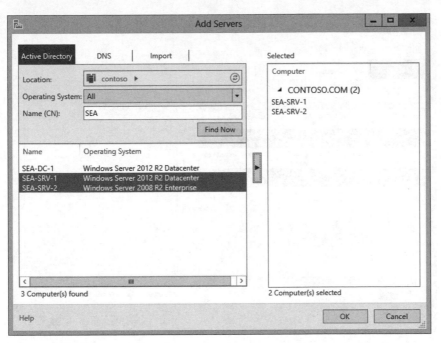

FIGURE 3-5 Add servers to the server pool.

Creating server groups

After you add all the servers you want to manage to the server pool, the next task you should perform is to create custom server groups for different kinds of servers. A *server group* is a logical subset of the server pool. You can use various criteria for deciding which server groups you want to create. For example, you could create server groups for grouping your organization's servers according to any of the following criteria:

- Business function (for example, Accounting servers)
- Geographical location (for example, Seattle servers)
- Role (for example, Hyper-V hosts running a particular version of Windows Server)
- Responsibility (for example, Bob's servers)

To create a new server group, do the following:

1. From any Server Manager page, click the Manage menu and then click Create Server Group to open the Create Server Group dialog box.

2. Type a descriptive name for the new server group.

3. Select the servers you want to add to the new server group from the list of servers in the server pool and click the control to add them to the server group. (See Figure 3-6.)

4. Alternatively, you can select servers by searching Active Directory, querying DNS, or importing a text file with a list of computer names as described in the previous topic.

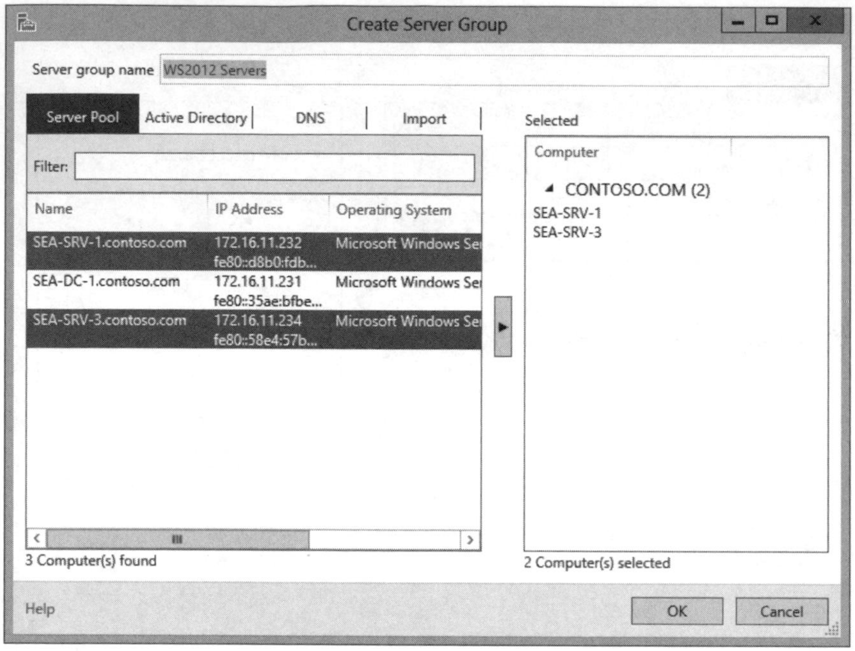

FIGURE 3-6 Add servers in the pool to a server group.

After you create your new server group, it appears as a separate page in Server Manager. (See Figure 3-7 in the next section.) To modify the membership of an existing server group or delete the server group, click the Tasks control in the Servers tile of the page for that server group.

> **NOTE SERVER GROUP MEMBERSHIP**
>
> A server can belong to more than one server group.

Restarting a server

After you group your servers according to the criteria you've decided upon, you can perform various management tasks on these servers directly from within Server Manager. For example, to restart a particular server in a particular server group, do the following:

1. Select the Server Manager page for that server group.

2. Right-click a particular server listed in the Servers tile of that page.

3. Select Restart Server from the context menu. (See Figure 3-7.)

Other management tasks are also available in the context menu, but note that some of these tasks require certain prerequisites before they will work. For example, Remote Desktop must be enabled on the remote server before you can open a Remote Desktop connection to that server.

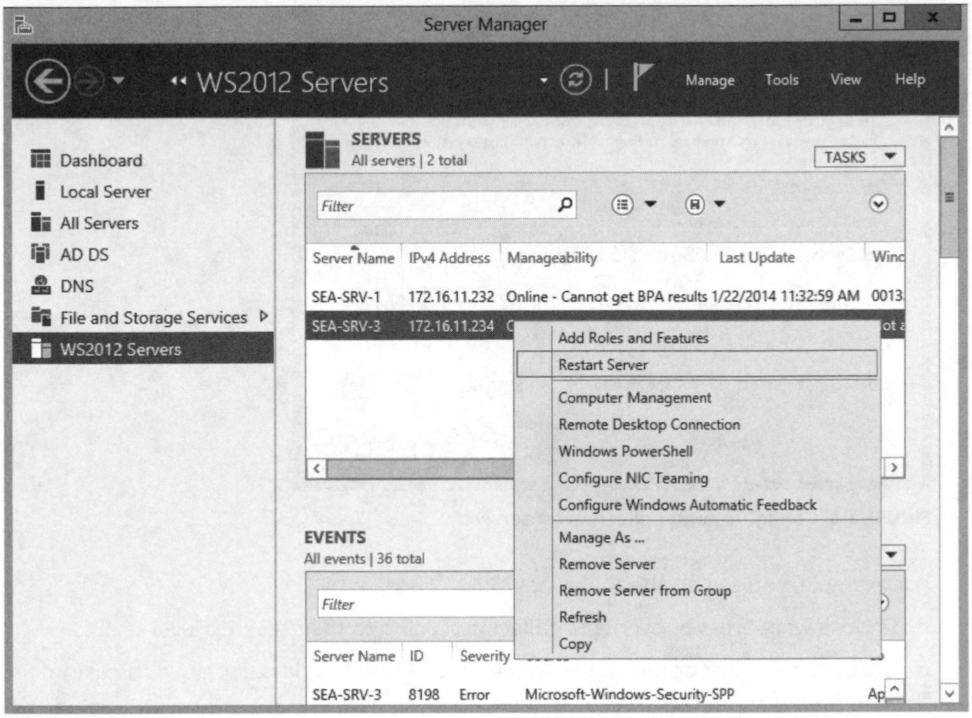

FIGURE 3-7 Restart a server in the selected server group.

Collecting events

You can use Server Manager to collect events from the event logs of remote servers and then display alerts on the Dashboard whenever certain event criteria are met.

Configuring event collection

You can configure event collection for the servers listed on any of these pages:

- Local Server
- All Servers
- Role-specific pages
- Pages for server groups you created

For example, to configure event collection for servers listed on the All Servers page, do the following:

1. Select the All Servers page in Server Manager.

2. In the Events tile, click Tasks and select Configure Event Data to open the Configure Event Data dialog box, shown in Figure 3-8.

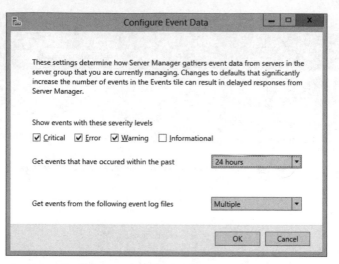

FIGURE 3-8 Configure event collection for servers.

For example, you can do the following:

- Choose what types of events to collect according to their severity level
- Collect events that occurred within the past 24 hours, 3 days, 7 days, or a custom time period expressed in days or hours
- Get events from all event logs or only specific event logs on the servers

When events have been collected from the servers, they are displayed in the Events tile of the selected Server Manager page. Selecting one server on that page displays all events collected from that server; selecting multiple servers displays all events collected from all selected servers.

By selecting a particular event, you can display a pane, like the one shown in Figure 3-9, with additional information concerning the event.

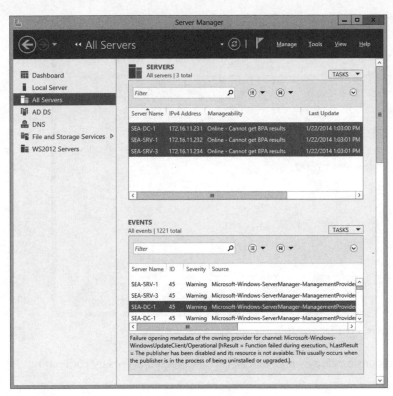

FIGURE 3-9 View information about a specific event.

Configuring alerts for events

When events are being collected for the servers listed on a particular page, you can configure the Dashboard tile for that page to display alerts whenever an event of a particular type has been collected. To continue the preceding example, you can configure the All Servers tile on the Dashboard to display alerts for specific types of events by doing the following:

1. Select the Dashboard in Server Manager.

2. In the All Servers tile, click Events to open the All Servers - Events Detail View dialog box shown in Figure 3-10.

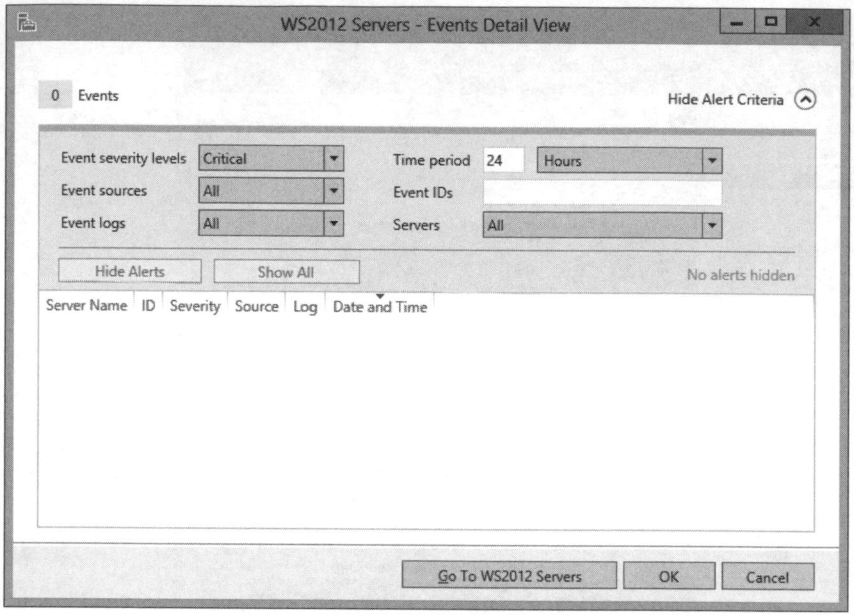

FIGURE 3-10 Configure alerts for events.

3. Specify the conditions for displaying event alerts for collected events by configuring the following:

- Whether critical, error, or warning events (or all three) should generate alerts. (By default, only critical events generate alerts.)

- The event sources for the events. (By default, this includes all event sources.)

- The event logs for the events. (By default, this includes all event logs.)

- The time period during which the event occurred. (By default, this is during the last 24 hours.)

- Specific event IDs that should generate alerts. For example, specifying 1–20, –13, 75 generates only alerts that have event IDs of 1–20 (except 13) or 75.

- The servers on which the events occurred. (Deselect any servers for which you don't want to use the Dashboard to generate event alerts.)

Event alerts are indicated by red numbers next to the Events thumbnail of tiles on the Dashboard. Click the Events thumbnail of any tile to see more information about the events that generated the alerts.

Monitoring services

You can use Server Manager to monitor services on remote servers and then display alerts on the Dashboard whenever a service meets certain criteria. You can also use Server Manager to start, stop, restart, pause, and resume services on remote servers. To configure other settings for services, open the Services MMC console from Administrative Tools.

Configuring service alerts

You can configure any tile on the Dashboard to display service alerts for the servers the tile represents by doing the following:

1. Select any tile on the Dashboard in Server Manager—for example, the All Servers tile.

2. Click the Services thumbnail in this tile to open the All Servers - Services Detail View dialog box for that server group, as shown in Figure 3-11.

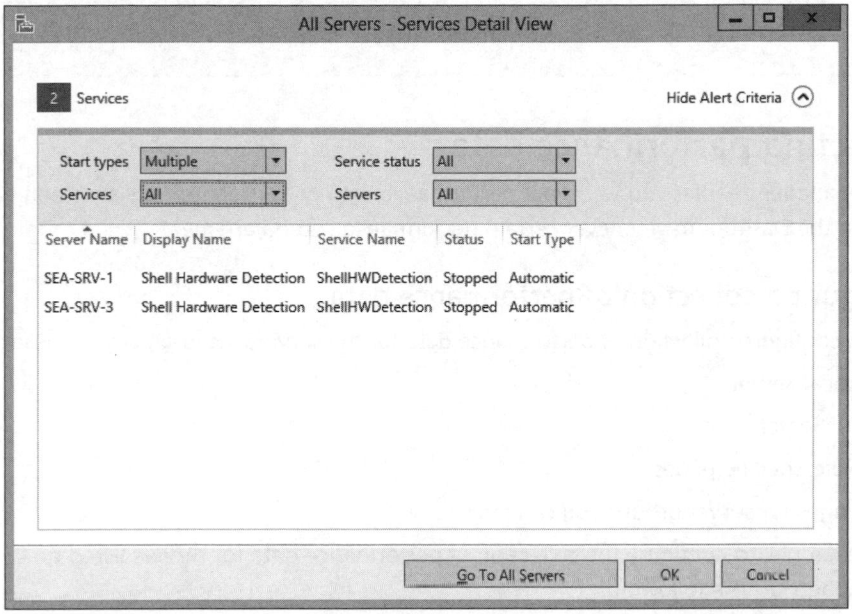

FIGURE 3-11 Configure service alerts for collected events.

3. Specify the conditions for displaying service alerts for collected events by configuring the following:

- Which service start types can generate alerts. (By default, only services configured to start automatically, or automatically with delayed start, are selected.)

- Which services can generate alerts. (By default, all services can generate alerts.)

- Which service status conditions can generate alerts. (All service status conditions can do this by default.)

- The servers on which the service issues occurred. (Deselect any servers for which you don't want to use the Dashboard to generate service alerts.)

Service alerts are indicated by red numbers next to the Services thumbnail of tiles on the Dashboard. Click the Services thumbnail of any tile to see more information about the services that generated the alerts.

Collecting performance data

Server Manager enables you to collect performance data on remote servers and then display alerts on the Dashboard whenever certain performance criteria are met.

Configuring collection of performance data

You can configure collection of performance data for the servers listed on any of these pages:

- Local Server
- All Servers
- Role-specific pages
- Pages for server groups you created

For example, to configure the collection of performance data for servers listed on the All Servers page, do the following:

1. Select the All Servers page in Server Manager.

2. In the Performance tile, right-click any servers that show Counter Status as Off and select Start Performance Counters from the context menu.

3. In the Performance tile, click Tasks and select Configure Performance Alerts to open the All Servers: Configure Performance Alerts dialog box, as shown in Figure 3-12.

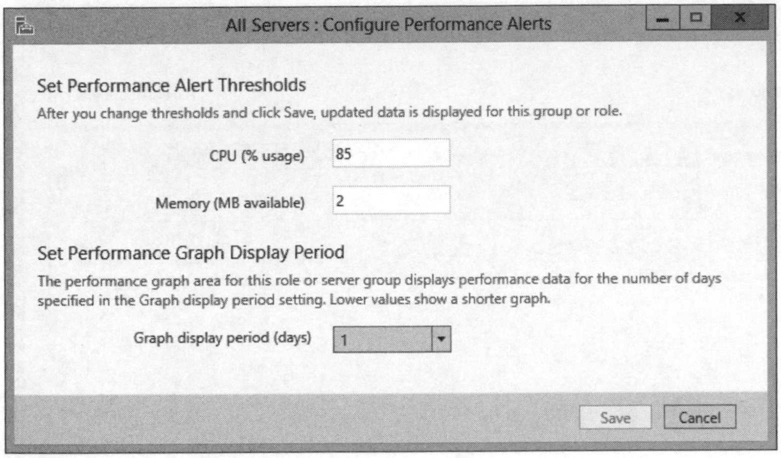

FIGURE 3-12 Collect performance data.

4. Specify performance alert thresholds for CPU usage and available memory and configure the graph display period in days.

Configuring performance alerts

When performance data is being collected for the servers listed on a particular page, you can configure the Dashboard tile for that page to display alerts whenever performance meets the specified criteria. To continue the preceding example, you can configure the All Servers tile on the Dashboard to display performance alerts by doing the following:

1. Select the Dashboard in Server Manager.

2. In the All Servers tile, click Performance to open the All Servers - Performance Detail View dialog box shown in Figure 3-13.

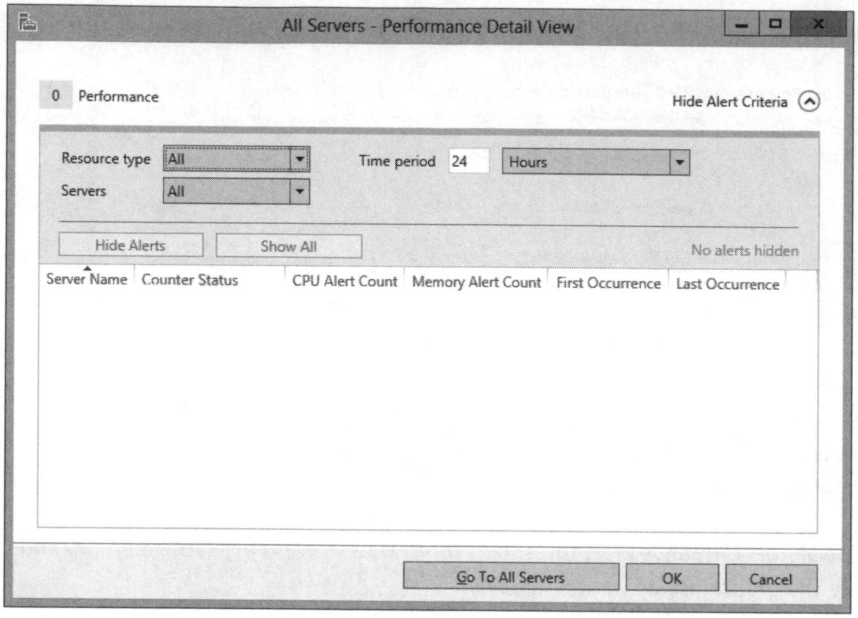

FIGURE 3-13 Configure performance alerts.

3. Specify the conditions for displaying performance alerts by configuring the following:

- Whether CPU or Memory can generate an alert. (By default, both can generate alerts.)

- The time period during which the performance condition occurred. (By default, this is during the last 24 hours.)

- The servers on which the performance condition occurred. (Deselect any servers for which you don't want to use the Dashboard to generate event alerts.)

Performance alerts are indicated by red numbers next to the Performance thumbnail of tiles on the Dashboard. Click the Performance thumbnail of any tile to see more information about the condition that generated the alerts.

Viewing status notifications

Status notifications about running tasks are indicated in two places in Server Manager:

- By a gray number icon beneath, a yellow warning icon beneath, or a red box around the Notification icon in the menu bar at the top of each page

- By a yellow or red message bar beneath the title bar of the appropriate tile

Figure 3-14 shows an example of both of these types of notifications.

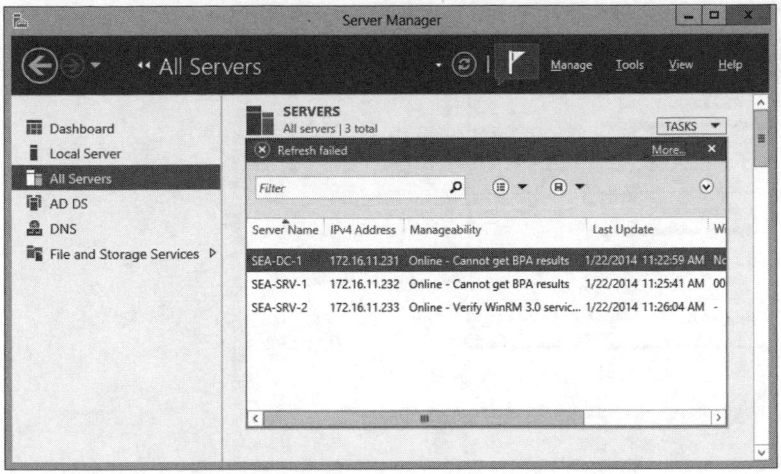

FIGURE 3-14 These are examples of status notifications.

Clicking the message bar in Figure 3-14 displays full details concerning any status notifications in a separate Task Details dialog box, like the one shown in Figure 3-15. Note that the lower pane of this dialog box shows examples of both error and warning notifications.

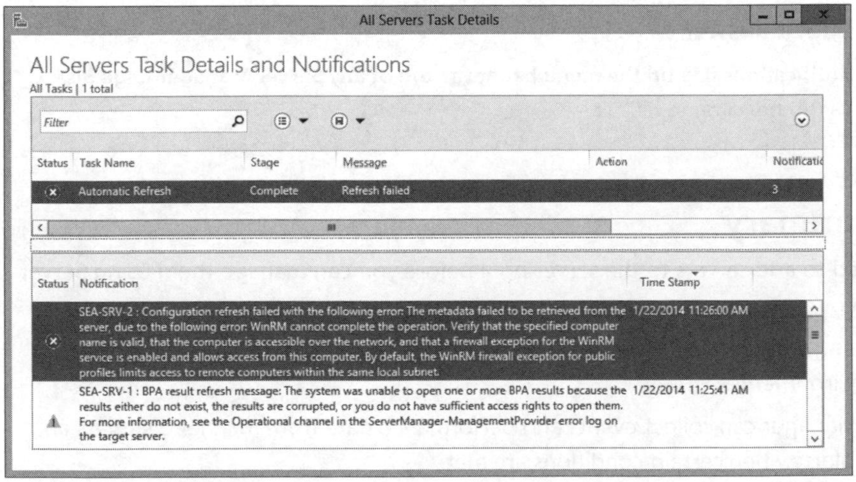

FIGURE 3-15 View full details of status notifications.

Clicking the Notifications flag displays brief summary information concerning any notifications that have been raised, as shown in Figure 3-16. Clicking Task Details at the bottom of this summary information opens the dialog box shown previously in Figure 3-15.

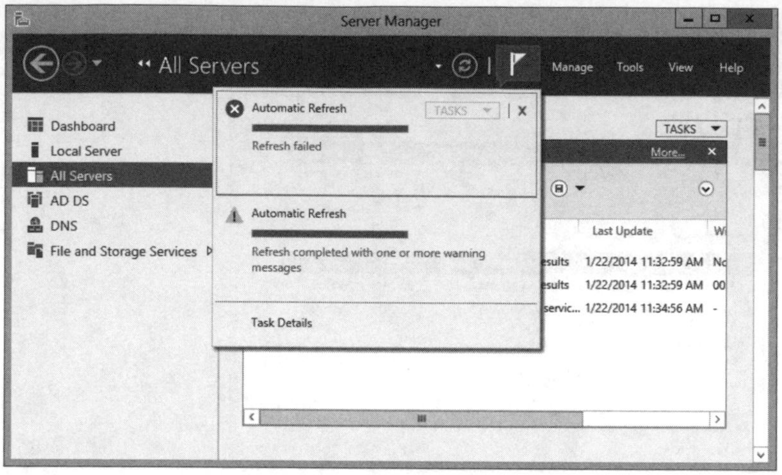

FIGURE 3-16 View brief summary information about status notifications.

✔ **Quick check**

- What type of indication does Server Manager display when a task has failed?

Quick check answer

- The Notifications flag on the menu bar at the top of any Server Manager page displays a red box around it.

Lesson summary

- You need to add servers to the server pool before you can manage them using Server Manager.
- Organizing servers into server groups makes them easier to manage in large, distributed environments.
- Server Manager can collect events and performance data from managed servers and display alerts when certain conditions are met.
- You can use Server Manager to perform some basic service management tasks.

Lesson review

Answer the following questions to test your knowledge of the information in this lesson. You can find the answers to these questions and explanations of why each answer choice is correct or incorrect in the "Answers" section at the end of this chapter.

1. Your organization has six servers running Windows Server 2012 in a domain environment. Only four of those servers are listed on the All Servers page of Server Manager. What should you do to ensure the remaining two servers are also listed on this page?

   A. Create a server group and add the two servers to the group.

   B. Create a server pool and add the two servers to the pool.

   C. Add the servers to an existing server group.

   D. Add the servers to your server pool.

2. Which of the following are *not* purposes for creating server groups in Server Manager? (Choose all that apply.)

   A. You can assign privileges to servers by adding them to server groups.

   B. You can use server groups to facilitate managing servers at different geographical locations.

   C. You can use server groups to facilitate the delegation of permissions for servers used by different departments in your organization.

   D. You can nest server groups to create a hierarchical collection of servers that mirrors the administrative responsibilities of your IT staff.

3. You configured the Performance tile on the All Servers page to set a performance alert threshold for CPU usage of 60 percent because when you opened the Performance tab of Task Manager on those servers, you noticed that several of your managed servers were experiencing heavy load. However, three hours later you notice that no alerts have been raised on the Performance tile of the All Servers page, even though the servers still appear to be under heavy load. Why? (Choose all that apply.)

   A. You neglected to enable performance counters on those servers.

   B. The minimum graph display period for performance alerts is one day, and that much time has not elapsed yet.

   C. You configured Server Manager properties to a refresh period of more than three hours.

   D. You have not yet added the servers to a custom server group.

4. Which of the following service management tasks can you *not* perform on remote servers by using a Services tile on one of the Server Manager pages?

   A. Stopping a service

   B. Pausing a service

   C. Starting a service

   D. Changing the Startup Type option of the service

Lesson 3: Installing roles and features

Roles and features provide additional functionality for Windows servers, such as the capability of using the server as a print server on your network. This lesson demonstrates how to install roles and features on a server running Windows Server 2012 or Windows Server 2012 R2 using both Server Manager and Windows PowerShell commands. Later chapters examine how to configure and manage specific roles, such as Active Directory Domain Services, DHCP Server, DNS Server, File And Storage Services, Hyper-V, and Print And Document Services.

> **After this lesson, you will be able to:**
> - Use Server Manager to install or remove roles and features on remote servers.
> - Use Windows PowerShell to install or remove roles and features on remote servers.
>
> **Estimated lesson time: 30 minutes**

Prerequisites for installing roles and features

To install a role or feature on a server running Windows Server 2012 or Windows Server 2012 R2, the server must have access to the binaries for installing that role or feature. As explained in Chapter 2, "Deploying servers," a capability called Features On Demand enables administrators to completely remove the binaries for roles and features from a server running Windows Server 2012 or Windows Server 2012 R2 to reduce the amount of disk space the operating system uses.

If the binaries for a particular role or feature you want to install on a server have previously been removed from the server's system drive, Windows Server 2012 and Windows Server 2012 R2 can obtain these binaries in several ways:

- By downloading them directly from Windows Update.
- By copying them from the side-by-side store (SxS) folder on a running installation of the same edition and service pack level as your server. To do this, share the SxS folder or a parent folder on the other server and then specify the UNC path to the shared SxS folder when using the Add Roles And Features Wizard or the Install-WindowsFeature cmdlet.
- By copying the entire SxS folder of an installation of the same edition and service pack level as your server to a shared folder on a file server on your network. Then specify the UNC path to this shared folder when using the Add Roles And Features Wizard or the Install-WindowsFeature cmdlet.
- By using a mounted Windows image from a Windows Image (WIM) file such as the Install.wim file in the \Sources folder on the Windows Server 2012 or Windows Server 2012 R2 product media (ISO file).

- By using a mounted virtual hard disk file that includes an installation of the same edition and service pack level as your server.

You can use the Group Policy Editor to control whether removed binaries are downloaded from Windows Update, and you can specify the path where the binaries can be found if their associated roles or features need to be installed. Browse to the policy setting for controlling this behavior:

Computer Configuration\Policies\Administrative Templates\System\Specify Settings For Optional Component Installation And Component Repair

Figure 3-17 shows the configuration options for this policy setting.

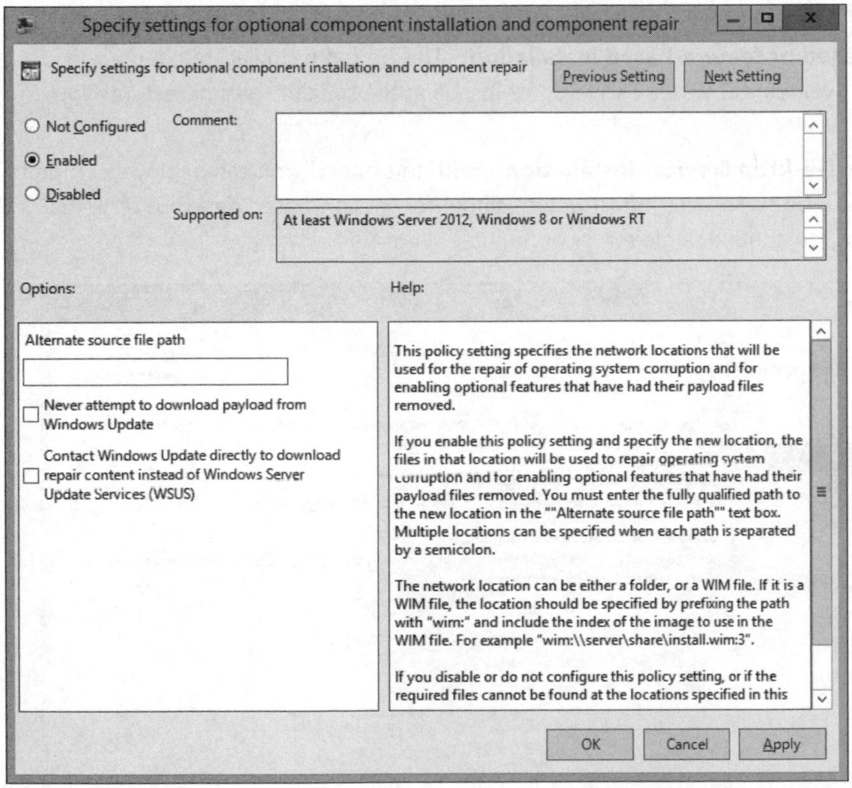

FIGURE 3-17 Specify Group Policy settings for controlling installation of previously removed role and feature binaries.

> **MORE INFO** **FEATURES ON DEMAND CAPABILITIES**
>
> Refer to Chapter 2 for more information about the Features On Demand capabilities in Windows Server 2012 and Windows Server 2012 R2.

Installing roles and features using Server Manager

In previous versions of Windows Server, you could use the Add Roles Wizard and Add Features Wizard to install roles and features, respectively, on the server. Windows Server 2012 introduced a single redesigned Add Roles And Features Wizard that provides greater flexibility and control for installing roles and features on servers. This wizard provides an easy way for administrators of small to midsized organizations to install roles and features on servers running Windows Server 2012 in their environment.

To use Server Manager to install a role or a feature on a server running Windows Server 2012, begin by clicking the Manage menu and selecting Add Roles And Features to open the Add Roles And Features Wizard. The Select Installation Type page of this wizard shown in Figure 3-18 offers two options for installing roles and features on the server:

- **Role-based or feature-based installation**   This option is similar to that used in previous versions of Windows Server for installing the specific roles or features you choose.

- **Remote Desktop Services installation**   With this option, you can deploy a complete Remote Desktop Services infrastructure, either for session-based desktops or virtual desktops, on either a single server or multiple servers.

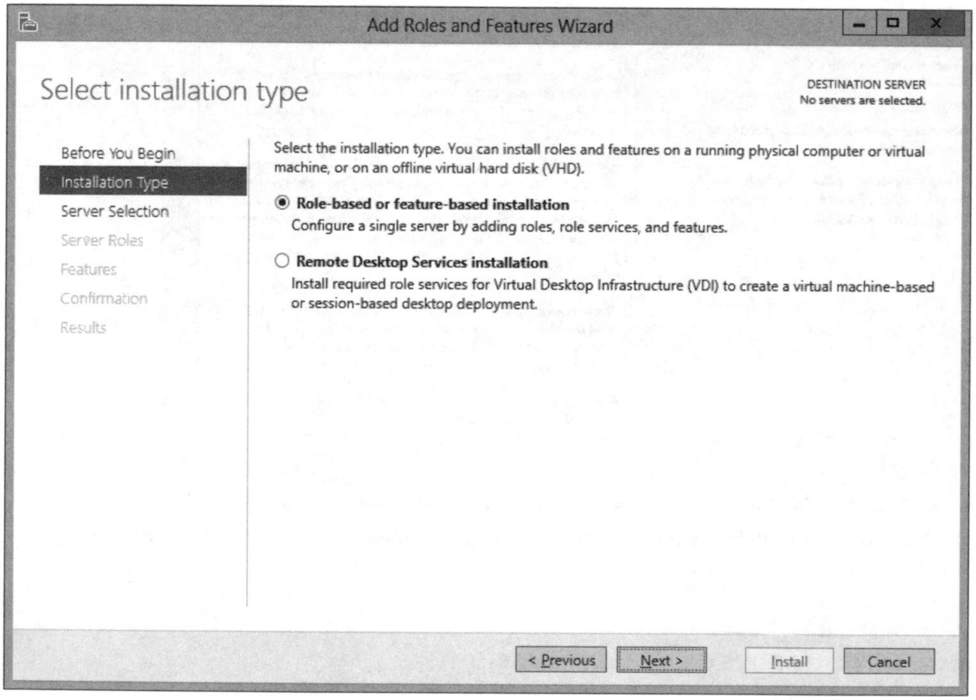

FIGURE 3-18 Windows Server 2012 offers two options for installing roles and features.

Choosing the first option on the Select Installation Type page opens the Select Destination Server page of the wizard (shown in Figure 3-19), which you use to choose a remote server from your server pool on which to install roles and features. Note that this page includes an option for selecting an offline virtual hard disk instead of an online server. In Windows Server 2012, you can install roles and features on offline virtual hard disks, and this capability is described further in Chapter 10, "Implementing Group Policy."

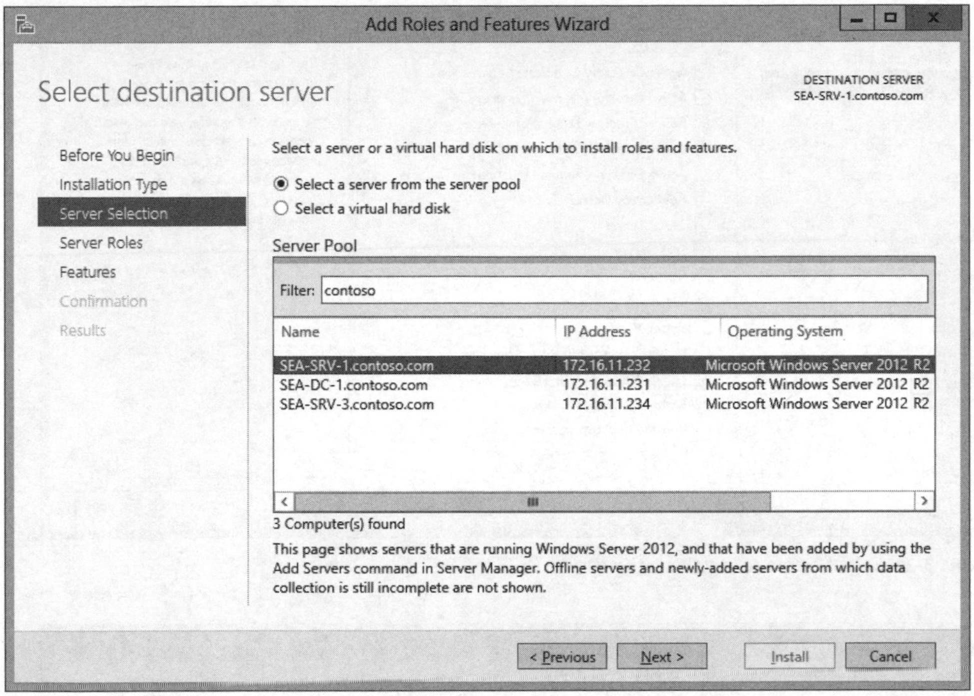

FIGURE 3-19 Select the server on which you want to install roles and features.

On the Select Server Roles page, shown in Figure 3-20, you can choose one or more roles to install on the selected server. When you do this, the wizard might prompt you to install the Remote Server Administration Tools for that role or feature plus any other management tools needed for managing the role or feature.

The Select Features Page is next, and you use it to choose features to install on your server. Additional wizard pages might also appear to provide you with additional information or configuration options for the roles and features you decide to install on the server or a list of role services from which to choose for the particular roles you are installing.

When you reach the Confirm Installation Selections page, shown in Figure 3-21, you can select the check box if you want the remote server to be restarted if this is needed to complete installation of the selected roles and features.

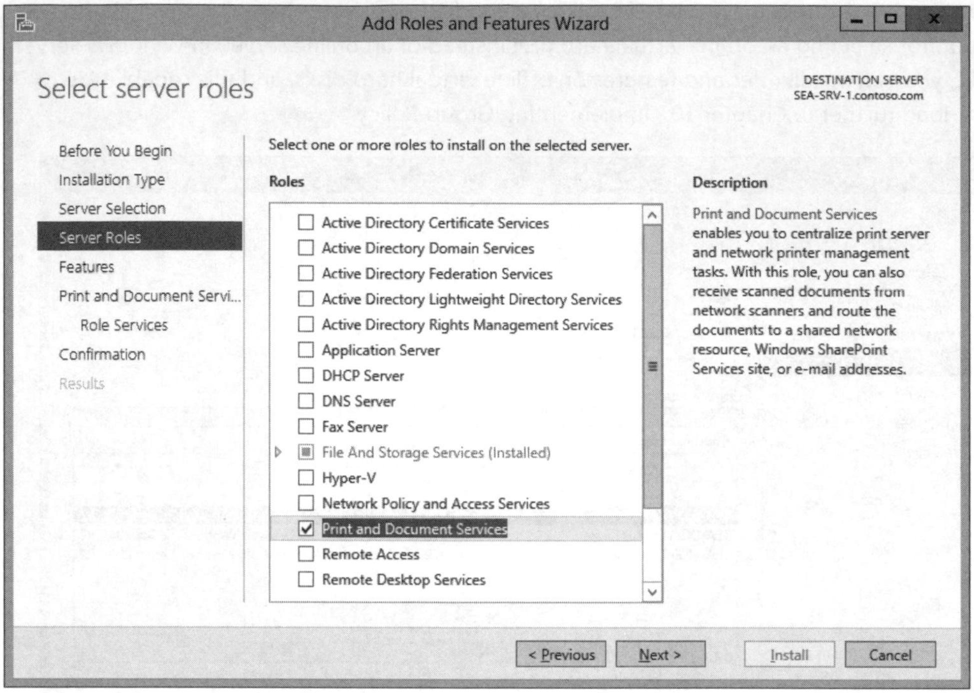

FIGURE 3-20 Select a role to install on the server.

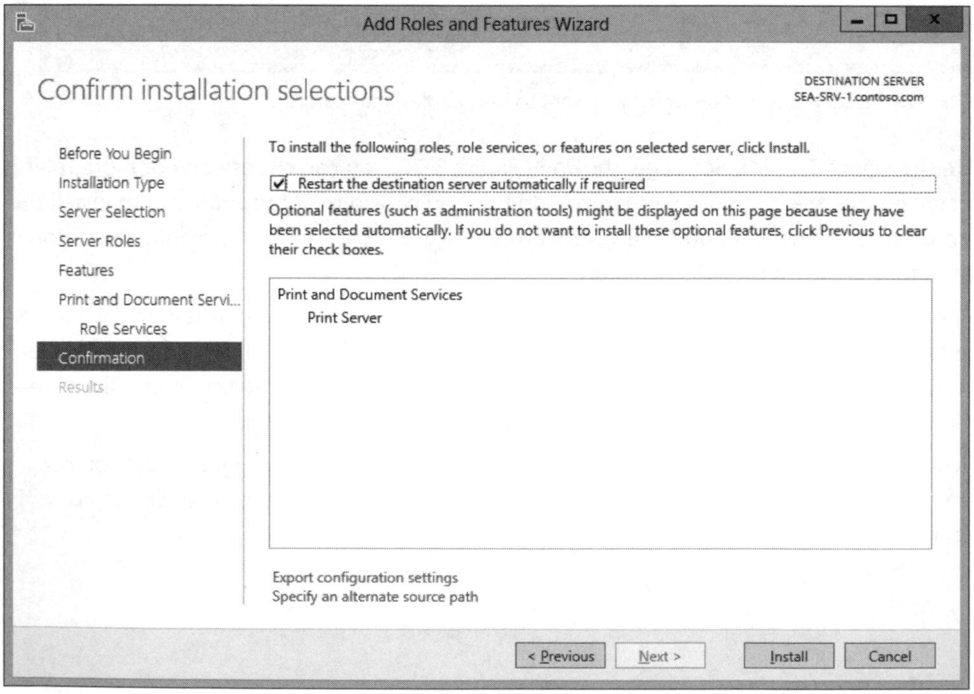

FIGURE 3-21 Confirm your installation selections and choose to restart the destination server if necessary.

At the bottom of the Confirm Installation Selections page shown in Figure 3-21 is a Specify An Alternate Source Path link. Click this link if you previously removed any of the binaries for the roles or features you are installing on the server. Clicking this link opens a Specify Alternate Source Path dialog box for specifying the UNC path to the location where you can find the binaries needed to install the roles or features.

When a new role is installed on the server, a new page for this role is added to Server Manager. For example, Figure 3-22 shows the Print Services page, which appears after the Print And Document Services role has been installed on one or more servers in your server pool. A new tile named Print Services also appears on the Dashboard so that you can monitor events, services, and the performance of your print servers and confirm their manageability.

The Notifications flag in the menu bar of Server Manager in Figure 3-22 indicates that one informational notification has been raised. Clicking this flag provides brief summary information concerning this notification, which indicates that installation of the selected feature has been successful.

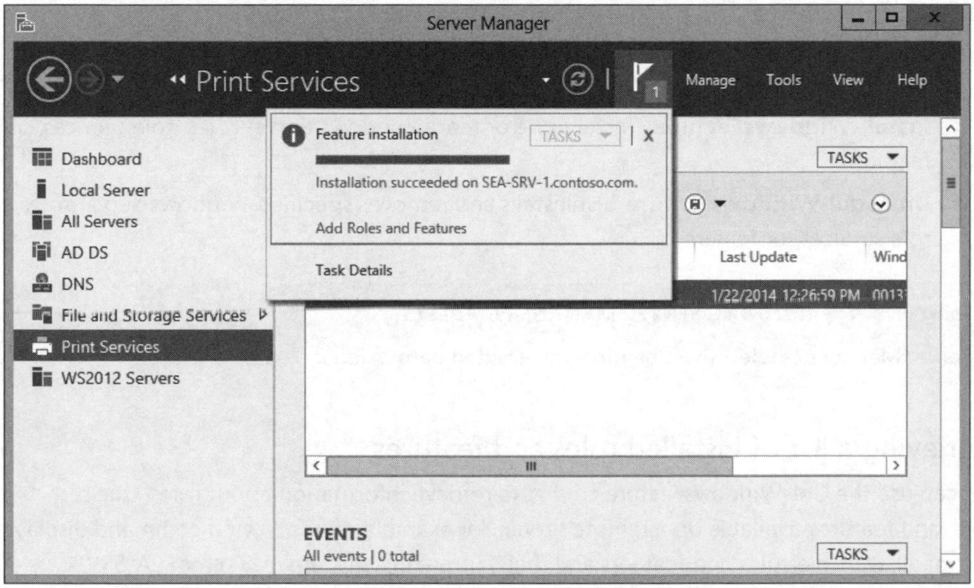

FIGURE 3-22 Each role on a managed server has its associated page in Server Manager.

> ✔ **Quick check**
> ■ What Group Policy setting can you use to specify an alternate source path for installing features whose binaries have been removed from a server?

Installing roles and features using Windows PowerShell

You can also install roles and features on servers running Windows Server 2012 or Windows Server 2012 R2 by using Windows PowerShell commands. This approach can be useful for administrators who work in midsized to large environments that have many servers deployed—for example, in a data center. You can also use Windows PowerShell to install roles and features on offline virtual disks.

You can use the following Server Manager cmdlets for managing roles and features using Windows PowerShell:

■ **Get-WindowsFeature** Retrieves information about Windows Server roles, role services, and features that are available

■ **Install-WindowsFeature** Installs one or more Windows Server roles, role services, or features

■ **Uninstall-WindowsFeature** Uninstalls and removes specified Windows Server roles, role services, or features

> *IMPORTANT* **RUNNING SERVER MANAGER CMDLETS**
>
> Server Manager cmdlets must be run with elevated permissions.

Retrieving a list of installed roles and features

You can use the Get-WindowsFeature cmdlet to retrieve information about roles, role services, and features available on a remote server. For example, the following command displays a list of all available roles and features and their current install state on server SEA-SRV-1:

```
Get-WindowsFeature -ComputerName SEA-SRV-1
```

To display a list of all installed roles and features on the server, pipe the output of the preceding command into the Where-Object cmdlet and use Where-Object to filter out everything except roles and features whose *InstallState* property is equal to *Installed*:

```
Get-WindowsFeature -ComputerName SEA-SRV-1 | Where-Object InstallState -eq Installed
```

You can narrow your results even further by using the *–name* parameter of the Get-WindowsFeature cmdlet to select only roles and features that begin with "Print," like this:

```
Get-WindowsFeature -Name Print* -ComputerName SEA-SRV-1 | Where-Object InstallState -eq
Installed
```

The output from running this command against server SEA-SRV-1 verifies that the Print Server role service of the Print And Document Services role is installed:

```
Display Name                       Name                Install State
------------                       ----                -------------
[X] Print and Document Services    Print-Services      Installed
[X] Print Server                   Print-Server        Installed
```

REAL WORLD **WINDOWS POWERSHELL 3.0 SIMPLIFIED SYNTAX**

One of the improvements introduced in Windows PowerShell 3.0 is the simplification of the syntax for the Where-Object cmdlet. If you are an administrator who already has some familiarity with using Windows PowerShell for managing Windows servers, you might have wondered about the syntax of some of the commands in this section. In particular, you might have wondered why the second example didn't look like this:

```
Get-WindowsFeature - ComputerName SEA-SRV-1 | Where-Object {$_.InstallState
-eq Installed}
```

The reason is because Windows PowerShell 3.0 and later let you eliminate the script block notation (the curly braces), the current object placeholder ($_), and the dot property notation. These improvements make Windows PowerShell code easier to understand.

Installing roles and features

You can use the Install-WindowsFeature cmdlet to install roles, role services, and features available on a remote server. You can also use the alias Add-WindowsFeature to invoke this command. For example, the following command installs the DHCP Server role on server SEA-SRV-1:

```
Install-WindowsFeature -Name DHCP -ComputerName SEA-SRV-1
```

The output from running the preceding command looks like this:

```
Success    Restart Needed    Exit Code     Feature Result
-------    --------------    ---------     --------------
True       No                Success       {DHCP Server}
```

To install the DHCP Server role with the management tools for this role, add the *–IncludeManagementTools* parameter to the preceding command. If a restart is required for the installation of a role or feature to install properly, you can force this to happen by including the *–Restart* parameter in the command.

To install all of the Remote Server Administration features on this server, use this command:

```
Install-WindowsFeature -Name RSAT -IncludeAllSubFeature -ComputerName SEA-SRV-1
```

MORE INFO For more examples of how to use the Install-WindowsFeature cmdlet, type **Get-Help Install-WindowsFeature –examples** in the Windows PowerShell console.

Installing roles and features on multiple servers

Although Server Manager can be used to install roles and features only on a single server at a time, you can use Windows PowerShell to install roles and features on multiple servers at the same time. You can do this by using the Invoke-Command cmdlet to run the Install-WindowsFeature command on multiple computers. For example, this command installs the XPS Viewer feature on servers SEA-SRV-1 and SEA-SRV-3:

```
Invoke-Command -ComputerName SEA-SRV-1,SEA-SRV-3 -ScriptBlock {Install-WindowsFeature
-Name XPS-Viewer}
```

The output from running the preceding command looks like this:

```
Success    Restart Needed    Exit Code    Feature Result    PSComputerName
-------    --------------    ---------    --------------    --------------
True       No                Success      {XPS Viewer}      SEA-SRV-1
True       No                Success      {XPS Viewer}      SEA-SRV-3
```

> **NOTE INSTALLING AND REMOVING ROLES OR FEATURES FROM MULTIPLE COMPUTERS**
>
> You can use the Invoke-Command with the Server Manager cmdlets to install or remove roles or features on up to 32 computers at a time. If you specify more than 32 computers, the additional computers will be queued. You can use the *–ThrottleLimit* parameter to override this behavior.

Installing roles and features for which the payload has been removed

If the binaries for the role or feature you want to install have been removed from the server, you can use the *–Source* parameter to specify the location of the binaries needed to install the role or feature. If you don't specify this parameter, the necessary binaries will be downloaded from Windows Update unless this behavior has been disabled using Group Policy. Note that downloading role or feature binaries from Windows Update can take some time.

> ✔ **Quick check**
> - What parameter of the Install-WindowsFeature cmdlet should you include if you want to force the targeted server to restart to complete the installation of a role or feature?
>
> **Quick check answer**
> - Include the *–Restart* parameter.

Removing roles and features

You can remove roles and features from a remote server by using either Server Manager or Windows PowerShell:

- To remove roles or features by using Server Manager, select Remove Roles And Features from the Manage menu and complete the steps of the Remove Roles And Features Wizard.

- To remove roles or features by using Windows PowerShell, use the Uninstall-WindowsFeature cmdlet or its alias Remove-WindowsFeature. For help on using this cmdlet, type **Get-Help Uninstall-WindowsFeature –Detailed** at a Windows PowerShell prompt.

Lesson summary

- If the binaries for roles or features are removed from a server, you can still install the role or feature as long as either Windows Update is available or the needed binaries are made available on your network.

- You can install and remove roles and features by using either Server Manager or Windows PowerShell.

- If you need to install or remove roles or features from multiple servers at the same time, you can do this by using Windows PowerShell.

Lesson review

Answer the following questions to test your knowledge of the information in this lesson. You can find the answers to these questions and explanations of why each answer choice is correct or incorrect in the "Answers" section at the end of this chapter.

1. Which of the following Windows PowerShell commands will *not* uninstall the Windows Server Backup feature?

   A. Uninstall-WindowsFeature –Name Windows-Server-Backup

   B. Remove-WindowsFeature –Name Windows-Server-Backup

   C. Get-WindowsFeature –Name *Backup* | Uninstall-WindowsFeature

   D. Invoke-Command –ScriptBlock {Delete-WindowsFeature –Name Windows-Server-Backup}

2. What action will the following command perform?

   ```
   Get-WindowsFeature -Computer SERVER9 | Where-Object InstallState -eq Installed |
   Uninstall-WindowsFeature
   ```

   A. The command will install all available roles and features on the remote server.

   B. The command will uninstall all available roles and features on the remote server.

C. The command will uninstall all installed roles and features on the remote server.

D. The command has incorrect syntax and will generate an error.

3. What action will the following command perform?

```
Add-WindowsFeature -Name Web-Server -IncludeAllSubFeature -ComputerName
SERVER5,SERVER6
```

A. Because Add-WindowsFeature is an alias for the Install-WindowsFeature cmdlet, this command will install the Web Server (IIS) role on the two remote servers indicated.

B. Because Add-WindowsFeature is an alias for the Install-WindowsFeature cmdlet, this command will install the Web Server (IIS) role and all of its subordinate role services and features on the two remote servers indicated.

C. Because Add-WindowsFeature is an alias for the Install-WindowsFeature cmdlet, this command will install the Web Server (IIS) role, all of its subordinate role services and features, and all applicable management tools for the role and its subordinate role services and features on the two remote servers indicated.

D. The command has incorrect syntax and will generate an error.

4. If the binaries for a feature have been removed from a server, which of the following conditions are likely to prevent the feature from being successfully installed on the server? (Choose all that apply.)

A. Internet connectivity is down, which prevents the needed binaries from being downloaded from Windows Update if no local source for these binaries is present on the network and configured to be used by Server Manager or the Install-WindowsFeature cmdlet.

B. Group Policy has been configured to prevent the needed binaries from being downloaded from Windows Update, and there is no local source for these binaries present on the network and configured to be used by Server Manager or the Install-WindowsFeature cmdlet.

C. Group Policy has been configured to prevent the needed binaries from being downloaded from Windows Update, and a local source for these binaries is present on the network but has been configured incorrectly to be used by Server Manager or the Install-WindowsFeature cmdlet.

D. The server is connected to the Internet, but the Windows Update site is temporarily down, which prevents the needed binaries from being downloaded if no local source for these binaries is present on the network and configured to be used by Server Manager or the Install-WindowsFeature cmdlet.

Lesson 4: Windows PowerShell automation

Automation is essential for managing data-center environments because it simplifies the job of performing and scheduling tasks on multiple servers. Windows PowerShell 2.0, which was introduced with Windows Server 2008 R2, included a feature called *background jobs* that made it easier to automate server management tasks. Windows PowerShell 3.0, which was included in Windows Server 2012, introduced additional features that made Windows PowerShell a more flexible platform for automating server management. And Windows PowerShell 4.0, which is new in Windows Server 2012 R2, provides even more powerful automation capabilities. This lesson provides an overview of some of the Windows PowerShell features included in Windows Server 2012 and Windows Server 2012 R2 and lists some resources for administrators who are not yet familiar with Windows PowerShell and want to learn more.

After this lesson, you will be able to:

- Use the background jobs feature in Windows PowerShell 2.0 and later.
- Use some of the automation improvements introduced in Windows PowerShell 3.0 in Windows Server 2012.
- Use some of the additional automation improvements introduced in Windows PowerShell 4.0 in Windows Server 2012 R2.
- Grow your Windows PowerShell skills with the help of additional resources.

Estimated lesson time: 30 minutes

Background jobs

Windows PowerShell 2.0 introduced a feature called background jobs, which are commands that can run asynchronously in the background. For example, the following command starts a background job that installs the XPS Viewer feature on server SEA-DC-1:

```
Start-Job -ScriptBlock {Install-WindowsFeature -name XPS-Viewer -ComputerName SEA-DC-1}
```

The output from this command looks like this:

```
Id   Name   PSJobTypeName   State     HasMoreData   Location   Command
--   ----   -------------   -----     -----------   --------   -------
4    Job4   BackgroundJob   Running   True          localhost  Install-WindowsFeature...

PS C:\Users\Administrator>
```

Note that once the job is started, it runs in the background and the command prompt returns immediately so that you can run another command.

After a short period of time, you can use the Get-Job cmdlet to verify that the job you started has successfully completed:

```
Get-Job -Name Job4
```

The output from this command indicates the state of the job as Completed:

```
Id  Name  PSJobTypeName  State      HasMoreData  Location   Command
--  ----  -------------  -----      -----------  --------   -------
4   Job4  BackgroundJob  Completed  True         localhost  Install-WindowsFeature...
```

A simpler way to verify that the job has completed is to select the job's State, like this:

```
Get-Job -Name Job4 | Select-Object State

State
-----
Completed
```

> **NOTE** **THE SELECT ALIAS**
>
> You can type **select** as an alias for the Select-Object cmdlet.

If you want to start a background job and also display any output generated by the job's commands, you can use the Receive-Job cmdlet to accomplish this:

```
$job = Start-Job -ScriptBlock {Install-WindowsFeature -name XPS-Viewer -ComputerName
SEA-DC-1}
Receive-Job -Job $job

Success  Restart Needed  Exit Code   Feature Result
-------  --------------  ---------   --------------
True     No              Success     {XPS Viewer}
```

Scheduled jobs

Windows PowerShell 3.0 introduced the capability of scheduling Windows PowerShell background jobs and managing them either with Windows PowerShell or the Windows Task Scheduler. Like tasks created with Task Scheduler, you can run scheduled jobs on a one-time basis, on a recurrent schedule, or in response to some action or event.

For example, to create a scheduled job that installs the XPS Viewer feature on server SEA-DC-1 at a specific time of the current day, you first use the New-JobTrigger cmdlet to create a job trigger for the scheduled job you're going to create:

```
$trigger = New-JobTrigger -Once -At 6:40PM
```

Then you use the Register-ScheduledJob cmdlet to create the new scheduled job:

```
Register-ScheduledJob -Name InstallXPS -ScriptBlock {Install-WindowsFeature
-Name XPS-Viewer -ComputerName SEA-DC-1} -Trigger $trigger
```

The output from the Register-ScheduledJob cmdlet looks like this:

```
Id    Name         JobTriggers   Command                                    Enabled
--    ----         -----------   -------                                    -------
1     InstallXPS   1             Install-WindowsFeature -Name XPS-View...   True
```

Figure 3-23 shows the Microsoft\Windows\PowerShell\ScheduledJobs folder in the Task Scheduler after the configured job trigger time has elapsed. The Last Run Result column in the upper-right pane confirms that the job has been successfully executed.

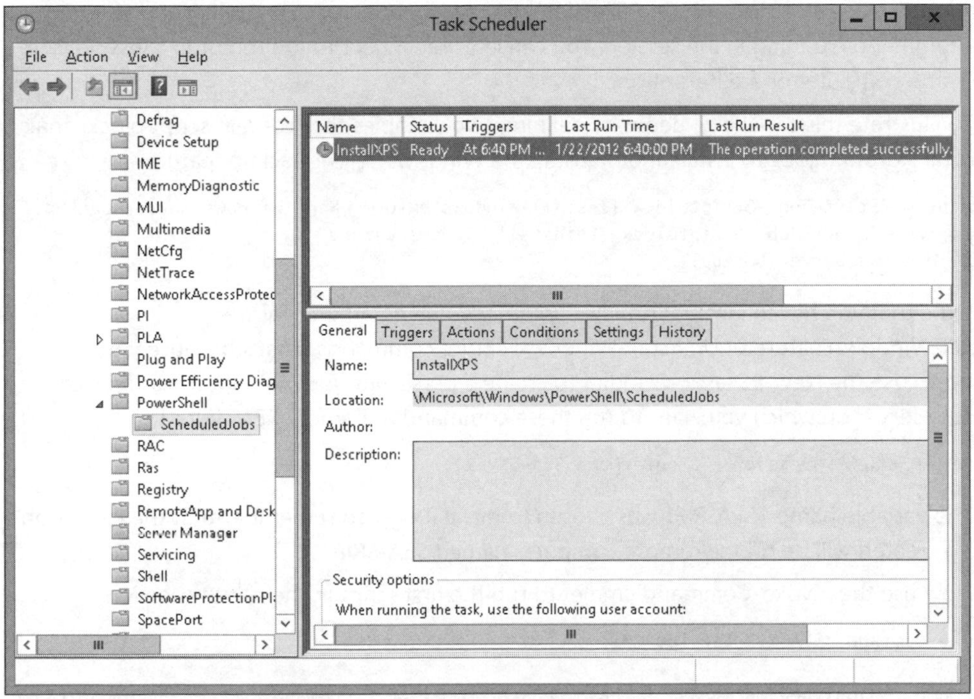

FIGURE 3-23 Use Task Scheduler to confirm the execution of a Windows PowerShell scheduled job.

A new feature of scheduled jobs in Windows PowerShell 4.0 is the *–RunNow* parameter that enables you to run a scheduled job immediately instead of configuring it to run later.

> **MORE INFO** **SCHEDULED JOB CMDLETS**
>
> For more information about Windows PowerShell scheduled job cmdlets, see *http://technet .microsoft.com/en-us/library/hh849778*.

Disconnected sessions

In Windows PowerShell 2.0 and earlier, you can use the New-PSSession cmdlet to create a Windows PowerShell session on a remote computer. When you create the new session, Windows PowerShell establishes a persistent connection to the remote computer. These persistent sessions are called PSSessions.

Windows PowerShell 3.0 introduced an enhancement to PSSessions so that any new sessions you create using the New-PSSession cmdlet are saved on the remote computer. Because of this, once you start the remote PSSession you can disconnect from it without disrupting any commands running in the session. You can later reconnect to the remote PSSession from the same computer or a different one.

To illustrate this capability, begin by defining two variables that contain script blocks that start background jobs to install and uninstall the Windows Server Backup feature:

```
$script = {Start-Job -ScriptBlock {Install-WindowsFeature -Name Windows-Server-Backup}}
$script2 = {Start-Job -ScriptBlock {Uninstall-WindowsFeature
-Name Windows-Server-Backup}}
```

Note that you haven't included the –*ComputerName* parameter for the Install-WindowsFeature or Uninstall-WindowsFeature commands. That's because you are going to use the New-PSSession cmdlet to create a persistent user-managed session to the remote server on which you want to run these commands—namely, SEA-SRV-1:

```
$SEASRV1 = New-PSSession -ComputerName SEA-SRV-1
```

The variable name $SEASRV1 was chosen to make it easy to remember that the PSSession being created will be on the remote computer named SEA-SRV-1.

Now use the Invoke-Command cmdlet to run the first script in the remote session:

```
Invoke-Command $SEASRV1 $script

Id  Name  PSJobTypeName  State    HasMoreData  Location  Command          PSComputerName
--  ----  -------------  -----    -----------  --------  -------          ---
1   Job1  BackgroundJob  Running  True         localhost Install-WindowsFeature... SEA
```

The output from this command shows that a background job that installs the Windows Server Backup feature is now running on the remote server, so you can use the Disconnect-PSSession cmdlet to disconnect from the remote session while leaving the background job running in it:

```
Disconnect-PSSession -Name $SEASRV1
```

At this point, the Get-WindowsFeature cmdlet enables you to confirm that the Windows Server Backup feature has been successfully installed on SEA-SRV-1:

```
Get-WindowsFeature -Name Windows-Server-Backup -ComputerName SEA-SRV-1

Display Name              Name                   Install State
------------              ----                   -------------
[X] Windows Server Backup Windows-Server-Backup  Installed
```

Next, uninstall the feature on the remote server. You begin by using the Connect-PSSession cmdlet to reconnect to the remote session, which is still running on SEA-SRV-1:

```
Connect-PSSession -Name $SEASRV1
```

You then use Invoke-Command again, this time to remove the feature from the remote server:

```
Invoke-Command $SEASRV1 $script2
```

By using Get-WindowsFeature again, you can confirm that the feature has been successfully removed from the remote computer.

Finally, because you're now finished managing the remote server, you pipe the output of the Get-PSSession cmdlet, which gets all PSSessions that were created during the current session, into the Remove-PSSession cmdlet, which closes the PSSessions:

```
Get-PSSession | Remove-PSSession
```

> **MORE INFO**   **CMDLETS**
>
> For more information about the cmdlets in this section, see *http://technet.microsoft.com /en-us/library/hh849695*.

✔ **Quick check**

- What cmdlet should you use to get all the Windows PowerShell sessions on the local and remote computers?

Quick check answer

- Use the Get-PSSession cmdlet.

Desired State Configuration

Probably the biggest new feature in Windows PowerShell 4.0 is Desired State Configuration (DSC), which is designed to enable you to specify what software should be installed on a server and how that software should be configured. DSC is still a work in progress, however, and its real power is likely to be unleashed in the next version of Windows Server.

DSC works as follows. You start by creating a Windows PowerShell script block that defines the desired configuration for the target server. The script block begins with the keyword Configuration followed by an identifier, and the rest of the script block is contained within braces, like this:

```
Configuration MyServers
{
```

```
...
}
```

Inside the configuration block, you include one or more node blocks that define the desired configuration for each node (server) in your environment. Node blocks start with the keyword Node followed by an identifier and braces:

```
Configuration MyServers
{
    Node "SEA-SRV-1"
    {
    ...
    }
    Node "SEA-SRV-2"
    {
    ...
    }
...
}
```

Inside each node block, you then define resource blocks that configure specific resources on the node. These resources can include server features, configuration settings, files and folders, registry keys, and more. Resource blocks start with the name of the resource followed by an identifier and braces:

```
Configuration MyServers
{
    Node "SEA-SRV-1"
    {
        WindowsFeature MyServerFeatures
        {
            Name = "Windows-Server-Backup"
            Ensure = "Present"
        }
    }
    Node "SEA-SRV-2"
    {
        File MyServerFiles
        {
            Type = "Directory"
            Ensure = "Present"
            DestinationPath = "C:\Scripts"
        }
    }
...
}
```

In the above example, the configuration block is designed to ensure that server SEA-SRV-1 has the Windows Server Backup feature installed and that a folder named Scripts is present in the root of C drive on server SEA-SRV-2. To invoke this configuration block, you just invoke it by name, like this:

```
PS C:\> MyServers
```

Invoking the configuration creates Microsoft Operations Framework (MOF) files that contain the configuration information for the target nodes. The MOF files are then saved in a new child directory of the current directory. The new child directory will have the same name as the configuration block (MyServers in this example).

Once the MOF files have been created, you can enact this configuration by running the following command:

```
Start-DscConfiguration -Wait -Verbose -Path .\MyServers
```

The *–Wait* parameter causes the command to run interactively. If you omit this parameter, the command creates and returns a job instead.

> **MORE INFO**   For more information on DSC, see *http://technet.microsoft.com/en-us /library/dn249912.aspx.*

Resources for learning Windows PowerShell

If you're new to Windows PowerShell, you can use its built-in help resources to learn about different cmdlets. There are also a number of helpful books you can learn from.

Using Windows PowerShell help

You can use the Get-Help cmdlet to display the syntax for other cmdlets and examples of how to use those cmdlets. For example, to display basic help for the Connect-PSSession cmdlet, use this command:

```
Get-Help Connect-PSSession
```

To show detailed help, use this command:

```
Get-Help Connect-PSSession -detailed
```

To show some examples of how to use Connect-PSSession, use this command:

```
Get-Help Connect-PSSession -examples
```

To show detailed help and examples, use this command:

```
Get-Help Connect-PSSession -full
```

Updatable help

Windows PowerShell 3.0 introduced the capability of downloading updated help files for the cmdlets in Windows PowerShell modules. To download the latest help files, use this command:

```
Update-Help
```

You can also use this cmdlet to download updated help files to a shared folder on your network so that you can install them on your servers without needing to allow those servers to connect to the Internet. To learn how to use the Update-Help cmdlet, use this command:

```
Get-Help Update-Help
```

Enhanced online help

Windows PowerShell 3.0 also introduced the ability to display the online version of the help for a cmdlet in your default Internet browser. To do this, include the *–Online* parameter with the Get-Help cmdlet, like this:

```
Get-Help Connect-PSSession -Online
```

Save-Help improvements

Windows PowerShell 3.0 introduced a cmdlet called Save-Help that you could use to download and save help content to your local computer. This made it somewhat easier to distribute help content for Windows PowerShell modules because instead of having to download the content to all your servers or workstations, you could just share the folder containing the content on your local machine. The catch, however, was that the Save-Help cmdlet could only download content for Windows PowerShell modules that are installed on the local machine. If you needed to distribute content for a module that wasn't installed on the local machine, you needed to download it from a server or client computer that already has that module installed and then copy it to your shared folder.

To make downloading and distributing help content easier, Windows PowerShell 4.0 enables you to save help content for modules that are installed on remote computers so you can copy them to your local computer even if your local computer doesn't have Internet connectivity.

For example, let's say that a server named SEA-SRV-8 has a Server Core installation of Windows Server 2012 R2 installed. Windows PowerShell 4.0 has a new module called ServerCore that includes two cmdlets not previously available in earlier Windows Server versions:

- **Get-DisplayResolution**   Shows the current display resolution for a Server Core server
- **Set-DisplayResolution**   Changes the display resolution for a Server Core server

You can verify this by using the Get-Command cmdlet on any Windows Server 2012 R2 installation, like this:

```
PS C:\> Get-Command -Module ServerCore

CommandType     Name                              ModuleName
-----------     ----                              ----------
Function        Get-DisplayResolution             ServerCore
Function        Set-DisplayResolution             ServerCore
```

Now, let's say you want to install the help content for these commands on your local machine by copying the content from the remote server SEA-SRV-8. To do this from your local machine, first use the New-PSSession cmdlet to create a persistent connection to the remote server and assign it to a variable, like this:

```
$a = New-PSSession -computer SEA-SRV-8
```

Next, use the Get-Module cmdlet to get the ServerCore module from the remote server and assign it to another variable:

```
$b = Get-Module ServerCore -PSSession $a -ListAvailable
```

Finally, use the Save-Help cmdlet to copy the help for the ServerCore module from the remote server to a folder on your local machine:

```
Save-Help -Module $b -DestinationPath C:\PShelp
```

Recommended books

The following are some books that Windows PowerShell experts at Microsoft have recommended. These are listed in order, starting with books for beginners and ending with books for advanced users:

- *Learn Windows PowerShell 3 in a Month of Lunches*, by Don Jones (Manning Publications, 2012)
- *Windows PowerShell 3.0 First Steps*, by Ed Wilson (Microsoft Press, 2014)
- *Windows PowerShell Cookbook, 3rd Edition*, by Lee Holmes (O'Reilly Media, 2013)
- *PowerShell in Depth: An Administrator's Guide* by Don Jones (Manning Publications, 2013)

More recommendations for learning about Windows PowerShell can be found in the Windows PowerShell Survival Guide in the TechNet Wiki at *http://social.technet.microsoft.com /wiki/contents/articles/183.windows-powershell-survival-guide-en-us.aspx*.

Lesson summary

- You can run Windows PowerShell background jobs asynchronously in the background to execute commands and scripts on remote servers.
- You can use Windows PowerShell scheduled jobs to schedule PowerShell execution of commands and scripts on remote servers.
- You can disconnect from a Windows PowerShell session running on a remote server and allow the commands and scripts in the session to continue to execute.
- You can reconnect to a disconnected Windows PowerShell session on a remote server.
- You can download updated help files for the cmdlets in Windows PowerShell modules.

Lesson review

Answer the following questions to test your knowledge of the information in this lesson. You can find the answers to these questions and explanations of why each answer choice is correct or incorrect in the "Answers" section at the end of this chapter.

1. Which of the following statements is *not* true about background jobs?

    A. You can view them by using the Get-ScheduledJob cmdlet.

    B. You can create them by using the Start-Job cmdlet.

    C. You can temporarily stop them by using the Suspend-Job cmdlet.

    D. You can delete them by using the Remove-Job cmdlet.

2. What action will typing the command **New-JobTrigger –Daily –At "4:15 AM" –DaysInterval 3** perform when it is run?

    A. It creates a new scheduled job that runs daily at 4:15 A.M. on the third day of each week.

    B. It creates a new scheduled job that runs daily at 4:15 A.M. every third day.

    C. It creates a new job trigger that can be used to run a scheduled job daily at 4:15 A.M. on the third day of each week.

    D. It creates a new job trigger that can be used to run a scheduled job daily at 4:15 A.M. every third day.

3. What two cmdlets would you use to create a scheduled job?

    A. New-Job and New-JobTrigger

    B. New-Job and New-ScheduledJob

    C. New-JobTrigger and New-ScheduledJob

    D. New-JobTrigger and Register-ScheduledJob

4. Which of the following is *not* true concerning PSSessions in Windows PowerShell 3.0?

    A. Any new sessions you create using the New-PSSession cmdlet are saved on the remote computer.

    B. Once you start the remote PSSession, you can disconnect from it using the Disconnect-PSSession cmdlet without disrupting any commands running in the session.

    C. You can later reconnect to a disconnected remote PSSession from the same or a different computer using the Connect-PSSession cmdlet.

    D. You should use PSSessions only when you need to run a single command on a remote server, not multiple commands that share data such as a function or the value of a variable.

Practice exercises

The goal of this section is to provide you with hands-on practice with the following:

- Installing roles and features
- Managing alerts with the Dashboard
- Scheduling tasks using Windows PowerShell jobs

To perform the exercises in this section, you need at least one clean installation of Windows Server 2012 R2 using the Server With A GUI installation option. The server should be a stand-alone server belonging to a workgroup, have Internet connectivity, and have no additional roles or features installed. You should be logged on interactively to the server using a user account that is a member of the local Administrators group but that is not the default Administrator account. For the purpose of these exercises, the name of the server is assumed to be SERVER1.

Exercise 1: Installing roles and features

In this exercise, you use both Server Manager and Windows PowerShell to install and remove roles and features from a server.

1. Open a Windows PowerShell console with administrative privileges using the Run As Administrator option.

2. Pipe the output of Get-WindowsFeature into Where-Object to display a list of currently installed roles and features. Note any roles and features that are installed by default on a clean installation using the Server With A GUI installation option.

3. Start Server Manager, switch to the All Servers page, and scroll down to the Roles And Features tile. Compare what you see in that tile with the output of the command in step 2.

4. Use Server Manager to launch the Add Roles And Features Wizard and install the DHCP Server role on the server, including the administration tools for this role.

5. Click the Notifications flag on the menu bar of the Dashboard to confirm that the feature installed successfully.

6. Run the command **Get-WindowsFeature –Name *DHCP*** to verify that both the DHCP Server role and DHCP Server Tools feature are now installed.

7. Pipe the output of the previous command into Uninstall-WindowsFeature to uninstall both the DHCP Server role and DHCP Server Tools feature from the server.

8. Notice the warning message that says you must restart the server to finish the removal process. Do not restart the server yet.

9. Run the command **Get-WindowsFeature –Name *DHCP*** again and examine the Install State of the DHCP Server role and DHCP Server Tools feature.

10. Use the **Shutdown** command to restart the server.

11. When you log on again, use the command **Get-WindowsFeature –Name *DHCP***
    again and note the Install State of the DHCP Server role and DHCP Server Tools
    feature.

12. Disconnect your server from the Internet.

13. Launch the Add Roles And Features Wizard again and select .NET Framework 3.5
    Features on the Select Features page.

14. Note the yellow warning message on the Confirm Installation Selections page and click
    Install.

15. Note the error message. The installation of this feature failed because the binaries for
    .NET Framework 3.5 (which includes .NET Framework 2.0 and .NET Framework 3.0) are
    not included in a Windows Server 2012 R2 installation and must either be downloaded
    from Windows Update or made available on your network. Read *http://technet*
    .microsoft.com/en-us/library/hh831809#BKMK_FoD for more information.

16. Close the Add Roles And Features Wizard and reconnect your server to the Internet.

Exercise 2: Managing alerts with the Dashboard

In this exercise, you configure and raise alerts on the Dashboard of Server Manager.

1. Open Server Manager and select the Dashboard page.

2. Click the Notifications flag on the menu bar at the top to display any error, warning, or
   information alerts that have been raised. Read the alerts and dismiss them by clicking
   Remove Task (the X button) at the upper right of each alert.

3. Switch to the All Servers page and review the events listed in the Events tile.

4. Click the Tasks control in the Events tile and configure the tile to display only Error
   events that occurred in the System event log during the last six hours.

5. Configure the Events tile again to display only Warning events that occurred in all
   event logs during the last six hours.

6. Filter the list of events by entering the event ID of one of the listed events into the
   Filter text box.

7. Click the right-side Query control, type a descriptive name for your query, and save
   your query.

8. Clear the filter you applied in step 6.

9. Click the left Query control and select your previously saved query.

10. Delete your saved query and clear the filter again.

11. Sort the list of services in the Service tile by Display Name.

12. Verify that the Print Spooler service is running and then right-click the service and
    stop it.

13. Switch to the Dashboard page and note the alert raised for the Services thumbnail in
    the Local Server tile.

14. Click on this alert, restart the Print Spooler service, and note that the alert previously raised has been removed.

15. Click on the Services thumbnail in the Local Server tile and configure the tile so that a stopped service will not raise an alert.

16. Return to the All Servers page and use the Services tile to stop the Print Spooler service again.

17. Return to the Dashboard and note that this time no alert has been raised in the Services tile.

18. Return to the All Servers page and restart the Print Spooler service.

Exercise 3: Scheduling tasks using Windows PowerShell jobs

In this exercise, you create a Windows PowerShell scheduled job to install a role on the server.

1. Run the **Get-ScheduledJob** command and verify that there are currently no Windows PowerShell scheduled jobs on the server.

2. Run the following command to create a new job trigger that will cause a scheduled job to run the next time the user logs on:

   ```
   $trigger = New-JobTrigger -AtLogon -RandomDelay 00:01:00
   ```

3. Find out what the *–RandomDelay* parameter does in the preceding command by reviewing the syntax of the New-JobTrigger cmdlet at *http://technet.microsoft.com /en-us/library/hh849759*.

4. Run the following command to create a scheduled job that will install all role services of the Web Server (IIS) role when the trigger condition you created in step 2 occurs:

   ```
   Register-ScheduledJob -Name MyJob -ScriptBlock {Install-WindowsFeature
   -Name Web-Server -IncludeAllSubFeature -IncludeManagementTools}
   -Trigger $trigger
   ```

5. Run the **Get-JobTrigger MyJob** command to display the trigger condition for the scheduled job you created in step 4.

6. Use the Tools menu of Server Manager to open Task Scheduler to verify the creation of the Windows PowerShell scheduled job you created and examine its properties. Then answer the following question:

   Question: What would happen if you right-clicked MyJob in Task Scheduler and selected Run?

   Answer: The job MyJob would run immediately to install the Web Server (IIS) role with all its role services on the server.

7. Close Task Scheduler and return to the Windows PowerShell console.

8. Log off the server and then log on again.

9. Open an elevated Windows PowerShell console and repeatedly run the command **Get-Job | Select-Object State** until the output shows *Running*, indicating that the scheduled job has begun to execute. (Hint: Press the Up arrow key followed by Enter to rerun the command without having to retype it.)

10. Continue running the command **Get-Job | Select-Object State** until the output shows *Completed*, indicating that the scheduled job has finished.

11. Run the command **Get-WindowsFeature –Name *Web*** and view the Install State of all role services and features associated with the Web Server (IIS) role.

12. Use Windows PowerShell to uninstall the Web Server (IIS) role and all role services and features associated with it, including the applicable management tools.

Suggested practice exercises

The following additional practice exercises are designed to give you more opportunities to practice what you've learned and to help you successfully master the lessons presented in this chapter.

- **Exercise 1**   If you have a domain controller available, join your two Windows Server 2012 R2 servers to the domain and try using the commands in the section "Disconnected sessions" in Lesson 4 to install the Windows Server Backup feature on SERVER2 by running Windows PowerShell commands on SERVER1.

- **Exercise 2**   If you don't have a domain controller available, try using the information found in the section "Add and manage servers in workgroups" at *http://technet .microsoft.com/en-us/library/hh831453* to use Server Manager on SERVER1 to add SERVER2 to the server pool.

- **Exercise 3**   If you have a server running Windows Server 2008 or Windows Server 2008 R2 available, try enabling remote management on that server using the information found at *http://technet.microsoft.com/en-us/library/hh921475* and then use Server Manager on SERVER1 to add the down-level server to the server pool.

- **Exercise 4**   Create a configuration block that ensures a role or feature is installed on your local server and then invoke the configuration by using the Start-DscConfiguration cmdlet.

Answers

This section contains the answers to the lesson review questions in this chapter.

Lesson 1

1. **Correct answers: B, C, and D**

    A. **Incorrect:** The Print Services page will be available in Server Manager as long as at least one of your print servers has been added to your server pool, even if all your print servers are currently offline.

    B. **Correct:** At least one server must be running the Print And Document Services role, and the server must have been added to your server pool for the Print Services page to be available in Server Manager.

    C. **Correct:** At least one server running the Print And Document Services role must be present in your server pool for the Print Services page to be available in Server Manager.

    D. **Correct:** At least one server running the Print And Document Services role must be present in your server pool for the Print Services page to be available in Server Manager, and servers running an earlier version of Windows Server must be configured for remote management before they can be added to the server pool.

2. **Correct answers: B and D**

    A. **Incorrect:** The Dashboard is used to display alerts and does not indicate whether remote management is enabled on the server.

    B. **Correct:** If the Remote Management setting on the Local Server page displays Enabled, remote management is enabled on the server.

    C. **Incorrect:** The All Servers page is used to add servers to the server pool, create server groups, configure event data, and perform other tasks, but it does not indicate whether remote management is enabled on the server.

    D. **Correct:** The output of this command indicates whether remote management is enabled on the server.

3. **Correct answer: B**

    A. **Incorrect:** Remote Server Administration Tools for Windows 8.1 includes tools for managing roles and features that run on Windows Server 2012 R2 and Windows Server 2012. In limited cases, you also can use the tools to manage roles and features that are running on Windows Server 2008 R2 or Windows Server 2008. So you won't be able to manage all roles and features on servers running Windows Server 2008 R2.

    B. **Correct:** Remote Server Administration Tools for Windows 8.1 includes tools for managing roles and features that run on Windows Server 2012 R2 and Windows Server 2012. In limited cases, you also can use the tools to manage roles and features that are running on Windows Server 2008 R2 or Windows Server 2008. So you will be able to manage some roles and features on servers running Windows Server 2008 R2.

C. **Incorrect:** Remote Server Administration Tools for Windows 8.1 includes tools for managing roles and features that run on Windows Server 2012 R2 and Windows Server 2012. In limited cases, you also can use the tools to manage roles and features that are running on Windows Server 2008 R2 or Windows Server 2008. So you can manage some roles and features on servers running Windows Server 2008 R2.

D. **Incorrect:** Remote Server Administration Tools for Windows 8.1 must be installed on Windows 8.1 and cannot be installed on earlier Windows versions.

Lesson 2

1. **Correct answer: D**

   A. **Incorrect:** To add a server to a server group, the server must first be present in your server pool. Because the two servers are not present in the server pool, this action cannot be performed.

   B. **Incorrect:** There is only one server pool, and it represents all the servers that are currently being managed using Server Manager. You cannot create an additional server pool, so this action cannot be performed.

   C. **Incorrect:** To add a server to a server group, the server must first be present in your server pool. Because the two servers are not present in the server pool, this action cannot be performed.

   D. **Correct:** Servers must be added to your server pool before you can manage them using Server Manager. Find the servers by querying Active Directory or your DNS servers or by importing their names in a text file and then add them to your server pool.

2. **Correct answers: B**

   A. **Incorrect:** Server groups cannot be used to assign privileges. They are simply a means of logically grouping managed servers in your environment.

   B. **Correct:** By creating different server groups for the different geographical locations of your organization, you can facilitate server management by making it easy to determine what servers are located where.

   C. **Incorrect:** Server groups cannot be used to delegate permissions. They are simply a means of logically grouping managed servers in your environment.

   D. **Incorrect:** Server groups cannot be nested.

3. **Correct answers: A and C**

   A. Correct: Performance counters must be started on a server before performance data can be collected from that server.

   B. Incorrect: When performance counters have been started on a server, performance data will be collected. It might take several minutes until that data is displayed. After three hours have elapsed, however, you should certainly see some performance data displayed in graph form.

   C. Correct: The refresh period for Server Manager can be configured in minutes from 1 minute to 14,400 minutes (10 days). If you configure the refresh period to be more than three hours, the Dashboard display will not change until a refresh occurs and you won't see any new alerts raised until it refreshes.

   D. Incorrect: Server groups are simply a means of logically grouping managed servers in your environment. They have no effect on any configuration you perform on the All Servers page.

4. **Correct answer: D**

   A. Incorrect: One or more running services can be stopped by right-clicking them in a Services tile and selecting Stop Services.

   B. Incorrect: One or more running services can be paused by right-clicking them in a Services tile and selecting Pause Services as long as their Startup Type is Manual.

   C. Incorrect: One or more stopped services can be started by right-clicking them in a Services tile and selecting Start Services as long as their Startup Type is not Disabled.

   D. Correct: You cannot change the Startup Type of services from a Services tile. To do this, you can use the Services MMC console, which you can launch from the Tools menu of Server Manager.

Lesson 3

1. **Correct answer: D**

   A. Incorrect: You can use the Uninstall-WindowsFeature cmdlet to uninstall features.

   B. Incorrect: Remove-WindowsFeature is an alias for the Uninstall-WindowsFeature cmdlet added for backward compatibility, and you can use it to uninstall features.

   C. Incorrect: Piping the output of the Get-WindowsFeature cmdlet into Uninstall-WindowsFeature like this will uninstall all features that match the wildcard *Backup*.

   D. Correct: Delete-WindowsFeature is not a Windows PowerShell cmdlet or standard alias, but if you change **Delete** to **Uninstall**, this command will work.

2. **Correct answer: C**

   A. **Incorrect:** The final command in the pipeline is Uninstall-WindowsFeature, which uninstalls features, not installs them.

   B. **Incorrect:** If a role or feature is available, it can be installed, not uninstalled.

   C. **Correct:** Typing the command **Get-WindowsFeature –Computer SERVER9 | Where-Object InstallState –eq Installed** will get all roles and features that are currently installed on the remote server. Piping the output of this command into the Uninstall-WindowsFeature cmdlet will then uninstall all installed roles and features on the server

   D. **Incorrect:** The syntax is valid; see answer C for the explanation.

3. **Correct answer: B**

   A. **Incorrect:** The presence of the *–IncludeAllSubFeature* parameter in this command indicates that the command will install not only the Web Server (IIS) feature but also all of its subordinate role services and features.

   B. **Correct:** The presence of the *–IncludeAllSubFeature* parameter in this command indicates that the command will install the Web Server (IIS) feature and all of its subordinate role services and features.

   C. **Incorrect:** The absence of the *–IncludeManagementTools* parameter in this command indicates that the command will install the Web Server (IIS) feature and all of its subordinate role services and features but none of the applicable management tools for the role and its subordinate role services and features.

   D. **Incorrect:** The syntax is valid; see answer B for the explanation.

4. **Correct answers: A, B, and C**

   A. **Correct:** If no local source for these binaries is present on the network and configured to be used by Server Manager or the Install-WindowsFeature cmdlet, and if Group Policy has not been configured to prevent the needed binaries from being downloaded from Windows Update, Windows will attempt to download the needed binaries from Windows Update unless Internet connectivity is down, in which case the install will fail.

   B. **Correct:** If Group Policy has been configured to prevent the needed binaries from being downloaded from Windows Update, and if there is no local source for these binaries present on the network and configured to be used by Server Manager or the Install-WindowsFeature cmdlet, the binaries for installing the role are not available and the install will fail.

   C. **Correct:** If Group Policy has been configured to prevent the needed binaries from being downloaded from Windows Update, and if a local source for these binaries is present on the network but has been configured incorrectly to be used by Server Manager or the Install-WindowsFeature cmdlet, the binaries for installing the role cannot be used to install the feature.

D. Incorrect: This scenario is possible but very unlikely because Microsoft tries to ensure that Windows Update is always available.

Lesson 4

1. **Correct answer: A**

    A. Correct: The Get-ScheduledJob cmdlet can be used to manage only scheduled jobs, not manually started background jobs.

    B. Incorrect: The Start-Job cmdlet can be used to start background jobs.

    C. Incorrect: The Suspend-Job cmdlet can be used to pause background jobs.

    D. Incorrect: The Remove-Job cmdlet can be used to delete background jobs.

2. **Correct answer: D**

    A. Incorrect: The New-JobTrigger cmdlet is used to create job triggers, not scheduled jobs.

    B. Incorrect: The New-JobTrigger cmdlet is used to create job triggers, not scheduled jobs.

    C. Incorrect: The *–DaysInterval* parameter specifies the number of days between occurrences on a daily schedule, not on a weekly schedule.

    D. Correct: The *–DaysInterval* parameter specifies the number of days between occurrences on a daily schedule. See *http://technet.microsoft.com/en-us/library /hh849759*.

3. **Correct answer: D**

    A. Incorrect: The New-JobTrigger cmdlet is needed to create a job trigger for your scheduled job, but the New-Job cmdlet can be used to create only background jobs, not scheduled jobs.

    B. Incorrect: The New-Job cmdlet can be used to create only background jobs, not scheduled jobs; however, New-ScheduledJob is not a valid Windows PowerShell cmdlet. See *http://technet.microsoft.com/en-us/library/hh849778*.

    C. Incorrect: The New-JobTrigger cmdlet is needed to create a job trigger for your scheduled job, but New-ScheduledJob is not a valid Windows PowerShell cmdlet. See *http://technet.microsoft.com/en-us/library/hh849778*.

    D. Correct: The New-JobTrigger cmdlet is needed to create a job trigger for your scheduled job, and the Register-ScheduledJob cmdlet is then used to create the scheduled job and associate it with the job trigger.

4. **Correct answer: D**

    A. Incorrect: In Windows PowerShell 3.0, any new sessions you create using the New-PSSession cmdlet are saved on the remote computer.

    B. Incorrect: You use the Disconnect-PSSession cmdlet to disconnect from a remote PSSession without disrupting any commands running in the session.

C. **Incorrect:** You use the Connect-PSSession cmdlet to reconnect to a disconnected remote PSSession from the same computer or a different one.

D. **Correct:** PSSessions can be used to run multiple commands that share data, such as a function or the value of a variable.

CHAPTER 4

Deploying domain controllers

Active Directory Domain Services (AD DS) provides a distributed database and directory service that stores and manages information about the users, computers, groups,
shares, printers, and other types of objects that comprise an organization's IT infrastructure.
With AD DS, you can create the following:

- A forest that acts as the security boundary for your organization

- One or more domains that define the scope of authority of administrators in your
  organization

- A hierarchical collection of organizational units (OUs) to simplify delegation of
  authority for managing directory objects

- Sites that map to the structure of your organization's network

Domain controllers are servers that host AD DS within your infrastructure, and the
process for deploying domain controllers has been enhanced in several ways beginning
with Microsoft Windows Server 2012. The Active Directory Domain Services Configuration
Wizard (dcpromo.exe) used in previous Windows Server versions has been replaced with
a new Active Directory Domain Services Configuration Wizard that simplifies the task
of deploying new domain controllers to help reduce the possibility of error. Windows
PowerShell now provides a way of scripting all aspects of domain controller deployment,
making it possible to automate the mass deployment of domain controllers in data center environments. Safeguards have also been introduced so that you can safely virtualize
domain controllers, which simplifies deployment of private and public cloud solutions.

Windows Server 2012 R2 introduced several more enhancements to Active Directory, the
most important of which is Workplace Join. Workplace Join enables information workers to
join their personal devices to the Active Directory infrastructure of their company to access
company resources and services from these devices. Workplace Join is enabled by means of
a new Device Registration Service (DRS) included in the Active Directory Federation Role in
Windows Server 2012 R2. Administrators can use Workplace Join to identify known devices
with device authentication and can then provide these devices with conditional access to
resources. The result for users is a more seamless Single Sign-On experience to company
resources from trusted devices.

This chapter describes how to prepare for the deployment of Windows Server 2012 and
Windows Server 2012 R2 domain controllers, how to deploy domain controllers using both
Server Manager and Windows PowerShell, and how to take advantage of domain-controller
virtualization.

Lessons in this chapter:

Before you begin

To complete the practice exercises in this chapter

- You need at least two servers that have a clean install of Windows Server 2012 R2 and are configured as stand-alone servers in a workgroup. They can be either physical servers or virtual machines, and their TCP/IP settings should be configured to provide connectivity with the Internet.

- You might need additional servers to perform some of the optional exercises in the "Suggested practice exercises" section. You might also need access to installation media for earlier Windows Server versions for some of these exercises.

- You should be familiar with basic AD DS concepts such as forests, domains, organizational units (OUs), sites, domain controllers, schema, replication, and so on.

- It will be helpful if you also have at least rudimentary knowledge of using Windows PowerShell.

Lesson 1: Preparing for deploying domain controllers

Careful planning is critical when you roll out or make changes to an AD DS environment by adding, replacing, or upgrading domain controllers. A number of different scenarios are possible, and you should identify best practices for each scenario you need to implement for your organization. This lesson describes some common AD DS deployment scenarios and the different ways that you can deploy domain controllers for these scenarios.

After this lesson, you will be able to:

- Describe some common AD DS deployment scenarios.
- Describe different ways Windows Server 2012 and Windows Server 2012 R2 domain controllers can be deployed in a new forest.
- Describe different ways Windows Server 2012 and Windows Server 2012 R2 domain controllers can be deployed in an existing forest running earlier versions of Windows Server.

Estimated lesson time: 30 minutes

AD DS deployment scenarios

There are two basic scenarios for AD DS deployment:

- Deploying a new forest based on AD DS in Windows Server 2012 or Windows Server 2012 R2
- Deploying domain controllers in an existing forest based on AD DS in an earlier version of Windows Server

The sections that follow describe the high-level differences between these scenarios.

New forest deployments

If your organization has not yet deployed AD DS, you're in luck: this is your opportunity to get it right. Although deploying a new forest based on Windows Server 2012 or Windows Server 2012 R2 AD DS is as simple as deploying your first domain controller (the forest root domain controller), there are numerous planning considerations you need to be aware of before you perform this task.

At a basic level, the technical requirements for deploying your forest root domain controller are straightforward:

- You must have local Administrator credentials on the server.
- You must have one or more local fixed NTFS volumes to store the directory database, log files, and SYSVOL share.
- You need to appropriately configure TCP/IP settings, including Domain Name Server (DNS) server addresses.
- You either need to use an existing DNS server infrastructure or deploy the DNS Server role with the Active Directory Domain Services role when you make your server a domain controller.

The preceding technical requirements, however, are only a small part of the overall AD DS planning process. The key at this stage is to plan the entire directory structure of your organization so that you won't need to make drastic changes later, like renaming domains or modifying your hierarchy of OUs. The details of such planning are well beyond the scope of this book, but for readers who are interested, the "More Info" topic in this section highlights some resources that can help you design an effective AD DS infrastructure and plan for its implementation.

After you create your forest by deploying the forest root domain controller, you can deploy additional controllers for the following purposes:

- Deploy additional domain controllers in your forest root domain for redundancy and load-balancing purposes.
- Deploy domain controllers that create additional domains within your forest based on your organization's administrative or geographical structure.
- Deploy read-only domain controllers (RODCs) at less secure, branch office sites within your organization.

- Deploy virtualized domain controllers to provide greater support for private and public cloud-computing environments.

MORE INFO   **RESOURCES FOR AD DS PLANNING AND DESIGN**

The following resources can be helpful if you are planning an implementation of AD DS for the first time:

- **Designing and Deploying Directory and Security Services**   This section of the Windows Server 2003 Deployment Guide on Microsoft TechNet—found at *http:// technet.microsoft.com/en-us/library/cc787010(v=WS.10).aspx*—is a bit dated, but it's still a good starting point to learn how to design and plan an AD DS environment. Be sure to supplement this resource, however, with the more recent resources that follow.

- **AD DS Design Guide**   This section of the TechNet Library—found at *http://technet .microsoft.com/en-us/library/cc754678(v=ws.10)*—provides updated guidance on how to design an AD DS environment based on Windows Server 2008, Windows Server 2008 R2, or Windows Server 2012. Apart from implementing new Windows Server 2012 R2 features like Workplace Join, the guidance in this document also applies to designing AD DS environments based on Windows Server 2012 R2.

- **Windows Server 2008 Active Directory Resource Kit from Microsoft Press**   This book provides an excellent introduction to basic AD DS concepts, design, and administration. The book is available from O'Reilly Media at *http://shop.oreilly.com /product/9780735625150.do* in various formats, including APK, DAISY, ePub, Mobi, PDF, and print-on-demand.

Finally, a good place to find answers to your AD DS questions is the Directory Services forum on TechNet at *http://social.technet.microsoft.com/Forums/windowsserver/en-us /home?forum=winserverDS*.

Best practices for new forest deployments

The actual number of domain controllers and the types needed for your environment depend on a number of factors, but here are some key best practices to keep in mind:

- Each domain should have at least two functioning writeable domain controllers to provide fault tolerance. If a domain has only one domain controller and this domain controller fails, users will not be able to log on to the domain or access any resources in the domain. And if you have only one writable domain controller in your domain and this domain controller fails, you won't be able to perform any AD DS management tasks.

- Each domain in each location should also have a sufficient number of domain controllers to service the needs of users for logging on and accessing network resources. The TechNet sections described in the earlier "More Info" topic include some recommendations on how to determine the number of domain controllers you need based on their hardware configuration and the number of users at the location.

- Domain controllers should be dedicated servers that are used only for hosting the AD DS and DNS Server roles. Their full attention should be directed to performing their main job, which is authenticating users and computers for client logons and for accessing network resources.

- The simplest forest design has one domain. The more domains you have, the more administrative overhead you will experience managing multiple service administrator groups, maintaining consistency among Group Policy settings that are common to different domains, maintaining consistency among access control and auditing settings that are common to different domains, and so on.

- If your organization has multiple sites, such as a head office and one or more remote branch offices, you should generally deploy at least one domain controller at each remote office to provide users with faster logon times and more efficient access to network resources. For best security, domain controllers at remote offices should be RODCs.

Existing forest deployments

Most readers of this book will likely deploy new Windows Server 2012 or Windows Server 2012 R2 domain controllers in an existing Active Directory infrastructure based on Windows Server 2008 R2, Windows Server 2008, or Windows Server 2003. There are several ways you can introduce such changes:

- Deploying new Windows Server 2012 or Windows Server 2012 R2 domain controllers in an existing forest whose domain controllers are running an earlier version of Windows Server

- Upgrading domain controllers running earlier versions of Windows Server to Windows Server 2012 or Windows Server 2012 R2

These scenarios will be discussed later in this lesson.

> ***IMPORTANT*** **END OF SUPPORT DATE FOR WINDOWS SERVER 2003**
>
> **Windows Server 2003 exited mainstream support in July 2010 and will exit extended support in July 2015, so if you are planning to upgrade your AD DS environment to Windows Server 2012 or Windows Server 2012 R2, you should do it before mainstream support ends unless you have an extended support agreement with Microsoft.**

New forest domain controller deployment

Depending on the administrative and geographical structure of your organization and the number of users to be supported, deploying a new forest based on Windows Server 2012 or Windows Server 2012 R2 AD DS might involve several of the following domain controller deployment scenarios:

- Deploying the first domain controller in a new forest (required)
- Deploying the first domain controller for a new domain (required if additional domains need to be created in the forest)
- Deploying additional domain controllers in each domain to provide fault tolerance and support the number of users at each location (recommended)
- Deploying read-only domain controllers (RODCs) at remote branch office locations (recommended)
- Deploying virtualized domain controllers (not recommended for most production environments)

The sections that follow provide some additional information on each of these deployment scenarios.

First domain controller in a new forest

Installing the first domain controller in a new forest requires that you be logged on as the local Administrator of the server. You can do this using either Server Manager or Windows PowerShell, as demonstrated in Lessons 2 and 3 of this chapter.

Regardless of which method you use for deploying the first domain controller in your forest root domain, you need to provide the following information:

- **Domain name**   Enter the fully qualified domain name (FQDN) for the root domain of your new forest—for example, corp.contoso.com.
- **Domain NetBIOS name**   Enter the NetBIOS name for your new forest (required if the FQDN prefix name is longer than 15 characters).
- **Forest functional level**   Select one of the following:
    - Windows Server 2003
    - Windows Server 2008
    - Windows Server 2008 R2
    - Windows Server 2012 (the default for Windows Server 2012)
    - Windows Server 2012 R2 (the default for Windows Server 2012 R2 and not available for Windows Server 2012)
- **Domain functional level**   Select one of the following:
    - Windows Server 2003
    - Windows Server 2008
    - Windows Server 2008 R2

- Windows Server 2012 (set to the selected forest functional level in Windows Server 2012)

- Windows Server 2012 R2 (set to the selected forest functional level in Windows Server 2012 R2 and not available for Windows Server 2012)

- **Directory Services Restore Mode (DSRM) password**   You must specify this at the time the server is promoted to a domain controller.

- **DNS Server**   Indicate whether the new domain controller should also be a DNS server (recommended).

- **Database folder**   Specify where the AD DS database is stored. (The default location is %windir%\NTDS.)

- **Log files folder**   Specify where the AD DS log files are stored. (The default location is %windir%\NTDS.)

- **SYSVOL folder**   Specify where the AD DS SYSVOL share is located. (The default is %windir%\SYSVOL.)

A new feature of deploying Windows Server 2012 and Windows Server 2012 R2 domain controllers is a validation phase that is performed just prior to the promotion process. As Figure 4-1 illustrates, this validation phase invokes a series of tests that check whether all necessary prerequisites have been met to ensure that the domain controller deployment operation will succeed. You can bypass this prerequisite check when deploying domain controllers using Windows PowerShell, but doing this is not recommended.

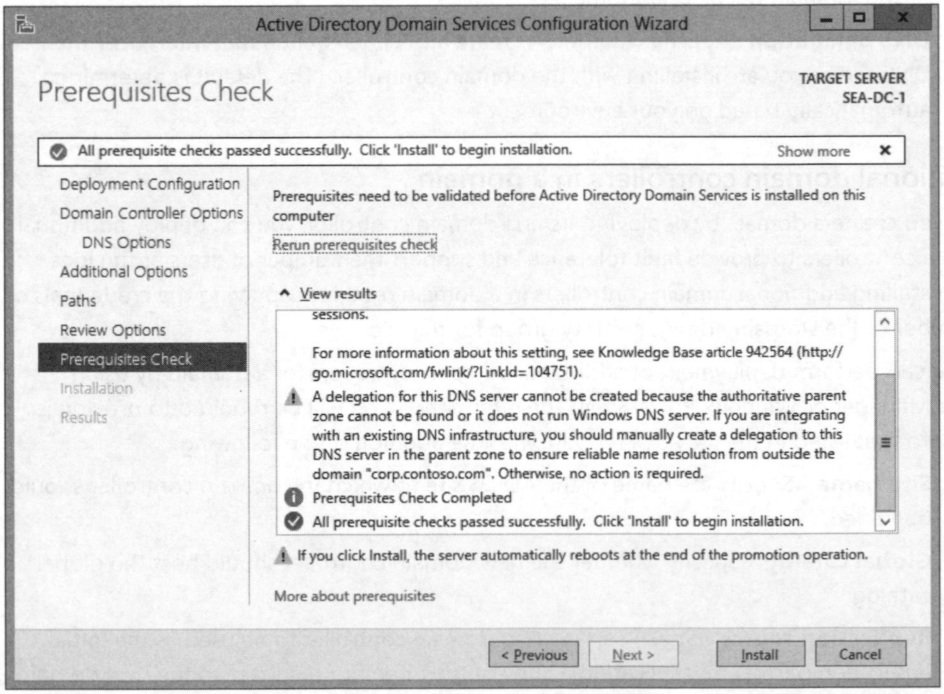

FIGURE 4-1 This is the new validation phase that occurs during domain controller promotion using Server Manager.

> **REAL WORLD** **DOMAIN CONTROLLERS AND DNS SERVERS**
>
> Unless your organization uses a third-party DNS server such as BIND on your internal network, you should always have all your domain controllers also function as DNS servers to ensure high availability in distributed environments. By default, when you install the AD DS role on a server and then promote the server to a domain controller, the DNS Server role is automatically installed and configured.

First domain controller in a new domain

After the first domain of the forest (that is, the forest root domain) has been created, new child domains or tree domains can be created if your AD DS design warrants doing so. Installing the first domain controller for a new child domain or tree domain requires supplying the credentials of a member of the Enterprise Admins security group, which is one of two new security groups (the other is the Schema Admins group) that AD DS creates when the forest root domain controller is deployed.

Deployment of domain controllers for new child domains or tree domains can be performed remotely using Server Manager or Windows PowerShell. The required information is similar to that listed in the previous section, with the addition of the following:

- **Domain type**   Specify whether to create a new child domain or a new tree domain.
- **Parent domain name**   Enter the name of the parent domain of which the new child or tree domain will be a subdomain.
- **DNS delegation**   Specify whether to create a DNS delegation that references the new DNS server you are installing with the domain controller. (The default is determined automatically based on your environment.)

Additional domain controllers in a domain

After you create a domain by deploying its first domain controller, you can deploy additional domain controllers to provide fault tolerance and support the number of users at the location. Installing additional domain controllers in a domain requires supplying the credentials of a member of the Domain Admins security group for that domain.

You can perform deployment of additional domain controllers for a domain by using Server Manager or Windows PowerShell. The information you will be required to provide is similar to that listed in the previous section, with the addition of the following:

- **Site name**   Specify the name of the AD DS site to which the domain controller should be added.
- **Global catalog**   Specify whether the new domain controller should host the global catalog.
- **Replication source**   Specify an existing domain controller to be used as the initial replication partner for replicating a copy of the directory database to the new domain controller. (The default is any available domain controller.)

- **Application partitions to replicate** Specify application partitions on existing domain controllers that should be replicated to the new domain controller.
- **Install from media path** You can choose to install the new domain controller using backed-up media by means of the Install From Media (IFM) deployment option.

REAL WORLD **DOMAIN CONTROLLERS AND THE GLOBAL CATALOG**

The global catalog contains a searchable, partial representation of every object in every domain in the forest. You can use the global catalog to quickly locate objects from any domain in the forest without having to know the name of the domain. All your domain controllers should also function as global catalog servers to ensure high availability in distributed environments. By default, when you promote a server to a domain controller, the new domain controller is automatically configured as a global catalog server.

Read-only domain controllers

Read-only domain controllers (RODCs) are additional domain controllers for a domain and are intended mainly for deployment in branch office environments that have relatively few users, few or no IT staff, and slow wide area network (WAN) connectivity with the head office, and in environments that lack the level of physical security controls available at a typical head office.

RODCs host read-only partitions of the AD DS database. Clients can authenticate against an RODC but cannot write directory changes to it. RODCs include additional safeguards that help ensure any information on the RODC remains confidential if it is stolen or if its security is compromised.

You can remotely perform deployment of an RODC by using Server Manager or Windows PowerShell. Deploying an RODC requires the following:

- Availability of credentials of a member of the Domain Admins for the domain
- A forest functional level of Windows Server 2003 or later
- At least one writable domain controller running Windows Server 2008 or later installed in the domain

---

MORE INFO **DEPLOYING RODCS**

More information on how to plan the deployment of RODCs can be found in the TechNet Library at *http://technet.microsoft.com/en-us/library/cc771744(v=ws.10)*.

REAL WORLD **RODC ON SERVER CORE INSTALLATIONS**

Beginning with Windows Server 2008 R2, RODCs can be deployed on Windows Server Core installations. Doing this helps further reduce the attack surface of your RODCs and lower their maintenance requirements. Refer to Chapter 2, "Deploying servers," for information on how to convert a Server With A GUI installation of Windows Server 2012 or Windows Server 2012 R2 to a Server Core installation.

Virtualized domain controllers

 Virtualized domain controllers are domain controllers running in virtual machines on Hyper-V hosts. Beginning with Windows Server 2012, new capabilities were introduced that help make domain controller virtualization much safer and less prone to problems than with previous Windows Server versions. For more information, see the following "Real World" topic.

REAL WORLD **VIRTUALIZING DOMAIN CONTROLLERS**

Windows Server 2012 and Windows Server 2012 R2 help enable cloud computing by making virtualized domain controllers both easier to deploy and less prone to problems. For example, you can deploy replica virtual domain controllers by cloning existing virtual domain controllers and then deploying them using Server Manager or Windows PowerShell. Virtualizing domain controllers is also much safer than it was with previous versions of Windows Server. That's because each virtual domain controller has a unique identifier called a GenerationID that is exposed to the hypervisor on the host machine. This helps protect the AD DS directory hosted by a virtual domain controller from unexpected rollback events caused by the accidental application of snapshots or other occurrences that caused duplicate directory objects and other issues in previous Windows Server versions.

For more information about these different improvements, see the section "Virtualization that just works" in the topic "What's New in Active Directory Domain Services (AD DS)" in the TechNet Library at *http://technet.microsoft.com/en-us/library/hh831477#BKMK _VirtualizationJustWorks*.

Quick check

- What are the minimum credentials you need to deploy an additional domain controller in an existing domain of a forest?

Quick check answer

- The minimum credentials you need are those for a member of the Domain Admins security group in the target domain. You could also use the credentials of a member of the Enterprise Admins or Schema Admins group, but these credentials should generally be used only for managing the forest root domain and schema.

Windows Azure Active Directory

Deploying your Active Directory infrastructure on-premises isn't the only option available for today's businesses. Windows Azure Active Directory (Windows Azure AD) is a cloud-based version of Active Directory that provides a subset of the functionality of the familiar Active Directory Domain Services (AD DS) that so many businesses around the world use as their identity and access control solution.

Windows Azure AD provides a cloud-based identity provider that can integrate into your on-premises AD DS deployments. Windows Azure AD is also the identity solution used by Microsoft Online Services such as Windows Azure, Microsoft Office 365, Dynamics CRM Online, and Windows Intune. Because of these things and because of its ability to integrate with web identity providers like Microsoft Account and popular third-party providers like Google, Yahoo!, and Facebook, Windows Azure AD can provide single sign-on for users across Microsoft Online Services, third-party cloud services, and applications built on Windows Azure.

Using Windows Azure AD

When you log on to the Windows Azure Management Portal for the first time and select the Active Directory tab on the left, an item called the Default Directory appears as Active for your subscription, as shown here:

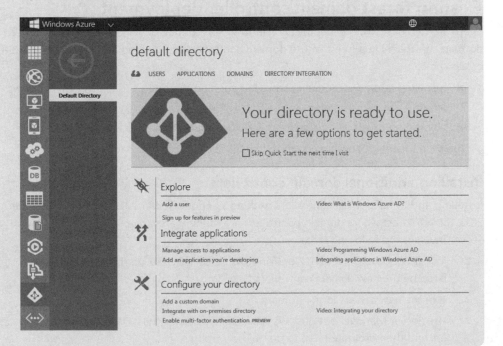

If you click Default Directory, a page similar to this opens:

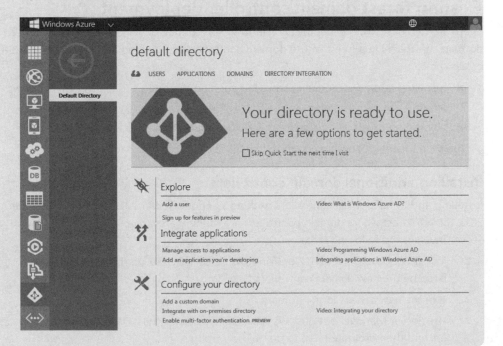

As you can see from the above screenshot, you can use this page of the Management Portal to create and manage new user accounts, add applications and manage access to them, and perform other identity management tasks.

For more detailed information on what Windows Azure Active Directory is and how to get started using it, see *http://www.windowsazure.com/en-us/documentation /services/active-directory/*.

Deploying Active Directory using Windows Azure Virtual Machines

Windows Azure also supports other ways of deploying Active Directory in the cloud. For example, you can deploy an entire Active Directory forest in a self-contained manner using Windows Azure Virtual Machines. Another identity and access control scenario that Windows Azure supports is a hybrid deployment in which you deploy an organization's domain controllers partly on-premises and partly on Windows Azure Virtual Machines.

For more information on these types of deployment scenarios, see "Guidelines for Deploying Windows Server Active Directory on Windows Azure Virtual Machines," which can be found at *http://msdn.microsoft.com/en-us/library/windowsazure /jj156090.aspx*.

Existing forest domain controller deployment

There are two basic ways of deploying Windows Server 2012 or Windows Server 2012 R2 domain controllers in a forest whose domain controllers are running Windows Server 2008 R2 or earlier:

- Installing additional domain controllers running Windows Server 2012 or Windows Server 2012 R2
- Upgrading existing domain controllers running earlier versions of Windows Server

The sections that follow provide more details about these approaches.

Installing additional domain controllers

Installing additional domain controllers running Windows Server 2012 or Windows Server 2012 R2 in a forest whose domain controllers are running an earlier version of Windows Server involves the following steps:

1. Install Windows Server 2012 or Windows Server 2012 R2 on the servers that will become the new domain controllers.
2. Join the new servers to the domain.
3. Use Server Manager or Windows PowerShell to install the AD DS role on the new servers and then promote them to domain controllers.

Once deployed, the new Windows Server 2012 or Windows Server 2012 R2 domain controllers can coexist with the domain controllers running earlier versions of Windows Server if you want them to. Alternatively, you can move the Flexible Single Master Operations (FSMO) roles from the earlier domain controllers that are running earlier versions of Windows Server to the new domain controllers that are running Windows Server 2012 or Windows Server 2012 R2. Then you can finally demote and retire the earlier domain controllers.

> *NOTE* **PREPARING THE SCHEMA**
>
> Introducing Windows Server 2012 or Windows Server 2012 R2 domain controllers into a forest whose domain controllers are running earlier versions of Windows Server automatically causes the AD DS schema to be extended to the latest version. See Lesson 2 for more information on extending the schema.

Upgrading domain controllers running Windows Server 2008 R2 or earlier

Upgrading all of a forest's existing domain controllers that are running Windows Server 2008 R2 or earlier to Windows Server 2012 or Windows Server 2012 R2 involves the following steps:

1. Prepare your forest and domains for an upgrade by using either the Windows Server 2012 or Windows Server 2012 R2 version of the Adprep.exe command-line tool (depending on which version of Windows Server you are upgrading to) to extend your Active Directory schema. (See Lesson 2 for more information about Adprep.)

2. Verify that the operating system of your existing domain controllers has a supported in-place upgrade path to Windows Server 2012 or Windows Server 2012 R2.

3. Verify all prerequisites for upgrading your existing domain controllers to Windows Server 2012 or Windows Server 2012 R2. For example, the drive that hosts the AD DS database (NTDS.DIT) must have at least 20 percent free disk space before you begin the operating system upgrade.

4. Perform an in-place upgrade of your existing domain controllers to Windows Server 2012 or Windows Server 2012 R2.

Upgrading Windows Server 2012 domain controllers to Windows Server 2012 R2

Upgrading all of a forest's existing domain controllers that are running Windows Server 2012 to Windows Server 2012 R2 involves the following steps:

1. Prepare your forest and domains for an upgrade by using the Windows Server 2012 R2 version of the Adprep.exe command-line tool to extend your Active Directory schema. (See Lesson 2 for more information about Adprep.)

2. Verify all prerequisites for upgrading your existing domain controllers to Windows Server 2012 R2. For example, the drive that hosts the AD DS database (NTDS.DIT)

must have at least 20 percent free disk space before you begin the operating system upgrade.

3. Perform an in-place upgrade of your existing domain controllers to Windows Server 2012 R2.

> **MORE INFO** **PREREQUISITES FOR UPGRADING DOMAIN CONTROLLERS**
>
> For more information about supported upgrade paths and other prerequisites for performing in-place upgrades of domain controllers running earlier versions of Windows Server to Windows Server 2012 and Windows Server 2012 R2, see the topic "Upgrade Domain Controllers to Windows Server 2012" in the TechNet Library at *http://technet.microsoft.com/en-us/library/hh994618*. See also "Determine Domain Controller Upgrade Order" at *http://technet.microsoft.com/en-us/library/cc732085(WS.10).aspx.*

Lesson summary

- The two main AD DS deployment scenarios are deploying new forests using Windows Server 2012 or Windows Server 2012 R2 and deploying domain controllers into existing forests running earlier versions of Windows Server.

- Be sure to gather the necessary information and credentials before deploying AD DS and complete any other steps needed to prepare your environment before deploying domain controllers.

- The process of promoting member servers running Windows Server 2012 or Windows Server 2012 R2 as domain controllers includes a prerequisites check to ensure the promotion process can succeed.

- The process of promoting member servers running Windows Server 2012 or Windows Server 2012 R2 as domain controllers automatically runs Adprep when needed to prepare a forest and domains running earlier versions of Windows Server.

- You still need to run Adprep manually if you are performing in-place upgrades of domain controllers running earlier versions of Windows Server.

Lesson review

Answer the following questions to test your knowledge of the information in this lesson. You can find the answers to these questions and explanations of why each answer choice is correct or incorrect in the "Answers" section at the end of this chapter.

1. Which of the following is *not* a best practice for performing new forest deployments?

   A. Ensure that each domain has at least two domain controllers to provide fault tolerance and ensure availability. Only one of these domain controllers needs to be writeable; the other can be an RODC.

   B. Make sure that each site in your domain has a sufficient number of domain controllers to service the needs of users for logging on and accessing network resources.

C. Whenever possible, keep the design of your forest simple by having only one domain.

D. Install only the AD DS and DNS Server roles on your domain controllers; do not install any other server roles.

2. Which of the following information should you obtain or decide upon during the planning stage of deploying the first Windows Server 2012 or Windows Server 2012 R2 domain controller in a new forest? (Choose all that apply.)

A. The fully qualified domain name (FQDN) for the root domain of your new forest

B. The forest and domain functional levels

C. The location for the AD DS database, log files, and SYSVOL folder

D. The credentials of a member of the Domain Admins security group

3. Which of the following is *not* true? (Choose all that apply.)

A. Creating a DNS delegation is a required step for all AD DS deployments.

B. All domain controllers in a domain should have the DNS Server role installed and configured to ensure high availability in distributed environments.

C. All domain controllers in a domain should be configured as global catalog servers to ensure high availability in distributed environments.

D. Read-only domain controllers require that there be at least one writeable domain controller running Windows Server 2003 or later installed in the domain.

Lesson 2: Deploying domain controllers using Server Manager

Server Manager provides an easy way to deploy Windows Server 2012 and Windows Server 2012 R2 domain controllers. Server Manager is mainly intended for managing small and mid-sized environments where the automation of domain controller deployment is not required. This lesson demonstrates how to use Server Manager to deploy domain controllers in both new and existing forests.

After this lesson, you will be able to:

- Use Server Manager to prepare your Windows Server 2012 or Windows Server 2012 R2 environment for domain controller deployment.

- Install the Active Directory Domain Services role using the Add Roles And Features Wizard of Server Manager.

- Promote servers to domain controllers using the Active Directory Domain Services Configuration Wizard of Server Manager.

- Verify the promotion of servers to domain controllers.
- Demote domain controllers and remove the Active Directory Domain Services role.

Estimated lesson time: 30 minutes

Preparing for domain controller deployment

The steps for preparing to deploy Windows Server 2012 or Windows Server 2012 R2 domain controllers using Server Manager differ depending on whether you are deploying the first domain controller in a new forest, deploying additional domain controllers in the new forest, or deploying domain controllers in an existing forest whose domain controllers are running an earlier version of Windows Server.

Preparing for deploying the first domain controller in a new forest

To deploy the first Windows Server 2012 or Windows Server 2012 R2 domain controller in a new forest using Server Manager, you should either log on locally to the server or connect to it using Remote Desktop. No other preparation is needed for this scenario.

Preparing for deploying additional domain controllers in the new forest

After you create a new forest by deploying your first Windows Server 2012 or Windows Server 2012 R2 domain controller, you can use Server Manager to deploy additional domain controllers in an existing domain, create new child domains, or create new tree domains. You can perform these tasks remotely by using Server Manager on any Windows Server 2012 or Windows Server 2012 R2 domain controller or member server or on a Windows 8 or Windows 8.1 client computer that has the appropriate version of the Remote Server Administration Tools (RSAT) installed.

The recommended steps for preparing to use Server Manager to deploy additional domain controllers are as follows:

1. Make sure you have the appropriate credentials for the task you are going to perform. For example, if you are going to add domain controllers to an existing domain, make sure you have Domain Admin credentials for that domain. If you are going to create a new child domain, make sure you have Enterprise Admin credentials.

2. Add the remote servers you'll be promoting to domain controllers to the server pool so that you can manage them remotely using Server Manager.

3. Create a new server group for the remote servers you'll be promoting to domain controllers and add the servers to the server group. Doing this makes it easier to promote multiple remote servers to domain controllers simultaneously.

Preparing for deploying domain controllers in an existing forest

Adding Windows Server 2012 or Windows Server 2012 R2 domain controllers to an existing forest or domain running an earlier version of Windows Server first requires that you extend the existing Active Directory schema. In previous versions of Windows Server, you used Adprep.exe for extending the schema. Adprep is a command-line tool that was available in the \support\adprep folder of Windows Server 2008 R2 installation media or in the \sources \adprep folder of Windows Server 2008 installation media. The Adprep command uses parameters such as */forestprep* and */domainprep* to prepare an existing forest for the intro-duction of a domain controller running a later version of Windows Server.

Beginning with Windows Server 2012, however, Adprep is run automatically as needed when you deploy a new Windows Server 2012 or Windows Server 2012 R2 domain controller in an existing forest or domain running an earlier version of Windows Server. This change sim-plifies the task of adding Windows Server 2012 or Windows Server 2012 R2 domain control-lers to an existing forest or domain running an earlier version of Windows Server because you no longer need to manually run Adprep before introducing the new domain controllers into your forest.

Adprep is also available as a stand-alone command-line tool in the \support\adprep folder of Windows Server 2012 and Windows Server 2012 R2 installation media. The stand-alone version of Adprep is required for certain scenarios, such as performing an in-place upgrade of your first Windows Server 2012 or Windows Server 2012 R2 domain controller. In this case, you must run Adprep manually to prepare your forest and its domains before you begin upgrading your existing domain controllers to Windows Server 2012 or Windows Server 2012 R2.

> *NOTE* **ADPREP SYNTAX**
>
> To display the syntax and usage examples for Adprep, type *<drive>*\support\adprep
> \adprep at a command prompt, where *drive* is the letter for the drive where your installa-
> tion media can be found.

You can use the Windows Server 2012 version of Adprep to extend the schema of an exist-ing forest whose domain controllers are running any of the following versions of Windows Server:

- Windows Server 2008 R2
- Windows Server 2008
- Windows Server 2003 R2
- Windows Server 2003

However, the following considerations apply when running the Windows Server 2012 ver-sion of Adprep:

- You must have the credentials of a member of the Enterprise Admins group to run the **Adprep /forestprep** command.

- Adprep can be run only on a server (domain controller, member server, or stand-alone server) that is running a 64-bit version of Windows Server 2008 or later. You cannot run Adprep on a server running Windows Server 2003 or a 32-bit version of Windows Server 2008.

- The server on which you run Adprep must have network connectivity to the schema master of the existing forest.

- The server on which you run Adprep must have network connectivity to the infrastructure master of the existing domain where you want to add a new Windows Server 2012 domain controller.

You can use the Windows Server 2012 R2 version of Adprep to extend the schema of an existing forest whose domain controllers are running any of the following versions of Windows Server:

- Windows Server 2012
- Windows Server 2008 R2
- Windows Server 2008
- Windows Server 2003 R2
- Windows Server 2003

Similar considerations apply when running the Windows Server 2012 R2 version of Adprep as when running the Windows Server 2012 version.

REAL WORLD **VERIFYING ADPREP**

You can use the Dsquery.exe command-line tool to verify whether Adprep has extended your forest's schema. For example, let's say your existing forest has domain controllers running Windows Server 2008 R2. To determine the current schema level of your forest, open a command prompt on one of your domain controllers and run the following command:

```
dsquery * cn=schema,cn=configuration,dc=fabrikam,dc=com -scope base
  -attr objectVersion
```

The output from this command looks like this:

```
objectVersion
47
```

Next, take a server running Windows Server 2012, join it to a domain in your forest, and use Server Manager to promote the server to a domain controller. After you finish introducing the new domain controller into your forest, rerun the preceding *dsquery* command on the domain controller on which you previously ran it. The output from the command looks like this:

```
objectVersion
56
```

The version number *56* indicates that the schema of your forest has been extended to include domain controllers running Windows Server 2012.

Finally, take a server running Windows Server 2012 R2, join it to a domain in your forest, and use Server Manager to promote the server to a domain controller. After you finish introducing the new domain controller into your forest, rerun the preceding *dsquery* command on the domain controller on which you previously ran it. The output from the command looks like this:

```
objectVersion
69
```

The version number *69* indicates that the schema of your forest has been extended to include domain controllers running Windows Server 2012 R2.

Quick check

- When deploying additional domain controllers in a forest using Server Manager, why should you create a server group using Server Manager for the remote servers you'll be promoting to domain controllers?

Quick check answer

- You should create a server group so that you can more easily promote them remotely as domain controllers and manage them.

Installing the AD DS role

Before you can promote a server to a domain controller, you must first install the AD DS role on the server. To do this using Server Manager, select Add Roles And Features from the Manage menu to launch the Add Roles And Features Wizard. On the Select Server Roles page of the wizard, select the Active Directory Domain Services role and confirm the installation of the tools for managing AD DS, as shown in Figure 4-2.

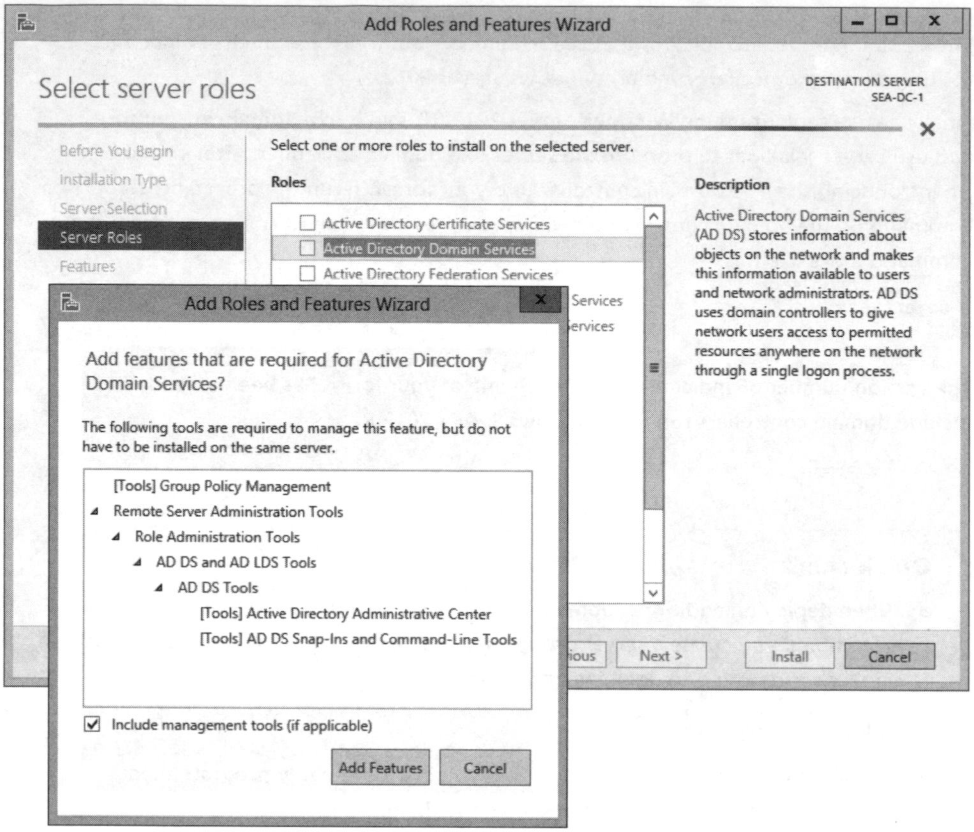

FIGURE 4-2 Install the AD DS role with the role-management tools.

Running the AD DS Configuration Wizard

When you complete the installation of the role, the final page of the AD DS Configuration Wizard prompts you to promote the server to a domain controller. If you close the wizard at this point, you can still access the link to promote the server from the Notifications menu of Server Manager, as shown in Figure 4-3.

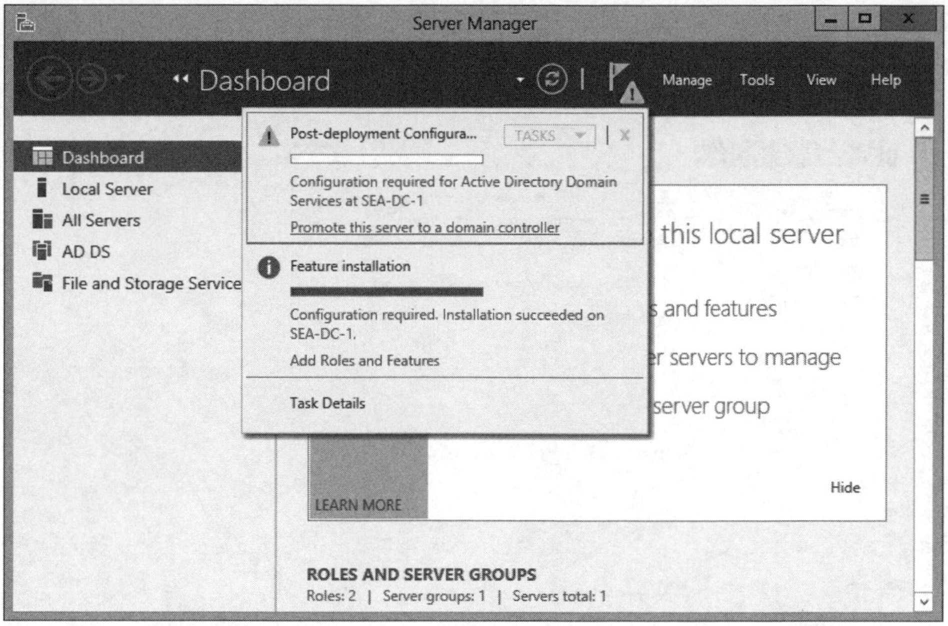

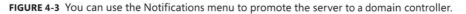

FIGURE 4-3 You can use the Notifications menu to promote the server to a domain controller.

Clicking the link to promote the server to a domain controller launches the AD DS Configuration Wizard. The steps of this wizard depend on which type of domain controller deployment scenario you are performing. The upcoming sections cover the following scenario types:

- First domain controller in new forest
- Additional domain controller in new domain
- First Windows Server 2012 or Windows Server 2012 R2 domain controller in existing forest

First domain controller in new forest

After you have added the AD DS role to the server, using the AD DS Configuration Wizard to promote the server to the first domain controller in a new forest involves the following steps:

1. On the Deployment Configuration page of the wizard, shown in Figure 4-4, select the Add A New Forest option and specify the root domain for your new forest. Then proceed through the wizard and perform the steps that follow.

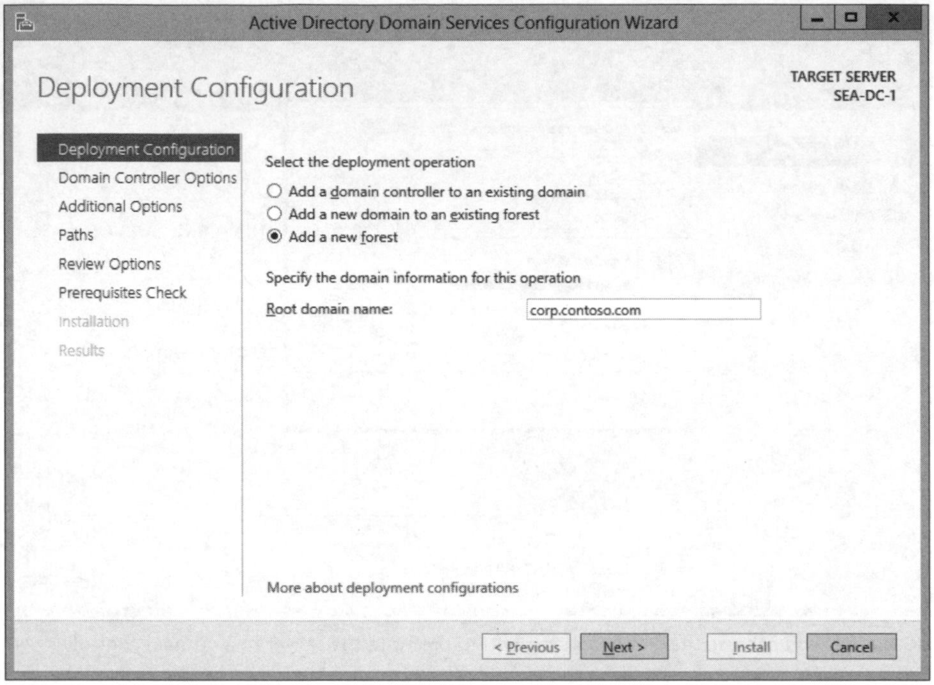

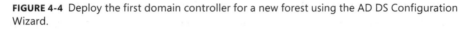

FIGURE 4-4 Deploy the first domain controller for a new forest using the AD DS Configuration Wizard.

2. On the Domain Controller Options page, specify a functional level for your new forest and root domain. The default forest and functional levels are Windows Server 2012 if your server is running Windows Server 2012 or Windows Server 2012 R2 if your server is running Windows Server 2012 R2. If you have no domain controllers running earlier versions of Windows Server in your environment, you should leave the defaults unchanged.

3. On the same page, specify whether your domain controller should also be a DNS server. Microsoft recommends that all domain controllers also be DNS servers to ensure AD DS availability.

4. On the same page, note that the first domain controller must be a global catalog server and that it cannot be an RODC.

5. On the same page, enter a password for the Directory Services Restore Mode (DSRM) administrator account.

6. On the DNS Options page, specify DNS delegation options if you are integrating AD DS with an existing DNS infrastructure. To do this, you can manually create a delegation for your new DNS server in its authoritative parent zone to ensure reliable name resolution from outside your AD DS environment. For example, if the root domain name of your new forest is corp.contoso.com, as shown in Figure 4-4, you create a

delegation for your DNS server in the authoritative parent zone on the DNS server that manages the public contoso.com domain for your organization.

7. On the Additional Options page, the wizard suggests a NetBIOS name for your forest root domain. You can either accept what the wizard suggests or specify a different name of up to 15 Internet-standard characters (A–Z, a–z, 0–9, and "-") but not entirely numeric.

8. On the Paths page, specify the location of the AD DS database, log files, and SYSVOL or accept the defaults.

9. The Review Options page displays the results of your selections.

10. The Prerequisites Check page verifies that all prerequisites have been met for successfully deploying the domain controller. See Figure 4-1 earlier in this chapter for an example of what this wizard page looks like.

11. Clicking Install promotes the server to a domain controller and automatically reboots the server at the end of the promotion operation.

REAL WORLD **WINDOWS POWERSHELL BEHIND THE WIZARD**

The AD DS Configuration Wizard is built entirely on Windows PowerShell. In other words, you can think of the wizard as a UI that simply runs a Windows PowerShell command whose parameters are determined by the selections you make on the different wizard pages. On the Review Options page of the wizard, you can click View Script to display the Windows PowerShell script in Notepad. For example, if you are deploying the first Windows Server 2012 R2 domain controller in a new forest whose forest root domain is corp.contoso.com, the script that performs this action looks like this:

```
#
# Windows PowerShell script for AD DS Deployment
#

Import-Module ADDSDeployment
Install-ADDSForest '
-CreateDnsDelegation:$false '
-DatabasePath "C:\Windows\NTDS" '
-DomainMode "Win2012R2" '
-DomainName "corp.contoso.com" '
-DomainNetbiosName "CORP" '
-ForestMode "Win2012R2" '
-InstallDns:$true '
-LogPath "C:\Windows\NTDS" '
-NoRebootOnCompletion:$false '
-SysvolPath "C:\Windows\SYSVOL" '
-Force:$true
```

Being able to view the script behind the wizard provides several benefits. First, it enables you to quickly learn the syntax of Windows PowerShell cmdlets for AD DS deployment. Second, you can copy these scripts, customize them, and use them to automate the deployment of other domain controllers in your environment.

MORE INFO NAMING YOUR NEW FOREST

For some recommendations on how to name the forest root domain of a new forest, see the topic "Selecting the Forest Root Domain" in the TechNet Library at *http://technet.microsoft.com/en-us/library/cc726016(v=WS.10).aspx.*

Additional domain controller in new domain

After you deploy the first domain controller in a new domain or forest, you should deploy at least one additional domain controller in the domain for fault tolerance. After adding the AD DS role to the server that will become the additional domain controller, you can use the AD DS Configuration Wizard to promote the server to be an additional domain controller for the domain by performing the following steps:

1. On the Deployment Configuration page of the wizard, shown in Figure 4-5, select the Add A Domain Controller To An Existing Domain option. Specify the domain to which you want to add the new domain controller, and if your current logon credentials have insufficient privileges to perform the option, click Change and specify suitable credentials.

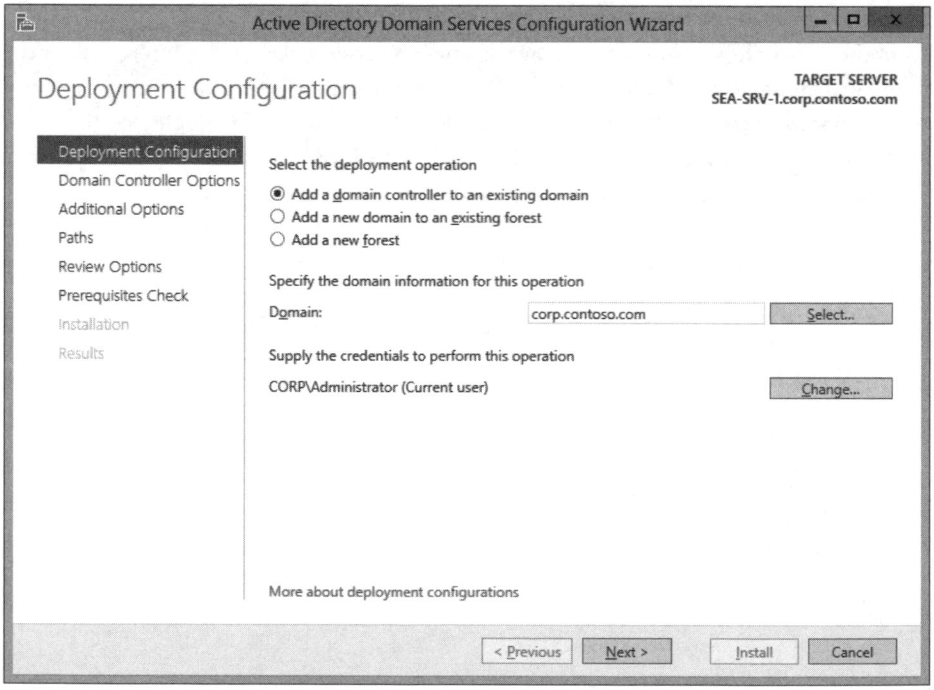

FIGURE 4-5 Deploy an additional domain controller to an existing domain.

2. On the Domain Controller Options page, specify whether your domain controller should also be a DNS server. (This option is selected by default.)

3. On the same page, specify whether your domain controller should also be a global catalog server. (This option is selected by default.)

4. On the same page, specify whether your domain controller should also be an RODC. You should have at least two writeable domain controllers in every domain in your forest, so do not select this option if this is the second domain controller in your domain.

5. On the same page, specify the name of the existing AD DS site to which the new domain controller should belong. (The default is Default-First-Site-Name.)

6. On the same page, enter a password for the DSRM administrator account.

7. On the DNS Options page, specify DNS delegation options if you are integrating AD DS with an existing DNS infrastructure.

8. On the Additional Options page, select the Install From Media (IFM) option if you used the Ntdsutil.exe tool to create installation media for additional domain controllers that you are deploying in the domain. You can use the Install From Media (IFM) option to minimize the replication of directory data over your network, which helps make deploying additional domain controllers at remote sites more efficient. If you are deploying additional domain controllers at your organization's hub site (its headquarters or central office), however, you generally will not use the IFM option.

9. On the same page, if you are not using the IFM option for deploying additional domain controllers, you can select which domain controller in your domain the new additional domain controller should use as an initial replication partner for pulling down a copy of the AD DS database. By default, your new domain controller replicates from any available domain controller in the domain, but you have the option of specifying a particular domain controller as its initial replication partner.

10. Complete the remaining steps of the wizard to deploy the additional domain controller in the domain.

> **MORE INFO**   **INSTALL FROM MEDIA**
>
> For more information about deploying domain controllers using the Install From Media (IFM) option, see the topic "Installing AD DS from Media" in the TechNet Library at *http://technet.microsoft.com/en-us/library/cc770654(v=WS.10).aspx*.

First Windows Server 2012 or Windows Server 2012 R2 domain controller in existing forest

You can also use the AD DS Configuration Wizard to deploy Windows Server 2012 or Windows Server 2012 R2 domain controllers in a forest or domain whose existing domain controllers are running Windows Server 2008 R2, Windows Server 2008, or Windows Server 2003. As explained earlier in this lesson, when you use the wizard to deploy the first Windows Server 2012 or Windows Server 2012 R2 domain controller in a domain of a forest whose domain controllers are running earlier Windows Server versions, the Adprep tool automatically runs to prepare the forest and domain by extending the schema to its latest version.

The procedure that follows demonstrates this scenario by deploying a Windows Server 2012 or Windows Server 2012 R2 domain controller named *VAN-SRV-3* in a forest root domain named *fabrikam.com* whose existing domain controllers are all running Windows Server 2008 R2. After you have added the AD DS role to server VAN-SRV-3, using the AD DS Configuration Wizard to add the server as the first Windows Server 2012 or Windows Server 2012 R2 domain controller in the fabrikam.com forest involves the following steps:

1. On the Deployment Configuration page of the wizard, shown in Figure 4-6, select the Add A Domain Controller To An Existing Domain option, specify fabrikam.com as the forest root domain, and specify suitable credentials for performing the operation.

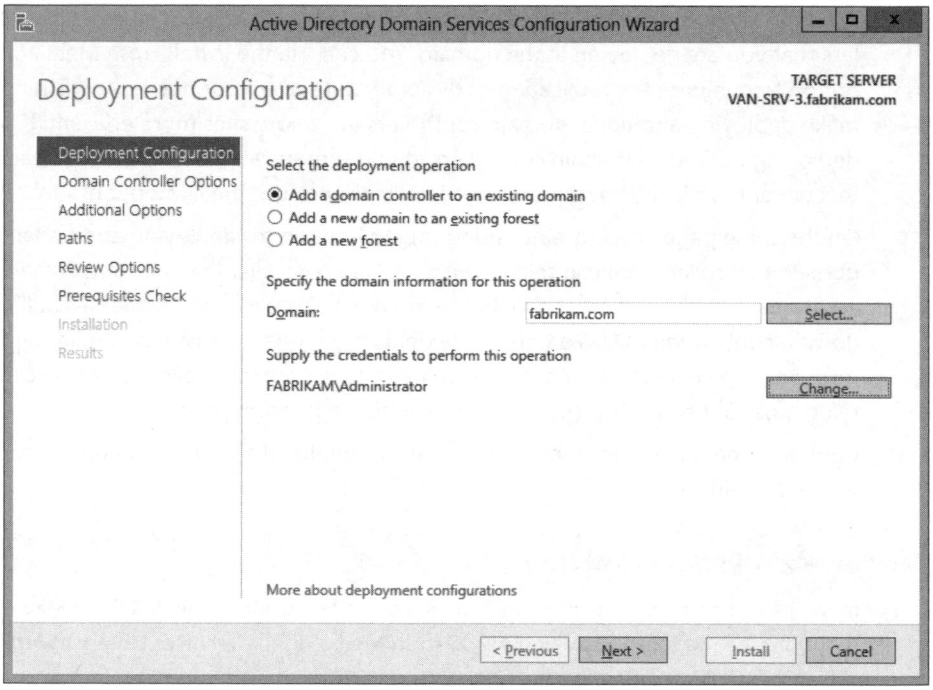

FIGURE 4-6 Promote the server named VAN-SRV-3 to be the first Windows Server 2012 or Windows Server 2012 R2 domain controller in the existing fabrikam.com forest root domain.

2. Proceed through the wizard as described in the previous section until you reach the Preparation Options page shown in Figure 4-7. This page informs you that performing this operation will prepare your forest and domain for Windows Server 2012 or Windows Server 2012 R2 domain controllers by extending the schema. If you do not want to extend the schema, cancel the operation and do not deploy the new domain controller.

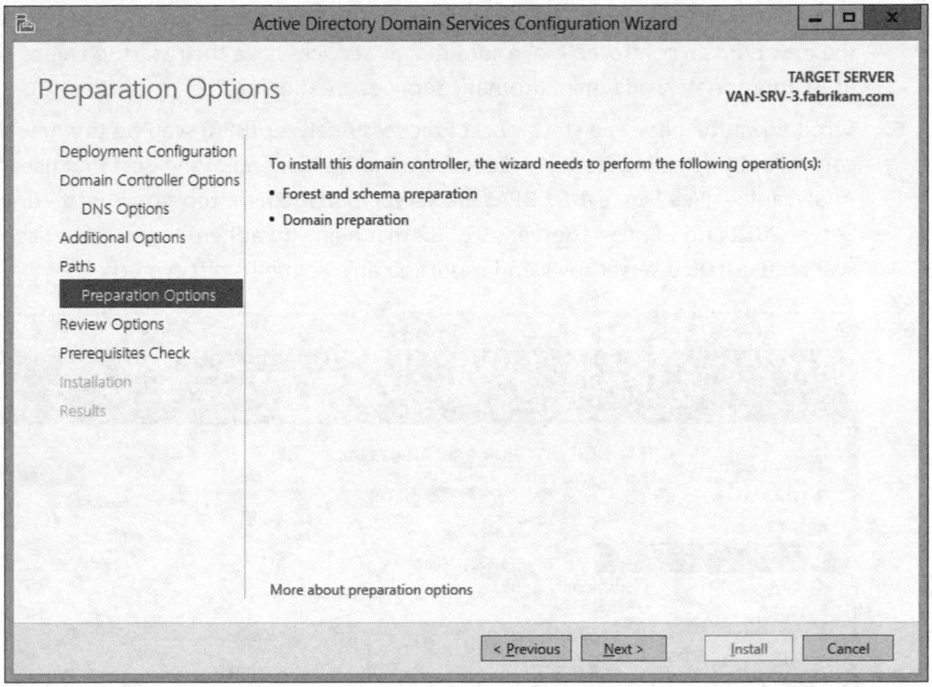

FIGURE 4-7 The wizard informs you that the forest schema will be extended if you perform this operation.

3. Complete the remaining steps of the wizard to deploy the domain controller and extend the schema. Note that you did not have to manually run Adprep to prepare your forest or domain for the domain controller running Windows Server 2012 or Windows Server 2012 R2.

Verifying the installation

After deploying a new domain controller running Windows Server 2012 or Windows Server 2012 by using Server Manager, you should verify the installation by performing the following steps:

1. Add the new domain controller to the server pool and to any server group you created for grouping together your Windows Server 2012 domain controllers.

2. Select the new domain controller from any applicable page of Server Manager.

3. Check for any alerts raised concerning the new controller on the Notifications menu.

4. Scroll down the page to the Events tile and review any events raised for the new domain controller. Pay special attention to any critical, error, or warning events raised and perform any additional configuration or remedial action needed to address these events.

5. Scroll down the page to the Services tile and review the condition of the services on the new domain controller. Make sure that all services have their startup values configured appropriately and that automatic services are running.

6. Scroll down the page and start a Best Practices Analyzer (BPA) scan on the new domain controller by selecting Start BPA Scan from the Tasks menu of the Best Practices Analyzer tile. (See Figure 4-8.) BPAs are server management tools built into Windows Server 2012 and Windows Server 2012 R2 that help you adhere to best practices by scanning installed server roles and reporting any violations discovered.

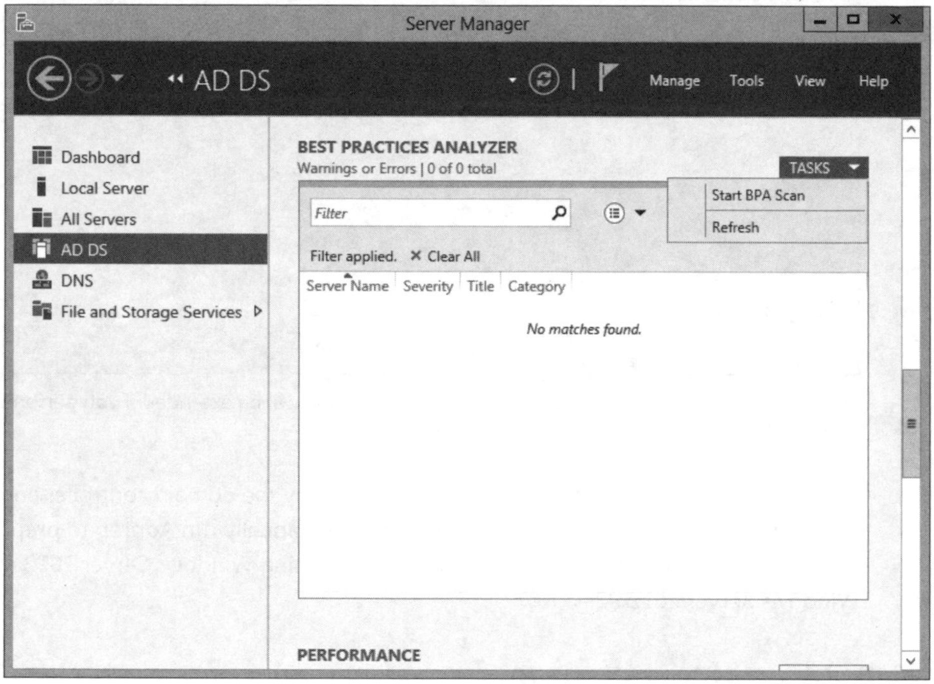

FIGURE 4-8 Start a BPA scan on a domain controller.

As an example, Figure 4-9 shows the results of running a BPA scan on two Windows Server 2012 or Windows Server 2012 R2 domain controllers deployed in a new forest. These domain controllers have been grouped together in Server Manager by creating a custom server group named Domain Controllers. The Error displayed in the Best Practices Analyzer tile indicates that domain controller SEA-DC-1 is the PDC Emulator operations master for the forest and needs to be able to synchronize its clock with a reliable time source on the Internet. After you run a BPA scan on your domain controllers, be sure to carefully review the results displayed in the tile.

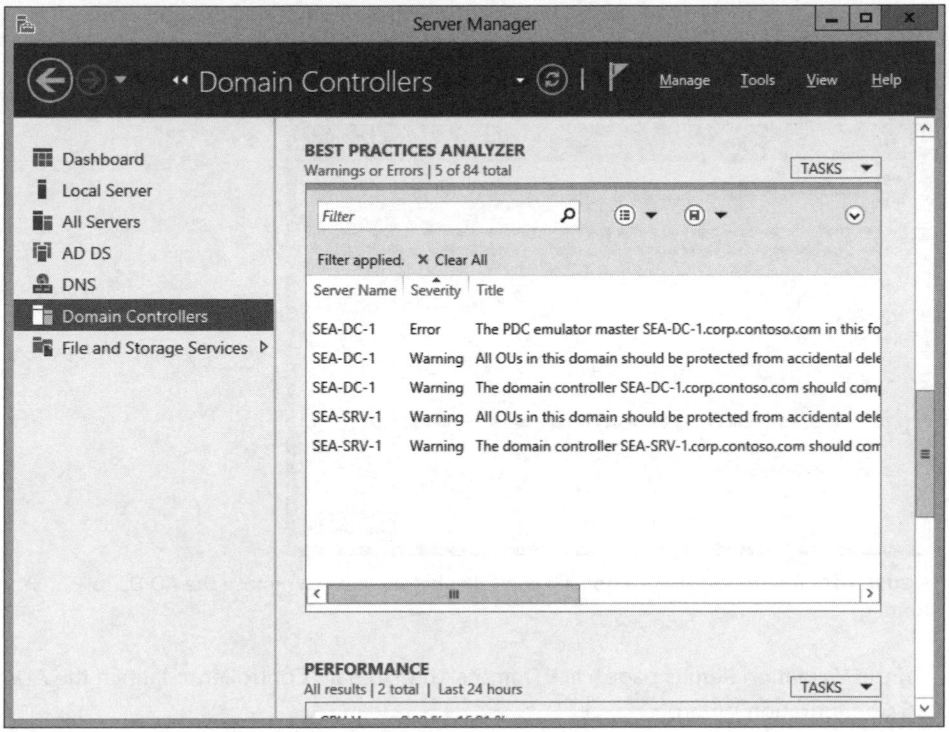

FIGURE 4-9 Review the results of a BPA scan performed on newly deployed domain controllers.

✔ Quick check

- You used Server Manager to install the AD DS role on a remote server, but you closed the Add Roles And Features Wizard without first promoting the server to a domain controller. How can you finish the job and promote the server?

Quick check answer

- Access the link to promote the server from the Notifications menu of Server Manager.

Uninstalling AD DS

If you need to retire a Windows Server 2012 or Windows Server 2012 R2 domain controller from your environment—for example, to repurpose its server hardware for some other role—you can do this using Server Manager by performing the following steps:

1. Launch the Remove Roles And Features Wizard from the Manage menu and select your server from the server pool.

2. On the Remove Server Roles page, deselect the Active Directory Domain Services check box. The Validation Results page appears, indicating that you must demote the domain controller before you can remove the AD DS role. (See Figure 4-10.)

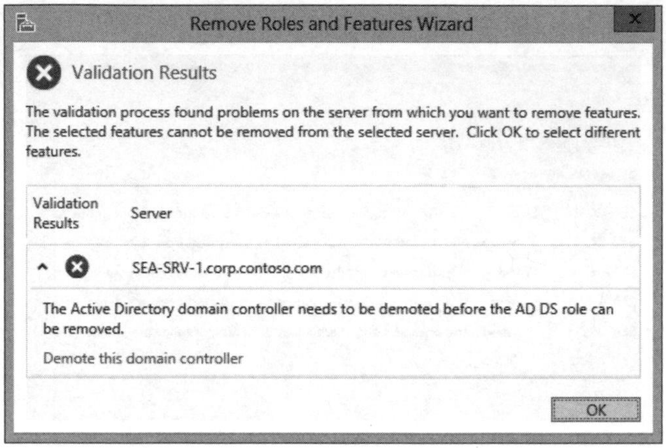

FIGURE 4-10 You must demote a domain controller before you can remove the AD DS role from it.

3. On the Validation Results page, click Demote This Domain Controller to launch the AD DS Configuration Wizard.

4. On the Credentials page, supply the necessary credentials to perform this operation if your current logon credentials have insufficient privileges. If previous attempts to remove AD DS from this domain controller failed, select the Force The Removal Of This Domain Controller check box on this page.

5. If you are demoting the last domain controller in the domain, make sure the Last Domain Controller In The Domain check box is selected to confirm that you want to remove the domain from your forest. Note that this check box is displayed only if the server is the last domain controller in the domain.

6. On the Warnings page, make sure the Proceed With Removal check box is selected to confirm your decision to perform the demotion. Note that this page is not displayed if you chose to force the removal of AD DS in the previous step.

7. On the Removal Options page, you have the option to remove any DNS delegations created in the authoritative parent zone. Note that you need to supply appropriate credentials to perform this action.

8. If you are demoting the last domain controller in the domain, you also have the options of removing the DNS zone and any application partitions from the domain. (See Figure 4-11.) By clicking View Partitions, you can display a list of any application partitions in AD DS.

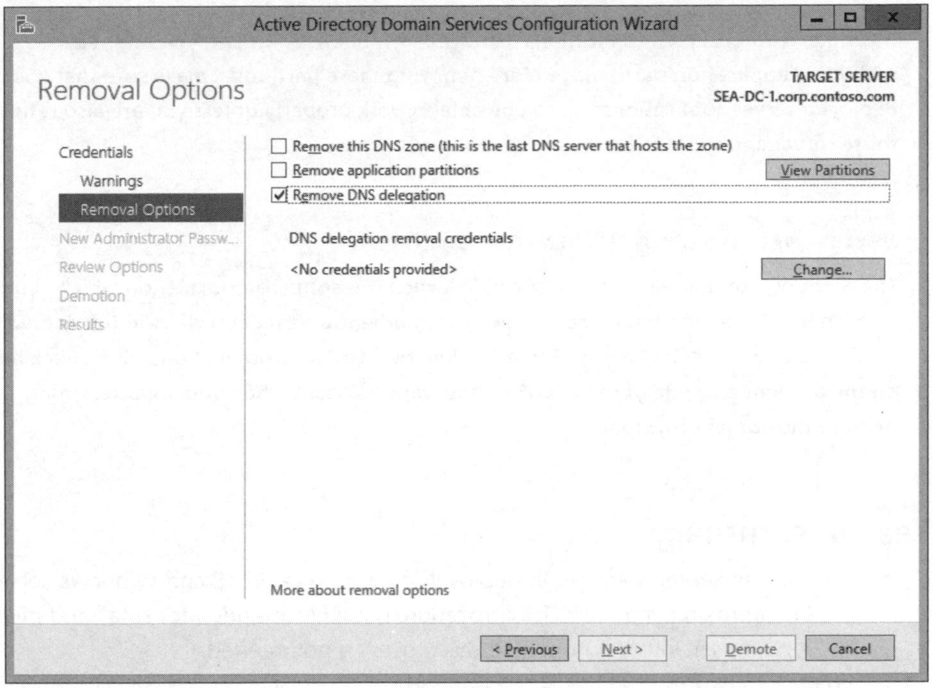

FIGURE 4-11 You have options for removing the DNS zone and application partitions when demoting the last domain controller in a domain.

9. On the New Administrator Password page, enter a password for the local Administrator account for the server.

10. On the Review Options page, click Demote. The server restarts, and you can log on using the local Administrator account and the new password you specified in the previous step.

11. Launch the Remove Roles And Features Wizard again from the Manage menu and select your server from the server pool.

12. On the Remove Server Roles page, deselect the Active Directory Domain Services and DNS Server check boxes. Finish running the wizard. When the server restarts, both the AD DS and DNS Server roles will have been removed.

IMPORTANT **REMOVING APPLICATION PARTITIONS**

When you demote the last domain controller in a domain using Server Manager, you have the option of removing any application partitions. At a minimum, when you do this you should see the default DNS application partitions—for example:

- DC=DomainDNSZones,DC=corp,DC=contoso,DC=com
- DC=ForestDNSZones,DC=corp,DC=contoso,DC=com

If you have other server applications deployed in your environment, you might see additional application partitions. Before removing these partitions, make sure that your deployed server applications will still be able to work properly unless you are also retiring those server applications from your environment.

REAL WORLD **FORCING THE REMOVAL OF AD DS**

The demotion of domain controllers can fail when the domain controller on which you are performing this action has no connectivity with other domain controllers in the domain. If this happens, try selecting the Force The Removal Of This Domain Controller check box on the Credentials page of the AD DS Configuration Wizard when you are attempting to demote the domain controller.

Lesson summary

- You can use Server Manager to deploy Windows Server 2012 and Windows Server 2012 R2 domain controllers. This procedure is mainly intended for small and midsized environments in which automating this process is not needed.

- After you use the Add Roles And Feature Wizard to install the AD DS role on a remote server, you can use the AD DS Configuration Wizard to promote the server to a domain controller.

- After you deploy a domain controller, you can use Server Manager to verify the installation by reviewing the Event logs, reviewing the state of services, and running a Best Practices Analyzer scan on the new domain controller.

- You can use the Remove Roles And Features Wizard to uninstall the AD DS role on a remote server, but you first need to demote the server from being a domain controller.

- Adprep is still available as a stand-alone command-line tool in the \support\adprep folder of Windows Server 2012 and Windows Server 2012 R2 installation media when you need to perform an in-place upgrade of your first Windows Server 2012 or Windows Server 2012 R2 domain controller.

Lesson review

Answer the following questions to test your knowledge of the information in this lesson. You can find the answers to these questions and explanations of why each answer choice is correct or incorrect in the "Answers" section at the end of this chapter.

1. Which of the following procedures for deploying the first Windows Server 2012 R2 domain controller in a new forest is correct? (Choose all that apply.)

   A. Install Windows Server 2012 R2 on your server and log on using the local Administrator account. Open Server Manager and run the AD DS Configuration Wizard to promote the server as a domain controller.

B. Install Windows Server 2012 R2 on your server and log on using the local Administrator account. Open Server Manager and run the Add Roles And Features Wizard to promote the server as a domain controller.

C. Install Windows Server 2012 R2 on your server and log on using the local Administrator account. Open Server Manager and run the Add Roles And Features Wizard to install the AD DS role on the server. Then run the AD DS Configuration Wizard to promote the server as a domain controller.

D. Install Windows Server 2012 R2 on your server and log on using the local Administrator account. Open Server Manager and run the AD DS Configuration Wizard to install the AD DS role on the server. Then run the Add Roles And Features Wizard to promote the server as a domain controller.

2. Which of the following statements is *not* correct concerning the deployment of the first Windows Server 2012 R2 domain controller in an existing forest running an earlier version of Windows Server? (Choose all that apply.)

A. You must prepare the forest and domain and extend the schema by manually running Adprep before you use Server Manager to deploy the first Windows Server 2012 R2 domain controller in an existing forest running an earlier version of Windows Server.

B. You must select the Add A Domain Controller To An Existing Domain option on the Deployment Configuration page of the AD DS Configuration Wizard to deploy the first Windows Server 2012 R2 domain controller in an existing forest running an earlier version of Windows Server.

C. You can use the Install From Media (IFM) deployment method to deploy the first Windows Server 2012 R2 domain controller in an existing forest running an earlier version of Windows Server.

D. If your current logon credentials have insufficient privileges to deploy the first Windows Server 2012 R2 domain controller in an existing forest running an earlier version of Windows Server, you can specify different credentials on the Deployment Configuration page of the AD DS Configuration Wizard.

3. Which of the following is the best syntax when using the Dsquery.exe command-line tool to verify that Adprep has successfully extended your forest's schema?

A. Dsquery * cn=schema,cn=configuration,dc=fabrikam,dc=com –attr objectVersion

B. Dsquery * cn=schema,cn=configuration,dc=fabrikam,dc=com –scope base –attr sAMAccountName

C. Dsquery * cn=schema,cn=configuration,dc=fabrikam,dc=com –scope base –attr *

D. Dsquery * cn=schema,cn=configuration,dc=fabrikam,dc=com –scope base –attr objectVersion

Lesson 3: Deploying domain controllers using Windows PowerShell

Windows PowerShell provides a way to automate the deployment of Windows Server 2012 and Windows Server 2012 R2 domain controllers. This approach to domain controller deployment can be particularly useful in large enterprise environments, data centers, and cloud-computing scenarios. This lesson demonstrates how to use Windows PowerShell to deploy domain controllers in both new and existing forests.

> **After this lesson, you will be able to:**
>
> - Prepare your environment for domain controller deployment using Windows PowerShell.
> - Use Windows PowerShell to verify the prerequisites for installing new forests, domains, and domain controllers.
> - Use Windows PowerShell to install AD DS on servers and promote them as domain controllers in both new and existing forests.
> - Use Windows PowerShell to demote domain controllers.
>
> **Estimated lesson time: 30 minutes**

Preparing for domain controller deployment

Like deploying domain controllers using Server Manager as described in the previous lesson, the steps for preparing to deploy Windows Server 2012 and Windows Server 2012 R2 domain controllers using Windows PowerShell differ depending on the scenario.

> **REAL WORLD**   **WINDOWS POWERSHELL AND SERVER CORE INSTALLATIONS**
>
> The Server Core installation option for Windows Server 2012 and Windows Server 2012 R2 is ideal for data center environments because of its smaller servicing footprint, disk space requirements, and attack surface. The Server Core installation option also supports installing the AD DS role, so using Windows PowerShell to deploy Server Core domain controllers is ideal for a data center.

Preparing for deploying the first domain controller in a new forest

To deploy the first Windows Server 2012 or Windows Server 2012 R2 domain controller in a new forest, you can run Windows PowerShell commands directly on the server by either logging on locally to the server or connecting to it using Remote Desktop. Another option is to use Windows PowerShell remoting, which enables you to run Windows PowerShell commands on one or more remote computers simultaneously by using the WS-Management protocol.

As explained previously in Chapter 3, "Server remote management," the remote management capability is enabled by default on Windows Server 2012 and Windows Server 2012 R2 to make it easy to remotely manage servers using both Server Manager and Windows PowerShell. For more information, see the section "Configuring remote management" in Lesson 4 of Chapter 3.

The difficulty, however, is that Windows PowerShell remoting is primarily intended for remotely managing domain-joined computers, and if you are preparing to deploy the first domain controller in a new forest there is no domain to join! In other words, the remote server that will be promoted to a domain controller is initially in a workgroup, not a domain. In addition, the local computer from which you will be performing the deployment might also be in a workgroup.

The solution is to prepare your environment by enabling the two stand-alone computers to talk to each other using the WS-Management protocol. If the computer from which you are performing the deployment is also running Windows Server 2012 or Windows Server 2012 R2, you just need to add the name of the remote server to the *TrustedHosts list* in the local computer's WinRM configuration. Doing this enables the local computer to connect to the remote server using NTLM as the authentication mechanism instead of Kerberos, which is used in domain-based environments.

> **IMPORTANT**   **ADDING REMOTE SERVERS TO THE TRUSTEDHOSTS LIST ON YOUR COMPUTER**
>
> When you add a remote server to the TrustedHosts list on your computer, you allow your credentials to be sent to the remote server without verifying the server's identity. So add remote servers to this list only if you are certain the network path from your computer to the remote server machine is completely secure.

To illustrate how to do this, consider a scenario in which you have two stand-alone servers running Windows Server 2012 or Windows Server 2012 R2: a local server named SEA-HOST-2 and a remote server named SEA-SRV-1. You want to use the Get-WindowsFeature cmdlet on the local server to display a list of installed and available roles and features on the remote server, but when you try to do this on the local server, you get the error indicated in the following code:

```
PS C:\> Get-WindowsFeature -ComputerName SEA-SRV-1 -Credential SEA-SRV-1\Administrator

Get-WindowsFeature : The WinRM client cannot process the request. If the authentication
scheme is different from Kerberos, or if the client computer is not joined to a domain,
then HTTPS transport must be used or the destination machine must be added to the
TrustedHosts configuration setting. Use winrm.cmd to configure TrustedHosts. Note that
computers in the TrustedHosts list might not be authenticated. You can get more
information about that by running the following command: winrm help config.

At line:1 char:1
+ Get-WindowsFeature -ComputerName SEA-SRV-1 -Credential SEA-SRV-1\Administrator
+ ~~~~~~~~~~~~~~~~~~~~~~~~~~~~~~~~~~~~~~~~~~~~~~~~~~~~~~~~~~~~~~~~~~~~~~~~~~~~~~~~~
```

```
+ CategoryInfo : DeviceError: (Microsoft.Manag...rDetailsHandle):CimException)
[Get-WindowsFeature], Exception + FullyQualifiedErrorId : UnSupportedTargetDevice,
Microsoft.Windows.ServerManager.Commands.GetWindowsFeatureCommand
```

The error occurs because the remote server SEA-SRV-1 is not domain-joined and therefore must be added to the TrustedHosts list on the local server before you can manage the remote server from the local server. You can use the Set-Item cmdlet to do this:

```
PS C:\> Set-Item wsman:\localhost\Client\TrustedHosts -Value SEA-SRV-1

WinRM Security Configuration.
This command modifies the TrustedHosts list for the WinRM client. The computers
in the TrustedHosts list might not be authenticated. The client might send credential
information to these computers. Are you sure that you want to modify this list?
[Y] Yes  [N] No  [S] Suspend  [?] Help (default is "Y"): y
```

You can then use the Get-Item cmdlet to verify the result:

```
PS C:\> Get-Item wsman:\\localhost\Client\TrustedHosts


   WSManConfig: Microsoft.WSMan.Management\WSMan::localhost\Client

Type             Name                    SourceOfValue   Value
----             ----                    -------------   -----
System.String    TrustedHosts                            SEA-SRV-1
```

Running the Get-WindowsFeature cmdlet now no longer throws an error:

```
PS C:\> Get-WindowsFeature -ComputerName SEA-SRV-1 -Credential SEA-SRV-1\Administrator

Display Name                                      Name                 Install State
------------                                      ----                 -------------
[ ] Active Directory Certificate Services         AD-Certificate       Available
    [ ] Certification Authority                   ADCS-Cert-Authority  Available
    [ ] Certificate Enrollment Policy Web Service ADCS-Enroll-Web-Pol  Available
...
```

> **NOTE** **TIPS FOR RUNNING SET-ITEM WSMAN:\LOCALHOST\CLIENT\TRUSTEDHOSTS**
>
> If you need to add another remote server to the TrustedHosts list on your local computer, include the *–Concatenate* parameter when you use Set-Item the second time so that you don't overwrite the current contents of the list. You can also suppress the Yes/No prompt with the Set-Item cmdlet by adding the *–Force* parameter to it.

Preparing for deploying additional domain controllers in the new forest

Deploying additional domain controllers in a new forest is easier than deploying the first domain controller because you already have a domain environment, which means Windows PowerShell remoting will work without any further configuration. By running your Windows PowerShell commands from an existing Windows Server 2012 or Windows Server 2012 R2 domain controller in your forest or from a Windows 8 or Windows 8.1 client computer on which the appropriate version of RSAT has been installed, you are able to deploy additional domain controllers to existing domains, install new child domains, and install new tree domains as long as you have the appropriate credentials for the task you are going to perform.

Preparing for deploying domain controllers in an existing forest

You can also deploy Windows Server 2012 or Windows Server 2012 R2 domain controllers in a forest whose domain controllers are running an earlier version of Windows Server by using Windows PowerShell as follows:

1. Install Windows Server 2012 or Windows Server 2012 R2 on a server and join the server to an existing domain.

2. Use the Install-WindowsFeature cmdlet to install the AD DS role with its role-management tools as follows:

   ```
   Install-WindowsFeature -name AD-Domain-Services -IncludeManagementTools
   ```

3. Run commands from the ADDSDeployment module on the server to remotely install AD DS on other domain-joined servers running Windows Server 2012 or Windows Server 2012 R2.

Using Windows PowerShell to deploy domain controllers

The Windows PowerShell cmdlets for installing a forest, installing domains, deploying domain controllers, and performing similar deployment tasks are found in the ADDSDeployment module. This Windows PowerShell module is installed by default when you add the AD DS role with its role-management tools on a server, regardless of whether the server has been promoted to a domain controller. To see a list of the available cmdlets in this module, use the Get-Command cmdlet as follows:

```
PS C:\> Get-Command -Module ADDSDeployment
```

CommandType	Name	ModuleName
Cmdlet	Add-ADDSReadOnlyDomainControllerAccount	ADDSDeployment
Cmdlet	Install-ADDSDomain	ADDSDeployment
Cmdlet	Install-ADDSDomainController	ADDSDeployment
Cmdlet	Install-ADDSForest	ADDSDeployment
Cmdlet	Test-ADDSDomainControllerInstallation	ADDSDeployment
Cmdlet	Test-ADDSDomainControllerUninstallation	ADDSDeployment
Cmdlet	Test-ADDSDomainInstallation	ADDSDeployment
Cmdlet	Test-ADDSForestInstallation	ADDSDeployment
Cmdlet	Test-ADDSReadOnlyDomainControllerAccountCreation	ADDSDeployment
Cmdlet	Uninstall-ADDSDomainController	ADDSDeployment

Verifying prerequisites

You can use the Test-ADDS* cmdlets to run a prerequisites check before attempting to install a new forest, install a new domain, deploy a writeable domain controller, or deploy an RODC in your environment. The output of this command will help you determine whether your environment is ready for the operation you intend to perform or whether additional configuration might be required. The example here shows some output from running the Test-ADDSForestInstallation cmdlet on a stand-alone server running Windows Server 2012 or Windows Server 2012 R2 to determine whether the server satisfies the prerequisites for becoming the first domain controller of the forest root domain of a new forest:

```
PS C:\> Test-ADDSForestInstallation -DomainName corp.adatum.com
SafeModeAdministratorPassword: ********
Confirm SafeModeAdministratorPassword: ********
WARNING: Windows Server 2012 Release Candidate domain controllers have a default for the
security setting named "Allow cryptography algorithms compatible with Windows NT 4.0"
that prevents weaker cryptography algorithms when establishing security channel
sessions.

For more information about this setting, see Knowledge Base article 942564
(http://go.microsoft.com/fwlink/?LinkId=104751).

WARNING: This computer has at least one physical network adapter that does not have
static IP address(es) assigned to its IP Properties. If both IPv4 and IPv6 are enabled
for a network adapter, both IPv4 and IPv6 static IP addresses should be assigned to both
IPv4 and IPv6 Properties of the physical network adapter. Such static IP address(es)
assignment should be done to all the physical network adapters for reliable Domain Name
System (DNS) operation.

WARNING: A delegation for this DNS server cannot be created because the authoritative
parent zone cannot be found or it  does not run Windows DNS server. If you are
integrating with an existing DNS infrastructure, you should manually create a delegation
to this DNS server in the parent zone to ensure reliable name resolution from outside
the domain "adatum.com". Otherwise, no action is required.


Message                         Context             RebootRequired    Status
-------                         -------             --------------    ------
Operation completed succes...   Test.VerifyDcPromo...              False   Success
```

To determine whether a remote server running Windows Server 2012 or Windows Server 2012 R2 satisfies these requirements, use the Invoke-Command cmdlet to execute the Test-ADDSForestInstallation cmdlet on the remote server as follows:

```
Invoke-Command -ComputerName SEA-SRV-1 {Test-ADDSForestInstallation -DomainName corp
.adatum.com}
```

First domain controller in new forest

Deploying the first domain controller running Windows Server 2012 or Windows Server 2012 R2 in a new forest is equivalent to installing a new forest and involves two steps:

1. Adding the AD DS role to the server
2. Promoting the server as a domain controller

Using Windows PowerShell, you can combine these actions into a single script you can execute on remote servers. The following scenario uses two stand-alone servers running Windows Server 2012 or Windows Server 2012 R2: a local server named SEA-HOST-2 and a remote server named SEA-SRV-1. The goal is to run a script on SEA-HOST-2 that will install a new forest, with SEA-SRV-1 being the first domain controller in the forest root domain. To accomplish this, you could proceed as follows:

1. Begin by logging on to a local server running Windows Server 2012 or Windows Server 2012 R2 using your administrator credentials and open an elevated Windows PowerShell prompt. (If you are logged on with the built-in Administrator account, any Windows PowerShell prompt you open will be elevated.)

2. Change the script execution policy on the local server to RemoteSigned by running the following command:

   ```
   Set-Execution Policy RemoteSigned
   ```

> **NOTE   DEFAULT EXECUTION POLICY**
>
> Beginning with Windows Server 2012 R2, the default execution policy for Windows PowerShell is RemoteSigned. This means that step 2 only has to be performed if the server is running the earlier version of Windows Server 2012.

3. Changing the execution policy enables you to run Windows PowerShell scripts (.ps1 files) on the local server. By using Windows PowerShell remoting, you are also able to run scripts on the remote server.

4. Open Notepad and type the following two commands:

   ```
   Install-WindowsFeature -Name AD-Domain-Services -IncludeManagementTools
   Install-ADDSForest -DomainName corp.adatum.com -InstallDNS
   ```

   The first command installs AD DS with the role-management tools on the targeted server. The second command promotes the targeted server as the first domain controller in the forest root domain corp.adatum.com. Note that the name of the targeted server has not been specified in this script. Use Notepad to save the script with the file name script1.ps1 in the folder C:\scripts or some other suitable location on the local server.

5. Run the following command on the local server to execute your script on the remote server SEA-SRV-1:

   ```
   Invoke-Command -ComputerName SEA-SRV-1 -FilePath C:\scripts\script1.ps1
   ```

6. When the AD DS role has finished installing on SEA-SRV-1, you will be prompted to specify a Safe Mode Administrator Password. This password is necessary because it enables you to log on to the new domain controller in Directory Services Recovery Mode when needed. After entering a password and confirming it, press Y and then ENTER to confirm that you want to promote the server as a domain controller. The promotion process begins, as shown in Figure 4-12. Note that you can eliminate the need to press Y and then ENTER by including the *–Force* parameter in the second line of your script.

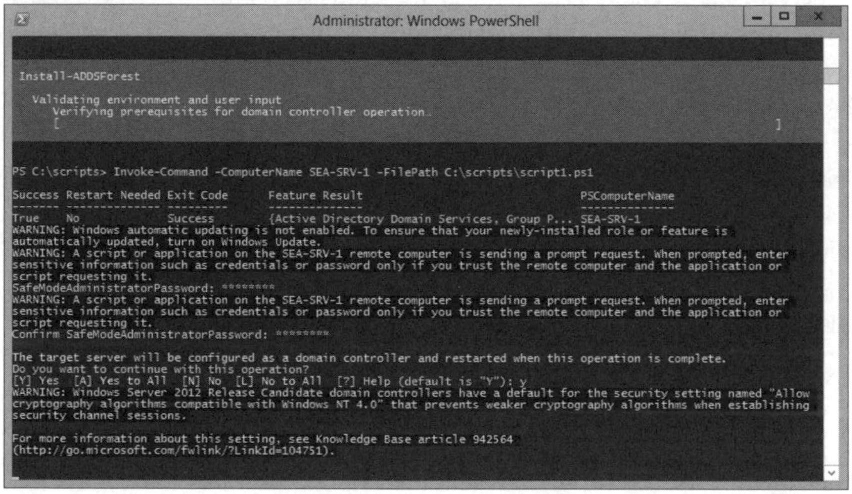

FIGURE 4-12 Remote server SEA-SRV-1 is being promoted to be the first domain controller in a new forest.

7. Command output like the following will be displayed if the promotion process is successful:

```
PSComputerName  : SEA-SRV-1
RunspaceId      : dd268942-f430-43c9-9830-7c547d1a4b73
Message         : Operation completed successfully
Context         : DCPromo.General.3
RebootRequired  : False
Status          : Success
```

The server will then be restarted to complete the promotion process. If the remote server is a Server With A GUI installation, logging on to the server and launching Server Manager will confirm that the AD DS and DNS Server roles have been installed and the server is the first domain controller in the corp.adatum.com forest.

Additional domain controller in domain

You can use the Install-ADDSDomainController cmdlet to install an additional domain controller in an existing domain. For example, the following command installs and promotes a new domain controller and DNS server in the corp.adatum.com domain using domain administrator credentials:

```
Install-ADDSDomainController -InstallDns -Credential '
(Get-Credential CORP\Administrator) -DomainName corp.adatum.com
```

You will be prompted to provide and confirm the Directory Services Restore Mode (DSRM) password during the installation process.

If you want to use local administrator credentials instead of domain administrator credentials for this process, omit the *–Credential* parameter as follows:

```
Install-ADDSDomainController -InstallDns -DomainName corp.adatum.com
```

If you want to be prompted to supply the credentials needed to install and promote the domain controller, use the following command instead:

```
Install-ADDSDomainController -InstallDns -Credential '
(Get-Credential) -DomainName corp.adatum.com
```

You can use the Invoke-Command cmdlet to install several additional domain controllers at once, like this:

```
Invoke-Command -ComputerName SEA-SRV-2, SEA-SRV-3 -ScriptBlock '
{Install-ADDSDomainController -InstallDns -DomainName corp.adatum.com}
```

> **NOTE** **MULTIPLE-LINE COMMANDS**
>
> The backtick character is an escape character in Windows PowerShell that is appended to a line to indicate that the command continues on the next line.

First domain controller in child or tree domain

You can use the Install-ADDSDomain cmdlet to install a new child or tree domain in an existing forest by deploying the first domain controller for the new domain. For example, to install and promote a server to be the first domain controller of a child domain *hq* in the parent domain *corp.adatum.com*, use this command:

```
Install-ADDSDomain -Credential (Get-Credential CORP\Administrator) '
-NewDomainName hq -ParentDomainName corp.adatum.com -DomainType ChildDomain '
-InstallDNS -CreateDNSDelegation
```

For more information on the syntax for this command, use the Get-Help cmdlet.

Read-only domain controllers

You can use the Add-ADDSReadOnlyDomainControllerAccount cmdlet to create an RODC account that can be used to install an RODC in your forest. After you have created the RODC account, you can use the Install-ADDSDomainController cmdlet with the *–ReadOnlyReplica* parameter to deploy a new RODC in an existing domain. For more information on these cmdlets, use the Get-Help cmdlet.

> **MORE INFO** **INSTALLING AND PROMOTING DOMAIN CONTROLLERS**
>
> For additional examples and guidance concerning the deployment of domain controllers in different scenarios, see the following topics in the TechNet Library:
>
> - "Install Active Directory Domain Services" at *http://technet.microsoft.com/en-us /library/hh472162*
> - "AD DS Deployment Cmdlets" at *http://technet.microsoft.com/en-us/library /hh974719*
>
> See also Lesson 4 of Chapter 3.

> ✔ **Quick check**
>
> - What do you need to do before you can use one stand-alone Windows Server 2012 R2 server to remotely execute Windows PowerShell commands on another stand-alone Windows Server 2012 R2 server?
>
> **Quick check answer**
>
> - Add the second server to the TrustedHosts list on the first server.

Verifying domain controller deployment

You can also use Windows PowerShell to verify the results of installing AD DS on remote servers and promoting them as domain controllers. For example, you can use the cmdlets of the BestPractices module to perform BPA scans on remote servers. To illustrate this and continue the preceding scenario, begin by using Invoke-Command on local server SEA-HOST-2 to execute the Invoke-BPAModule cmdlet on remote server SEA-SRV-1:

```
PS C:\> Invoke-Command -ComputerName SEA-SRV-1 -ScriptBlock '
{Invoke-BpaModel -ModelId Microsoft/Windows/DirectoryServices}


ModelId           : Microsoft/Windows/DirectoryServices
SubModelId        :
Success           : True
ScanTime          : 6/20/2012 9:30:05 PM
ScanTimeUtcOffset : -07:00:00
Detail            : {SEA-SRV-1, SEA-SRV-1}
```

You can then execute the Get-BPAResult cmdlet on the remote server to display the results of the scan you performed by using this command:

```
PS C:\> Invoke-Command -ComputerName SEA-SRV-1 -ScriptBlock '
{Get-BpaResult Microsoft/Windows/DirectoryServices}
```

The output from this command will be quite extensive, so you might try piping it into the Where-Object cmdlet to display only results whose severity level is Error:

```
PS C:\Users\Administrator> Invoke-Command -ComputerName SEA-SRV-1 -ScriptBlock '
{Get-BpaResult Microsoft/Windows/DirectoyServices} | Where-Object Severity -eq Error
```

```
ResultNumber  : 28
ResultId      : 513979436
ModelId       : Microsoft/Windows/DirectoryServices
SubModelId    :
RuleId        : 36
ComputerName  : SEA-SRV-1
Context       :
Source        : SEA-SRV-1
Severity      : Error
Category      : Configuration
Title         : The PDC emulator master SEA-SRV-1.corp.adatum.com in this forest should
                be configured to correctly synchronize time from a valid time source
Problem       : The primary domain controller (PDC) emulator operations master in this
                forest is not configured to correctly synchronize time from a valid
                time source.
Impact        : If the PDC emulator master in this forest is not configured to
                correctly synchronize time from a valid time source, it might use its
                internal clock for time synchronization. If the PDC emulator master in
                this forest fails or otherwise becomes unavailable (and if you have not
                configured a reliable time server (GTIMESERV) in the forest root
                domain), other member computers and domain controllers in the forest
                will not be able to synchronize their time.
Resolution    : Set the PDC emulator master in this forest to synchronize time with a
                reliable external time source. If you have not configured a reliable
                time server (GTIMESERV) in the forest root domain, set the PDC emulator
                master in this forest to synchronize time with a hardware clock that is
                installed on the network (the recommended approach). You can also set
                the PDC emulator master in this forest to synchronize time with an
                external time server by running the w32tm /config /computer:SEA-SRV-
                1.corp.adatum.com /manualpeerlist:time.windows.com
                /syncfromflags:manual /update command. If you have configured a
                reliable time server (GTIMESERV) in the forest root domain, set the PDC
                emulator master in this forest to synchronize time from the forest root
                domain hierarchy by running w32tm /config
                /computer:SEA-SRV-1.corp.adatum.com /syncfromflags:domhier /update.
Compliance    :
Help          : http://go.microsoft.com/fwlink/?LinkId=142195
Excluded      : False
PSComputerName : SEA-SRV-1
```

Uninstalling AD DS

Finally, you can use the Uninstall-ADDSDomainController cmdlet to remove the AD DS role and demote a domain controller to a member server in the domain. You will be prompted to set and confirm the local Administrator password before the completion of the removal process. For more information on using this cmdlet, use the Get-Help cmdlet.

Lesson summary

- You can use Windows PowerShell to deploy domain controllers running Windows Server 2012 or Windows Server 2012 R2. This procedure is mainly intended for large enterprises, data centers, and cloud-computing environments in which automation of this process is a requirement.

- You can use Windows PowerShell to install and promote a remote stand-alone server running Windows Server 2012 or Windows Server 2012 R2 to a domain controller after taking some preparatory steps to enable Windows PowerShell remoting to work properly in a workgroup environment.

- To use Windows PowerShell to install the AD DS role on a remote server, use the Invoke-Command cmdlet to remotely execute the Install-WindowsFeature cmdlet.

- To use Windows PowerShell to promote a remote server that already has the AD DS role installed, use the Invoke-Command cmdlet to remotely execute the appropriate cmdlet from the ADDSDeployment module.

- To use Windows PowerShell to run a prerequisites check before attempting to install a new forest, install a new domain, deploy a writeable domain controller, and use the Test-ADDS* cmdlets from the ADDSDeployment module.

- To use Windows PowerShell to run a Best Practices Analyzer (BPA) scan on remote servers after installing AD DS and promoting them to domain controllers, use the Invoke-Command cmdlet to remotely execute the appropriate cmdlet from the BestPractices module.

Lesson review

Answer the following questions to test your knowledge of the information in this lesson. You can find the answers to these questions and explanations of why each answer choice is correct or incorrect in the "Answers" section at the end of this chapter.

1. Which of the following Windows PowerShell commands adds the remote server SRV-A to the TrustedHosts list on the local server?

   A. Get-Item wsman:\localhost\Client\TrustedHosts –Value SRV-A

   B. Set-Item wsman:\localhost\Client\TrustedHosts –Value SRV-A

   C. Get-Item wsman:\localhost\Server\TrustedHosts –Value SRV-A

   D. Set-Item wsman:\localhost\Server\TrustedHosts –Value SRV-A

2. Which of the following is *not* a cmdlet from the ADDSDeployment module?

   A. Install-ADDSDomain

   B. Install-ADDSDomainController

   C. Uninstall-ADDSDomainController

   D. Get-ADForest

3. Which Windows PowerShell command should you use to run a prerequisites check before attempting to deploy an additional domain controller in an existing forest?

   A. Install-ADDSDomainController –Prerequisites

   B. Invoke-BpaModel –ModelId Microsoft/Windows/DirectoryServices

   C. Test-ADDSDomainControllerInstallation

   D. Install-ADDSDomainController –Whatif

Practice exercises

The goal of this section is to provide you with hands-on practice with the following:

- Deploying domain controllers using Server Manager
- Deploying domain controllers using Windows PowerShell

To perform the following exercises, you need two clean installations of Windows Server 2012 R2: one installed using the Server With A GUI installation option and the other installed using the Server Core installation option. The servers should be stand-alone servers belonging to a workgroup, have Internet connectivity, and have no additional roles or features installed. For the purposes of these exercises, the name of the first server (the Server With A GUI installation) is assumed to be SERVER1 and the name of the second server (the Server Core installation) is assumed to be SERVER2. You should be logged on interactively to SERVER1 using the built-in local Administrator account.

> **NOTE** **SWITCHING TO SERVER CORE**
>
> If your SERVER2 is a Server With A GUI installation, you can switch it to a Server Core installation by running the following Windows PowerShell command on it:
>
> ```
> Uninstall-WindowsFeature Server-Gui-Mgmt-Infra –Restart
> ```

Exercise 1: Installing a new forest using Server Manager

In this exercise, you install a new forest named corp.contoso.com by using Server Manager to install AD DS on SERVER1 and promote the server as a domain controller.

1. Log on to SERVER1 using the built-in Administrator account and open Server Manager if it doesn't open automatically.

2. Use the Dashboard to verify that SERVER1 is in a healthy state before proceeding.

3. Use Server Manager to launch the Add Roles And Features Wizard and install the Active Directory Domain Services role on the server, including the administration tools for this role. Close the Add Roles And Features Wizard upon completion of the role installation.

4. Use the Notifications flag on the Server Manager menu to perform the post-deployment configuration task of promoting the server to a domain controller using the Active Directory Domain Services Configuration Wizard.

5. Select the Add A New Forest option on the first page of the AD DS Configuration Wizard and create a new forest root domain named corp.contoso.com. Make appropriate selections for the remaining items in the wizard pages.

6. On the Review Options page, click View Script and examine the Windows PowerShell script that the wizard will be executing. Look up the help page for the command in the TechNet Library to make sure you understand the syntax of the command.

7. After reviewing the results on the Prerequisites Check page, click Install to promote SERVER1 to be the first domain controller in the new forest.

8. After the server reboots, log on using the default domain administrator account and open Server Manager if it doesn't open automatically.

9. Use the Dashboard to examine any alerts that are raised for your new domain controller.

10. Select the AD DS page of Server Manager and review the Roles And Features tile at the bottom of the page to verify that the AD DS role has been installed on SERVER1.

11. Also on the AD DS page, review any critical, error, or warning events raised in the Events tile.

12. Also on the AD DS page, review the status of the services on SERVER1.

13. Also on the AD DS page, initiate a BPA scan of SERVER1 and review the results of this scan when it finishes.

14. Close Server Manager when you are finished.

Exercise 2: Remotely adding an additional domain controller using Windows PowerShell

In this exercise, you join SERVER2 to the corp.contoso.com domain and then use Windows PowerShell from SERVER1 to remotely deploy SERVER2 as an additional domain controller in your domain.

1. Log on locally to SERVER2 using the built-in local Administrator account. A command prompt window should be visible.

2. Type **Sconfig** in the command prompt window and press Enter to run the Server Configuration Tool (Sconfig.cmd).

3. Type **8** and press Enter to access the Network Adapter Settings page of the Configuration Tool. You are presented with a list of available network adapters that are attached to the server.

4. Type the index number of the adapter that you want to configure and then press Enter. You are presented with the current configuration for the network adapter that you selected.

5. Type **2** and press Enter to configure DNS Server settings for the selected network adapter.

6. Type the IP address for SERVER1 as the new preferred DNS server and press Enter. Then click OK in the dialog box that appears.

7. Press Enter to indicate that you will not be specifying an alternate DNS server.

8. The Configuration Tool returns you to the Network Adapter Settings page. Review the information on this page and make sure it is correct before proceeding. Then type **4** and press Enter to return to the Main Menu page.

9. Type **1** and press Enter and then type **D** and press Enter to indicate that you want to join SERVER2 to a domain.

10. Type **corp.contoso.com** as the name of the domain you want SERVER2 to join and then press Enter.

11. Type **CORP\Administrator** as the name of an authorized user for performing the domain join operation and then press Enter. (If you specified a different NetBIOS name for your domain in Exercise 1, use that name instead of CORP.)

12. In the new command prompt that opens, type the password associated with the user account you specified in the previous step and press Enter.

13. In the Change Computer Name dialog box that opens, click No.

14. In the Restart dialog box that opens, click Yes.

15. After SERVER2 has restarted, log on again using the local Administrator account and run the Server Configuration Tool again to verify that the server has successfully joined the domain. Then exit the Configuration Tool and switch to using SERVER1 for the remainder of this exercise.

16. Log on to SERVER1 with the default domain administrator account and close Server Manager if it opens automatically.

17. Open a Windows PowerShell prompt on SERVER1.

18. Use the Invoke-Command cmdlet with the Get-WindowsFeature cmdlet to remotely review the installed roles and features on SERVER2. Verify that the AD DS role is not yet installed on SERVER2.

19. Use Invoke-Command with Install-WindowsFeature to remotely install the AD DS role on SERVER2. Once this is done, use Get-WindowsFeature to confirm the installation.

20. Use the following command to remotely run a prerequisites check on SERVER2 to make sure the server is ready to be promoted to a domain controller:

```
Invoke-Command -ComputerName SERVER2 -ScriptBlock '
{Test-ADDSDomainControllerInstallation -DomainName corp.contoso.com '
-Credential (Get-Credential CORP\Administrator)}
```

Review the results the prerequisites check returns before proceeding.

21. Use the following command to remotely promote SERVER2 as an additional domain controller in the corp.contoso.com domain:

```
Invoke-Command -ComputerName SERVER2 '
{Install-ADDSDomainController -InstallDNS '
-Credential (Get-Credential CORP\Administrator) '
-DomainName corp.contoso.com}
```

22. When the promotion operation finishes, wait for SERVER2 to reboot. Then open Server Manager on SERVER1 and add SERVER2 to the server pool.

23. Use the Tools menu of Server Manager to launch the Active Directory Users And Computers console, select the Domain Controllers container under corp.contoso.com, and verify that SERVER2 is now a domain controller for this domain.

Suggested practice exercises

The following additional practice exercises are designed to give you more opportunities to practice what you've learned and to help you successfully master the lessons presented in this chapter.

- **Exercise 1**   Continue with the preceding exercises by first using Windows PowerShell to demote SERVER2 and remove AD DS and then using Server Manager to demote SERVER1 and remove AD DS to retire the forest.

- **Exercise 2**   Perform a clean install of Windows Server 2008 R2, Windows Server 2008, or Windows Server 2003, add the AD DS role, and promote the server as the first domain controller in the new forest root domain adatum.com. Use the Adprep.exe tool on your Windows Server 2012 R2 installation media to update the schema and prepare the forest for deploying Windows Server 2012 R2 domain controllers. Then perform an in-place upgrade of the first domain controller to Windows Server 2012 R2.

Answers

This section contains the answers to the lesson review questions in this chapter.

Lesson 1

1. **Correct answer: A**

    A. **Correct:** Having only one writeable domain controller in a domain is not a best practice. You should have at least two writeable domain controllers in each domain so that if one of them fails, users will still be able to log on and you will still be able to perform AD DS management tasks.

    B. **Incorrect:** Making sure that each site in your domain has a sufficient number of domain controllers to service the needs of users for logging on and accessing network resources is a best practice.

    C. **Incorrect:** Keeping the design of your forest simple by having only one domain is a best practice.

    D. **Incorrect:** Installing only the AD DS and DNS Server roles on your domain controllers is a best practice.

2. **Correct answers: A, B, and C**

    A. **Correct:** The fully qualified domain name (FQDN) for the root domain of your new forest is required information when planning the deployment of the first domain controller in a new forest.

    B. **Correct:** The forest and domain functional levels are required information when planning the deployment of the first domain controller in a new forest.

    C. **Correct:** The location for the AD DS database, log files, and SYSVOL folder is required information when planning the deployment of the first domain controller in a new forest.

    D. **Incorrect:** There is no Domain Admins security group if you haven't yet deployed the first domain controller in a new forest. Instead, you need the credentials of a member of the local Administrators security group on the server you are promoting to a domain controller.

3. **Correct answers: A and D**

    A. **Correct:** Creating a DNS delegation is not a required step for AD DS deployments if no external DNS servers will be used to reference the FQDN of your organization's internal forest.

    B. **Incorrect:** A best practice is for all domain controllers in a domain to have the DNS Server role installed and configured to ensure high availability in distributed environments.

    C. **Incorrect:** A best practice is for all domain controllers in a domain to be configured as global catalog servers to ensure high availability in distributed environments.

D. **Correct:** Read-only domain controllers require that there be at least one write-able domain controller running Windows Server 2008 or later installed in the domain. Having only writeable domain controllers running Windows Server 2003 is insufficient.

Lesson 2

1. **Correct answer: C**

   A. **Incorrect:** You need to run the Add Roles And Features Wizard to install the AD DS role on the server before you can run the AD DS Configuration Wizard to promote the server to a domain controller.

   B. **Incorrect:** The Add Roles And Features Wizard is used to install the AD DS role on a server, not to promote the server to a domain controller.

   C. **Correct:** This is the correct procedure.

   D. **Incorrect:** The Add Roles And Features Wizard is used to install the AD DS role on a server, not to promote the server to a domain controller. The AD DS Configuration Wizard is used to promote a server to a domain controller, not to install the AD DS role on the server.

2. **Correct answers: A and C**

   A. **Correct:** When you use the AD DS Configuration Wizard to deploy the first Windows Server 2012 R2 domain controllers in a domain of a forest whose domain controllers are running earlier Windows Server versions, the Adprep tool automati-cally runs to prepare the forest and domain by extending the schema to its latest version.

   B. **Incorrect:** Add A Domain Controller To An Existing Domain is the correct option to select on the Deployment Configuration page of the AD DS Configuration Wizard to deploy the first Windows Server 2012 R2 domain controller in an existing forest running an earlier version of Windows Server.

   C. **Correct:** Install From Media (IFM) is a supported deployment method to deploy the first Windows Server 2012 R2 domain controller in an existing forest running an earlier version of Windows Server.

   D. **Incorrect:** You can specify different credentials on the Deployment Configuration page of the AD DS Configuration Wizard if your current logon credentials have insufficient privileges to deploy the first Windows Server 2012 R2 domain control-ler in an existing forest running an earlier version of Windows Server.

3. **Correct answer: D**

   A. **Incorrect:** This command is missing the *–scope* base parameter and therefore does not return the correct result.

   B. **Incorrect:** This command returns the value of the *sAMAccountName* attribute, which has nothing to do with the schema level.

C. **Incorrect:** This command works because it returns the values of all attributes for the specified LDAP path, including the desired attribute *objectVersion*, but it is not the best syntax because it returns too much unnecessary information.

D. **Correct:** This is the correct command syntax to verify that Adprep has successfully extended your forest's schema.

Lesson 3

1. **Correct answer: B**

   A. **Incorrect:** This command displays the contents of the TrustedHosts list on the local server.

   B. **Correct:** This is the correct command syntax.

   C. **Incorrect:** You need to use Set-Item, not Get-Item, to configure the TrustedHosts list on the local server. In addition, the wsman:\ path is incorrect in this command—it should be wsman:\localhost\Client\TrustedHosts.

   D. **Incorrect:** The wsman:\ path is incorrect in this command—it should be wsman:\ localhost\Client\TrustedHosts.

2. **Correct answer: D**

   A. **Incorrect:** Install-ADDSDomain is a cmdlet from the ADDSDeployment module.

   B. **Incorrect:** Install-ADDSDomainController is a cmdlet from the ADDSDeployment module.

   C. **Incorrect:** Uninstall-ADDSDomainController is a cmdlet from the ADDSDeployment module.

   D. **Correct:** Get-ADForest is not a cmdlet from the ADDSDeployment module; it is a cmdlet from the ActiveDirectory module.

3. **Correct answer: C**

   A. **Incorrect:** The Install-ADDSDomainController cmdlet doesn't have a *–Prerequisites* parameter.

   B. **Incorrect:** This command performs a BPA scan on the server and is intended for use after the server has been promoted as a domain controller, not before.

   C. **Correct:** This is the correct command because it runs only the prerequisites check for deploying a domain controller.

   D. **Incorrect:** This command only summarizes the changes that would occur during the deployment process; it doesn't actually test whether those changes are possible given the current environment like the Test-ADDSDomainControllerInstallation command does.

CHAPTER 5

Active Directory administration

The day-to-day job of Active Directory administration involves such tasks as creating, configuring, maintaining, monitoring, and deleting user accounts, groups, computer accounts, and other directory objects. In addition, there are some tasks that need to be performed only infrequently or perhaps only once, such as creating a forest and its various domains; raising forest and domain functional levels; creating hierarchies of organizational units (OUs); delegating administrative control over OUs and the objects they contain; creating and configuring sites, site links, and subjects; and so on.

This chapter demonstrates the capabilities of the two primary tools used for administering Active Directory environments based on Windows Server 2012 or Windows Server 2012 R2. One of these tools is the Active Directory Administrative Center (ADAC), a GUI-based tool intended for tasks that need to be performed only occasionally, for the administration of smaller environments, and for use by administrators who are unfamiliar with command-line scripting. The other tool is the Active Directory module for Windows PowerShell, which enables administrators of large environments, such as data centers, to script Active Directory administration tasks for automation purposes.

Lessons in this chapter:

Before you begin

To complete the practice exercises in this chapter

- You need at least one server that has a clean install of Windows Server 2012 R2 and is configured as a domain controller. The server can be either a physical server or a virtual machine, and its TCP/IP settings should be configured to provide connectivity with the Internet.

- You should know how to use tools like the Active Directory Users And Computers MMC snap-in to perform common Active Directory administration tasks such as creating users, groups, and organizational units in Active Directory environments based on previous versions of Windows Server.

- You also should have at least rudimentary knowledge of using Windows PowerShell.

Lesson 1: Administering Active Directory objects using ADAC

Active Directory Administrative Center (ADAC) is the primary tool for performing day-to-day tasks in the administration of an Active Directory environment. This lesson provides an overview of the ADAC user-interface features and demonstrates how to locate and manage directory objects using ADAC.

After this lesson, you will be able to:

- Describe the user-interface features of ADAC.
- Use ADAC to locate Active Directory objects so that you can administer them.
- Create and configure users, groups, computers, organizational units, and other directory objects.
- Perform additional Active Directory management tasks using ADAC.
- Identify some Active Directory management tasks that cannot be performed using ADAC.

Estimated lesson time: 30 minutes

Overview of ADAC

ADAC was first introduced in Windows Server 2008 R2 as a tool for managing directory objects, such as users, groups, computers, organizational units, and domains. ADAC was designed to supersede the Active Directory Users And Computers snap-in for the Microsoft Management Console (MMC) by providing an enhanced management experience that uses a rich graphical user interface (GUI).

> *NOTE* **KERBEROS TICKET-GRANTING TICKET LIFETIME**
>
> Beginning with Windows Server 2012 R2, you can configure the default lifetime setting of four hours for Kerberos ticket-granting tickets (TGTs) using Authentication Policies and Silos accessed through ADAC. This means that when four hours has passed, the user must authenticate again. This appears to be the only significant change in ADAC in this latest version of Windows Server.

Built upon a foundation of Windows PowerShell, ADAC was enhanced in Windows Server 2012 with new functionality, including the Windows PowerShell History Viewer, which makes it easier to transition from GUI-based administration of Active Directory to automated management using Windows PowerShell scripting.

> **MORE INFO** **WINDOWS POWERSHELL HISTORY VIEWER**
>
> The Windows PowerShell History Viewer is demonstrated in the section "Creating users" later in this chapter.

User-interface features

The different user-interface features of ADAC, shown in Figure 5-1, include the following:

- **Breadcrumb bar**   Displays the location of the currently selected object within Active Directory. You can use this bar to quickly navigate to any container within Active Directory by specifying the container's path in one of the following forms:

    - A Lightweight Directory Access Protocol (LDAP) path, such as LDAP://ou=Seattle Users OU,ou=Seattle OU OU,dc=corp,dc=contoso,dc=com

    - A distinguished name (DN), such as ou=Seattle Users OU,ou=Seattle OU OU,dc=corp,dc=contoso,dc=com

    - A hierarchical path, such as Active Directory Domain Services\corp (local)\Seattle OU\Seattle Users OU

- **Navigation pane**   Enables you to browse Active Directory using either the list or tree view, as described in the next sections.

- **Management list**   Displays the contents of the container that is currently selected in the navigation pane.

- **Preview pane**   Displays various information about the object or container that is currently selected in the management list.

- **Tasks pane**   Enables you to perform different tasks on the object or container that is currently selected in the management list.

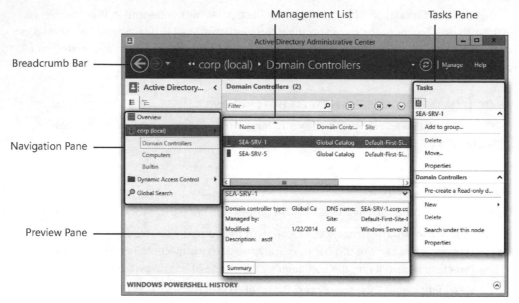

FIGURE 5-1 Active Directory Administrative Center shows various user-interface features.

List view

List view is one of two views available in the ADAC navigation pane. You can use it to browse Active Directory for the objects or containers you want to administer. In list view, you can use Column Explorer, shown in Figure 5-2, to quickly explore the contents of containers within the hierarchical structure of Active Directory.

FIGURE 5-2 You can use Column Explorer in list view in ADAC.

List view also maintains a Most Recently Used (MRU) list of the last three containers you accessed. Figure 5-2 indicates that the most recently accessed container was the Domain Controllers container in the corp.contoso.com domain, followed by the Computers and Builtin containers in the same domain. You can use the MRU list to quickly return to a container in which you were working just by selecting the appropriate MRU list item in the navigation pane.

You can also customize list view by adding nodes you might need to frequently access, similar to how you can use favorites in Internet Explorer or in the File Open/Save dialog box of Windows Explorer. Customizing ADAC list view is demonstrated later in this lesson.

Tree view

Tree view, shown in Figure 5-3, is the other view available in the ADAC navigation pane. Tree view presents a hierarchical representation of directory containers similar to that used in the Active Directory Users And Computers MMC snap-in.

FIGURE 5-3 This is the Overview page of tree view in ADAC.

Figure 5-3 shows the Overview page of ADAC, which includes the following tiles:

- **Welcome tile** Provides links you can click to learn more about using ADAC and administering an Active Directory environment built on Windows Server 2012 or Windows Server 2012 R2, to ask your questions in an online forum on TechNet, and to access other useful resources

- **Reset Password tile**   Enables you to quickly reset the password for a user account
- **Global Search tile**   Enables you to quickly search the selected container or the global catalog for objects and containers you need to administer

Searching Active Directory

Although using ADAC to browse the hierarchy of containers within Active Directory is one way of locating the objects you need to administer, a more efficient method is to use the query-building search and filtering capabilities that are built into ADAC. For example, say you are the Active Directory administrator for Contoso Ltd. and the Human Resources department has informed you that the user account for Marie Dubois needs to be disabled until further notice. To do this, you might proceed as follows:

1. Launch ADAC and select the Overview page in either list or tree view.

2. Type **marie** in the search box in the Global Search tile:

3. Select corp (local) as the scope for your search and press Enter.

The results of this query are shown in Figure 5-4. By right-clicking the user object Marie Dubois and selecting Disable, you can disable Marie's account.

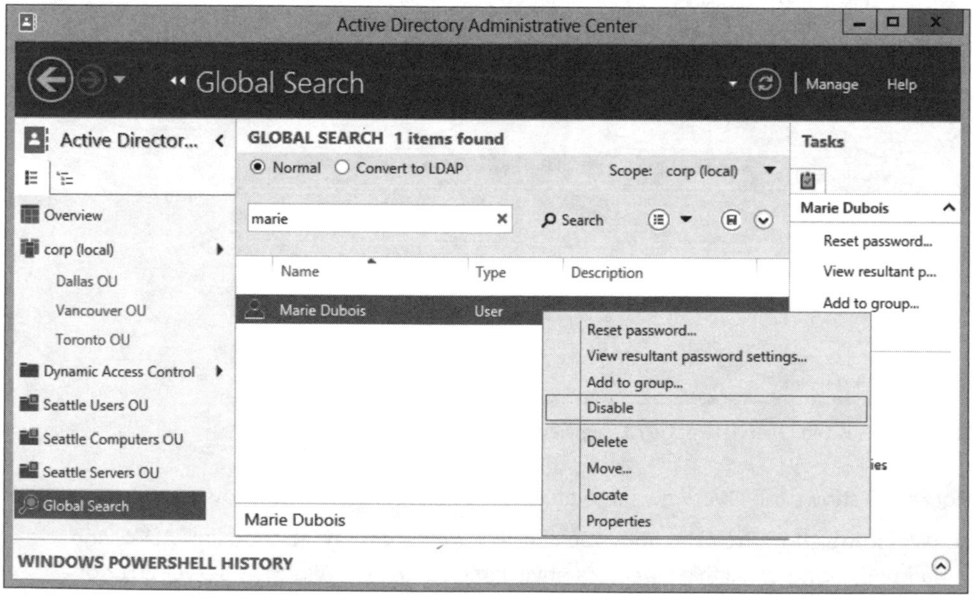

FIGURE 5-4 Disable the user account for a user you located using the Global Search tile.

You can broaden or narrow your search by selecting one or more navigation nodes. To do this, perform the following steps:

1. Click the down arrow at the right of the Scope item on the Global Search tile to display the Navigation Nodes explorer:

2. Select or deselect the nodes you want to include in your query.

You can make your query more specific by including additional search criteria. To do this, perform the following steps:

1. Click the small caret icon (^) beneath the small triangle referenced earlier. Doing this displays the Add Criteria control.

2. Click the Add Criteria control to display a list of criteria you can add to your search:

3. Select the criteria you want to add to your search and click Add.

Common administration tasks

Common administrative tasks you can perform using ADAC include creating, configuring, and managing the following types of objects:

- Organizational units (OUs)
- User accounts
- Computer accounts
- Groups

Creating organizational units

Creating a new organizational unit (OU) using ADAC involves the following steps:

1. Right-click the desired parent domain or OU, select New, and then select Organizational Unit:

2. Enter the necessary data and make the required selections on the different sections of the Create Organizational Unit properties page, as shown in Figure 5-5.

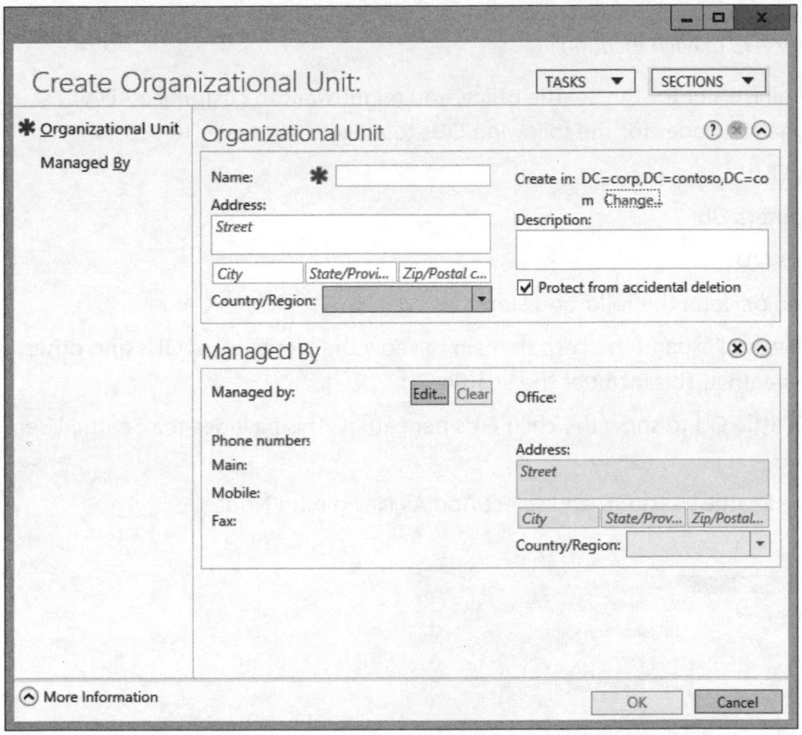

FIGURE 5-5 Make selections on the Create Organizational Unit properties page.

ADAC properties pages like this include several features that make them easy to use:

- Required information is indicated with a large red asterisk.

- You can hide or restore to view different sections in the page by selecting the Sections control at the upper right of the page. By hiding sections you never use, you can make the page easier to navigate.

- The Tasks control at the upper right of the page enables you to quickly perform certain tasks associated with the object or container type represented by the page. For example, you can move or delete the selected OU by using the Tasks control on the properties page for the OU.

- The same properties pages are used for both creating new objects or containers and modifying the properties of existing objects or containers.

One of the benefits of using ADAC list view is that you can customize this view by adding nodes representing Active Directory containers you frequently need to access to perform administration tasks on the objects in those containers. For example, consider the following scenario:

Contoso Ltd. has offices in several North American cities, including Seattle, Dallas, and Vancouver. The Active Directory structure for this organization consists of a single domain named corp.contoso.com, with top-level OUs for each city and second-level OUs for users, computers, and servers at each location.

If you are the administrator for the Seattle office, you might want to customize ADAC list view by adding navigation nodes for the following OUs to make them easier to access:

- Seattle Users OU
- Seattle Computers OU
- Seattle Servers OU

To do this, you can perform the following steps:

1. Select tree view and expand the corp domain to show the hierarchy of OUs and other containers beneath it. This includes the Seattle OU.

2. Expand the Seattle OU to show the child OUs beneath it. This includes the Seattle Users OU.

3. Right-click the Seattle Users OU and select Add As Navigation Node:

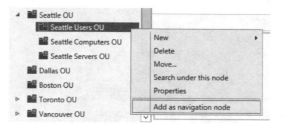

4. Repeat step 3 for the Seattle Computers OU and Seattle Servers OU.

Figure 5-6 shows what list view might look like after you add these three new navigation nodes. Note that you can rearrange your custom nodes by right-clicking them and selecting Move Up or Move Down. Any actions you perform on these navigation nodes have the same effect as acting directly upon the Active Directory containers they represent.

You can also add navigation nodes directly by right-clicking any blank area of the navigation pane in list view and selecting Add Navigation Nodes. Doing this opens the Add Navigation Nodes explorer shown in Figure 5-7.

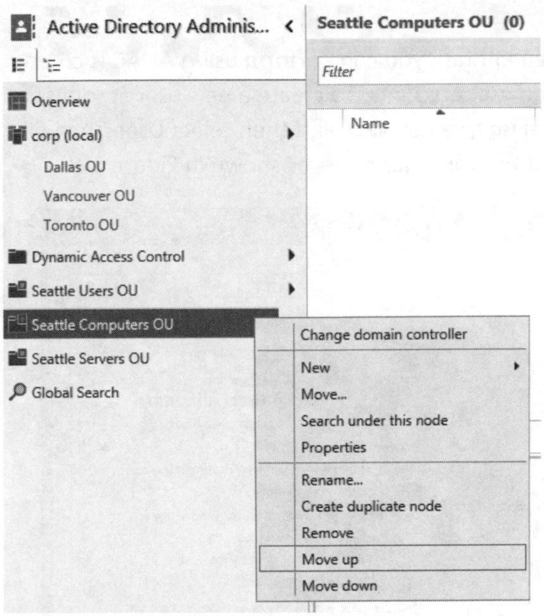

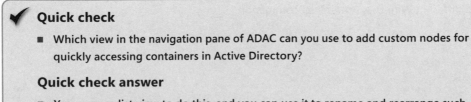

FIGURE 5-6 You can rearrange any custom navigation nodes you add to ADAC list view.

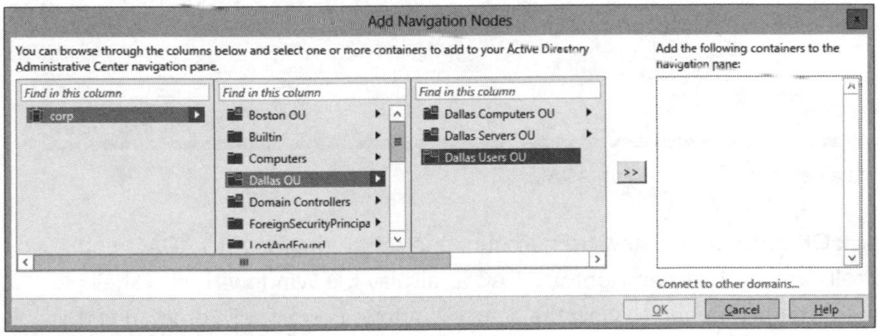

FIGURE 5-7 The Add Navigation Nodes explorer opens.

> ✓ **Quick check**
>
> ■ Which view in the navigation pane of ADAC can you use to add custom nodes for quickly accessing containers in Active Directory?
>
> **Quick check answer**
>
> ■ You can use list view to do this, and you can use it to rename and rearrange such nodes to help simplify the administration of your Active Directory environment.

Creating users

A second common Active Directory management task you can perform using ADAC is creating new user accounts and managing existing user accounts. To create a new user account, just right-click the appropriate organizational unit, select New, and then select User. Then fill in the necessary information on the Create User properties page, as shown in Figure 5-8.

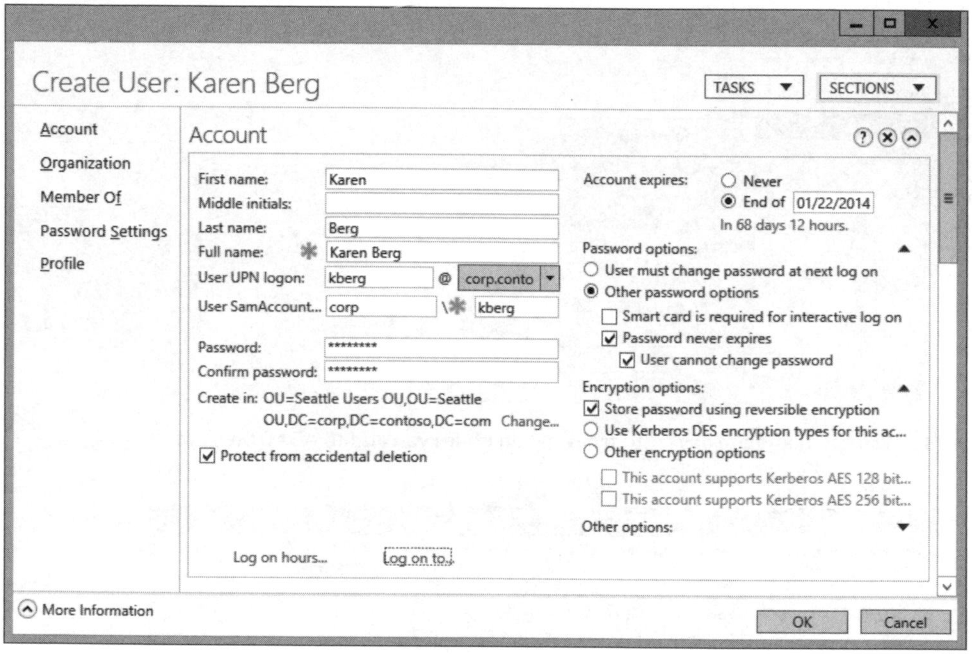

FIGURE 5-8 Create a new user account using ADAC.

After you click OK to create the new user account and return the focus to ADAC, you can click the small caret at the lower right of ADAC to display the Windows PowerShell History Viewer, which enables you to view the actual Windows PowerShell commands that are executed whenever you perform administrative tasks with ADAC. Figure 5-9 shows the commands involved during the creation of the new user account for Karen Berg shown in Figure 5-8. Note that a simple task like creating a single new user might require executing several different Windows PowerShell commands.

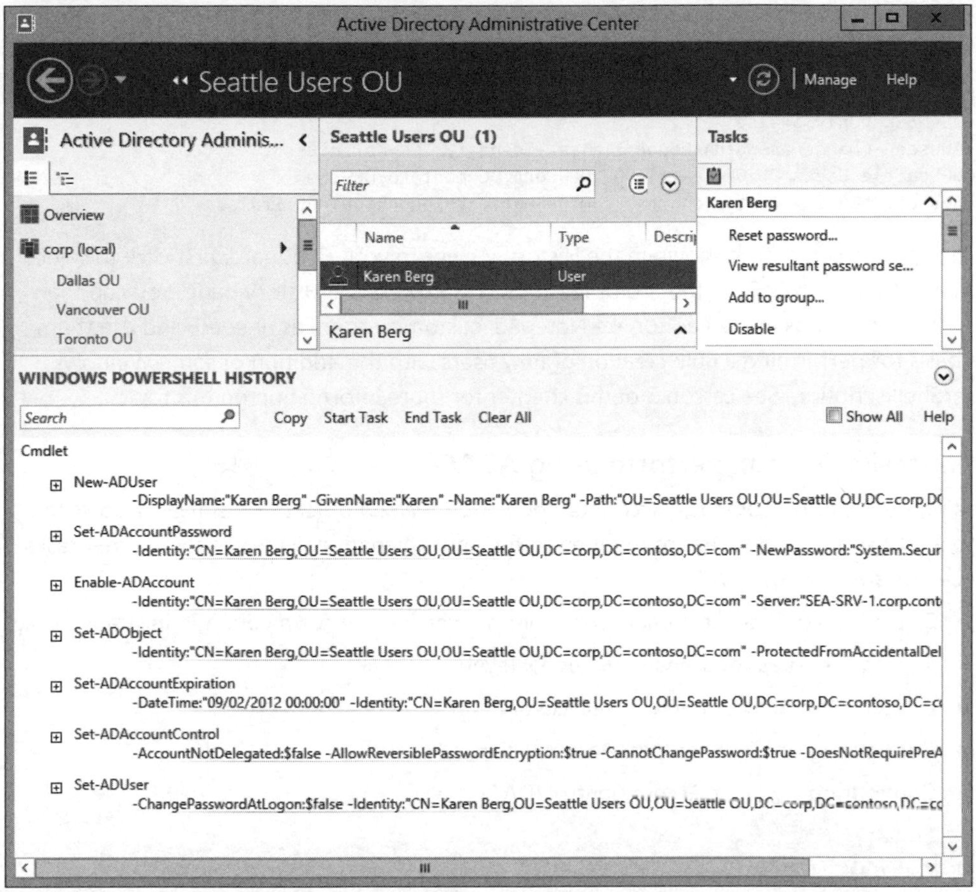

FIGURE 5-9 Review the Windows PowerShell History Viewer contents after creating new user Karen Berg.

The actual Windows PowerShell commands needed to create the new user Karen Berg in the preceding example are as follows:

```
New-ADUser -DisplayName:"Karen Berg" -GivenName:"Karen" -Name:"Karen Berg"
    -Path:"OU=Seattle Users OU,OU=Seattle OU,DC=corp,DC=contoso,DC=com"
    -SamAccountName:"kberg" -Server:"SEA-SRV-1.corp.contoso.com"
    -Surname:"Berg" -Type:"user" -UserPrincipalName:kberg@corp.contoso.com
Set-ADAccountPassword -Identity:"CN=Karen Berg,OU=Seattle Users OU,
    OU=Seattle OU,DC=corp,DC=contoso,DC=com" -NewPassword:"System.Security.SecureString"
    -Reset:$null -Server:"SEA-SRV-1.corp.contoso.com"
Enable-ADAccount -Identity:"CN=Karen Berg,OU=Seattle Users OU,
    OU=Seattle OU,DC=corp,DC=contoso,DC=com" -Server:"SEA-SRV-1.corp.contoso.com"
Set-ADObject -Identity:"CN=Karen Berg,OU=Seattle Users OU,
    OU=Seattle OU,DC=corp,DC=contoso,DC=com" -ProtectedFromAccidentalDeletion:$true
    -Server:"SEA-SRV-1.corp.contoso.com"
Set-ADAccountExpiration -DateTime:"09/02/2012 00:00:00" -Identity:"CN=Karen Berg,
    OU=Seattle Users OU,OU=Seattle OU,DC=corp,DC=contoso,DC=com"
    -Server:"SEA-SRV-1.corp.contoso.com"
Set-ADAccountControl -AccountNotDelegated:$false
```

```
    -AllowReversiblePasswordEncryption:$true
    -CannotChangePassword:$true -DoesNotRequirePreAuth:$false
    -Identity:"CN=Karen Berg,OU=Seattle Users OU,OU=Seattle OU,DC=corp,DC=contoso,
    DC=com" -PasswordNeverExpires:$true -Server:"SEA-SRV-1.corp.contoso.com"
    -UseDESKeyOnly:$false
Set-ADUser -ChangePasswordAtLogon:$false -Identity:"CN=Karen Berg,
    OU=Seattle Users OU,OU=Seattle OU,DC=corp,DC=contoso,DC=com"
    -Server:"SEA-SRV-1.corp.contoso.com" -SmartcardLogonRequired:$false
```

To copy the commands shown in the History Viewer to your Clipboard, first click to select them and then click Copy at the top of the Windows PowerShell History pane. You can then paste the commands into an editor like Notepad, customize them as needed, and use them as a basis for performing a bulk creation of new users with the addition of some Windows PowerShell scripting. See Lesson 3 of this chapter for more information on this topic.

Other tasks you can perform using ADAC

Creating new groups, computer accounts, and *InetOrgPerson* objects is a similar process to the one just shown and therefore requires no further explanation. Here are some other tasks you can perform using ADAC:

- Selecting a domain or domain controller on which to perform your administrative tasks
- Raising the forest or domain functional level
- Enabling the Active Directory Recycle Bin
- Configuring fine-grained password policies
- Configuring Dynamic Access Control (DAC)

> *MORE INFO* **DYNAMIC ACCESS CONTROL**
>
> Dynamic Access Control (DAC) is another feature of Active Directory in Windows Server 2012 and Windows Server 2012 R2. You use DAC to implement a claims-based authorization solution. In this type of solution, you use central access policies, rules, and claim types to enable the use of file-classification information in authorization decisions. By using DAC, you can define access and audit policies in a simple and flexible way that can significantly reduce the number of groups you need to manage in your Active Directory environment. For more information on DAC, see the post "Introduction to Windows Server 2012 Dynamic Access Control" on the Windows Server Blog at *http://blogs.technet.com/b/windowsserver /archive/2012/05/22/introduction-to-windows-server-2012-dynamic-access-control.aspx*.

Tasks you cannot perform using ADAC

There are a number of Active Directory management tasks you cannot perform using ADAC, such as the following:

- Delegate administrative control over Active Directory OUs and the objects they contain
- Create and manage sites, site links, subnets, and similar objects

- Create trusts between domains or forests
- Directly edit the configuration, schema, or application directory partitions

To perform such tasks, you need to use the following familiar tools:

- Active Directory Users And Computers
- Active Directory Sites And Services
- Active Directory Domains And Trusts
- ADSI Edit

Choosing a forest or domain functional level

Functional levels determine the capabilities of an Active Directory environment. The forest functional level specifies the highest functional level available for domains in your forest. Domain functional level is configured on a per-domain basis and cannot be higher than the forest functional level.

Raising the functional level of a domain generally adds new functionality for servers and client computers that are members of the domain. However, it can also result in the loss of certain functionality, such as changes to or loss of support for certain earlier versions of Windows.

Generally, you want to specify the highest possible forest functional level for your environment. You might, however, want to keep the domain functional level for some domains lower than your forest functional level; for example, if you are still running domain controllers running earlier versions of Windows Server like Windows Server 2003.

Lesson summary

- Active Directory Administrative Center (ADAC) is the primary GUI-based tool for managing user accounts, groups, computer accounts, and organizational units (OUs).
- Some of the features that make ADAC a useful tool for managing Active Directory environments include its list and tree views, its search and filtering capabilities, and the Windows PowerShell History Viewer.
- Because ADAC is built upon a foundation of Windows PowerShell, you can view and customize the Windows PowerShell commands executed when you perform a task using ADAC. By customizing these commands, you can automate many Active Directory management tasks.

- Using the version of ADAC introduced in Windows Server 2012, you also can enable and use the Active Directory Recycle Bin, configure fine-grained password policies, and configure Dynamic Access Control (DAC).

Lesson review

Answer the following questions to test your knowledge of the information in this lesson. You can find the answers to these questions and explanations of why each answer choice is correct or incorrect in the "Answers" section at the end of this chapter.

1. What feature of ADAC enables you to quickly access the last three containers you accessed? (Choose all that apply.)

   A. Column Explorer

   B. Navigation pane

   C. Navigation nodes

   D. MRU list

2. Which of the following types of directory objects can you *not* create using ADAC? (Choose all that apply.)

   A. Sites

   B. Domains

   C. Trusts

   D. Groups

3. Which of the following Active Directory administration tasks can you *not* perform using ADAC? (Choose all that apply.)

   A. Raising the forest functional level

   B. Delegating administrative control over an OU and the objects it contains

   C. Enabling the Active Directory Recycle Bin

   D. Configuring fine-grained password policies

Lesson 2: Enabling advanced features using ADAC

Two advanced features for Active Directory administration that you can configure using ADAC in Windows Server 2012 and Windows Server 2012 R2 are the Active Directory Recycle Bin and fine-grained password policies. This lesson demonstrates how to enable and use these two features using ADAC.

Enabling and using the Active Directory Recycle Bin

Administrators of Active Directory environments sometimes make mistakes—for example, deleting the user account for a user who still needs access to the corporate network. The effects of such mistakes can range from lost end-user productivity to broken network functionality.

Windows Server 2008 R2 introduced a feature called the *Active Directory Recycle Bin* (AD Recycle Bin) to provide administrators with a way to recover directory objects that were accidentally deleted. However, using the AD Recycle Bin in Windows Server 2008 R2 environments proved difficult for some administrators because enabling and using this feature could be performed only from the command-line, either by using the Ldp.exe utility or Windows PowerShell cmdlets. Windows Server 2012 and Windows Server 2012 R2 simplify this task—now you can use the GUI-based ADAC for both enabling the AD Recycle Bin and recovering deleted objects.

Understanding the AD Recycle Bin

To understand the limitations of the AD Recycle Bin, you need to know how it works. When the AD Recycle Bin feature is enabled in an Active Directory environment, directory objects can be in one of the following four states (illustrated in Figure 5-10):

- **Live** The object is functioning in Active Directory and is located in its proper container within the directory. As an example, a user account object in the live state is one that a user can utilize for logging on to the network.

- **Deleted** The object has been moved to the Deleted Objects container within Active Directory. The object is no longer functioning in Active Directory, but the object's link-valued and non-link-valued attributes are preserved, allowing the object to be recovered by restoring it from the AD Recycle Bin if the lifetime of the deleted object has not yet expired. (By default, when the AD Recycle Bin is enabled, the deleted object lifetime is configured as 180 days.) For example, a user account in the deleted state cannot be used for logging on to the network, but if the user account is restored to its live state, it can again be used for logon purposes.

- **Recycled** The deleted object lifetime has expired for the object. The object remains in the Deleted Objects container, but most of its attributes are stripped away. The object can no longer be recovered by restoring it from the AD Recycle Bin or by taking other steps, such as reanimating Active Directory tombstone objects.

- **Removed** The recycled object lifetime has expired for the object. The Active Directory garbage collection process has physically removed the object from the directory database.

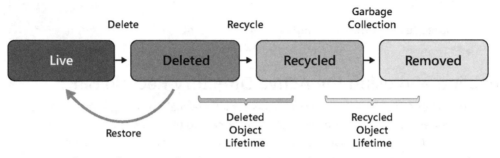

FIGURE 5-10 There are four states of Active Directory objects when the AD Recycle Bin is enabled.

Enabling the AD Recycle Bin

By default, the AD Recycle Bin feature is disabled until you choose to enable it. Enabling the AD Recycle Bin in your environment requires that the forest functional level be Windows Server 2008 R2 or higher. This means that all domain controllers in your forest must be running Windows Server 2008 R2 or later.

To enable the AD Recycle Bin using ADAC, perform the following steps:

1. Log on using credentials of an account that belongs to the Enterprise Admins or Schema Admins group.

2. Right-click the forest root domain in the navigation pane and select Raise The Forest Functional Level:

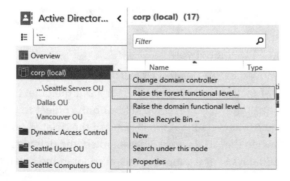

3. Ensure that the forest functional level for your environment is Windows Server 2008 R2 or higher.

4. Right-click the forest root domain again and select Enable Recycle Bin.

5. Review the warning and click OK to proceed with enabling the AD Recycle Bin.

6. Refresh ADAC and wait until all domain controllers in the forest have replicated the configuration change before attempting to use the AD Recycle Bin to restore deleted objects.

NOTE **USING WINDOWS POWERSHELL TO ENABLE THE AD RECYCLE BIN**

You can also use Windows PowerShell to perform all of the actions required to enable the AD Recycle Bin for your environment. For example, you can use the Set-ADForestMode cmdlet to raise the forest functional level to Windows Server 2008 R2 or higher. You can use the Enable-ADOptionalFeature cmdlet to enable the AD Recycle Bin feature. Use the Get-Help cmdlet to display the syntax and examples for each of these cmdlets.

IMPORTANT **ENABLING THE AD RECYCLE BIN IS AN IRREVERSIBLE DECISION**

Although enabling the AD Recycle Bin is a recommended best practice for Active Directory administration, after you enable this feature you cannot disable it. So plan carefully before taking this step because you will be unable to roll back the forest functional level after you have done it. For more information on rolling back the forest functional level, see the topic titled "Understanding Active Directory Domain Services (AD DS) Functional Levels" in the TechNet Library at *http://technet.microsoft.com/en-us/library/understanding-active -directory-functional-levels(WS.10).aspx.*

Using the AD Recycle Bin

After the AD Recycle Bin is enabled, using it to restore deleted directory objects is straight-forward as long as the deleted object lifetime of the objects has not expired. For example, Figure 5-11 shows how to restore the user account for Marie Dubois after it was accidentally deleted. The following menu options are available:

- **Restore**   Restore the deleted object to its original location within Active Directory.
- **Restore To**   Restore the deleted object to a container you specify using Column Explorer.
- **Locate Parent**   Display the container where the deleted object originally resided.
- **Properties**   Display or modify the properties of the deleted object.

NOTE **RESTORING MULTIPLE DELETED OBJECTS**

You can restore multiple deleted objects in one action by multiselecting them in the Deleted Objects container and choosing the appropriate menu option.

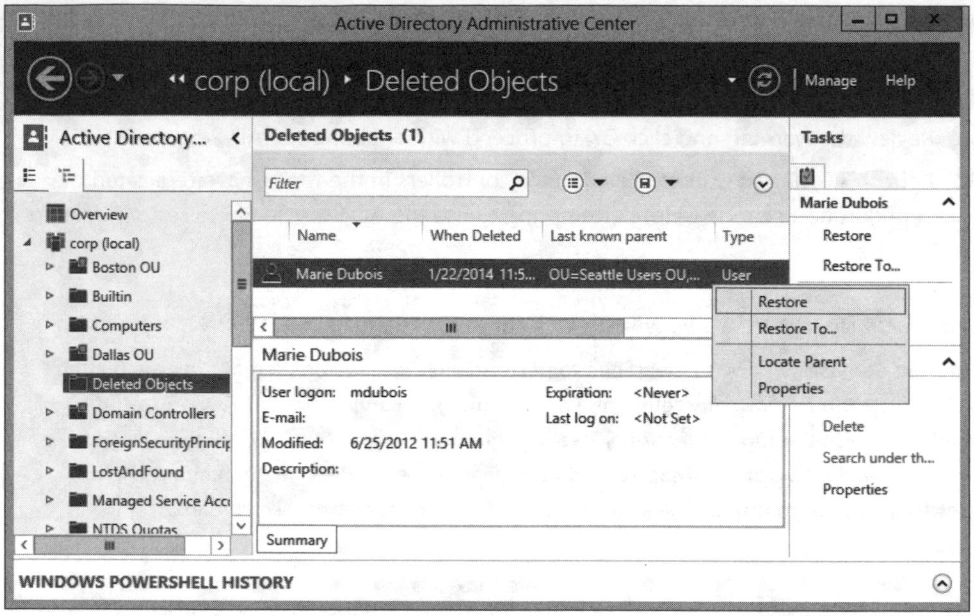

FIGURE 5-11 Restore a deleted object using the AD Recycle Bin.

NOTE **USING WINDOWS POWERSHELL TO RESTORE DELETED OBJECTS**

After you have enabled the AD Recycle Bin for your environment, you can also use Windows PowerShell to restore directory objects you accidentally deleted. You can do this using the Restore-ADObject cmdlet. Use the Get-Help cmdlet to display the syntax and examples for this cmdlet.

✔ **Quick check**

- If a directory object is in the Recycled state, can you still recover it using the AD Recycle Bin?

Quick check answer

- No. If an object is in the Recycled state, its deleted object lifetime has expired. The object is still in the Deleted Objects container, but because most of its attributes have been stripped away you can no longer recover it by restoring it from the AD Recycle Bin.

Configuring fine-grained password policies

In Windows Server 2003 and earlier, you could have only a single password policy and account lockout policy governing all user accounts in a domain. You could configure this password policy by editing the Default Domain Policy Group Policy Object (GPO)—specifically, the six policy settings found under

Computer Configuration\Policies\Windows Settings\Security Settings\Account Policies\Password Policy

Each domain also had three account lockout policy settings, found under

Computer Configuration\Policies\Windows Settings\Security Settings\Account Policies\Account Lockout Policy

Windows Server 2008 introduced a feature called *fine-grained password policies* that you could use to configure multiple password policies and account lockout policies for each domain. This provided Active Directory administrators with greater flexibility because they could create different policies for different groups of users. The problem, however, was that you needed to use ADSI Edit and the Ldifde command-line utility to create fine-grained password policies on the earlier platform. This task is simplified in Windows Server 2012 and Windows Server 2012 R2 because you can use the GUI-based ADAC for creating fine-grained password policies. In addition, you can use ADAC to view the resultant password settings for particular users in your environment to ensure fine-grained password policies have been configured as intended.

Understanding fine-grained password policies

You can assign fine-grained password policies to users or groups. If a user belongs to more than one group that has a fine-grained password policy assigned to it, the precedence value of each policy is used to determine which policy applies to members of the group. The precedence value of a policy must be an integer value of 1 or greater. If multiple policies apply to the same user, the policy having the lowest precedence value takes effect.

> **REAL WORLD** **UNDERSTANDING POLICY PRECEDENCE**
>
> Consider a scenario in which a user named Karen Berg in the corp.contoso.com domain is a member of two groups: the Marketing group and the Sales group. Fine-grained password policies have been configured as follows:
>
> - A fine-grained password policy having a precedence value of 1 has been created and assigned to the Marketing group.
> - A fine-grained password policy having a precedence value of 2 has been created and assigned to the Sales group.
>
> Because Karen belongs to both groups, both policies apply to her, but the one with the lowest precedence value (the policy assigned to the Marketing group) is the one that takes effect.

Note that if two fine-grained password policies have the same precendence value and both policies are applied to the same user, the policy with the smallest globally unique identifier (GUID) takes effect.

Best practices for implementing fine-grained password policies

When planning to implement fine-grained password policies within your Active Directory environment, you should follow these best practices:

- Assign policies to groups instead of individual users for easier management.
- Assign a unique precedence value to each fine-grained password policy you create within a domain.
- Create a fallback policy for the domain so that users who don't belong to any groups that specifically have fine-grained password policies assigned to them still have password and account lockout restrictions apply when they try to log on to the network. This fallback policy can be either of the following:
  - The password and account lockout policies defined in the Default Domain Policy GPO
  - A fine-grained password policy that has a higher precedence value than any other policy

REAL WORLD **IMPLEMENTING A FALLBACK POLICY FOR YOUR DOMAIN**

Consider a scenario in which the corp.contoso.com domain has three groups: Marketing, Sales, and Human Resources. Fine-grained password policies have been configured as follows:

- A fine-grained password policy having a precedence value of 1 has been created and assigned to the Marketing group.
- A fine-grained password policy having a precedence value of 2 has been created and assigned to the Sales group.
- No fine-grained password policy has been assigned to the Human Resources group.

To ensure that password and account lockout restrictions apply when members of the Human Resources group try to log on to the network, you can do either of the following:

- Configure password and account lockout policy settings in the Default Domain Policy GPO for the domain.
- Create a fine-grained password policy that has a precedence value of 100 and assign this policy to the Domain Users group.

Note that the second option is the recommended approach because Default Domain Policy is a legacy feature dating back to the Windows NT era and fine-grained password policies are the future.

Creating fine-grained password policies

Before you can create fine-grained password policies for a domain, you must ensure that the domain functional level is Windows Server 2008 or higher. You can do this by using either ADAC or Windows PowerShell as described in the previous topic in this lesson.

> **NOTE DOMAIN FUNCTIONAL LEVEL**
>
> **Domain Admin credentials or greater are required to raise the domain functional level for a domain.**

Fine-grained password policies for a domain are stored in the Password Settings Container, which is found under System, as shown in Figure 5-12.

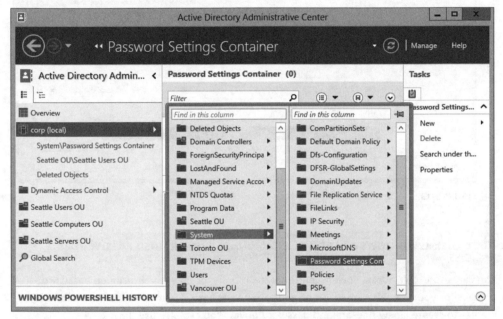

FIGURE 5-12 Fine-grained password policies are stored in the Password Settings Container.

To create a new fine-grained password policy using ADAC, follow these steps:

1. Display the Password Settings Container in either the navigation pane or the management list pane.

2. Right-click the Password Settings Container and select New. Then select Password Settings.

3. Fill in the appropriate information on the Create Password Settings properties page, as shown in Figure 5-13.

4. Click Add and locate the group or groups to which you want the policy to apply. Then click OK to create the new policy.

5. Repeat the preceding steps to create additional fine-grained password policies as needed for your environment.

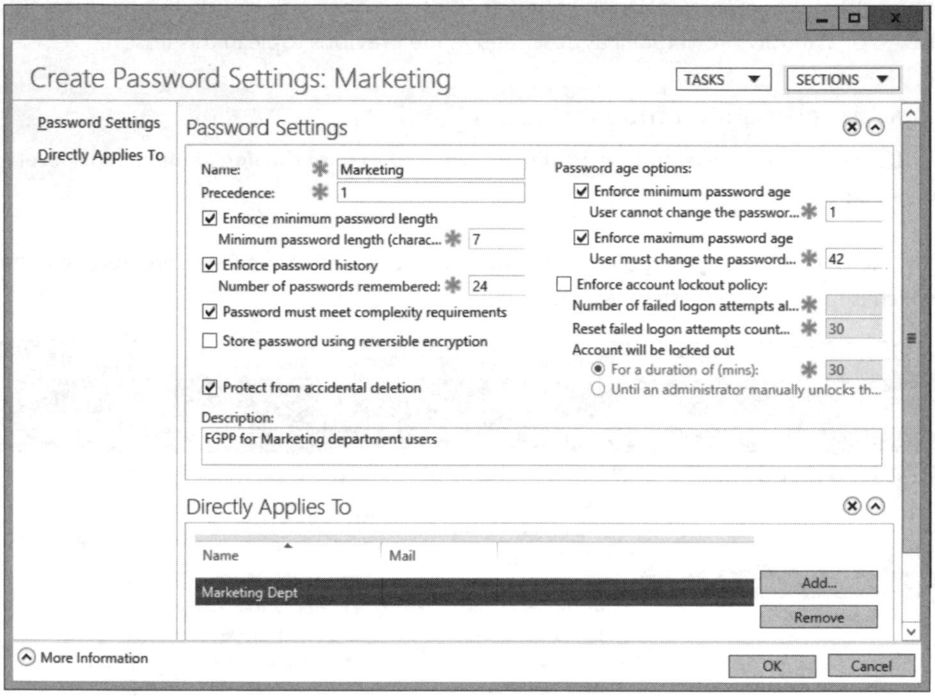

FIGURE 5-13 Create a new fine-grained password policy.

> **NOTE** **USING WINDOWS POWERSHELL TO MANAGE FINE-GRAINED PASSWORD POLICIES**
>
> You can also use Windows PowerShell to create, modify, or delete fine-grained password policies for your domain. For example, you can use the New-ADFineGrainedPasswordPolicy cmdlet to create a new fine-grained password policy. You can also use the Set-ADFineGrainedPasswordPolicy cmdlet to modify an existing fine-grained password policy. And you can use the Remove-ADFineGrainedPasswordPolicy cmdlet to delete a fine-grained password policy that is no longer needed in your environment. Use the Get-Help cmdlet to display the syntax and examples for each of these cmdlets.

Viewing the resultant password settings for a user

You can also use ADAC to view the resultant password settings for users in a domain. This is useful both for ensuring that you have created and assigned fine-grained password policies as you intended for your environment and also for troubleshooting problems with policies not being applied as expected.

To view the resultant password settings for a particular user, first locate the user in Active Directory either by browsing using the navigation pane or by using the Global Search tile. Then right-click the user account and select View Resultant Password Settings, as shown in Figure 5-14. The fine-grained password policy that is displayed is the one that applies to the user who has the lowest precedence value.

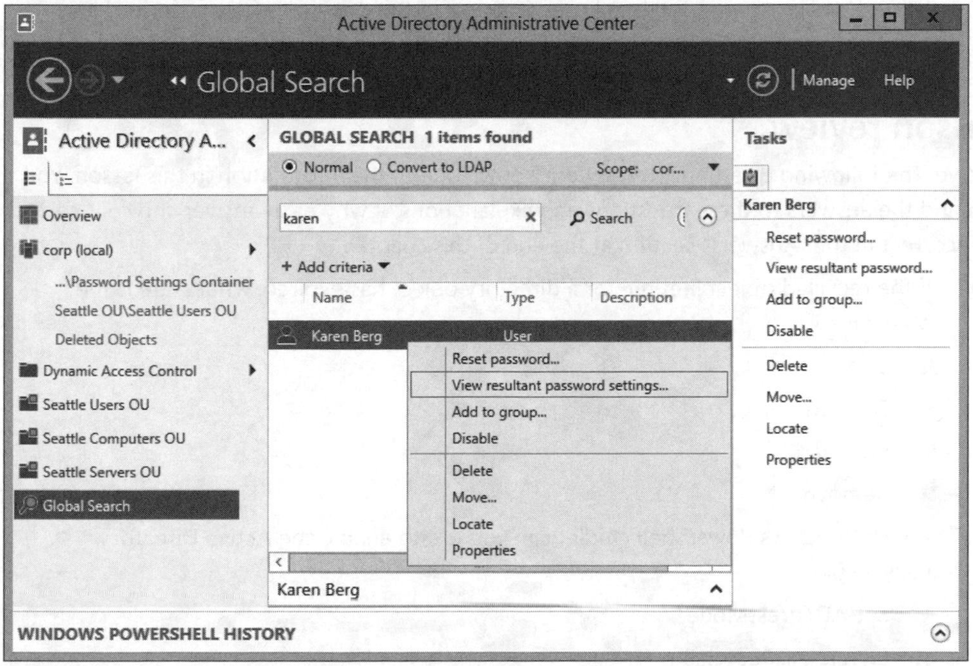

FIGURE 5-14 View the resultant set of policies for a user.

> **NOTE** **USING WINDOWS POWERSHELL TO VIEW THE RESULTANT SET OF POLICIES**
>
> You can also use Windows PowerShell to view the resultant password settings for a user. You can do this using the Get-ADUserResultantPasswordPolicy cmdlet. Use the Get-Help cmdlet to display the syntax and examples for this cmdlet.

Lesson summary

- You can use ADAC to enable the Active Directory Recycle Bin and recover deleted objects by restoring them to the same location or a different location in the directory.
- Directory objects in an Active Directory forest that has been set to the Windows Server 2012 or Windows Server 2012 R2 forest functional level can be in one of four states: Live, Deleted, Recycled, or Removed. Only objects that are still in the Deleted state can be restored from the AD Recycle Bin.

- You can use ADAC to configure fine-grained password policies for a domain and also view the resultant set of policies.

- Fine-grained password policies are intended as the replacement for the password and account policy settings found in the Default Domain Policy GPO.

- When configuring fine-grained password policies for a domain, you should create a fallback policy to ensure that all user accounts in the domain have a password and account lockout policy applied.

Lesson review

Answer the following questions to test your knowledge of the information in this lesson. You can find the answers to these questions and explanations of why each answer choice is correct or incorrect in the "Answers" section at the end of this chapter.

1. If the recycled object lifetime for a directory object has expired, what state is the object in?

   A. Live

   B. Deleted

   C. Recycled

   D. Removed

2. Which Windows PowerShell cmdlet can you use to enable the Active Directory Recycle Bin?

   A. Set-ADForestMode

   B. Enable-ADRecycleBin

   C. Enable-ADOptionalFeature

   D. New-ADFineGrainedPasswordPolicy

3. Which of the following are best practices for implementing fine-grained password policies in a domain? (Choose all that apply.)

   A. Assign fine-grained password policies to users instead of groups.

   B. Ensure that each fine-grained password policy has its own unique preference value.

   C. Ensure that each group has at least one fine-grained password policy assigned to it.

   D. Make sure you have configured a fallback policy for the domain. This can be either a fine-grained password policy that has a higher precedence value than any other policy or the password and account lockout settings defined in the Default Domain Policy GPO.

Lesson 3: Administering Active Directory using Windows PowerShell

Although ADAC can be useful for performing some Active Directory management tasks, especially in smaller environments, using Windows PowerShell to automate Active Directory administration is the preferred approach when you must repeat such tasks frequently—for example, when you need to create user accounts in bulk. This chapter demonstrates some of the different ways that you can use Windows PowerShell commands to perform common Active Directory management tasks. The chapter also demonstrates some of the more advanced administration tasks you can perform on your Active Directory environment using Windows PowerShell.

After this lesson, you will be able to:

- Demonstrate different ways of using Windows PowerShell to perform common Active Directory management tasks, such as creating and managing user accounts singly and in bulk.

- Find Windows PowerShell cmdlets that you can use for managing different aspects of Active Directory.

- Perform an advanced Active Directory administration task that involves creating a new site and site link followed by moving a domain controller to the new site.

Estimated lesson time: 30 minutes

Managing user accounts with Windows PowerShell

Creating and managing user accounts is a common Active Directory administration task. Windows PowerShell provides considerable flexibility in how this can be done in Windows Server 2012 and Windows Server 2012 R2. Typing **Get-Command *ADUser** at a Windows PowerShell prompt shows there are four cmdlets for managing user accounts:

- **New-ADUser**   Creates a new Active Directory user
- **Get-ADUser**   Gets one or more Active Directory users so that you can perform some action with them
- **Set-ADUser**   Modifies the properties of an existing Active Directory user
- **Remove-ADUser**   Removes the specified user from Active Directory

Any administration of user accounts using Windows PowerShell involves using one or more of these cmdlets. The following sections demonstrate some of the ways you can create new user accounts using the New-ADUser cmdlet. The approach you choose depends on the particular needs of your situation.

Example 1: Create a single new user account

To create a new user account for Phil Gibbins using *pgibbins* for the user's SAM account name and *pgibbins@corp.contoso.com* for the user's UPN logon, you can use the New-ADUser cmdlet as follows:

```
PS C:\> New-ADUser -Name "Phil Gibbins" -GivenName Phil -Surname Gibbins `
-SamAccountName pgibbins -UserPrincipalName pgibbins@corp.contoso.com
```

Note that there is no output if the command runs successfully. The resulting properties of the new user account when it is opened in ADAC are shown in Figure 5-15. Note that there are numerous other properties you could have specified when creating the account. Each of these additional properties has a parameter associated with it when using the New-ADUser cmdlet.

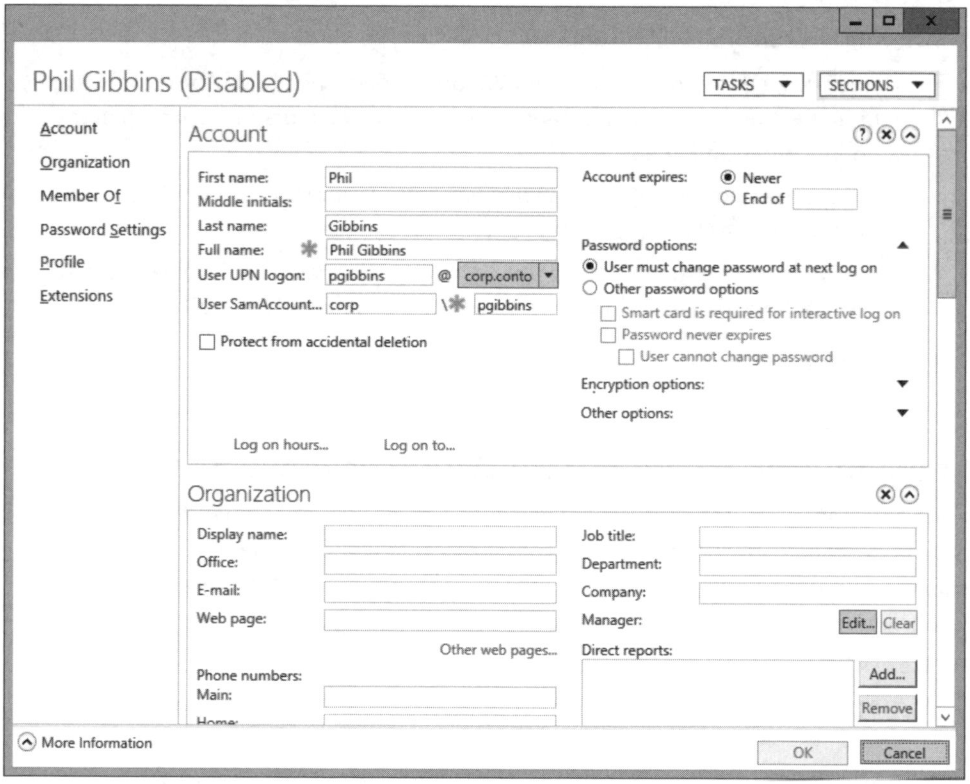

FIGURE 5-15 Create a new user account using the New-ADUser cmdlet.

> **NOTE   WHERE NEW USERS ARE CREATED**
>
> If you try the preceding example, you'll discover that the user account for Phil Gibbins is created in the Users container of the domain. To create a user account in a different location, you must specify the *–Path* parameter with this command. For

example, to create this account in the location ou=Seattle Users OU,ou=Seattle OU OU,dc=corp,dc=contoso,dc=com in Active Directory, you could append *–Path "ou=Seattle Users OU,ou=Seattle OU OU,dc=corp,dc=contoso,dc=com"* to the command used in the preceding example.

Example 2: Create a new user account and specify a password

To specify a password when you create the user account for Phil Gibbins, you can use the Read-Host cmdlet. With this cmdlet, you enter a password when you run the command, as shown by the highlighted code in the following example:

```
PS C:\> New-ADUser -Name "Phil Gibbins" -GivenName Phil -Surname Gibbins `
-SamAccountName pgibbins -UserPrincipalName pgibbins@corp.contoso.com `
-AccountPassword (Read-Host -AsSecureString "AccountPassword")
```

Example 3: Create and enable a new user account

When you use the New-ADUser cmdlet to create a user account, the new account is disabled and cannot be enabled unless either of the following has occurred:

- A valid password has been set for the account.
- The *–PasswordNotRequired* parameter has been set to *true*.

To create a user account for Phil Gibbins, specify a password, and enable the new account, you can use the following command:

```
PS C:\> New-ADUser -Name "Phil Gibbins" -GivenName Phil -Surname Gibbins `
-SamAccountName pgibbins -UserPrincipalName pgibbins@corp.contoso.com `
-AccountPassword (Read-Host -AsSecureString "AccountPassword") `
-PassThru | Enable-ADAccount
```

The *–PassThru* parameter, which has been added to the New-ADUser command just shown, returns the newly created user account object so that it can be piped into the Enable-ADAccount cmdlet to enable the new account.

Example 4: Bulk-create new user accounts /0

A good example of how you can use Windows PowerShell to automate a common Active Directory management task is the bulk creation of users. For example, you can combine the previous examples with the Import-Csv cmdlet, which enables you to read in data from a comma-separated values (CSV) file to create multiple user accounts in a single operation.

To illustrate this, the file new-users.csv contains a line of header information followed by attributes for three user accounts as follows:

```
Name,GivenName,Surname,SamAccountName,UserPrincipalName
Arno Bost,Arno,Bost,abost,abost@corp.contoso.com
Peter Fischer,Peter,Fischer,pfischer,pfischer@corp.contoso.com
Manish Chopra,Manish,Chopra,mchopra,mchopra@corp.contoso.com
```

The following command first reads the CSV file and pipes its contents into the New-ADUser cmdlet, then sets the password for each user account as Pa$$w0rd, and finally enables the accounts:

```
PS C:\> Import-Csv C:\data\new-users.csv | New-ADUser -PassThru | `
Set-ADAccountPassword -Reset `
-NewPassword (ConvertTo-SecureString -AsPlainText 'Pa$$w0rd' -Force) `
-PassThru | Enable-ADAccount
```

The highlighted portion of this command takes the string *"Pa$$w0rd"* and converts it from plain text to a secure string so that it can be used by the *–NewPassword* parameter of the Set-ADAccountPassword cmdlet. The *–Force* parameter is needed to suppress the confirmation prompt generated by use of the *–AsPlainText* parameter.

> **REAL WORLD** **BULK ACCOUNT CREATION**
>
> Bulk creation of user accounts, computer accounts, groups, and other types of directory objects involves two steps:
>
> - Creating the source file with the information for the accounts that need to be created
> - Creating the command or script that takes the source file and uses it to bulk-create the new accounts
>
> The CSV format used in the example in this section is a universal format supported by numerous applications, including Microsoft Excel, Microsoft Access, and even Microsoft SQL Server. By using a program like Excel to create the source information and save it in CSV format, you can quickly and easily bulk-create accounts in Active Directory.

Example 5: Create new user accounts from a template account

A template account is an account you use as a basis for creating other accounts. By configuring template account properties that are common to the other accounts you need to create, you can reduce the amount of information you need to provide for creating the additional accounts.

For example, you could configure properties like the account expiration date and password options in a template account if these will be the same for the other user accounts you need to create. You may also configure properties like Company, Address, City, and Country in the template account. By doing this, you won't need to specify these properties when you create the other user accounts.

One of the practice exercises at the end of this chapter demonstrates how you can create a template account and then use it as a basis for creating additional user accounts.

Finding Active Directory administration cmdlets

The Get-Command cmdlet, which is new in Windows PowerShell 3.0, can be helpful when you need to find cmdlets to perform some administration task on Active Directory. For example, typing **Get-Command New-AD*** lists all cmdlets used for creating new Active Directory objects. The output from running this command looks like this:

CommandType	Name	ModuleName
Cmdlet	New-ADCentralAccessPolicy	ActiveDirectory
Cmdlet	New-ADCentralAccessRule	ActiveDirectory
Cmdlet	New-ADClaimTransformPolicy	ActiveDirectory
Cmdlet	New-ADClaimType	ActiveDirectory
Cmdlet	New-ADComputer	ActiveDirectory
Cmdlet	New-ADDCCloneConfigFile	ActiveDirectory
Cmdlet	New-ADFineGrainedPasswordPolicy	ActiveDirectory
Cmdlet	New-ADGroup	ActiveDirectory
Cmdlet	New-ADObject	ActiveDirectory
Cmdlet	New-ADOrganizationalUnit	ActiveDirectory
Cmdlet	New-ADReplicationSite	ActiveDirectory
Cmdlet	New-ADReplicationSiteLink	ActiveDirectory
Cmdlet	New-ADReplicationSiteLinkBridge	ActiveDirectory
Cmdlet	New-ADReplicationSubnet	ActiveDirectory
Cmdlet	New-ADResourceProperty	ActiveDirectory
Cmdlet	New-ADResourcePropertyList	ActiveDirectory
Cmdlet	New-ADServiceAccount	ActiveDirectory
Cmdlet	New-ADUser	ActiveDirectory

The function of each command is self-explanatory, given the names of these commands. To see the syntax and usage examples for each command, use the Get-Help cmdlet.

As a second example of finding Active Directory administration cmdlets, typing **Get-Command *ADAccount*** displays all cmdlets used for managing Active Directory accounts. The output of this command is as follows:

CommandType	Name	ModuleName
Cmdlet	Clear-ADAccountExpiration	ActiveDirectory
Cmdlet	Disable-ADAccount	ActiveDirectory
Cmdlet	Enable-ADAccount	ActiveDirectory
Cmdlet	Get-ADAccountAuthorizationGroup	ActiveDirectory
Cmdlet	Get-ADAccountResultantPasswordReplicationPolicy	ActiveDirectory
Cmdlet	Search-ADAccount	ActiveDirectory
Cmdlet	ccountControl	ActiveDirectory

```
Cmdlet          Set-ADAccountExpiration                ActiveDirectory
Cmdlet          Set-ADAccountPassword                  ActiveDirectory
Cmdlet          Unlock-ADAccount                       ActiveDirectory
```

Again, the names of these cmdlets provide clear insight into the actions they perform, such as enabling, disabling, and unlocking accounts; setting passwords for accounts; setting and clearing the expiration date for accounts; and so on.

Finally, the Get-Help cmdlet can be useful for both finding cmdlets and learning what you can do with them. For example, typing **Get-Help *ADUser*** displays some of the cmdlets used for managing Active Directory user accounts and describes what they do. The output of this command is as follows:

```
Name                            Category  Module          Synopsis
----                            --------  ------          --------
Get-ADUser                      Cmdlet    ActiveDirectory Gets one or more Active
                                                          Directory users.

Get-ADUserResultantPasswordPolicy Cmdlet  ActiveDirectory Gets the resultant
                                                          password policy for a
                                                          user.

New-ADUser                      Cmdlet    ActiveDirectory Creates a new Active
                                                          Directory user.

Remove-ADUser                   Cmdlet    ActiveDirectory Removes an Active
                                                          Directory user.

Set-ADUser                      Cmdlet    ActiveDirectory Modifies an Active
                                                          Directory user.
```

From the previous examples, you can see that typing **Get-Help *ADAccount*** provides information about more cmdlets used for managing Active Directory user accounts.

> **REAL WORLD** **LEARNING HOW TO USE WINDOWS POWERSHELL TO MANAGE ACTIVE DIRECTORY**
>
> There is a total of 135 different cmdlets in the Active Directory module for Windows PowerShell in Windows Server 2012. In addition, 12 new cmdlets were added in Windows Server 2012 R2 to provide new capabilities for automating Active Directory management tasks using Windows PowerShell. These new cmdlets focus on new credentials protection and management functionalities called authentication policy and authentication policy silos. Active Directory in Windows Server 2012 R2 introduces the concept of forest-based authentication policies that apply to accounts in a domain that is running at Windows Server 2012 R2 domain functional level. These authentication policies enable you to control which hosts a user can use to sign in, and they work in conjunction with the Protect Users security group. You can then apply access control conditions that can isolate accounts to constrain the scope of the network visible to them. The new cmdlets for these functionalities are as follows:
>
> - Get-ADAuthenticationPolicy
> - New-ADAuthenticationPolicySilo
> - Set-ADAccountAuthenticationPolicySilo

- Get-ADAuthenticationPolicySilo
- Remove-ADAuthenticationPolicy
- Set-ADAuthenticationPolicy
- Grant-ADAuthenticationPolicySiloAccess
- Remove-ADAuthenticationPolicySilo
- Set-ADAuthenticationPolicySilo
- New-ADAuthenticationPolicy
- Revoke-ADAuthenticationPolicySiloAccess
- Show-ADAuthenticationPolicyExpression

To learn more about each of these cmdlets, you can review their TechNet pages, *such as http://technet.microsoft.com/en-us/library/dn528538.aspx*. However, the only way you can learn how to effectively work with all 147 Active Directory cmdlets in Windows Server 2012 R2 is by trying them out to perform different kinds of administration tasks in a safe test environment.

Performing an advanced Active Directory administration task

To conclude this lesson, here is an example of how to perform an advanced Active Directory administration task using Windows PowerShell. The scenario is as follows:

Contoso Ltd. is in the process of rolling out its Active Directory environment at its headquarters in Seattle. So far, two domain controllers have been deployed at this location. A new branch office is going to be set up in Bellevue, and the Contoso administrator has decided to move one of the existing domain controllers to this new location.

Here are the steps that the administrator will perform:

1. Create a new site named Branch-Office-One for the Bellevue location.
2. Create a new site link named Hub-to-Branch-Office-One to enable replication to occur between the two sites.
3. Move one of the two domain controllers from Default-First-Site-Name to Branch-Office-One.

This is how these tasks can be done using Windows PowerShell:

1. List all the sites that currently exist in the domain:

```
PS C:\> Get-ADReplicationSite -Filter * | ft Name

Name
----
Default-First-Site-Name
```

2. List all the domain controllers in the domain:

```
PS C:\> Get-ADDomainController -Filter * | ft Hostname

Hostname
--------
SEA-SRV-1.corp.contoso.com
SEA-SRV-5.corp.contoso.com
```

3. Create a new site named Branch-Office-One:

```
PS C:\> New-ADReplicationSite Branch-Office-One
```

4. Verify the creation of the new site:

```
PS C:\> Get-ADReplicationSite -Filter * | ft Name

Name
----
Default-First-Site-Name
Branch-Office-One
```

5. Create a new site link between the two sites and enable the change-notification process for replication:

```
PS C:\> New-ADReplicationSiteLink 'Hub-to-Branch-Office-One' `
-SitesIncluded Default-First-Site-Name,Branch-Office-One `
-OtherAttributes @{'options'=1}
```

6. Specify the cost and replication frequency for the new site link:

```
PS C:\> Set-ADReplicationSiteLink Hub-to-Branch-Office-One `
-Cost 100 -ReplicationFrequencyInMinutes 15
```

7. Verify the results by viewing the properties of the new site link:

```
PS C:\> Get-ADReplicationSiteLink -Filter {Name -eq "Hub-to-Branch-Office-One"}

Cost                          : 100
DistinguishedName             : CN=Hub-to-Branch-Office-One,CN=IP,CN=Inter-Site
                                Transports,CN=Sites,CN=Configuration,
                                DC=corp,DC=contoso,DC=com
Name                          : Hub-to-Branch-Office-One
ObjectClass                   : siteLink
ObjectGUID                    : f9df8b3c-f8bc-4ca9-b082-09655e14c80b
ReplicationFrequencyInMinutes : 15
SitesIncluded                 : {CN=Branch-Office-One,CN=Sites,CN=Configuration,
                                DC=corp,DC=contoso,DC=com,CN=Default-First-
                                Site-Name,CN=Sites,CN=Configuration,DC=corp,
                                DC=contoso,DC=com}
```

8. Move domain controller SEA-SRV-5 from the hub site to the branch office site:

```
PS C:\> Get-ADDomainController SEA-SRV-5.corp.contoso.com | `
Move-ADDirectoryServer -Site Branch-Office-One
```

9. Verify that the domain controller has been moved to the branch office site:

```
PS C:\> Get-ADDomainController -Filter * | ft Hostname,Site

Hostname                      Site
--------                      ----
SEA-SRV-1.corp.contoso.com    Default-First-Site-Name
SEA-SRV-5.corp.contoso.com    Branch-Office-One
```

Finally, opening the Active Directory Sites And Services MMC console shows the expected configuration of sites, site links, and domain controllers. (See Figure 5-16.)

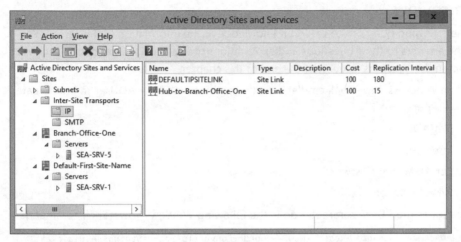

FIGURE 5-16 This MMC console confirms what the Windows PowerShell cmdlets accomplished.

Lesson summary

- The Active Directory module in Windows Server 2012 includes 135 Windows PowerShell cmdlets you can use for performing Active Directory administration tasks from the command line or by using scripts. Windows Server 2012 R2 adds 12 more Active Directory cmdlets for a total of 147 cmdlets.

- You should become familiar with the syntax of cmdlets such as New-ADUser, New-ADOrganizationalUnit, and others in the Active Directory Windows PowerShell module so that you can use them to automate the creation of user accounts, organizational units, and other types of directory objects in your Active Directory environment.

- You can use cmdlets such as New-ADUser in different ways to create user accounts appropriately for the needs of each Active Directory administration scenario. The same is true when using Windows PowerShell to create other types of directory objects like groups, computer accounts, and organizational units.

- You can combine cmdlets such as New-ADUser with other Windows PowerShell cmdlets to create user accounts in different ways, such as from a template account or in bulk. The same is true when using Windows PowerShell to create other types of directory objects like groups, computer accounts, and organizational units.

- You can use the new Get-Command cmdlet to quickly identify the Active Directory administration cmdlets you need to perform a specific task.

- You can use Windows PowerShell to perform advanced Active Directory administration tasks that previously required using MMC snap-ins like Active Directory Sites And Services.

Lesson review

Answer the following questions to test your knowledge of the information in this lesson. You can find the answers to these questions and explanations of why each answer choice is correct or incorrect in the "Answers" section at the end of this chapter.

1. Which Windows PowerShell cmdlet can you combine with New-ADUser to bulk-create new user accounts?

    A. Get-ADUser

    B. Import-Csv

    C. Set-ADAccountPassword

    D. Where-Object

2. What does the *–Force* parameter do in the following Windows PowerShell command?

    ```
    Set-ADAccountPassword -Reset -NewPassword (ConvertTo-SecureString -AsPlainText
    "Pa$$w0rd" -Force)
    ```

    A. It forces the specified password to be converted from plain text to a secure string.

    B. It forces the specified password to be encrypted.

    C. It suppresses the confirmation prompt that the user normally would have to respond to when performing this action.

    D. It forces the user to respond to a confirmation prompt when performing this action.

3. What commands can you use to find Windows PowerShell cmdlets for managing Active Directory groups? (Choose all that apply.)

    A. Get-Command –Module ActiveDirectory

    B. Get-Command *ADGroup*

    C. Get-Help *ADGroup*

    D. Get-Help ActiveDirectory

Practice exercises

The goal of this section is to provide you with hands-on practice with the following:

- Creating organizational units using Windows PowerShell
- Creating user accounts using Windows PowerShell

To perform the following exercises, you need at least one clean installation of Windows Server 2012 R2 using the Server With A GUI installation option. The server is assumed to be a domain controller in the corp.contoso.com domain and have Internet connectivity. You should be logged on interactively to the server using a user account that is a member of the Domain Administrators group. For the purposes of these exercises, the name of the server is assumed to be DC-1. You can modify the exercises as needed if the name of your server and domain are different from the ones given here.

Exercise 1: Creating organizational units using Windows PowerShell

In this exercise, you create and run a Windows PowerShell script that creates a hierarchy of organizational units in the corp.contoso.com domain.

1. Log on to DC-1 using an account that is a member of the Domain Admins account for the corp.contoso.com domain.

2. Create a folder named Data in the root of your C drive.

3. Open Notepad and type the following lines:

```
New-ADOrganizationalUnit -Name "Montreal" `
-Path "dc=corp,dc=contoso,dc=com"
New-ADOrganizationalUnit -Name "Montreal Users" `
-Path "ou=Montreal,dc=corp,dc=contoso,dc=com"
New-ADOrganizationalUnit -Name "Montreal Computers" `
-Path "ou=Montreal,dc=corp,dc=contoso,dc=com"
New-ADOrganizationalUnit -Name "Montreal File Servers" `
-Path "ou=Montreal,dc=corp,dc=contoso,dc=com"
New-ADOrganizationalUnit -Name "Montreal Terminal Servers" `
-Path "ou=Montreal,dc=corp,dc=contoso,dc=com"
New-ADOrganizationalUnit -Name "Montreal Administrators" `
-Path "ou=Montreal,dc=corp,dc=contoso,dc=com"
```

4. Select File, select Save As, and type **new-OUs.ps1** as the file name. Click the Save As type control, select All Files, and save the script in your C:\Data folder.

5. Open the Windows PowerShell console using elevated privileges by right-clicking the Windows PowerShell taskbar icon and selecting Run As Administrator.

6. Type **Get-ExecutionPolicy** to view the current script-execution policy on the server. This will likely be Restricted, which means that no scripts can be run and Windows PowerShell can be used only in interactive mode.

7. Type **Set-ExecutionPolicy Unrestricted** to change the execution policy on the server to Unrestricted, which means that all Windows PowerShell scripts can be run with no restrictions (that is, both signed and unsigned scripts can be run).

8. Type **C:\Data\new-OUs.ps1** to run the script you created earlier.

9. Type the following command to verify that the new organizational units were created as expected:

```
Get-ADOrganizationalUnit -Filter 'Name -like "Montreal*"' | `
Format-Table Name,DistinguishedName
```

10. Open ADAC, navigate to the corp.contoso.com domain, and verify that the hierarchy of organizational units was successfully created. You might need to refresh ADAC if it was already open to see the OUs.

11. Add the new OUs as navigation nodes in ADAC list view and rearrange them as desired.

Exercise 2: Creating user accounts using Windows PowerShell

In this exercise, you create a template user account that will be used as a starting point for creating other user accounts. You then create a new user account based on your template account.

1. Log on to DC-1 using an account that is a member of the Domain Admins account for the corp.contoso.com domain.

2. Open the Windows PowerShell console using elevated privileges by right-clicking the Windows PowerShell taskbar icon and selecting Run As Administrator.

3. Use the New-ADOrganizationalUnit cmdlet to create a new OU named "Denver" in the corp.contoso.com domain.

4. Use the New-ADOrganizationalUnit cmdlet again to create a new OU named "Denver Users" in the "Denver" OU you created in the previous step.

5. Run the following command to create a template user named DenverTemplateUser that expires at 2 A.M. on December 30, 2014, and that has its City property set to Denver:

```
New-ADUser -Name DenverTemplateUser `
-AccountExpirationDate "12/30/2014 2:00:00 AM" -City "Denver"
```

6. Open ADAC, navigate to the default Users container in the corp.contoso.com domain, and verify that the template user was successfully created. You might need to refresh ADAC if it was already open to see the new user.

7. Open the properties of the template user in ADAC and verify that the Account Expiration Date and City properties were configured properly.

8. Switch back to the Windows PowerShell console and use the Get-ADUser cmd-let to retrieve the default properties of the template user you just created with the two custom properties you configured. Then assign the result to a variable named *$templateDenverUser* by running this command:

```
$templateDenverUser = Get-ADUser `
-Identity "cn=DenverTemplateUser,cn=Users,dc=corp,dc=contoso,dc=com" `
-Properties AccountExpirationDate,City
```

9. Type **$templateDenverUser** and verify that the properties of the template account are correct.

10. Execute the following command to create a new user account for Tony Madigan that is based on the template user you created earlier. Note that the backtick character is used here to enable you to enter this long command in several lines to make it easier to understand:

```
New-ADUser -Name "Tony Madigan" `
   -GivenName Tony -Surname Madigan `
  -SamAccountName tmadigan `
  -UserPrincipalName tmadigan@corp.contoso.com `
  -Path "ou=Denver Users,ou=Denver,dc=corp,dc=contoso,dc=com" `
  -Instance $templateDenverUser `
  -AccountPassword (ConvertTo-SecureString -AsPlainText "Pa$$w0rd" -Force)
```

11. Note the *–Instance* parameter in the preceding command. This is used to specify an instance of an existing object that is to be used as a template for a new object. Refer to *http://technet.microsoft.com/en-us/library/hh852238* if you want to learn more about how to use the *–Instance* parameter with the New-ADUser cmdlet.

12. Run the following command to get the configured properties of the new user account with the two custom properties that were retrieved from the template account:

```
Get-ADUser -Identity tmadigan -Properties `
Name,GivenName,Surname,SamAccountName,UserPrincipalName,AccountExpirationDate,City
```

13. Verify from the output of the preceding command that the new user account has the correct properties.

14. Switch back to ACAC, navigate to the Denver Users OU beneath the Denver OU, open the properties of Tony Madigan's user account, and verify that the properties were configured as expected.

Suggested practice exercises

The following additional practice exercises are designed to give you more opportunities to practice what you've learned and to help you successfully master the lessons presented in this chapter:

- **Exercise 1**   Create a Windows PowerShell script that takes an existing template account and uses it as a basis for bulk-creating new user accounts whose unique properties have been specified in a CSV file you created using Microsoft Excel.

- **Exercise 2**   Create a series of Windows PowerShell commands that create three new groups, add some users to each group from the bulk users created in the previous practice, and configure and assign a unique fine-grained password policy to each group.

Answers

This section contains the answers to the lesson review questions in this chapter.

Lesson 1

1. **Correct answer: D**

   A. **Incorrect:** Column Explorer simplifies browsing through the levels of your Active Directory hierarchy by displaying all the child containers of the parent container (the container for which you opened Column Explorer) in a single column. It does not, however, enable you to quickly access the last three containers you accessed.

   B. **Incorrect:** The navigation pane is the left pane of ADAC and enables you to browse through Active Directory by using the tree view, which is similar to the Active Directory Users And Computers console tree, or by using the new list view, which you can customize by adding navigation nodes. It does not, however, enable you to quickly access the last three containers you accessed.

   C. **Incorrect:** Navigation nodes are custom nodes you can add to the new list view of ADAC to provide a quick way of accessing specific containers within the directory. It does not, however, enable you to access the last three containers you accessed.

   D. **Correct:** The Most Recently Used (MRU) list automatically appears under a navigation node when you visit at least one container in this navigation node. The MRU list always contains the last three containers you visited in a particular navigation node. Every time you select a particular container, this container is added to the top of the MRU list and the last container in the MRU list is removed from it.

2. **Correct answers: A, B, and C**

   A. **Correct:** To create sites, you can use either Windows PowerShell or the Active Directory Sites And Services MMC snap-in.

   B. **Correct:** To create domains in your forest, you can use either Windows PowerShell or Server Manager to install the Active Directory Domain Services role on a server and promote the server as the first domain controller in a new child domain or tree domain.

   C. **Correct:** To create explicit trusts with domains in your forest or in another forest, you can use either Windows PowerShell or the Active Directory Domains And Trusts MMC snap-in.

   D. **Incorrect:** You can use either ADAC or Windows PowerShell to create new groups in Active Directory.

3. **Correct answer: B**

   A. **Incorrect:** You can use ADAC to raise the forest functional level by right-clicking the forest root domain.

B. **Correct:** You cannot use ADAC to delegate administrative control over an OU and the objects it contains. You must use the Active Directory Users And Computers MMC snap-in to perform this task.

C. **Incorrect:** You can use ADAC to enable and use the Active Directory Recycle Bin.

D. **Incorrect:** You can use ADAC to configure fine-grained password policies and view the results of a policy application on user accounts.

Lesson 2

1. **Correct answer: D**

   A. **Incorrect:** An object in the Live state is functioning in Active Directory. Its recycled object lifetime has not expired.

   B. **Incorrect:** An object in the Deleted state has been moved to the Deleted Objects container in Active Directory and will remain in this container for the deleted object lifetime, which is configure by default as 180 days. As long as it remains in the Deleted state, its recycled object lifetime has not expired.

   C. **Incorrect:** When an object is in the Recycled state, its deleted object lifetime has expired. It remains in the Recycled state until its recycled object lifetime has expired.

   D. **Correct:** When an object is in the Removed state, its recycled object lifetime has expired. The Active Directory garbage-collection process physically removes such an object from the directory database.

2. **Correct answer: C**

   A. **Incorrect:** You can use the Set-ADForestMode cmdlet to raise the forest functional level to Windows Server 2008 R2 or higher, which is a requirement before enabling the AD Recycle Bin in your environment. However, this cmdlet does not enable the AD Recycle Bin feature.

   B. **Incorrect:** This is not a Windows PowerShell cmdlet.

   C. **Correct:** You can use the Enable-ADOptionalFeature cmdlet to enable the AD Recycle Bin feature and other optional features of Active Directory.

   D. **Incorrect:** You can use the New-ADFineGrainedPasswordPolicy cmdlet to create a new fine-grained password policy. It has nothing to do with the AD Recycle Bin feature.

3. **Correct answers: B and D**

   A. **Incorrect:** Assigning fine-grained password policies to individual users is not a best practice. Assigning fine-grained password policies to groups makes such policies much easier to manage.

   B. **Correct:** You should ensure that each fine-grained password policy has its own unique precedence value to prevent policy conflicts that can lead to unexpected results.

C. **Incorrect:** Although you can choose to ensure that each group has at least one fine-grained password policy assigned to it, this is not necessary if you have a fallback policy configured for the domain.

D. **Correct:** You should make sure you have configured a fallback policy for the domain. This can be either a fine-grained password policy that has a higher precedence value than any other policy or the password and account lockout settings defined in the Default Domain Policy GPO.

Lesson 3

1. **Correct answer: B**

   A. **Incorrect:** You can use Get-ADUser to retrieve one or more user accounts. It is useful, for example, when you need to retrieve an existing user account to use as a template account for creating additional user accounts. You also need to use other cmdlets if you want to bulk-create user accounts.

   B. **Correct:** The Import-Csv cmdlet enables you to read in data from a comma-separated values (CSV) file to create multiple user accounts in a single operation.

   C. **Incorrect:** The Set-ADAccountPassword cmdlet enables you to set the password for a user account. You also need to use other cmdlets if you want to bulk-create user accounts.

   D. **Incorrect:** The Where-Object cmdlet enables you to filter data returned by other cmdlets. You also need to use other cmdlets if you want to bulk-create user accounts.

2. **Correct answer: C**

   A. **Incorrect:** The ConvertTo-SecureString cmdlet converts an encrypted standard string to a secure string. It can also convert plain text to a secure string.

   B. **Incorrect:** The ConvertFrom-SecureString cmdlet converts a secure string to an encrypted standard string.

   C. **Correct:** The –*Force* parameter confirms that you understand the implications of using the *AsPlainText* parameter of the ConvertTo-SecureString cmdlet and still want to use it. When the –*Force* parameter is specified, no confirmation prompt is displayed when you use the ConvertTo-SecureString cmdlet.

   D. **Incorrect:** When the –*Force* parameter is specified, no confirmation prompt is displayed when you use the ConvertTo-SecureString cmdlet. In other words, the –*Force* parameter suppresses the prompt instead of displaying it.

3. **Correct answers: B and C**

   A. **Incorrect:** Get-Command –Module ActiveDirectory lists all of the cmdlets in the Active Directory Windows PowerShell module.

   B. **Correct:** Get-Command *ADGroup* lists cmdlets you can use for managing Active Directory groups.

C. **Correct:** Get-Help *ADGroup* lists cmdlets you can use for managing Active Directory groups and gives a brief summary of what each cmdlet does.

D. **Incorrect:** Get-Help ActiveDirectory lists all of the cmdlets in the Active Directory Windows PowerShell module and gives a brief summary of what each cmdlet does.

CHAPTER 6

Network administration

The network is the foundation of an organization's information system and enables computers and other devices to communicate with one another and with the Internet. Network services such as Dynamic Host Configuration Protocol (DHCP) servers and Domain Name System (DNS) servers simplify the configuration and management of IP address information and network names. To adequately fulfill these roles, such services must be available for clients that need them and be secure from attack.

Microsoft Windows Server 2012 and Windows Server 2012 R2 include enhancements to the DHCP Server and DNS Server roles that can help increase DHCP availability and safeguard DNS name resolution from being compromised or misused. Windows Server 2012 and Windows Server 2012 R2 also include added support for managing different aspects of Windows Server–based networks using Windows PowerShell. This chapter demonstrates how to implement these capabilities to ensure the availability and security of these critical network services and to manage Windows Server–based networks more efficiently. In addition, this chapter describes how to configure Internet Protocol version 6 (IPv6) networking and interoperability between IPv6 and IPv4.

Lessons in this chapter:

Before you begin

To complete the practice exercises in this chapter

- You should be familiar with basic networking concepts and administration tasks, including TCP/IP addressing concepts, how DHCP and DNS work, and how to configure DHCP and DNS servers using the Microsoft Management Console (MMC) snap-ins for these services.

- You need to know how to deploy Windows Server 2012 R2, create an Active Directory forest, and add roles and features using Windows PowerShell.
- It will be helpful if you also have at least rudimentary knowledge of using Windows PowerShell on earlier versions of Windows Server.

Lesson 1: Ensuring DHCP availability

DHCP provides a way to dynamically assign IP addresses and other parameters to hosts on a TCP/IP network. DHCP is designed to work automatically and relieves much of the management overhead associated with manually assigning static addresses to network hosts. DHCP servers play a critical role in ensuring hosts such as servers, clients, and printers on a TCP/IP network can communicate with one another.

Because DHCP leases addresses for only a specified amount of time, these leases need to be periodically renewed if the hosts are to continue communicating on the network. Although the DHCP lease renewal process has some degree of tolerance for DHCP server downtime built into it, ensuring the availability of DHCP servers on your network is nevertheless essential so that they can respond in a timely manner to lease renewal requests from network hosts. Otherwise, it is possible that some hosts might not be able to renew their addresses and therefore won't be able to participate on the network.

> **After this lesson, you will be able to:**
> - Compare and contrast the different methods of ensuring DHCP availability on Windows Server–based networks.
> - Explain the two failover modes of DHCP servers running Windows Server 2012 or Windows Server 2012 R2.
> - Implement DHCP failover using the DHCP console.
> - Describe the tasks involved in managing a DHCP failover solution.
>
> **Estimated lesson time: 30 minutes**

Previous approaches to implementing DHCP availability

Traditionally, DHCP server availability has been implemented on Windows Server–based networks using one or more of the following methods:

- **Split scopes**   This approach involves splitting the IP address pool of a scope between two DHCP servers, typically by assigning the primary server 80 percent of the addresses in the scope and the secondary server the remaining 20 percent of the addresses. That way, if the primary server goes offline for any reason, DHCP clients on the subnet can still respond to lease renewal requests from the secondary server.

- **Server cluster** This approach involves using the Failover Clustering feature of Windows Server 2008 or Windows Server 2008 R2 to cluster DHCP servers so that if the primary DHCP server in a cluster fails, the secondary server can take up the slack and continue leasing addresses to clients.

- **Standby server** This approach uses a hot standby DHCP server with scopes and options configured identically to your production DHCP server.

Each of the preceding approaches has the following disadvantages, which make them of limited usefulness in ensuring DHCP server availability:

- The split-scope approach provides limited IP availability during outages. As a result, some clients might not receive addresses during a long-term DHCP server outage. In addition, if your DHCP server scope is currently running at high utilization—which is common for Internet Protocol version 4 (IPv4) networks—splitting the scope might not be feasible.

- The DHCP server-cluster approach has only one DHCP database located on the cluster shared storage. That means there is a single point of failure for DHCP services on your network. In addition, implementing Failover Clustering requires relatively complex setup processes and maintenance tasks.

- The standby server approach requires both careful configuration of the standby DHCP server and manual intervention on the part of the administrator to ensure the failover transition when your production DHCP server fails or goes offline. There is additional complexity in this approach when DHCP is configured to automatically update DNS records, as is recommended in an Active Directory environment.

Understanding DHCP failover

DHCP failover is a new approach to ensuring DHCP availability that was introduced in Windows Server 2012. With this approach, two DHCP servers can be configured to provide leases from the same pool of addresses. The two servers then replicate lease information between them, which enables one server to assume responsibility for providing leases to all clients on the subnet when the other server is unavailable. The goal of implementing this approach is to ensure DHCP service availability at all times, which is a key requirement for enterprise networks.

The current implementation of DHCP failover in Windows Server 2012 and Windows Server 2012 R2 has the following limitations:

- It only supports using a maximum of two DHCP servers.

- The failover relationship is limited to IPv4 scopes and subnets.

You can implement DHCP server failover in two different configurations:

- **Load-balance mode** Leases are issued from both servers equally, which ensures availability and provides load balancing for your DHCP services. (This is the default DHCP server failover configuration.)

- **Hot-standby mode** Leases are issued from the primary server until it fails, then the lease data is automatically replicated to the secondary server, which assumes the load.

Load-balance mode

A typical scenario for implementing load-balance mode is when you want to have two DHCP servers at the same physical site. If the site has a single subnet, all you need to do is enable DHCP failover in its default configuration. If there are multiple subnets, deploy both DHCP servers in the same subnet, configure your routers as DHCP relay agents (or deploy additional DHCP relay agents in subnets), and enable DHCP server failover in its default configuration.

Hot-standby mode

When implementing hot-standby mode, you can configure a DHCP server so that it acts as the primary server for one subnet and as the secondary server for other subnets. One scenario in which you might implement this approach is in organizations that have a central hub site (typically, the data center at the head office) connected via wide area network (WAN) links to multiple remote branch-office sites. Figure 6-1 shows an example of an organization that has DHCP servers deployed at each branch office and at the head office. Branch-office servers are configured to lease addresses to clients at their branch offices, and the central server leases addresses to clients at the head office. Each branch-office server has a failover relationship with the central server, with the branch-office server assuming the role as primary and the central server as secondary. That way, if a DHCP server fails at a branch office, the central server can take up the slack for the remote site. For example, the DHCP server at Branch Office A is the primary server for the scope 10.10.0.0/16 and the DHCP server at the Head Office is the secondary server for that scope.

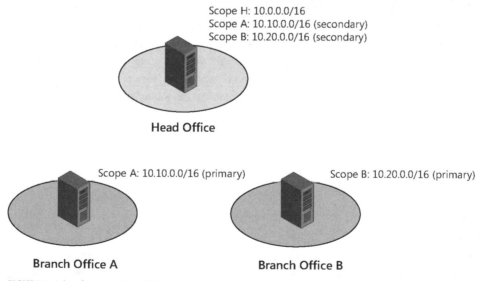

FIGURE 6-1 Implement DHCP failover in hot-standby mode in a hub-and-spoke site scenario.

> *NOTE* **DHCP PACKETS OVER MULTIPLE SUBNETS**
>
> Routers usually block DHCP packets from being forwarded from one subnet to another because DHCP packets are broadcast traffic. If an organization's network consists of multiple subnets, using DHCP for dynamic address assignment requires one of the following:
>
> ■ Deploying a DHCP server on each subnet of your network
>
> ■ Enabling forwarding of DHCP traffic on your routers by configuring them as DHCP relay agents
>
> In general, the first approach is recommended because it provides a greater degree of fault tolerance. For more information, see *http://support.microsoft.com/kb/120932*.

Implementing DHCP failover

To enable DHCP failover, begin by installing two DHCP servers running Windows Server 2012 or Windows Server 2012 R2, designating one of them as the primary server and the other as the secondary server. If the DHCP servers are domain members, they must be authorized in Active Directory. However, you can also implement DHCP failover on stand-alone DHCP servers in a workgroup.

After deploying your two DHCP servers, create and configure scopes on the primary DHCP server for the DHCP clients in your environment. Then perform the following steps:

1. Open the DHCP console and add the primary server. Then right-click a scope and select Configure Failover:

2. In the Configure Failover Wizard, select an available scope.

3. Add the partner server that will be used as the secondary server for the host server (the primary server).

4. Configure the new failover relationship for either load-balance mode (shown in Figure 6-2) or standby mode (shown in Figure 6-3). Adjust the mode settings to meet the needs of your environment.

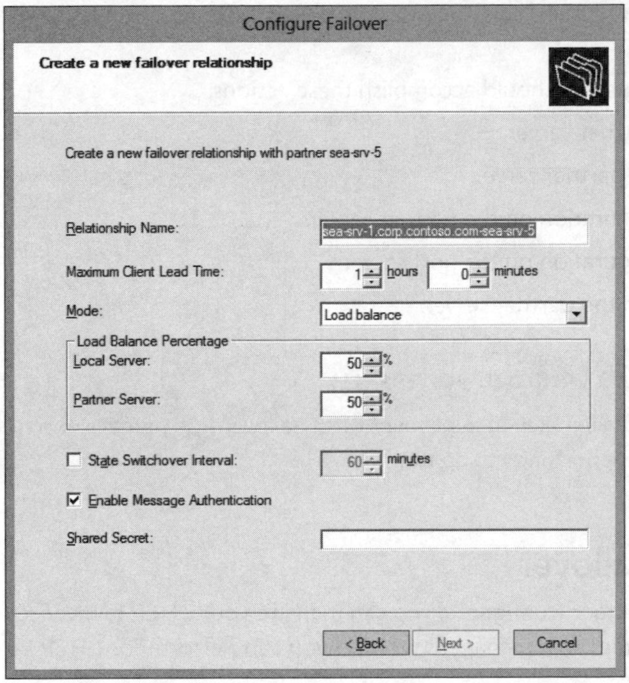

FIGURE 6-2 Create a new DHCP server failover relationship using load-balance mode.

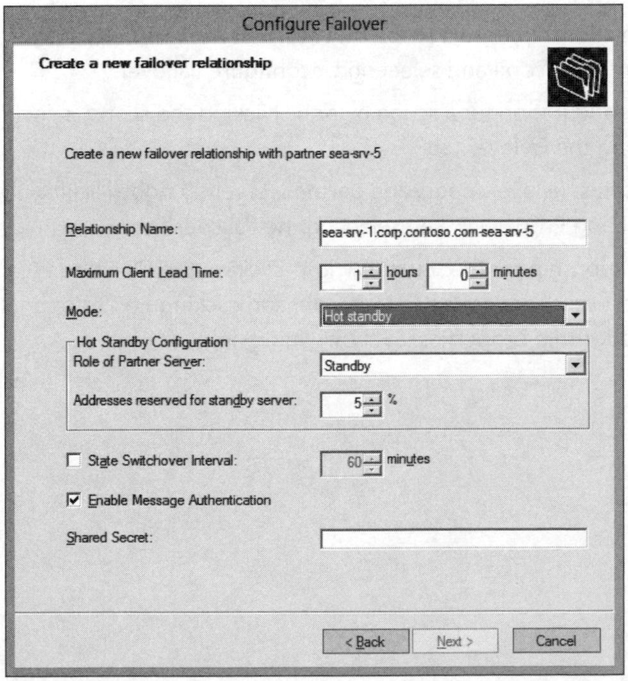

FIGURE 6-3 Create a new DHCP server failover relationship using hot-standby mode.

5. Complete the wizard and make sure the progress dialog indicates success for all operations.

Completing the preceding steps should accomplish these actions:

1. Add scopes on the partner server.

2. Disable scopes on the partner server.

3. Create a failover configuration on the partner server.

4. Create a failover configuration on the host server.

5. Activate the scopes on the partner server.

> **NOTE   DHCP FAILOVER AND WINDOWS POWERSHELL**
>
> You can also use Windows PowerShell to implement DHCP failover. The practice exercises in this chapter give you an opportunity to do this.

Managing DHCP failover

After DHCP failover is enabled and configured, you can manage your DHCP failover solution using the DHCP console. Examples of management tasks you can perform for DHCP server failover include the following:

- Configuring a new failover relationship by right-clicking either another scope or the IPv4 node for the server and selecting Configure Failover

- Removing a failover relationship from a scope that has previously been configured for failover by right-clicking the scope and selecting Deconfigure Failover

- Viewing the failover configuration for a scope by right-clicking the scope, selecting Properties, and selecting the Failover tab

- Viewing the failover status, failover mode, and partner server by right-clicking the IPv4 node for a server, selecting Properties, and selecting the Failover tab

- Editing the failover relationship for the server by right-clicking the IPv4 node for a server, selecting Properties, selecting the Failover tab, and clicking Edit to open the View/Edit Failover Relationship properties (as shown in Figure 6-4)

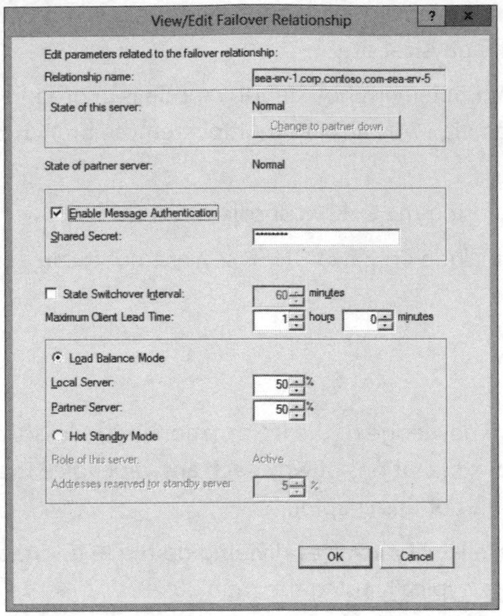

FIGURE 6-4 Modify the properties of a DHCP server failover relationship.

- Forcing the replication of a scope in a failover relationship to the partner server for that relationship by right-clicking the scope and selecting Replicate Scope

- Forcing the replication of all scopes in a failover relationship to the partner server for that relationship by right-clicking the scope and selecting Replicate Relationship

- Forcing the replication of all scopes in all failover relationships to the partner servers for those relationships by right-clicking the IPv4 node for the server and selecting Replicate Failover Scopes

> *NOTE* **FORCING REPLICATION**
>
> Replication of DHCP database information should occur automatically when DHCP servers have been configured for failover. Manually forcing replication generally needs to be performed only when you are troubleshooting replication issues.

Lesson summary

- DHCP availability solutions for previous Windows Server versions each have advantages and disadvantages.
- DHCP failover is a new approach to ensuring DHCP server availability that was introduced in Windows Server 2012.
- DHCP failover is supported only for IPv4 scopes.
- DHCP failover can be implemented in two different configurations: load-balance mode or hot-standby mode.

- A typical scenario in which you might implement load-balance mode is when you want to have two DHCP servers at the same physical site.

- A typical scenario in which you might implement hot-standby mode is in organizations that have a central hub site connected via WAN links to multiple remote branch-office sites.

- You can implement DHCP failover by using the DHCP console or Windows PowerShell.

- Each DHCP failover relationship can include only two DHCP servers, but it can apply to multiple scopes on the servers.

Lesson review

Answer the following questions to test your knowledge of the information in this lesson. You can find the answers to these questions and explanations of why each answer choice is correct or incorrect in the "Answers" section at the end of this chapter.

1. Which approach to ensuring DHCP availability involves dividing up the IP address pool of a scope between two DHCP servers, typically using the ratio 80:20?

   A. Server cluster

   B. Split scope

   C. Standby server

   D. DHCP failover

2. Which of the following is true concerning DHCP failover in Windows Server 2012 and Windows Server 2012 R2? (Choose all that apply.)

   A. DHCP failover only supports using a maximum of two DHCP servers.

   B. DHCP failover is supported for both IPv4 and IPv6 scopes and subnets.

   C. DHCP failover can be implemented in two ways: load-balance mode or hot-standby mode.

   D. DHCP failover requires that the DHCP servers be domain members and authorized in Active Directory.

3. Which of the following scenarios might be appropriate for implementing DHCP failover in hot-standby mode? (Choose all that apply.)

   A. Your organization has a hub-and-spoke site topology.

   B. You want to use the DHCP server in your data center as a standby in case a DHCP server at one of your remote branch offices goes offline.

   C. Your organization has a hub-and-spoke site topology, but you have a limited budget for deploying additional servers as standbys for existing servers in your environment.

   D. Your organization has only one physical site.

Lesson 2: Implementing DNSSEC

DNS provides a user-friendly way of naming hosts and services on a TCP/IP network. DNS servers perform name resolution to convert DNS names into IP addresses so that DNS clients can access network services. DNS servers thus play a critical role in enabling users and applications to locate hosts and services on the network or on the Internet. However, no authentication or integrity checking is done when name resolution is being performed using traditional DNS. As a result, communication between DNS clients and servers is inherently insecure. By spoofing DNS traffic or otherwise poisoning the DNS cache on clients, an attacker could hijack network communications and redirect users and applications to malicious sites and services.

To help organizations address these problems, Windows Server 2012 and Windows Server 2012 R2 include enhanced support for *DNS Security Extensions (DNSSEC)*, a suite of extensions that add security to the DNS protocol by enabling DNS servers to validate DNS responses. In a practical sense, this enables users to be confident that the site they are accessing on their corporate intranet is in fact the site they believe it to be and not some malicious site masquerading as a legitimate site. This lesson helps you understand the benefits of DNSSEC, how it works, and how to implement it in an Active Directory environment based on Windows Server 2012 or Windows Server 2012 R2.

After this lesson, you will be able to:

- Explain what types of security DNSSEC provides and describe its benefits for organizations.
- Compare and contrast DNSSEC functionality in Windows Server 2012 and Windows Server 2012 R2 with that in previous Windows Server versions.
- Describe how DNSSEC works as part of the name-resolution process.
- Explain DNSSEC concepts such as zone signing, key master, and trust anchors.
- List the different kinds of DNSSEC resource records and describe what they are used for.
- Deploy DNSSEC in a Windows Server 2012 or Windows Server 2012 R2 Active Directory environment using the DNS Manager MMC console.

Estimated lesson time: 30 minutes

Benefits of DNSSEC

DNS is used for locating resources on a TCP/IP network and the Internet. For example, when a user types **www.bing.com** into the address bar of Internet Explorer, the DNS client on the user's computer sends a name query request to a DNS server. The DNS server then either responds with the IP address for the site being accessed (Bing) or forwards the query to another DNS server for consideration. When the client has the site's IP address, it can access the site to download content.

But this question arises: How can the user or application be confident that the site being accessed is genuine and not some fake site masquerading as the real one? To a certain extent, the Secure Sockets Layer (SSL) protocol already does this. SSL is used whenever the user or application accesses a resource using Secure HTTP (HTTPS). SSL does this by authenticating the site being accessed and encrypting the data returned over the network. However, SSL is of no use if the DNS server being queried returns a spoofed IP address instead of the real one. This could be accomplished, for example, if a malicious DNS server intercepted name-resolution traffic and inserted a spoofed response to a query from a DNS client or a recursive DNS server. Not only could such an attack hijack a particular DNS session, it also would also poison the local DNS cache on the client server, recursive server, or both, which could lead to further erroneous responses to name-resolution requests until the cache data expired.

To address these issues, the Internet Engineering Task Force (IETF) developed DNSSEC to add a layer of security to the inherently insecure DNS protocol. Specifically, DNSSEC helps prove two things:

- The information the client is accessing is coming from the correct source. In other words, it confirms the *authority* of the originator of the data that a DNS server returns.

- The information you receive is the same as the information that was sent. In other words, it confirms the *integrity* of the data that a DNS server returns.

DNSSEC also provides *authenticated denial of existence* when the information the client is trying to access does not exist. In other words, it provides proof that the site being requested really doesn't exist.

What DNSSEC does *not* provide is *confidentiality* of the data that a DNS server returns. In other words, it does not guarantee that the data hasn't been intercepted and examined while en route to the client. DNSSEC also does not provide any protection against a distributed denial-of-service (DDoS) attack against an organization's DNS infrastructure. So although DNSSEC provides two of the requirements of the information security CIA triad (Confidentiality, Integrity, and Availability), it is not in itself a complete solution to the problem of protecting an organization's DNS infrastructure and traffic.

> **MORE INFO HOW DNS WORKS**
>
> For a detailed look at how the DNS name-resolution process works, see "How DNS Works" at *http://technet.microsoft.com/en-us/library/dd197446(v=WS.10).aspx*.

> **REAL WORLD WHY YOU SHOULD DEPLOY DNSSEC**
>
> There are several reasons why organizations today need to consider deploying DNSSEC in their Windows Server–based environments:

- DNSSEC provides protection from DNS cache poisoning and other types of attacks that can compromise an organization's security.

- DNSSEC provides an additional layer of security for enterprises that have private clouds deployed or use extranets for business communications.

- Revision 3 of National Institute of Standards and Technology (NIST) Special Publication (SP) 800-53 mandates the requirement of DNSSEC for internal DNS zone signing on U.S. federal government information systems.

In addition, DNSSEC is likely to become a regulatory requirement for some industries, such as finance and banking.

DNSSEC in previous Windows Server versions

Basic support for DNSSEC was introduced in Windows Server 2003 to enable DNS servers to act as secondary DNS servers for existing DNSSEC-compliant secure zones. Windows Server 2003 DNS servers, however, were not capable of signing zones and resource records or validating the *Signature (SIG) resource records*. In addition, all DNSSEC configuration had to be performed by editing the registry on DNS servers.

Support for DNSSEC was enhanced in Windows Server 2008 R2 but was limited because it was intended as a solution only for file-backed, static zones and not for dynamic Active Directory–integrated zones. The DNS server command-line management tool (Dnscmd .exe) could be used to perform offline key generation and zone-signing capability through a signing tool. Windows PowerShell scripts were later released through the TechNet Script Center for performing DNSSEC administration tasks such as signing zones and for adding, rolling over, and verifying trust anchors. However, the DNS client in Windows 7 and Windows Server 2008 R2 is DNSSEC-aware but nonvalidating. In other words, the DNS client can examine a response received from a DNS server to determine whether the response has been validated by the DNS server, but the client cannot itself validate the response it receives from the DNS server. This means that you must use some other method, such as Internet Protocol security (IPsec), to secure the last mile between the client and its local DNS server, even when DNSSEC has been configured on DNS servers running Windows Server 2008 R2.

Windows Server 2012 and Windows Server 2012 R2 include full DNSSEC support for Active Directory–integrated DNS scenarios, including DNS dynamic updates in DNSSEC signed zones, automated trust-anchor distribution through Active Directory, automated trust-anchor rollover support per RFC 5011, and validation of records signed with updated DNSSEC standards (NSEC3, RSA/SHA-2). An updated user interface with deployment and management wizards and full Windows PowerShell support for configuring and managing DNSSEC are also included. However, the DNS client in Windows 8, Windows 8.1, Windows Server 2012, and Windows Server 2012 R2 is still DNSSEC-aware but nonvalidating, which means you should still use IPsec to secure the network connecting the client to its local DNS server.

How DNSSEC works

DNSSEC works by combining public key infrastructure (PKI) cryptography with DNS to use digital signatures and cryptographic keys to sign DNS zones and validate that DNS responses are authentic. Figure 6-5 shows the steps involved in the name-resolution process when DNSSEC has been implemented in a Windows Server–based network. The basic steps involved are as follows:

1. A client such as a Windows 8 computer issues a DNS query to its local DNS server.

2. The client's local DNS server has DNSSEC enabled but is not authoritative for the zone being queried, so it issues a recursive query to the authoritative server for the zone to request an authoritative response.

3. The authoritative server has DNSSEC enabled and is the authoritative server for the zone being queried. This means that the zone has been digitally signed on this server. When the authoritative server receives the recursive query, it returns an authoritative response to the client's local server. This response includes one or more DNSSEC resource records, which can include the following types:

   - **Resource Record Signature (RRSIG)**   These resource records contain digital signatures for all records in a zone.

   - **DNS Public Key (DNSKEY)**   These resource records contain the public keys for a particular zone.

   - **Delegation Signer (DS)**   These resource records indicate the public key for a child zone.

   - **Next Secure (NSEC or NSEC3)**   These resource records allow the validation of a negative response.

4. The local server uses the public key of the signed zone on the authoritative server to validate the response it received from the authoritative server.

5. The local server returns the requested response to the client that issued the query. The client can now access the network resource represented by the name for which it was querying.

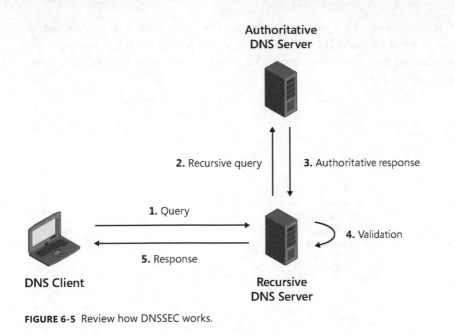

Authoritative
DNS Server

2. Recursive query   **3.** Authoritative response

1. Query

4. Validation

5. Response

DNS Client   **Recursive
DNS Server**

FIGURE 6-5 Review how DNSSEC works.

✔ **Quick check**

■ When DNSSEC is implemented on a Windows Server–based network, where is vali-
    dation performed for the response to a client's DNS query?

Quick check answer

■ On the client's local DNS server, not on the client itself

Deploying DNSSEC

Deploying DNSSEC using Windows Server 2012 or Windows Server 2012 R2 into an existing
Active Directory environment involves performing the following steps:

1. Begin by introducing Windows Server 2012 or Windows Server 2012 R2 domain
   controllers into your environment. These domain controllers should also have the DNS
   Server role installed and be configured to use Active Directory–integrated zones. Note
   that the schema must be updated to Windows Server 2012 level or higher to support
   the DNSSEC extensions.

2. DNSSEC is implemented by signing zones on your DNS servers. After deciding which DNS zone to implement DNSSEC on, sign the zone by opening the DNS Manager console, selecting the DNS server, right-clicking the zone, selecting DNSSEC, and then selecting Sign The Zone:

3. Follow the prompts of the Zone Signing Wizard to complete the process of signing the zone. The simplest approach is to use the default settings to sign the zone:

For example, selecting this option when signing the corp.contoso.com zone on your first Windows Server 2012 R2 domain controller DC-1.corp.contoso.com would have the following results:

- The domain controller becomes the key master for the corp.contoso.com zone. The *key master* is the DNS server that generates and manages signing keys for a zone that is protected with DNSSEC.

- A *key signing key (KSK)* with a length of 2048 bits is generated using the RSA/SHA-256 cryptographic algorithm. The KSK is an authentication key that signs all of the DNSKEY records at the root of the zone, and it is part of the chain of trust. By default, the KSK has a rollover frequency of 755 days and any DNSKEY records signed using the key have a signature validity of 168 hours. Key rollover and signature refresh are enabled by default on Windows Server 2012 R2 DNS servers.

- A *zone signing key (ZSK)* with a length of 1024 bits is generated using the RSA/SHA-256 algorithm. The ZSK is used to sign zone data, such as the SOA, NS, and A resource records found in a typical zone. By default, the ZSK has a rollover frequency of 90 days and any zone resource records signed using the key have a signature validity of 240 hours. Key rollover and signature refresh are enabled by default on Windows Server 2012 R2 DNS servers.

- NSEC3 is used by default for providing authenticated denial of existence. The NSEC3 hash algorithm used is RSA/SHA-1 with 50 iterations and a salt length of 8.

Trust anchors are not distributed. A *trust anchor* is a preconfigured public key associated with a specific zone. The trust anchor enables DNS servers to validate DNSKEY resource records for the corresponding zone and establish a chain of trust to child zones, if any exist. Validating DNS servers must be configured with one or more trust anchors to perform DNSSEC validation. If the DNS server is running on a domain controller, trust anchors are stored in the forest directory partition in Active Directory.

1. If the zone you signed is an Active Directory–integrated zone, private zone signing keys now replicate automatically to all domain controllers hosting the zone through Active Directory replication. Each zone owner signs its own copy of the zone when it receives the key as long as the zone owner is a domain controller running Windows Server 2012 or Windows Server 2012 R2.

   Most of the key-management process is automated for DNSSEC in Windows Server 2012 and Windows Server 2012 R2. After the key rollover frequency has been configured for a zone using the Zone Signing Wizard, the key master automatically generates new keys and replicates through Active Directory. The zone owner rolls over keys and re-signs the zone, and secure delegations from the parent are also automatically updated within the same forest.

2. At this point, the zone has been signed and contains the necessary RRSIG, DNSKEY, DS, and NSEC3 resource records to support DNSSEC validation:

3. When zone data is updated by a client sending a DNS dynamic update to an authoritative DNS server, that DNS server updates its own copy of the zone and generates the required signatures. The unsigned update is then securely replicated to all other authoritative servers, and each DNS server adds the update to its copy of the zone and generates the required signatures.

4. *Trust anchors* must then be distributed to the DNS servers in your environment to enable the DNSSEC validation process to be performed by nonauthoritative (recursive or caching) DNS servers. If the DNS servers are running on domain controllers, trust anchors are stored in the forest directory partition in Active Directory and are replicated to all domain controllers in the forest. On stand-alone DNS servers, trust anchors are stored in a file named TrustAnchors.dns and can be manually imported to these servers using the DNS Manager console or Windows PowerShell.

For example, the stand-alone DNS server running Windows Server 2012 R2 shown next displays its configured trust anchors in the DNS Manager console tree in the Trust Points container. Note that two DNSKEY trust points are displayed: one for the active key and one for the standby key.

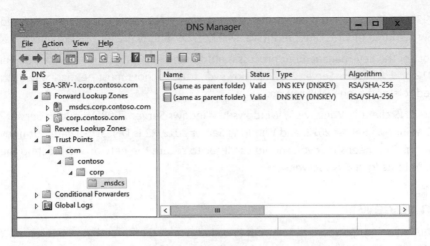

5. Trust Anchor updates are then automatically replicated through Active Directory to all servers in the forest, and automated Trust Anchor rollover is used to keep trust anchors up to date.

6. The final step in deploying DNSSEC is to ensure security between the nonvalidating DNS clients (which can be computers running Windows 7, Windows 8, Windows Server 2008 R2, Windows Server 2012, or Windows Server 2012 R2) and their local DNS servers. The recommended way to do this is to use IPsec to protect the last mile between the client and its local DNS server. The DNS clients must also be configured to check that responses have been validated by their local DNS server, and you do this by configuring the Name Resolution Policy Table (NRPT) on the clients. The NRPT is a table that contains rules you can configure to specify DNS settings or special behavior for names or namespaces. You can configure the NRPT by using either Group Policy or Windows PowerShell.

Lesson summary

- DNSSEC is a suite of extensions that add security to the DNS protocol by enabling DNS servers to validate DNS responses.
- DNSSEC confirms the authority of the originator and the integrity of the data being returned.
- DNSSEC provides authenticated denial of existence when the information the client is trying to access does not exist. In other words, it provides proof that the site being requested really doesn't exist.
- DNSSEC does not provide confidentiality for the data a DNS server returns.
- DNSSEC works by combining public key infrastructure (PKI) cryptography with DNS to use digital signatures and cryptographic keys to sign DNZ zones and validate that DNS responses are authentic.

- DNSSEC is implemented by signing zones on your DNS servers. Signing a zone adds new resource records of types RRSIG, DNSKEY, DS, and NSEC (or NSEC3) into the zone.

- Most of the key-management process is automated for DNSSEC in Windows Server 2012 and Windows Server 2012 R2. However, trust anchors must be manually distributed to stand-alone DNS servers.

- The DNS client in Windows 7, Windows 8, Windows Server 2008, Windows Server 2008 R2, Windows Server 2012, and Windows Server 2012 R2 is DNSSEC-aware but nonvalidating. This means that you should use IPsec to secure the network connecting the client to its local DNS server.

Lesson review

Answer the following questions to test your knowledge of the information in this lesson. You can find the answers to these questions and explanations of why each answer choice is correct or incorrect in the "Answers" section at the end of this chapter.

1. Which of the following is *not* a correct explanation of a DNSSEC term or concept?

   A. DNSKEY resource records contain the public keys for a particular zone.

   B. Only zones that are authoritative can be signed.

   C. The key signing key (KSK) is used to sign all of the DNSKEY records at the root of the zone.

   D. When zone data is updated by a client sending a DNS dynamic update to an authoritative DNS server, the entire zone must be re-signed.

2. In a Windows Server–based DNS infrastructure in which DNSSEC has been implemented, where is the validation of the response to a query performed?

   A. On an authoritative DNS server in the forest root domain

   B. On an authoritative DNS server in a child or tree domain

   C. On a recursive DNS server that is not authoritative for the zone being queried

   D. On the client computer issuing the name query

3. When you want to implement DNSSEC in an Active Directory environment in which all DNS servers are domain controllers and use only Active Directory–integrated zones, which of the following steps in the DNSSEC deployment process is *not* correct?

   A. Begin by introducing Windows Server 2012 or Windows Server 2012 R2 domain controllers into your environment.

   B. After deciding which DNS zone to implement DNSSEC on, sign the zone.

   C. Use Robocopy.exe to replicate the private zone signing keys to all domain controllers hosting the zone.

   D. Use IPsec to protect the last mile between the nonvalidating DNS client and its local DNS server.

Lesson 3: Managing networking using Windows PowerShell

Managing network settings and services is a core task for administrators of Windows Server–based networks. Examples of network configuration tasks include configuring interfaces, IP addresses, default gateways, routes, and metrics; configuring ISATAP and Teredo for IPv4/IPv6 interoperability; and similar tasks. Examples of network service tasks include configuring DHCP scopes, options, and reservations; creating different types of DNS zones; configuring DNS root hints and forwarders; creating resource records; and similar tasks.

In earlier versions of Windows Server, such tasks usually had to be performed using a combination of GUI tools and various command-line utilities. But with the significantly increased Windows PowerShell capabilities built into Windows Server 2012 and Windows Server 2012 R2, you can perform most network-administration tasks from the Windows PowerShell command line or by running Windows PowerShell scripts. This lesson demonstrates how to identify network components that have Windows PowerShell support and how to perform common network-administration tasks and troubleshooting using Windows PowerShell.

> **After this lesson, you will be able to:**
> - Identify possible Windows PowerShell cmdlets that you can use for performing specific network-management tasks.
> - Use the Show-Command cmdlet to learn the syntax of other cmdlets.
> - Configure TCP/IP address settings using Windows PowerShell.
> - Manage different aspects of network adapters using Windows PowerShell.
> - Manage DHCP servers using Windows PowerShell.
> - Manage DNS servers using Windows PowerShell.
> - Troubleshoot networking problems using Windows PowerShell.
>
> **Estimated lesson time: 40 minutes**

Identifying networking cmdlets

In Windows Server 2012 and Windows Server 2012 R2, there are hundreds of Windows PowerShell cmdlets that you can use to view, configure, and monitor different networking components and services in the platform. The tasks you can perform using these cmdlets range from the common (such as configuring static IP addresses or DHCP reservations for servers) to the more specialized (such as configuring quality-of-service parameters) to the settings related to virtual environments (such as configuring the Hyper-V extensible switch). There is obviously too much to learn here in a single lesson or even a single book, and many administrators might perform some tasks only occasionally, or even not at all. So let's begin with a more practical approach to the problem of administering a Windows Server 2012 or Windows Server 2012 R2 networking environment using Windows PowerShell by asking a simple question: How can you find the right cmdlet (if there is a cmdlet) to perform a particular networking task?

Using Get-Command

You could start by using the Get-Command cmdlet to search for all Windows PowerShell cmdlets and functions that have the string "net" in their names. This generates a lot of output, however, as shown here:

```
PS C:\> Get-Command *net*

CommandType     Name                                            ModuleName
-----------     ----                                            ----------
Function        Add-NetIPHttpsCertBinding                       NetworkTransition
Function        Add-NetLbfoTeamMember                           NetLbfo
Function        Add-NetLbfoTeamNic                              NetLbfo
Function        Add-NetSwitchTeamMember                         NetSwitchTeam
Function        Copy-NetFirewallRule                            NetSecurity
Function        Copy-NetIPsecMainModeCryptoSet                  NetSecurity
Function        Copy-NetIPsecMainModeRule                       NetSecurity
Function        Copy-NetIPsecPhase1AuthSet                      NetSecurity
Function        Copy-NetIPsecPhase2AuthSet                      NetSecurity
Function        Copy-NetIPsecQuickModeCryptoSet                 NetSecurity
Function        Copy-NetIPsecRule                               NetSecurity
Function        Disable-NetAdapter                              NetAdapter
Function        Disable-NetAdapterBinding                       NetAdapter
Function        Disable-NetAdapterChecksumOffload               NetAdapter
Function        Disable-NetAdapterEncapsulatedPacketTaskOffload NetAdapter
Function        Disable-NetAdapterIPsecOffload                  NetAdapter
...
```

From the preceding output, you can see there are several Windows PowerShell modules that perform network-related actions. To see this more clearly, the following commands take the preceding output, sort it by module name, and remove duplicates:

```
PS C:\> Get-Command *net* | Sort-Object ModuleName | Format-Table ModuleName `
-HideTableHeaders | Out-String | Out-File c:\data\test.txt
PS C:\> Get-Content C:\data\test.txt | Get-Unique


ActiveDirectory
BranchCache
DnsServer
MsDtc
NetAdapter
NetConnection
NetLbfo
NetQos
NetSecurity
NetSwitchTeam
NetTCPIP
```

```
NetworkTransition
NFS
SmbShare
```

To investigate the NetTCPIP module further, you can use the *–Module* parameter of Get-Command to list all cmdlets and functions contained in this module:

```
PS C:\> Get-Command -Module NetTCPIP | Sort-Object Name | Format-Table Name

Name
----
Get-NetIPAddress
Get-NetIPConfiguration
Get-NetIPInterface
Get-NetIPv4Protocol
Get-NetIPv6Protocol
Get-NetNeighbor
Get-NetOffloadGlobalSetting
Get-NetPrefixPolicy
Get-NetRoute
Get-NetTCPConnection
Get-NetTCPSetting
Get-NetTransportFilter
Get-NetUDPEndpoint
Get-NetUDPSetting
New-NetIPAddress
New-NetNeighbor
New-NetRoute
New-NetTransportFilter
Remove-NetIPAddress
Remove-NetNeighbor
Remove-NetRoute
Remove-NetTransportFilter
Set-NetIPAddress
Set-NetIPInterface
Set-NetIPv4Protocol
Set-NetIPv6Protocol
Set-NetNeighbor
Set-NetOffloadGlobalSetting
Set-NetRoute
Set-NetTCPSetting
Set-NetUDPSetting
```

Using Show-Command

At this point, you can begin using Get-Help to learn about the syntax of NetTCPIP cmdlets in which you're interested and to see some examples of their usage. Unfortunately for administrators who are not very familiar with Windows PowerShell, the syntax displayed when you use Get-Help with a cmdlet can appear daunting. For example, consider a scenario in which you have a web server running Windows Server 2012 or Windows Server 2012 R2 and you want to add a second IP address to a network adapter on the server.

You might guess from the output of *Get-Command –Module NetTCPIP* shown previously that New-NetIPAddress is the cmdlet you use to perform this task, and you would be correct. But to the Windows PowerShell beginner, the syntax from *Get-Help New-NetIPAddress* might look quite confusing:

```
Parameter Set: ByInterfaceAlias
New-NetIPAddress -InterfaceAlias <String> [-AddressFamily <AddressFamily> ] [-AsJob]
[-CimSession <CimSession[]> ] [-DefaultGateway <String> ] [-IPv4Address <String> ]
[-IPv6Address <String> ] [-PassThru] [-PreferredLifetime <TimeSpan> ]
[-PrefixLength <Byte> ] [-PrefixOrigin <PrefixOrigin> ] [-SkipAsSource <Boolean> ]
[-Store <Store> ] [-SuffixOrigin <SuffixOrigin> ] [-ThrottleLimit <Int32> ]
[-Type <Type> ] [-ValidLifetime <TimeSpan> ] [-Confirm] [-WhatIf] [ <CommonParameters>]

Parameter Set: ByIfIndexOrIfALias
New-NetIPAddress [-AddressFamily <AddressFamily> ] [-AsJob]
[-CimSession <CimSession[]> ] [-DefaultGateway <String> ] [-InterfaceAlias <String> ]
[-InterfaceIndex <UInt32> ] [-IPv4Address <String> ] [-IPv6Address <String> ]
[-PassThru] [-PreferredLifetime <TimeSpan> ] [-PrefixLength <Byte> ]
[-PrefixOrigin <PrefixOrigin> ] [-SkipAsSource <Boolean> ] [-Store <Store> ]
[-SuffixOrigin <SuffixOrigin> ] [-ThrottleLimit <Int32> ] [-Type <Type> ]
[-ValidLifetime <TimeSpan> ] [-Confirm] [-WhatIf] [ <CommonParameters>]
```

Fortunately, the new Show-Command cmdlet introduced in Windows Server 2012 can help make the syntax of Windows PowerShell cmdlets easier to understand and use. Start by typing the following command:

```
PS C:\> Show-Command New-NetIPAddress
```

> **NOTE USING SHOW-COMMAND ON SERVER CORE**
>
> To use the Show-Command cmdlet on a Windows Server Core installation, you must first install the Windows PowerShell ISE feature on the server.

When you run the preceding command, the properties page shown in Figure 6-6 opens to show you the different parameters you can use with the New-NetIPAddress cmdlet. Parameters such as *InterfaceAlias* and *IPAddress* that are marked with an asterisk are mandatory; those not marked this way are optional.

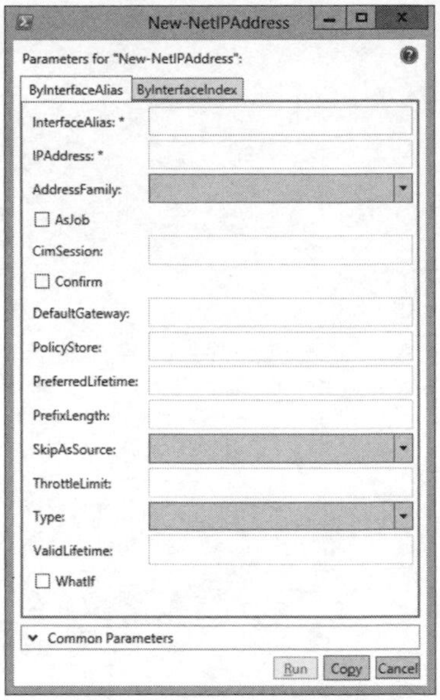

FIGURE 6-6 The Show-Command properties page for the New-NetIPAddress cmdlet shows you the parameters you can use.

To add a new IP address, you first need to know the alias or index of the network interface to which you want to add the address. To find the interfaces on the system, you could use **Get-Command *interface*** to find all cmdlets that include "interface" in their name. Of the eight cmdlets displayed when you run this command, the cmdlet Get-NetIpInterface is the one you are looking for, and running this cmdlet displays a list of all interfaces on the server:

```
PS C:\> Get-NetIPInterface

ifIndex InterfaceAlias               AddressFamily NlMtu(Bytes) InterfaceMetric Dhcp
------- --------------               ------------- ------------ --------------- ----
12      Ethernet                     IPv6                  1500               5 Disabled
14      Teredo Tunneling Pseudo...   IPv6                  1280              50 Disabled
13      isatap.{4B8DC8AE-DE20-4...   IPv6                  1280              50 Disabled
1       Loopback Pseudo-Interfa.     IPv6            4294967295              50 Disabled
12      Ethernet                     IPv4                  1500               5 Disabled
1       Loopback Pseudo-Interfa.     IPv4            4294967295              50 Disabled
```

From the preceding command output, you can see that the interface you are looking for is identified by the alias Ethernet. To view the existing TCP/IP configuration of this interface, you can use the *–InterfaceAlias* parameter with the Get-NetIPAddress cmdlet as follows:

```
PS C:\> Get-NetIPAddress -InterfaceAlias Ethernet


IPAddress          : fe80::cf8:11a1:2e3:d9bc%12
InterfaceIndex     : 12
InterfaceAlias     : Ethernet
AddressFamily      : IPv6
```

```
Type               : Unicast
PrefixLength       : 64
PrefixOrigin       : WellKnown
SuffixOrigin       : Link
AddressState       : Preferred
ValidLifetime      : Infinite ([TimeSpan]::MaxValue)
PreferredLifetime  : Infinite ([TimeSpan]::MaxValue)
SkipAsSource       : False
PolicyStore        : ActiveStore

IPAddress          : 172.16.11.236
InterfaceIndex     : 12
InterfaceAlias     : Ethernet
AddressFamily      : IPv4
Type               : Unicast
PrefixLength       : 24
PrefixOrigin       : Manual
SuffixOrigin       : Manual
AddressState       : Preferred
ValidLifetime      : Infinite ([TimeSpan]::MaxValue)
PreferredLifetime  : Infinite ([TimeSpan]::MaxValue)
SkipAsSource       : False
PolicyStore        : ActiveStore
```

The preceding command output shows that the Ethernet interface currently has 172.16.11.236/24 as its IPv4 address and Classless Interdomain Routing (CIDR) prefix.

Returning to the open properties page displayed by **Show-Command New-NetIPAddress**, you can add a second IP address to the interface by specifying the parameter values shown in Figure 6-7.

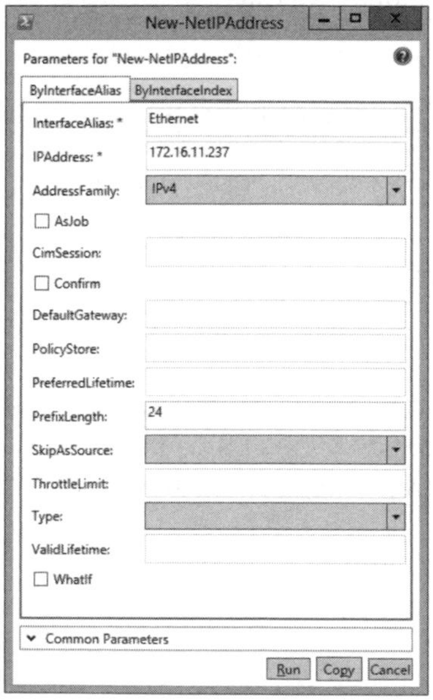

FIGURE 6-7 Add the address 172.16.11.237/24 to the interface named Ethernet.

If you click Copy in the properties page shown in Figure 6-7, the command is copied to the clipboard. The resulting command looks like this:

```
New-NetIPAddress -InterfaceAlias Ethernet -IPAddress 172.16.11.237 `
-AddressFamily IPv4 -PrefixLength 24
```

If you click Run, the command executes. By using *–InterfaceAlias* with the Get-NetIPAddress cmdlet again, you can verify that the command accomplished the desired result:

```
PS C:\> Get-NetIPAddress -InterfaceAlias Ethernet


IPAddress           : fe80::cf8:11a1:2e3:d9bc%12
InterfaceIndex      : 12
InterfaceAlias      : Ethernet
AddressFamily       : IPv6
Type                : Unicast
PrefixLength        : 64
PrefixOrigin        : WellKnown
SuffixOrigin        : Link
AddressState        : Preferred
ValidLifetime       : Infinite ([TimeSpan]::MaxValue)
PreferredLifetime   : Infinite ([TimeSpan]::MaxValue)
SkipAsSource        : False
PolicyStore         : ActiveStore

IPAddress           : 172.16.11.237
InterfaceIndex      : 12
InterfaceAlias      : Ethernet
AddressFamily       : IPv4
Type                : Unicast
PrefixLength        : 24
PrefixOrigin        : Manual
SuffixOrigin        : Manual
AddressState        : Preferred
ValidLifetime       : Infinite ([TimeSpan]::MaxValue)
PreferredLifetime   : Infinite ([TimeSpan]::MaxValue)
SkipAsSource        : False
PolicyStore         : ActiveStore

IPAddress           : 172.16.11.236
InterfaceIndex      : 12
InterfaceAlias      : Ethernet
AddressFamily       : IPv4
Type                : Unicast
PrefixLength        : 24
PrefixOrigin        : Manual
SuffixOrigin        : Manual
AddressState        : Preferred
ValidLifetime       : Infinite ([TimeSpan]::MaxValue)
PreferredLifetime   : Infinite ([TimeSpan]::MaxValue)
SkipAsSource        : False
PolicyStore         : ActiveStore
```

Opening the Advanced TCP/IP Settings for the interface from the Network Connections folder confirms the result. (See Figure 6-8.)

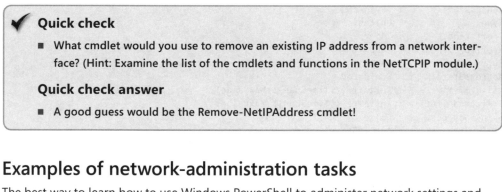

FIGURE 6-8 The Advanced TCP/IP Settings dialog box confirms that the second IP address was successfully added to the interface.

> **✓ Quick check**
>
> - What cmdlet would you use to remove an existing IP address from a network interface? (Hint: Examine the list of the cmdlets and functions in the NetTCPIP module.)
>
> **Quick check answer**
>
> - A good guess would be the Remove-NetIPAddress cmdlet!

Examples of network-administration tasks

The best way to learn how to use Windows PowerShell to administer network settings and services on Windows Server 2012 and Windows Server 2012 R2 is to experiment with performing different tasks in a test environment. The following sections provide some examples of what you can do in this area, and the practice and suggested practice exercises included in this chapter present you with further challenges for learning these skills.

Displaying network adapters with 100 Mbps link speed

You can use the Get-NetAdapter cmdlet to display all network adapters on the server that have a link speed of 100 megabits per second (Mbps) like this:

```
PS C:\> Get-NetAdapter | Where-Object -FilterScript {$_.LinkSpeed -eq "100 Mbps"}

Name        InterfaceDescription      ifIndex Status  MacAddress         LinkSpeed
----        --------------------      ------- ------  ----------         ---------
Ethernet 2  Broadcom NetXtreme Gig... 13 Up           A4-BA-DB-0A-96-0C  100 Mbps
Ethernet    Broadcom NetXtreme Gig... 12 Up           A4-BA-DB-0A-96-0B  100 Mbps
```

The output of this command consists of objects that can be passed through the pipeline to other cmdlets. For example, you could pipe the output into the Set-NetIPInterface cmdlet to assign a metric value of 5 to all interfaces having a link speed of 100 Mbps as follows:

```
PS C:\> Get-NetAdapter | Where-Object -FilterScript {$_.LinkSpeed -eq "100 Mbps"} | `
Set-NetIPInterface -InterfaceMetric 5
```

Disabling a binding on a network adapter

You can enable and disable bindings on a network adapter using Windows PowerShell. For example, start by using the Get-NetAdapterBinding cmdlet to display the bindings for the specified interface:

```
PS C:\> Get-NetAdapterBinding -InterfaceAlias "Ethernet 2"

Name        DisplayName                                       ComponentID   Enabled
----        -----------                                       -----------   -------
Ethernet 2  Hyper-V Extensible Virtual Switch                 vms_pp        False
Ethernet 2  Link-Layer Topology Discovery Responder           ms_rspndr     True
Ethernet 2  Link-Layer Topology Discovery Mapper I/O Driver   ms_lltdio     True
Ethernet 2  Microsoft Network Adapter Multiplexor Protocol    ms_implat     False
Ethernet 2  Client for Microsoft Networks                     ms_msclient   True
Ethernet 2  Windows Network Virtualization Filter driver      ms_netwnv     False
Ethernet 2  QoS Packet Scheduler                              ms_pacer      True
Ethernet 2  File and Printer Sharing for Microsoft Networks   ms_server     True
```

```
Ethernet 2  Internet Protocol Version 6 (TCP/IPv6)        ms_tcpip6    True
Ethernet 2  Internet Protocol Version 4 (TCP/IPv4)        ms_tcpip     True
```

To disable a specific binding such as QoS Packet Scheduler, you can use the DisableNetAdapterBinding cmdlet like this:

```
PS C:\> Disable-NetAdapterBinding -Name "Ethernet 2" -ComponentID ms_pacer
```

You can use the Enable-NetAdapterBinding cmdlet to reenable the binding.

Disabling a network adapter

You can disable a specific network adapter or even all network adapters using Windows PowerShell. For example, the following command disables the adapter named Ethernet 2 with no confirmation prompt displayed:

```
PS C:\> Disable-NetAdapter -Name "Ethernet 2" -Confirm:$false
```

To disable all network adapters on the server, you can use this command:

```
PS C:\> Disable-NetAdapter -Name *
```

Note that all remote connectivity with the server will be lost if you do this.

To enable any network adapters that are disabled, you can use the Enable-NetAdapter cmdlet.

Creating a DHCP server scope

You can manage Windows Server 2012 or Windows Server 2012 R2 DHCP servers using Windows PowerShell. Common DHCP server-management tasks include creating scopes, creating exclusion ranges, creating reservations, configuring scope and server options, and so on.

For example, begin by viewing all the scopes currently configured on the DHCP server:

```
PS C:\> Get-DhcpServerv4Scope

ScopeId        SubnetMask      Name  State  StartRange   EndRange      LeaseDuration
-------        ----------      ----  -----  ----------   --------      -------------
172.16.11.0    255.255.255.0   test  Active 172.16.11.35 172.16.11.39  8.00:00:00
```

Note that there is currently only one active scope on the DHCP server. Now add a second scope for the IP address range 172.16.12.50 through 172.16.11.100. Leave the scope inactive until you finish configuring exclusions and reservations for it:

```
PS C:\> Add-DhcpServerv4Scope -EndRange 172.16.12.100 -Name test2 `
-StartRange 172.16.12.50 -SubnetMask 255.255.255.0 -State InActive
```

Note that in this cmdlet the order in which you specify the parameters doesn't matter because you specified the end of the address range before specifying its beginning.

Running Get-DdhpServerv4Scope again indicates that adding the new scope was successful:

```
PS C:\> Get-DhcpServerv4Scope

ScopeId       SubnetMask      Name    State     StartRange      EndRange       LeaseDuration
-------       ----------      ----    -----     ----------      --------       -------------
172.16.11.0   255.255.255.0   test    Active    172.16.11.35    172.16.11.39   8.00:00:00
172.16.12.0   255.255.255.0   test2   Inactive  172.16.12.50    172.16.12.100  8.00:00:00
```

Now exclude the range 172.16.12.70 through 172.16.12.75 from the new scope:

```
PS C:\> Add-DhcpServerv4ExclusionRange -EndRange 172.16.12.75 -ScopeId 172.16.12.0 `
    -StartRange 172.16.12.70
```

Also add a reservation for a file server:

```
PS C:\> Add-DhcpServerv4Reservation -ClientId EE-05-B0-DA-04-00 `
-IPAddress 172.16.12.88  -ScopeId 172.16.12.0 `
-Description "Reservation for file server"
```

Here, EE-05-B0-DA-04-00 represents the MAC address of the file server's network adapter.

Configure a default gateway address for the new scope by creating a scope option as follows:

```
PS C:\> Set-DhcpServerv4OptionValue -Router 172.16.12.1 -ScopeId 172.16.12.0
```

If you want to create a server option instead of a scope option, you could do this by omitting the *–ScopeID* parameter from the preceding command.

Now you're done creating and configuring the new scope, so finish by activating it:

```
PS C:\> Set-DhcpServerv4Scope -State Active
```

> **NOTE** **WHY DOESN'T GET-COMMAND DISPLAY THE EXPECTED RESULTS?**
>
> If you run the command **Get-Command *dhcp*** on a clean install of Windows Server 2012 or Windows Server 2012 R2, you won't get any results. That's because Get-Command can display commands only for Windows PowerShell modules that are installed on the server, and the module for DHCP isn't installed until you add the DHCP Server role to your server.

Creating DNS resource records

You can manage Windows Server 2012 or Windows Server 2012 R2 DNS servers using Windows PowerShell. Common DNS server-management tasks include adding resource records to zones, configuring forwarders, configuring root hints, and so on.

For example, view a list of zones on a DNS server that is also a domain controller for the corp.contoso.com domain:

```
PS C:\> Get-DnsServerZone
```

```
ZoneName                    ZoneType  IsAutoCreated  IsDsIntegrated  IsRever...  IsSigned
--------                    --------  -------------  --------------  ----------  --------
_msdcs.corp.contoso.com     Primary   False          True            False       True
0.in-addr.arpa              Primary   True           False           True        False
127.in-addr.arpa            Primary   True           False           True        False
255.in-addr.arpa            Primary   True           False           True        False
corp.contoso.com            Primary   False          True            False       False
TrustAnchors                Primary   False          True            False       False
```

To view a list of resource records of type A (address) in the corp.contoso.com zone, you can pipe the output of the Get-DnsServerResourceRecord cmdlet into the Where-Object cmdlet, like this:

```
PS C:\> Get-DnsServerResourceRecord -ZoneName corp.contoso.com | Where-Object
    {$_.RecordType -eq "A"}

HostName         RecordType Timestamp              TimeToLive   RecordData
--------         ---------- ---------              ----------   ----------
@                A          7/8/2012 12:00:00 PM   00:10:00     172.16.11.36
@                A          7/8/2012 1:00:00 PM    00:10:00     172.16.11.232
DomainDnsZones   A          7/8/2012 12:00:00 PM   00:10:00     172.16.11.36
DomainDnsZones   A          7/8/2012 12:00:00 PM   00:10:00     172.16.11.232
ForestDnsZones   A          7/8/2012 12:00:00 PM   00:10:00     172.16.11.36
ForestDnsZones   A          7/8/2012 12:00:00 PM   00:10:00     172.16.11.232
sea-srv-1        A          0                      01:00:00     172.16.11.232
SEA-SRV-5        A          0                      01:00:00     172.16.11.36
```

To add a new A resource record for a test server, you can use the Add-DnsServerResourceRecordA cmdlet, like this:

```
PS C:\> Add-DnsServerResourceRecordA -IPv4Address 172.16.11.239 -Name SEA-TEST `
-ZoneName corp.contoso.com
```

You can also add other types of resource records—such as PTR, CN, or MX records—using the preceding cmdlet. And you can use the Remove-DnsServerResourceRecord cmdlet to remove resource records from a zone.

There are over 100 different cmdlets in the DnsServer module for Windows PowerShell in Windows Server 2012 and Windows Server 2012 R2. Table 6-1 shows the cmdlets you can use to perform some common DNS administration tasks. You'll get some hands-on experience with using some of these cmdlets in the practice exercises for this chapter.

TABLE 6-1 Common DNS server-administration tasks and Windows PowerShell cmdlets you can use to perform them

Task	Cmdlet
Configure forwarders	Add-DnsServerForwarder
Create a stub zone	Add-DnsServerStubZone
Display the contents of the DNS server cache	Show-DnsServerCache
Clear the DNS server cache	Clear-DnsServerCache

Task	Cmdlet
Display full configuration details of the DNS server	Get-DnsServer
Display statistics for the DNS server	Get-DnsServerStatistics
Import root hints	Import-DnsServerRootHint
Configure the DNS server cache settings	Set-DnsServerCache
Configure DNS server scavenging	Set-DnsServerScavenging
Initiate scavenging	Start-DnsServerScavenging

Troubleshooting networking problems

Both Windows Server 2012 and Windows Server 2012 R2 introduce new Windows PowerShell cmdlets that can help you troubleshoot network connection problems when they occur. We've already briefly examined the Get-NetAdapter and Get-NetIPAddress cmdlets that were introduced in Windows Server 2012. We now look at some additional capabilities of these two cmdlets, some other cmdlets, and a few new cmdlets introduced in Windows Server 2012 R2.

Get-NetAdapter and Get-VMNetworkAdapter

The Get-NetAdapter cmdlet was first introduced in Windows Server 2012 to enable you to retrieve the configuration of all physical network adapters in the server. If you're experiencing what might be a networking issue with one of your servers, the first thing you probably want to check is the configuration of the network adapters. For example, see what happens when you run this command on a Hyper-V host named SERVER1.contoso.com that is running Windows Server 2012 R2:

```
PS C:\> Get-NetAdapter

Name                   InterfaceDescription              ifIndex Status
----                   --------------------              ------- ------
vEthernet (Broadcom Ne... Hyper-V Virtual Ethernet Adapter #2    18 Up
Ethernet               Broadcom NetXtreme Gigabit Ethernet    12 Di...
Ethernet 2             Broadcom NetXtreme Gigabit Ethernet #2  13 Up
```

Because this is a Hyper-V host, there are probably some virtual machines running on it. On Hyper-V hosts running Windows Server 2012 and later, you can use the Get-VMNetworkAdapter cmdlet to collect configuration information for the network adapters for these virtual machines. For example, the following command retrieves information about all virtual machine network adapters on the host:

```
PS C:\> Get-VMNetworkAdapter *

Name             IsManagementOs VMName       SwitchName
----             -------------- ------       ----------
Network Adapter  False          SRV-STANDARD Broadcom NetXtreme Gigabit Ether...
Network Adapter  False          SRV2012R2    Broadcom NetXtreme Gigabit Ether...
Network Adapter  False          SRV2012R2
```

```
Network Adapter False          SRV2012        Broadcom NetXtreme Gigabit Ether...
Network Adapter False          SRV2012        Broadcom NetXtreme Gigabit Ether...
Network Adapter False          Gen2Test       Broadcom NetXtreme Gigabit Ether...
```

You can also use Get-VMNetworkAdapter with the *-VMName* parameter to display network adapters for a specific virtual machine on the host.

Get-NetIPAddress

The Get-NetIPAddress cmdlet was first introduced in Windows Server 2012 to enable you to retrieve the IP addresses configured on the system's network adapters. You can use the Get-NetIPAddress cmdlet both on physical servers and within virtual machines. For example, you can run this command on SERVER1 described above:

```
PS C:\> Get-NetIPAddress


IPAddress          : fe80::8843:1e98:a8a6:6fab%12
InterfaceIndex     : 12
InterfaceAlias     : Ethernet
AddressFamily      : IPv6
Type               : Unicast
PrefixLength       : 64
PrefixOrigin       : WellKnown
SuffixOrigin       : Link
AddressState       : Deprecated
ValidLifetime      : Infinite ([TimeSpan]::MaxValue)
PreferredLifetime  : Infinite ([TimeSpan]::MaxValue)
SkipAsSource       : False
PolicyStore        : ActiveStore

IPAddress          : fe80::1905:8ae1:5bfd:7b8e%18
InterfaceIndex     : 18
InterfaceAlias     : vEthernet (Broadcom NetXtreme Gigabit Ethernet #2 -
                     Virtual Switch)
AddressFamily      : IPv6
Type               : Unicast
PrefixLength       : 64
PrefixOrigin       : WellKnown
SuffixOrigin       : Link
AddressState       : Preferred
ValidLifetime      : Infinite ([TimeSpan]::MaxValue)
PreferredLifetime  : Infinite ([TimeSpan]::MaxValue)
SkipAsSource       : False
PolicyStore        : ActiveStore

IPAddress          : fe80::5efe:172.16.11.30%14
InterfaceIndex     : 14
InterfaceAlias     : isatap.{3D53D3DC-9209-4C7F-8AAE-AD8ADCBD93FC}
AddressFamily      : IPv6
Type               : Unicast
PrefixLength       : 128
PrefixOrigin       : WellKnown
SuffixOrigin       : Link
```

```
AddressState        : Deprecated
ValidLifetime       : Infinite ([TimeSpan]::MaxValue)
PreferredLifetime   : Infinite ([TimeSpan]::MaxValue)
SkipAsSource        : False
PolicyStore         : ActiveStore

IPAddress           : ::1
InterfaceIndex      : 1
InterfaceAlias      : Loopback Pseudo-Interface 1
AddressFamily       : IPv6
Type                : Unicast
PrefixLength        : 128
PrefixOrigin        : WellKnown
SuffixOrigin        : WellKnown
AddressState        : Preferred
ValidLifetime       : Infinite ([TimeSpan]::MaxValue)
PreferredLifetime   : Infinite ([TimeSpan]::MaxValue)
SkipAsSource        : False
PolicyStore         : ActiveStore

IPAddress           : 169.254.111.171
InterfaceIndex      : 12
InterfaceAlias      : Ethernet
AddressFamily       : IPv4
Type                : Unicast
PrefixLength        : 16
PrefixOrigin        : WellKnown
SuffixOrigin        : Link
AddressState        : Tentative
ValidLifetime       : Infinite ([TimeSpan]::MaxValue)
PreferredLifetime   : Infinite ([TimeSpan]::MaxValue)
SkipAsSource        : False
PolicyStore         : ActiveStore

IPAddress           : 172.16.11.30
InterfaceIndex      : 18
InterfaceAlias      : vEthernet (Broadcom NetXtreme Gigabit Ethernet #2 -
                      Virtual Switch)
AddressFamily       : IPv4
Type                : Unicast
PrefixLength        : 24
PrefixOrigin        : Manual
SuffixOrigin        : Manual
AddressState        : Preferred
ValidLifetime       : Infinite ([TimeSpan]::MaxValue)
PreferredLifetime   : Infinite ([TimeSpan]::MaxValue)
SkipAsSource        : False
PolicyStore         : ActiveStore

IPAddress           : 127.0.0.1
InterfaceIndex      : 1
InterfaceAlias      : Loopback Pseudo-Interface 1
AddressFamily       : IPv4
Type                : Unicast
PrefixLength        : 8
```

```
PrefixOrigin      : WellKnown
SuffixOrigin      : WellKnown
AddressState      : Preferred
ValidLifetime     : Infinite ([TimeSpan]::MaxValue)
PreferredLifetime : Infinite ([TimeSpan]::MaxValue)
SkipAsSource      : False
PolicyStore       : ActiveStore
```

You can see that Get-NetIPAddress returns a lot of useful information that you can parse or pipe into other commands for further processing.

Get-NetIPConfiguration

The Get-NetIPConfiguration cmdlet was first introduced in Windows Server 2012 to enable you to retrieve able network interfaces, IP addresses, and DNS servers configured on a system. The key value of Get-NetIPConfiguration is that it gives you the big picture of the system's network configuration in a concise way. For example, see what happens when you run this command on SERVER1 without specifying any further options:

```
PS C:\> Get-NetIPConfiguration


InterfaceAlias          : vEthernet (Broadcom NetXtreme Gigabit Ethernet #2 -
                          Virtual Switch)
InterfaceIndex          : 18
InterfaceDescription    : Hyper-V Virtual Ethernet Adapter #2
NetProfile.Name         : contoso.com
IPv4Address             : 172.16.11.30
IPv6DefaultGateway      :
IPv4DefaultGateway      : 172.16.11.1
DNSServer               : 172.16.11.50

InterfaceAlias          : Ethernet
InterfaceIndex          : 12
InterfaceDescription    : Broadcom NetXtreme Gigabit Ethernet
NetAdapter.Status       : Disconnected
```

To make things even easier, you can use the alias GIP instead of typing Get-NetIPConfiguration at the command line. For example, say you want to retrieve only the DNS Server configuration of the network adapter whose alias begins with vEthernet as shown above. Here's how you can do this:

```
PS C:\> $a = GIP 'v*'
PS C:\> $a.DNSServer

InterfaceAlias                Interface Address ServerAddresses  PSComputerName
                              Index     Family
--------------                --------- ------- ---------------  --------------
vEthernet (Broadcom NetXt...         18 IPv6    {}
vEthernet (Broadcom NetXt...         18 IPv4    {172.16.11.50}
```

Get-NetIPConfiguration can also provide verbose output if you specify the *-Detailed* parameter as shown here:

```
PS C:\> GIP -Detailed

ComputerName                    : SERVER1
InterfaceAlias                  : vEthernet (Broadcom NetXtreme Gigabit Ethernet
                                  #2 - Virtual Switch)
InterfaceIndex                  : 18
InterfaceDescription            : Hyper-V Virtual Ethernet Adapter #2
NetAdapter.LinkLayerAddress     : 00-24-E8-50-17-F3
NetAdapter.Status               : Up
NetProfile.Name                 : contoso.com
NetProfile.NetworkCategory      : DomainAuthenticated
NetProfile.IPv6Connectivity     : LocalNetwork
NetProfile.IPv4Connectivity     : Internet
IPv6LinkLocalAddress            : fe80::1905:8ae1:5bfd:7b8e%18
IPv4Address                     : 172.16.11.30
IPv6DefaultGateway              :
IPv4DefaultGateway              : 172.16.11.1
NetIPv6Interface.N1MTU          : 1500
NetIPv4Interface.N1MTU          : 1500
NetIPv6Interface.DHCP           : Enabled
NetIPv4Interface.DHCP           : Disabled
DNSServer                       : 172.16.11.50

ComputerName                    : SERVER1
InterfaceAlias                  : Ethernet
InterfaceIndex                  : 12
InterfaceDescription            : Broadcom NetXtreme Gigabit Ethernet
NetAdapter.LinkLayerAddress     : 00-24-E8-50-17-F4
NetAdapter.Status               : Disconnected
```

Test-NetConnection

The Test-NetConnection cmdlet has been introduced in Windows Server 2012 R2 to enable
you to perform ICMP and TCP connectivity tests. To see how this cmdlet can be used, perform
some tests from a Windows PowerShell prompt on the same server named SERVER1.contoso
.com described previously.

First, test network connectivity between SERVER1 and another server named SERVER2 on
the network:

```
PS C:\> Test-NetConnection SERVER2.contoso.com


ComputerName            : SERVER2.contoso.com
RemoteAddress           : 172.16.11.50
InterfaceAlias          : vEthernet (Broadcom NetXtreme Gigabit Ethernet #2 -
                          Virtual Switch)
SourceAddress           : 172.16.11.30
PingSucceeded           : True
PingReplyDetails (RTT)  : 0 ms
```

You can also use the Test-NetConnection cmdlet to test network connectivity with hosts on remote networks and over the Internet. For example, see if SERVER1 can establish network connectivity with the Microsoft Xbox website:

```
PS C:\> Test-NetConnection www.xbox.com


ComputerName            : www.xbox.com
RemoteAddress           : 184.29.219.150
InterfaceAlias          : vEthernet (Broadcom NetXtreme Gigabit Ethernet #2 -
                          Virtual Switch)
SourceAddress           : 172.16.11.30
PingSucceeded           : True
PingReplyDetails (RTT)  : 26 ms
```

You can also use the -*TraceRoute* parameter to trace the exact network route used to establish connectivity with the remote site:

```
PS C:\> Test-NetConnection www.xbox.com -TraceRoute


ComputerName            : www.xbox.com
RemoteAddress           : 184.29.219.150
InterfaceAlias          : vEthernet (Broadcom NetXtreme Gigabit Ethernet #2 -
                          Virtual Switch)
SourceAddress           : 172.16.11.30
PingSucceeded           : True
PingReplyDetails (RTT)  : 29 ms
TraceRoute              : 172.16.11.1
                          142.161.5.200
                          142.161.5.65
                          4.28.68.21
                          4.69.158.146
                          4.69.138.166
                          4.68.111.70
                          184.29.219.150
```

You can also use Test-NetConnection to test connectivity on a specific TCP port by including the -*Port* parameter in your command. For example, you can verify that the Xbox website can be accessed on the standard HTTP port, which is TCP port 80:

```
PS C:\> Test-NetConnection www.xbox.com -Port 80


ComputerName            : www.xbox.com
RemoteAddress           : 184.29.219.150
RemotePort              : 80
InterfaceAlias          : vEthernet (Broadcom NetXtreme Gigabit Ethernet #2 -
                          Virtual Switch)
SourceAddress           : 172.16.11.30
PingSucceeded           : True
PingReplyDetails (RTT)  : 28 ms
TcpTestSucceeded        : True
```

You can also use an alias like RDP to verify TCP connectivity with the well-known port for the Remote Desktop Protocol (RDP), which is TCP port 3389. For example, you can see if SERVER1 can establish connectivity to TCP port 3389 on SERVER2:

```
PS C:\> Test-NetConnection SERVER2 RDP
```

```
ComputerName            : SERVER2
RemoteAddress           : 172.16.11.50
RemotePort              : 3389
InterfaceAlias          : vEthernet (Broadcom NetXtreme Gigabit Ethernet #2 -
                          Virtual Switch)
SourceAddress           : 172.16.11.30
PingSucceeded           : True
PingReplyDetails (RTT) : 0 ms
TcpTestSucceeded        : True
```

The success of the above test indicates that Remote Desktop is enabled on the server SERVER2.

Test-NetConnection also lets you use other aliases besides RDP for testing connectivity with well-known TCP ports. For example, you can also use the following:

- SMB

- HTTP

- PING

Now see what happens when you try the RDP test against the server HOST40 on the network:

```
PS C:\> Test-NetConnection HOST40 RDP
WARNING: Ping to HOST40 failed -- Status: TimedOut
```

```
ComputerName            : HOST40
RemoteAddress           : 172.16.11.61
RemotePort              : 3389
InterfaceAlias          : vEthernet (Broadcom NetXtreme Gigabit Ethernet #2 -
                          Virtual Switch)
SourceAddress           : 172.16.11.30
PingSucceeded           : False
PingReplyDetails (RTT) : 0 ms
TcpTestSucceeded        : True
```

Note that RDP connectivity succeeded but pinging the server failed. This indicates that the server's firewall is active and blocking the inbound ICMP messages that are being sent by SERVER1.

The Test-NetConnection cmdlet also supports an -*InformationLevel* parameter that enables you to gather more detailed information concerning the connectivity test being performed:

```
PS C:\> Test-NetConnection SERVER2 RDP -InformationLevel Detailed
```

```
ComputerName              : SERVER2
RemoteAddress             : 172.16.11.50
RemotePort                : 3389
AllNameResolutionResults  : 172.16.11.50
                            fe80::396f:7162:ab64:fa82
MatchingIPsecRules        :
NetworkIsolationContext   : Private Network
InterfaceAlias            : vEthernet (Broadcom NetXtreme Gigabit Ethernet #2 -
                            Virtual Switch)
SourceAddress             : 172.16.11.30
NetRoute (NextHop)        : 0.0.0.0
PingSucceeded             : True
PingReplyDetails (RTT)    : 0 ms
TcpTestSucceeded          : True
```

You also can use -*InformationLevel* to suppress all output except whether the desired test was successful:

```
PS C:\> Test-NetConnection HOST40 RDP -InformationLevel Quiet
WARNING: Ping to HOST40 failed -- Status: TimedOut
True
PS C:\>
```

One final note about Test-NetConnection is that you can also run it with no parameters, like this:

```
PS C:\> Test-NetConnection
```

```
ComputerName             : internetbeacon.msedge.net
RemoteAddress            : 131.253.3.197
InterfaceAlias           : vEthernet (Broadcom NetXtreme Gigabit Ethernet #2 -
                           Virtual Switch)
SourceAddress            : 172.16.11.30
PingSucceeded            : True
PingReplyDetails (RTT)   : 49 ms
```

Doing this just tests whether your server has a network connection with the Internet by testing connectivity with a remote server belonging to the DNS domain msedge.net, which is registered by Microsoft.

Lesson summary

- The Get-Command cmdlet can help identify possible cmdlets for performing a specific administration task.
- The Show-Command cmdlet is useful for learning the syntax of other cmdlets.
- You can view and configure the TCP/IP configuration of a network interface, including its IP address settings, by using Windows PowerShell.
- You can identify, configure, manage, enable, and disable network adapters by using Windows PowerShell.

- You can display, configure, and manage DHCP server properties, scopes, exclusion ranges, reservations, and options by using Windows PowerShell.
- You can display, configure, and manage DNS server properties, zones, resource records, forwarders, cache settings, and replication by using Windows PowerShell.

Lesson review

Answer the following questions to test your knowledge of the information in this lesson. You can find the answers to these questions and explanations of why each answer choice is correct or incorrect in the "Answers" section at the end of this chapter.

1. When you use Show-Command to open a properties page for a cmdlet, what does an asterisk (*) mean when you find one beside a parameter?

   A. The parameter is optional.

   B. The parameter is mandatory.

   C. The parameter does not apply to that cmdlet.

   D. The parameter can be specified only from the command line.

2. Which cmdlet can you use to disable a binding on a network adapter?

   A. Get-NetAdapterBinding

   B. Remove-NetAdapterBinding

   C. Disable-NetAdapterBinding

   D. Disable-NetAdapter

3. What action does the following command perform?

   ```
   Set-DhcpServerv4OptionValue -Router 10.10.0.1 -ScopeId 10.10.20.0
   ```

   A. Configures a DHCP server option that assigns the address 10.10.0.1 as the default gateway on any DHCP client whose IPv4 address is on the 10.10.20.0 subnet

   B. Configures a DHCP scope option that assigns the address 10.10.0.1 as the default gateway on any DHCP client whose IPv4 address is on the 10.10.20.0 subnet

   C. Configures a DHCP server option that assigns the address 10.10.0.1 to a router on the 10.10.20.0 subnet

   D. Configures a DHCP scope option that assigns the address 10.10.0.1 to a router on the 10.10.20.0 subnet

Lesson 4: Configuring IPv6/IPv4 interoperability

An increasingly important part of the administrator's role is to prepare the organization's network for migration to Internet Protocol version 6 (IPv6). The reasons for this include the exponential growth of the Internet, the proliferation of mobile devices that need to be able to connect to the corporate network, and the impending exhaustion of the IPv4 address space.

Unfortunately, many administrators still lack an understanding of basic IPv6 concepts and the necessary skills. This lesson provides an overview of IPv6 concepts and technologies as they relate to Windows-based networks and describes how to implement several IPv6 transition technologies as part of an overall IPv6 migration plan.

After this lesson, you will be able to:

- Understand basic IPv6 concepts and terminology.
- Understand the dual IP layer architecture of the TCP/IP networking stack and how to disable IPv6 functionality.
- Understand how IPv6 addressing works and the different types of IPv6 addresses.
- Understand the different ways IPv6 addresses can be assigned, including manual addressing, stateless address autoconfiguration, and stateful address autoconfiguration.
- Configure a DHCPv6 server for stateless and stateful address autoconfiguration.
- Describe the different IPv6 transition technologies.
- Configure Intra-Site Automatic Tunnel Addressing Protocol (ISATAP).

Estimated lesson time: 30 minutes

IPv6 concepts and terminology

Although some IPv6 concepts and terminology are similar to those for IPv4, others are quite different. The following list is a brief summary of some of the important IPv6 terminology with which you should be familiar when you begin developing an IPv6 migration plan for your organization. Figure 6-9 illustrates how many of these concepts are interrelated. Additional IPv6 terminology is introduced later in this lesson when appropriate.

- **Node** A device that can be configured with an IPv6 address. Examples of nodes include hosts and routers.
- **Host** A node that can be either the source of or a destination for IPv6 traffic. Hosts are not able to forward IPv6 packets that are explicitly addressed to them. Instead, they silently discard such packets.
- **Router** A node that is able to forward IPv6 packets not explicitly addressed to itself. Routers advertise their presence on a network. They also advertise host configuration information.
- **Link** A collection of network interfaces that use the same 64-bit IPv6 unicast address prefix, which includes hosts but not routers. Links are bounded by routers and are also referred to as *network segments* or *subnets*.

- **Interface** A representation for how a node is attached to a link. An interface can be either of the following:
  - **Physical** For example, a network adapter in a server
  - **Logical** For example, a tunnel interface that encapsulates IPv6 packets inside an IPv4 header to send IPv6 traffic over an IPv4-only network
- **Address** An identifier that designates either the source of or destination for an IPv6 packet. IPv6 addresses are assigned at the IPv6 layer of an interface. The different types of IPv6 addresses are described later in this lesson.
- **Neighbors** Nodes connected to the same link. In IPv6, neighbors are able to detect and monitor reachability with one another by using a process called Neighbor Discovery.
- **Network** Two or more links connected by routers.
- **Site** An autonomously operated IPv6 network that is connected to the IPv6 Internet.

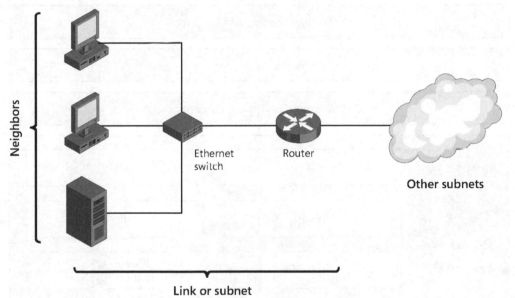

FIGURE 6-9 Review basic IPv6 networking concepts.

IPv6 and the TCP/IP protocol architecture

As Figure 6-10 illustrates, the TCP/IP protocol networking stack on the Microsoft Windows platform is implemented using a dual IP layer approach. This means, for example, that

- Only a single implementation of transport layer protocols—such as Transmission Control Protocol (TCP) and User Datagram Protocol (UDP)—is needed for both IPv4 and IPv6 communications.

- Only a single implementation of framing layer protocols—such as Ethernet (802.3), Point-to-Point Protocol (PPP), and mobile broadband (802.11)—is needed for both IPv4 and IPv6 communications.

This dual IP layer TCP/IP stack is implemented on the following Windows platforms:

- Windows 8.1
- Windows 8
- Windows 7
- Windows Vista
- Windows Server 2012 R2
- Windows Server 2012
- Windows Server 2008 R2
- Windows Server 2008

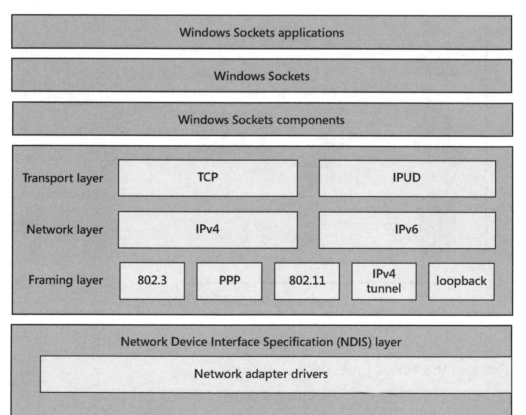

FIGURE 6-10 The TCP/IP protocol stack is implemented using a dual IP layer approach.

NOTE IPV6 ON WINDOWS PLATFORMS

Because IPv6 functionality is essentially the same on Windows 8.1, Windows 8, Windows 7, Windows Vista, Windows Server 2012 R2, Windows Server 2012, Windows Server 2008 R2, and Windows Server 2008, all information presented in the remainder of this lesson applies to these specific Windows platforms unless explicitly stated otherwise. IPv6 functionality in earlier Windows platforms, such as Windows XP and Windows 2003, is more limited and therefore is not covered in this lesson.

Default IPv6 functionality

On Windows platforms, IPv6 is installed by default and cannot be uninstalled because it is a fundamental component of Tcpip.sys, the TCP/IP driver file on these platforms. IPv6 is also enabled by default for all connections in the Network Connections folder on a Windows computer. To verify this, open the properties of a network connection, select the Networking tab, and check that Internet Protocol Version 6 (TCP/IPv6) is selected, as shown in Figure 6-11.

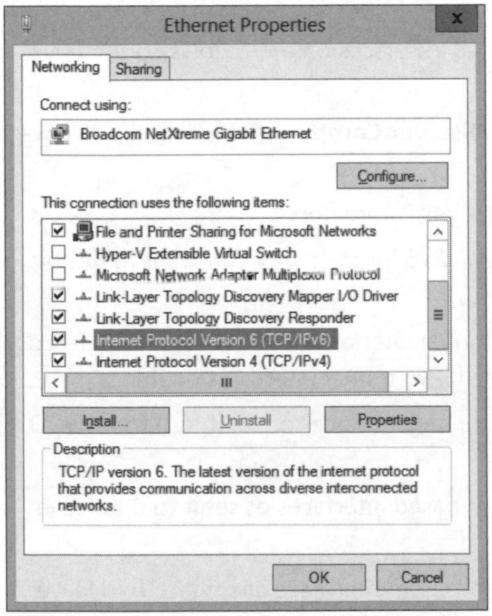

FIGURE 6-11 IPv6 is enabled by default on Windows Server 2012 and Windows Server 2012 R2.

IPv6 is also preferred over IPv4 for network communications by Windows computers. For example, if a DNS server returns both IPv4 and IPv6 addresses in response to a name query, Windows will first try to communicate with the remote host using IPv6. If this fails, Windows will then attempt to use IPv4.

Disabling IPv6

Although you cannot uninstall IPv6 on Windows platforms, you can disable it if desired. However, Microsoft does not recommend disabling IPv6 for the following reasons:

■ During the development of Windows platforms by Microsoft, services and applications were tested only with IPv6 enabled. As a result, Microsoft cannot predict the possible consequences of disabling IPv6 on Windows.

■ Some Windows features will not function if IPv6 is disabled. Examples of such features include DirectAccess and Remote Assistance.

By leaving IPv6 enabled, you ensure that your Windows computers are fully supported and that all network-enabled features can work as intended. However, if you decide you need to disable IPv6 on a Windows computer for some reason, there are several ways you can do this. For example, if you want to disable IPv6 for a specific local area network (LAN) interface on a Windows computer, you can do so by deselecting Internet Protocol Version 6 (TCP/IPv6) on the Networking tab of the connection's properties, as shown previously in Figure 6-11. Note, however, that performing this action does not disable IPv6 for either the loopback interface or any tunnel interfaces on the computer.

To disable specific types of IPv6 functionality for all interfaces on a Windows computer, perform the following steps:

1. Create a new DWORD registry value named **DisabledComponents** under the following registry key:

    HKLM\SYSTEM\CurrentControlSet\Services\tcpip6\Parameters\

2. Create an 8-bit binary that defines the types of IPv6 functionality you want to disable by using the following information:

    ■ **Bit 0** Set this bit to 1 to disable all IPv6 tunnel interfaces, including ISATAP, Teredo, 6to4, and IP-HTTPS, or set it to 0 to leave all IPv6 tunnel interfaces enabled.

    ■ **Bit 1** Set this bit to 1 to disable all 6to4 tunnel interfaces or set it to 0 to leave all 6to4 tunnel interfaces enabled.

    ■ **Bit 2** Set this bit to 1 to disable all ISATAP-based interfaces or set it to 0 to leave all ISATAP-based interfaces enabled.

    ■ **Bit 3** Set this bit to 1 to disable all Teredo-based interfaces or set it to 0 to leave all Teredo-based interfaces enabled.

    ■ **Bit 4** Set this bit to 1 to disable IPv6 for all nontunnel interfaces, including LAN and PPP interfaces, or set it to 0 to leave all nontunnel interfaces enabled.

    ■ **Bit 5** Set this bit to 1 to configure the default prefix table so that IPv4 is preferred over IPv6 when attempting to establish a network connection or set it to 0 to leave IPv6 as the preferred network layer protocol.

    ■ **Bit 6** Leave this bit set to 0 because it is reserved for future use.

    ■ **Bit 7** Set this bit to 1 to disable all IP-HTTPS-based interfaces or set it to 0 to leave all IP-HTTPS-based interfaces enabled.

3. Convert the binary number you created into hexadecimal form and assign it as the value for the DisabledComponents registry value. Remember that bit 7 is the leftmost bit and bit 0 is the rightmost bit of the binary number.

4. Restart the computer to have the changes take effect.

For example, say you want to disable both Teredo and 6to4 on a Windows computer but leave ISATAP and all other IPv6 functionality enabled. To do this, you need to assign values to bits 0 through 7 as follows:

- Bit 0   0
- Bit 1   1
- Bit 2   0
- Bit 3   1
- Bit 4   0
- Bit 5   0
- Bit 6   0
- Bit 7   0

The binary number 00001010 converted to hexadecimal form is 0xA, and this is the value you would assign to the DisabledComponents registry value.

> ✔ **Quick check**
>
> - What effect will the value 0x21 have when it is assigned to a newly created DisabledComponents registry value on a Windows computer?
>
> **Quick check answer**
>
> - The hexadecimal number 0x21 converted to binary form is 00100001, which means that bits 0 and 5 have the value 1. Assigning this value to the DisabledComponents registry value will do two things. First, it will cause IPv4 to be preferred over IPv6 when the computer attempts to establish network communications. Second, it will disable all IPv6 tunnel interfaces on the computer.

IPv6 addressing

In contrast to the 32-bit (4-byte) addresses used by the IPv4 protocol, IPv6 uses 128-bit (16-byte) addresses. Using addresses that are four times longer increases the theoretically usable address space from 232 addresses (approximately 4 billion addresses) to 2128 addresses (approximately 3.4 × 1038 addresses). The actual address space for IPv6 is smaller, however, because of the hierarchical way that IPv6 addresses are constructed. Specifically, each 128-bit IPv6 address consists of two parts:

- A 64-bit IPv6 prefix that indicates the address type, how packets containing the address should be routed, the subnet on which the interface having the address resides, or some combination of these types of information

- A 64-bit IPv6 interface identifier that identifies the interface on the subnet

IPv6 address representation

IPv4 addresses are usually represented in the familiar dotted-decimal form, such as 65.55.58.201, in which each number represents 8 bits of the 32-bit address. By contrast, the much longer IPv6 addresses are typically represented by dividing the 128-bit address into 16-bit (4-byte) segments. Each segment is then converted from binary format to a 4-bit hexadecimal number and these numbers are separated by using colons.

For example, when expressed in binary form, the following IPv6 address spans two lines of text on this page:

```
0010000000000001000011011011100000111111101010010000000000000000
0000000000000000000000000000000000000000110100111001110001011010
```

When converted into colon hexadecimal notation, the address is much shorter:

```
2001:0DB8:3FA9:0000:0000:0000:00D3:9C5A
```

The preceding address can be further compressed by suppressing leading zeros as follows:

```
2001:DB8:3FA9:0:0:0:D3:9C5A
```

Even further compression can be achieved by representing contiguous blocks of hexadecimal zeros as double colons as follows:

```
2001:DB8:3FA9::D3:9C5A
```

> **NOTE DOUBLE-COLON NOTATION**
> To ensure unambiguous representation, you can use only one double colon when representing an IPv6 address.

IPv6 prefixes

The first 64 bits of a 128-bit IPv6 address represent the IPv6 prefix for the address. An IPv6 prefix can be used to

- Specify the type of the IPv6 address.

- Define a summarized route.

- Indicate a subnet.

For example, the IPv6 prefix portion of the IPv6 address 2001:DB8:3FA9::D3:9C5A used in the previous section is 2001:DB8:3FA9:0.

IPv6 prefixes are expressed using an <address>/<prefix_length> format that is similar to the Classless Interdomain Routing (CIDR) notation used on IPv4 networks. The value of <prefix_length> can vary as follows:

- Subnets always have a prefix length of 64.
- Summarized routes always have a prefix length of less than 64.

For example, an IPv6 prefix of 2001:DB8:3FA9::/48 represents a summarized route.

IPv6 address types

IPv4 addresses can be unicast, multicast, or broadcast addresses. IPv6 addresses, by comparison, can be any of the following:

- **Unicast** This type of IPv6 address identifies a single interface within a region of an IPv6 network over which the address is unique.
- **Multicast** This type of IPv6 address identifies zero or more interfaces on the same host or different hosts and is used for one-to-many communications with delivery to multiple interfaces.
- **Anycast** This type of IPv6 address identifies multiple interfaces and is used for one-to-one-of-many communications with delivery to a single interface.

Unicast IPv6 addresses can be further categorized as one of the following:

- Global unicast addresses
- Link-local addresses
- Unique local addresses
- Special addresses
- Transition addresses

The sections that follow go into greater detail about unicast address types. Note that there are no broadcast addresses in IPv6. Instead, multicast addresses are used when broadcast functionality is required over a portion of an IPv6 network.

Global unicast addresses

Global unicast addresses are IPv6 addresses that are globally routable and therefore are reachable on the IPv6 Internet. Global unicast addresses for IPv6 are the equivalent of public addresses for IPv4.

A global unicast address is always structured as follows:

- The first 3 bits of the address are always 001 in binary format.
- The next 45 bits represent the global routing prefix for the organization's site. Taken with the three predefined high-order bits, they define the 48-bit site prefix, which

routers on the IPv6 Internet use to identify IPv6 packets that should be forwarded to the routers of the organization's site.

- The next 16 bits are used to identify the subnet within the site. Because 16 bits are available for defining subnets, each site can have up to 216, or 65,536, subnets.

- The final 64 bits specify the interface on the indicated subnet within the site.

> **NOTE INTERFACES VS. NODES**
>
> IPv6 unicast addresses always indicate interfaces (not nodes) on an IPv6 network.

Link-local addresses

Link-local addresses are IPv6 addresses that are used whenever a node needs to communicate with a neighbor (another node on the same link). For example, if a site has no routers and therefore only one subnet, all network communications between hosts can take place using link-local addresses.

On Windows platforms, IPv6 link-local addresses are always configured automatically on all interfaces even if no other unicast IPv6 addresses are configured. The IPv4 equivalents to these addresses are IPv4 link-local addresses, which are addresses in the range 169.254.0.0/16 that are dynamically configured on interfaces when no Dynamic Host Configuration Protocol (DHCP) server is available. On Windows platforms, IPv4 link-local addresses are assigned using Automatic Private IP Addressing (APIPA).

A link-local address is always structured as follows:

- The first 64 bits are always 11111110 10000000 00000000 00000000 in binary format. This means that a link-local address always begins with FE80 and has a prefix identifier of FE80::/64.

- The final 64 bits specify the interface on the local link.

> **NOTE LINK-LOCAL ADDRESSES AND ROUTERS**
>
> IPv6 routers never forward packets addressed to link-local addresses beyond the local link.

Unique local addresses

Unique local addresses are IPv6 addresses that are private to an organization in the same way that private addresses—such as 10.x.x.x, 192.168.x.x, or 172.16.0.0 - 172.31.255.255—can be used on an IPv4 network. Unique local addresses therefore are not routable on the IPv6 Internet in the same way that an address like 10.20.100.55 is not routable on the IPv4 Internet.

A unique local address is always structured as follows:

- The first 8 bits are always 11111101 in binary format. This means that a unique local address always begins with FD and has a prefix identifier of FD00::/8.

- The next 40 bits represent the global identifier, which represents a specific site within the organization. This global identifier is randomly generated.

- The next 16 bits are used to identify the subnet within the site. Because 16 bits are available for defining subnets, each site can have up to 216, or 65,536, subnets.

- The final 64 bits specify the interface on the indicated subnet within the site.

Special addresses

The following two addresses have special significance in IPv6:

- The address 0:0:0:0:0:0:0:0, which is commonly represented as a double colon (::), indicates the absence of an IPv6 address. The IPv4 equivalent to this address is 0.0.0.0.

- The loopback address 0:0:0:0:0:0:0:1, which is commonly represented as ::1, is assigned to the loopback interface on a node. The loopback address is used whenever a node needs to send a packet to itself. The IPv4 equivalent to this address is 127.0.0.1.

Transition addresses

Transition addresses are IPv6 addresses used by IPv6 transition technologies such as ISATAP, Teredo, and 6to4. Transition addresses enable the coexistence of IPv4 and IPv6 hosts on the same network. IPv6 transition technologies are described in more detail later in this lesson.

Multicast addresses

Multicasting on IPv6 networks works essentially the same way that it does on IPv4 networks. An IPv6 multicast address always begins with 11111111 or FF and includes additional structure that identifies the scope of the address and the multicast group to which the interface belongs. IPv6 multicast addresses therefore are always of the form FF00::/8. In comparison, IPv4 multicast addresses are always of the form 224.0.0.0/4.

As indicated earlier in this lesson, IPv6 does not have broadcast addresses and instead uses certain multicast addresses whenever some form of broadcast functionality is required. Examples of this usage include the following multicast addresses:

- **FF01::1** This address is an all-nodes multicast address that has interface-local scope.

- **FF02::1** This address is an all-nodes multicast address that has link-local scope.

- **FF01::2** This address is an all-routers multicast address that has interface-local scope.

- **FF02::2** This address is an all-routers multicast address that has link-local scope.

- **FF05::2** This address is an all-routers multicast address that has site-local scope.

For example, the equivalent of IPv6 address FF02::1 on an IPv4 network is 255.255.255.255.

IPv6 address assignment

On IPv4 networks, you can assign addresses to interfaces in three ways: manually by using static addresses, dynamically by using DHCP, or automatically by using APIPA. Administrators of small networks often configure IPv4 addresses manually, and midsize to large organizations usually use DHCP. Automatic address configuration using APIPA is usually done only on very small networks, such as a home or office LAN that connects to the Internet using a DSL router.

Address assignment on IPv6 networks is somewhat different. IPv6 addresses can be assigned to an interface by doing the following:

- Manually configuring one or more IPv6 addresses on the interface
- Stateful address autoconfiguration using a DHCPv6 server
- Stateless address autoconfiguration based on the receipt of Router Advertisement messages
- Both stateful and stateless address autoconfiguration

In addition, a link-local address is always automatically configured on an interface regardless of whether stateful or stateless address autoconfiguration is being used.

The main difference, however, between address assignment in IPv6 and in IPv4 is that the IPv6 protocol was designed to be autoconfiguring. This means that in most cases, you will neither need to assign addresses manually nor deploy a DHCPv6 server; instead, you can use stateless address autoconfiguration for most of your network hosts. This means that in contrast to physical interfaces (network adapters) on IPv4 hosts, which are usually single-homed (have only a single address assigned), most physical interfaces on IPv6 hosts are multihomed (have multiple addresses assigned). Specifically, a physical IPv6 interface usually has at least two addresses:

- An automatically generated link-local address, which is used for traffic on the local link
- An additional unicast address (either a global address or a unique local address), which is used for traffic that needs to be routed beyond the local link

Manual address assignment

Manual assignment of IPv6 addresses is generally done only in two scenarios:

- For certain servers on your network
- On most router interfaces

On a computer running Windows Server 2012 or Windows Server 2012 R2, you can manually configure an IPv6 address using any of the following methods:

- By opening the Internet Protocol Version 6 (TCP/IPv6) Properties dialog box from the properties of an interface in the Network Connection folder and configuring the IPv6 address, subnet prefix length, default gateway, and DNS server addresses as shown in Figure 6-12
- By using the New-NetIPAddress and Set-DnsClientServerAddress cmdlets of Windows PowerShell
- By using commands from the netsh interface ipv6 context of the Netsh.exe command-line utility

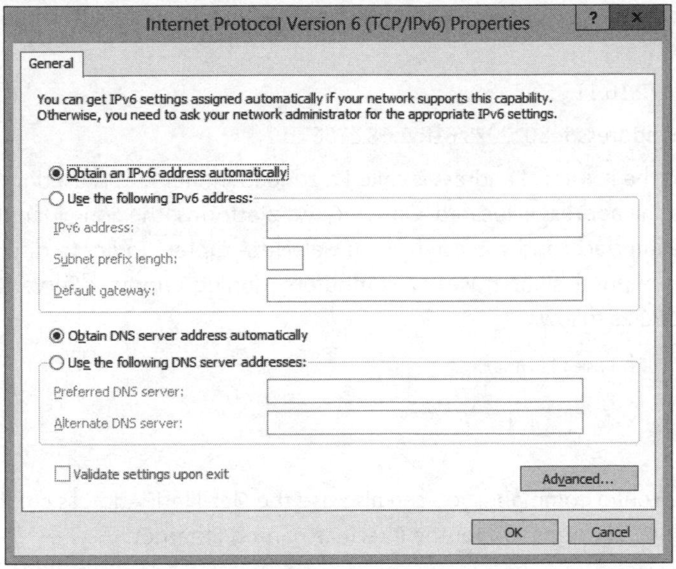

FIGURE 6-12 Manually configure an IPv6 address in Windows Server 2012 or Windows Server 2012 R2.

The following is an example of using Windows PowerShell to manually configure an IPv6 address on a physical interface of a computer running Windows Server 2012 or Windows Server 2012 R2. First, here is the output from running the Ipconfig command on the server:

```
PS C:\> ipconfig

Windows IP Configuration

Ethernet adapter Ethernet:

   Connection-specific DNS Suffix  . :
   Link-local IPv6 Address . . . . . : fe80::2025:61fb:b68:c266%12
   IPv4 Address. . . . . . . . . . . : 172.16.11.75
   Subnet Mask . . . . . . . . . . . : 255.255.255.0
   Default Gateway . . . . . . . . . : 172.16.11.1

Tunnel adapter isatap.{DD59BFFD-706A-4685-9073-647788046335}:

   Media State . . . . . . . . . . . : Media disconnected
   Connection-specific DNS Suffix  . :

Tunnel adapter Teredo Tunneling Pseudo-Interface:

   Media State . . . . . . . . . . . : Media disconnected
   Connection-specific DNS Suffix  . :
```

From the preceding command, you can see that the physical interface named Ethernet has two addresses assigned:

- The IPv4 address 172.16.11.75
- The link-local IPv6 address fe80::2025:61fb:b68:c266%12

The %12 appended to the link-local address is called a zone identifier and is used to specify the link on which the address is located. On Windows platforms, the zone identifier is equal to the index of the interface, and you can use the Get-NetAdapter cmdlet to display a list of names and indexes of physical interfaces on computers running Windows Server 2012 or Windows Server 2012 R2 as follows:

```
PS C:\> Get-NetAdapter | fl Name,ifIndex

Name    : Ethernet
ifIndex : 12
```

Instead of using the Ipconfig command, you can also use the Get-NetIPAddress cmdlet as follows to display the address information for the interface named Ethernet:

```
PS C:\> Get-NetIPAddress | where {$_.InterfaceAlias -eq "Ethernet"}

IPAddress          : fe80::2025:61fb:b68:c266%12
InterfaceIndex     : 12
InterfaceAlias     : Ethernet
AddressFamily      : IPv6
Type               : Unicast
PrefixLength       : 64
PrefixOrigin       : WellKnown
SuffixOrigin       : Link
AddressState       : Preferred
ValidLifetime      : Infinite ([TimeSpan]::MaxValue)
PreferredLifetime  : Infinite ([TimeSpan]::MaxValue)
SkipAsSource       : False
PolicyStore        : ActiveStore

IPAddress          : 172.16.11.75
InterfaceIndex     : 12
InterfaceAlias     : Ethernet
AddressFamily      : IPv4
Type               : Unicast
PrefixLength       : 24
PrefixOrigin       : Manual
SuffixOrigin       : Manual
AddressState       : Preferred
ValidLifetime      : Infinite ([TimeSpan]::MaxValue)
PreferredLifetime  : Infinite ([TimeSpan]::MaxValue)
SkipAsSource       : False
PolicyStore        : ActiveStore
```

Note how the preceding cmdlet output is more informative than the output from the Ipconfig command.

You can use the NewNetIPAddress cmdlet to assign a new global unicast IPv6 address with prefix length 64 and also a default gateway address to the Ethernet interface as follows:

```
PS C:\> New-NetIPAddress -InterfaceAlias "Ethernet" -IPAddress 2001:DB8:3FA9::D3:9C5A `
-PrefixLength 64 -DefaultGateway 2001:DB8:3FA9::0C01

IPAddress          : 2001:db8:3fa9::d3:9c5a
InterfaceIndex     : 12
InterfaceAlias     : Ethernet
AddressFamily      : IPv6
Type               : Unicast
PrefixLength       : 64
PrefixOrigin       : Manual
SuffixOrigin       : Manual
AddressState       : Tentative
ValidLifetime      : Infinite ([TimeSpan]::MaxValue)
PreferredLifetime  : Infinite ([TimeSpan]::MaxValue)
SkipAsSource       : False
PolicyStore        : ActiveStore

IPAddress          : 2001:db8:3fa9::d3:9c5a
InterfaceIndex     : 12
InterfaceAlias     : Ethernet
AddressFamily      : IPv6
Type               : Unicast
PrefixLength       : 64
PrefixOrigin       : Manual
SuffixOrigin       : Manual
AddressState       : Invalid
ValidLifetime      : Infinite ([TimeSpan]::MaxValue)
PreferredLifetime  : Infinite ([TimeSpan]::MaxValue)
SkipAsSource       : False
PolicyStore        : PersistentStore
```

To verify the result, you can use the Get-NetIPAddress cmdlet with the *–AddressFamily* parameter to display only IPv6 addressing information as follows:

```
PS C:\> Get-NetIPAddress -AddressFamily IPv6 | where {$_.InterfaceAlias -eq "Ethernet"}

IPAddress          : fe80::2025:61fb:b68:c266%12
InterfaceIndex     : 12
InterfaceAlias     : Ethernet
AddressFamily      : IPv6
Type               : Unicast
PrefixLength       : 64
PrefixOrigin       : WellKnown
SuffixOrigin       : Link
AddressState       : Preferred
ValidLifetime      : Infinite ([TimeSpan]::MaxValue)
PreferredLifetime  : Infinite ([TimeSpan]::MaxValue)
SkipAsSource       : False
PolicyStore        : ActiveStore

IPAddress          : 2001:db8:3fa9::d3:9c5a
InterfaceIndex     : 12
```

```
InterfaceAlias     : Ethernet
AddressFamily      : IPv6
Type               : Unicast
PrefixLength       : 64
PrefixOrigin       : Manual
SuffixOrigin       : Manual
AddressState       : Preferred
ValidLifetime      : Infinite ([TimeSpan]::MaxValue)
PreferredLifetime  : Infinite ([TimeSpan]::MaxValue)
SkipAsSource       : False
PolicyStore        : ActiveStore
```

The interface is now multihomed because it has one link-local IPv6 address and one global IPv6 address. Opening the Internet Protocol Version 6 (TCP/IPv6) Properties dialog box displays the expected manually configured address information, as shown in Figure 6-13.

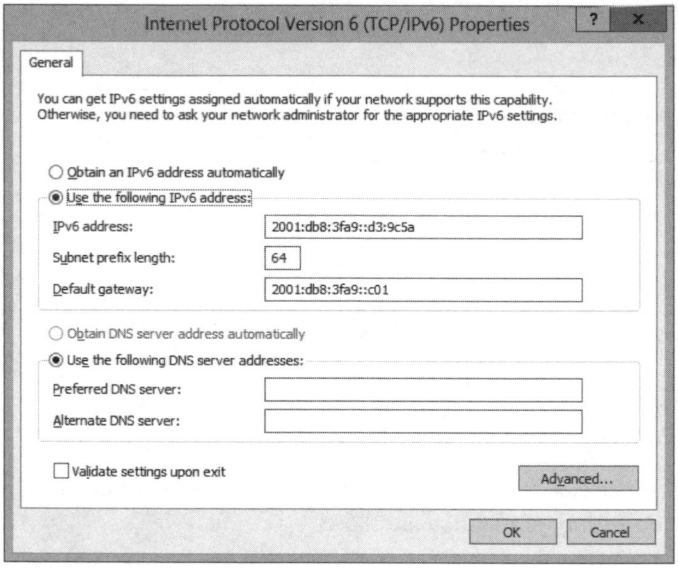

FIGURE 6-13 Verify IPv6 address settings configured using Windows PowerShell.

To configure preferred and alternate DNS servers for this interface, use the Set-DnsClientServerAddress cmdlet. For more information on Net TCP/IP and DNS client cmdlets, see the following TechNet Library pages:

- *http://technet.microsoft.com/en-us/library/hh826123.aspx*
- *http://technet.microsoft.com/en-us/library/jj590772.aspx*

Stateless address autoconfiguration

Stateless address autoconfiguration is one of the most valuable aspects of IPv6 because it enables IPv6 nodes to communicate on a network without the need to manually assign addresses to them or deploy a DHCP server. The automatic assignment of link-local addresses to interfaces on an IPv6 host is one example of stateless address autoconfiguration at work, and it enables hosts on the same link to communicate with one another. This type of address autoconfiguration is called *stateless* because it does not make use of an address configuration protocol such as DHCP.

Another example of stateless address configuration at work is when an IPv6 host uses router discovery to automatically configure additional addresses, such as global or unicast local addresses, a default gateway address, and other IPv6 configuration parameters. What typically happens is this:

1. The host (which here is a computer running Windows Server 2012 or Windows Server 2012 R2) sends out a Router Solicitation message to request a Router Advertisement message from any router listening on the host's link.

2. A router (either an IPv6 router or an ISATAP router) on the host's link responds to the host's message by sending a Router Advertisement message to the host.

3. The host uses the information in the Router Advertisement message to assign a tentative address to the host along with any additional settings specified. IPv6 addresses that have been autoconfigured can be in any of the following states:

   - **Tentative**   The address still needs to be verified as unique by performing duplicate address detection. Tentative addresses cannot receive unicast traffic until they have been verified as valid.

   - **Valid**   The address is unique. A valid address is also either preferred or deprecated.

   - **Preferred**   The address is valid and therefore can be used for sending or receiving unicast traffic.

   - **Deprecated**   The address is valid and therefore can be used for sending or receiving unicast traffic, but it should not be used to initiate any new communication.

   - **Invalid**   The address can no longer be used for sending or receiving unicast traffic.

4. The time during which an address is in a particular state is determined by information provided by the router.

> *NOTE* **ADDRESS AUTOCONFIGURATION IS NOT FOR ROUTERS**
>
> Apart from configuring link-local addresses, address autoconfiguration is used only to assign addresses to hosts. Addresses for routers must be configured using a different method, such as manual address assignment.

Stateful address autoconfiguration

Stateful address autoconfiguration is based on the use of an address-resolution protocol. On IPv4 networks, DHCP is such a protocol and it can be used for dynamically assigning IP addresses and other configuration settings to interfaces on hosts. The infrastructure for DHCP consists of DHCP servers, DHCP clients, and DHCP relay agents that can relay DHCP messages between clients and servers on different subnets.

The IPv6 version of this protocol is called DHCPv6, and it uses a similar infrastructure of DHCPv6 servers, DHCPv6 clients, and DHCPv6 relay agents. However, DHCPv6 can provide IPv6 hosts with both stateful address configuration and stateless address configuration settings. This can be a problem because it can result in additional addresses being assigned to hosts, but you can prevent this by configuring your IPv6 routers appropriately so that hosts are assigned only stateful addresses by DHCPv6 servers.

One reason for deploying a DHCPv6 server on an IPv6 network is because Windows does not support stateless address autoconfiguration of DNS server settings using Router Advertisement messages. This means that a DHCPv6 server is required if your Windows computers need to be able to perform DNS name resolution using IPv6.

DHCPv6 client software is built into the following versions of Windows:

- Windows 8.1
- Windows 8
- Windows 7
- Windows Vista
- Windows Server 2012 R2
- Windows Server 2012
- Windows Server 2008 R2
- Windows Server 2008

Configuring a DHCPv6 server

The DHCP Server service in the following versions of Windows Server supports both stateful and stateless address autoconfiguration through DHCPv6:

- Windows Server 2012 R2
- Windows Server 2012
- Windows Server 2008 R2
- Windows Server 2008

You can configure a computer running Windows Server 2012 or Windows Server 2012 R2 as either a DHCPv6 stateless server or a DHCPv6 stateful server by performing the following steps:

1. Begin by installing the DHCP Server role on your server.
2. Assign static IPv6 addresses to the DHCPv6 server interfaces that will be listening for incoming DHCPv6 request messages.
3. Open the DHCP snap-in and expand the IPv6 node beneath the server node.

4. To configure DHCPv6 options for stateless address autoconfiguration, right-click the Server Options node beneath the IPv6 node and select Configure Options as shown here:

Then configure the DHCPv6 server options as desired. For example, you could configure option 23 DNS Recursive Name Server IPv6 Address List as shown here:

5. To configure DHCPv6 options for stateful address autoconfiguration, right-click the IPv6 node and select New Scope as shown here:

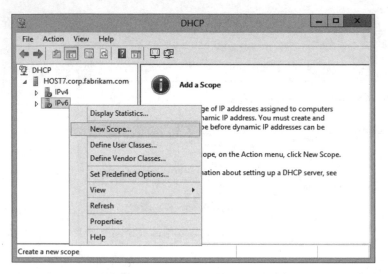

Then use the New Scope Wizard to specify a name and description for the scope, an IPv6 subnet prefix, and the other information required.

IPv6 transition technologies

The ultimate goal of IPv6 is for IPv4 to eventually be retired and all nodes on all TCP/IP networks to use only IPv6. However, such a goal might take years, or even decades, to achieve. In the meantime, IPv4 and IPv6 nodes must be able to interoperate on the same network so that communications will not be disrupted, and IPv6 transition technologies make this possible. Windows platforms can be used to implement the following IPv6 transition technologies:

- **ISATAP**   This transition technology enables IPv6/IPv4 nodes on an IPv4-only intranet to use IPv6 to communicate with each other and across the IPv6 Internet.

- **6to4**   This transition technology provides automatic tunneling that enables IPv6/IPv4 hosts to establish IPv6 connectivity with each other across the IPv4 Internet. However, implementing 6to4 requires that the edge device (router) use a public IPv4 address.

- **Teredo**   This transition technology provides automatic tunneling that enables IPv6/IPv4 hosts to establish IPv6 connectivity with each other across the IPv4 Internet even when IPv4 network address translation (NAT) devices need to be traversed. Because of this capability, Teredo is more suitable than 6to4 for small office/home office (SOHO) environments that use NATs to hide their private IPv4 addresses from the Internet.

In addition, Windows platforms support the following IPv6-to-IPv4 traffic translation technologies:

- **NAT64**   This technology is used to enable IPv6-only nodes to access IPv4-only hosts. The DirectAccess features of Windows Server 2012 and Windows Server 2012 R2 use

NAT64 to enable DirectAccess clients (which act as IPv6-only nodes) to access hosts on an IPv4 corporate network.

- **DNS64**   This technology is used to map IPv6-only address record (AAAA) name queries to IPv4 address record (A) name queries. Using DNS64 with NAT64 enables IPv6 nodes to initiate communication with IPv4-only nodes with no changes to either node.

- **PortProxy**   This technology enables IPv4/IPv6 TCP traffic to be proxied to IPv4/IPv6 TCP traffic at a different address. The technology is useful when nodes cannot communicate using either IPv4 or IPv6.

The following section describes one of these transition technologies (ISATAP) in more detail.

ISATAP

ISATAP enables unicast communication between IPv6/IPv4 hosts across the IPv4-only Internet. ISATAP works by encapsulating IPv6 packets with an IPv4 header so that the IPv6 packet can be sent over an IPv4-only network. This approach is called IPv6-over-IPv4 tunneling, and ISATAP uses automatic tunneling that does not require any manual configuration.

ISATAP addresses

ISATAP addresses are assigned by ISATAP hosts to their ISATAP tunnel interfaces. An ISATAP address consists of a valid 64-bit unicast address prefix and a 64-bit interface identifier. The interface identify can be either ::0:5efe:w.x.y.z or ::200:5efe:w.x.y.z, where *w.x.y.z* is either a private or public IPv4 address, respectively.

On Windows platforms, IPv6 automatically creates a separate ISATAP tunneling interface for each LAN interface that has a unique DNS suffix. A link-local ISATAP address is then automatically configured on these ISATAP interfaces to enable IPv6 communication over an IPv4-only network without the need to assign global or unique local ISATAP addresses to the interfaces.

In Windows Server 2012 and Windows Server 2012 R2, you can use the Get-NetIPInterface cmdlet to list the interfaces on the computer (the command output has been truncated for display reasons):

```
PS C:\> Get-NetIPInterface -AddressFamily IPv6

ifIndex InterfaceAlias               NlMtu(Bytes) InterfaceMetric ConnectionState
------- ---------------              ------------ --------------- ---------------
12      Ethernet                             1500               5 Connected
14      Teredo Tunneling Pseudo-Inte...      1280              50 Disconnected
13      isatap.{DD59BFFD-706A-4685-9...      1280              50 Disconnected
1       Loopback Pseudo-Interface 1    4294967295              50 Connected
```

From the preceding output, you can see that the index number of the ISATAP interface is 13, which allows you to display more detailed information about the interface as follows:

```
PS C:\> Get-NetIPInterface -AddressFamily IPv6 -ifIndex 13 | fl
```

```
InterfaceIndex                      : 13
InterfaceAlias                      : isatap.{DD59BFFD-706A-4685-9073-647788046335}
AddressFamily                       : IPv6
Forwarding                          : Disabled
Advertising                         : Disabled
NlMtu(Bytes)                        : 1280
AutomaticMetric                     : Enabled
InterfaceMetric                     : 50
NeighborDiscoverySupported          : Yes
NeighborUnreachabilityDetection     : Disabled
BaseReachableTime(ms)               : 30000
ReachableTime(ms)                   : 23000
RetransmitTime(ms)                  : 1000
DadTransmits                        : 0
RouterDiscovery                     : Enabled
ManagedAddressConfiguration         : Disabled
OtherStatefulConfiguration          : Disabled
WeakHostSend                        : Disabled
WeakHostReceive                     : Disabled
IgnoreDefaultRoutes                 : Disabled
AdvertisedRouterLifetime            : 00:30:00
AdvertiseDefaultRoute               : Disabled
CurrentHopLimit                     : 0
ForceArpNdWolPattern                : Disabled
DirectedMacWolPattern               : Disabled
EcnMarking                          : AppDecide
Dhcp                                : Disabled
ConnectionState                     : Disconnected
PolicyStore                         : ActiveStore
```

ISATAP components

As shown in Figure 6-14, an ISATAP infrastructure includes the following components:

- **ISATAP subnets**   An ISATAP subnet is a portion of an IPv4-only network on which ISATAP will be used for IPv6-over-IPv4 tunneling.

- **ISATAP hosts**   An ISATAP host has an ISATAP tunneling interface, which it can use to communicate with other ISATAP hosts on the same ISATAP subnet. Windows computers can function as ISATAP hosts using link-local, unique local, or global ISATAP addresses.

- **ISATAP routers**   An ISATAP router is used to enable communication between ISATAP hosts on an ISATAP subnet and IPv6 hosts on an IPv6-capable network. Computers running Windows Server 2012 or Windows Server 2012 R2 can function as ISATAP routers by configuring their LAN interfaces with appropriate IPv6 addresses, routes, and other settings.

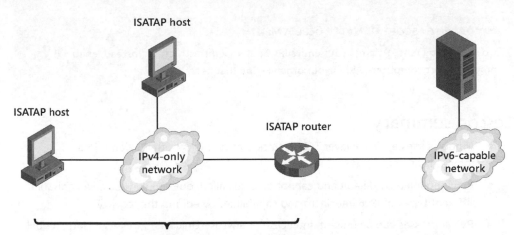

FIGURE 6-14 Review the components of an ISATAP deployment.

You can configure a Windows computer to use an ISATAP router in the following ways:

- By using Group Policy, as shown in Figure 6-15
- By using the Set-NetIsatapConfiguration cmdlet
- By using the Netsh interface isatap set router command

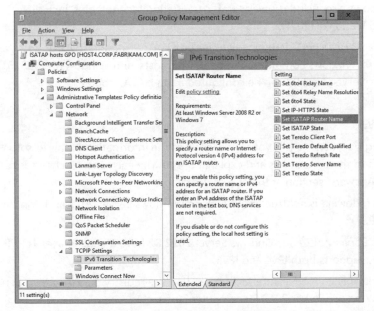

FIGURE 6-15 Configure a Windows computer to use an ISATAP router by using Group Policy settings.

Lesson summary

- Windows uses a dual IP layer TCP/IP stack that supports both IPv4 and IPv6 communications.
- IPv6 is enabled by default and cannot be uninstalled, but you can selectively disable different types of IPv6 interfaces and capabilities by editing the registry.
- IPv6 addresses can be unicast, multicast, or anycast. Unicast addresses include global, link-local, unique local, special, and transition addresses.
- You can often determine the type of an IPv6 address by its prefix.
- You can assign IPv6 addresses manually or by using stateless or stateful address autoconfiguration.
- You can configure Windows Server 2012 and Windows Server 2012 R2 as a stateless or stateful DHCPv6 server.
- Windows includes several IPv6 transition technologies, including ISATAP, 6to4, and Teredo. Windows also includes several traffic translation technologies, including NAT64, DNS64, and PortProxy.
- The components of an ISATAP deployment include ISATAP subnets, ISATAP hosts, and ISATAP routers. Windows computers can be ISATAP hosts, and Windows Server 2012 and Windows Server 2012 R2 can be configured as an ISATAP router.

Lesson review

Answer the following questions to test your knowledge of the information in this lesson. You can find the answers to these questions and explanations of why each answer choice is correct or incorrect in the "Answers" section at the end of this chapter.

1. Which of the following is *not* true about IPv6 on Windows Server 2012 and Windows Server 2012 R2?

   A. Windows Server 2012 and Windows Server 2012 R2 have a dual IP layer TCP/IP stack that supports both IPv4 and IPv6.

   B. You can disable IPv6 on all interfaces by editing the registry on a Windows Server 2012 or Windows Server 2012 R2 computer.

   C. You can use Windows Server 2012 and Windows Server 2012 R2 as a DHCPv6 server for stateless address autoconfiguration.

   D. You can use Windows Server 2012 and Windows Server 2012 R2 as an ISATAP router.

2. The IPv6 address assigned to an interface has a prefix identifier of FE80::/64. What type of address is it?

   A. Global address

   B. Unique local address

   C. Link-local address

   D. Multicast address

3. Which Windows PowerShell cmdlet can you use to display the address information for an interface?

   A. Ipconfig

   B. Get-NetAdapter

   C. Get-NetIPAddress

   D. Get-NetIPInterface

4. What do you need to do or use for Windows computers on an IPv4-only network to be able to communicate with Windows computers on a different network that is IPv6-capable?

   A. You need to do nothing because Windows computers automatically assign IPv6 addresses to their LAN interfaces using stateless address autoconfiguration.

   B. You need to deploy Windows Server 2012 or Windows Server 2012 R2 as an ISATAP router and use it to forward traffic between the IPv4-only and IPv6-capable networks.

   C. You need to deploy Windows Server 2012 or Windows Server 2012 R2 as a Teredo server and use it to forward traffic between the IPv4-only and IPv6-capable networks.

   D. You need to deploy Windows Server 2012 or Windows Server 2012 R2 as a DHCPv6 server and use it to assign global IPv6 addresses to the computers on the IPv4-only network.

Practice exercises

The goal of this section is to provide you with hands-on practice with the following:

- Implementing DHCP failover using Windows PowerShell
- Configuring a caching-only DNS server using Windows PowerShell

To perform the following exercises, you need at least two installations of Windows Server 2012 R2 that were deployed using the Server With A GUI installation option. The first server should be the first domain controller in the forest root domain corp.contoso.com and should have the DNS Server role installed and configured in the default manner using Active Directory–integrated zones. The second server should be a member server in the contoso .com domain and have no server roles installed. Both servers should have static IP addresses assigned and have Internet connectivity. You should be logged on interactively to each server using a user account that is a member of the Domain Admins group.

You also need one workstation running Windows Vista, Windows 7, Windows 8 or Windows 8.1. The workstation should be a stand-alone computer that belongs to a workgroup. The workstation should have its IP address assigned dynamically using DHCP or Automatic Private IP Addressing (APIPA). You should be logged on interactively to the workstation using a user account that is a member of local Administrators group on the computer. The workstation should be turned off until you are instructed to turn it on.

For the purposes of these exercises, the name of the first server is assumed to be SERVER1, the second server is SERVER2, and the workstation is CLIENT1. In addition, the IP addresses of SERVER1 and SERVER 2 are assumed to be 10.10.0.1 and 10.10.0.2, respectively. If your computers or domains are named differently or if you have different IP addresses assigned to your servers, you should modify the steps in these exercises accordingly.

Exercise 1: Implementing DHCP failover using Windows PowerShell

In this exercise, you ensure DHCP availability for clients in the corp.contoso.com domain by using Windows PowerShell to install the DHCP Server role on both servers, create a scope on SERVER1, and configure and verify DHCP failover.

1. Log on to SERVER1, open Server Manager, select the All Servers page, and make sure that both servers are displayed in the Servers tile. If SERVER2 is not displayed, add it to the server pool.

2. Open a Windows PowerShell prompt and run the following command to install the DHCP Server role on both servers:

   ```
   Invoke-Command -ComputerName SERVER1,SERVER2 -ScriptBlock `
   {Install-WindowsFeature -Name DHCP -IncludeManagementTools -Restart}
   ```

   Note that although you specified the *–Restart* parameter, the servers did not restart after role installation because a restart was determined to be unnecessary.

3. Authorize both DHCP servers in Active Directory by executing the following commands:

   ```
   Add-DhcpServerInDC -DnsName SERVER1
   Add-DhcpServerInDC -DnsName SERVER2
   ```

4. Use the Get-DhcpServerInDC cmdlet to verify that the servers have been authorized in Active Directory.

5. Create a new scope on SERVER1 and activate the scope by running the following command:

   ```
   Add-DhcpServerv4Scope -ComputerName SERVER1 -StartRange 10.10.0.50 `
   -EndRange 10.10.0.100 -Name "corp clients" -SubnetMask 255.255.0.0 -State Active
   ```

6. Use the Get-DhcpServerv4Scope cmdlet to verify that the new scope has been created on SERVER1 and is active.

7. Use **Get-DhcpServerv4Scope –ComputerName SERVER2** to verify that SERVER 2 currently has no scopes on it.

8. Run the following command to create a DHCP failover relationship in load-balance mode between the two servers with SERVER 2 as the partner server and failover implemented for the newly created scope:

```
Add-DhcpServerv4Failover -Name "SERVER1 to SERVER2" -ScopeId 10.10.0.0 `
-PartnerServer SERVER2 -ComputerName SERVER1 -LoadBalancePercent 50 `
-AutoStateTransition $true
```

9. Use the Get-DhcpServerv4Failover cmdlet to view the properties of the new failover relationship.

10. Use **Get-DhcpServerv4Scope –ComputerName SERVER2** to verify that the scope has been replicated from SERVER1 to SERVER2.

11. Turn on CLIENT1 and log on to the client computer.

12. Open a command prompt and use the **ipconfig** command to view the current IP address of the computer. If the client computer is currently using an address in the APIPA range (169.254.x.y), use **ipconfig /renew** to acquire an address from a DHCP server on your network. Verify that the address acquired comes from the scope you created earlier.

13. Verify that the client computer's address is recorded as leased in the DHCP database of SERVER1 by executing the following command:

```
Get-DhcpServerv4Lease -ComputerName SERVER1 -ScopeId 10.10.0.0
```

14. Verify that the client computer's address is recorded as leased in the DHCP database of SERVER2 by executing the following command:

```
Get-DhcpServerv4Lease -ComputerName SERVER2 -ScopeId 10.10.0.0
```

Exercise 2: Configuring a caching-only DNS server using Windows PowerShell

In this exercise, you configure a caching-only DNS server using Windows PowerShell. You then configure a forwarder on your caching-only DNS server to improve its name-resolution performance.

1. Log on to SERVER1, open Server Manager, select the All Servers page, and make sure that both servers are displayed in the Servers tile. If SERVER2 is not displayed, add it to the server pool.

2. Open a Windows PowerShell prompt and run the following command to install the DNS Server role on SERVER2:

```
Install-WindowsFeature -Name DNS -ComputerName SERVER2 -IncludeManagementTools
-Restart
```

Note that although you specified the *–Restart* parameter, the servers did not restart after role installation because a restart was determined to be unnecessary.

3. SERVER2 is now configured as a caching-only DNS server. It is not authoritative for any domains and can only perform queries, cache the answers, and return the results. Caching-only DNS servers can be useful at locations such as branch-office sites and use root hints to identify the authoritative DNS servers for the root zone of your organization's DNS namespace.

4. SERVER2 is currently using root hints for recursively performing name resolution. To view the root hints configured on SERVER2, run the following command:

```
Get-DnsServerRootHint -ComputerName SERVER2
```

5. Display the contents of the DNS server cache on SERVER2 by running the following command:

```
Show-DnsServerCache -ComputerName SERVER2
```

6. Use the nslookup command-line utility to attempt to use SERVER2 for resolving the IP address for the fully qualified domain name (FQDN) www.bing.com as follows:

```
nslookup www.bing.com SERVER2
```

7. Note that one or more DNS server timeouts might occur when you perform this name query. This is because name resolution is being performed recursively, beginning with the root name servers on the Internet, which can take several seconds to complete. If no response is received to your query, repeat running the preceding command until a nonauthoritative response is received.

8. Use the command **Show-DnsServerCache –ComputerName SERVER2** and note that the DNS server cache now contains numerous entries relating to the name query you performed using nslookup.

9. Clear the DNS server cache on SERVER2 by running the following command:

```
Clear-DnsServerCache -ComputerName SERVER2
```

10. Display the contents of the DNS server cache on SERVER2 again by running this command:

```
Show-DnsServerCache -ComputerName SERVER2
```

11. Note that the cache entries relating to the name query you performed using nslookup have now been deleted. The only entries that remain in the cache are those for the root hints configured on the server.

12. To speed up name resolution on your caching-only name server, configure SERVER1 as a forwarder on SERVER2. After you do this, any name query sent to SERVER2 will be forwarded to SERVER1, which will then use its external forwarders at your Internet Service Provider (ISP) for resolving the query.

13. Configure SERVER1 as a forwarder on SERVER2 by running the following command:

```
Add-DnsServerForwarder -IPAddress 10.10.0.1 -ComputerName SERVER2
```

14. Verify the result by displaying the forwarders configured on SERVER2 as follows:

```
Get-DnsServerForwarder -ComputerName SERVER2
```

15. Use nslookup to perform another name query against SERVER2 for the FQDN www.bing.com. The response should be received almost immediately, with no DNS server timeouts occurring. This is because the query was forwarded to SERVER1, which then forwarded it to your ISP's DNS servers for resolution. This approach is generally much faster than using the Internet root name servers to recursively resolve the requested FQDN.

16. Display the contents of the DNS server cache on SERVER2 again. Note the cache entries relating to your name query and note also that there are considerably fewer cache entries than when root hints alone were used for performing recursive name resolution.

Suggested practice exercises

The following additional practice exercises are designed to give you more opportunities to practice what you learned and to help you successfully master the lessons presented in this chapter.

- **Exercise 1** Modify the steps in the Exercise 2 so that when a client computer at the branch office issues a name query to the caching-only DNS server located at that branch office, the following happens:

    - If the queried FQDN is for something on the corporate intranet, the query is forwarded to the DNS server located at the central office.

    - If the queried FQDN is for something on the Internet, the query is forwarded to the DNS servers at the organization's ISP.

    Hint: You need to use conditional forwarding. See *http://technet.microsoft.com/en-us /library/cc794735(v=WS.10).aspx* for more information.

- **Exercise 2** Create a Windows PowerShell script that runs a series of commands that removes the static IP address, subnet mask, default gateway, and DNS server settings from the network adapter of a server and then assigns a different static IP address, subnet mask, default gateway, and DNS server settings to the adapter.

- **Exercise 3** Create a Windows PowerShell script that runs a series of commands that assigns static IP addresses to two network adapters on a server and then adds static routes to the router table to enable the server to be used as a router to join two subnets.

Answers

This section contains the answers to the lesson review questions in this chapter.

Lesson 1

1. **Correct answer: B**

    A. Incorrect: The server-cluster approach involves using the Failover Clustering feature of Windows Server 2008 or Windows Server 2008 R2 to cluster DHCP servers so that if the primary DHCP server in a cluster fails, the secondary server can take up the slack and continue leasing addresses to clients.

    B. Correct: The split-scope approach involves splitting the IP address pool of a scope between two DHCP servers, typically by assigning the primary server 80 percent of the addresses in the scope and the secondary server the remaining 20 percent of the addresses. That way, if the primary server goes offline for any reason, DHCP clients on the subnet can still respond to lease renewal requests from the secondary server.

    C. Incorrect: The standby-server approach uses a hot-standby DHCP server with scopes and options configured identically to your production DHCP server.

    D. Incorrect: The DHCP-failover approach involves configuring two DHCP servers to provide leases from the same pool of addresses. The two servers then replicate lease information between them, which enables one server to assume responsibility for providing leases to all clients on the subnet when the other server is unavailable.

2. **Correct answers: A and C**

    A. Correct: DHCP failover only supports using a maximum of two DHCP servers.

    B. Incorrect: DHCP failover relationships are limited to IPv4 scopes and subnets.

    C. Correct: DHCP failover can be implemented in two ways: using load-balance mode or hot-standby mode. In load-balance mode, leases are issued from both servers equally, which ensures availability and provides load balancing for your DHCP services. In hot-standby mode, leases are issued from the primary server until it fails, whereupon the lease data is automatically replicated to the secondary server, which assumes the load.

    D. Incorrect: If the DHCP servers for which you want to implement DHCP failover are domain members, they must be authorized in Active Directory. However, you can also implement DHCP failover on stand-alone DHCP servers in a workgroup.

3. **Correct answers: A, B, and C**

    A. Correct: One scenario in which you might implement hot-standby mode is for organizations that have a central hub site (typically the data center at the head office) connected via WAN links to multiple remote branch-office sites.

B. **Correct:** A common implementation of hot-standby mode is when each branch-office DHCP server has a failover relationship with the central-office DHCP server, with the branch office assuming the role as primary and the central server as secondary. That way, if a DHCP server fails at a branch office, the central server can take up the slack for the remote site.

C. **Correct:** Budget should not be a consideration when implementing hot-standby mode because you can use the existing DHCP server in your data center as the standby for DHCP servers in your branch offices. In other words, no new servers need to be deployed if you want to implement DHCP failover in hot-standby mode.

D. **Incorrect:** DHCP failover in load-balance mode is a more appropriate solution for organizations that have only one physical site.

Lesson 2

1. Correct answer: D

A. **Incorrect:** DNSKEY resource records contain the public keys for a particular zone. Other types of DNSSEC resource records include RRSIG, DS, and NSEC (or NSEC3).

B. **Incorrect:** Only zones that are authoritative can be signed. Zones that are not authoritative cannot be signed.

C. **Incorrect:** The KSK is an authentication key with a length of 2048 bits that is generated using the RSA/SHA-256 cryptographic algorithm. The KSK is used to sign all of the DNSKEY records at the root of the zone, and it is part of the chain of trust. By default, the KSK has a rollover frequency of 755 days and any DNSKEY records signed using the key have a signature validity of 168 hours.

D. **Correct:** When zone data is updated by a client sending a DNS dynamic update to an authoritative DNS server, that DNS server updates its own copy of the zone and generates the required signatures. The unsigned update is then securely replicated to all other authoritative servers, and each DNS server adds the update to its copy of the zone and generates the required signatures.

2. Correct answer: C

A. **Incorrect:** When an authoritative server receives the recursive query, it returns an authoritative response to the client's local server.

B. **Incorrect:** When an authoritative server receives the recursive query, it returns an authoritative response to the client's local server.

C. **Correct:** The local server uses the public key of the signed zone on the authoritative server to validate the response it received from the authoritative server.

D. **Incorrect:** The DNS client on all supported versions of Microsoft Windows is DNSSEC-aware but nonvalidating.

3. **Correct answer: C**

   A. **Incorrect:** You should begin by introducing Windows Server 2012 or Windows Server 2012 R2 domain controllers into your environment. These domain controllers should also have the DNS Server role installed and be configured to use Active Directory–integrated zones.

   B. **Incorrect:** After deciding which DNS zone to implement DNSSEC on, sign the zone by opening the DNS Manager console, selecting the DNS server, right-clicking the zone, selecting DNSSEC, and then selecting Sign The Zone.

   C. **Correct:** If the zone you signed is an Active Directory–integrated zone, private zone-signing keys now replicate automatically to all domain controllers hosting the zone through Active Directory replication. Each zone owner signs its own copy of the zone when it receives the key as long as the zone owner is a domain controller running Windows Server 2012 or Windows Server 2012 R2.

   D. **Incorrect:** The final step in deploying DNSSEC is to ensure security between the nonvalidating DNS client and its local DNS servers. The recommended way to do this is to use IPsec to protect the last mile between the client and its local DNS server. The DNS clients must also be configured to check that responses have been validated by their local DNS server, and you do this by configuring the Name Resolution Policy Table (NRPT) on the clients. The NRPT can be configured by using either Group Policy or Windows PowerShell.

Lesson 3

1. **Correct answer: B**

   A. **Incorrect:** Parameters that are marked with an asterisk (*) are mandatory; those not marked this way are optional.

   B. **Correct:** Parameters that are marked with an asterisk (*) are mandatory; those not marked this way are optional.

   C. **Incorrect:** All parameters that Show-Command displays in the properties page for a cmdlet apply to that cmdlet.

   D. **Incorrect:** All parameters that Show-Command displays in the properties page for a cmdlet can have values specified for them on that properties page.

2. **Correct answer: C**

   A. **Incorrect:** You can use the Get-NetAdapterBinding cmdlet to display the bindings for the specified interface.

   B. **Incorrect:** There is no cmdlet called Remove-NetAdapterBinding.

   C. **Correct:** You can use the Disable-NetAdapterBinding cmdlet to disable the specified binding.

   D. **Incorrect:** You can use the Disable-NetAdapter cmdlet to disable the specified network adapter.

3. **Correct answer: B**

   A. Incorrect: If the *–ScopeId* parameter is used with this cmdlet, the result is to configure a scope option, not a server option.

   B. Correct: This command configures a DHCP scope option that assigns the address 10.10.0.1 as the default gateway on any DHCP client whose IPv4 address is on the 10.10.20.0 subnet.

   C. Incorrect: DHCP is not used to assign TCP/IP settings to routers.

   D. Incorrect: DHCP is not used to assign TCP/IP settings to routers.

Lesson 4

1. **Correct answer: B**

   A. Incorrect: A dual-layer TCP/IP stack has been a standard feature on Windows platforms since Windows Vista and Windows Server 2008.

   B. Correct: You can disable IPv6 on most interfaces by editing the registry, but you cannot disable the loopback interface (::1) on a Windows computer.

   C. Incorrect: The DHCP role can be configured for both stateless and stateful DHCPv6 address autoconfiguration.

   D. Incorrect: Windows Server 2012 and Windows Server 2012 R2 computers can function as ISATAP routers by configuring their LAN interfaces with appropriate IPv6 addresses, routes, and other settings.

2. **Correct answer: C**

   A. Incorrect: The first 3 bits of a global address are always 001 in binary format. This means that the first byte of the address can be 0x2 (binary 0010) or 0x3 (binary 0011) in hexadecimal format.

   B. Incorrect: The first 8 bits of a unique local address are always 11111101 in binary format. This means that a unique local address always begins with FD and has a prefix identifier of FD00::/8.

   C. Correct: The first 64 bits of a link-local address are always 11111110 10000000 00000000 00000000 in binary format. This means that a link-local address always begins with FE80 and has a prefix identifier of FE80::/64.

   D. Incorrect: A multicast address always begins with 11111111 or FF.

3. **Correct answer: C**

   A. Incorrect: You can use Ipconfig to display the address information for an interface, but it is not a Windows PowerShell cmdlet.

   B. Incorrect: You can use Get-NetAdapter to get the basic network adapter properties.

   C. Correct: You can use Get-NetIPAddress to get information about IP address configuration.

D. Incorrect: You can use Get-NetIPInterface to get information about the IP interface properties.

4. **Correct answer: B**

   A. Incorrect: Windows computers automatically assign IPv6 addresses to their LAN interfaces using stateless address autoconfiguration, but these addresses are link-local addresses that can be used only for communications between computers on the same link.

   B. Correct: An ISATAP router is used to enable communication between ISATAP hosts on an ISATAP subnet and IPv6 hosts on an IPv6-capable network. Computers running Windows Server 2012 or Windows Server 2012 R2 can function as ISATAP routers by configuring their LAN interfaces with appropriate IPv6 addresses, routes, and other settings.

   C. Incorrect: Teredo is an IPv6 transition technology that provides automatic tunneling that enables IPv6/IPv4 hosts to establish IPv6 connectivity with each other across the IPv4 Internet even when IPv4 network address translation (NAT) devices need to be traversed.

   D. Incorrect: Using a DHCPv6 server to assign IPv6 addresses to computers on an IPv4-only network will not help them communicate with computers on a different network that is IPv6-capable.

CHAPTER 7

Hyper-V virtualization

Virtualization is rapidly becoming the essential foundation for today's data center environments. Both private and public cloud computing are based on virtualization technologies, as is the emerging Virtual Desktop Infrastructure (VDI) paradigm that can provide benefits beyond those provided by traditional desktop computing for certain scenarios. Being able to implement and manage a virtualization infrastructure, therefore, is becoming a key job role for data center administrators.

The Hyper-V server role of Microsoft Windows Server provides an out-of-the-box platform for virtualizing both server workloads and desktops. The numerous enhancements and improvements made to Hyper-V in Windows Server 2012 and Windows Server 2012 R2 make it easier than ever to deploy, configure, manage, and maintain an organization's virtualized computing infrastructure. This chapter demonstrates how to deploy and manage virtualization hosts and virtual machines by using both the GUI administration tools and Windows PowerShell cmdlets included in Windows Server 2012 and Windows Server 2012 R2.

Lessons in this chapter:

Before you begin

To complete the practice exercises in this chapter

- You need to know how to perform a clean install of Windows Server 2012 R2 and perform initial configuration tasks like configuring the server's TCP/IP settings for Internet connectivity.

- You should have some familiarity with using Hyper-V Manager to manage hosts running Windows Server 2008 R2 or Windows Server 2008.

- You also should have at least rudimentary knowledge of using Windows PowerShell.

Lesson 1: Deploying and configuring Hyper-V hosts

The first step in implementing a virtualization infrastructure is deploying and configuring the servers that will host your virtualized workloads. For the Windows Server platform, this means planning, installing, and configuring Hyper-V hosts. This lesson helps you understand the issues and considerations involved in planning host deployment. The lesson also demonstrates how to configure storage and networking for Hyper-V hosts.

> **After this lesson, you will be able to:**
> - Describe the various considerations involved in planning the deployment of Windows Server 2012 and Windows Server 2012 R2 Hyper-V hosts.
> - Describe some of the scalability, availability, mobility, security, management, and disaster-recovery improvements in Hyper-V.
> - Describe the different types of virtual switches you can create on Hyper-V hosts.
> - Describe the different types of storage devices that hosts can use.
> - Install the Hyper-V role by using either Server Manager or Windows PowerShell on any installation option of Windows Server 2012 or Windows Server 2012 R2.
> - Configure virtual machine storage for hosts.
> - Create and configure virtual switches on hosts.
> - Perform additional host-configuration tasks.
>
> **Estimated lesson time: 30 minutes**

Planning Hyper-V deployment

Successful deployment requires careful planning ahead of time to ensure problems don't arise during or after the deployment process. The following issues should be considered when planning the deployment of Hyper-V hosts within your data center:

- Hardware
- Licensing
- Networking
- Storage
- Management
- Security
- Scalability
- Availability
- Mobility
- Disaster recovery

You should consider each of these issues from both the host and virtual machine perspective before you begin to deploy Hyper-V hosts within your data center. Although the sections that follow focus mainly on considerations relating to planning for host machines, some mention of planning for virtual machines is included where appropriate, especially when it directly relates to host-planning issues.

> **REAL WORLD** **DATA CENTER DESIGN**
>
> Although the discussion below focuses on issues relating to the features and capabilities of the Windows Server platform, there are other matters that you need to carefully consider before you begin deploying servers in your data center. These include power and cooling requirements, physical security, role-based administration, network and storage infrastructure design, and the use of virtualization, automation, and monitoring. There are helpful resources on many of these things in various presentations found on Microsoft TechNet; to find them, use Bing to search for "how Microsoft does IT." In addition, if you will be deploying third-party server applications you should check the vendors' hardware, software, virtualization, and licensing requirements for their applications.

Hardware

A key hardware requirement for a Hyper-V host is that the underlying host system support hardware-assisted virtualization such as Intel Virtualization Technology (Intel VT) or AMD Virtualization (AMD-V) technologies. In addition, hardware-enforced Data Execution Prevention (DEP) must be available and enabled on the host system. Specifically, this means that the Intel XD bit (the execute disable bit) or AMD NX bit (the no execute bit) must be enabled.

Although you can install the Hyper-V role on a Windows Server 2012 or Windows Server 2012 R2 server that meets the minimum system requirements of a single-core, 1.4-gigahertz (GHz) CPU and 512 MBs of RAM, you probably won't be able to run any virtual machines on that host machine. This is mainly because each virtual machine you run on a host requires a minimum amount of RAM that depends on the guest operating system installed in the virtual machine. In other words, the number of virtual machines and types of virtualized workloads you can run on Hyper-V hosts directly relate to the available hardware resources of the host.

To plan your host hardware, you should be aware of the maximum supported processor and memory capabilities of Windows Server 2012 and Windows Server 2012 R2, which are as follows:

- Up to 64 physical processors (sockets) per host
- Up to 320 logical processors (cores) per host
- Up to 4 terabytes (TBs) of physical memory per host

Next, you should consider the maximum supported processor and memory capabilities for virtual machines running on Windows Server 2012 or Windows Server 2012 R2 Hyper-V hosts. These are as follows:

- Up to 64 virtual processors per virtual machine (up to a total of 2048 virtual processors per host)
- Up to 1 TB of physical memory per virtual machine
- Up to 1024 active virtual machines running on the host

Finally, you must decide how many virtual machines you want to run on each host. In deciding this, you must consider the following:

- How many cores you can afford when you purchase your host systems
- How much physical memory you can afford for your host systems
- How much processing power and physical memory your virtualized workloads will need to meet the performance requirements of your service level agreement (SLA)

> **REAL WORLD PLANNING THE HOST PROCESSOR AND MEMORY**
>
> As an example, let's say you wanted to run two file servers and a Microsoft SQL Server database server on a single Hyper-V host in your data center. You've determined that the file servers will each require two virtual processors and 4 GBs of RAM to perform as intended and the database server will require four virtual processors and 12 GBs of RAM for optimal performance. The total processor and memory requirements of your virtual machines will therefore be
>
> (2 × 2) + 4 = 8 virtual processors
>
> (2 × 4) + 12 = 20 GBs RAM
>
> By including the minimum processor and memory requirements of the underlying host operating system plus room for growth, you might decide that a rack-mounted system with dual Intel Xeon E5-2430 processors and 24 GBs of RAM can meet your needs. The Intel Xeon E5-2430 is a six-core processor, so two of them give you 12 cores, which easily meets the requirements of eight dedicated virtual processors needed by the virtual machines. And the 24 GBs of RAM provides several GBs of RAM overhead on the host in case extra memory needs to be assigned to the database server workload.

Licensing

Your decision concerning how many virtualized workloads to run on a host might also influence your decision about which edition of Windows Server 2012 R2 to purchase. There are no technical differences between the capabilities of the Standard and Datacenter editions of Windows Server 2012 R2. Both editions support up to 64 physical processors and 4 TBs of physical memory. Both editions also support installing the same set of roles and features. The only differences between these editions are the virtualization rights included in their licensing and the price of the editions.

The virtualization rights included with the licensing for each edition are as follows:

- The Standard edition includes two instances of Windows Server.
- The Datacenter edition includes unlimited instances of Windows Server.

As a result, you should choose the Standard edition if you need to deploy Windows Server 2012 R2 as a workload on bare metal in a nonvirtualized environment and choose the Datacenter edition if you need to deploy Windows Server 2012 Hyper-V hosts for a virtualized data center or private-cloud scenario.

The licensing model for Windows Server 2012 R2 has also been simplified to make it easier for you to plan the budget for your IT department. Specifically, the Datacenter edition is licensed in increments of two physical processors. This means, for example, that if you want to deploy the Datacenter edition onto a system that has eight processors, you need to purchase four licenses of the product.

> **MORE INFO** **COMPARING EDITIONS**
>
> For more information on how Windows Server 2012 R2 editions compare and for current pricing information, see the Windows Server 2012 R2 home page at *http://www.microsoft.com/en-us/server-cloud/products/windows-server-2012-r2/* and click Buy.

Networking

Hyper-V networking requires careful planning to ensure reliable and secure network connectivity and management of both hosts and virtual machines. At a minimum, your host machines should have at least two physical network adapters configured as follows:

- One network adapter to allow virtualized workloads to communicate with other systems on your production network
- One network adapter dedicated for the management of your Hyper-V hosts and connected to a dedicated network used by your systems management platform

You might need more physical network adapters if you have additional services or special requirements. For example, you might need additional network adapters for the following:

- Providing connectivity between hosts and Internet SCSI (iSCSI) storage
- Deploying a failover cluster
- Using Cluster Shared Volumes (CSV) shared storage
- Performing live migrations of running virtual machines
- Increasing available bandwidth using Windows NIC Teaming

> **REAL WORLD** **PLANNING HOST NETWORKING**
>
> As an example, let's say you want to deploy Hyper-V to run a number of mission-critical server workloads for your organization. You decide that your hosts should be clustered and use CSV for performing live migration. You also decide that a single 1-gigabit Ethernet

(GbE) network adapter will have insufficient bandwidth to allow clients to access the workloads. So you decide to use Windows NIC Teaming, a feature introduced in Windows Server 2012, to allow two network adapters to provide 2 gigabits per second (Gbps) of network connectivity between your host cluster and the 10 GbE backbone of your production network. Finally, you plan on using your Fibre Channel storage area network (SAN) to provide storage for your host machines. How many physical network adapters will each host machine need?

- One NIC to provide dedicated connectivity to your management network
- Two NICs teamed together to provide connectivity between the virtualized workloads and your production network
- One NIC dedicated to the private network for failover clustering
- One NIC dedicated for use by CSV shared storage
- One NIC dedicated to live migration traffic

That's six network adapters in total that are needed for each host. Note that no network adapter is required for SAN connectivity because you're using Fibre Channel, not iSCSI.

In addition to deciding how many network adapters your hosts will need, you must also consider what types of virtual switches you will need for your environment. A Hyper-V virtual switch is a layer 2 network switch that works like a physical Ethernet switch but is implemented in software on the host. Hyper-V enables you to create three different kinds of virtual switches:

- **Private** This type of virtual switch allows virtual machines running on the host to communicate only with each other and not with the operating system of the host. A private virtual switch is not bound to any physical network adapter on the host, which means that the virtual machines on the host cannot communicate with any other system on any physical network connected to the host.

- **Internal** This type of virtual switch allows virtual machines running on the host to communicate with each other and with the operating system of the host. An internal virtual switch is not bound to any physical network adapter on the host, which means that the virtual machines on the host cannot communicate with any other system on any physical network connected to the host.

- **External** Unlike the other two types of virtual switches listed, this type is bound to a physical network adapter on the host. The result is that an external virtual switch allows virtual machines running on the host to communicate with each other, with the operating system of the host, and with other systems on the physical network connected to the host through that adapter. In addition, the external virtual switch can be bound to the physical network adapter by means of miniports in one of three ways:

- By using a single miniport representing a single physical network adapter
- By using a single miniport representing multiple physical network adapters
- By using multiple miniports representing a single physical network adapter

The Hyper-V virtual switch was enhanced in Windows Server 2012 with extensibility features that allow independent software vendors (ISVs) to add functionality for filtering, forwarding, and monitoring network traffic through virtual switches. These virtual-switch extensions can be implemented using two kinds of drivers:

- **NDIS filter drivers** These extensions can be used to perform network packet inspection, network packet filtering, and network forwarding. They are based on the Network Driver Interface Specification (NDIS) 6.0 specification, which was introduced in Windows Server 2012.

- **WFP callout drivers** These extensions are based on the Windows Filtering Platform (WFP) and can be used to provide virtual firewall functionality, connection monitoring, and filtering traffic that is protected using Internet Protocol security (IPsec).

If your virtualized infrastructure requires any of the preceding functionalities to be implemented at the virtual-switch level on Windows Server 2012 or Windows Server 2012 R2 Hyper-V hosts, you can search for an ISV that provides a software solution that meets your needs.

Storage

Different organizations have different requirements and different budgets for their IT operations, and Windows Server 2012 R2 provides a wide range of physical storage options for Hyper-V hosts. Choosing the storage solution that meets your needs and cost parameters is an important part of the host-deployment planning process.

Hyper-V hosts can use the following types of physical storage for storing virtual machine configuration files and disks:

- **Direct Attached Storage (DAS)** With DAS solutions, the storage is directly attached to the management operating system. Hyper-V supports the following DAS technologies:
  - Serial Advanced Technology Attachment (SATA)
  - External SATA (eSATA)
  - Small Computer System Interface (SCSI)
  - Serial Attached SCSI (SAS)
  - Parallel Advanced Technology Attachment (PATA)
  - Universal Serial Bus (USB)
  - FireWire

- **Storage area network (SAN)** With SAN solutions, the storage is provided by a set of interconnected devices that are connected to a common communication and data-transfer infrastructure, commonly known as the *storage fabric*. Hyper-V supports the following types of storage fabrics:

  - Fibre Channel
  - Internet SCSI (iSCSI)
  - Serial Attached SCSI (SAS)

- **Scale-Out File Servers** New features of version 3.0 of the Server Message Block (SMB) protocol allow file servers running Windows Server 2012 or Windows Server 2012 R2 to provide continuously available and scalable storage for CSVs. This allows you to use a file share on a Windows Server 2012 or Windows Server 2012 R2 file server to provide storage for Hyper-V host clusters.

> **NOTE NAS AND HYPER-V**
>
> Network-attached storage (NAS) is not supported for Hyper-V hosts.

Deciding whether to use SAN or DAS as your host storage solution depends on a number of factors. For example, the advantages of the SAN approach include the following:

- SAN allows multiple servers access to a pool of storage. This means SAN provides flexibility by allowing any server to access any storage unit in the SAN array.

- Because SAN is a centralized storage solution, it is easier to manage than DAS. This might be an important consideration if you will be deploying many Hyper-V hosts.

- SAN has a more scalable architecture than the DAS approach.

The disadvantages of the SAN approach include the following:

- SANs are usually more costly than DAS solutions, and depending on your business priorities, this factor might weigh heavily in your decision.

- DAS solutions typically have lower latency than SANs. So if application I/O or service latency is a priority, DAS might be the route to take.

Management

Once you deploy your Hyper-V hosts, you need to be able to manage them efficiently. Choosing the right management solution, therefore, is a key aspect of the host-deployment process.

Hyper-V includes two in-box tools for configuring and managing host machines:

- **Hyper-V Manager** This Microsoft Management Console (MMC) snap-in has been enhanced with additional functionality in Windows Server 2012 and Windows Server 2012 R2, but it basically provides the same level of host-management capability as in previous versions of Windows Server. You can use this tool to manage any number of host machines, but as the number of managed hosts increases, the amount of work to manage them scales accordingly.

- **Windows PowerShell**   The Hyper-V module in Windows Server 2012 and Windows Server 2012 R2 includes over a hundred new Windows PowerShell cmdlets that you can use to manage both Hyper-V hosts and virtual machines running on these hosts. Because of its flexibility and support for automation, Windows PowerShell is the preferred in-box tool for managing Hyper-V hosts and virtual machines in large environments such as data centers and cloud-computing environments.

> *NOTE* **MANAGING HYPER-V ON DIFFERENT WINDOWS SERVER VERSIONS**
>
> You can use the Hyper-V Manager snap-in to manage Windows Server 2012 and Windows Server 2012 R2 Hyper-V hosts from either a Server With A GUI or Minimal Server Interface installation that has the Hyper-V management tools installed or from a Windows 8.1 administrator workstation that has the Remote Server Administration Tools (RSAT) for Windows 8.1 installed. However, you cannot manage Hyper-V hosts running earlier versions of Windows Server by using these tools. Such hosts must be managed by using an earlier version of Hyper-V Manager. This means that you might need multiple sets of management tools to manage a mixed environment that has Hyper-V hosts running different Windows Server versions. The alternative is to use System Center 2012 Virtual Machine Manager R2, which allows you to manage all versions of Hyper-V hosts.

You can use Windows PowerShell to manage hosts and virtual machines by using one-off commands issued from the Windows PowerShell console, by using Windows PowerShell scripts, and by using the following capabilities introduced in Windows PowerShell 3.0 in Windows Server 2012:

- **Windows PowerShell workflows**   These allow you to create sequences of multi-computer management activities that are long-running, repeatable, frequent, parallelizable, interruptible, stoppable, and restartable. Windows PowerShell workflows can be suspended and resumed after a network outage, machine restart, or power loss. Windows PowerShell workflows are also portable and can be exported and imported as XAML files.

- **Windows PowerShell scheduled jobs**   These allow you to schedule Windows PowerShell background jobs and manage them in Windows PowerShell and in Task Scheduler. Windows PowerShell scheduled jobs run asynchronously in the background. You can create, edit, manage, disable, and re-enable them; create scheduled job triggers; and set scheduled job options by using Windows PowerShell cmdlets.

Windows PowerShell 4.0 in Windows Server 2012 R2 also includes Desired State Configuration (DSC), which is designed to allow you to specify what software should be installed on a server and how that software should be configured. For more information on

DSC, you can refer to the section titled "Desired State Configuration" in Chapter 3, "Server remote management."

In addition to using the preceding in-box tools for managing Hyper-V hosts and virtual machines that are included in Windows Server 2012 and Windows Server 2012 R2, organizations that need to deploy and manage large numbers of hosts or virtual machines can benefit from the following products from the Microsoft System Center platform:

- **System Center Virtual Machine Manager**   Allows you to configure and deploy virtual machines and centrally manage your physical and virtual infrastructure from one console

- **System Center Configuration Manager**   Allows you to assess, deploy, and update servers, client computers, and devices across physical, virtual, distributed, and mobile environments

> *NOTE* **SYSTEM CENTER AND WINDOWS SERVER 2012 R2 HYPER-V**
>
> System Center 2012 R2 is required for managing Hyper-V hosts running Windows Server 2012 R2. For more information, see the System Center 2012 R2 home page at *http://www .microsoft.com/en-us/server-cloud/system-center/default.aspx*.

Security

It's important to consider the security of your Hyper-V hosts as you prepare your host deployment plan. To begin, you should apply the same principles, processes, and practices for securing Hyper-V hosts that you would apply to any other Windows Server components within your environment. In addition to adhering to such best practices, you should also do the following:

- Deploy the Server Core installation option on your Hyper-V hosts instead of the Server With A GUI installation option. Server Core is the default installation option when installing Windows Server 2012 or Windows Server 2012 R2 because of its smaller attack surface and reduced servicing footprint. If needed, you can still use the Hyper-V Manager snap-in to manage Server Core hosts as long as you do so from either a server that has the Server With A GUI installation option installed or a client machine that has the Remote Server Administration Tools (RSAT) for Windows 8 installed.

- Do not install any server roles on your hosts other than the Hyper-V role. Your Hyper-V hosts should be dedicated servers whose only function is to host the virtualized workloads that run on them. Installing additional roles on hosts not only uses additional server resources (processor, memory, disk, and network) but also can also increase the server's attack surface and maintenance (updating) requirements. The exception to this is the File And Storage Services role because the role services for this role can be used for configuration storage pools for virtual machine storage. For more information on the File And Storage Services role, see Chapter 8, "File services and storage."

For more information on securing Hyper-V hosts and the virtual machines that run on them, see "Planning for Hyper-V Security" at *http://technet.microsoft.com/en-us/library/dd283088(v=ws.10)* and "Planning for Hyper-V Security" at *http://technet.microsoft.com/en-us/library/cc974516.aspx*.

Scalability, availability, and mobility

The section titled "Hardware" earlier in this lesson described some of the scalability enhancements for processor and memory resources on Hyper-V hosts and virtual machines in Windows Server 2012 and Windows Server 2012 R2. *Scalability* is the ability of a system or technology to expand to meet business needs, and it is therefore an important consideration when planning the deployment of Hyper-V hosts.

Availability is another important consideration for deployment planning and is related to scalability. *Availability* is the degree to which clients perceive a system or technology to be available so that they can access it. Systems that are available are considered resilient for two reasons. First, they minimize the occurrence of service-affecting incidents that can interrupt access by clients. Second, they allow effective actions to be performed when a service-affecting incident does happen.

The Failover Clustering feature of Windows Server 2012 and Windows Server 2012 R2 can provide both high availability and increased scalability for Hyper-V hosts and for the virtualized workloads that run on such hosts. A failover cluster is a group of servers that work together to increase the availability of applications and services running on those servers. The clustered servers, also called *nodes*, are connected by both physical cables and software such that if one of the cluster nodes fails, another node can begin providing service by using a process known as *failover*.

Failover Clustering was enhanced in a number of ways in Windows Server 2012:

- It has improved scalability. Hyper-V host clusters can scale up to 64 nodes with up to 4000 virtual machines per cluster and up to 1024 virtual machines per node.

- A priority setting can be assigned to each virtual machine in a Hyper-V host cluster to control the order in which virtual machines are started when a failover event occurs.

- CSV storage can be located on a SMB 3.0 file share on a Scale-Out File Server, which can potentially help reduce the cost of storage for Hyper-V host cluster solutions.

- CSV storage can be encrypted with BitLocker Drive Encryption to provide greater security for host deployments outside secure data centers.

- Cluster-Aware Updating (CAU) allows software updates to be applied automatically to each node in a host cluster while maintaining availability during the update process.

Besides improving availability, implementing Failover Clustering with Hyper-V hosts also provides mobility by allowing the migration of running virtual machines from one node to another in a host cluster. Live migration can help organizations create a dynamic and flexible IT environment that responds to changing business needs, so understanding and planning for virtual machine mobility is an important aspect of host-deployment planning.

Live migration improvements in Windows Server 2012 include the following:

- Live migrations of multiple running virtual machines can be performed concurrently, which helps minimize service interruption when a cluster node needs to be taken down for maintenance.

- Live migrations can be implemented using SMB 3.0 shared storage on a Scale-Out File Server even if the Hyper-V hosts involved are not members of a host cluster. In this scenario, the virtual hard disks of the virtual machines on the hosts reside and remain on the same file server and only the running state of the virtual machine is migrated from one host to another.

- Live migrations can even be performed without shared storage if the hosts involved belong to the same domain. In this scenario, the storage of a running virtual machine is first mirrored on the destination host. Once everything is synchronized, the mirror is broken and the storage on the source host is deleted.

- A feature called Storage Migration allows you to move the storage of a running virtual machine without any downtime. This enables new scenarios—for example, the ability to add more physical disk storage to a clustered or nonclustered Hyper-V host and then move the virtual machines to the new storage while the virtual machines continue to run.

For more information on these and other availability and mobility enhancements in Windows Server 2012, see "What's New in Failover Clustering in Windows Server 2012" at *http://technet.microsoft.com/en-US/library/hh831414.aspx* and "Virtual Machine Live Migration" at *http://technet.microsoft.com/en-us/library/hh831435.aspx*.

Disaster recovery

Preparing for disaster to ensure business continuity is a critical component of any deployment plan. Essential to any disaster-recovery planning is the ability to create and restore from reliable backups. With Hyper-V, you have to consider backing up the following:

- The management operating system on the Hyper-V host itself

- The configuration, virtual hard disks, checkpoints, and other files associated with each virtual machine running on the host

Performing backups of disk volumes on Windows servers uses the Volume Shadow Copy Service (VSS), which is a set of COM interfaces that implements a framework to enable volume backups to be performed while applications and services running on the server continue to write to the volumes being backed up. VSS provides an underlying framework that the following Windows features and applications use:

- **Windows Server Backup** An optional feature that uses VSS and block-level backup technology to provide basic backup and recovery functionality. Windows Server Backup can be managed using an MMC snap-in, command-line tools, or Windows PowerShell.

- **Shadow Copies of Shared Folders** A feature that provides point-in-time copies of files stored on file shares on file servers. Shadow Copies of Shared Folders allows users to view and access shadow copies, which are shared files and folders as they existed at different points of time in the past. By accessing previous versions of files and folders, users can compare versions of a file while working and recover files that were accidentally deleted or overwritten.

- **System Restore** A client-only feature that is available in Windows 8 and Windows 8.1 but not in Windows Server 2012 or Windows Server 2012 R2, System Restore creates restore points you can use to return a computer to its previous state for troubleshooting purposes.

In addition, VSS is used by System Center Data Protection Manager (DPM), which enables disk-based and tape-based data protection and recovery for Windows servers, including Hyper-V hosts and the virtualized workloads running on such hosts. In addition, you can use DPM to centrally manage system state and bare metal recovery (BMR).

> *NOTE* **SYSTEM CENTER DPM AND WINDOWS SERVER 2012 R2 HYPER-V**
>
> System Center 2012 Data Protection Manager Service R2 is required for managing Hyper-V hosts running Windows Server 2012 R2. For more information, see the System Center 2012 R2 home page at *http://www.microsoft.com/en-us/server-cloud/system-center/default.aspx*.

A new feature of VSS introduced in Windows Server 2012 was VSS for SMB File Shares, which allows VSS-aware backup applications such as System Center DPM to create shadow copies of VSS-aware server applications that store their data on SMB 3.0 file shares, such as file shares on a Scale-Out File Server. On previous versions of Windows Server, VSS only supported creating shadow copies of data stored on local volumes. Because Windows Server 2012 and Windows Server 2012 R2 Hyper-V hosts can use SMB 3.0 shared storage for storing virtual machine files, VSS for SMB File Shares is needed to ensure that virtual machines running on hosts using SMB 3.0 shared storage can reliably back up such virtual machine files.

Windows Server Backup does not support VSS for SMB File Shares functionality, but the Diskshadow.exe command-line utility included in Windows Server 2012 and Windows Server 2012 R2 that exposes the functionality offered by VSS does support it. For more information on VSS for SMB File Shares and how to configure it for use with Diskshadow.exe or System Center DPM, see the post "VSS for SMB File Shares" by Claus Joergensen, Principal Program Manager on the Windows File Server Team, on his TechNet blog at *http://blogs.technet.com /b/clausjor/archive/2012/06/14/vss-for-smb-file-shares.aspx*. For information on the syntax of the Diskshadow.exe command, see "Command-Line Reference for Windows Server 2012" at *http://technet.microsoft.com/en-us/library/hh831799(WS.11).aspx*.

Whether you are using Windows Server Backup, System Center DPM, or a third-party backup product, the recommended approach for backing up Hyper-V hosts is to perform full backups from the host operating system itself. Such backups will include all virtual machine files, including virtual hard disks, checkpoint files, and virtual machine configuration files. Virtual switches are not included in such backups, however, and after a host has been restored you need to re-create the host's virtual switches and reconnect the virtual network adapters in each virtual machine to the appropriate virtual switch. Because of this, you should make sure that you carefully document the configuration of all virtual switches on your Hyper-V hosts as part of your disaster-recovery plan.

The preceding approach to backing up Hyper-V hosts will not work, however, in scenarios in which the host storage does not support the Hyper-V VSS writer. An example of this is when virtual machine files are being stored on a SMB 3.0 file share on a Scale-Out File Server. In such scenarios, you should augment the preceding approach by also running the backup program from within the guest operating system of each virtual machine.

A new feature of Hyper-V introduced in Windows Server 2012 that can provide additional options for disaster-continuity scenarios is Hyper-V Replica, which you can use to replicate all changes on a virtual machine to a counterpart virtual machine running on a different host. For example, for an organization with a single head office and multiple branch offices whose IT infrastructure has been implemented in a hub-and-spoke topology, you can use Hyper-V Replica to replicate virtual machines running on hosts deployed at headquarters to standby hosts deployed at each branch office. This way, if wide area network (WAN) connectivity is lost between a branch office and headquarters, the standby host at that branch office can take over the workload from the host at the head office. For more information on Hyper-V Replica, see "Hyper-V Replica Overview" at *http://technet.microsoft.com/en-us/library /jj134172*.

> **IMPORTANT USING CHECKPOINTS IN PLACE OF BACKUPS**
>
> Microsoft recommends that you do not use virtual machine checkpoints (previously called snapshots in Windows Server 2012 and earlier versions of Hyper-V) in place of backups because of the risk of unintended data loss associated with using them for such purposes. Checkpoints are intended primarily for development and test purposes, and you should avoid using them in production environments.

✔ Quick check

- Which of the following *cannot* be used as virtual machine storage for Hyper-V hosts?

    - SAN

    - NAS

    - DAS

    - Scale-Out File Server

Quick check answer

- NAS, or network-attached storage, is not supported for this purpose.

Installing the Hyper-V role

Once you have planned the deployment of your Hyper-V hosts, you are ready to install the Hyper-V role on the servers you plan to use for this purpose. As with other server roles in Windows Server 2012 and Windows Server 2012 R2, you can install the Hyper-V role on a server by using either of the following:

- Server Manager
- Windows PowerShell

Using Server Manager

You can use Server Manager to install the Hyper-V role on a server as follows:

1. On either the All Servers page or a custom server group page in Server Manager, right-click the remote server on which you want to install the Hyper-V role and select Add Roles And Features to launch the Add Roles And Features Wizard.

2. On the Installation Type Wizard page, select Role-Based Or Feature-Based Installation.

3. On the Server Roles page, select the Hyper-V role. At this point, you will be prompted to install the GUI and Windows PowerShell management tools for the Hyper-V role. If the server on which you are installing the Hyper-V role is a Server Core installation, clear the Include Management Tools check box.

4. Proceed through the remaining wizard pages to install the role and restart the remote server when prompted.

> **NOTE** **INSTALLING MANAGEMENT TOOLS ON SERVER CORE**
>
> If you are using Server Manager to install the Hyper-V role on a remote server, you might want to select the Hyper-V Module For Windows PowerShell on the Features page of the Add Roles And Features Wizard to install this module locally on the server. That way, if at some future time you are unable to manage the Hyper-V role on the remote server by using either the Hyper-V Manager snap-in or Windows PowerShell you might still be able to establish a Remote Desktop session with the remote server so that you can run Windows PowerShell commands locally on the server.
>
> Alternatively, you might decide to install the Hyper-V role on a Windows Server 2012 or Windows Server 2012 R2 instance that has been configured with the Minimal Server Interface installation option, which will allow you to install both the Hyper-V Management snap-in and Hyper-V Module For Windows PowerShell while retaining some of the security and servicing advantages of the Server Core installation option. When the Hyper-V role is installed on a server that has the Minimal Server Interface installation, you can launch the Hyper-V Management snap-in locally on the server by entering **virtmgmt.msc** at the command prompt. Note that Minimal Server Interface is not available on the stand-alone Windows Server 2012 or Windows Server 2012 R2 Hyper-V product, which has only the Server Core installation option.

Using Windows PowerShell

You can also use Windows PowerShell to install the Hyper-V role on a server. The command you use depends on the installation option used when the remote server was deployed. For example, if the remote server is a Server With A GUI installation, you can install the Hyper-V role with the management tools for the role by using the following command:

```
Install-WindowsFeature -Name Hyper-V -ComputerName <name> -IncludeManagementTools
-Restart
```

Here, *<name>* is the NetBIOS name, an IP address, or fully qualified domain name (FQDN) of the remote server. For example, to see what happens if this command is run against a server named HOST4, you can include the *–WhatIf* parameter as follows:

```
PS C:\> Install-WindowsFeature -Name Hyper-V -ComputerName HOST4 -IncludeManagementTools
-Restart -WhatIf
What if: Continue with installation?
What if: Performing installation for "[Hyper-V] Hyper-V".
What if: Performing installation for "[Remote Server Administration Tools] Hyper-V
Module for Windows PowerShell".
What if: Performing installation for "[Remote Server Administration Tools] Hyper-V
Management Tools".
What if: Performing installation for "[Remote Server Administration Tools] Role
Administration Tools".
What if: Performing installation for "[Remote Server Administration Tools] Remote Server
Administration Tools".
What if: Performing installation for "[Remote Server Administration Tools] Hyper-V GUI
Management Tools".
What if: The target server may need to be restarted after the installation completes.

Success Restart Needed Exit Code    Feature Result
------- -------------- ---------    --------------
True    Maybe          Success      {Hyper-V, Hyper-V Module for Windows Power...
```

Run the command again without the *–WhatIf* parameter to install the Hyper-V role on the remote server. After the remote server has restarted, you can use the Get-WindowsFeature cmdlet to verify installation of the Hyper-V role and associated management features:

```
PS C:\> Get-WindowsFeature -Name *Hyper-V* -ComputerName HOST4 | `
ft DisplayName,InstallState

DisplayName                                             InstallState
-----------                                             ------------
Hyper-V                                                 Installed
Hyper-V Management Tools                                Installed
Hyper-V GUI Management Tools                            Installed
Hyper-V Module for Windows PowerShell                   Installed
```

> **NOTE ADVANTAGES OF THE GUI APPROACH**
>
> Although using the Install-WindowsFeature cmdlet of Windows PowerShell is the preferred method for installing most roles and features on remote servers running Windows Server 2012 or Windows Server 2012 R2, there might be some advantage to using the Add Roles

And Features Wizard when you want to install the Hyper-V role on a server. This is because the wizard presents you with four Hyper-V configuration options that you would have to configure separately using different cmdlets after role installation if you were using Windows PowerShell to install the role. These four configuration options are as follows:

- Configuring the default location for virtual disk files
- Configuring the default location for virtual machine configuration files
- Creating a new virtual switch
- Enabling live migration

If you configure these settings during the installation of the role using the wizard, you won't need to configure them later as part of the post-installation configuration of the host.

Configuring Hyper-V hosts

After you have installed the Hyper-V role on a server, you still need to configure the role to meet the needs of your environment. Configuring a Hyper-V host involves steps such as the following:

- Configuring virtual machine storage
- Creating virtual switches
- Performing other configuration tasks

Hyper-V hosts can also be configured using either the Hyper-V Manager snap-in or Windows PowerShell cmdlets. To view the configuration of a host using the Hyper-V Manager snap-in, right-click the host in the console tree and select Hyper-V Settings to display the Hyper-V Settings dialog box shown in the screen shots in this section. To view the configuration of a host using Windows PowerShell, use the Get-VMHost cmdlet as shown here:

```
PS C:\> Get-VMHost -ComputerName HOST4

Name  LogicalProcessorCount MemoryCapacity(M) VirtualMachineMigrationEnabled
----  --------------------- ----------------- ------------------------------
HOST4 4                     24570.2421875     False
```

To view all configuration settings associated with the specified host, pipe the output of the preceding command into the Format-List cmdlet and specify a wildcard:

```
PS C:\> Get-VMHost -ComputerName HOST4 | Format-List *

ComputerName            : HOST4
VirtualHardDiskPath     : C:\Users\Public\Documents\Hyper-V\Virtual Hard Disks
VirtualMachinePath      : C:\ProgramData\Microsoft\Windows\Hyper-V
FullyQualifiedDomainName : WORKGROUP
Name                    : HOST4
MacAddressMinimum       : 00155D0BE600
MacAddressMaximum       : 00155D0BE6FF
```

```
MaximumStorageMigrations                      : 2
MaximumVirtualMachineMigrations               : 2
VirtualMachineMigrationEnabled                : False
VirtualMachineMigrationAuthenticationType     : CredSSP
UseAnyNetworkForMigration                     : False
FibreChannelWwnn                              : C003FF0000FFFF00
FibreChannelWwpnMaximum                       : C003FF68F816FFFF
FibreChannelWwpnMinimum                       : C003FF68F8160000
LogicalProcessorCount                         : 4
MemoryCapacity                                : 25763766272
ResourceMeteringSaveInterval                  : 01:00:00
NumaSpanningEnabled                           : True
HostNumaStatus                                : {HOST4}
NumaStatus                                    :
InternalNetworkAdapters                       : {CONTOSO Virtual Switch}
ExternalNetworkAdapters                       : {CONTOSO Virtual Switch_External}
IovSupport                                    : False
IovSupportReasons                             : {Ensure that the system has chipset...
```

Note that the configuration of virtual switches on a host is not included in the output of the Get-VMHost cmdlet. To view a list of virtual switches that have been created on the host, use the Get-VMSwitch cmdlet as shown here:

```
PS C:\> Get-VMSwitch

Name                    SwitchType NetAdapterInterfaceDescription
----                    ---------- ------------------------------
CONTOSO Virtual Switch  External   Broadcom NetXtreme Gigabit Ethernet #2
```

To view all of the properties of all virtual switches on the host, use the following command:

```
PS C:\> Get-VMSwitch | Format-List *

ComputerName                       : HOST4
Name                               : CONTOSO Virtual Switch
Id                                 : cffd5106-2735-4c54-b9e1-1cad8944e8c0
Notes                              :
SwitchType                         : External
AllowManagementOS                  : True
NetAdapterInterfaceDescription     : Broadcom NetXtreme Gigabit Ethernet #2
AvailableVMQueues                  : 0
NumberVmqAllocated                 : 0
IovEnabled                         : False
IovVirtualFunctionCount            : 0
IovVirtualFunctionsInUse           : 0
IovQueuePairCount                  : 0
IovQueuePairsInUse                 : 0
AvailableIPSecSA                   : 0
NumberIPSecSAAllocated             : 0
BandwidthPercentage                : 10
BandwidthReservationMode           : Absolute
DefaultFlowMinimumBandwidthAbsolute : 10000000
DefaultFlowMinimumBandwidthWeight  : 0
Extensions                         : {Microsoft NDIS Capture, Microsoft Windows
Filtering Platform}
```

```
IovSupport                              : False
IovSupportReasons                       : {Ensure that the system has chipset support...
IsDeleted                               : False
```

Configuring virtual machine storage

Figure 7-1 shows the default location where a Hyper-V host stores the virtual hard disk files for its virtual machines. Such files might include the following:

- VHD or VHDX, which can be the system drive or data drives for each virtual machine
- AVHD files, which are the differencing disk files used for virtual machine checkpoints

As part of the post-installation configuration of your Hyper-V hosts, you should change this location to the volume where you want the virtual hard disk files stored. This volume will depend on the type of storage solution that you have decided to use for your Hyper-V hosts, as described earlier in this lesson in the section titled "Storage."

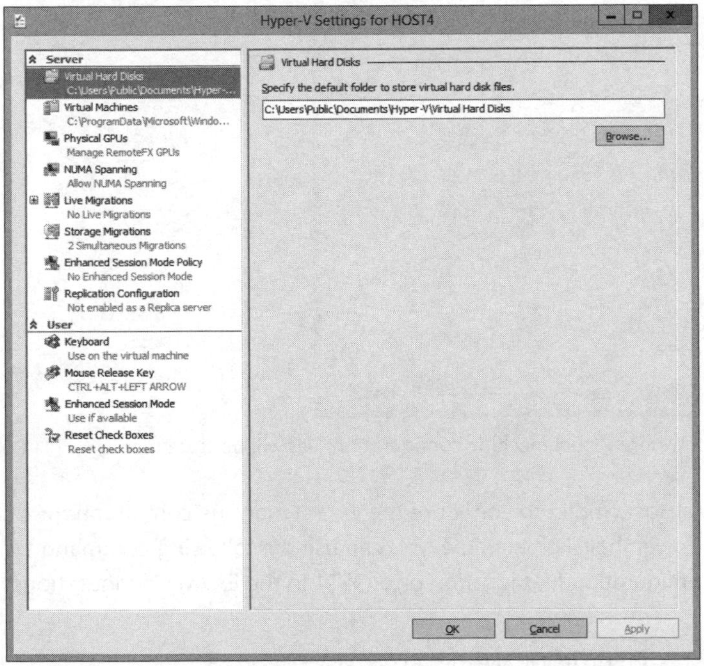

FIGURE 7-1 Configure the location where virtual hard disk files will be stored.

You can also use the Set-VMHost cmdlet to configure the virtual hard disk location using Windows PowerShell. For example, you can use the following command to change the virtual hard disk location on HOST4 to the E:\VM Storage folder:

```
Set-VMHost -ComputerName HOST4 -VirtualHardDiskPath "E:\VM Storage"
```

Figure 7-2 shows the default location where a Hyper-V host stores its virtual machine configuration files. Such files can include the following:

- XML files named with the globally unique identifier (GUID) used to internally identify a virtual machine or checkpoint
- BIN files containing the memory of a virtual machine or checkpoint
- VSV files containing the saved state from the devices associated with a virtual machine

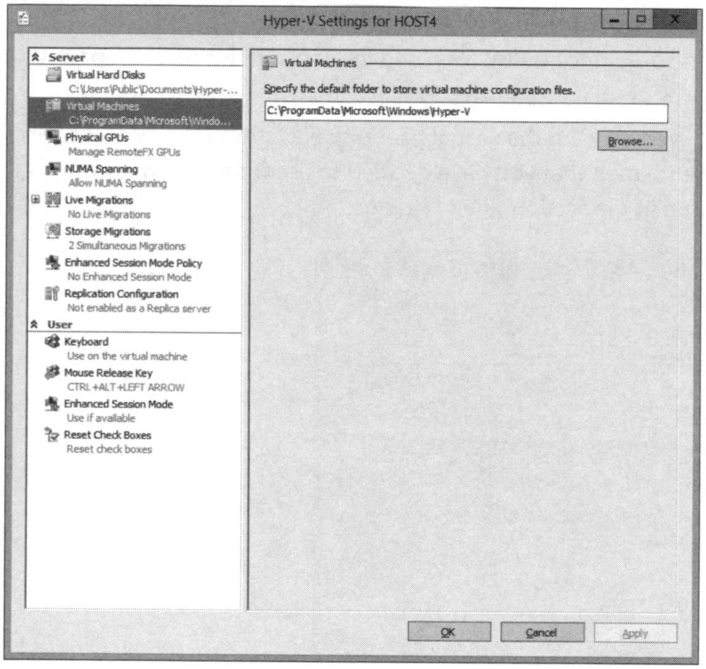

FIGURE 7-2 Configure the location where virtual machine configuration files will be stored.

You can also use the Set-VMHost cmdlet to configure the virtual machine configuration files location using Windows PowerShell. For example, you can use the following command to change the virtual machine configuration files location on HOST4 to the E:\VM Configurations folder:

```
Set-VMHost -ComputerName HOST4 -VirtualMachinePath "E:\VM Configurations"
```

REAL WORLD **PREVENTING PROBLEMS**

Everyone knows that it's better to prevent problems from happening than to try to deal with things after they go wrong. That's why it's important to make sure you configure your default Hyper-V storage locations appropriately before you start creating new virtual machines on a Hyper-V host or importing existing virtual machines onto the host. Ben Armstrong, a Program Manager on the Hyper-V team at Microsoft, indicates in his "Virtual PC Guy Blog" that one of the top support-call generators for Hyper-V is when customers run out of space on their host. This is because the default location for storing virtual hard disks and virtual machine configuration files is the system drive on the host, and if this drive becomes filled the host can fail to function. Because of the problems that can arise if this default location remains unchanged, some changes were made to the Add Roles And Features Wizard to ensure that customers think about the potential impact of this issue when they are installing the Hyper-V role. For more information, see "Default Hyper-V Storage Paths in Windows Server 2012" at *http://blogs.msdn.com/b/virtual_pc_guy /archive/2012/06/19/default-hyper-v-storage-paths-in-windows-server-2012.aspx*.

Creating virtual switches

Figure 7-3 shows the New Virtual Network Switch page of the Virtual Switch Manager dialog box for a Hyper-V host. You can use this page to create virtual switches of the external, internal, and private types described earlier in this lesson in the section titled "Networking."

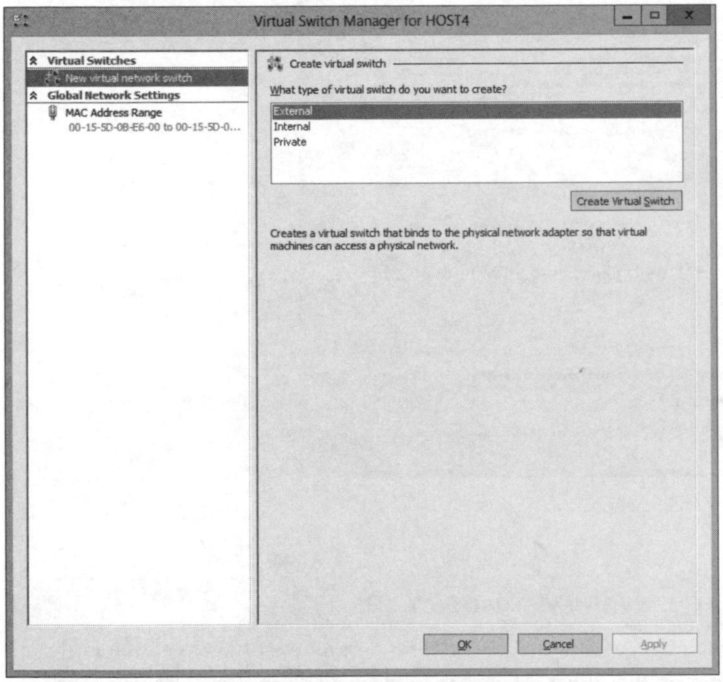

FIGURE 7-3 Create a new virtual switch in Hyper-V Manager.

Clicking Create Virtual Switch, shown in Figure 7-3, creates a new virtual switch of the type selected (here, External), and you can now configure the properties of the new virtual switch as shown in Figure 7-4. The key properties to configure are these:

■ Specifying a descriptive name for the new switch

■ Selecting the connection type (External, Internal, or Private) if you decide to change your initial choice

If you select External as the connection type, you must assign a physical network adapter on the host to the new switch. In that case, you also have the option of allowing the management operating system on the host to share the selected network adapter. If you are using a separate physical network for host management and the host has another physical network adapter connected to the management network, you can clear the check box shown as selected in Figure 7-4. Additionally, you have the option of enabling single-root I/O virtualization (SR-IOV) if the selected network adapter supports this feature. SR-IOV is described later in this chapter. Finally, if you are using virtual local area networks (VLANs) to segment traffic on your production network, you can enable this feature and specify a VLAN identifier here.

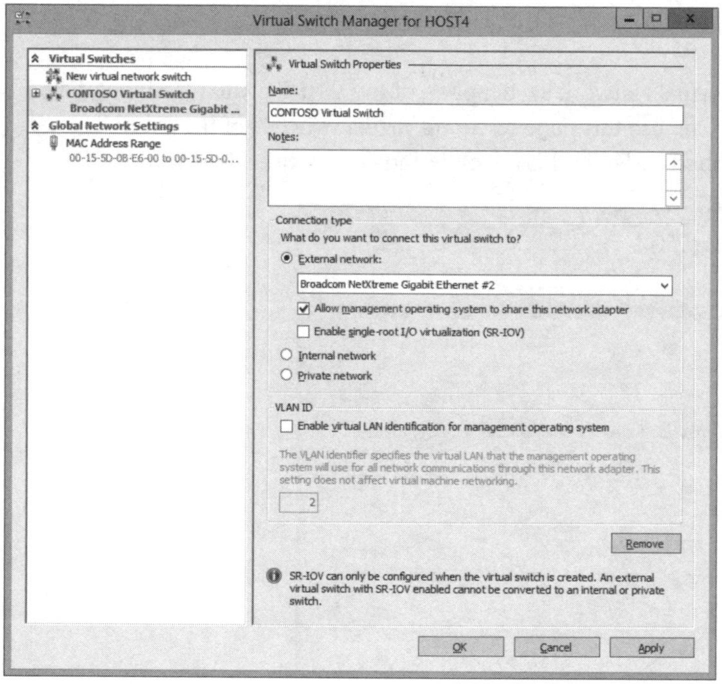

FIGURE 7-4 Configure the new virtual switch.

> ***NOTE*** **NETWORK CONNECTIONS AND VIRTUAL SWITCHES**
>
> **Creating a new virtual switch of type External also creates a new network connection in the Network Connections folder on the server, which can be displayed using the Network And Internet utility in Control Panel. The new network connection is typically named *vEthernet (<name of virtual switch>)*, and the TCP/IP settings assigned to the physical network adapter associated with the switch become the TCP/IP settings of the new connection.**

You can also use the New-VMSwitch cmdlet to create new virtual switches using Windows PowerShell. For example, you could use the following command to create the CONTOSO Virtual Switch shown in Figure 7-4:

```
New-VMSwitch -Name "CONTOSO Virtual Switch" `
-NetAdapterName "Broadcom NetXtreme Gigabit Ethernet #2" -ComputerName HOST4
```

For help with the syntax of this cmdlet, use the Get-Help New-VMSwitch command.

> **IMPORTANT** **NETWORK CONNECTIVITY WITH THE HOST**
>
> Creating or reconfiguring a virtual switch results in changes that might disrupt network connectivity with the host. If you are managing the host remotely using Remote Desktop Connection, you might need to close and reopen the connection after making such changes. In addition, loss of network connectivity by the host when the changes are applied might affect any network operations in progress. This is one reason why it's a best practice for a Hyper-V host to have at least two physical network adapters with one adapter being used for host and virtual machine management and the other for inbound and outbound traffic.

In addition to creating and configuring virtual switches on your hosts, you can configure the range of media access control (MAC) addresses that the host can use to dynamically assign MAC addresses to the virtual network adapters of virtual machines on the host. Figure 7-5 shows the default range of MAC addresses used for this purpose. Although this default range might suffice when only a few hosts are being deployed, it's generally a good idea to assign a different MAC address range to each host to ensure that duplicate MAC addresses cannot be assigned to virtual machines on different hosts, which could cause network problems for the guest operating systems of such virtual machines.

You can also use the Set-VMHost cmdlet to configure the range of MAC addresses that the host can assign to virtual network adapters of virtual machines on the host. For example, you can use the following command to change the MAC address range on HOST4 to span from 00-00-04-00-00-00 to 00-00-04-FF-FF-FF:

```
Set-VMHost -ComputerName HOST4 -MacAddressMinimum 000004000000 `
-MacAddressMaximum 000004FFFFFF
```

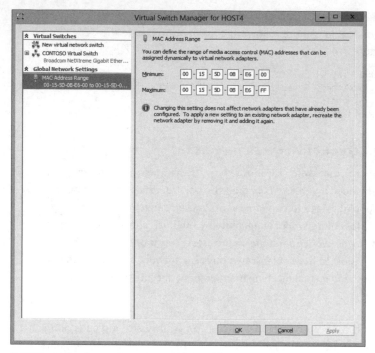

FIGURE 7-5 Configure the range of MAC addresses that the host can assign to virtual network adapters.

Other configuration steps

Additional steps needed for configuring your Hyper-V hosts depend on what types of functionality you want to enable on them. For example, by using the Hyper-V Settings dialog box, you can:

- Enable live migrations on the host and configure the authentication protocol used for live migration, how many live migrations can be performed simultaneously, and which network or IP address can be used for incoming live migrations.

- Configure how many simultaneous storage migrations can be performed on the host.

- Enable Hyper-V Replica functionality on the host and the authentication protocol and ports used for replication and choose whether replication will be allowed from any authenticated server or from a list of specified servers.

- Enable *NUMA spanning*, a new feature of Hyper-V introduced in Windows Server 2012 that allows virtual machines to span non-uniform memory architecture (NUMA) nodes on NUMA-capable hosts. NUMA spanning works by projecting a virtual NUMA topology to the guest operating system in a way that is optimized to match the NUMA topology of the underlying physical host machine. This provides virtual machines with additional computing resources for high-performance server applications such as Microsoft SQL Server and modern server operating systems such as Windows Server 2012 and Windows Server 2012 R2 that include built-in NUMA optimizations.

You can also use Windows PowerShell to perform these additional configuration steps on your hosts. For example, you can use the Set-VMHost cmdlet to enable live migration, configure it to use CredSSP for authentication, and configure it to allow incoming live migrations using any available network as follows:

```
Set-VMHost –VirtualMachineMigrationEnabled $true `
-VirtualMachineMigrationAuthenticationType CredSSp –UseAnyNetworkForMigration $true
```

> **MORE INFO HYPER-V CMDLETS**
>
> For information about the syntax of the Hyper-V cmdlets and for usage examples, see "Hyper-V Cmdlets in Windows PowerShell" at *http://technet.microsoft.com/en-us/library /hh848559.*

Lesson summary

- Key considerations for planning the deployment of Hyper-V hosts include hardware, licensing, networking, storage, management, security, scalability, availability, mobility, and disaster recovery.
- You can install and configure the Hyper-V role using either the Hyper-V Manager snap-in or Windows PowerShell.
- Whenever possible, you should deploy Hyper-V on Server Core installations and manage your hosts by using Windows PowerShell.
- Configuring virtual machine storage for a host involves specifying the location where virtual machine configuration files and virtual hard disk files will be stored.
- Configuring virtual networking for a host involves creating and configuring virtual switches of the type and number needed by your environment.

Lesson review

Answer the following questions to test your knowledge of the information in this lesson. You can find the answers to these questions and explanations of why each answer choice is correct or incorrect in the "Answers" section at the end of this chapter.

1. Which edition and installation option of Windows Server 2012 R2 are the best choices for deploying Hyper-V hosts in a data center environment?

   A. Standard edition on Server Core

   B. Standard edition on Server With A GUI

   C. Datacenter edition on Server Core

   D. Datacenter edition on Server With A GUI

2. You want to use a Server Core installation of Windows Server 2012 R2 as a Hyper-V host. The server has been joined to an Active Directory domain and resides in your

data center. Because you do not yet feel confident managing servers from the command line, you want to manage the host using the Hyper-V Manager snap-in. Given that security is a concern and you also want to keep the servicing overhead low for your servers while managing them conveniently, which of the following would be the best approach for you to pursue?

A. Log on to the local console of the server, type **powershell** at the command prompt, and type **Install-WindowsFeature –Server-Gui-Mgmt-Infra –Restart** to convert your Server Core installation to a Minimal Server Interface installation. Now log on again to the local console of the server and launch the Hyper-V Manager snap-in to manage the Hyper-V host and its virtual machines.

B. Enable Remote Desktop on the server and configure it to allow only remote clients that use Network Level Authentication to connect to the server. Now log on to an administrator workstation running Windows 8.1, use Remote Desktop Connection to connect to the remote host, and manage the host from your workstation.

C. Log on to the local console of the server, type **powershell** at the command prompt, and type **Install-WindowsFeature –Server-Gui-Mgmt-Infra –Restart** to convert your Server Core installation to a Minimal Server Interface installation. Enable Remote Desktop on the server and configure it to allow only remote clients that use Network Level Authentication to connect to the server. Now log on to an administrator workstation running Windows 8, use Remote Desktop Connection to connect to the remote host, and manage the host from your workstation.

D. Install the RSAT for Windows 8 on an administrator workstation running Windows 8, launch the Hyper-V Manager snap-in, connect to the remote host, and manage the host from your workstation.

3. Which Windows PowerShell cmdlet can you use to configure the default storage location for virtual machine files on a Hyper-V host?

A. Get-VMHost

B. Set-VMHost

C. Add-VMStoragePath

D. Set-VM

Lesson 2: Deploying and configuring virtual machines

After deploying and configuring your Hyper-V hosts, the next step in implementing your virtualization infrastructure is deploying and configuring the virtual machines that will be used to virtualize your server workloads. This lesson helps you understand the issues and considerations involved in planning virtual machine deployment and how to create and configure virtual machines.

After this lesson, you will be able to:

- Describe the different ways that virtual machines can be deployed on Hyper-V hosts.
- Describe the various considerations involved in planning the deployment of virtual machines on Hyper-V hosts.
- Explain the difference between Generation 1 and Generation 2 virtual machines.
- Describe the different types of virtual hard disks and their purposes and limitations.
- Explain why using checkpoints is not recommended in production environments.
- Describe the different choices involved when importing virtual machines onto a host.
- Create new virtual machines using the Hyper-V Manager snap-in and Windows PowerShell.
- Create new virtual disks and add them to virtual machines using the Hyper-V Manager snap-in and Windows PowerShell.
- Add new virtual network adapters to virtual machines and configure the adapters.
- Configure virtual hardware and management settings for virtual machines.

Estimated lesson time: 40 minutes

Planning virtual machine deployment

Depending on the scenario being envisioned, deploying a virtual machine can mean different things, such as

- Creating a new virtual machine and installing a guest operating system and applications on it.
- Importing an existing virtual machine that already has a guest operating system and applications installed on it.
- Performing a physical-to-virtual (P2V) conversion of a physical server to migrate the server's operating system and applications into a virtual machine.
- Performing a virtual-to-virtual (V2V) conversion by converting another vendor's virtual machine to a Hyper-V virtual machine.

You can perform the first two types of virtual-machine deployments by using the in-box management tools of the Hyper-V role of Windows Server 2012 and Windows Server 2012 R2—specifically, the Hyper-V Manager and the Hyper-V module for Windows PowerShell. Deploying new virtual machines by performing P2V or V2V conversions requires additional tools, such as System Center Virtual Machine Manager or third-party utilities.

MORE INFO   **VMM AND P2V**

Performing P2V conversions using Virtual Machine Manager (VMM) is beyond the scope of this book. For more information on how to use VMM for performing P2V conversion, see the topic "How to Convert Physical Computers to Virtual Machines" at *http://technet .microsoft.com/en-us/library/hh427286.aspx*.

The following issues should be considered when creating new virtual machines on a Hyper-V host:

- Virtual machine generation
- Location of configuration files
- Startup memory
- Dynamic Memory
- Virtual processors
- Virtual networking
- Virtual hard disks
- Guest operating system deployment
- Automatic virtual machine activation
- Performing checkpoints

Note that these issues apply mainly to the creation of new virtual machines. Importing existing virtual machines entails a different set of conditions that are described later in this section.

Virtual machine generation

Windows Server 2012 and earlier versions of Hyper-V supported only a single type (generation) of virtual machines. Such virtual machines had the following characteristics:

- They used a standard set of emulated hardware devices to ensure compatibility running all versions of Windows. These emulated devices include an AMI BIOS, Intel 440BX chipset motherboard, S3 Trio graphics display adapter, Intel/DEC 21140 network adapter, and other virtual devices.
- They included a legacy network adapter virtual device, which you had to use for PXE-based installation of a guest operating system.
- They could only boot from integrated development environment (IDE) disks (virtual disks attached to the virtual machine using the IDE controller).

Windows Server 2012 R2 introduces a new kind of virtual machine called a Generation 2 virtual machine. The characteristics of Generation 2 virtual machines include the following:

- They comply with the Unified Extensible Firmware Interface (UEFI) standard and enable virtual machines to use Secure Boot.

- Many of the emulated devices have been removed and replaced with synthetic drivers and software-based devices as summarized in Table 7-1.
- The legacy network adapter device is no longer required (or even supported) by Generation 2 virtual machines. Instead, you can PXE-boot a Generation 2 virtual machine using a standard network adapter.
- They can boot directly from SCSI disks (virtual disks attached to the virtual machine using the SCSI controller). In fact, Generation 2 virtual machines don't even have an IDE controller and they can also boot from a SCSI virtual DVD. The SCSI controller performs much better than the legacy IDE controller in the previous generation of virtual machines. This means, for example, that installing a supported guest operating system in a Generation 2 virtual machine takes about half as long as installing the same guest operating system in a previous-generation virtual machine.

Because of all these hardware changes, Generation 2 virtual machines only support the following versions of Windows as guest operating systems:

- 64-bit versions of Windows 8 and Windows Server 2012
- 64-bit versions of Windows 8.1 and Windows Server 2012 R2

TABLE 7-1 Hardware device changes in Generation 2 virtual machines

Legacy Devices Removed	Replacement Devices	Enhancements
IDE controller	Virtual SCSI controller	Boot from VHDX (64 TB max size, online resize)
IDE CD-ROM	Virtual SCSI CD-ROM	Hot add/remove
Legacy BIOS	UEFI firmware	Secure Boot
Legacy NIC	Synthetic NIC	Network boot with IPv4 and IPv6
Floppy & DMA Controller	No floppy support	
UART (COM ports)	Optional UART for debugging	Faster and more reliable
i8042 keyboard controller	Software-based input	No emulation – reduced resources
PS/2 keyboard	Software-based keyboard	No emulation – reduced resources
PS/2 mouse	Software-based mouse	No emulation – reduced resources
S3 video	Software-based video	No emulation – reduced resources
PCI bus	VMBus	
Programmable Interrupt Controller (PIC)	No longer required	
Programmable Interrupt Timer (PIT)	No longer required	
Super I/O device	No longer required	

Inside a Generation 2 virtual machine

As the screenshot below shows, Windows Server 2012 R2 Hyper-V supports both Generation 1 and Generation 2 virtual machines. You must choose the generation of a virtual machine when you create the virtual machine, and you cannot change its generation after you create it.

Once the Generation 2 virtual machine has Windows Server 2012 R2 installed as the guest operating system, opening Device Manager reveals the various synthetic and software-based devices attached to the VMBus. Note that unlike first-generation virtual machines, there is no PCI-to-ISA bridge running in ISA mode, no PS/2 keyboard, no PS/2 mouse, no COM ports, and so on. The next screenshot compares Device Manager for Generation 1 virtual machines (left) with Device Manager for Generation 2 virtual machines (right):

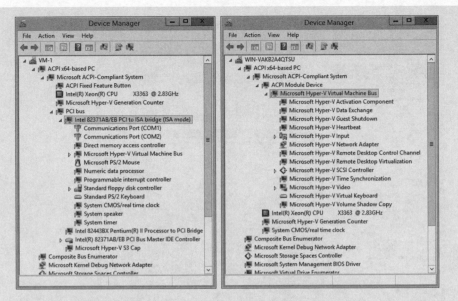

The key benefits of using Generation 2 virtual machines as opposed to Generation 1 virtual machines are twofold. First, as mentioned previously, Generation 2 virtual machines can be quickly provisioned because they can boot from a SCSI device or a standard network adapter. This can be useful in scenarios in which you need to quickly deploy new virtual machines to scale out a cloud-based application to meet rapidly increasing demand.

The second main benefit of Generation 2 virtual machines is in the area of security. Because Generation 2 virtual machines are UEFI-based and support Secure Boot, unauthorized operating systems, drivers, and firmware can be prevented from running when the virtual machine starts. For this to apply, however, Secure Boot must be enabled for the virtual machine. As the screenshot below shows, you can enable or disable Secure Boot on a Generation 2 virtual machine by opening the Settings of the virtual machine, selecting Firmware under Hardware, and selecting or clearing the Enable Secure Boot checkbox. By default, Secure Boot is enabled when you create a new Generation 2 virtual machine:

For more information about UEFI Secure Boot, see the post titled "Protecting the pre-OS environment with UEFI" in the Building Windows 8 blog at *http://blogs .msdn.com/b/b8/archive/2011/09/22/protecting-the-pre-os-environment-with -uefi.aspx*.

Location of configuration files

Although the default location where virtual machine configuration files are stored can be configured at the host level, you have the option of overriding this default when you create a new virtual machine. You might do this, for example, if you are creating a virtual machine for high availability—that is, a clustered virtual machine on a failover cluster of Hyper-V hosts that uses CSV shared storage. In such a scenario, you need to specify the CSV under the ClusterStorage folder in Failover Cluster Manager as the location where the virtual machine will be stored. Another scenario in which you might override the default configuration file storage location is when you are creating a virtual machine that will be stored on a SMB 3.0 file share on a Scale-Out File Server. In this case, you would specify the client access point that is configured in the failover cluster for the Scale-Out File Server as the location where the virtual machine will be stored. For an example of this second scenario, see "Configure Hyper-V to use Scale-Out File Server" at *http://technet.microsoft.com/en-us/library/hh831463.aspx*.

Startup memory

The memory that each new virtual machine will need is an important consideration when planning the creation of new virtual machines. Physical host systems have a fixed amount of physical memory, and this memory must be shared in an appropriate way among the different virtual machines that run on the host. (The host itself also requires some physical memory to function with optimum performance.) Planning the amount of physical memory to be allocated to a new virtual machine you will create involves two considerations:

- Deciding upon the amount of startup memory to be assigned to the virtual machine. The guest operating system installed in a virtual machine must have access to sufficient memory; otherwise, the virtual machine might not be able to start. The recommended startup memory varies based on the guest operating system involved and also on whether Dynamic Memory is enabled on the host. Some recommended values for startup memory include the following:

  - 512 MBs for Windows Server 2008 R2 and Windows 7

  - 128 MBs for Windows Server 2003

- Deciding whether to enable Dynamic Memory on the virtual machine. Dynamic Memory manages physical memory on the host as a shared resource that can be automatically reallocated among running virtual machines based on changes in memory demand and values you can specify. Dynamic Memory is discussed in more detail in Lesson 3 of this chapter.

Virtual processors

Some workloads can require additional processor resources to perform optimally. Hyper-V allows you to assign one or more virtual processors to each virtual machine running on the host, up to the maximum number of logical processors supported by the guest operating system installed in the virtual machine. You can also use Hyper-V to keep a reserve of the processor resources available to a virtual machine, specify a limit to the amount of processor resources the virtual machine can use, and configure how Hyper-V allocates processor resources when multiple running virtual machines on a host compete for the host's processor resources. For more information on resource control settings for virtual processors, see "Configure Memory and Processors" at *http://technet.microsoft.com/en-us/library /cc742470.aspx*.

Virtual networking

Virtual networking involves creating virtual network adapters in virtual machines and assigning these adapters to virtual switches on the host. The following considerations apply when planning virtual networking for virtual machines:

- Each virtual machine can have up to 12 virtual network adapters installed in it. Of these 12 virtual network adapters, up to 8 can be the *network adapter* type and up to

4 can be the *legacy network adapter* type. These two types of virtual network adapters are discussed in more detail later in this lesson.

- Each virtual network adapter can be configured with either a static MAC address or a dynamic MAC address that is automatically assigned from the configured MAC address range on the host.

- Each virtual network can be assigned a unique VLAN channel to segment or isolate network traffic.

- Up to 512 virtual machines can be assigned to each virtual switch on the host.

> *NOTE* **HYPER-V AND WIRELESS NETWORKING**
>
> Virtual switches on a Hyper-V host cannot be connected to a wireless network adapter on the host system.

Virtual hard disks

When you create a new virtual machine, you have three options concerning the virtual hard disks associated with the new virtual machine:

- You can create a new virtual hard disk when you create the new virtual machine.

- You can assign an existing virtual hard disk to the new virtual machine you are creating.

- You can create a new virtual machine with no virtual hard disk and then assign a virtual hard disk to it afterward.

Another planning consideration concerning virtual hard disks is the type of storage controller used for the disk. Virtual machines include both IDE and SCSI controllers, and you can add virtual hard disks to either type of controller. And although the startup (boot) disk of a virtual machine must be connected to the IDE controller, the underlying physical storage used for the virtual IDE device can be any of the storage types described in the section titled "Storage" in Lesson 1 earlier in this chapter.

Another planning consideration is the type of virtual disk to use—namely, one of the following types:

- **Fixed-size**   This type of virtual hard disk has its image file preallocated on the physical storage device for the maximum size requested when the disk is created. For example, a 250 GB, fixed-size virtual hard disk will occupy 250 GBs of space on the host's storage device.

- **Dynamically expanding**   This type of virtual hard disk uses only as much physical storage space as it needs to store the actual data that the disk currently contains. The size of the virtual disk's image file then grows as additional data is written to it. For example, the image file for a dynamic virtual hard disk of a newly created virtual machine that has no operating system installed on it has a size of only 4 MBs even though its maximum size is configured with the default value of 127 GBs. Once

Windows Server 2012 or Windows Server 2012 R2 has been installed as the guest operating system, however, the size of the virtual disk's image file will grow to more than 8 GBs. See Lesson 3 in this chapter for information on how to expand, compact, or shrink dynamically expanding disks.

- **Differencing** This type of virtual hard disk allows you to make changes to a parent virtual hard disk without modifying the parent disk. For example, the parent disk could have a clean install of Windows Server 2012 R2 as its guest operating system and the differencing disk could contain changes to the parent. The changes can be reverted if needed by merging the differencing disk with the parent. Hyper-V checkpoints use such differencing disk technology.

REAL WORLD **PASS-THROUGH DISKS**

Another type of disk that a Hyper-V virtual machine can use is the pass-through disk, which is not really a virtual disk at all. Instead, with pass-through disks the virtual machine is directly attached to a physical disk on the host's storage system and the physical disk on the host is dedicated for use by the virtual machine only. With the performance improvements that have been made to both fixed-size and dynamically expanding virtual hard disks in recent versions of Hyper-V and given the added flexibility that virtual hard disks can provide, pass-through disks no longer offer any performance benefits beyond those provided by virtual hard disks and should not be used anymore.

Some additional planning considerations relating to virtual hard disks include the following:

- Whether to use virtual hard disks that use the VHD disk format used by previous versions of Hyper-V or the newer VHDX format introduced in Windows Server 2012. Although the older VHD format supported virtual hard disks up to 2040 GBs in size, the newer VHDX format supports virtual hard disks up to 64 TBs in size. VHDX also includes other enhancements, such as improved alignment to make the format work well on large-format disks, larger block sizes for dynamic and differencing disks, support for trim, support for 4 KB logical sector virtual disks, improved safeguards against data corruption when power interruptions occur, and other features. For more information on VHDX improvements, see "Hyper-V Virtual Hard Disk Format Overview" at *http://technet.microsoft.com/en-us/library/hh831446.aspx*.

- If the storage capacity provided by a single virtual hard disk is not sufficient for the needs of the virtual machine's workload, you can create additional virtual disks and attach them to the virtual machine using the IDE controller, SCSI controller, or both controllers.

- The maximum supported storage for a single virtual machine is 512 TBs for all types.

- If your Hyper-V hosts are using a SAN for their storage, you can improve storage performance by taking advantage of the Offloaded Data Transfer (ODX) functionality included in Windows Server 2012 and Windows Server 2012 R2. ODX can help minimize latency, maximize array throughput, and reduce processing and network resource usage on Hyper-V hosts by transparently offloading file-transfer operations from the host to the SAN. For more information, see "Windows Offloaded Data Transfers Overview" at *http://technet.microsoft.com/en-us/library/hh831628.aspx*.

- If your virtual machines need to be able to access storage on a Fibre Channel SAN, they can take advantage of the *virtual Fibre Channel* feature introduced in Windows Server 2012 Hyper-V. This feature provides Fibre Channel ports within the guest operating system so that you can directly connect virtual machines to SAN storage. The benefits of virtual Fibre Channel include being able to virtualize workloads that require direct SAN connectivity and being able to cluster guest operating systems over Fibre Channel. Implementing virtual Fibre Channel requires that the host bus adapter (HBA) on the host have an updated driver that supports virtual Fibre Channel and that the HBA ports be configured with a Fibre Channel topology that supports N_Port ID Virtualization (NPIV). For more information, see "Hyper-V Virtual Fibre Channel Overview" at *http://technet.microsoft.com/en-us/library/hh831413.aspx*.

Online VHDX resize

New in Windows Server 2012 R2 Hyper-V is the ability to increase or decrease the size of a virtual hard disk attached to a virtual machine while that virtual machine is still running on the host. This means that if the workload running on a virtual machine requires more space, you can expand the virtual hard disk without interrupting any applications accessing the workload. And if you want to reallocate storage space from one virtual machine to another, you can shrink the virtual hard disk attached to the first virtual machine (provided that there is sufficient unpartitioned space on the disk) to free up space for expanding the disk on the second machine.

Online resizing of virtual hard disks requires that these disks be using the newer VHDX virtual hard disk format first introduced in Windows Server 2012. VHDX was designed to address the growing technological demands of today's enterprises and provides greater storage capacity, built-in data protection, and support for large-sector hard disk drives. In addition, online resizing requires that the virtual disk be attached to the virtual machine's SCSI bus.

For example, you can take the following steps to use Hyper-V Manager to expand the size of a running virtual machine:

1. In Hyper-V Manager, right-click the virtual machine and select Settings.

2. In the Settings dialog box for the virtual machine, click the Hard Drive node under SCSI Controller for the virtual hard disk you want to expand and then click the Edit button to launch the Edit Virtual Hard Disk Wizard.

3. Select the Expand option on the Choose Action page, click Next, type the new size you want the virtual hard disk to have (see the screenshot below), and then click Next followed by Finish.

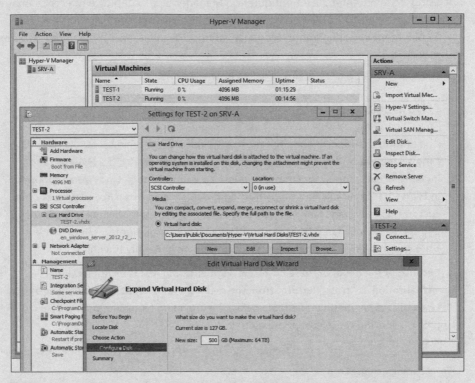

Once you've expanded a virtual hard disk, the option to shrink it will be displayed the next time you use the Edit Virtual Hard Disk Wizard. Of course, you can also resize online virtual disks by using Windows PowerShell.

Guest operating system deployment

You can install guest operating systems in virtual machines the same way you install them on physical systems. For example, you could do the following:

- Manually install the guest operating system by attaching an ISO image of the product media to the virtual machine's virtual DVD drive and then walk through the steps of the installation process.

- Perform a Lite Touch Installation (LTI) deployment of the guest operating system by booting the virtual machine from a server that has the Windows Deployment Services role installed and then stepping through (or automating) the Windows Deployment

Wizard of Microsoft Deployment Toolkit (MDT) 2012 Update 1. For more information, see Chapter 2, "Deploying servers."

- Perform a Zero Touch Installation (ZTI) deployment of the guest operating system by using System Center 2012 Configuration Manager SP1 to deploy a reference image created using MDT 2012 Update 1. For more information, see "Operating System Deployment in Configuration Manager" at *http://technet.microsoft.com/en-us/library /gg682018.*

Linux as a guest

In addition to supporting the full range of Windows client and server operating systems as guest operating systems, Windows Server 2012 R2 Hyper-V also includes broad support for Linux as a guest operating system. Linux guest support in Hyper-V is especially desired by hosting providers who often like to provide their customers with a wide range of platform options for running their web applications and services. Linux (and UNIX) support in Hyper-V is also important in the enterprise space in which heterogeneous IT solutions are generally the norm.

Because of the needs of these customer segments, Microsoft envisions Hyper-V virtualization as "cross-platform from the metal up" and supports a wide range of Linux distros, as shown in the table below, by providing Linux Integration Services (LIS) for specific versions of popular distros.

Distro	Version	LIS Availability
Red Hat Enterprise Linux	5.7, 5.8, 6.0–6.3	Download LIS from Microsoft
	5.9, 6.4	LIS built-in and certified by Red Hat
SUSE Linux Enterprise Server	11 SP2	LIS built-in
CentOS	5.7, 5.8, 6.0–6.3	Download LIS from Microsoft
	5.9, 6.4	LIS built-in
Ubuntu Server	12.04, 12.10, 13.04	LIS built-in
Debian	7.0	LIS built-in

As part of Microsoft's continuing commitment to making Hyper-V the best all-around virtual platform for hosting providers, Linux support for Hyper-V in Windows Server 2012 R2 has been enhanced in the following ways:

- **Improved video** A virtualized video driver is now included for Linux virtual machines to provide an enhanced video experience with better mouse support.

- **Dynamic Memory** Dynamic Memory is now fully supported for Linux virtual machines, including both hot-add and remove functionality. This means you can now run Windows and Linux virtual machines side by side on the same host machine while using Dynamic Memory to ensure fair allocation of memory resources to each virtual machine on the host.

- **Online VHDX resize**   Virtual hard disks attached to Linux virtual machines can now be resized while the virtual machine is running.

- **Online backup**   You can now back up running Linux virtual machines to Windows Azure by using the Windows Azure Online Backup capabilities of the in-box Windows Server Backup utility, System Center Data Protection Manager, or any third-party backup solution that supports backing up Hyper-V virtual machines.

Microsoft also includes robust Linux/UNIX capabilities across the entire System Center family of products and in Windows Azure. Linux/UNIX support is an integral part of all of these platforms, not merely an extension of Windows-centric functionality.

Automatic virtual machine activation

Beginning with Windows Server 2003 R2 with Service Pack 2, the Datacenter edition of Windows Server has provided unlimited virtualization rights for servers to allow organizations to deploy as many virtual machines as they need in their environments. Until now, however, this benefit has come with the cost of the administrative overhead of deploying a key management infrastructure for licensing and activating these virtual machines.

Beginning with Windows Server 2012 R2, the task of managing product keys for virtual machines can be simplified by using a new capability called Automatic Virtual Machine Activation (AVMA). It works like this:

1. To start, the Hyper-V host on which your virtual machines will be deployed must have Windows Server 2012 R2 Datacenter edition installed on it as the host operating system.

2. Next, to avoid having to activate virtual machines and manage their product keys, the virtual machines must have Windows Server 2012 R2 Standard, Windows Server 2012 R2 Datacenter, or Windows Server 2012 R2 Essentials installed on them as their guest operating systems.

3. Once the guest operating system is installed in a virtual machine and the virtual machine is started, you can log on to the virtual machine, open an elevated command prompt, and install the AVMA key in the virtual machine by running this command:

```
slmgr /ipk <AVMA_key>
```

Doing this automatically activates the license for the virtual machine against the host.

4. Alternatively, you can use the AVMA key in an unattend.xml answer file and completely automate the activation of the virtual machine when an unattended installation of the guest operating system is performed on the virtual machine.

AVMA greatly reduces the time and effort that large enterprises and hosters need for managing licensing and activation of large numbers of virtual machines in their environment. Regardless of whether your Hyper-V hosts are OEM machines or are running a volume-licensed version of Windows Server activated using Key Management Service (KMS) or Multiple Activation Key (MAK), if the host machine is running Windows Server 2012 R2 Datacenter edition and is activated then all virtual machines running any Windows Server 2012 R2 edition as a guest operating system are automatically activated.

In addition, AVMA is completely secure with respect to your existing key management infrastructure because no keys are used to activate the virtual machines. So if you copy or move one of your virtual machines to someone else's environment—for example, for demonstration purposes—your keys won't be exposed. Of course, the other environment must also be using hosts running an activated copy of a Datacenter edition of Windows Server.

Performing checkpoints

Although checkpoints (called snapshots in Windows Server 2012 and earlier versions of Hyper-V but now called checkpoints to harmonize with System Center Virtual Machine Manager terminology) are not recommended for use in production environments, they might have value in certain limited scenarios. For example, you might consider performing a checkpoint of a production virtual machine just before you apply a critical software update to the guest operating system of the virtual machine. That way, if something goes wrong after applying the update you can quickly revert the virtual machine to its previous state (that is, before the update was applied). However, there are certain scenarios in which you should never perform checkpoints, specifically the following:

- Don't perform checkpoints on virtualized domain controllers.
- Don't perform checkpoints on virtualized workloads that run time-sensitive services.
- Don't perform checkpoints on virtualized workloads that use data distributed across multiple databases.

Also, don't try to restore checkpoints older than 30 days because the computer password for the guest operating system might have expired, which will cause the guest to *disjoin* itself from the domain.

Finally, if you do plan on performing checkpoints, make sure the host has sufficient storage for all the checkpoint files you might create. Checkpoints can consume a lot of disk space, and you could end up running out of storage space if you perform too many of them.

Considerations for importing virtual machines

Although the process of importing an existing virtual machine onto a Hyper-V host has been simplified in Windows Server 2012 and Windows Server 2012 R2, there are still a number of issues that you should consider before you perform the import. The following improvements were made to the virtual machine import process beginning with Windows Server 2012:

- The import process has been updated so that configuration problems that might prevent the import from being successful are detected and resolved. For example, if you are importing the virtual machine onto a target host that has a different set of virtual switches from those on the source host, the Import Virtual Machine Wizard, which can be launched from Hyper-V Manager, prompts you to choose a virtual switch to connect to the virtual network adapter on the virtual machine.

- Virtual machines can be directly imported from the virtual machine's configuration file without first exporting the virtual machine. You can do this by manually copying the virtual machine files instead of exporting them. In fact, when you export a virtual machine in Windows Server 2012 or Windows Server 2012 R2, all that happens is that a copy of the virtual machine's files is created.

- Hyper-V includes Windows PowerShell cmdlets that you can use to export and import virtual machines.

The following issues might be important to consider when planning the import of virtual machines onto your hosts:

- When you import a virtual machine, you have the choice of either of the following approaches:

    - Registering the virtual machine in-place and assigning the GUID of the existing virtual machine to the new virtual machine (the default). You can choose this option if the virtual machine's files are already in the location where they need to be to run on the target host and you just want to begin running the virtual machine from where it is located.

    - Restoring the virtual machine and assigning the GUID of the existing virtual machine to the new virtual machine. You can use this option if the virtual machine's files are stored on a file share or removable storage device and you want to move them to the default storage location on the target host.

    - Copying the virtual machine and generating a new GUID for the new virtual machine. You can use this option if you want to use the existing virtual machine as a template that you will be importing multiple times to create new virtual machines— for example, for test or development work.

- If you are migrating the virtual machines from a host running an earlier version of Windows Server such as Windows Server 2008 R2, you can use the Compare-VM cmdlet to generate a compatibility report that lists any incompatibilities that the virtual machine might have with the target host. You can then use this report to take steps to resolve such issues so that when you use the Import-VM cmdlet later the import process will go smoothly.

- If you are importing virtual machines from a nonclustered host to a clustered host, there might be additional considerations, such as whether you need to import the virtual machines to the shared storage used by the failover cluster.

Live export

New in Windows Server 2012 R2 is the ability to export a complete copy of a running virtual machine or to export any checkpoint of a running virtual machine. You also can use Virtual Machine Manager 2012 R2 to clone a running virtual machine, which basically involves exporting and then importing a virtual machine to create a new virtual machine that is based on the existing virtual machine. You can even export snapshots (checkpoints) associated with a virtual machine while the virtual machine is running.

One scenario in which live export can be helpful is when a running virtual machine in your environment begins to exhibit some instability but is still performing its expected workload. Previously, you had to choose between the lesser of two evils:

- Stop the virtual machine or take it offline and try to troubleshoot the problem. Unfortunately, while the virtual machine is stopped or offline its workload will no longer be available to users, which can result in loss of either business or productivity.

- Let the virtual machine continue to run and hope it doesn't fail. This approach allows the virtual machine's workload to continue to be available, but instability often causes the application or guest operating system to crash, which means a probable interruption in workload will occur. Once again, this is likely to result in loss of either business or productivity.

With live export, however, you can now clone a copy of your unstable virtual machine without shutting down the virtual machine. You can then let your production virtual machine continue to run while you perform troubleshooting steps on the cloned workload to see if you can resolve the issue causing the instability. Once you determine how to fix the problem by working with the cloned virtual machine, you might be able to repair your production virtual machine without needing to reboot the guest operating system or restart its running applications, depending on the issue causing the instability.

Some other scenarios in which being able to export running virtual machines can be useful include troubleshooting problems with applications running in virtual machines, performing tests prior to moving a virtual machine from your private cloud to a hosted or public cloud environment (or vice versa), and duplicating your existing production environment to create a test lab.

Creating virtual machines

You can create new virtual machines on a Hyper-V host by using either Hyper-V Manager or Windows PowerShell.

Using Hyper-V Manager

You create a new virtual machine using Hyper-V Manager in the same way as in previous versions of Windows Server. The steps in this process are as follows:

1. Launch the New Virtual Machine Wizard by right-clicking the host in Hyper-V Manager and selecting New and then Virtual Machine.

2. Specify a descriptive name for the new virtual machine and optionally specify a different location for storing the virtual machine's files (configuration files, virtual hard disks, and checkpoints) if the default storage locations for the host are not the ones you want to use.

3. Specify the amount of startup memory to be used by the virtual machine's guest operating system and specify whether Dynamic Memory is to be used for the virtual machine.

4. Select an existing virtual switch on the host that should be connected to the virtual network adapter on the virtual machine or leave the virtual machine unconnected from any virtual switches on the host.

5. Create a new virtual disk as the system volume on the virtual machine, attach an existing virtual disk for this purpose, or create the virtual machine without any virtual hard disks attached so that you can attach one later. If you choose the first option, you can specify whether to install the guest operating system later; install it from the virtual CD/DVD drive, ISO image file, or virtual floppy disk; or install it from a network-based installation server (if you have connected the virtual network adapter to a virtual switch).

Using Windows PowerShell

You can also use the New-VM cmdlet to create a new virtual machine using Windows PowerShell. For example, to create a new virtual machine named SRV-A on HOST4, assign the virtual machine 1 GB of startup memory, attach it to the virtual switch named CONTOSO Virtual Switch, create a new virtual hard disk (VHDX file) of 500 GBs in the default location, and make the virtual CD drive the default boot device, use the following command:

```
PS C:\> New-VM -ComputerName HOST4 -Name SRV-A -MemoryStartupBytes 1GB `
-BootDevice CD -SwitchName "CONTOSO Virtual Switch" -NewVHDSizeBytes 500GB `
-NewVHDPath SRV-A.vhdx

Name   State CPUUsage(%) MemoryAssigned(M) Uptime   Status
----   ----- ----------- ----------------- ------   ------
SRV-A  Off   0           0                 00:00:00 Operating normally
```

Importing virtual machines

You can also import existing virtual machines onto a Hyper-V host by using either Hyper-V Manager or Windows PowerShell. For example, to import a virtual machine by using Hyper-V Manager, select the target host and click Import Virtual Machine in the Actions pane. This launches the Import Virtual Machine Wizard. As Figure 7-6 shows, you can use this wizard to perform the various import scenarios described earlier in this lesson.

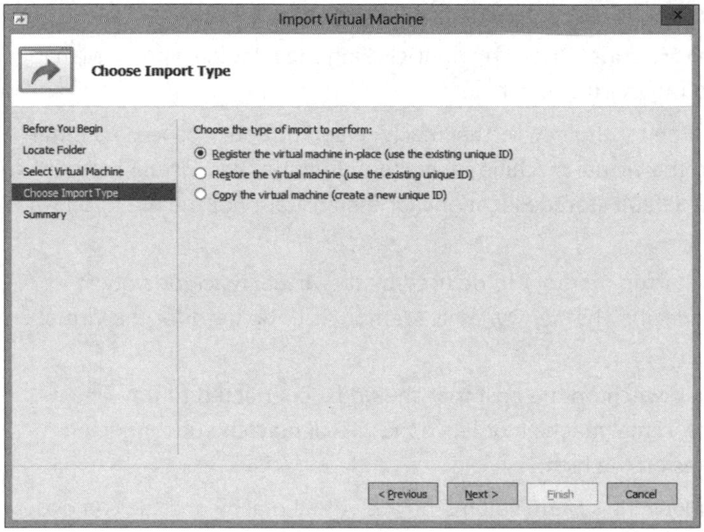

FIGURE 7-6 Use the Import Virtual Machine Wizard.

To import virtual machines by using Windows PowerShell, use the Import-VM cmdlet. For help on using this cmdlet, see the examples at the end of the "Import-VM" topic at *http://technet.microsoft.com/en-us/library/hh848495*.

✔ **Quick check**

- You want to use an existing virtual machine as a template for creating new virtual machines on a Hyper-V host in your test environment. Should you register, restore, or copy the virtual machine when you import it onto a host?

Quick check answer

- You should copy it. This generates a new GUID for each new virtual machine you create with the import process.

Configuring virtual machines S

Once you have created a virtual machine, you might need to further configure its virtual hardware and management settings. You can do this either by opening the virtual machine's settings in Hyper-V Manager or by using Windows PowerShell. For example, to view or modify the settings for a virtual machine by using Hyper-V Manager, right-click the virtual machine and select Settings. Doing this displays a Settings dialog box such as the one shown in Figure 7-7.

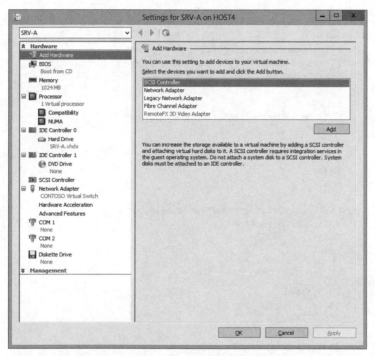

FIGURE 7-7 Configure virtual hardware for a virtual machine.

To view the settings of the same virtual machine by using Windows PowerShell, you can use the Get-VM cmdlet as shown here:

```
PS C:\> Get-VM -Name SRV-A | Format-List *

VMName                     : SRV-A
VMId                       : cabb9f25-1d4a-4ce0-884a-a04520ed0880
Id                         : cabb9f25-1d4a-4ce0-884a-a04520ed0880
Name                       : SRV-A
State                      : Off
OperationalStatus          : {Ok}
PrimaryOperationalStatus   : Ok
SecondaryOperationalStatus :
StatusDescriptions         : {Operating normally}
PrimaryStatusDescription   : Operating normally
SecondaryStatusDescription :
```

```
Status                          : Operating normally
Heartbeat                       :
ReplicationState                : Disabled
ReplicationHealth               : NotApplicable
ReplicationMode                 : None
CPUUsage                        : 0
MemoryAssigned                  : 0
MemoryDemand                    : 0
MemoryStatus                    :
SmartPagingFileInUse            : False
Uptime                          : 00:00:00
IntegrationServicesVersion      :
ResourceMeteringEnabled         : False
ConfigurationLocation           : C:\ProgramData\Microsoft\Windows\Hyper-V
SnapshotFileLocation            : C:\ProgramData\Microsoft\Windows\Hyper-V
AutomaticStartAction            : StartIfRunning
AutomaticStopAction             : Save
AutomaticStartDelay             : 0
SmartPagingFilePath             : C:\ProgramData\Microsoft\Windows\Hyper-V
NumaAligned                     :
NumaNodesCount                  : 1
NumaSocketCount                 : 1
IsDeleted                       : False
ComputerName                    : HOST4
Notes                           :
Path                            : C:\ProgramData\Microsoft\Windows\Hyper-V
CreationTime                    : 8/13/2012 8:16:47 AM
IsClustered                     : False
SizeOfSystemFiles               : 28464
ParentSnapshotId                :
ParentSnapshotName              :
MemoryStartup                   : 1073741824
DynamicMemoryEnabled            : False
MemoryMinimum                   : 536870912
MemoryMaximum                   : 1099511627776
ProcessorCount                  : 1
RemoteFxAdapter                 :
NetworkAdapters                 : {Network Adapter}
FibreChannelHostBusAdapters     : {}
ComPort1                        : Microsoft.HyperV.PowerShell.VMComPort
ComPort2                        : Microsoft.HyperV.PowerShell.VMComPort
FloppyDrive                     : Microsoft.HyperV.PowerShell.VMFloppyDiskDrive
DVDDrives                       : {DVD Drive on IDE controller number 1 at location 0}
HardDrives                      : {Hard Drive on IDE controller number 0 at location 0}
VMIntegrationService            : {Time Synchronization, Heartbeat, Key-Value Pair Exchange,
Shutdown...}
```

To modify these virtual machine settings, you can use the Set-VM cmdlet and other Hyper-V cmdlets. In the sections that follow, we examine only a few of these different virtual machine settings and how to configure them. For additional information on configuring virtual machine settings, search the TechNet Library for the appropriate topic.

Adding virtual disks

You can use the IDE Controller 0, IDE Controller 1, and SCSI Controller pages of the virtual machine Settings dialog box in Hyper-V Manager to add new virtual disks to a virtual machine. You can also use subpages of these pages to inspect, browse, or edit an existing virtual hard disk; remove a virtual disk that is attached to the virtual machine; or attach a physical disk on the host's storage system to the virtual machine.

When you add a virtual disk using the New Virtual Hard Disk Wizard, you have a choice of using either the VHDX or VHD format for the new disk. (The default is VHDX.) The New Virtual Hard Disk Wizard also lets you configure a name for the new disk, the disk type (the default is dynamically expanding), the maximum size for the disk (the default is 127 GBs), and whether the new disk should be blank or contain the data on a physical disk on the host or on an existing virtual disk, as shown in Figure 7-8.

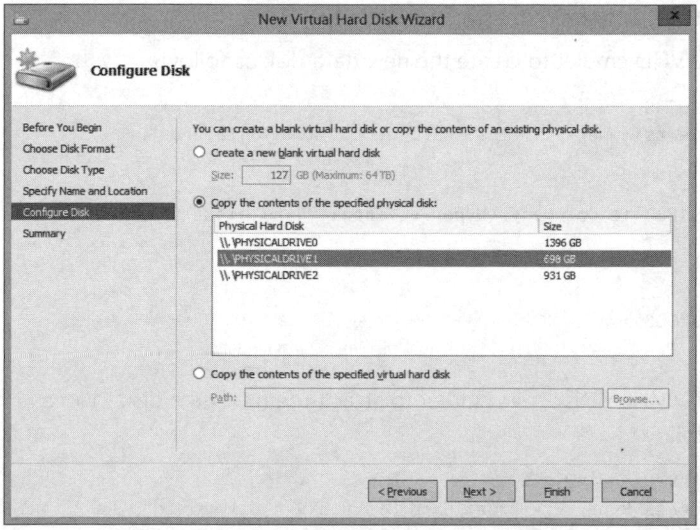

FIGURE 7-8 Configure a new virtual disk to copy its data from a physical disk on the host.

You can also use the Add Hardware page of the virtual machine Settings dialog box to add SCSI controllers to your virtual machine so that you can connect more virtual disks to the virtual machine.

You can also use Windows PowerShell to create new virtual disks and add them to your virtual machines. For example, say you want to create and attach a 500 GB dynamically expanding data disk to virtual machine SRV-A on HOST4. You can begin by using the Get-VHD command to display a list of disks attached to SRV-A as follows:

```
PS C:\> Get-VM -VMName SRV-A | Select-Object VMId | Get-VHD | `
Format-List Path,VhdFormat,VhdType,Size

Path                     : C:\Users\Public\Documents\Hyper-V\Virtual Hard Disks\SRV-A.vhdx
VhdFormat                : VHDX
```

```
VhdType            : Dynamic
Size               : 536870912000
```

The preceding command takes advantage of the pipeline capabilities of Windows PowerShell and works like this:

1. The command Get-VM –VMName SRV-A returns an object representing virtual machine SRV-A.

2. The output of the preceding command is then piped into the command Select-Object VMId, which returns an object representing the GUID for SRV-A.

3. The GUID for SRV-A is then piped into the Get-VHD command to indicate which virtual machine is to be queried for its virtual disks.

4. The output of the Get-VHD command is then formatted as a list to display only those properties of interest—namely, the path and file name of the virtual disk file, the format it uses, the disk's type, and the disk's size.

Next you can use the New-VHD cmdlet to create the new data disk as follows:

```
PS C:\> New-VHD -SizeBytes 500GB `
-Path "C:\Users\Public\Documents\Hyper-V\Virtual Hard Disks\SRV-A-data.vhdx"

ComputerName       : HOST4
Path               : C:\Users\Public\Documents\Hyper-V\Virtual Hard Disks\SRV-A-data.vhdx
VhdFormat          : VHDX
VhdType            : Dynamic
FileSize           : 4194304
Size               : 536870912000
...
```

Then you can use the Add-VMHardDiskDrive cmdlet to attach the new data disk to location 1 on IDE controller 0 as follows:

```
PS C:\> Add-VMHardDiskDrive -VMName SRV-A `
-Path "C:\Users\Public\Documents\Hyper-V\Virtual Hard Disks\SRV-A-data.vhdx" `
-ControllerType IDE -ControllerNumber 0 -ControllerLocation 1
```

You can then use the Get-VHD cmdlet as before to verify the result:

```
PS C:\> Get-VM -VMName SRV-A | Select-Object VMId | Get-VHD | `
Format-List Path,VhdFormat,VhdType,Size

Path        : C:\Users\Public\Documents\Hyper-V\Virtual Hard Disks\SRV-A.vhdx
VhdFormat   : VHDX
VhdType     : Dynamic
Size        : 536870912000

Path        : C:\Users\Public\Documents\Hyper-V\Virtual Hard Disks\SRV-A-data.vhdx
VhdFormat   : VHDX
VhdType     : Dynamic
Size        : 536870912000
```

Alternatively, you can use the Get-VMHardDiskDrive cmdlet to display all disks connected to the IDE controllers on the virtual machine:

```
PS C:\> Get-VMHardDiskDrive -VMName SRV-A | `
Format-List ControllerNumber,ControllerLocation,Path

ControllerNumber   : 0
ControllerLocation : 0
Path               : C:\Users\Public\Documents\Hyper-V\Virtual Hard Disks\SRV-A.vhdx

ControllerNumber   : 0
ControllerLocation : 1
Path               : C:\Users\Public\Documents\Hyper-V\Virtual Hard Disks\SRV-A-data.
vhdx
```

Viewing the IDE 0 Controller page and its subpages in the Settings dialog box for the virtual machine also confirms that the procedure was successful.

Adding and configuring virtual network adapters

You can use the Add Hardware page of the virtual machine Settings dialog box in Hyper-V Manager to add new virtual network adapters to your virtual machine. You can choose from two types of virtual network adapters:

- **Network adapter** Originally called a *synthetic network adapter* in the first version of Hyper-V, this type of virtual network adapter relies on Integration Components being installed in the virtual machine to ensure optimal performance. Operating systems such as Windows Server 2008 R2 and later have Integration Components built into them. When you use older operating systems for the guest, you might need to install Integration Components in the virtual machine.

- **Legacy network adapter** This type of virtual network adapter emulates a multiport DEC 21140 10/100TX 100 MB Ethernet adapter and is provided for three main reasons:

  - To support legacy guest operating systems that do not support the installation of Integration Components.

  - To support non-Windows guest operating systems for which Hyper-V does not provide Integration Components.

  - To support network-based installations. (Legacy network adapters have the ability to boot to the Pre-Boot Execution Environment [PXE] to start the network-based installation process.)

> *NOTE* **SUPPORT FOR LEGACY NETWORK ADAPTERS**
>
> Legacy network adapters are not supported in the 64-bit edition of Windows Server 2003 or the Windows XP Professional x64 edition.

Once a virtual network adapter has been added to your virtual machine, you can configure the adapter by selecting the appropriate page in the virtual machine Settings dialog box as shown in Figures 7-9, 7-10, and 7-11. The configuration settings available for the network adapter type of virtual network adapter are as follows:

- **Virtual Switch**   You can connect the virtual network adapter to a different virtual switch on the host or even remove all connectivity if needed.

- **Virtual LAN Identification**   You can enable VLAN identification and specify a VLAN ID to segment or isolate network traffic for the virtual network adapter.

- **Bandwidth Management**   You can specify how much network bandwidth the virtual network adapter should use for communications over the connected virtual switch.

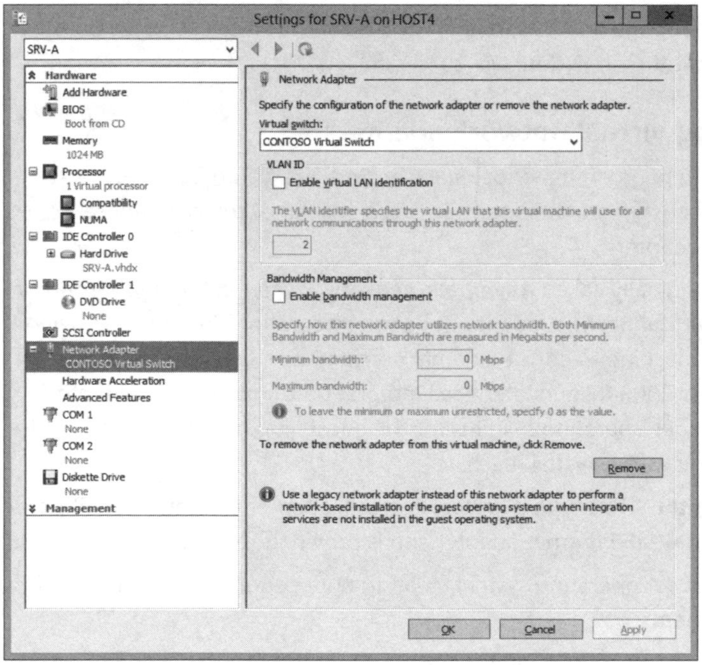

FIGURE 7-9 The Settings dialog box shows the configuration settings available for virtual network adapters.

- **Virtual Machine Queue (VMQ)**   This technology allows supported network adapters to use hardware packet filtering to deliver packet data from an external virtual machine network directly to the virtual machine. This reduces the overhead of routing and copying packets from the management operating system to the virtual machine. VMQ is enabled by default on new virtual network adapters.

- **IPsec Task Offloading**   This technology allows supported network adapters to perform IPsec processing to reduce the processing load on the host. IPsec task offloading is enabled by default on new virtual network adapters.

- **Single-Root I/O Virtualization** You can assign SR-IOV-capable network adapters directly to a virtual machine to maximize network throughput while minimizing network latency and the CPU overhead required for processing network traffic. Implementing SR-IOV requires host firmware, such as Intel VT-d, that supports SR-IOV and an SR-IOV-capable network adapter and driver installed in both the management operating system and the virtual machine.

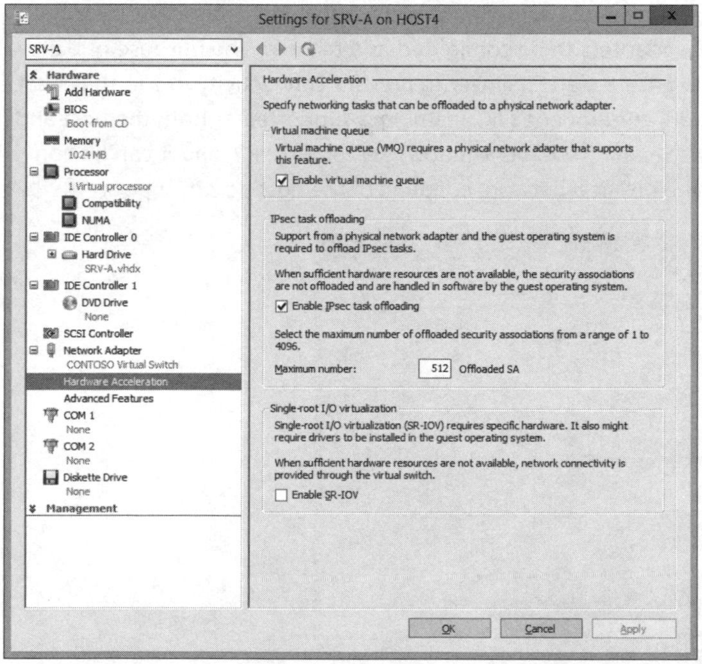

FIGURE 7-10 The Settings dialog box also shows the hardware acceleration settings available for virtual network adapters.

- **MAC Address** You can configure a virtual network adapter to obtain its MAC address dynamically from the pool of available MAC addresses configured on the host, or you can assign a static MAC address to the adapter.

- **MAC Address Spoofing** This feature helps protect the virtual machine against attempts to use ARP spoofing to steal IP addresses from the virtual machine by allowing the virtual machine to change the source MAC address in outgoing packets to an address that is not assigned to it.

- **DHCP Guard** This feature helps protect the virtual machine against Dynamic Host Configuration Protocol (DHCP) man-in-the-middle attacks by dropping DHCP server messages from unauthorized virtual machines pretending to be DHCP servers.

- **Router Guard** This feature helps safeguard the virtual machine against unauthorized routers by dropping router advertisement and redirection messages from unauthorized virtual machines pretending to be routers.

- **Protected Network** In a Failover Clustering environment, this feature causes the virtual machine to move to another cluster node if a network disconnection is detected. This setting is new in Windows Server 2012 R2 Hyper-V.

- **Port Mirroring** This feature copies traffic sent to or from a Hyper-V virtual switch port to a mirror port so that third-party network diagnostic and performance tools can monitor the switch port.

- **NIC Teaming** Also known as *load balancing and failover (LBFO)*, this feature allows multiple virtual network adapters to be configured as a team for the purpose of bandwidth aggregation or to ensure traffic failover to prevent connectivity loss in the event of the failure of a network component. NIC Teaming is supported at both the host and guest levels in Windows Server 2012 and Windows Server 2012 R2, and it can be configured in the guest if the physical network adapters of the host do not support it.

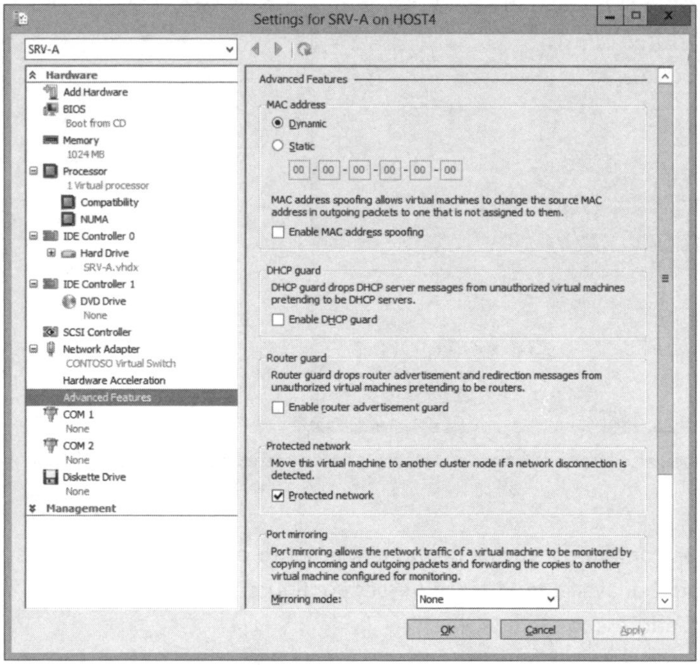

FIGURE 7-11 Additional configuration settings are available for virtual network adapters.

You can also use Windows PowerShell to view, add, remove, and configure virtual network adapters of both the network adapter type and the legacy network adapter type. For example, say you want to add a second virtual network adapter to a virtual machine, connect it to a virtual switch on the host, and enable both DHCP Guard and Router Guard on the adapter. To do this, you can begin by using the Get-VMNetworkAdapter cmdlet to display a list of virtual network adapters installed on the virtual machine:

```
PS C:\> Get-VMNetworkAdapter -VMName SRV-B
```

```
Name                    IsManagementOs VMName SwitchName      MacAddress    Status IPAddresses
----                    -------------- ------ ----------      ----------    ------ -----------
Network Adapter False                  SRV-B  CONTOSO Virtua... 00155D0BE600          {}
```

Next you can use the Add-VMNetworkAdapter to create the new adapter and connect it to the desired virtual switch:

```
PS C:\> Add-VMNetworkAdapter -VMName SRV-B -VMNetworkAdapterName "Network Adapter 2" `
-SwitchName "MANAGEMENT Virtual Switch"
```

You can then use the Get-VMNetworkAdapter again to verify the result:

```
PS C:\> Get-VMNetworkAdapter -VMName SRV-B
```

```
Name                     IsManagementOs VMName SwitchName      MacAddress    Status IPAddresses
----                     -------------- ------ ----------      ----------    ------ -----------
Network Adapter   False                 SRV-B  CONTOSO Virt... 00155D0BE600          {}
Network Adapter 2 False                 SRV-B  MANAGEMENT V... 000000000000          {}
```

You can pipe the output of the preceding command into the Format-List cmdlet to determine whether DHCP Guard and Router Guard are already enabled on the adapter:

```
PS C:\> Get-VMNetworkAdapter -VMName SRV-B -VMNetworkAdapterName "Network Adapter 2" `
| Format-List DhcpGuard,RouterGuard
```

```
DhcpGuard   : Off
RouterGuard : Off
```

Now use the Set-VMNetworkAdapter to enable both of these features on the adapter:

```
PS C:\> Set-VMNetworkAdapter -VMName SRV-B -VMNetworkAdapterName "Network Adapter 2" `
-DhcpGuard On -RouterGuard On
```

Running Get-VMNetworkAdapter again verifies the result:

```
PS C:\> Get-VMNetworkAdapter -VMName SRV-B -VMNetworkAdapterName "Network Adapter 2" `
| Format-List DhcpGuard,RouterGuard
```

```
DhcpGuard   : On
RouterGuard : On
```

Configuring other hardware settings

Some of the other virtual hardware settings you might want to configure include the following:

- BIOS settings—for example, to modify the boot device order or turn on Num Lock
- Memory settings—for example, to change the amount of startup RAM or enable Dynamic Memory on the virtual machine
- Processor settings—for example, to configure the number of virtual processors that the virtual machine uses, enable processor compatibility to allow live migrations to hosts having a different processor architecture, or configure the NUMA topology on a NUMA-capable host

These settings and others can be configured using either Hyper-V Manager or Windows PowerShell, and you can search the TechNet Library for more information about what they do and how to configure them.

Configuring virtual machine management

In addition to configuring the virtual hardware for a new virtual machine, you might need to configure some of its management settings. As with virtual hardware, you can do this either by opening the virtual machine's Settings dialog box in Hyper-V Manager as shown in Figure 7-12 or by using Windows PowerShell.

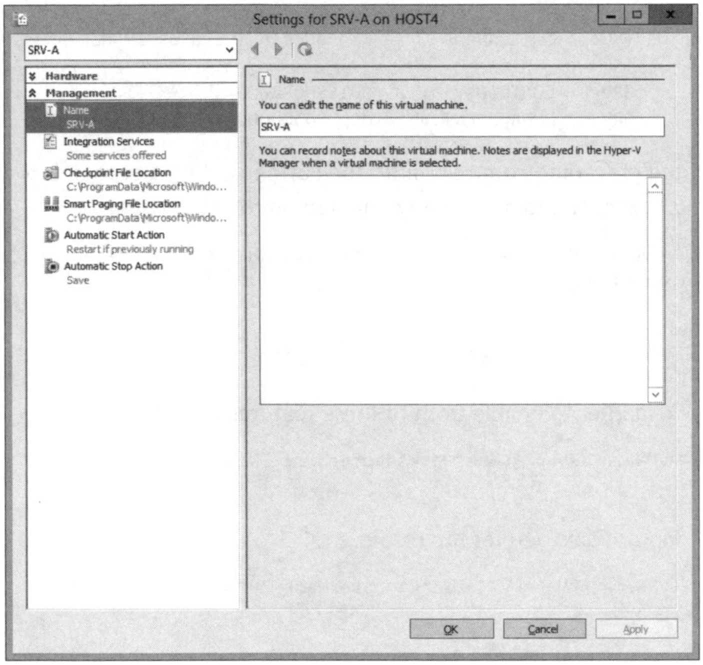

FIGURE 7-12 Configure management settings for a virtual machine.

The management settings you can configure for a virtual machine are as follows:

- **Name** If you want, you can change the name of the virtual machine as displayed in Hyper-V Manager and used with Windows PowerShell cmdlets. However, changing the name of the virtual machine does not change the names of the virtual machine's configuration files and virtual hard disk files.

- **Integration Services** By default, all Integration Services are offered to the virtual machine. However, if you need to, you can disable some or all of these services—for example, if the guest operating system doesn't support some of them.

- **Checkpoint File Location** By default, checkpoint files are stored in subfolders of the default location where virtual machine configuration files are stored. If you frequently perform checkpoints and are running out of storage space on the host storage device, you might want to change the checkpoint files location to a different storage device.

- **Smart Paging File Location** This new feature introduced in Windows Server 2012 Hyper-V allows a virtual machine that is being restarted to temporarily use disk resources on the host as a source for any additional memory needed to successfully restart the virtual machine. Then, after the virtual machine has been restarted and its memory requirements have lessened, Smart Paging releases the previously used disk resources because of the performance hit that such use can create. Smart Paging is used only when a virtual machine is restarted and there is no free physical memory on the host and no memory can be reclaimed from other running virtual machines. Smart Paging is not used if you just try to start a virtual machine that's in a stopped state or if a virtual machine is failing over in a cluster.

- **Automatic Start Action** This setting allows you to specify what the virtual machine should do when the host machine boots up. You can choose to automatically start the virtual machine if it was running when the VMM service on the host stopped (the default), to always start the virtual machine automatically, or to do nothing. You can also specify a startup delay in seconds to reduce resource content between different virtual machines starting up on the host.

- **Automatic Stop Action** This setting allows you to specify what the virtual machine should do when host machine shuts down. You can choose to save the virtual machine state (the default), turn off the virtual machine, or shut down the guest operating system.

You can also use Set-VM cmdlet of Windows PowerShell to configure the preceding virtual machine management settings. For example, to change the name of virtual machine SRV-A on HOST4 to SQL Workload, you would use this command:

```
Set-VM -Name SRV-A -NewVMName "SQL Workload" -ComputerName HOST4
```

Lesson summary

- Key considerations when planning the deployment of virtual machines include the location of configuration files, startup memory, Dynamic Memory, virtual networking, virtual hard disks, guest operating system deployment, and performing checkpoints.

- Different types of virtual disks have advantages and disadvantages that make them suitable for different scenarios.

- Generally, you should not use checkpoints in production environments.

- You can create and configure new virtual machines by using the Hyper-V Manager snap-in or Windows PowerShell.

- You can create new virtual disks and attach them to virtual machines by using the Hyper-V Manager snap-in or Windows PowerShell.

- You can create and configure new virtual network adapters on virtual machines by using the Hyper-V Manager snap-in or Windows PowerShell.

- Hyper-V virtual network adapters in Windows Server 2012 and Windows Server 2012 R2 have many advanced features that can provide security, control bandwidth, reduce processor overhead, and provide other benefits.

Lesson review

Answer the following questions to test your knowledge of the information in this lesson. You can find the answers to these questions and explanations of why each answer choice is correct or incorrect in the "Answers" section at the end of this chapter.

1. Which of the following is *not* true concerning virtual network adapters?

    A. Each virtual machine can have up to 12 virtual network adapters installed in it.

    B. Each virtual network adapter can be configured with either a static MAC address or a dynamic MAC address.

    C. Each virtual network can be assigned a unique VLAN channel.

    D. Virtual switches on a Hyper-V host can be connected to a wireless network adapter on the host system.

2. Why are pass-through disks no longer recommended for Hyper-V virtual machines? (Choose all that apply.)

    A. Pass-through disks are no longer being manufactured and therefore are difficult to obtain.

    B. Tests have demonstrated that fixed-size virtual hard disks perform almost as well as pass-through disks and also provide the flexibility benefits of virtual hard disks.

    C. Tests have demonstrated that dynamically expanding virtual hard disks perform almost as well as pass-through disks and also provide the flexibility benefits of virtual hard disks.

    D. Configuring a virtual machine to use a pass-through disk is a complex task that might introduce errors.

3. Although performing checkpoints is not recommended in production environments, they are sometimes used. Which of the following checkpoint actions should you never take? (Choose all that apply.)

    A. Performing checkpoints on virtualized domain controllers

    B. Performing checkpoints on a virtual machine just before applying a critical software update to the guest operating system

    C. Performing checkpoints on virtualized workloads that use data distributed across multiple databases

    D. Restoring checkpoints older than 30 days on domain-joined virtual machines

4. You want to enable DHCP Guard on a virtual network adapter on virtual machine SRV-B running on host HOST4. To do this, you run the following command:

```
Set-VMNetworkAdapter -ComputerName HOST4 -VMName SRV-B -DhcpGuard:$true
```

Unfortunately, running this command returns the following error:

```
Set-VMNetworkAdapter : Cannot bind parameter 'DhcpGuard'. Cannot convert value
"True" to type "Microsoft.HyperV.PowerShell.OnOffState". Error: "Invalid cast from
'System.Boolean' to 'Microsoft.HyperV.PowerShell.OnOffState'."
At line:1 char:67
+ Set-VMNetworkAdapter -ComputerName HOST4 -VMName SRV-B -DhcpGuard:$true
+                                                                  ~~~~~
    + CategoryInfo          : InvalidArgument: (:) [Set-VMNetworkAdapter],
ParameterBindingException
    + FullyQualifiedErrorId :
CannotConvertArgumentNoMessage,Microsoft.HyperV.PowerShell.Commands.
SetVMNetworkAdapterCommand
```

What is the reason for this error?

A. The virtual network adapter does not support DHCP Guard.

B. You forgot to include the *–VMName* parameter in your command to specify which virtual network adapter you want to configure on the virtual machine.

C. You should have specified *–DhcpGuard ok* instead of *–DhcpGuard:$true* in your command.

D. You should have specified *–DhcpGuard 1* instead of *–DhcpGuard:$true* in your command.

Lesson 3: Managing virtual machines 6

Once you have deployed virtual machines onto the Hyper-V hosts in your environment, you need to manage and maintain those virtual machines. This lesson focuses on a few key management tasks you can perform using built-in tools in Windows Server 2012 and Windows Server 2012 R2, such as optimizing workload consolidation, optimizing network performance, optimizing virtual disks, managing checkpoints, and monitoring virtual machines.

> **After this lesson, you will be able to:**
>
> - Optimize workload consolidation on Hyper-V hosts by configuring Dynamic Memory on virtual machines.
> - Optimize network performance of virtual machines by configuring bandwidth management.
> - Optimize virtual hard disks by compacting, converting, expanding, or shrinking them as needed.

- Manage checkpoints by using the Hyper-V Manager snap-in or Windows PowerShell.

- Monitor virtual machines by using the Hyper-V Manager snap-in or Windows PowerShell.

Estimated lesson time: 30 minutes

Optimizing workload consolidation

One of the key benefits of server virtualization is that it allows businesses to better utilize their hardware resources. For example, in a traditional (nonvirtualized) environment, you might have a dozen servers at your head office location with each server performing some specialized role, such as file server, print server, database server, DHCP server, and so on. Many of these server roles can incur low average processing overhead, and this means that much of the system hardware in your server room might be significantly underutilized. For example, a dedicated DHCP server might have an average CPU usage of less than 10 percent.

By virtualizing your server workloads, you might be able to consolidate most—or even all—of your existing physical servers as virtual machines running on a single two-mode failover cluster of Hyper-V hosts. This reduces the number of physical servers in your environment from a dozen to only two, which not only simplifies your physical infrastructure but also might lead to significant cost savings because of the reduced power requirements. By using P2V conversion using the tools available in System Center Virtual Machine Manager or a third-party product, you have a dozen virtualized server workloads to manage instead of a dozen physical systems. And by carefully analyzing the processor and memory requirements of your original servers, you can choose appropriate system hardware for your two Hyper-V hosts to ensure that they have enough processing and memory resources to run all these virtual machines with optimal performance.

This leads to the question of how many virtual machines one can actually run on a Hyper-V host. This question was previously discussed in Lesson 1 in a Real World reader aid titled "Planning the host processor and memory" to demonstrate a simple way of determining how many virtual machines a host can run if each virtual machine is assigned a fixed amount of physical memory from the host. But in the real world, the memory requirements of a server (either physical or virtual) can vary significantly over time depending on the load incurred by clients accessing the operating system and applications running on the server. By adjusting the memory allocated to each virtual machine on a host so that the virtual machine has just enough memory to perform optimally, you might be able to significantly increase the number of virtual machines that can simultaneously run on the host. Achieving higher virtual machine consolidation ratios through this approach can result in cost savings by eliminating the need for costly memory upgrades or even more costly purchases of additional host systems.

This capability is what *Dynamic Memory* is all about. Dynamic Memory was first introduced for Hyper-V in Windows Server 2008 R2 as a way of enabling Hyper-V hosts to make more effective use of physical memory allocated to virtual machines running on the host. Dynamic Memory works by adjusting the amount of memory available to a virtual machine in real time. These adjustments in memory allocation are based on how much memory the virtual machine needs and how Dynamic Memory settings have been configured for the virtual machine.

Although it can provide some benefit when virtualizing server workloads, Dynamic Memory is especially valuable for Virtual Desktop Infrastructure (VDI) scenarios, in which it can provide scalability and performance benefits that can result in significant cost savings. This is because at any given time in a VDI environment, some of the virtual machines running on the host tend either to be idle or to have a relatively low load. By using Dynamic Memory, you can consolidate greater numbers of virtual machines on your Hyper-V hosts. This means that you'll need fewer hosts for provisioning virtual desktops to your user population, which means you won't need to procure as much high-end server hardware and can therefore save money.

Configuring Dynamic Memory

As shown in Figure 7-13, you can use the Memory page of the virtual machine Settings dialog box in Hyper-V Manager to enable and configure Dynamic Memory for a virtual machine. You can only enable and configure Dynamic Memory on a per-virtual machine basis. Once it is enabled for a virtual machine, the settings you can configure for Dynamic Memory include the following:

- **Minimum RAM**   This setting specifies the minimum amount of memory that the virtual machine can use while it is running.

- **Maximum RAM**   This setting specifies the maximum amount of memory that the virtual machine can use while it is running.

- **Memory Buffer**   This setting specifies the amount of memory (as a percentage of the amount that the virtual machine actually needs to perform its workload) that can be allocated to the virtual machine when there is sufficient memory available on the host.

- **Memory Weight**   This setting is a parameter that determines how available memory on the host is allocated among the different virtual machines running on the host.

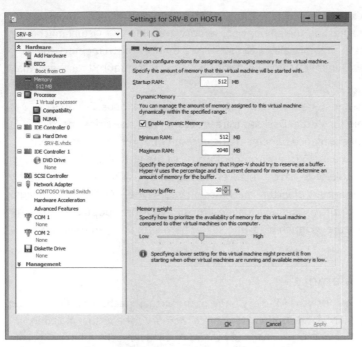

FIGURE 7-13 Configure Dynamic Memory for a virtual machine.

REAL WORLD **UNDERSTANDING THE MEMORY BUFFER**

You can think of the Memory Buffer setting for Dynamic Memory as a memory reserve for the virtual machine. For example, if you configure the buffer to have a value of 50 percent, an additional amount of memory of up to 50 percent of the committed memory can be allocated to the virtual machine when needed.

One common scenario in which this can provide benefits is when the virtual machine is running a workload that makes heavy use of the disk cache. In this case, increasing the buffer setting will result in additional memory being allocated to the virtual memory from the pool of idle memory on the host. In such scenarios, begin by raising the buffer setting from its default value of 20 percent to something like 30 or 40 percent and observe the change in the performance of the workload. Then, if additional tuning is required, try raising the buffer setting a little further. Just don't suddenly bump it up to 300 percent, because you might end up starving the other workloads on the host!

The Minimum RAM setting was introduced in Windows Server 2012 Hyper-V because Windows generally needs more memory when starting than it does when idle and running. As a result of this change, you can specify sufficient startup RAM to enable the virtual machine to start quickly and then a lesser amount of memory (the minimum RAM) for when the virtual machine is running. That way, a virtual machine can get some extra memory so that it can start properly, and then once it's started Windows reclaims the unneeded memory so that other virtual machines on the host can use the reclaimed memory if needed.

Another change in the way you can configure Dynamic Memory in Windows Server 2012 and Windows Server 2012 R2 is that you can modify the Maximum RAM and Minimum RAM settings while the virtual machine is running. In Windows Server 2008 R2, you could modify the Maximum RAM setting only when the virtual machine was in a stopped state. This change gives you a new way of quickly provisioning more memory to a critical virtual machine when needed.

You can also use the Set-VM cmdlet to enable and configure Dynamic Memory for a virtual machine using Windows PowerShell. For example, say you wanted to enable Dynamic Memory for a virtual machine named SRV-B that is running on HOST4 and configure the maximum RAM as 4 GBs. To do this, you first have to stop the virtual machine because you cannot enable or disable Dynamic Memory while the virtual machine is running. You can use the Stop-VM cmdlet to do this as follows:

```
PS C:\> Stop-VM -Name SRV-B -ComputerName HOST4
```

Next you can use the Set-VM cmdlet to enable Dynamic Memory for the virtual machine and set the maximum RAM to 4 GBs as follows:

```
PS C:\> Set-VM -Name SRV-B -ComputerName HOST4 -DynamicMemory -MemoryMaximumBytes 4GB
```

Now you can use Start-VM to restart the stopped virtual machine:

```
PS C:\> Start-VM -Name SRV-B -ComputerName HOST4
```

Finally, you can use Get-VM to verify the result:

```
PS C:\> Get-VM -Name SRV-B -ComputerName HOST4 | `
Format-List DynamicMemoryEnabled,MemoryMaximum

DynamicMemoryEnabled : True
MemoryMaximum        : 4294967296
```

Now say that you decide later that 3 GBs would be a better value for maximum RAM than 4 GBs. By using the –*Passthru* parameter, which specifies that an object is to be passed through to the pipeline, you can make the change and verify the result by using a single Windows PowerShell command as follows:

```
PS C:\> Stop-VM -Name SRV-B -ComputerName HOST4 -Passthru | Set-VM -DynamicMemory `
-MemoryMaximumBytes 3GB -Passthru | Start-VM -Passthru | Get-VM | `
Format-List DynamicMemoryEnabled,MemoryMaximum

DynamicMemoryEnabled : True
MemoryMaximum        : 3221225472
```

> **MORE INFO** **USING THE –*PASSTHRU* PARAMETER**
>
> For more information on using the –*Passthru* parameter, see "Use the PowerShell Passthru Parameter and Get Back Objects" at *http://blogs.technet.com/b/heyscriptingguy/archive /2011/11/18/use-the-powershell-passthru-parameter-and-get-back-objects.aspx.*

Configuring host reserved memory

Although Dynamic Memory can help you consolidate more virtualized workloads on a host, it's important that the host itself have enough memory. If the host has insufficient memory, the management operating system might stop responding or crash, resulting in all virtual machines being stopped unexpectedly and possible data loss.

To prevent this from happening, Hyper-V automatically reserves some of the host's physical memory for the management operating system. With Hyper-V in Windows Server 2008 R2 SP1, you could also manually specify how much memory should be reserved for the host by using Registry Editor to create a REG_DWORD registry value named MemoryReserve in the following location:

HKLM\Software\Microsoft\Windows NT\CurrentVersion\Virtualization

You could then use MemoryReserve to specify the amount of physical memory in MBs that should be reserved for the parent partition, with 2 GBs (2048 MBs) being the recommended value. The host then had to be rebooted for the change to take effect.

With Hyper-V in Windows Server 2012 and Windows Server 2012 R2, however, the management operating system on the host reserves more memory than in previous versions of Hyper-V to ensure greater reliability and responsiveness. In addition, manually configuring the MemoryReserve registry value as just described can have undesirable results in some circumstances. For example, a combination of management activity, background processes, scheduled tasks, and other activity on the host might cause memory usage by the management operating system to temporarily rise above the value you manually configured by using the MemoryReserve registry value. Should this occur, the management operating system might stop responding or crash, resulting in service interruption and possible data loss. As a result, Microsoft no longer recommends manually configuring the MemoryReserve registry value. Instead, you should allow Hyper-V itself to ensure enough memory is always reserved for the host.

Optimizing network performance

Good network performance is also important between your virtualized workloads and clients accessing them. Windows Server 2012 and Windows Server 2012 R2 networking features were described previously in the section titled "Adding and configuring virtual network adapters" in Lesson 2. The following sections describe which of these features can help optimize network performance for virtual machines.

Configuring bandwidth management

You can use the main page for a virtual network adapter in the virtual machine Settings dialog box to enable and configure bandwidth management for the adapter. Bandwidth management, also known as *Hyper-V quality of service (Hyper-V QoS)*, is a new feature introduced in Windows Server 2012 that enables you to guarantee network traffic levels for virtual network adapters and virtual switches. In the previous version of Hyper-V, you could configure only the maximum bandwidth allowed for a virtual network adapter. Also new in Windows Server 2012 Hyper-V is the ability to also configure a minimum bandwidth for a virtual network adapter, as shown in Figure 7-14.

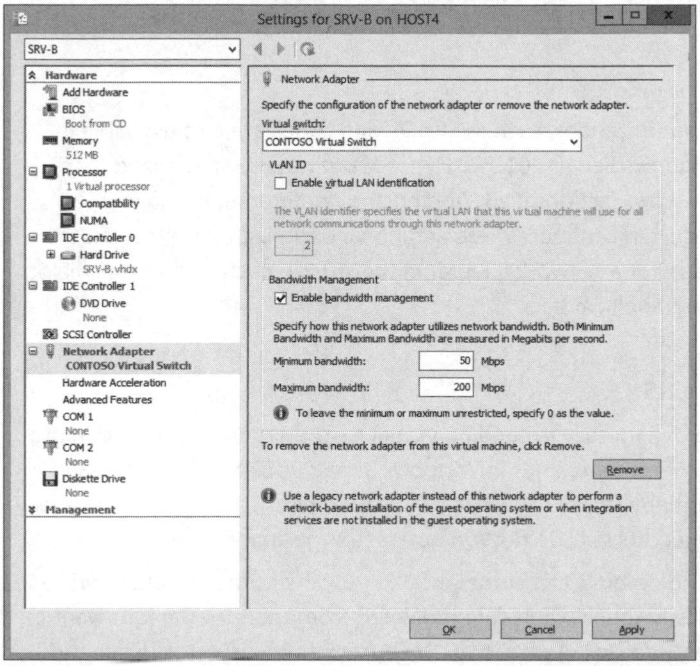

FIGURE 7-14 Configure maximum and minimum bandwidth for a virtual network adapter.

You can also use the Set-VMNetworkAdapter cmdlet to configure bandwidth management settings for a virtual network adapter using Windows PowerShell. The Set-VMNetworkAdapter cmdlet enables you to specify maximum and minimum bandwidth in either megabits per second (Mbps) or in terms of a relative weight between 0 and 100. You can use the latter approach to control how much bandwidth the virtual network adapter can have compared to other virtual network adapters connected to the same virtual switch. For example, you can use the following command to implement bandwidth fair-sharing, in which every virtual network adapter for the specified virtual machines is assigned the same minimum bandwidth weight:

```
PS C:\> Get-VMNetworkAdapter –VMName SRV-A,SRV-B,SRV-C | Set-VMNetworkAdapter `
-MinimumBandwidthWeight 1
```

You can also configure a minimum bandwidth (either absolute or relative) for a virtual switch by using the Set-VMSwitch cmdlet. You can also do this when you create a new virtual switch using the New-VMSwitch cmdlet. You cannot configure this setting using Hyper-V Manager.

Other optimizations

Other network performance optimizations, such as SR-IOV and VMQ, are also available in Windows Server 2012 and Windows Server 2012 R2 Hyper-V but require specialized hardware, as described previously in the section titled "Adding and configuring virtual network adapters" in Lesson 2. You can configure these additional optimizations either on the Hardware Acceleration subpage for a network adapter in the virtual machine Settings dialog box or by using Windows PowerShell cmdlets.

Optimizing virtual disks

Although both fixed-size and dynamically expanding virtual hard disks are supported in production environments, Microsoft recommends in Windows Server 2012 and Windows Server 2012 R2 Hyper-V that you continue to use fixed-size virtual hard disks to ensure that virtualized workloads on your production hosts do not run out of storage space.

Because dynamically expanding disks can automatically grow over time as data is written to them but do not automatically shrink when data is deleted from them, you might want to shrink such disks to reclaim unused storage space on the host so that you can allocate the reclaimed space to other virtual machines. And because fixed-size disks can fill up over time, you might need to expand such disks to make more room so that the guest operating system and applications can continue to perform optimally. Hyper-V enables you to perform different kinds of actions on virtual hard disks to help maintain or optimize their performance:

- **Compacting virtual disks**   This action reclaims empty disk space and reduces the size of the virtual hard disk. Such empty disk space is left behind when files are deleted on the disk. You should defragment the guest operating system before you compact the disk. Both dynamically expanding and differencing disks can be compacted; fixed-size disks cannot be compacted.

- **Converting virtual disks**   You can use this action to convert between different virtual hard disk formats (VHD and VHDX), between different virtual hard disk types (dynamically expanding and fixed-size), or both. During the conversion process, all data is retained and the guest operating system is not changed. You cannot convert dynamically expanding or fixed-size disks to or from differencing disks.

- **Expanding virtual disks**   You can use this action to expand an existing virtual hard disk instead of creating a new disk and manually migrating the data. You can expand all types of virtual hard disks provided you have free storage space on the host.

- **Shrinking virtual disks** This action was introduced in Windows Server 2012 Hyper-V to allow you to reduce the storage capacity of a virtual hard disk. You can shrink all types of virtual hard disks provided you have first freed up space in them.

> *IMPORTANT* **SHRINKING A VIRTUAL HARD DISK**
>
> Before you use either Windows PowerShell or Hyper-V Manager to shrink a VHD or VHDX file, you should log on to the Windows guest operating system and use the Disk Management snap-in to shrink the volume on the virtual disk you want to shrink. For more information, see "Shrinking a virtual hard disk in Windows 8" at *http://blogs.msdn.com/b /virtual_pc_guy/archive/2012/05/07/shrinking-a-virtual-hard-disk-in-windows-8.aspx*.

There are also two actions you can perform only on differencing disks:

- **Merging differencing disks** You can use this action to combine the changes stored in a differencing disk with the contents of its parent disk. You can do this either by copying the contents of the parent disk and differencing disk into a new virtual hard disk, leaving the two source disks intact, or by applying the changes contained in the differencing disk to the parent disk.

- **Reconnecting differencing disks** This action is available only when you select a differencing disk and the parent disk cannot be located. If the disks involved belong to a chain of differencing disks, this action is available only if none of the disks in the chain can be found.

> *IMPORTANT* **AVOIDING DATA LOSS**
>
> Do not compact, convert, expand, shrink, or merge a virtual hard disk when any of the following conditions apply:
>
> - The disk is associated with a virtual machine that has checkpoints.
> - The disk is associated with a virtual machine that has replication enabled.
> - The disk is associated with a chain of differencing disks.
>
> If you perform any of these actions under such conditions, data loss or corruption might occur.

Using Hyper-V Manager

You can use Hyper-V Manager to compact, convert, expand, shrink, merge, and perform other actions on virtual hard disks. The actions that are available will depend on the type of virtual disk you select. To perform any of these actions, click Edit Disk in the Actions pane to launch the Edit Virtual Hard Disk Wizard. Then after browsing to select the disk you want to edit, you can choose the action you want to perform on the disk as shown in Figure 7-15.

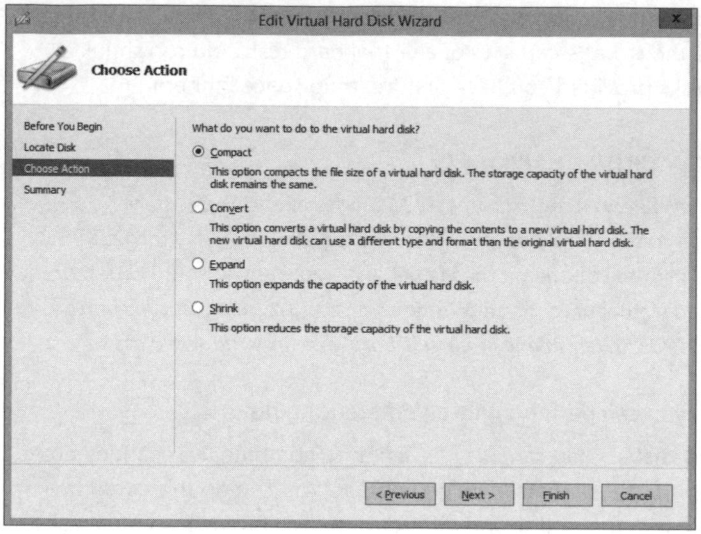

FIGURE 7-15 Edit a virtual hard disk using Hyper-V Manager.

Using Windows PowerShell

You can also use Windows PowerShell to compact, convert, expand, shrink, merge, and perform other actions on virtual hard disks. For example, you can use the Optimize-VHD cmdlet to compact a virtual disk, the Resize-VHD cmdlet to expand or shrink a virtual disk, and the Convert-VHD cmdlet to change the format version or type of a virtual disk. For help with any of these cmdlets, use the Get-Help cmdlet.

> ✔ **Quick check**
>
> ■ Which type of virtual hard disk cannot be compacted?
>
> **Quick check answer**
>
> ■ Fixed-size virtual hard disks

Managing checkpoints

As described earlier in this chapter, performing checkpoints on virtual machines is not recommended in production environments. Checkpoints are commonly used in test and development environments, however, so it's important to be able to manage them properly. Hyper-V enables you to perform the following kinds of actions concerning virtual machine checkpoints:

■ **Performing checkpoints**   You can perform checkpoints on a virtual machine to create point-in-time images of the virtual machine to which you can return later if needed. You can perform checkpoints on both running and stopped virtual machines and with any guest operating system installed. There is no interruption to running virtual machines when checkpoints are performed on them.

- **Applying checkpoints**   This action copies the virtual machine state from the selected checkpoint to the virtual machine. As a result, any unsaved data in the virtual machine will be lost. If the checkpoint was originally performed when the virtual machine was running, the virtual machine will be in a saved state after the checkpoint has been applied. If the checkpoint was originally performed when the virtual machine was stopped, the virtual machine will be in a stopped state after the checkpoint has been applied.

- **Reverting virtual machines**   This action takes the virtual machine back to the last checkpoint that was taken or applied, which is indicated in the Checkpoints pane of Hyper-V Manager by a green arrow with the word "Now" beside it as shown in Figure 7-16. The action also deletes any changes that have been made to the virtual machine since that checkpoint was performed.

- **Deleting checkpoints**   This action deletes the files associated with the checkpoint. As a result, you will no longer be able to restore the virtual machine to the point in time represented by the deleted checkpoint.

- **Deleting a checkpoints tree**   This action deletes the selected checkpoint and also any checkpoints underneath it in the hierarchy of checkpoints of the virtual machine.

- **Exporting checkpoints**   This action exports the selected checkpoint as a separate and independent virtual machine, which can then be imported onto another Hyper-V host if desired.

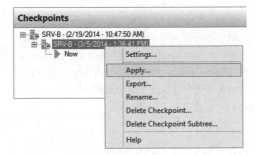

FIGURE 7-16 Apply a checkpoint to a virtual machine.

REAL WORLD **RENAMING CHECKPOINTS**

You can also rename checkpoints, and this is generally a good idea. Give each checkpoint you perform a name that describes either the purposes of the checkpoint or the state of the virtual machine just before the checkpoint was performed.

Using Hyper-V Manager

You can use Hyper-V Manager to perform, apply, delete, revert, or export checkpoints of virtual machines. To perform a checkpoint or revert a virtual machine, right-click the appropriate virtual machine in the Virtual Machines pane of Hyper-V Manager as shown in Figure 7-17. To apply, export, rename, or delete a checkpoint or checkpoint tree, right-click the appropriate checkpoint in the Checkpoint pane as shown in Figure 7-16 earlier.

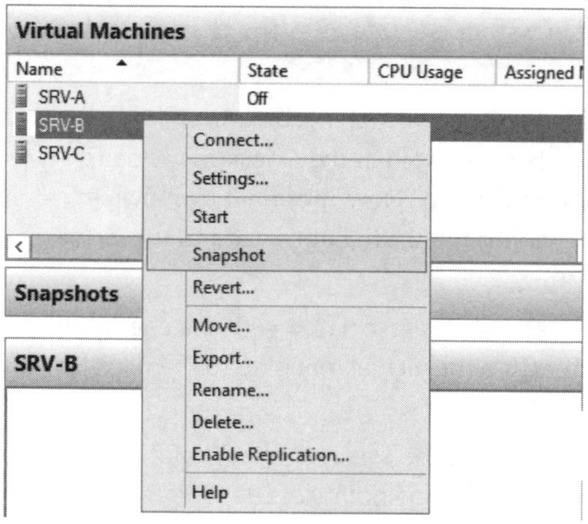

FIGURE 7-17 Perform a checkpoint on a virtual machine.

Using Windows PowerShell

You can also use Windows PowerShell to perform, apply, rename, export, or delete checkpoints and to revert virtual machines. You can use the Checkpoint-VM cmdlet to perform a checkpoint on a virtual machine, the Get-VMSnapshot cmdlet to display a list of checkpoints of a virtual machine, the RemoveVMSnapshot cmdlet to delete a checkpoint or checkpoint tree, and so on. For example, here is some output from running Get-VMSnapshot for a virtual machine on which a critical software update is being tested:

```
PS C:\> Get-VMSnapshot -VMName SRV-B -ComputerName HOST4

VMName Name                       SnapshotType CreationTime           ParentSnapshotName
------ ----                       ------------ ------------           ------------------
SRV-B  Before installing update ... Standard   8/13/2012 8:48:15 PM
SRV-B  After reconfiguring firew... Standard   8/13/2012 9:18:57 PM Before installi...
```

Monitoring virtual machines

Although the best tools for monitoring virtual machines running on Hyper-V hosts are those of the System Center family of products, you can monitor certain aspects of virtual machines by using Hyper-V Manager or Windows PowerShell. For example, Figure 7-18 shows the lower-center pane in Hyper-V Manager when a virtual machine named SRV-B is selected in the upper-center Virtual Machines pane. By selecting the Memory tab on this pane, you can view the current values for assigned memory and memory demand for virtual machines on which Dynamic Memory has been enabled.

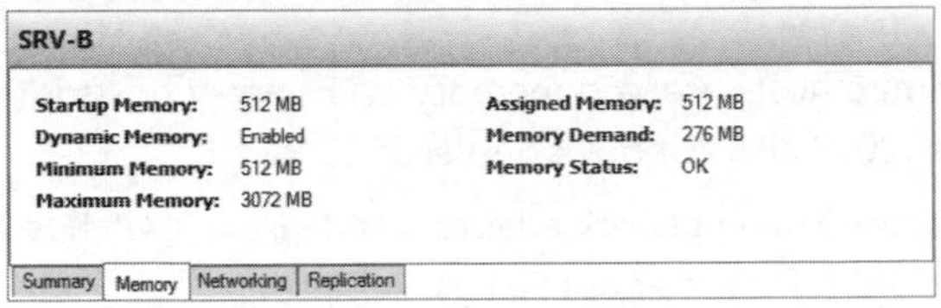

SRV-B			
Startup Memory:	512 MB	**Assigned Memory:**	512 MB
Dynamic Memory:	Enabled	**Memory Demand:**	276 MB
Minimum Memory:	512 MB	**Memory Status:**	OK
Maximum Memory:	3072 MB		

Summary | Memory | Networking | Replication

FIGURE 7-18 View Dynamic Memory in real time for a virtual machine.

You can also monitor virtual machines by using resource metering, a new feature of Hyper-V introduced in Windows Server 2012 that enables you to use Windows PowerShell to collect and report on historical resource usage of the following metrics:

- Average CPU usage by a virtual machine
- Average physical memory usage by a virtual machine
- Minimum physical memory usage by a virtual machine
- Maximum physical memory usage by a virtual machine
- Maximum amount of disk space allocated to a virtual machine
- Total incoming network traffic for a virtual network adapter
- Total outgoing network traffic for a virtual network adapter

In addition, you can collect these metrics in a consistent fashion even when the virtual machines are moved between hosts using live migration or when their storage is moved using storage migration. Organizations that use Hyper-V to build cloud-computing solutions can also use resource metering for such purposes as tracking the resources business units or customers are consuming to bill them for their use of these resources.

For example, you can use the Enable-VMResourceMetering cmdlet to enable resource metering on a virtual machine as follows:

```
PS C:\> Enable-VMResourceMetering -VMName SRV-B
```

Use the Get-VM cmdlet to verify the result:

```
PS C:\> Get-VM SRV-B | Format-List ResourceMeteringEnabled

ResourceMeteringEnabled : True
```

You can now use the Measure-VM cmdlet to display real-time resource usage by the virtual machine:

```
PS C:\> Measure-VM -Name SRV-B

VMName  AvgCPU(MHz) AvgRAM(M) MaxRAM(M) MinRAM(M) TotalDisk(M) NetworkIn... NetworkOut...
------  ----------- --------- --------- --------- ------------ ------------ -------------
SRV-B   176         512       512       512       130469       2            1
```

For more information on using these cmdlets, use the Get-Help cmdlet.

Lesson summary

- You can use Dynamic Memory to achieve higher virtual machine consolidation ratios on Hyper-V hosts.
- Editing the registry to manually configure host-reserved memory on Hyper-V hosts is not recommended in Windows Server 2012 and Windows Server 2012 R2.
- You can configure Hyper-V QoS on both virtual network adapters and virtual switches to guarantee minimum network bandwidth for the adapter or switch port.
- You can optimize virtual hard disks by compacting, expanding, shrinking, or converting them. Different types of virtual disks support different types of optimizations.
- You can use the Hyper-V Manager snap-in or Windows PowerShell to perform, apply, delete, or export checkpoints or to revert a virtual machine.
- You can use resource metering to monitor resource usage by a virtual machine using Windows PowerShell.

Lesson review

Answer the following questions to test your knowledge of the information in this lesson. You can find the answers to these questions and explanations of why each answer choice is correct or incorrect in the "Answers" section at the end of this chapter.

1. You have three virtual machines running on a Hyper-V host that has 16 GBs of physical memory. The guest operating system installed in all three virtual machines is Windows Server 2008 R2, and none of the virtual machines is a file server. Dynamic Memory is enabled on all three machines and is configured as follows:

   - VM-1 has 1 GB minimum RAM, 4 GBs maximum RAM, and 20 percent memory buffer.
   - VM-2 has 2 GBs minimum RAM, 8 GBs maximum RAM, and 30 percent memory buffer.
   - VM-3 has 1 GB minimum RAM, 6 GBs maximum RAM, and 100 percent memory buffer.

   Over time, you find that the performance of VM-1 and VM-2 is becoming sluggish. Why?

   A. The minimum RAM assigned to VM-1 is probably too low.

   B. The maximum RAM assigned to VM-2 is probably too high.

   C. The memory buffer for both VM-1 and VM-2 is probably too low.

   D. The memory buffer for VM-3 is probably too high.

2. In which of these scenarios might you try to optimize a virtual hard disk by compacting, expanding, shrinking, or merging it?

   A. When the disk is associated with a virtual machine that has checkpoints

   B. When you need to free up storage space on the host

C. When the disk is associated with a virtual machine that has replication enabled

D. When the disk is associated with a chain of differencing disks

3. Which of the following is *not* true concerning checkpoints? (Choose all that apply.)

A. Performing checkpoints creates point-in-time images of the virtual machine to which you can return later if needed. There is no interruption to running virtual machines when checkpoints are performed on them.

B. When you apply a checkpoint, any unsaved data in the virtual machine will be lost.

C. You can perform checkpoints only when the virtual machine is stopped.

D. Exporting checkpoints is not supported in Hyper-V.

Practice exercises

The goal of this section is to provide you with hands-on practice with the following:

- Installing and configuring Hyper-V on Server Core
- Creating and configuring virtual machines

To perform the following exercises, you need at least one clean installation of Windows Server 2012 R2 performed using the Server Core installation option. The server should be a stand-alone server belonging to a workgroup, have at least two physical hard disk drives with the second drive formatted as a data volume, have at least two physical network adapters with both configured with static TCP/IP settings, have Internet connectivity, and have no additional roles or features installed. You should be logged on interactively to the server using the default Administrator account. For the purposes of these exercises, the name of the server is assumed to be HOST7 and the data volume is the E drive.

If you want, you can perform these exercises remotely from another computer by enabling Remote Desktop on HOST7 and using Remote Desktop Connection on your computer. If you do this, note that certain actions (such as creating new virtual switches) might temporarily disrupt Remote Desktop connectivity with the remote host.

Exercise 1: Installing and configuring Hyper-V on Server Core

In this exercise, you use Windows PowerShell to install the Hyper-V role, configure virtual machine storage locations, and create virtual switches.

1. Log on to HOST7 and type **powershell** at the command prompt to open a Windows PowerShell prompt.

2. Use the Get-WindowsFeature cmdlet to verify that the Hyper-V role and Hyper-V Module For Windows PowerShell are available for installation but the Hyper-V GUI Management Tools are removed and not available for installation.

3. Use the Install-WindowsFeature cmdlet to install the Hyper-V role and Hyper-V Module For Windows PowerShell. You can use the *–IncludeManagementTools* parameter to do this using a single command. Make sure you include the *–Restart* parameter.

4. Once the server has restarted, log on as Administrator, type **powershell** at the command prompt, and use the Get-WindowsFeature cmdlet to verify that the Hyper-V role and Hyper-V Module For Windows PowerShell have been successfully installed.

5. Type **mkdir E:\vmstorage** to create a new directory on the data drive.

6. Use the Get-VMHost cmdlet to display the values of the *VirtualHardDiskPath* and *VirtualMachinePath* properties.

7. Use the Set-VMHost cmdlet to change the values of the preceding two properties to E:\vmstorage.

8. Use the Get-VMHost cmdlet to verify the change you made to the default storage location for virtual machine files.

9. Use the Get-VMSwitch cmdlet to verify that there are no virtual switches configured on the host.

10. Type **Get-NetAdapter** and note the names of the two physical network adapters on the host.

11. Use the New-VMSwitch cmdlet to create a new virtual switch of External type named CONTOSO. Ensure that the new switch is connected to one of the network adapters on the host.

12. Use the New-VMSwitch cmdlet to create a second virtual switch of External type named MANAGEMENT. Ensure that the new switch is connected to the other network adapter on the host.

13. Use the Get-VMSwitch cmdlet to verify that both virtual switches have been successfully created.

14. Leave yourself logged on to HOST7 and proceed to the next exercise.

Exercise 2: Creating and configuring virtual machines

In this exercise, you use Windows PowerShell to create a new virtual machine, enable and configure Dynamic Memory on the virtual machine, change the number of virtual processors on the virtual machine, enable and configure bandwidth management on the network adapter, and perform a checkpoint of the virtual machine.

1. Type **New-VM –Name SERVER8 –Path E:\vmstorage –NewVHDPath server8 .vhdx –NewVHDSizeBytes 100GB –SwitchName CONTOSO** to create a new virtual machine named SERVER8 that has a dynamically expanding virtual hard disk of size 100 GBs and a virtual network adapter connected to the CONTOSO virtual switch.

2. Type **Get-VM | fl ConfigurationLocation** and verify that the configuration files for the virtual machine are stored in the E:\vmstorage\SERVER8 directory.

3. Type **dir "E:\vmstorage\SERVER8\Virtual Hard Disks"** and verify that a file named server8.vhdx exists in this location.

4. Type **Set-VM –Name SERVER8 –MemoryStartupBytes 2GB** to configure the Startup RAM setting as 2 GBs.

5. Type **Set-VM –Name SERVER8 –DynamicMemory** to enable the Dynamic Memory feature on the virtual machine.

6. Type **Set-VM –Name SERVER8 –MemoryMinimumBytes 1GB** to configure the Dynamic Memory Minimum RAM setting as 1 GB.

7. Type **Set-VM –Name SERVER8 –MemoryMaximumBytes 4GB** to configure the Dynamic Memory Maximum RAM setting as 4 GBs.

8. Type **Set-VMMemory –VMName SERVER8 –Buffer 40** to configure the Dynamic Memory Memory Buffer setting as 40 percent.

9. Type **Get-WmiObject Win32_Processor | fl NumberOfLogicalProcessors** to view the number of logical processors on the host system.

10. Type **Get-VMProcessor –VMName SERVER8 | fl Count** to view the number of virtual processors currently configured on the virtual machine. (This should be one processor.)

11. Type **Set-VMProcessor –VMName SERVER8 –Count 2** to change the number of virtual processors on the virtual machine from one to two processors.

12. Type **Get-VMProcessor –VMName SERVER8 | fl Count** again to confirm the change.

13. Type **Get-VMNetworkAdapter –VMName SERVER8** to view information about the virtual network adapter on the virtual machine. Make a note of the name of the adapter. (It should be named Network Adapter.)

14. Type **Set-VMNetworkAdapter –VMName SERVER8 –Name "Network Adapter" –MinimumBandwidthAbsolute 50000000** to assign a minimum bandwidth value of 50 Mbps to the virtual machine's virtual network adapter.

15. Type **Set-VMNetworkAdapter –VMName SERVER8 –Name "Network Adapter" –MaximumBandwidth 200000000** to assign a maximum bandwidth value of 200 Mbps to the virtual machine's virtual network adapter.

16. Type **Checkpoint-VM –VMName SERVER8 –SnapshotName "Guest OS not installed"** to perform a checkpoint of the virtual machine.

17. Type **dir "E:\vmstorage\SERVER8\Snapshots"** and verify that the checkpoint files have been created.

18. The remaining steps in this practice exercise are optional because of the amount of time it might take to perform them.

19. Type **Install-WindowsFeature –Name Server-Gui-Mgmt-Infra –Restart** to convert your Server Core installation to a Minimal Server Interface installation. Because the feature binaries will need to be installed from Windows Update, this step might take some time to complete.

20. Once the server has restarted and you have logged on again, Server Manager should automatically open. When it opens, launch the Add Roles And Features Wizard and install the Hyper-V GUI Management Tools feature, which is found under Role Administration Tools\Hyper-V Management Tools on the Features page of the wizard.

21. Select the Hyper-V page in Server Manager, right-click HOST7, and select Hyper-V Manager to open the Hyper-V Manager snap-in.

22. Use the Hyper-V Manager snap-in to verify all of the configuration steps you performed in the two practice exercises in this chapter.

Suggested practice exercises

The following additional practice exercises are designed to give you more opportunities to practice what you've learned and to help you successfully master the lessons presented in this chapter.

- **Exercise 1**   Modify the two practice exercises so that they use as few Windows PowerShell commands as possible to perform all the configuration actions required.

- **Exercise 2**   Build on the second practice exercise by adding a second virtual network adapter to the virtual machine, connecting the second adapter to the second virtual switch on the host, and configuring NIC Teaming for the virtual machine.

- **Exercise 3**   Modify the second practice exercise to create and configure a Generation 2 virtual machine.

- **Exercise 4**   Start a virtual machine and resize its virtual hard disk while it is still running. Then try exporting the live virtual machine and importing it onto another host.

Answers

This section contains the answers to the lesson review questions in this chapter.

Lesson 1

1. **Correct answer: C**

   A. **Incorrect:** You should choose the Standard edition if you need to deploy Windows Server 2012 R2 as a workload on bare metal in a nonvirtualized environment.

   B. **Incorrect:** You should choose the Standard edition if you need to deploy Windows Server 2012 R2 as a workload on bare metal in a nonvirtualized environment.

   C. **Correct:** The Datacenter edition is the best choice if you need to deploy Windows Server 2012 R2 Hyper-V hosts for a virtualized data center or private-cloud scenario. The Server Core installation option is the best choice for Hyper-V hosts because of its smaller attack surface and reduced servicing footprint.

   D. **Incorrect:** The Datacenter edition is the right choice if you need to deploy Windows Server 2012 R2 Hyper-V hosts for a virtualized data center or private-cloud scenario. However, you should deploy the Server Core installation option on your Hyper-V hosts instead of the Server With A GUI installation option because of the smaller attack surface and reduced servicing footprint of the Server Core installation option.

2. **Correct answer: D**

   A. **Incorrect:** Installing the Minimal Server Interface might increase the attack surface of the host and increase its servicing overhead. Because you are concerned about security and servicing overhead, this might not be the best approach. In addition, if the server is located in a data center, it is usually not convenient to manage the server from its local console.

   B. **Incorrect:** Using Remote Desktop to remotely manage servers has the benefit of convenience, especially when the servers are located in a data center. However, using Remote Desktop to manage a Server Core installation still presents you with only a command line for management purposes.

   C. **Incorrect:** Using Remote Desktop to remotely manage servers has the benefit of convenience, especially when the servers are located in a data center. However, installing the Minimal Server Interface might increase the attack surface of the host and increase its servicing overhead. Because you are concerned about security and servicing overhead, this might not be the best approach.

   D. **Correct:** Remote management is enabled by default on servers running Windows Server 2012 R2. By installing RSAT for Windows 8.1 on an administrator workstation running Windows 8, you can launch Hyper-V Manager, connect to a remote host, and manage the host from the convenience of your workstation.

3. **Correct answer: B**

   A. **Incorrect:** Get-VMHost can be used only to view host configuration settings, not to configure them.

   B. **Correct:** Set-VMHost can be used to configure settings for a Hyper-V host.

   C. **Incorrect:** Add-VMStoragePath is used to add a path to a storage resource pool. It cannot be used to configure the default storage location for virtual machine files on a Hyper-V host.

   D. **Incorrect:** Set-VM can be used to configure settings for virtual machines, not for hosts.

Lesson 2

1. **Correct answer: D**

   A. **Incorrect:** Each virtual machine can have up to 12 virtual network adapters installed in it. Of these 12 virtual network adapters, up to 8 can be the network adapter type and up to 4 can be the legacy network adapter type.

   B. **Incorrect:** Each virtual network adapter can be configured with either a static MAC address or a dynamic MAC address that is automatically assigned from the configured MAC address range on the host.

   C. **Incorrect:** Each virtual network can be assigned a unique VLAN channel to segment or isolate network traffic.

   D. **Correct:** Virtual switches on a Hyper-V host cannot be connected to a wireless network adapter on the host system.

2. **Correct answers: B and C**

   A. **Incorrect:** A pass-through disk is a physical disk on the host that is attached to a virtual machine. Pass-through disks are thus just standard hard drives, which are easily obtained.

   B. **Correct:** Tests by Microsoft have indeed demonstrated that fixed-size virtual hard disks perform almost as well as pass-through disks and also provide the flexibility benefits of virtual hard disks.

   C. **Correct:** Tests by Microsoft have indeed demonstrated that dynamically expanding virtual hard disks perform almost as well as pass-through disks and also provide the flexibility benefits of virtual hard disks.

   D. **Incorrect:** Configuring a virtual machine to use a pass-through disk is no more difficult than configuring it to use a virtual hard disk.

3. **Correct answers: A, C, and D**

   A. **Correct:** You should never perform checkpoints on virtualized domain controllers.

   B. **Incorrect:** You might consider performing a checkpoint of a production virtual machine just before you apply a critical software update to the guest operating system of the virtual machine. That way, if something goes wrong after applying the update, you can quickly revert the virtual machine to its previous state (that is, before the update was applied).

C.   **Correct:** You should never perform checkpoints on virtualized workloads that use data distributed across multiple databases.

D.   **Correct:** You should never restore checkpoints older than 30 days on domain-joined virtual machines.

4.   **Correct answer: D**

A.   **Incorrect:** All virtual network adapters (except legacy network adapters) support DHCP Guard.

B.   **Incorrect:** Although you should include the *–VMName* parameter in your command to specify which virtual network adapter you want to configure on the virtual machine, this is unnecessary if the virtual machine has only one adapter installed.

C.   **Incorrect:** Specifying *–DhcpGuard ok* also generates an error.

D.   **Correct:** Specifying *–DhcpGuard 1* works, as does specifying *–DhcpGuard On*. The clue is in the string *"Microsoft.HyperV.PowerShell.OnOffState"*, which indicates the data type accepted by this parameter.

Lesson 3

1.   **Correct answer: D**

A.   **Incorrect:** 1 GB is a reasonable amount for the Minimum RAM setting for VM-1 when Windows Server 2008 R2 is the guest operating system.

B.   **Incorrect:** 8 GBs is a reasonable amount for the Maximum RAM setting for VM-2 when compared with the Maximum RAM setting configured for the other two virtual machines.

C.   **Incorrect:** Memory buffer generally needs to be increased only for file servers that make heavy use of the disk cache. Because none of the virtual machines are file servers, keeping this setting close to its default value of 20 percent is reasonable.

D.   **Correct:** Memory buffer generally needs to be increased only for file servers that make heavy use of the disk cache. Because VM-3 is not a file server, it is probably not a good idea to configure such a high memory buffer value for this virtual machine.

2.   **Correct answer: B**

A.   **Incorrect:** Do not compact, convert, expand, shrink, or merge a virtual hard disk when the disk is associated with a virtual machine that has checkpoints. If you perform any of these actions under such conditions, data loss or corruption might occur.

B. Correct: The ability to shrink a virtual hard disk is new in Windows Server 2012 Hyper-V and can be used to reduce the storage capacity of a virtual hard disk. You can shrink all types of virtual hard disks provided you have first freed up space in them.

C. Incorrect: Do not compact, convert, expand, shrink, or merge a virtual hard disk when the disk is associated with a virtual machine that has replication enabled. If you perform any of these actions under such conditions, data loss or corruption might occur.

D. Incorrect: Do not compact, convert, expand, shrink, or merge a virtual hard disk when the disk is associated with a chain of differencing disks. If you perform any of these actions under such conditions, data loss or corruption might occur.

3. **Correct answers: C and D**

    A. Incorrect: Performing checkpoints creates point-in-time images of the virtual machine to which you can return later if needed.

    B. Incorrect: Applying a checkpoint copies the virtual machine state from the selected checkpoint to the virtual machine. As a result, any unsaved data in the virtual machine will be lost. If the checkpoint was originally performed when the virtual machine was running, the virtual machine will be in a saved state after the checkpoint has been applied. If the checkpoint was originally performed when the virtual machine was stopped, the virtual machine will be in a stopped state after the checkpoint has been applied.

    C. Correct: Checkpoints can be performed on both running and stopped virtual machines and with any guest operating system installed.

    D. Correct: Exporting a checkpoint exports it as a separate and independent virtual machine, which can then be imported onto another Hyper-V host if desired.

CHAPTER 8

File services and storage

Provisioning and managing storage is a key role for IT administrators in organizations of all sizes. Data is a business asset that must be available, accessible, and secure; otherwise, the business won't survive in today's competitive marketplace.

In traditional IT infrastructures, managing storage can be a complex task because data is often stored using a wide range of storage technologies that might include an iSCSI storage area network (SAN), network-attached storage (NAS) devices, direct-attached storage (DAS) devices, Just a Bunch of Disks (JBOD) enclosures, and even removable storage devices such as USB drives. Some of these technologies, such as SANs, might require special expertise to administer, which can further complicate the task of storage administration.

Fortunately, Microsoft Windows Server 2012 and Windows Server 2012 R2 can help alleviate much of the burden and cost of acquiring, deploying, and administering storage by using Storage Spaces. This chapter explains how to deploy Storage Spaces in your environment and how to use Storage Spaces to provision storage for various needs and in different scenarios. The chapter also explains how to configure iSCSI storage using the built-in Internet Small Computer System Interface (iSCSI) Target Server role and iSCSI initiator in Windows Server 2012 and Windows Server 2012 R2.

Lessons in this chapter:

Before you begin

To complete the practice exercises in this chapter

- You need to know how to perform a clean install of Windows Server 2012 R2 and perform initial configuration tasks, such as configuring the server's TCP/IP settings for Internet connectivity.
- You also should have at least rudimentary knowledge of using Windows PowerShell.

Lesson 1: Deploying Storage Spaces

Virtualization of storage resources is nothing new to administrators of large enterprises that have SANs deployed within their network infrastructures. Until now, however, storage virtualization has required purchasing proprietary third-party solutions that are expensive and require you to use their own set of management tools. Such solutions not only add to the cost of your network but also require special training to implement, manage, and maintain.

Storage Spaces, introduced in Windows Server 2012 and enhanced in Windows Server 2012 R2, is designed to make storage virtualization affordable, even for small businesses. Storage Spaces is easy to deploy and manage, and it can provide your business with shared storage that can grow on demand to meet your organization's evolving needs. This lesson explains how Storage Spaces works, describes its capabilities, and demonstrates how to implement it using common, off-the-shelf storage hardware.

> **After this lesson, you will be able to:**
> - Understand the basic concepts and benefits of Storage Spaces.
> - Explain the difference between fixed and thin provisioning.
> - Describe the different resiliency options available with Storage Spaces.
> - Describe the different considerations involved in planning for a Storage Spaces deployment.
> - Implement Storage Spaces using both Server Manager and Windows PowerShell.
>
> **Estimated lesson time: 30 minutes**

Understanding Storage Spaces

Storage virtualization basically involves doing two things:

- Taking physical storage devices and creating virtual pools of storage from them
- Provisioning shared storage from these pools as the need arises

For example, a storage virtualization solution might allow you to pool several internal and externally connected hard drives into a single pool of storage. You could then provision portions of this storage for your various file servers without being concerned about which drives are being used by each file server or where on the drives any particular data is being stored. The benefits of this approach are obvious to experienced administrators and include the following:

- **Increased flexibility**   You can create new pools and expand existing ones without adding any new physical storage devices.
- **Increased scalability**   You can easily add and use physical storage when needed to meet increasing business demands.

- **Increased elasticity** You can preallocate storage capacity by using thin provisioning. Capacity can be increased to meet growing demand even when the underlying physical storage is insufficient.

- **Increased efficiency** You can reclaim storage capacity when it is no longer needed to use physical storage resources more efficiently.

- **Lower cost** By using low-cost, commodity-based hard drives, you can create large pools of storage. These pools can easily meet the needs of small and midsized businesses.

Windows Server 2012 introduced support for storage virtualization through a feature called Storage Spaces, which enables you to aggregate internal and external physical disks into pools of low-cost storage that can have different levels of resiliency. These pools are simple to administer, can be allocated either manually or automatically, can be delegated for administration purposes, and can be delivered using either thin or fixed provisioning.

Concepts and terminology

To implement and use Storage Spaces, you first need to understand its basic concepts and terminology. The following is a list of terminology associated with Storage Spaces:

- **Storage Management Application Programming Interface (SMAPI)** A collection of Windows Management Instrumentation (WMI) interfaces for platform-neutral and vendor-neutral management of storage that are included in Windows Server 2012, Windows Server 2012 R2, System Center 2012 Virtual Machine Manager, and System Center 2012 R2 Virtual Machine Manager.

- **Storage Management Provider (SMP)** An interface that provides a mechanism for discovering, managing, and provisioning storage. Windows Server 2012 and Windows Server 2012 R2 include support for the following types of SMPs:

  - **Storage Spaces provider** This SMP is used for implementing storage virtualization using Storage Spaces.

  - **Storage Management Initiative Specification (SMI-S) providers** These providers support the Storage Management Initiative Specification (SMI-S) standard of the Storage Network Industry Association (SNIA) and can be used for platform-neutral and vendor-neutral implementation of storage virtualization using third-party storage solutions such as SANs.

- **Storage subsystem** A storage subsystem uses an SMP to expose physical storage devices so that they can be virtualized into storage pools.

- **Storage pool** A collection of physical disks that can be used to create virtual disks. A single storage pool can consist of physical disks having different sizes and using different storage interconnects. For example, you could mix and match Small Computer System Interface (SCSI) and Serial Attached SCSI (SAS) hard drives to create a pool.

  You can create and delete storage pools to manage virtualized storage in your environment. Each physical disk can be included in only one storage pool at a time, and once you add a physical disk to a pool the disk is no longer exposed in Disk Management for directly creating partitions or volumes on it.

- **Primordial storage pool** The default pool that contains all physical storage devices in a storage system that the Storage Spaces provider is able to enumerate, regardless of whether these devices have been added to other pools. Physical disks are displayed in the primordial pool only when they have no partitions or volumes created on them. If there are no available unused disks connected to your file server, the primordial pool is not displayed in Server Manager.

- **Virtual disk** A logical unit number (LUN) that has been provisioned from a storage pool. Virtual disks behave like physical disks but have increased flexibility, scalability, and elasticity because they represent virtualized storage instead of physical storage. Virtual disks are also sometimes referred to as *spaces*.

- **Volume** A portion of a virtual disk that has been formatted with a file system such as NTFS.

- **Share** A folder in the file system of a volume that has been made accessible over the network to users who have appropriate permissions.

MORE INFO **THE SMI-S STANDARD**

For more info on the SMI-S standard, see "Introduction to SMI-S" at *http://blogs.technet .com/b/filecab/archive/2012/06/25/introduction-to-smi-s.aspx*. For information on how to use the Windows Standards-Based Storage Management feature introduced in Windows Server 2012 to implement storage virtualization with third-party SANs and other storage solutions, see "Getting started with SMI-S on Windows Server 2012" at *http://blogs.technet .com/b/filecab/archive/2012/07/05/getting-started-with-smi-s-on-windows-server-2012 .aspx*. For an example of implementing storage virtualization using SMI-S with EMC stor- age arrays, see "Using the EMC SMI-S provider with Windows Server 2012 and SCVMM" at *http://blogs.technet.com/b/filecab/archive/2012/07/16/using-the-emc-smi-s-provider-with -windows-server-2012-and-scvmm.aspx*.

IMPORTANT **DYNAMIC DISKS AND STORAGE SPACES**

In previous versions of Windows Server, you could use dynamic disks for implementing software RAID 0 or RAID 1 redundancy for the boot volume and data volumes. Dynamic disks were first introduced in Windows Server 2003 and were implemented using the Virtual Disk Service (VDS) API included in that platform. Beginning with Windows Server 2012, however, the VDS API was superseded by SMAPI. This means that dynamic disks are considered deprecated for all usages except mirroring the boot volumes. You should use Storage Spaces instead of dynamic disks when you need to provide resiliency for data volumes. In addition, the following tools that rely on the VDS API should also be considered deprecated:

- DiskPart command
- DiskRAID command
- Disk Management MMC snap-in

Note that you can still use these commands on Windows Server 2012 and Windows Server 2012 R2, but they will not work with Storage Spaces or with any SMAPI components or tools. For more information, see "Virtual Disk Service is transitioning to Windows Storage Management API" at *http://msdn.microsoft.com/en-us/library/windows/desktop /hh848071(v=vs.85).aspx.*

Fixed vs. thin provisioning

Once you've aggregated physical disks into a storage pool, you can provision storage from that pool by creating virtual disks. Storage Spaces supports two ways of provisioning virtual disks:

- **Fixed provisioning**   The size of the virtual disk is the actual amount of physical storage space allocated from the pool.
- **Thin provisioning**   The size of the virtual disk represents the maximum amount of physical storage space that can be allocated from the pool. No space is actually used until data is stored on a volume on the virtual disk, and the amount of space used will grow or shrink as data is written to or deleted from the disk.

The difference between these two types of provisioning can be explained using the following example. Figure 8-1 shows a storage pool named Storage Pool 1 that has been created from three 2-terabyte (TB) physical hard drives. If you use fixed provisioning to create virtual disks from this pool, you could create, for example, one virtual disk that is 4 TBs in size and a second virtual disk that is 2 TBs in size for a total of 6 TBs, which equals the physical storage space available in the pool. At this point, because all available storage in the pool has been provisioned, no new virtual disks can be created unless additional physical disks are added to the pool.

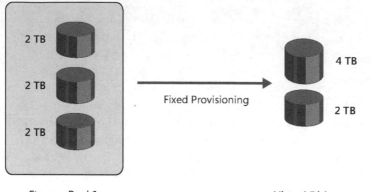

Storage Pool 1   **Virtual Disks**

FIGURE 8-1 Create virtual disks from a storage pool using fixed provisioning.

In contrast, Figure 8-2 shows thin provisioning being used to create virtual disks from the same storage pool of physical disks. Two virtual disks have been created: one 20 TBs in size and the other 10 TBs in size for a total of 30 TBs. You could now create volumes on these virtual disks and use the volumes to store data. For example, you could create three volumes of sizes 10 TBs, 5 TBs, and 5 TBs on the 20 TB virtual disk and create a single 10 TB volume on the 10 TB virtual disk. If you discover that the volumes you created are insufficient to meet the needs of your environment, you could perform either of the following actions:

- Create additional thinly provisioned virtual disks from the same storage pool
- Extend one (or more) of your existing virtual disks to create more room on it and then create additional volumes on the extended disk (or disks)

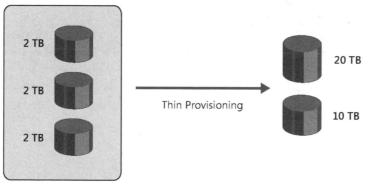

Storage Pool 1   **Virtual Disks**

FIGURE 8-2 Create virtual disks from a storage pool using thin provisioning.

How can 6 TBs of physical storage space be used to create 30 TBs of NTFS-formatted volumes for storing data? With fixed provisioning, this is not possible. However, with thin provisioning, the data volumes use space on the physical disks only when you store some data on the volumes.

What happens, then, if you begin copying large amounts of data onto the two volumes shown in Figure 8-2? Once you begin to approach the actual available physical capacity of the storage pool, a notification message will be displayed to alert you to the situation. At that point, you can either stop copying data to the volumes or add more physical disks to your storage pool.

> **NOTE HOW STORAGE SPACE STORES DATA ON PHYSICAL DISKS**
>
> Storage Space stores data for a volume on a virtual disk by striping the data across all physical disks in the pool. Data is interleaved in 256 MB segments called *slabs*. Storage Spaces then keeps track of which slab on which disk corresponds to which portion of each volume on each virtual disk provisioned from the pool. For detailed information on how this works, see "Virtualizing storage for scale, resiliency, and efficiency" at *http://blogs.msdn.com/b /b8/archive/2012/01/05/virtualizing-storage-for-scale-resiliency-and-efficiency.aspx*.

Resiliency

You can use Storage Spaces to provide resilient storage similar (but not identical) to RAID 0 (disk striping) and RAID 1 (mirroring) that you can implement using hardware RAID solutions. As long as your storage pool has a sufficient number of physical disks in it, you can use Storage Spaces to create virtual disks whose storage layout is any of the following three types:

- **Simple**   The data on volumes created on this type of virtual disk is striped across all physical disks in the pool. You can use simple virtual disks to provision the maximum amount of storage from the pool, but they provide no resiliency against physical disk failure.

- **Mirror**   The data on volumes created on this type of virtual disk is striped across all physical disks in the pool. Each segment of data is also duplicated on either two or three physical disks, as specified when the mirrored virtual disk is created, so that a copy of all data will still be available if a physical disk fails in the pool. Mirror virtual disks provide resiliency to help protect you from data loss arising from the failure of a physical disk in the pool. The degree of resiliency provided depends on the number of physical disks in the pool—for example:

  - You can use a pool containing two physical disks to create mirror virtual disks that are resilient against the failure of a single physical disk.

  - You can use a pool containing five physical disks to create mirror virtual disks that are resilient against the failure of two physical disks.

- **Parity**   The data on volumes created on this type of virtual disk, with parity information that you can use to facilitate automatic reconstruction of data in the event of a physical disk failure, is striped across all physical disks in the pool. Parity virtual disks also provide resiliency to help protect you from data loss arising from the failure of a physical disk in the pool, but they perform better with large sequential disk writes than with random I/O.

When a physical disk fails in a pool being used to provision resilient (mirror or parity) virtual disks, Storage Spaces will continue to provide access to data stored on volumes on the virtual disk and will automatically regenerate data copies for all affected virtual disks as long as there are sufficient alternate physical disks available in the pool. When you add a physical disk to a storage pool, you have a choice of two ways to allocate the disk to the pool:

- **Automatic** The pool will automatically use the disk for storing data written to any volumes created on the disk.
- **Hot-spare** The pool will hold the disk in reserve so that it can be used if another physical drive in the pool fails.

✔ Quick check

- You need to create a 5 TB file share for archiving your company's presentations and media files. Your file server is running Windows Server 2012 R2, but you currently have only two data disks in your file server with each disk having a capacity of 2 TBs. You've ordered an external SATA (eSATA) card and a Serial Advanced Technology Attachment (SATA) JBOD with four 2 TB disks, but the shipment is on backorder and is not expected to arrive for several weeks. Is there anything you can do in the meantime that will enable you to begin archiving your content?

Quick check answer

- Yes! If you implemented Storage Spaces, you can use thin provisioning to create a virtual disk 5 TBs in size even though you currently have only 4 TBs of available physical storage for your file server. You can then create a 5 TB volume on this virtual disk and start archiving content to the volume. When the extra storage hardware you ordered arrives, you can add the new storage to the storage pool on your server and finish archiving your content.

Planning a Storage Spaces deployment

Successful deployment requires careful planning to ensure problems don't arise during or after the deployment process. You should consider the following issues when planning the deployment of Storage Spaces for your organization:

- Hardware
- Performance
- Resiliency
- Availability
- Management
- Scalability

Hardware

The hardware requirements for implementing Storage Spaces define the kinds of physical storage devices and formats that you can use for creating storage pools. These hardware requirements vary depending on whether the Failover Clustering feature is being used to provide high availability for your storage pools.

If you are deploying Storage Spaces without Failover Clustering, the supported types of physical storage devices are as follows:

- Serial ATA (SATA) hard drives, including solid state drives (SSDs)
- Serial Attached SCSI (SAS) hard drives, including SSDs

> **NOTE USB DRIVES AND STORAGE SPACES**
>
> Although using USB 2.0 hard drives with Storage Spaces is supported, it is not recommended because of the performance limitations of using USB 2.0 to perform simultaneous reads and writes to multiple connected USB drives.

In addition, you can connect these devices to a server running Windows Server 2012 or Windows Server 2012 R2 in the following ways:

- Internal connection using SATA or SAS controllers
- External connection to a JBOD enclosure of SATA disks
- External connection to a SAS storage array

If you are deploying a highly available (HA) Storage Spaces solution, the requirements are as follows:

- Two servers running Windows Server 2012 or Windows Server 2012 R2 with the Failover Clustering feature installed and configured to use Cluster Shared Volumes (CSVs).

- SAS-connected JBODs that comply with the Certified for Windows Server 2012 or Windows Server 2012 R2 logo requirements.
- You cannot use iSCSI storage devices for an HA Storage Spaces solution.

> **NOTE STORAGE SPACES AND HARDWARE RAID**
>
> You cannot use Storage Spaces in conjunction with hardware RAID. Choosing between hardware RAID and Storage Spaces depends on several factors:
>
> - Choose Storage Spaces when you want to be able to virtualize and deploy shared storage of data using thin provisioning and save money by using low-cost, commodity hard drives and ensuring a level of resiliency similar to what RAID can provide.
> - Choose a hardware RAID solution for a server when you need to ensure data integrity, fault tolerance, and high performance—for example, a RAID 5 or RAID 6 solution implemented using a RAID controller card. You should also choose hardware RAID when you want to ensure data integrity and fault tolerance for a server's boot volume—for example, by configuring the boot volume as a RAID 1 or RAID 10 volume.
>
> If a server has a RAID controller card and multiple hard drives and you want to use Storage Spaces to pool these drives, you need to configure the RAID card to expose each drive separately to the operating system.

> **REAL WORLD SES SAS JBODS**
>
> SCSI Enclosure Services (SES) is a protocol that allows the controller to send diagnostic information to and receive it from connected storage devices. For example, a SAS JBOD enclosure that supports SES has a series of LED lights on the enclosure, with each LED corresponding to one of the SAS hard drives in the enclosure. When Storage Spaces is implemented using SAS JBODs that support SES, Storage Spaces can use SES to light up the LED of a drive that has failed so that you can quickly determine which drive needs to be replaced in the enclosure when Storage Spaces notifies you that a drive in a storage pool has failed.
>
> Search the Windows Server Catalog at *http://windowsservercatalog.com* to find Certified for Windows Server 2012 or Windows Server 2012 R2 SAS JBODs that support the SES version 3 protocol. Then go to the vendor's website and confirm that the devices support SES.

Performance

To ensure optimal performance of Storage Spaces, make sure you consider the following:

- Use enterprise-level SAS disks if you can afford them to get optimum performance from your Storage Spaces solution. Make sure you also use top-quality SAS controller cards. Most SAS controller cards are backward compatible for connecting to SATA disks, so you can use these if your budget is limited. If top performance is needed and money is no object, consider using SSDs.

- Create different storage pools for the different performance needs of your environment and populate the pools with appropriate kinds of physical disks. For example, a storage pool for a high-speed file server might contain a mix of SSDs and 15,000 RPM SAS disks, and another storage pool used mainly for archiving multimedia presentations could use cheaper 7200 RPM SATA disks.

Resiliency

Provisioning the right type of virtual disk from a storage pool involves the following considerations:

- For general-purpose file servers and similar uses, use mirror virtual disks to ensure resiliency against the failure of one or two physical disks in the pool.

- For archival data and streaming media, use parity virtual disks. Because of the higher overhead they require when performing random I/O, do not use parity virtual disks for general-purpose file servers.

- For temporary storage such as scratch files for data-editing applications, you can implement simple virtual disks.

> **NOTE RESILIENT FILE SYSTEM**
>
> You can gain additional resiliency by formatting volumes using the Resilient File System (ReFS) in Windows Server 2012 and Windows Server 2012 R2. ReFS provides automatic data-integrity maintenance and can be used to add a layer of resiliency beyond what mirror or parity virtual disks can provide. For more information on ReFS, see "Building the next generation file system for Windows: ReFS" at *http://blogs.msdn.com/b/b8/archive/2012/01/16/building-the-next-generation-file-system-for-windows-refs.aspx*.
>
> Note that some storage features of Windows Server 2012 and Windows Server 2012 R2—such as data deduplication, which enables greater amounts of data to be stored on disks—are not supported by ReFS-formatted volumes. For more information on this aspect of ReFS, see "Plan to Deploy Data Deduplication" at *http://technet.microsoft.com/en-us/library/hh831700.aspx*.

Availability

You can deploy Storage Spaces with the Failover Clustering feature of Windows Server 2012 and Windows Server 2012 R2. You can use such a scenario to deliver continuously available shared storage for your environment by allowing shared storage to transparently fail over to a different node in a clustered file server when necessary. You can also integrate Storage Spaces with CSVs to implement a Scale-Out File Server that incorporates the benefits of using Storage Spaces.

You should keep the following considerations in mind when deploying Storage Spaces with Failover Clustering:

- You need a minimum of three physical disks.
- Physical disks must be SAS, not SATA.
- Physical disks must support persistent reservations.
- Physical disks must pass the failover cluster validation tests.
- Only fixed provisioning can be used, not thin provisioning.

> **MORE INFO** **IMPLEMENTING STORAGE SPACES WITH FAILOVER CLUSTERING**
>
> For more information on how to configure Storage Spaces with Failover Clustering, see "How to Configure a Clustered Storage Space in Windows Server 2012" at *http://blogs .msdn.com/b/clustering/archive/2012/06/02/10314262.aspx.*

Management

After you have implemented Storage Spaces in your environment, you can manage it in the following ways:

- Using the File And Storage Services role page in Server Manager
- Using cmdlets in the Storage module of Windows PowerShell

For smaller deployments, Server Manager offers a simple way of managing storage pools, virtual disks, volumes, and shares. For larger deployments—for example, when Storage Spaces is used for Hyper-V shared storage in a data center or cloud environment—Windows PowerShell provides a way to automate management tasks using scripts.

> **NOTE** **STORAGE SPACES AND WMI**
>
> You can also use WMI directly to manage Storage Spaces using SMAPI—for example, by writing a utility that does this.

Scalability

The scalability of Storage Spaces makes it suitable for various scenarios, ranging from deploying file servers for small businesses to implementing a private-cloud solution for a midsized organization. For example, a single stand-alone file server using Storage Spaces with a dozen connected physical disks might be used for any of the following purposes:

- A general-purpose file server for a small business or department
- An archival storage solution for infrequently accessed documents or media files
- Virtual machine storage for a Hyper-V host used for test or development

As a second example, you can combine Storage Spaces with Failover Clustering to deploy a highly available, two-node, clustered file server that you can use to provide shared storage for virtual machines running on clustered Hyper-V hosts in your production environment. Such a scenario is possible because the Windows Server 2012 and Windows Server 2012 R2 versions of Hyper-V support host-clustering using Server Message Block (SMB) 3.0 shares for storing your virtual machine files. The file server in this scenario could conceivably scale up to using several hundred disks deployed in rack-mounted SATA or SAS enclosures, and you could use such a file server as the storage for your organization's private-cloud solution.

REAL WORLD **SCALING BEYOND STORAGE SPACES**

If your organization's storage requirements are very large, you can implement Windows Server 2012 or Windows Server 2012 R2 file server clusters that use Fibre Channel for shared storage to take advantage of advanced storage-networking features such as SMB Scale-Out and SMB Direct. You could use such an infrastructure to provide shared storage for dozens, or even hundreds, of Hyper-V host clusters. If you use Fibre Channel for connectivity between the storage array and the file-server clusters, you should also use 10 gigabyte Ethernet (GbE) or InfiniBand for connectivity between the Hyper-V host clusters and the file-server clusters to ensure optimal performance. For more information on the SMB 3.0 capabilities included in Windows Server 2012 and Windows Server 2012 R2, see "Server Message Block overview" at *http://technet.microsoft.com/en-us/library /hh831795.aspx.*

Implementing Storage Spaces

Implementing a stand-alone Storage Spaces solution in your environment basically involves doing two things:

- Installing the File Server role service
- Connecting additional physical storage to your server if needed

You can perform the first step by using either Server Manager or Windows PowerShell, as the following sections demonstrate. You can add physical storage at any time, either by installing more internal disks in the server or by connecting external storage enclosures to the server. You can also add more physical storage either before or after you install the File Server role service.

NOTE **IMPLEMENTING HA STORAGE SPACES**

Implementing a highly available Storage Spaces solution using Failover Clustering is beyond the scope of this book. Search the TechNet Library for more information on this scenario if it is necessary for your organization.

Using Server Manager

You can use Server Manager to implement Storage Spaces on a server running Windows Server 2012 or Windows Server 2012 R2. To do this, launch the Add Roles And Features Wizard from the Manage menu on the Server Manager toolbar. Then select the File Server role service, which is located under the File And iSCSI Services role services in the File And Storage Services role as shown in Figure 8-3.

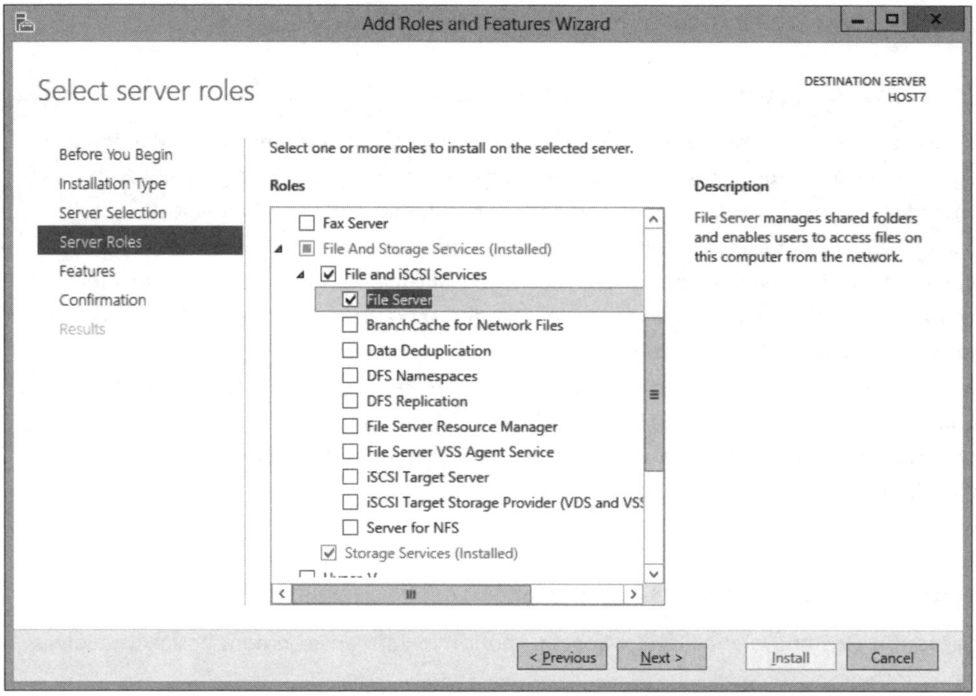

FIGURE 8-3 Installing the File Server role service implements Storage Spaces on the server.

> *NOTE* **STORAGE SERVICES**
>
> The Storage Services role service of the File And Storage Services role is always installed by default whenever you install Windows Server 2012 or Windows Server 2012 R2 on a server. This is because the Storage Services role service provides storage-management functionality that is needed by any other roles you might install on the server.

Using Windows PowerShell

You can also use Windows PowerShell to implement Storage Spaces on a server running Windows Server 2012 or Windows Server 2012 R2. You can use the Get-WindowsFeature cmdlet to display the install state of the different role services of the File And Storage Services role on a clean install of Windows Server 2012 or Windows Server 2012 R2 as follows:

```
[X] File And Storage Services            FileAndStorage-Services    Installed
    [ ] File and iSCSI Services          File-Services              Available
        [ ] File Server                  FS-FileServer              Available
        [ ] BranchCache for Network Files FS-BranchCache            Available
        [ ] Data Deduplication           FS-Data-Deduplication      Available
        [ ] DFS Namespaces               FS-DFS-Namespace           Available
        [ ] DFS Replication              FS-DFS-Replication         Available
        [ ] File Server Resource Manager FS-Resource-Manager        Available
        [ ] File Server VSS Agent Service FS-VSS-Agent              Available
        [ ] iSCSI Target Server          FS-iSCSITarget-Server      Available
        [ ] iSCSI Target Storage Provider (... iSCSITarget-VSS-VDS  Available
        [ ] Server for NFS               FS-NFS-Service             Available
    [X] Storage Services                 Storage-Services           Installed
```

For example, you can use the following command to implement Storage Spaces on server HOST7 by installing the File Server role service:

```
Install-WindowsFeature -Name FS-FileServer -ComputerName HOST7 - Restart
```

Afterward, you can use the following command to verify installation of the role service:

```
PS C:\> Get-WindowsFeature -ComputerName HOST7 | where DisplayName -eq "File Server"

Display Name                    Name                    Install State
------------                    ----                    -------------
    [X] File Server             FS-FileServer               Installed
```

Lesson summary

- Storage Spaces enables you to virtualize commodity physical disks into pools from which you can provision volumes and shares for different purposes.
- Storage Spaces supports both thin and fixed provisioning of storage.
- Storage Spaces can provide resiliency similar to hardware RAID 0 and RAID 1 solutions.
- When planning the deployment of Storage Spaces, you should consider hardware, performance, resiliency, availability, management, and scalability.
- You can implement Storage Spaces using either Server Manager or Windows PowerShell.

Lesson review

Answer the following questions to test your knowledge of the information in this lesson. You can find the answers to these questions and explanations of why each answer choice is correct or incorrect in the "Answers" section at the end of this chapter.

1. Which of the following might be true if the primordial pool is not visible in the Storage Pools tile on the Storage Pools subpage of the File And Storage Services page of Server Manager? (Choose all that apply.)

   A. A new storage pool has been created on the server.

   B. The server has only one connected physical disk (the boot disk).

   C. The physical disks are already allocated to storage pools on the server.

   D. The physical disks already have volumes on them.

2. Which of the following storage-management utilities is deprecated as of Windows Server 2012 R2? (Choose all that apply.)

   A. DiskPart

   B. DiskRAID

   C. The Disk Management MMC snap-in

   D. WMI

3. You have used Windows PowerShell to create two 5 TB data volumes on your file server. The total free space on all connected physical disks is only 2 TBs. What feature of Storage Spaces makes this possible?

   A. Thin provisioning

   B. Fixed provisioning

   C. Mirror resiliency

   D. Parity resiliency

4. Which of the following is *not* true when deploying Storage Spaces with Failover Clustering? (Choose all that apply.)

   A. A minimum of two physical disks is required.

   B. Physical disks must be SATA disks.

   C. Physical disks must pass the failover cluster validation tests.

   D. Thin provisioning must be used.

Lesson 2: Provisioning and managing shared storage

Provisioning and managing shared storage is an important part of the system administrator's job. In the previous lesson, you learned how Storage Spaces, which was introduced in Windows Server 2012, can enable you to implement low-cost, flexible storage solutions using commodity-based disk hardware. This lesson demonstrates how to use Storage Spaces to provision, manage, and maintain shared storage using both Server Manager and Windows PowerShell.

> **After this lesson, you will be able to:**
> - Create storage pools using Server Manager or Windows PowerShell.
> - Create virtual disks using Server Manager or Windows PowerShell.
> - Create volumes using Server Manager or Windows PowerShell.
> - Describe the different types of SMB shares you can create and their various configuration options.
> - Create SMB shares using Server Manager or Windows PowerShell.
> - Manage storage pools, virtual disks, volumes, and SMB shares using Server Manager or Windows PowerShell.
>
> **Estimated lesson time: 30 minutes**

Provisioning shared storage

Provisioning shared storage using Storage Spaces involves performing the following steps:

1. Create one or more storage pools.
2. Create virtual disks from your storage pools.
3. Create volumes on your virtual disks.

Once you complete the preceding steps, you are ready to create SMB file shares on the volumes you created. Provisioning SMB file shares is covered in the section titled "Provisioning SMB shares" later in this chapter.

Creating a storage pool

The first step in provisioning storage is to create one or more *storage pools*. Before you create a new storage pool, make sure that you have

- At least one available physical disk in your primordial pool if you plan on creating simple volumes.
- At least two available physical disks in your primordial pool if you plan on creating resilient volumes.
- At least three available physical disks in your primordial pool if you plan on creating resilient volumes in a failover cluster containing two file servers.

Figure 8-4 shows the primordial storage pool on a server named HOST7 in Server Manager. The Physical Disks tile of the Storage Pools page indicates that there are three physical disks available. These disks are SAS disks, and each one has a capacity of 233 GBs. You could create different pool configurations from these disks—for example:

- Three storage pools, with each pool created using a single physical disk. This configuration would allow you to create only simple (nonresilient) volumes.

- Two storage pools, with one pool using two of the physical disks and the second pool using the remaining physical disk. In this configuration, the first pool would allow you to create both simple and resilient volumes and the second pool would allow you to create only simple volumes.

- One storage pool that uses all three physical disks to support the creation of simple or resilient volumes.

FIGURE 8-4 The primordial storage pool on this server has three physical disks.

To create a new storage pool using Server Manager, perform the following steps:

1. Launch the New Storage Pool Wizard—for example, by right-clicking the Primordial storage pool item shown as selected in Figure 8-4.

2. Give your new storage pool a descriptive name, such as "Archive Pool," that identifies the purpose of the new pool—for example, to provide archival storage for presentations and media files for your company.

3. Select the physical disks in the primordial pool that you want to assign to your new pool. When you select a physical disk, you have the option of choosing Automatic, Hot Spare, or Manual as the allocation method for the disk. The configuration shown in Figure 8-5 will make two physical disks available for the creation of new virtual disks from the pool and keep an additional physical disk in reserve as a hot spare in case one of the other two disks fails.

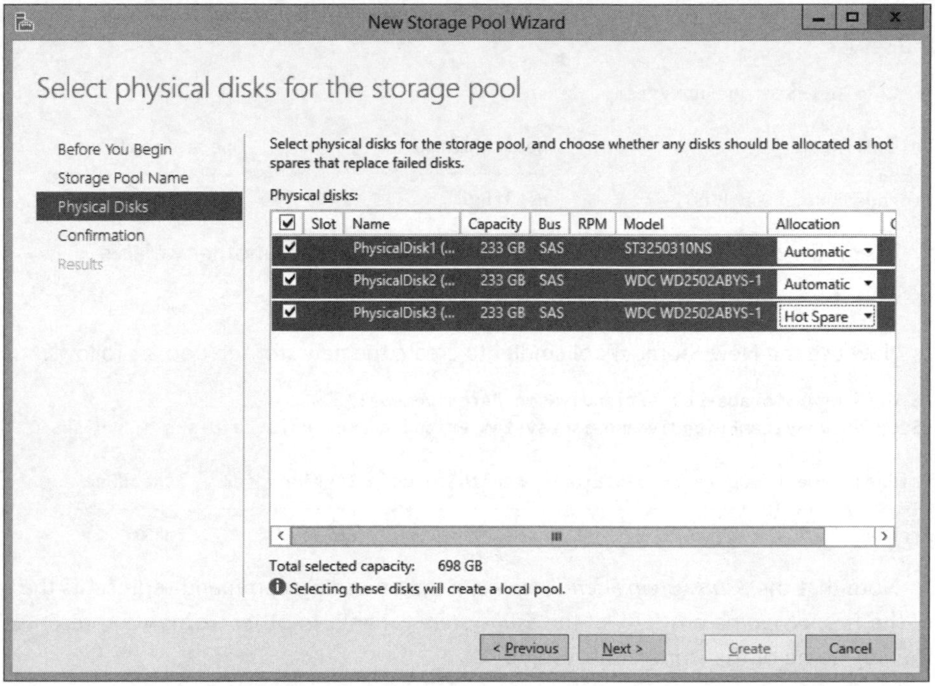

FIGURE 8-5 Assign physical disks to a new storage pool.

4. Click Next and then Create to create the new pool.

Alternatively, you could use Windows PowerShell to create the same storage pool. Begin by using the Get-StoragePool cmdlet to display a list of storage pools on the server:

```
PS C:\> Get-StoragePool

FriendlyName    OperationalStatus    HealthStatus    IsPrimordial    IsReadOnly
------------    -----------------    ------------    ------------    ----------
Primordial      OK                   Healthy         True            False
```

Next, use the Get-PhysicalDisk cmdlet to display a list of physical disks connected to the server:

```
PS C:\> Get-PhysicalDisk

FriendlyName    CanPool    OperationalStatus    HealthStatus    Usage          Size
------------    -------    -----------------    ------------    -----          ----
PhysicalDisk0   False      OK                   Healthy         Auto-Select    232.83 GB
PhysicalDisk1   True       OK                   Healthy         Auto-Select    232.83 GB
PhysicalDisk2   True       OK                   Healthy         Auto-Select    232.83 GB
PhysicalDisk3   True       OK                   Healthy         Auto-Select    232.83 GB
```

Only disks that have their *CanPool* property set to *True* are available for assigning to new storage pools you create. Use Get-PhysicalDisk again to assign such disks to a variable:

```
PS C:\> $phydisks = (Get-PhysicalDisk | where CanPool -eq True)
```

Next, use the Get-StorageSubSystem cmdlet to display the available storage subsystem on the server:

```
PS C:\> Get-StorageSubSystem

FriendlyName                      HealthStatus              OperationalStatus
------------                      ------------              -----------------
Storage Spaces on HOST7           Healthy                   OK
```

Assign the object that is the output from this command to another variable:

```
PS C:\> $subsystem = (Get-StorageSubSystem)
```

Now use the New-StoragePool cmdlet to create the new storage pool as follows:

```
PS C:\> New-StoragePool -FriendlyName "Archive Pool" `
-StorageSubSystemFriendlyName $subsystem.FriendlyName -PhysicalDisks $phydisks

FriendlyName   OperationalStatus   HealthStatus   IsPrimordial   IsReadOnly
------------   -----------------   ------------   ------------   ----------
Archive Pool   OK                  Healthy        False          False
```

Note that the *$subsystem.FriendlyName* in the preceding command represents the value of the *FriendlyName* property of the *$subsystem* variable. In other words, it represents the friendly name of the storage subsystem.

Finally, you can use Get-StoragePool again to verify the result:

```
PS C:\> Get-StoragePool

FriendlyName   OperationalStatus   HealthStatus   IsPrimordial   IsReadOnly
------------   -----------------   ------------   ------------   ----------
Primordial     OK                  Healthy        True           False
Archive Pool   OK                  Healthy        False          False
```

And if you want detailed information about the new storage pool, you can use this command:

```
PS C:\> Get-StoragePool -FriendlyName "Archive Pool" | fl *

Usage                        : Other
OperationalStatus            : OK
HealthStatus                 : Healthy
ProvisioningTypeDefault      : Fixed
SupportedProvisioningTypes   : {Thin, Fixed}
...
```

Creating virtual disks

Before you can create a *virtual disk*, you must create at least one storage pool on your file server. Continuing the procedure that was started in the previous section, Figure 8-6 shows that file server HOST7 now has a storage pool named Archive Pool that has a capacity of 696 GBs but no virtual disks yet.

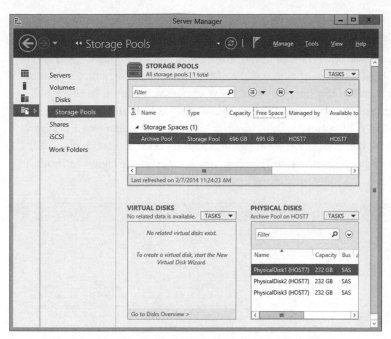

FIGURE 8-6 The storage pool named Archive Pool has no virtual disks yet.

To create a new virtual disk from a storage pool using Server Manager, perform the following steps:

1. Launch the New Virtual Disk Wizard—for example, by right-clicking the Archive Pool item shown as selected in Figure 8-6. Alternatively, you can select "Create a virtual disk when this wizard closes" at the end of the New Storage Pool wizard.

2. Select the storage pool from which you want to create your new virtual disk. In this example, you are using Archive Pool.

3. Give your new virtual disk a descriptive name, such as "Archive Disk," that identifies the purpose of the new disk, which in this case will be long-term storage of archival information for Contoso, Ltd.

4. If you want to use storage tiers to enable automatic movement of the most frequently accessed files to faster storage, select the check box labeled Create Storage Tiers On This Virtual Disk. This check box will be unavailable (grayed out) if the storage pool you

selected does not have at least one physical disk of each media type (SSD and HDD), as is the case in this walkthrough in which only SAS HDDs are being used.

5. Select the storage layout you want to use for the new virtual disk. Because Archive Pool has three physical disks with one being reserved as a hot spare, you can choose either Simple or Mirror as the storage layout for your new virtual disk. To choose Parity, you would need a minimum of three physical disks available, in which case you would need to have configured the third physical disk as Automatic instead of Hot Spare when you created your pool. Because the disk in this example will be used to archive valuable company information, select Mirror for its storage layout as shown in Figure 8-7.

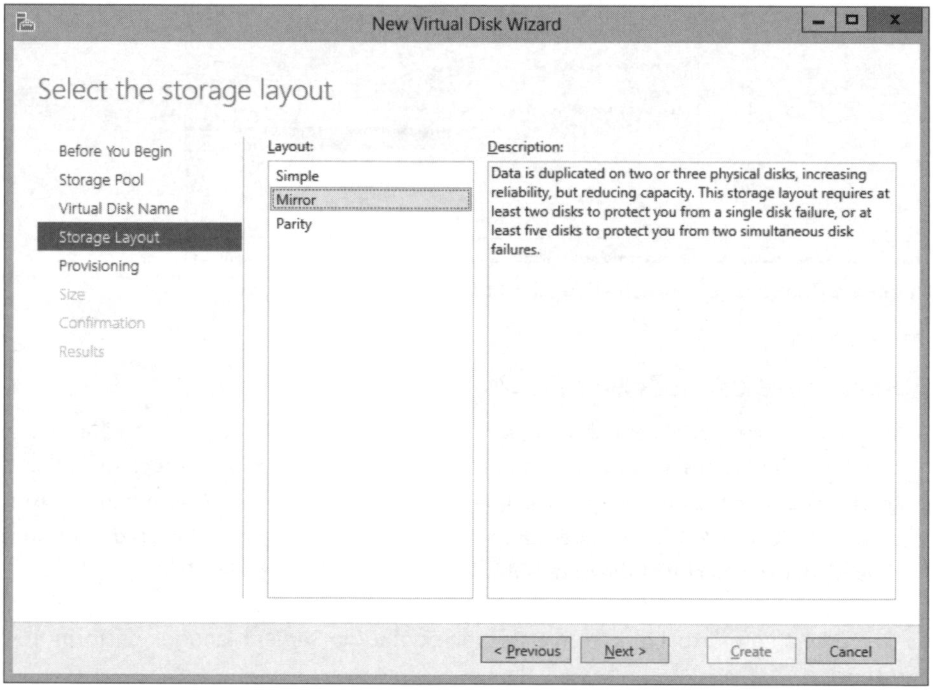

FIGURE 8-7 Specify the storage layout for the new virtual disk.

6. Select the provisioning type you want to use for the new virtual disk. Because the disk in this example will be used for archival storage of company information that might grow over time, select Thin for the provisioning type.

7. Specify the size of the new virtual disk you are creating as shown in Figure 8-8. The possible size you can specify depends on the type of provisioning, as follows:

   ■ If you selected Fixed as the provisioning type, you can either select Maximum Size to allow Storage Spaces to create a virtual disk that has the maximum capacity of the storage pool or you can specify your desired disk size in MBs, GBs, or TBs. Note that the virtual disk you are creating might use additional space from the pool to create a write-back cache.

- If you selected Thin as the provisioning type, you only have the option of specifying your desired disk size in MBs, GBs, or TBs. Once again, your virtual disk might take additional space to create a write-back cache.

In this example, specify 2 TBs as the maximum size of the new virtual disk. This large value is possible for this server only because you selected Thin as the provisioning type.

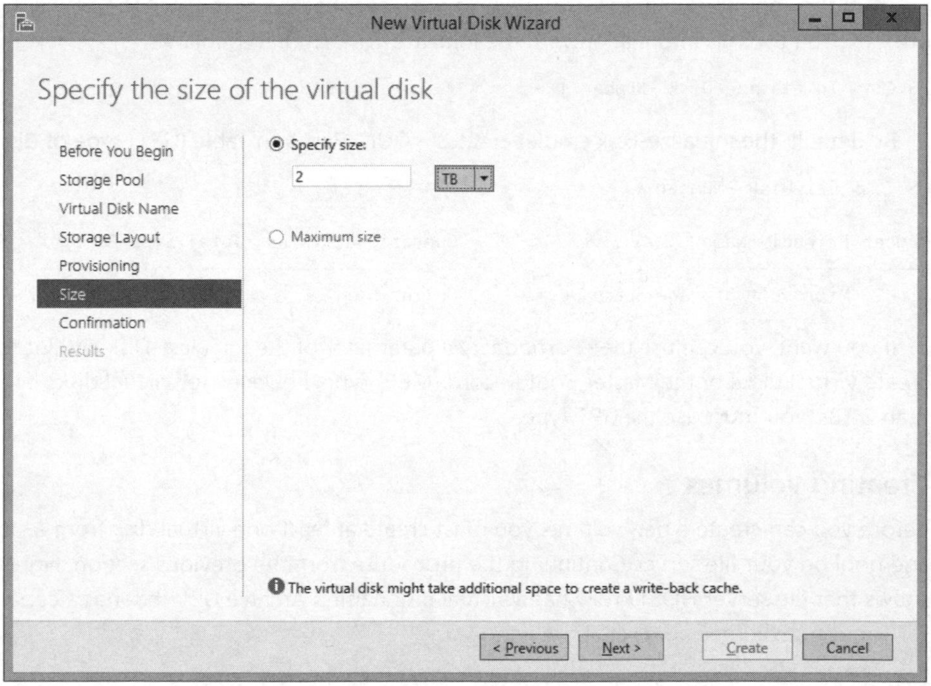

FIGURE 8-8 Specify the size of the new virtual disk.

8. Click Create to create the new virtual disk.

Alternatively, you could use Windows PowerShell to create the same virtual disk. Begin by using the New-VirtualDisk cmdlet to create the new virtual disk:

```
PS C:\> New-VirtualDisk -StoragePoolFriendlyName "Archive Pool" `
-FriendlyName "Archive Disk" -ResiliencySettingName Mirror -ProvisioningType Thin `
-Size 2TB

FriendlyName ResiliencySettingName OperationalStatus  HealthStatus IsManualAttach Size
------------ --------------------- -----------------  ------------ -------------- ----
Archive Disk Mirror                OK                 Healthy      False          2 TB
```

Any new virtual disk created this way must then be initialized (brought online) before it can be used. You can use the Get-Disk cmdlet to display more information about the disks (physical and virtual) on the server:

```
PS C:\> Get-Disk

Number Friendly Name                       OperationalStatus Total Size Partition Style
------ -------------                       ----------------- ---------- ---------------
0      ATA ST3250310NS SCSI Disk Device    Online            232.83 GB  MBR
4      Microsoft Storage Space Device      Offline           2 TB       RAW
```

From the command output just shown, you can see that the number of the new virtual disk is 4. You use this information with the Initialize-Disk cmdlet as follows:

```
PS C:\> Initialize-Disk -Number 4
```

By default, the Initialize-Disk cmdlet creates a GUID Partition Table (GPT) type of disk:

```
PS C:\> Get-Disk -Number 4

Number Friendly Name                       OperationalStatus Total Size Partition Style
------ -------------                       ----------------- ---------- ---------------
4      Microsoft Storage Space Device      Online            2 TB       GPT
```

If you want, you can use the *–PartitionStyle* parameter of the Initialize-Disk cmdlet to create virtual disks of the Master Boot Record (MBR) type; however, for virtual disks larger than 2 TBs, you must use the GPT type.

Creating volumes

Before you can create a new volume, you must create at least one virtual disk from a storage pool on your file server. Continuing the procedure from the previous section, Figure 8-9 shows that file server HOST7 now has a virtual disk named Archive Disk that has a capacity of 2 TBs but no volumes on it yet.

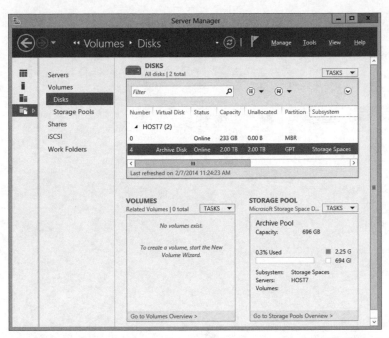

FIGURE 8-9 The virtual disk named Archive Disk has no volumes on it yet.

To create a new volume from a virtual disk using Server Manager, perform the following steps:

1. Launch the New Volume Wizard—for example, by right-clicking the Archive Disk item shown as selected in Figure 8-9. Alternatively, you can select "Create A Volume When This Wizard Closes" at the end of the New Virtual Disk wizard.

2. Select the virtual disk from which you want to create your new volume and the server to which you want to provision the volume. In this example, you are using Archive Disk to provision a new volume to HOST7.

3. Specify the size of the new volume you are creating as shown in Figure 8-10. The maximum size you can select here is the size of the virtual disk you selected in the previous step.

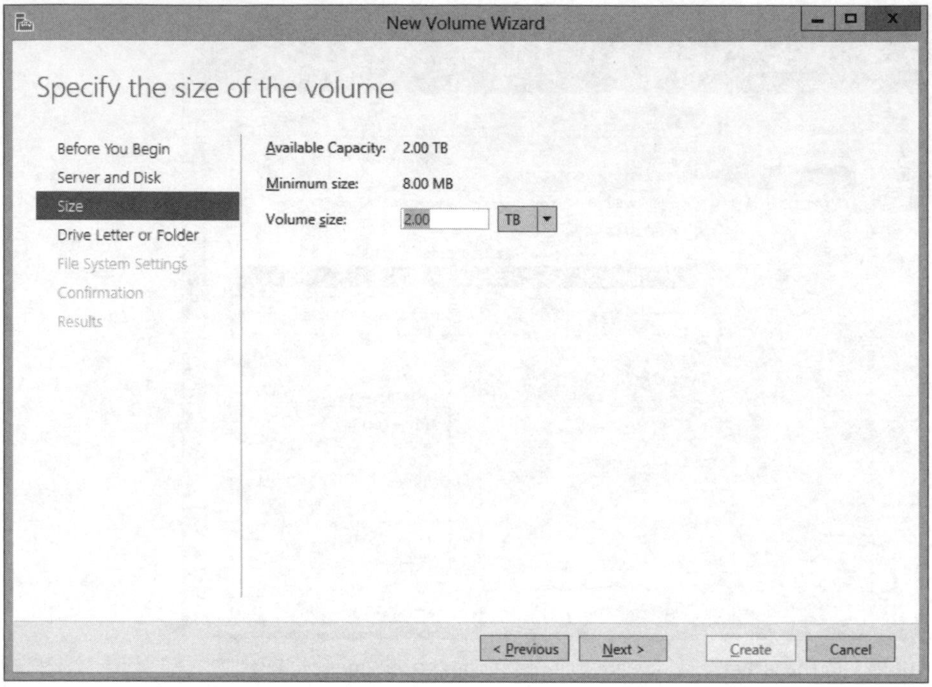

FIGURE 8-10 Specify the size for the new volume.

4. Assign the new volume a drive letter, a folder, or neither. If you assign a folder (for example, C:\Data), the volume will appear in the file system as a folder (Data) within a drive (C:).

5. Select the file system (NTFS or ReFS) for the new volume.

6. Either leave the allocation unit size for the file system as Default or select one of the available values.

7. Specify a descriptive volume name for the new volume.

8. Specify whether to generate short (8.3) file names for the new volume. Short file names are usually needed only to support legacy applications, such as 16-bit programs. Generating short file names is not recommended because it will make file operations slower.

9. Click Create to create the new volume.

Alternatively, you could use Windows PowerShell to create the same volume. Begin by using the Get-Volume cmdlet to display a list of volumes on the file server:

```
PS C:\> Get-Volume

DriveLetter FileSystemLabel FileSystem DriveType HealthStatus SizeRemaining Size
----------- --------------- ---------- --------- ------------ ------------- ----
            System Reserved NTFS       Fixed     Healthy      108.69 MB     350 MB
C                           NTFS       Fixed     Healthy      219.48 GB     232.49 GB
D                                      CD-ROM    Healthy      0 B           0 B
```

To create a new volume on your virtual disk, which you saw in the previous section is disk number 4 on the server, you use the New-Partition cmdlet as follows:

```
PS C:\> New-Partition -DiskNumber 4 -UseMaximumSize -AssignDriveLetter

    Disk Number: 4

PartitionNumber DriveLetter Offset    Size Type
--------------- ----------- ------    ---- ----
2               E           135266304 2 TB Basic
```

Once you create the new volume, you can use the Format-Volume cmdlet to format it as follows:

```
PS C:\> Format-Volume -DriveLetter E -FileSystem NTFS

Confirm
Are you sure you want to perform this action?
Warning, all data on the volume will be lost!
[Y] Yes  [A] Yes to All  [N] No  [L] No to All  [S] Suspend  [?] Help (default is "Y"):
y

DriveLetter  FileSystemLabel  FileSystem  DriveType  HealthStatus  SizeRemaining  Size
-----------  ---------------  ----------  ---------  ------------  -------------  ----
E                             NTFS        Fixed      Healthy       2 TB           2 TB
```

> **MORE INFO**   **STORAGE MODULE FOR WINDOWS POWERSHELL**
>
> For more information about New-StoragePool, New-VirtualDisk, and other cmdlets in the Storage module for Windows PowerShell, see "Storage Cmdlets in Windows PowerShell" at *http://technet.microsoft.com/en-us/library/hh848705.aspx*.

> ✔ **Quick check**
>
> - Why should you usually initialize your virtual disks as GPT disks instead of MBR disks?
>
> **Quick check answer**
>
> - GPT disks support volumes larger than 2 TBs. For more information about the advantages of using GPT rather than MBR, see "Using GPT Drives" at *http://msdn .microsoft.com/en-us/library/windows/hardware/gg463524.aspx*.

Provisioning SMB shares

After you create volumes using Storage Spaces, you can create shared storage for various purposes by provisioning new file shares. Storage Spaces supports the provisioning of two types of shares:

- **SMB shares**   Server Message Block (SMB) is a network file-sharing protocol that allows SMB clients to read and write to files and to request services from SMB servers on the network. Windows Server 2012 and Windows Server 2012 R2 support version 3.0 of the SMB protocol, which includes numerous enhancements in performance, security, and scalability. Using SMB 3.0 enables you to implement new file-server scenarios, such as storing Hyper-V virtual machines and Microsoft SQL Server databases on SMB file shares. SMB 3.0 also helps reduce latency over branch-office wide area network (WAN) connections and can help protect data from eavesdropping attacks. For more information on SMB 3.0 in Windows Server 2012 and Windows Server 2012 R2, see "Server Message Block overview" at *http://technet.microsoft.com/en-us /library/hh831795*.

- **NFS shares**   Network File System (NFS) enables file sharing in heterogeneous environments that include both Windows and non-Windows computers. Windows Server 2012 and Windows Server 2012 R2 include two NFS components:

  - **Server for NFS**   This component enables Windows Server 2012 or Windows Server 2012 R2 to act as a file server for non-Windows client computers.

  - **Client for NFS**   This component enables Windows Server 2012 or Windows Server 2012 R2 to access files that are stored on a non-Windows NFS server.

  Server for NFS has also been enhanced in Windows Server 2012 and Windows Server 2012 R2 to support continuous availability. This makes possible new scenarios, such as running VMware ESX virtual machines from file-based storage over the NFS protocol instead of using more expensive SAN storage. This improvement enables Windows Server 2012 and Windows Server 2012 R2 to provide continuous availability for VMware virtual machines, making it easier for organizations to integrate their VMware infrastructure with the Windows platform. Using Server for NFS as a data store for VMware virtual machines requires using VMware ESX 4.1. You also need a management server with VMware vSphere Client version 4.1 installed. You can use PowerShell to provision and configure shared files on your Server for NFS data store. For more information, see "Server for NFS Data Store" at *http://technet.microsoft.com/en-us /library/hh831653*.

Because NFS is useful only for certain types of scenarios, the remainder of this section focuses on provisioning SMB shares.

Configuration options for SMB shares

When you create a new SMB share, you can select from the following configuration options:

- **Enable Access-Based Enumeration**   When you enable this option, users who access a share can see only files and folders they have permission to access. When you disable access-based enumeration for a share, users can see all of the files and folders in the share even if they don't have permission to read or modify the files and folders. Implementing access-based enumeration helps reduce user confusion that might be caused when users are unable to access some of the files and folders in a share.

- **Allow Caching Of Share**   Enabling this option makes the contents of the share available to offline users. This ensures that users can access the files in the share even when they are working offline without access to the network.

- **Enable BranchCache**   By enabling this option, you allow computers in a branch office to use BranchCache to cache any files downloaded from the shared folder. The computers can then securely serve the files to other computers in the branch office. You can enable this option only if you also have enabled the Allow Caching Of Share option.

- **Encrypt Data Access**   Enabling this option causes remote file access to the share to be encrypted to protect against eavesdropping attacks.

- **Folder Usage**   You can use this option to specify the purpose of the share and the kinds of files stored in it. Folder Usage is used by data-management policies, such as when specifying the classification rules for the new File Classification Infrastructure feature of Windows Server 2012 and Windows Server 2012 R2.

- **Quota**   You can use this option to limit the space allowed for a volume or folder. You can also define quota templates that can be automatically applied to new volumes or folders.

> **NOTE   FILE SERVER RESOURCE MANAGER**
>
> Configuring the Folder Usage and Quota options requires that the File Server Resource Manager feature be installed on a Windows Server 2012 or Windows Server 2012 R2 file server in your environment.

Types of SMB shares

You can provision new SMB shares in your environment using either Server Manager or Windows PowerShell. As Figure 8-11 shows, you have three options from which to choose when creating SMB shares by using the New Share Wizard:

- **Quick**   Choose this option if you need to create a general-purpose SMB share for file sharing. This option enables caching of the share by default and allows you to enable access-based enumeration and to encrypt data access if desired. You can also enable BranchCache on the share if the BranchCache feature is installed on the server.

- **Advanced**   Choose this option if you need to configure quotas on your share or implement file classification. This option also enables caching of the share by default and allows you to enable access-based enumeration and to encrypt data access if desired. You can also enable BranchCache on the share if the BranchCache feature is installed on the server.

- **Applications**   Choose this option if the share will be used by Hyper-V hosts for shared storage, by a database application, or by other server applications. This option allows you to encrypt data access if desired, but you cannot enable caching or enable access-based enumeration on the share.

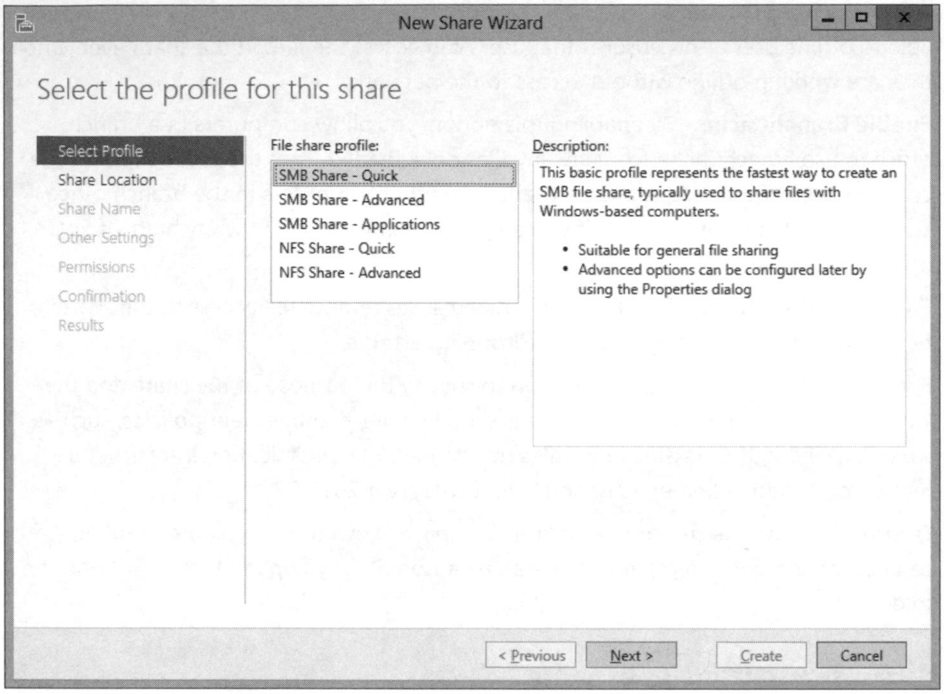

FIGURE 8-11 Choose the type of SMB share to create.

Creating general-purpose SMB shares

To create a new general-purpose SMB share on a volume by using Server Manager, perform the following steps:

1. Launch the New Share Wizard—for example, by right-clicking the volume named Archive Volume in Figure 8-12.

2. Select the SMB Share - Quick option shown previously in Figure 8-11.

3. Select a volume on a file server—for example, the 2 TB volume named Archive Volume that was provisioned using Storage Spaces in the previous section of this lesson.

4. Type a name for the new share. By default, a new local folder will be created for the share in the following location:

   <volume>\Shares\<share_name>

   For example, if you specify Archive Share as the name for the new share being created on the E volume, the following local folder will be created for the new share:

   E:\Shares\Archive Share

5. If access-based enumeration is desired, enable it on the share.

6. If you want, disable caching on the share. (Caching is enabled by default.) If you leave caching enabled and the BranchCache feature is installed on the server, you can enable BranchCache on the share if desired.

7. If you want, enable encrypted data access on the share.

8. Review the permissions for the new share. If you want, open the Advanced Security Settings dialog box and modify the permissions as needed.

9. Click Next and then click Create to create the new share.

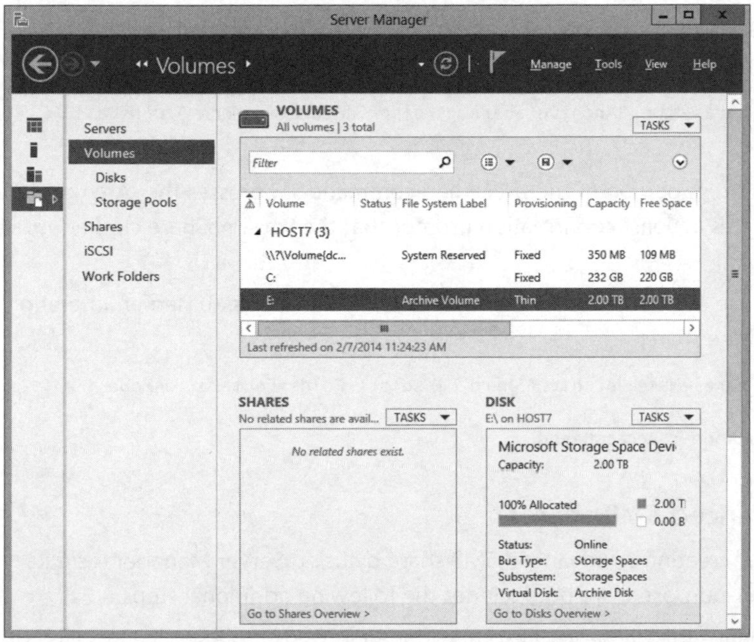

FIGURE 8-12 You can right-click volume E to create a new share on the volume.

You can also use Windows PowerShell to create new general-purpose SMB shares on a volume. For example, you could start by using the New-Item cmdlet to create a local folder named E:\Shares\Archived Content for your new share:

```
PS C:\> New-Item -Path "E:\Shares\Archived Content" -ItemType Directory

    Directory: E:\Shares

Mode          LastWriteTime      Length Name
----          -------------      ------ ----
d----     8/20/2012   8:55 PM           Archived Content
```

You could then use the New-SmbShare cmdlet to create a new share named Archive Share that maps to the local folder and assign the shared folder permission Change to the CONTOSO\Sales group as follows:

```
PS C:\> New-SmbShare -Name "Archive Share" -Path "E:\Shares\Archived Content" `
-ChangeAccess CONTOSO\Sales


Name              ScopeName      Path                          Description
----              ---------      ----                          -----------
Archive Share     *              E:\Shares\Archived Content
```

If you later decide you want to enable access-based enumeration on your new share, you could use the Set-SmbShare cmdlet as follows:

```
PS C:\> Set-SmbShare -Name "Archive Share" -FolderEnumerationMode AccessBased `
-Confirm:$false
```

The *–Confirm:$false* portion of the preceding command suppresses the "Are you sure you want to perform this action?" confirmation prompt that the Set-SmbShare cmdlet usually displays.

You can then use the Get-SmbShare cmdlet to verify that access-based enumeration has been enabled on the share:

```
PS C:\> Get-SmbShare -Name "Archive Share" | select FolderEnumerationMode | fl

FolderEnumerationMode : AccessBased
```

Creating advanced SMB shares

The procedure for creating an advanced SMB share by using Server Manager is similar to creating a general-purpose share but includes the following additional steps:

- You must have the File Server Resource Manager (FSRM) role service installed on the server before you can create an advanced SMB share.

- You can use the options on the Management Properties page to specify the type of usage for the folder. You can select one or more of the following values:
  - User Files
  - Group Files
  - Application Files
  - Backup And Archival Files

- You can also specify one or more email addresses for the folder owner or owners.

The Quota page shown in Figure 8-13 lets you apply a quota to the folder by selecting from a list of available templates.

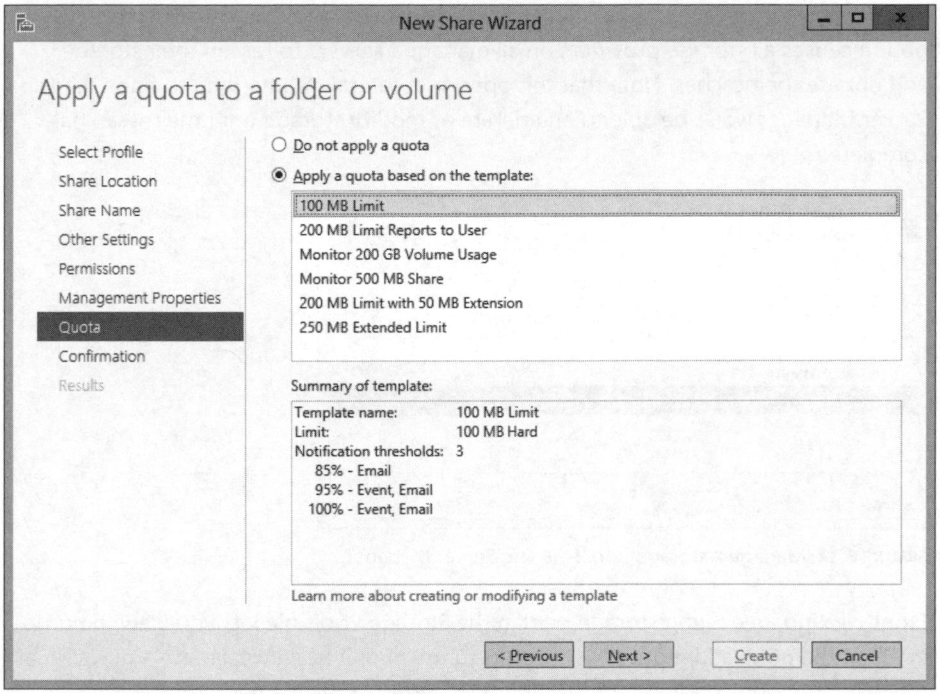

FIGURE 8-13 Configure a quota on a new share.

Managing shared storage

After you provision shared storage using Storage Spaces, you need to manage your shared storage. You can use both Server Manager and Windows PowerShell to manage shared storage in your environment. Your management tasks will include the following:

- Managing storage pools
- Managing virtual disks
- Managing volumes
- Managing shares

The sections that follow focus on using Server Manager for managing shared storage. For help with using Windows PowerShell to manage shared storage, see "Storage Cmdlets in Windows PowerShell" at *http://technet.microsoft.com/en-us/library/hh848705*.

Managing storage pools

You can use the Storage Pools subpage of the File And Storage Services page in Server Manager to manage your storage pools—for example:

- Clicking the Tasks control of the Storage Pools tile or right-clicking open space in the Storage Pools tile (see Figure 8-14) allows you to create new storage pools, refresh the current view, or rescan storage on managed file servers. Selecting the Rescan Storage option causes all storage providers on all managed servers to rescan their storage and update their caches. Note that this operation can take some time to finish, and Server Manager won't be able to enumerate or modify storage until the rescan has completed.

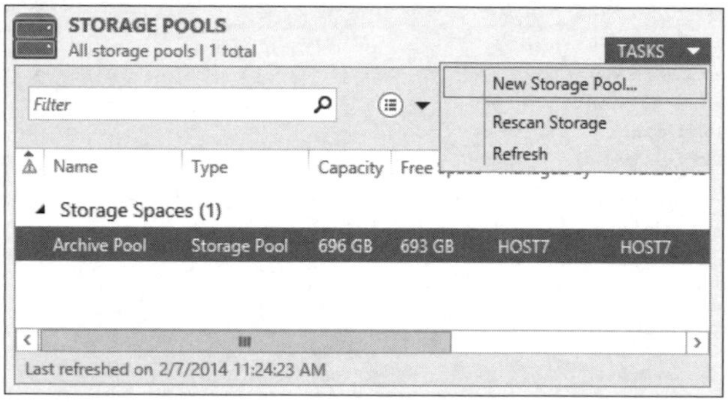

FIGURE 8-14 Manage a storage pool by using Server Manager.

- Right-clicking an existing storage pool in the Storage Pools tile lets you view the properties of the pool, add more physical disks to the pool if available, create a new virtual disk from the pool, upgrade the storage pool version, create a new storage pool, or delete the selected storage pool if all of its virtual disks have been deleted.

  You can also use the Storage Pool tile on the Disks subpage to quickly determine how much capacity has been used in a storage pool.

Managing virtual disks

You can use the Storage Pools subpage of the File And Storage Services page in Server Manager to manage your virtual disks. For example, by right-clicking a virtual disk in the Virtual Disks tile as shown in Figure 8-15, you can perform tasks such as creating a new volume on the disk, repairing the disk, extending the disk, or deleting the disk. Some options might be unavailable, depending on such things as the status of the disk and the availability of free space on the disk.

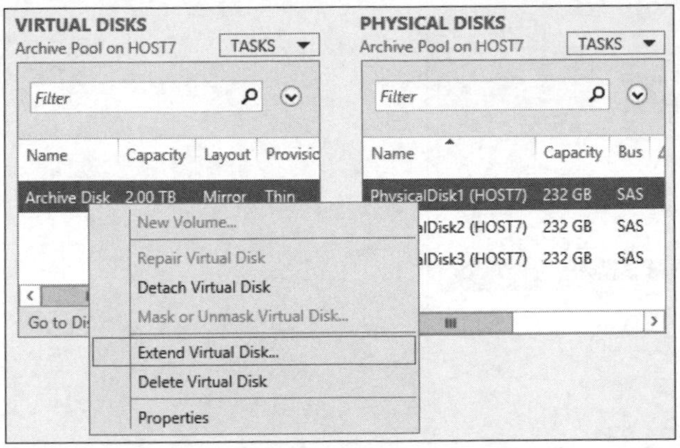

FIGURE 8-15 Extend a virtual disk from the Storage Pools subpage.

You can use the Disks subpage of the File And Storage Services page to manage both physical and virtual disks connected to the file server. For example, right-clicking a virtual disk in the Disks tile as shown in Figure 8-16 lets you take the disk offline, bring it back online, or reset the disk. The Disk tile also lets you view the status of your physical disks and their capacity, partition format, and other information.

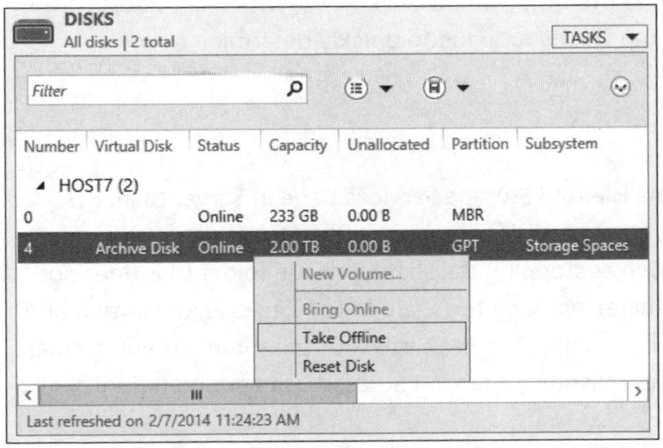

FIGURE 8-16 Take a virtual disk offline from the Disks subpage.

You can also use the Disk tile on the Volumes subpage to quickly determine how much capacity has been allocated on a physical or virtual disk.

Managing volumes

You can use the Volumes subpage of the File And Storage Services page in Server Manager to manage your volumes. For example, by right-clicking a volume in the Volumes tile as shown in Figure 8-17, you can perform tasks such as creating a new share on the volume, formatting the volume, extending the volume, or scanning the volume's file system for errors.

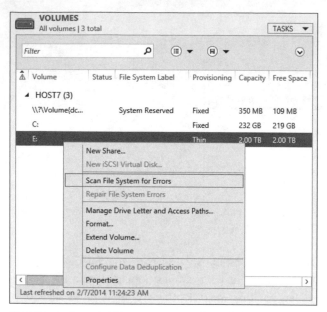

FIGURE 8-17 Scan the file system on a volume for errors.

You can also perform the same tasks from the Volumes tile on the Disks subpage. In addition, you can use the Volume tile on the Shares subpage to quickly determine how much capacity has been used on a volume.

Managing shares

You can use the Shares subpage of the File And Storage Services page in Server Manager to manage your shares. For example, by right-clicking a share in the Shares tile as shown in Figure 8-18, you can perform tasks such as stopping the sharing of the folder (this does not delete the underlying folder for the share), opening the share in File Explorer, or viewing and modifying the properties for the share. Opening the properties for the share lets you further configure the share by modifying its permissions, enabling access-based enumeration, configuring folder usage, and so on.

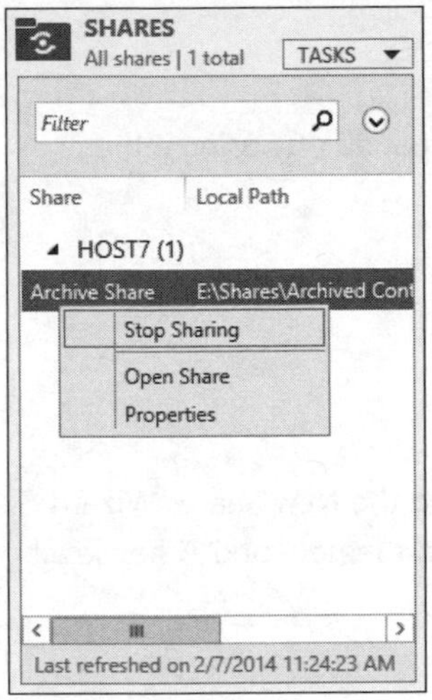

FIGURE 8-18 Manage a share.

Lesson summary

- You can create and manage storage pools, virtual disks, volumes, and shares by using both Server Manager and Windows PowerShell.
- You can create both SMB and NFS shares with Storage Spaces.
- SMB shares have various configuration options, some of which are available only when additional components such as File Server Resource Manager (FSRM) are installed on a file server.

Lesson review

Answer the following questions to test your knowledge of the information in this lesson. You can find the answers to these questions and explanations of why each answer choice is correct or incorrect in the "Answers" section at the end of this chapter.

1. What is the minimum number of physical disks required for a storage pool that will be used to provision resilient volumes for a failover cluster consisting of two file servers?

   A. One

   B. Two

   C. Three

   D. Four

2. Which Windows PowerShell cmdlet can you use to view the health status for Storage Spaces on your file server?

   A. Get-StoragePool

   B. Get-VirtualDisk

    C. Get-PhysicalDisk

    D. Get-StorageSubSystem

3. Which of the following tasks cannot be performed on a virtual disk by using either Server Manager or Windows PowerShell?

    A. Extending the virtual disk

    B. Shrinking the virtual disk

    C. Detaching the virtual disk

    D. Deleting the virtual disk

4. Which of the following profiles should you select when using the New Shares Wizard to create a share for storing Hyper-V virtual machine files on the network? (Choose all that apply.)

    A. SMB Share - Quick

    B. SMB Share - Advanced

    C. SMB Share - Application

    D. NFS Share

Lesson 3: Configuring iSCSI storage

Businesses are always looking for ways to keep costs under control. This can be especially true of departments like IT that are often viewed as cost centers more than as sources of revenue. Part of your role, then, as an administrator is to find innovative ways to cut costs in your department while maintaining services and quality. The built-in iSCSI storage features of Windows Server 2012 and Windows Server 2012 R2 are one avenue to explore in this direction.

> **After this lesson, you will be able to:**
>
> - Understand iSCSI storage benefits, uses, concepts, and terminology.
> - Understand the management tools and deployment considerations for implementing iSCSI storage using Windows Server 2012 or Windows Server 2012 R2.
> - Configure a server running Windows Server 2012 or Windows Server 2012 R2 as an iSCSI Target server.
> - Create iSCSI targets and iSCSI virtual disks on a target server.
> - Configure the iSCSI initiator on a server running Windows Server 2012 or Windows Server 2012 R2.
> - Use the iSCSI initiator to connect to a target on a target server and provision storage by creating volumes on the initiator computer.
>
> **Estimated lesson time: 30 minutes**

Understanding iSCSI storage

The Internet Small Computer System Interface (iSCSI) protocol is an industry-standard protocol that enables sharing of block storage over a TCP/IP network. iSCSI is designed to transmit and receive Small Computer System Interface (SCSI) commands and data encapsulated as TCP packets. This enables computers to utilize storage on an iSCSI-based storage device such as an iSCSI storage area network (SAN) even when the computers and SAN are located a long distance apart.

Benefits and uses ↙

A key benefit of iSCSI-based storage is cost. A typical Fibre Channel SAN can be prohibitively expensive as a storage solution for a small or midsized business. In contrast with Fibre Channel, iSCSI technology requires no special-purpose cabling because the storage can be transmitted and received over a simple Ethernet network. This enables iSCSI storage to be deployed using an organization's existing network infrastructure, which helps keep the cost of this solution low.

A second advantage of iSCSI-based storage is that it allows administrators to locate the storage in a data center where it can be centrally managed and easily backed up. From the perspective of the user on the computer consuming iSCSI storage, however, the storage appears as a locally installed drive even though it is actually located on an iSCSI SAN or storage server located in a remote data center. Users can thus copy and save files to iSCSI storage in the same way they would to hard drives installed in their computers, which leads to the third benefit of iSCSI-based storage—namely, transparency and ease of use.

Windows Server 2012 and Windows Server 2012 R2 include a built-in role service (iSCSI Target Server) and client component (iSCSI Initiator) that you can use to implement an iSCSI-based storage solution without the need to deploy a third-party iSCSI SAN. By using these features, you can gain the benefits of iSCSI storage without the need to purchase any additional hardware or software. Some of the possible uses of iSCSI storage include

- Deploying diskless servers that boot from iSCSI virtual disks over the network.
- Providing block storage to applications that require or can benefit from it.
- Creating iSCSI storage test environments in which you can validate applications before deploying them onto a third-party iSCSI SAN.

Because Microsoft iSCSI technologies are based on industry standards, you can also deploy Microsoft iSCSI storage solutions with third-party solutions in a heterogeneous environment.

Concepts and terminology

Before you can deploy a Microsoft iSCSI storage solution based on Windows Server 2012 or Windows Server 2012 R2 technologies, you first need to understand the following iSCSI concepts and terminology (which are illustrated in Figure 8-19):

- **iSCSI target server** This is the server or device (for example, SAN) that shares the storage so that users or applications running on a different computer can consume it. A target server is sometimes called a *target portal* or simply a *portal*. In Windows Server 2012 and Windows Server 2012 R2, a role service named iSCSI Target Server is used to implement this functionality.

- **iSCSI target**   This is an object created on the target server that allows an iSCSI initiator to establish a connection. The target also keeps track of the initiators that are allowed to connect to it and any iSCSI virtual disks that are associated with it.

- **iSCSI virtual disk**   This refers to storage backed by a virtual hard disk (VHD) file on the target server. The virtual disk appears as locally attached storage on the target server. The disk can also be mounted by the iSCSI initiator on the computer consuming the storage so that new volumes can be provisioned from it. An iSCSI virtual disk is sometimes called an *iSCSI LUN* (logical unit number) or simply a *LUN*.

- **iSCSI initiator**   This is a service running on a computer that enables users or applications to consume storage shared by a target server. In Windows Server 2012 and Windows Server 2012 R2, a built-in feature named iSCSI Initiator provides this functionality by a Windows service called the Microsoft iSCSI Service.

- **Connection**   This is a TCP connection between an initiator and a target. Connections transmit and receive control messages, SCSI commands, parameters, and data. Typically, an initiator can establish a connection with only one target. This limitation is in place to prevent multiple simultaneous read/writes from corrupting the file system on a volume provisioned from a virtual disk associated with the target. However, in clustering scenarios it is common for multiple initiators to form connections with the same target, although only one initiator is allowed to access the virtual disk at any one time.

- **Session**   This refers to the collection of TCP connections linking an initiator with a target. A session can have one or more connections, and you can add or remove connections from a session.

- **IQN**   The iSCSI Qualified Name (IQN) is a unique identifier for a target or initiator. In the Windows Server 2012 and Windows Server 2012 R2 implementation of an iSCSI target server, a target IQN looks like this:

```
iqn.1991-05.com.microsoft:<target_server_name>-<target-name>-target
```

For example, if a target named fabrikam-db is created on a target server named HOST7, the IQN for this target would be

```
iqn.1991-05.com.microsoft:host7-fabrikam db-target
```

Similarly, in the Windows Server 2012 and Windows Server 2012 R2 implementation of iSCSI initiator, an initiator IQN looks like this:

```
iqn.1991-05.com.microsoft:<initiator_server_FQDN>
```

For example, if the iSCSI initiator is running on a server named HOST4.corp.fabrikam.com, the IQN for this initiator would be

```
iqn.1991-05.com.microsoft:host4.corp.fabrikam.com
```

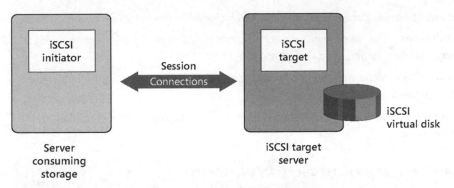

FIGURE 8-19 Understand basic iSCSI concepts and terminology.

iSCSI Target Server enhancements

iSCSI Target Server role service has been enhanced in several important ways in Windows Server 2012 R2:

■ VHDX support is now included, which enables the provisioning of larger LUNs, up to 64 TB in size. VHDX support also means you can expand or shrink iSCSI LUNs while they are online and dynamically grow them for greater scalability and flexibility. VHDX is now the default virtual disk format when creating new iSCSI LUNs.

■ iSCSI Target Server can be fully managed using SMI-S. This means that you can per-form end-to-end management of your iSCSI storage system by using System Center 2012 R2 Virtual Machine Manager.

For more information on using iSCSI Target Server with Virtual Machine Manager, see the post titled "iSCSI Target Server in Windows Server 2012 R2 for VMM Rapid Provisioning" on the File Cabinet Blog of the Storage Team at Microsoft at *http:// blogs.technet.com/b/filecab/archive/2013/10/08/iscsi-target-server-in-windows -server-2012-r2-for-vmm-rapid-provisioning.aspx.*

Management tools

Windows Server 2012 and Windows Server 2012 R2 include the following tools for managing the built-in iSCSI initiator and the iSCSI Target Server role services:

■ Server Manager, specifically the File And Storage Services page and subpages. This is the same user interface used to manage the Storage Spaces feature described earlier in this chapter.

- Windows PowerShell, specifically the cmdlets included in the following two modules:
  - **iscsitarget** This module includes commands for configuring and managing iSCSI target servers, targets, and virtual disks.
  - **iscsi** This module includes commands for configuring and managing iSCSI initiators, connections, and sessions.

You can use the *Get-Command –Module* command to display a list of cmdlets for each of these modules.

> **IMPORTANT** **MANAGING HETEROGENEOUS ENVIRONMENTS**
>
> Organizations that have previously downloaded and deployed the free Microsoft iSCSI Software Target 3.3 for Windows Server 2008 R2 need to be aware that if you need to manage a heterogeneous environment that includes target servers and initiators for Windows Server 2012 R2, Windows Server 2012, and Windows Server 2008 R2, you might need to use separate management tools for doing this. For example, you cannot use the iSCSI Target MMC snap-in for Windows Server 2008 R2 to manage target servers running Windows Server 2012 or Windows Server 2012 R2. Furthermore, you might need to modify Windows PowerShell commands and Windows Management Instrumentation (WMI) scripts used for managing the Microsoft iSCSI Software Target 3.3 if you want to use these commands and scripts to manage the iSCSI Target Server capabilities in Windows Server 2012 or Windows Server 2012 R2.

Deployment considerations

Although enabling iSCSI Target Server to provide block storage for your environment requires no hardware other than your existing Ethernet network and a server running Windows Server 2012 or Windows Server 2012 R2, there are some additional considerations you need to be aware of:

- You cannot host iSCSI virtual disks on physical disks that have been added to a storage pool on the server. In other words, iSCSI Target Server in Windows Server 2012 and Windows Server 2012 R2 is not compatible with Storage Spaces.
- iSCSI virtual disks can be backed only by VHD files, not by the newer VHDX files that Hyper-V uses by default in Windows Server 2012 and Windows Server 2012 R2.
- You can create new iSCSI virtual disks only on NTFS volumes, not on volumes formatted using the new Resilient File System (ReFS) in Windows Server 2012 and Windows Server 2012 R2.

Configuring iSCSI Target Server

This section describes how to perform the following tasks for iSCSI Target Server on Windows Server 2012 and Windows Server 2012 R2:

- Enabling iSCSI Initiator
- Installing the iSCSI Target Server role service
- Creating iSCSI virtual disks

The section shows how to perform these tasks using both Server Manager and Windows PowerShell.

Enabling iSCSI Initiator

Before you configure iSCSI Target Server, you should enable the iSCSI Initiator feature on the computer that will be connecting to the Target server. The following procedure shows how to enable the iSCSI Initiator feature on a server running Windows Server 2012 or Windows Server 2012 R2:

1. Open Server Manager and select iSCSI Initiator from the Tools menu.
2. When the Microsoft iSCSI dialog box appears, click Yes to start the Microsoft iSCSI Service and close the dialog box:

3. When the iSCSI Initiator Properties dialog box opens, click OK to close it.

You can also enable the iSCSI initiator by using Windows PowerShell to start the Microsoft iSCSI Service and change the service startup type to Automatic by running these two commands:

```
Start-Service msiscsi
Set-Service msiscsi -startuptype "automatic"
```

Installing the iSCSI Target Server role

As you saw in the previous lesson in this chapter, installing the File And iSCSI Services role service of the File And Storage Services role on a server running Windows Server 2012 or Windows Server 2012 R2 introduces a new File And Storage Services page to Server Manager. Selecting this page displays a number of subpages, including one named iSCSI, but if you select this iSCSI page you will see a message in the iSCSI Virtual Disks tile as shown in Figure 8-20. This message indicates you must install iSCSI Target Server before you can use the page to manage iSCSI storage.

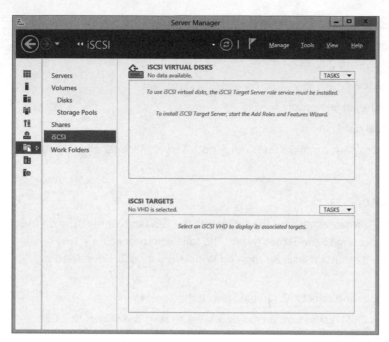

FIGURE 8-20 The iSCSI Target Server role service has not yet been installed on this server.

You can install the iSCSI Target Server role by using either Server Manager or Windows PowerShell. To install iSCSI Target Server by using Server Manager, launch the Add Roles And Features Wizard from the Manage menu. On the Select Server Roles page of this wizard, you will see two iSCSI role services as shown in Figure 8-21:

- **iSCSI Target Server**   Installing this role service installs services and management tools for iSCSI Targets.

- **iSCSI Target Storage Provider (VDS And VSS Hardware Providers)**   Installing this role service enables applications on a server that is connected to an iSCSI target to perform volume shadow copies of data on iSCSI virtual disks.

> *NOTE* **ISCSI TARGET STORAGE PROVIDER AND VDS**
>
> Installing the iSCSI Target Storage Provider (VDS And VSS Hardware Providers) role service also enables you to manage iSCSI virtual disks using management tools that use the deprecated Virtual Disk Service (VDS). Such tools include the Disk Management MMC snap-in, the Diskpart command, and the Diskraid command.

> *IMPORTANT* **WHERE TO INSTALL ISCSI TARGET STORAGE PROVIDER**
>
> You should not install the iSCSI Target Storage Provider role service on a server that has the iSCSI Target Server role service installed. Instead, install the iSCSI Target Storage Provider on the server you use to centrally manage storage for your environment.

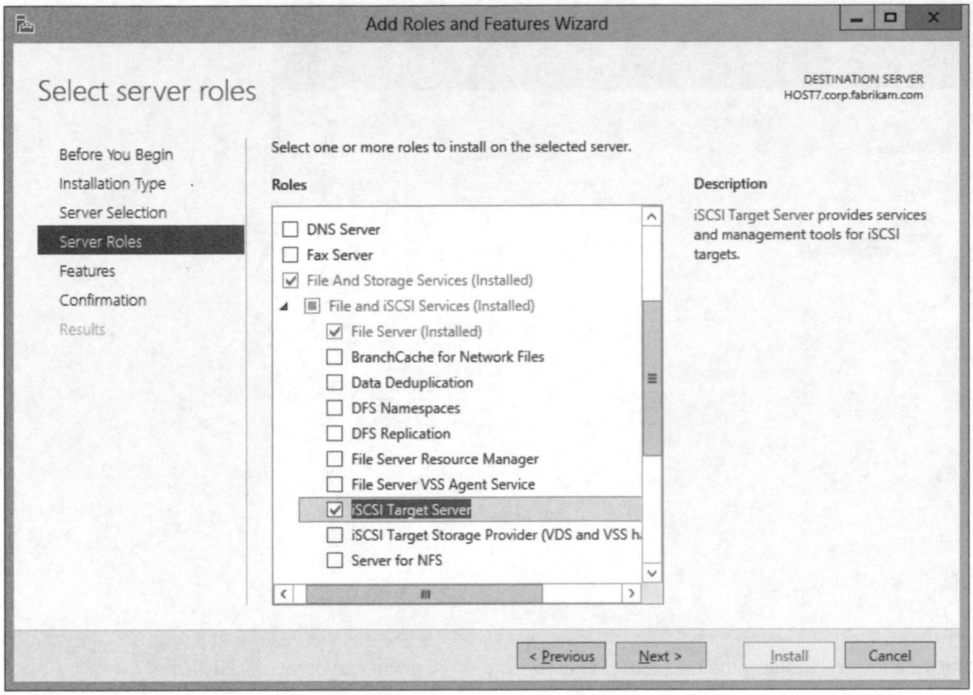

FIGURE 8-21 Add the iSCSI Target Server role service to the server.

You can also use Windows PowerShell to install iSCSI Target Server. You can do this by using the Add-WindowsFeature cmdlet like this:

```
Add-WindowsFeature –Name FS-iSCSITarget-Server
```

No restart is needed after installing this role service.

Creating iSCSI virtual disks

Once you finish installing the iSCSI Target Server role service by using the Add Roles And Feature Wizard, the message in the iSCSI Virtual Disks tile on the iSCSI page of Server Manager indicates that you can now create an iSCSI virtual disk. (See Figure 8-22.) Creating iSCSI virtual disks is the first step in provisioning iSCSI storage to applications that require or can use block storage.

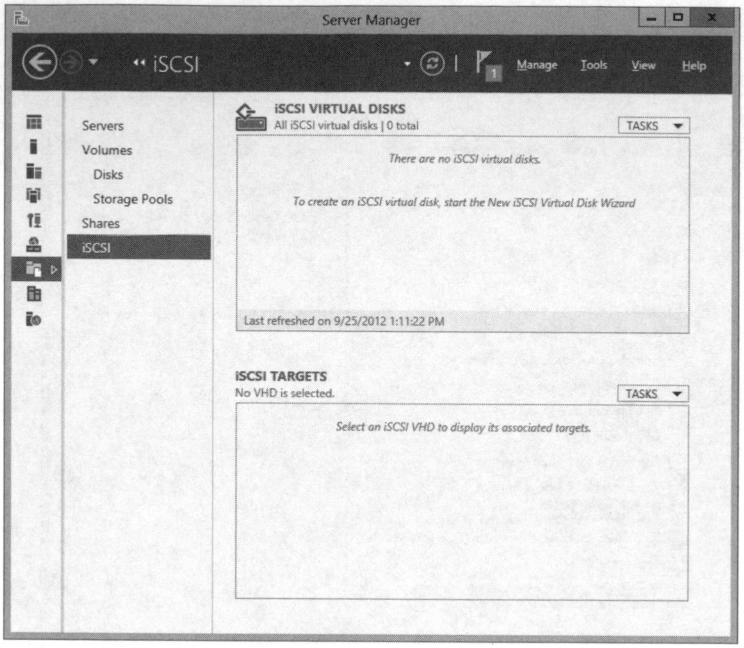

FIGURE 8-22 After installing the iSCSI Target Server role service you can create iSCSI virtual disks.

You can create a new iSCSI virtual disk by using either Server Manager or Windows PowerShell. To create a new iSCSI virtual disk by using Server Manager, do any of the following:

- Click the message in the iSCSI Virtual Disks tile on the iSCSI page.

- Select New iSCSI Virtual Disk from the Tasks menu of this iSCSI Virtual Disks tile on the iSCSI page.

- Right-click any NTFS volume in the Volumes tile on the Disks page or the Volumes page and select New iSCSI Virtual Disk.

Performing any of these actions will launch the New iSCSI Virtual Disk Wizard, which you can use to create your new iSCSI virtual disk as follows:

1. On the Select iSCSI Virtual Disk Location page, select a target server. The list of available servers shows those on which Server Manager has determined that the iSCSI Target Server role has been installed.

2. After you select an iSCSI Target server, select an NTFS-formatted volume on the server that has sufficient free space to host your new iSCSI virtual disk:

The New iSCSI Virtual Disk Wizard window titled "Select iSCSI virtual disk location" showing:

- Navigation steps on the left: iSCSI Virtual Disk Location, iSCSI Virtual Disk Name, iSCSI Virtual Disk Size, iSCSI Target, Target Name and Access, Access Servers, Enable authentication ser..., Confirmation, Results

Server:

Server Name	Status	Cluster Role	Owner Node
HOST7	Online	Not Clustered	

ⓘ The list is filtered to show only servers with the iSCSI Target Server role installed.

Storage location:
◉ Select by volume:

Volume	Free Space	Capacity	File System
C:	222 GB	232 GB	NTFS
X:	233 GB	233 GB	NTFS
Y:	233 GB	233 GB	NTFS
Z:	232 GB	233 GB	ReFS

The iSCSI virtual disk will be saved at \iSCSIVirtualDisk on the selected volume.

○ Type a custom path:

[Browse...]

[< Previous] [Next >] [Create] [Cancel]

3. In the preceding screenshot, volume X on server HOST7 is selected for hosting the new iSCSI virtual disk. The new disk will be backed by a VHD file that will be stored in a folder named iSCSIVirtualDisks in the root of X drive.

4. On the Specify iSCSI Virtual Disk Name page, type a name and optional description for the new iSCSI virtual disk. For example, if you name the disk "Database," a file named Database.vhd will be created in the location X:\iSCSIVirtualDisks on HOST7. This VHD file will be used to back the new iSCSI virtual disk you are creating.

5. On the Specify iSCSI Virtual Disk Size page, specify a size for the new iSCSI virtual disk. The maximum possible size of the disk depends on the amount of free space available on the selected volume.

6. On the Assign iSCSI Target page, select New iSCSI Target because this is the first iSCSI virtual disk you are creating. You can also assign the new disk to an existing target if any already exist in your environment.

7. On the Specify Target Name page, type a name and optional description for the new target:

8. On the Specify Access Servers page, click Add to specify the iSCSI initiator that will access your iSCSI virtual disk. Doing this opens the Add Initiator ID dialog box, which provides three ways of identifying iSCSI initiators:

- By querying a computer on which the iSCSI initiator has been enabled for its Initiator ID. This method is supported only in Windows Server 2012, Windows Server 2012 R2, Windows 8, and Windows 8.1.

- By selecting an available Initiator ID from the list of cached IDs on the Target server. This method works only if there are entries in the initiator cache on the Target server.

- By manually specifying the IQN for the initiator.

For example, say that the initiator computer is a server named HOST4 that is running Windows Server 2012 R2. To query for the Initiator ID on HOST4, select the first option in the preceding list and either type **HOST4** or click Browse to search Active Directory for the initiator computer and then click OK to return to the Specify Access Servers page of the New iSCSI Virtual Disk Wizard. At this point, the IQN for the initiator will be displayed as shown here:

New iSCSI Virtual Disk Wizard

Specify access servers

iSCSI Virtual Disk Location
iSCSI Virtual Disk Name
iSCSI Virtual Disk Size
iSCSI Target
Target Name and Access
Access Servers
Enable authentication ser...
Confirmation
Results

Click Add to specify the iSCSI initiator(s) that will access this iSCSI virtual disk.

Type	Value
IQN	iqn.1991-05.com.microsoft:host4.corp.fabrikam.com

Add...   Remove

Learn more about access servers

< Previous   Next >   Create   Cancel

> **NOTE ALLOWING ANY INITIATOR TO CONNECT TO THE TARGET**
>
> If you want to allow any iSCSI initiator to connect to the target, select the third option on the Specify Access Servers page and type **IQN:*** as the initiator IQN.

9. On the Enable Authentication page, you can optionally enable one or both of the following authentication protocols:

   - **CHAP**   You can use the Challenge Handshake Authentication Protocol (CHAP) to authenticate initiator connections.
   - **Reverse CHAP**   You can use this protocol to allow the initiator to authenticate the iSCSI target.

10. If you enable either of these protocols, you must specify a user name and password for each of them.

At this point, you should review the information on the Confirm Selections page to make sure you don't need to change anything. Once you are satisfied, click Create to create the new iSCSI virtual disk, create the target (if needed), and assign the disk to the target.

After you create your iSCSI virtual disk and target, you can view and manage them on the iSCSI subpage of the File And Storage Services page of Server Manager as shown in Figure 8-23.

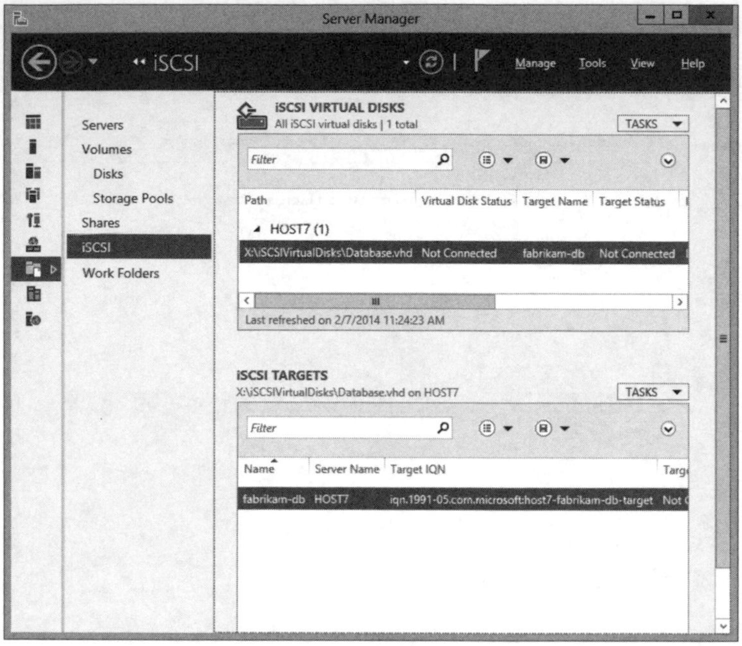

FIGURE 8-23 The new iSCSI target and virtual disk are displayed in Server Manager.

You can also use Windows PowerShell to create new iSCSI virtual disks and iSCSI targets and to assign iSCSI virtual disks to targets. For example, you can begin by opening a Windows PowerShell console on the iSCSI Target server HOST7 and using the Get-IscsiVirtualDisk cmdlet to display a list of existing iSCSI virtual disks on the server:

```
PS C:\> Get-IscsiVirtualDisk

ClusterGroupName    :
ComputerName        : HOST7.corp.fabrikam.com
Description         : iSCSI virtual disk for Fabrikam database server
DiskType            : Fixed
HostVolumeId        : {DD1FDED1-3C51-4A33-850A-23C06A555FE5}
LocalMountDeviceId  :
OriginalPath        :
ParentPath          :
Path                : X:\iSCSIVirtualDisks\Database.vhd
SerialNumber        : C9EACA53-B17D-4BCF-836B-9EF168G7B866
Size                : 161061273600
SnapshotIds         :
Status              : NotConnected
VirtualDiskIndex    : 1795469856
```

Note that the value of the *Path* property in the preceding command output is what you would expect based on what you saw earlier in the iSCSI Virtual Disks tile in Figure 8-23.

Next you can use the New-IscsiVirtualDisk cmdlet to create a new iSCSI virtual disk that is 50 GBs in size and is backed by a file named data.vhd:

```
PS C:\> New-IscsiVirtualDisk -Path X:\iSCSIVirtualDisks\data.vhd -Size 50GB

ClusterGroupName      :
ComputerName          : HOST7.corp.fabrikam.com
Description           :
DiskType              : Fixed
HostVolumeId          : {DD1FDED1-3C51-4A33-850A-23C06A555FE5}
LocalMountDeviceId    :
OriginalPath          :
ParentPath            :
Path                  : X:\iSCSIVirtualDisks\data.vhd
SerialNumber          : A6403147-E3E0-433E-88B4-403549244CB4
Size                  : 53687091200
SnapshotIds           :
Status                : NotConnected
VirtualDiskIndex      : 1884425455
```

Now you can either assign this new iSCSI virtual disk to the existing target you created earlier using Server Manager or you can create a new target and assign the disk to it. In this example, use the second approach but first use the Get-IscsiServerTarget cmdlet to display a list of targets on the iSCSI Target server:

```
PS C:\> Get-IscsiServerTarget

ChapUserName                  :
ClusterGroupName              :
ComputerName                  : HOST7.corp.fabrikam.com
Description                   : iSCSI target for use by Fabrikam database server
EnableChap                    : False
EnableReverseChap             : False
EnforceIdleTimeoutDetection   : True
FirstBurstLength              : 65536
IdleDuration                  : 00:15:00
InitiatorIds                  : {Iqn:iqn.1991-05.com.microsoft:host4.corp.fabrikam.com}
LastLogin                     :
LunMappings                   : {TargetName:fabrikam-db;VHD:"X:\iSCSIVirtualDisks\
                                Database.vhd";LUN:0}
MaxBurstLength                : 262144
MaxReceiveDataSegmentLength   : 65536
ReceiveBufferCount            : 10
ReverseChapUserName           :
Sessions                      : {}
Status                        : NotConnected
TargetIqn                     : iqn.1991-05.com.microsoft:host7-fabrikam-db-target
TargetName                    : fabrikam-db
```

Note that the value of the *TargetName* property in the preceding command output is what you would expect based on what you saw earlier in the iSCSI Targets tile in Figure 8-23.

Now use the New-IscsiServerTarget cmdlet to create a new target named fabrikam-data that will use the same Initiator ID used by your existing fabrikam-db target:

```
PS C:\> New-IscsiServerTarget -TargetName fabrikam-data `
-InitiatorIds "IQN:iqn.1991-05.com.microsoft:host4.corp.fabrikam.com"
```

```
ChapUserName                   :
ClusterGroupName               :
ComputerName                   : HOST7.corp.fabrikam.com
Description                    :
EnableChap                     : False
EnableReverseChap              : False
EnforceIdleTimeoutDetection    : True
FirstBurstLength               : 65536
IdleDuration                   : 00:00:00
InitiatorIds                   : {Iqn:iqn.1991-05.com.microsoft:host4.corp.fabrikam.com}
LastLogin                      :
LunMappings                    : {}
MaxBurstLength                 : 262144
MaxReceiveDataSegmentLength    : 65536
ReceiveBufferCount             : 10
ReverseChapUserName            :
Sessions                       : {}
Status                         : NotConnected
TargetIqn                      : iqn.1991-05.com.microsoft:host7-fabrikam-data-target
TargetName                     : fabrikam-data
```

Note that the *LunMappings* property in the preceding command indicates that no iSCSI virtual disks have yet been assigned to this target. You can assign your data.vhd virtual disk to your fabrikam-data target by using the Add-IscsiVirtualDiskTargetMapping cmdlet like this:

```
PS C:\> Add-IscsiVirtualDiskTargetMapping -TargetName fabrikam-data `
-Path X:\iSCSIVirtualDisks\data.vhd
```

Finally, to verify that the mapping was created, you can use the Get-IScsiServerTarget cmdlet again, like this:

```
PS C:\> Get-IscsiServerTarget -TargetName fabrikam-data | fl LunMappings

LunMappings: {TargetName:fabrikam-data;VHD:"X:\iSCSIVirtualDisks\data.vhd";LUN:0}
```

> ### ✔ Quick check
>
> - How does the IQN of an iSCSI target differ from the IQN of an iSCSI initiator?
>
> ### Quick check answer
>
> - A target IQN includes the hostname of the iSCSI target server hosting the target and the name you assigned when you created the target. An initiator IQN includes the fully qualified domain name (FQDN) of the computer on which the initiator resides.

Work Folders ⟨

As Figure 8-23 and a number of other figures in this lesson indicate, you can use Server Manager to manage a number of different file server and storage features, including storage pools, physical and virtual disks, volumes, shares, iSCSI targets and virtual disks, and something else: Work Folders. Work Folders is a new storage feature introduced in Windows Server 2012 R2 that can help organizations address the Bring Your Own Device (BYOD) scenario that so many of them are currently facing as the workplace evolves.

Work Folders provides a consistent way for users to access their work files from their personal computers and devices anywhere from centrally managed file servers on the corporate network. Work Folders can be also deployed alongside existing deployments of other Microsoft data synchronization solutions such as Folder Redirection (FR), Offline Files (also known as client-side caching or CSC), and even home folders.

The table below compares Work Folders with other Microsoft sync solutions including FR/CSC, OneDrive (formerly SkyDrive), and OneDrive for Business (formerly SkyDrive Pro):

Sync Solution	Technical Details
Work Folders	Intended use: Work data for users BYOD support: Yes Access protocol: HTTPS Data location: File server
FR/CSC	Intended use: Work data for users BYOD support: Yes Access protocol: SMB Data location: File server
OneDrive	Intended use: Personal data for users BYOD support: No Access protocol: HTTPS Data location: Public cloud
OneDrive for Business	Intended use: Work data for users and teams BYOD support: Yes Access protocol: HTTPS Data location: SharePoint Online in Office 365 or on-premises SharePoint 2013

For more information on how to set up and configure Work Folders, see the series of posts on the File Cabinet Blog from the Storage Team at Microsoft starting with "Introducing Work Folders on Windows Server 2012 R2" at *http://blogs.technet .com/b/filecab/archive/2013/07/09/introducing-work-folders-on-windows-server -2012-r2.aspx*.

Using iSCSI Initiator

This section describes how to perform the following tasks for iSCSI Initiator on Windows Server 2012 and Windows Server 2012 R2:

- Configuring iSCSI Initiator
- Discovering targets
- Establishing a connection
- Creating volumes

The section shows how to perform these tasks using both Server Manager and Windows PowerShell.

Configuring iSCSI Initiator

Before you can connect to an iSCSI target to provision and use iSCSI storage, you must configure the iSCSI initiator on your computer. To configure the initiator on a server running Windows Server 2012 or Windows Server 2012 R2, open Server Manager and select iSCSI Initiator from the Tools menu to open the iSCSI Initiator Properties dialog box as shown in Figure 8-24. Note that if you haven't previously enabled the initiator on the computer, you will first be prompted to start the Microsoft iSCSI Service as described in the section "Enabling iSCSI Initiator" earlier in this lesson.

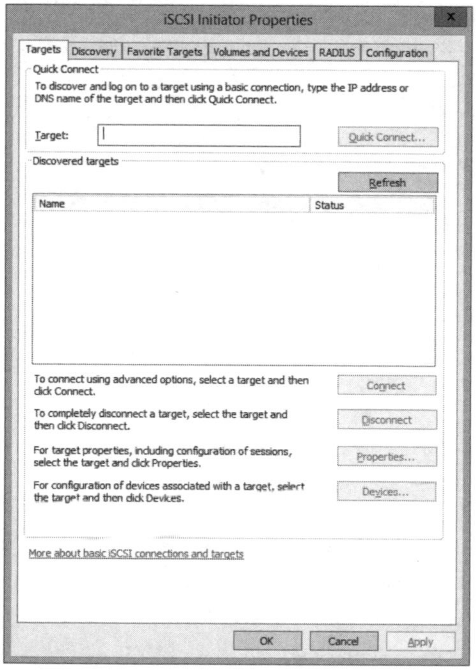

FIGURE 8-24 The iSCSI Initiator Properties dialog box has six tabs of settings for configuring the iSCSI initiator.

You can use the different settings on the six tabs of the iSCSI Initiator Properties dialog box to configure the initiator. Configuration might be required before you can connect your computer to iSCSI targets in your environment. The following list describes the six tabs that are available:

- **Targets**   You use this tab to view and connect to discovered targets, configure advanced connection settings, disconnect from targets, view session configuration settings, or view the configuration of devices associated with a target. You can also use Quick Connect to discover and log on to a target and add it to your list of favorite targets.

- **Discovery**   You can use this tab to discover, view, or remove target portals (iSCSI target devices) and Internet Storage Name Service (iSNS) servers in your environment. An iSNS server functions similarly to a Domain Name System (DNS) server. The computer running initiator asks the iSNS server for available iSCSI targets. Adding an iSNS server enables automatic discovery of all iSCSI targets available to the computer.

- **Favorite Targets**   You use this tab to add a target to the list of favorite targets, view details of a target, or remove a target from the favorites list. When you do this, the initiator uses saved login information to always attempt to reconnect to a target whenever the computer is rebooted.

- **Volumes And Devices**   You use this tab to view a list of the volumes and devices bound by the initiator. If a volume in the list is currently mounted, the drive letter and mount point are shown. You can also use this tab to automatically configure all available devices and to manually add or remove devices.

- **RADIUS**   You use this tab to configure Remote Authentication Dial-In User Service (RADIUS) authentication by adding a RADIUS server. Unlike CHAP authentication, which is performed between peers, RADIUS authentication is performed between a RADIUS server and a RADIUS client. To use RADIUS, you must have a RADIUS server on your network.

- **Configuration**   This tab displays the IQN for the initiator, and you can use its settings to modify the initiator name, configure a CHAP secret for the initiator, configure IPsec tunnel mode addresses for the initiator, or generate a report of all connected targets and devices on the system.

You can also use Windows PowerShell cmdlets such as Set-IscsiChapSecret and Register-IscsiSession to configure certain aspects of the iSCSI initiator.

Discovering targets

After you configure your iSCSI initiator, the next step is to discover available iSCSI targets in your environment. You can do this by performing the following steps:

1. Click the Discover tab of the iSCSI Initiator Properties dialog box and click Discover Portal to open the Discover Target Portal dialog box:

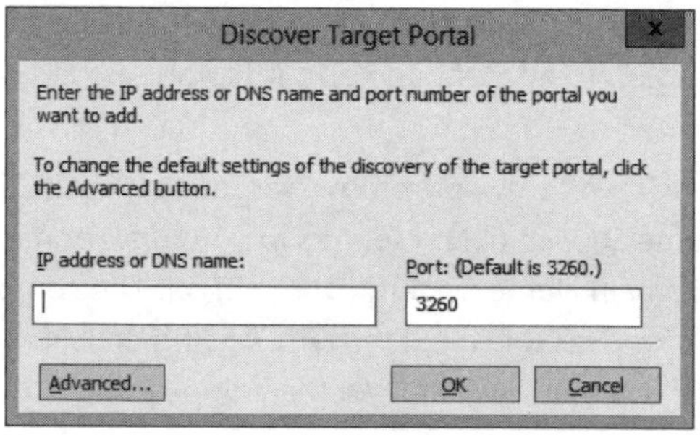

2. Type the IP address or DNS name (hostname or FQDN) for the target portal (iSCSI Target Server) that hosts the target to which you want to connect and then click OK. If additional configuration is required to discover the target portal, click Advanced.

3. After you click OK, the target portal you specified will be displayed in the Target Portals list on the Discover tab.

   If you now switch to the Targets tab, the Discovered Targets list should display all the available targets to which the initiator can connect on the portal. (See Figure 8-25.)

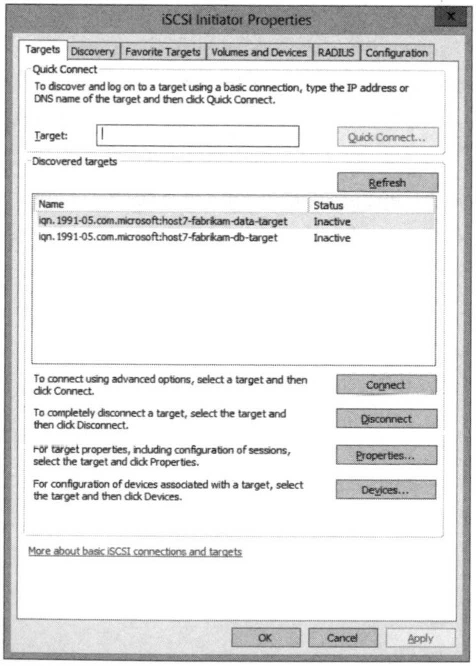

FIGURE 8-25 Two targets have been discovered on the target portal named HOST7.

Establishing a connection

After you discover the targets available on a target portal, you can use the initiator to connect to a target so that you can provision storage from the target. For example, Figure 8-25 shows two targets available on HOST7. To connect to the first target in this list, do the following:

1. Select the first target listed on the Targets tab of your initiator and click Connect. This displays the Connect To Target dialog box, which displays the name (IQN) of the target:

Note that by default, connecting to the target will also add the connection to the list of targets on the Favorite Targets tab so that each time the initiator computer starts, it will automatically attempt to restore the connection to the target.

2. Selecting the Enable Multi-Path option in the Connect To Target dialog box allows the initiator to use MultiPath IO (MPIO), which allows the use of multiple paths to iSCSI storage for redundancy and fault tolerance.

3. Clicking Advanced opens the Advanced Settings dialog box, which allows you to specify or configure the following:

   - The local adapter or initiator IP address
   - CRC/Checksum settings for data or the header digest

- CHAP logon information, including whether to use RADIUS
- IPsec settings

When you are ready to connect to the target, click OK. If the connection attempt is successful, the Status column will display Connected for the selected target. (See Figure 8-26.)

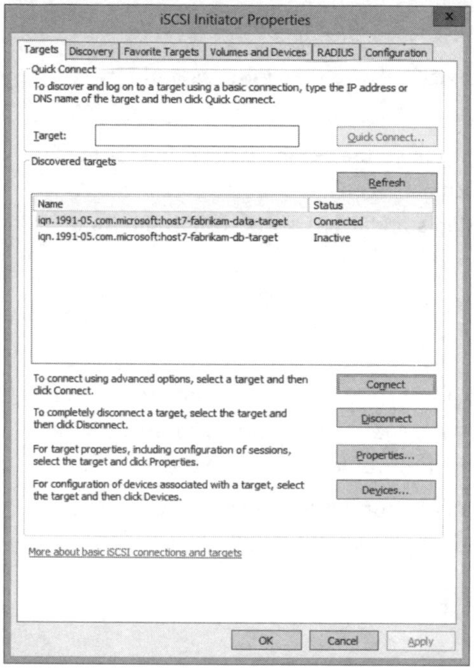

FIGURE 8-26 The initiator has established a connection with one of the targets on HOST7.

You can also use Windows PowerShell to establish a connection between an initiator and a target. As an example, start by using the Get-IscsiConnection cmdlet to display a list of active connections on the initiator computer:

```
PS C:\> Get-IscsiConnection

ConnectionIdentifier : fffffa80144a8020-1
InitiatorAddress     : 0.0.0.0
InitiatorPortNumber  : 34815
TargetAddress        : 172.16.11.240
TargetPortNumber     : 3260
PSComputerName       :
```

To view information about the session for this connection, you can get the connection using the Get-IscsiConnection cmdlet and pipe the connection into the Get-IscsiSession cmdlet like this:

```
PS C:\> Get-IscsiConnection -ConnectionIdentifier "fffffa80144a8020-1" | `
Get-IscsiSession
```

```
AuthenticationType      : NONE
InitiatorInstanceName   : ROOT\ISCSIPRT\0000_0
InitiatorNodeAddress    : iqn.1991-05.com.microsoft:host4.corp.fabrikam.com
InitiatorPortalAddress  : 0.0.0.0
InitiatorSideIdentifier : 400001370000
IsConnected             : True
IsDataDigest            : False
IsDiscovered            : False
IsHeaderDigest          : False
IsPersistent            : True
NumberOfConnections     : 1
SessionIdentifier       : fffffa80144a8020-4000013700000002
TargetNodeAddress       : iqn.1991-05.com.microsoft:host7-fabrikam-data-target
TargetSideIdentifier    : 0100
PSComputerName          :
```

Note that the value of the *TargetNodeAddress* property in the preceding command output is what you would expect based on what you saw earlier in the Discovered Targets list in Figure 8-26.

Now establish a connection to the second target shown in Figure 8-26. To do this, begin by using the Get-IscsiTarget cmdlet to display a list of available targets that have been discovered on the target portal:

```
PS C:\> Get-IscsiTarget | fl

IsConnected    : False
NodeAddress    : iqn.1991-05.com.microsoft:host7-fabrikam-db-target
PSComputerName :

IsConnected    : True
NodeAddress    : iqn.1991-05.com.microsoft:host7-fabrikam-data-target
PSComputerName :
```

You already established a connection with the target named fabrikam-data, so try to establish a connection with target fabrikam-db instead. To do this, use the Connect-IscsiTarget cmdlet and specify the IQN of target fabrikam-db like this:

```
PS C:\> Connect-IscsiTarget -NodeAddress `
"iqn.1991-05.com.microsoft:host7-fabrikam-db-target"

AuthenticationType      : NONE
InitiatorInstanceName   : ROOT\ISCSIPRT\0000_0
InitiatorNodeAddress    : iqn.1991-05.com.microsoft:host4.corp.fabrikam.com
InitiatorPortalAddress  : 0.0.0.0
InitiatorSideIdentifier : 400001370000
IsConnected             : True
IsDataDigest            : False
IsDiscovered            : False
IsHeaderDigest          : False
IsPersistent            : False
NumberOfConnections     : 1
SessionIdentifier       : fffffa80144a8020-4000013700000003
TargetNodeAddress       : iqn.1991-05.com.microsoft:host7-fabrikam-db-target
```

```
TargetSideIdentifier     : 0200
PSComputerName           :
```

The *IsConnected* property in the preceding command output indicates that your connection attempt succeeded, but the value of the *IsPersistent* property indicates that your connection won't persist across reboots. To fix this, you can use the Register-IscsiSession cmdlet with the *SessionIdentifier* taken from the preceding command output:

```
PS C:\> Register-IscsiSession -SessionIdentifier "fffffa80144a8020-4000013700000003"
```

If you now view the value of the *IsPersistent* property for this session, you can see that the session has been configured to persist across reboots:

```
PS C:\> Get-IscsiSession -SessionIdentifier "fffffa80144a8020-4000013700000003" | `
fl IsPersistent

IsPersistent : True
```

Creating volumes

Once you have configured your iSCSI targets and created iSCSI virtual disks on them, enabled and configured your iSCSI initiators, and established connections and sessions between initiators and targets, you are ready to provision iSCSI storage by creating new volumes. I'll conclude this lesson by walking you through an example of how to create a new volume on HOST4 (the server that has the initiator) from a target and virtual disk on HOST7 (the server with the iSCSI Target Server installed):

1. Begin by opening Server Manager on HOST4 and selecting the File And Storage Services page.

2. Because previously in this lesson you created two iSCSI virtual disks that are 50 and 150 GBs in size, these disks are displayed in the Disks tile on the Disks subpage. To create a new volume on HOST4 from the 50 GB iSCSI virtual disk on HOST7, you begin by right-clicking the 50 GB disk and selecting New Volume:

3. Doing this launches the New Volume Wizard, which was demonstrated previously in Lesson 2 of this chapter. Because you want the new volume to appear as a local drive on your initiator server (HOST4), you select HOST4 in the Server list on the Select The Server And Disk page of this wizard:

4. Proceed through the remaining steps of the wizard until you have clicked Create. At this point, an Offline Or Uninitialized Disk dialog box appears because the selected disk (the disk selected in the earlier screenshot of the Disks tile) has Unknown as its partition style. Clicking OK in this dialog box brings the disk online and initializes it as a GPT disk.

Once the new volume has been created, opening File Explorer on HOST4 shows the disk as a local volume even though the actual iSCSI storage is located elsewhere on HOST7. You can now copy or save files to the new volume as if it were a locally installed disk on the computer.

You can also create new volumes by using Windows PowerShell as described previously in Lesson 2 of this chapter.

Storage QoS

Storage Quality of Service (QoS) is another new feature of file-based storage introduced in Windows Server 2012 R2. Storage QoS is enabled at the VHDX layer and allows you to limit the maximum IOPS allowed to a virtual disk on a Hyper-V host. It can also allow you to set triggers to send notifications when a specified minimum IOPS is not met for a virtual disk. Possible usage scenarios for this feature include the following:

- Configuring different service-level agreements (SLAs) for different types of storage operations within your infrastructure. For example, a hoster might use this feature to configure Bronze, Silver, and Gold SLAs for storage performance available for different classes of tenants. You can even set alerts that trigger when virtual machines are not getting enough IOPS for storage access.

- Restricting the disk throughput for overactive or disruptive virtual machines within your environment that are saturating the storage array. Hosting providers will especially love this capability because it means they won't have to worry about one tenant consuming excessive storage fabric resources at the expense of other tenants.

As the above screenshot shows, you can configure Storage QoS by using Hyper-V manager even while the virtual machine is running. This gives organizations a lot of flexibility in how they manage access to the storage fabric from workloads running in their cloud environments.

Lesson summary

- To provision iSCSI storage, the iSCSI initiator on a computer must establish a connection to an iSCSI target on an iSCSI target server.
- iSCSI initiators and targets in an environment can be uniquely identified by their iSCSI Qualified Name (IQN).
- Configuring iSCSI Target Server involves installing the iSCSI Target Server role service and creating iSCSI virtual disks.
- Provisioning storage using an iSCSI initiator involves configuring the initiator, discovering targets, establishing connections, and creating volumes.

Lesson review

Answer the following questions to test your knowledge of the information in this lesson. You can find the answers to these questions and explanations of why each answer choice is correct or incorrect in the "Answers" section at the end of this chapter.

1. In an environment in which the iSCSI Target Server role service of Windows Server 2012 R2 has been deployed, what might the following string mean?

   iqn.1991-05.com.microsoft:srv4-finance-target

   A. This is the IQN of the iSCSI initiator on a computer named srv4.

   B. This is the IQN of the iSCSI initiator on a computer named finance.

   C. This is the IQN of an iSCSI target on a target portal named srv4.

   D. This is the IQN of an iSCSI target on a target portal named finance.

2. What steps can you take to make your iSCSI storage environment more secure? (Choose all that apply.)

   A. Enable and configure CHAP and Reverse CHAP on your iSCSI targets.

   B. Deploy a RADIUS server and configure your iSCSI initiators to use it for authentication.

   C. Configure IPsec tunnel mode addresses for the initiator.

   D. Configure your iSCSI targets to allow connections from initiators with an IQN of IQN:*.

3. Which of the following Windows PowerShell cmdlets produces output that you can use to determine the LUN mapping for an iSCSI target?

   A. Get-IscsiConnection

   B. Get-IscsiServerTarget

   C. Register-IscsiSession

   D. Get-IscsiTarget

Practice exercises

The goal of this section is to provide you with hands-on practice with the following:

- Provisioning and managing shared storage using Server Manager
- Provisioning and managing shared storage using Windows PowerShell

To perform the following exercises, you need at least one clean installation of Windows Server 2012 using the Server With A GUI installation option. The server should be a stand-alone server belonging to a workgroup, have Internet connectivity, and have no additional roles or features installed. In addition to the boot volume, the server should have at least two additional physical disks (either internally or externally connected) of a type supported by the Storage Spaces feature (for example, SAS or SATA disks). These disks should initially have no volumes on them.

You should be logged on interactively to the server using a user account that is a member of the local Administrators group but that is not the default Administrator account. You should also create a second user account named Test User that is a member of the built-in Users local group on the server. For the purposes of these exercises, the name of the server is assumed to be HOST7.

If you want, you can perform these exercises remotely from another computer by enabling Remote Desktop on HOST4 and using Remote Desktop Connection on your computer. If you do this, note that certain actions, such as creating new virtual switches, might temporarily disrupt Remote Desktop connectivity with the remote host.

Exercise 1: Provisioning and managing shared storage using Server Manager

In this exercise, you use Server Manager to create a new storage pool, create virtual disks from the pool, create volumes on the virtual disks, create SMB shares on the volumes, and manage various aspects for your shared storage.

1. Launch the Add Roles And Features Wizard from Server Manager and install the File Server role service of the File And Storage Services role on your server.

2. Select the Storage Pools subpage of the File And Storage Services page in Server Manager and verify that you have at least two available physical disks in the primordial pool on your server. If you have fewer than two physical disks in the primordial pool, connect additional physical disks to your server.

3. Click the Tasks control in the Physical Disks tile of the Storage Pools subpage and select New Storage Pool to launch the New Storage Pool Wizard.

4. Specify Pool 1 as the name for the new pool.

5. Add the first physical disk to the new pool, leaving the Allocation option as Automatic.

6. Complete the remaining steps of the New Storage Pool Wizard to create the new pool.

7. Right-click Pool 1 in the Storage Pools tile on the Storage Pools subpage and select New Virtual Disk to launch the New Virtual Disk Wizard.

8. Select Pool 1 as the storage pool from which you will create the new virtual disk.

9. Type **Simple Disk** as the name for the new virtual disk.

10. Select Simple as the storage layout for the new virtual disk.

11. Select Thin as the provisioning type for the new virtual disk.

12. Specify a value equal to 10 times the amount of free space in Pool 1 for the size of the new virtual disk.

13. Complete the remaining steps of the New Virtual Disk Wizard to create the new virtual disk. The New Volume Wizard will launch automatically.

14. Select Simple Disk as the virtual disk on which you will create the new volume.

15. Specify a value equal to half the available capacity of Simple Disk as the size for the new volume.

16. Specify S as the drive letter for the new volume.

17. Specify NTFS as the file system for the new volume.

18. Type **Simple Volume** as the label for the new volume.

19. Complete the remaining steps of the New Volume Wizard to create the new volume.

20. Right-click Simple Disk in the Virtual Disks tile on the Storage Pools subpage and select Extend Virtual Disk.

21. Specify a new size that will double the current size of Simple Disk.

22. Right-click Pool 1 in the Storage Pools tile on the Storage Pools subpage and select Add Physical Disk.

23. Select an available physical disk and add it to Pool 1, leaving the Allocation option set to Automatic.

24. Right-click Pool 1 in the Storage Pools tile on the Storage Pools subpage and select New Virtual Disk to launch the New Virtual Disk Wizard.

25. Select Pool 1 as the storage pool from which you will create the new virtual disk.

26. Type **Mirror Disk** as the name for the new virtual disk.

27. Select Mirror as the storage layout for the new virtual disk.

28. Select Fixed as the provisioning type for the new virtual disk.

29. Select Maximum Size for the size of the new virtual disk.

30. Complete the remaining steps of the New Virtual Disk Wizard to create the new virtual disk. The New Volume Wizard will launch automatically.

31. Select Mirror Disk as the virtual disk on which you will create the new volume.

32. Specify a value equal to the available capacity of Simple Disk as the size for the new volume.

33. Specify W as the drive letter for the new volume.

34. Specify ReFS as the file system for the new volume.

35. Type **Mirror Volume** as the label for the new volume.

36. Complete the remaining steps of the New Volume Wizard to create the new volume.

37. Select Simple Disk in the Disks tile on the Disks subpage. Verify that volume S is displayed in the Volumes tile on this page.

38. Select Mirror Disk in the Disks tile on the Disks subpage. Verify that volume W is displayed in the Volumes tile on this page.

39. Read the information displayed in the Storage Pool tile on the Disks subpage.

40. Select volume S in the Volumes tile on the Volumes subpage. Read the information displayed in the Disk tile on this page.

41. Select volume W in the Volumes tile on the Volumes subpage. Read the information displayed in the Disk tile on this page.

42. Right-click S in the Volumes tile on the Volumes subpage and select Extend Volume.

43. Specify a new size equal to half the maximum possible size for the volume.

44. Right-click S in the Volumes tile on the Volumes subpage and select New Share.

45. Select SMB Share - Quick as the profile for the new share.

46. Select S as the volume on which the new share will be created.

47. Type **Simple Share** as the name for the new share.

48. Select the check box to enable access-based enumeration for the new share.

49. Complete the remaining steps of the New Share Wizard to create the new share.

50. Press Windows key + R and type **S:\Shares\Simple Share** to open the folder in File Explorer.

51. Right-click in the open folder, select New Folder, and type **ABE_TEST** as the name for the new folder.

52. Right-click the ABE_TEST folder and select Properties, select the Security tab, and click Advanced to open the Advanced Security Settings For ABE_TEST dialog box.

53. On the Permissions tab, click Disable Inheritance and select Convert Inherited Permissions Into Explicit Permissions On This Object.

54. Select the two permission entries for the built-in Users local group and click Remove to remove them. Then click Apply.

55. Click the Effective Access tab, click Select A User, type **Administrator**, click OK, and click View Effective Access. Note the effective access that the built-in Administrator account will have when accessing the share both locally and over the network.

56. Click Select A User again, type **Test User**, click OK, and click View Effective Access. Note the effective access that Test User will have when accessing the share both locally and over the network.

57. Close File Explorer, press Windows logo key+R, and type **\\HOST7\Simple Share** to access the share using File Explorer. Verify that Administrator can open the ABE_TEST folder but cannot create new files in it because the share permissions for Simple Share are configured as Everyone has Read permission.

58. Log off as Administrator and log on as Test User.

59. Press Windows key+R and type **\\HOST7\Simple Share** to access the share using File Explorer. Verify that Test User cannot see the ABE_TEST folder because access-based enumeration has been configured on Simple Share and the Users group has no permission to access the ABE_TEST folder.

60. Log off as Test User and log on as an administrator.

61. Right-click Simple Share in the Shares tile on the Shares subpage and select Stop Sharing.

62. Right-click S in the Volumes tile on the Volumes subpage and select Delete Volume. Repeat this step to delete W.

63. Right-click Simple Disk in the Virtual Disks tile on the Storage Pools subpage and select Delete Virtual Disk. Repeat this step to delete Mirror Disk.

64. Right-click Pool 1 in the Storage Pools tile on the Storage Pools subpage and select Delete Storage Pool. Verify that the primordial pool is displayed and that there are at least two physical disks available in the Physical Disks tile. You are now ready to begin the next practice exercise.

Exercise 2: Provisioning and managing shared storage using Windows PowerShell

In this exercise, you use Windows PowerShell to create a new storage pool, create virtual disks from the pool, create volumes on the virtual disks, and create SMB shares on the volumes.

1. Use the Get-PhysicalDisk cmdlet to verify that at least two physical disks connected to your server have the *CanPool* property set to *True*.

2. Type **(Get-StorageSubsystem).FriendlyName** to display the value of the *FriendlyName* property of the storage subsystem on the server.

3. Type the following command to create a new storage pool named Pool 2 that includes all available physical disks in the primordial pool and uses both thin provisioning and mirror resiliency by default when creating new virtual disks:

```
New-StoragePool `
-FriendlyName "Pool 2" `
-StorageSubSystemFriendlyName (Get-StorageSubSystem).FriendlyName `
-PhysicalDisks (Get-PhysicalDisk | where CanPool -eq True) `
-ProvisioningTypeDefault Thin `
-ResiliencySettingNameDefault Mirror
```

4. Type the following command to create a new virtual disk named vDisk 1 that is 5 TBs in size and uses the default provisioning and resiliency settings for Pool 2:

```
New-VirtualDisk `
-FriendlyName "vDisk 1" `
-StoragePoolFriendlyName "Pool 2" `
-Size 5TB
```

5. Use the New-VirtualDisk cmdlet again to create a second virtual disk named vDisk 2 that is 10 TBs in size and uses the default provisioning and resiliency settings for Pool 2.

6. Use the Get-VirtualDisk cmdlet to verify that the virtual disks are 5 TBs and 10 TBs in size, respectively.

7. Type **Get-Disk | where Bustype –eq Spaces** to display information about the two virtual disks. Note that the virtual disks are both offline and have the partition style RAW.

8. Use the following command to initialize both virtual disks and set their partition style to GPT:

```
(Get-Disk | where BusType -eq Spaces) | Initialize-Disk -PartitionStyle GPT
```

9. Use Get-Disk to verify that the two disks are now online and have the partition style GPT.

10. Use the following command to create a new volume on each virtual disk, with each new volume being as large as possible and having a drive letter automatically assigned to it:

```
New-Partition `
-DiskNumber (Get-Disk | where BusType -eq Spaces).Number `
-UseMaximumSize -AssignDriveLetter | Format-Volume `
-FileSystem NTFS -Confirm:$false
```

11. Verify the result from the output of the preceding command and note the drive letters assigned to the new volumes.

12. Use the New-Item cmdlet to create a folder named Shares on each new volume and subfolders named Folder 1 and Folder 2, respectively, on each volume.

13. Use the New-SmbShare cmdlet to create new SMB shares named Share 1 and Share 2 that map to the two local folders you created in the previous step.

14. Use the Set-SmbShare cmdlet to enable access-based enumeration on Share 2.

15. Refresh the view in Server Manager and verify that all of the tasks you performed using Windows PowerShell achieved their intended result.

Suggested practice exercises

The following additional practice exercises are designed to give you more opportunities to practice what you've learned and to help you successfully master the lessons presented in this chapter.

- **Exercise 1**   Use the SMB Share - Advanced option in the New Share Wizard to create a share that has a quota assigned. Verify the quota settings by copying files to the share until a notification is issued.

- **Exercise 2**   Create a Windows PowerShell script (.ps1 file) that performs all the tasks in the second exercise in this chapter. Run the script to provision a storage pool, virtual disks, volumes, and shares.

- **Exercise 3**   Remove all shares, volumes, virtual disks, and storage pools you created in exercises 1 and 2 of this chapter. Then use your setup to deploy an iSCSI storage solution as described in Lesson 3 and configure and manage the environment using both Server Manager and Windows PowerShell.

Answers

This section contains the answers to the lesson review questions in this chapter.

Lesson 1

1. **Correct answers: B, C, and D**

    A. **Incorrect:** You can create a new storage pool using one, several, or all of the physical disks in the primordial pool on the server.

    B. **Correct:** If there are no available unused disks connected to your file server, the primordial pool is not displayed in Server Manager.

    C. **Correct:** If there are no available unused disks connected to your file server, the primordial pool is not displayed in Server Manager.

    D. **Correct:** Physical disks are displayed in the primordial pool only when they have no partitions or volumes created on them.

2. **Correct answers: A, B, and C**

    A. **Correct:** DiskPart relies on the Virtual Disk Service (VDS), which is deprecated beginning with Windows Server 2012. You can still use this utility in Windows Server 2012 and Windows Server 2012 R2, but it will not work with Storage Spaces or with any SMAPI components or tools.

    B. **Correct:** DiskRAID relies on the Virtual Disk Service (VDS), which is deprecated beginning with Windows Server 2012. You can still use this utility in Windows Server 2012 and Windows Server 2012 R2, but it will not work with Storage Spaces or with any SMAPI components or tools.

    C. **Correct:** The Disk Management MMC snap-in relies on the Virtual Disk Service (VDS), which is deprecated beginning with Windows Server 2012. You can still use this utility in Windows Server 2012 and Windows Server 2012 R2, but it will not work with Storage Spaces or with any SMAPI components or tools.

    D. **Incorrect:** The v1 namespace for WMI is deprecated beginning with Windows Server 2012. You should use WMIv2-based Windows Storage Management APIs and utilities for managing storage in Windows Server 2012 and Windows Server 2012 R2.

3. **Correct answer: A**

    A. **Correct:** With thin provisioning, the size of the virtual disk represents the maximum amount of physical storage space that can be allocated from the pool. No space is actually used, however, until data is stored on a volume on the virtual disk, and the amount of space used will grow or shrink as data is written to or deleted from the disk.

    B. **Incorrect:** With fixed provisioning, the size of the virtual disk is the actual amount of physical storage space allocated from the pool.

C. Incorrect: With mirror resiliency, the data on volumes created on this type of virtual disk is striped across all physical disks in the pool. Each segment of data is also duplicated on either two or three physical disks, as specified when the mirrored virtual disk is created, so that a copy of all data will still be available if a physical disk in the pool fails.

D. Incorrect: With parity resiliency, the data on volumes created on this type of virtual disk and parity information that can be used to facilitate automatic reconstruction of data if a physical disk fails is striped across all physical disks in the pool.

4. **Correct answers: A, B, and D**

   A. Correct: You must use a minimum of three physical disks when deploying Storage Spaces twith Failover Clustering.

   B. Correct: Physical disks must be SAS when deploying Storage Spaces with Failover Clustering.

   C. Incorrect: Physical disks must pass the failover cluster validation tests when deploying Storage Spaces with Failover Clustering.

   D. Correct: You can use only fixed provisioning when deploying Storage Spaces with Failover Clustering.

Lesson 2

1. **Correct answer: C**

   A. Incorrect: With one physical disk in the pool, you can provision only simple volumes. At least three physical disks are needed if you plan on creating resilient volumes in a failover cluster containing two file servers.

   B. Incorrect: With two physical disks in the pool, you can provision resilient volumes, but at least three physical disks are needed if you plan on creating resilient volumes in a failover cluster containing two file servers.

   C. Correct: At least three physical disks are needed if you plan on creating resilient volumes in a failover cluster containing two file servers.

   D. Incorrect: At least three physical disks are needed if you plan on creating resilient volumes in a failover cluster containing two file servers. The fourth volume can be used but is not required.

2. **Correct answer: D**

   A. Incorrect: The Get-StoragePool cmdlet returns either a specific storage pool or a set of *StoragePool* objects from all storage subsystems across all storage providers. Optionally, it returns a filtered subset based on specific parameters.

   B. Incorrect: The Get-VirtualDisk cmdlet returns a list of *VirtualDisk* objects across all storage pools and across all providers. Optionally, it returns a filtered subset based on provided criteria.

C. **Incorrect:** The Get-PhysicalDisk cmdlet returns a list of all *PhysicalDisk* objects visible across any available Storage Management providers. Optionally, it returns a filtered list.

D. **Correct:** The Get-StorageSubsystem cmdlet returns a single *StorageSubsystem* object or a set of *Subsystem* objects, depending on the parameters given. The returned information includes the friendly name, health status, and operational status of each storage subsystem on the server.

3. **Correct answers: A, C, and D**

   A. **Correct:** You can use either Server Manager or Windows PowerShell to extend a virtual disk.

   B. **Incorrect:** You cannot shrink a virtual disk.

   C. **Correct:** You can use either Server Manager or Windows PowerShell to detach a virtual disk.

   D. **Correct:** You can use either Server Manager or Windows PowerShell to delete a virtual disk.

4. **Correct answer: C**

   A. **Incorrect:** Use the SMB Share - Quick option if you need to create a general-purpose SMB share for file sharing.

   B. **Incorrect:** Use the SMB Share - Advanced option if you need to configure quotas on your share or implement file classification.

   C. **Correct:** Use the SMB Share - Application option if the share will be used by Hyper-V hosts for shared storage, by a database application, or by other server applications.

   D. **Incorrect:** Create an NFS share if you need to use file sharing in heterogeneous environments that include both Windows and non-Windows computers.

Lesson 3

1. **Correct answer: C**

   A. **Incorrect:** In the Windows Server 2012 implementation of an iSCSI initiator, the initiator IQN looks like this:

   ```
   iqn.1991-05.com.microsoft:<initiator_server_FQDN>
   ```

   Because srv4-finance-target is not in the proper form for a FQDN, the string cannot be the IQN of the iSCSI initiator.

   B. **Incorrect:** In the Windows Server 2012 implementation of iSCSI Initiator, the initiator IQN looks like this:

   ```
   iqn.1991-05.com.microsoft:<initiator_server_FQDN>
   ```

   Because srv4-finance-target is not in the proper form for a FQDN, the string cannot be the IQN of the iSCSI initiator.

C. Correct: In the Windows Server 2012 implementation of an iSCSI target server, the target IQN looks like this:

```
iqn.1991-05.com.microsoft:<target_server_name>-<target-name>-target
```

Because srv4-finance-target is of this form, the string is the IQN of an iSCSI target named finance on a target portal named srv4.

D. Incorrect: In the Windows Server 2012 implementation of an iSCSI target server, the target IQN looks like this:

```
iqn.1991-05.com.microsoft:<target_server_name>-<target-name>-target
```

Because srv4-finance-target is of this form, the string is the IQN of an iSCSI target. However, finance is the name of the target, not the target portal. The name of the target portal is srv4.

2. **Correct answers: A, B, and C**

   A. Correct: Challenge Handshake Authentication Protocol (CHAP) is a basic level of iSCSI security that is used to authenticate the peer of a connection and is based on the peers sharing a secret.

   B. Correct: Remote Authentication Dial-In User Service (RADIUS) is a standard used for maintaining and managing user authentication and validation. Unlike CHAP, authentication with RADIUS is not performed between peers but between a RADIUS server and a client. To use this level of security with iSCSI, either you must have a RADIUS server running on your network or you must deploy one.

   C. Correct: Internet Protocol security (IPsec) is a protocol that enforces authentication and data encryption at the IP packet layer. You can use IPsec in addition to CHAP or RADIUS authentication to provide an added level of security for iSCSI.

   D. Incorrect: Configuring your iSCSI targets to allow connections from initiators with an IQN of IQN:* actually weakens the security of your environment because it allows any initiator to access the target.

3. **Correct answer: B**

   A. Incorrect: The Get-IscsiConnection cmdlet gets information about connected iSCSI initiator connections. The output of this command does not include the LUN mapping for an iSCSI target.

   B. Correct: The Get-IscsiServerTarget cmdlet obtains iSCSI targets and their associated properties from the local server or specified computer. The output of this command includes the LUN mapping for the iSCSI targets on the target server.

   C. Incorrect: The Register-IscsiSession cmdlet registers an active iSCSI session to be persistent using the session identifier as input. The output of this command does not include the LUN mapping for an iSCSI target.

   D. Incorrect: The Get-IscsiTarget cmdlet returns information about connected iSCSI targets. The output of this command does not include the LUN mapping for an iSCSI target.

CHAPTER 9

Print and document services

Managing printers and print servers isn't one of the more exciting jobs of the IT administrator, but it's an important one. The so-called paperless office might never arrive, despite the numerous advances in both computer hardware and software in recent years. As a result, administrators still need to know how to deploy, configure, and manage Microsoft Windows print servers in enterprise environments. And that's what this chapter is all about.

Lessons in this chapter:

Before you begin

To complete the practice exercises in this chapter

- You need to know how to perform a clean install of Windows Server 2012 R2 and perform initial configuration tasks like configuring the server's TCP/IP settings for Internet connectivity.

- You need to know how to promote a server running Windows Server 2012 R2 as a domain controller.

- You also should have at least rudimentary knowledge of using Windows PowerShell.

Lesson 1: Deploying and managing print servers

You can use Server Manager to centralize the deployment of Windows Server 2012 and Windows Server 2012 R2 print servers. Once you have installed the Print And Document Services role on remote servers, you can use the Print Management console to configure and manage your print servers, printers, and printer drivers. You can also use the console to deploy and manage printer connections for clients on your network.

Deploying print servers

Deploying print servers in an enterprise environment involves performing the following tasks:

- Installing the Print Server role service and optionally other role services of the Print And Document Services role on target servers in your environment.
- Installing the Print And Document Services Tools feature on the computer or computers you will be using to manage the print servers and printers in your environment.

The following sections show how to perform these tasks using Server Manager.

Installing the Print Server role service

You can use the Add Roles And Features Wizard to deploy print servers on the local server or on remote servers running Windows Server 2012 or Windows Server 2012 R2. For example, to configure the local server as a print server, perform the following tasks:

1. Launch the Add Roles And Features Wizard from the Manage menu on the Server Manager toolbar.
2. Select Role-Based Or Feature-Based Installation and then select the local server from the server pool.
3. On the Select Server Roles page, select the Print And Document Services role and click OK when prompted to install the management tools for this role.
4. On the Select Role Services page, select the Print Server role service and proceed through the remaining steps of the wizard.

To use Server Manager to configure a remote server as a print server, perform these steps:

1. Make sure the remote server has been added to the server pool on the computer on which you are running Server Manager.

2. Launch the Add Roles And Features Wizard from the Manage menu on the Server Manager toolbar and select Role-Based Or Feature-Based Installation.

3. Select the remote server from the server pool and then proceed through the remaining steps of the wizard.

> **NOTE DEPLOYING REMOTE PRINT SERVERS**
>
> When you configure a remote server as a print server, you don't need to install the management tools for the Print And Document Services role on the remote server if you plan on administering all the print servers in your environment from a central location.

Installing other role services

As Figure 9-1 shows, there are additional role services of the Print And Document Services role that you can install when you configure a server running Windows Server 2012 or Windows Server 2012 R2 as a print server. These other role services are optional and provide the following capabilities:

- **Distributed Scan Server** This role service can receive scanned documents from network scanners and route the documents to their correct destinations. When you install this role service, the Scan Management snap-in is also installed and you can use this snap-in to manage network scanners and configure scan processes. Because a snap-in is installed with this role service, you cannot install Distributed Scan Server on a Server Core installation of Windows Server 2012 or Windows Server 2012 R2.

  Distributed Scan Server was introduced in Windows Server 2008 R2 and has not significantly changed in Windows Server 2012 or Windows Server 2012 R2. For more information on this feature, see "Install Distributed Scan Server" at *http://technet.microsoft .com/en-us/library/jj134196*.

- **Internet Printing** This role service installs the Web Server (IIS) role and creates a new website that users can use to manage their print jobs. Internet Printing also allows users who have the Internet Printing Client installed on their computers to use a web browser to open http://<*server_name*>/printers to connect and print to shared printers on a Windows print server using the Internet Printing Protocol (IPP). Client computers running Windows 7 and later can install Internet Printing Client as an optional in-box feature.

  Internet Printing and IPP were introduced in Windows Server 2003. The feature was enhanced in Windows Server 2008 and has not significantly changed since then. For more information on this feature, see "Internet Printing and Resulting Internet Communication in Windows 7 and Windows Server 2008 R2" at *http://technet .microsoft.com/en-us/library/ee126092(v=WS.10).aspx*.

- **Line Printer Daemon (LPD) Service** This role service enables UNIX-based and Linux-based computers to use the Line Printer Remote (LPR) service to print to shared printers on a Windows print server. LPD and LPR were introduced in Windows 2000 Server as part of the Print Services for UNIX component. For information on using LPD and LPR, see "Printing with UNIX Clients and Servers Using LPR/LPD" at *http://technet .microsoft.com/en-us/library/cc976747.aspx*.

Beginning with Windows Server 2012, the LPD and LPR services are deprecated. This means that support for these services will likely be removed in future versions of Windows Server.

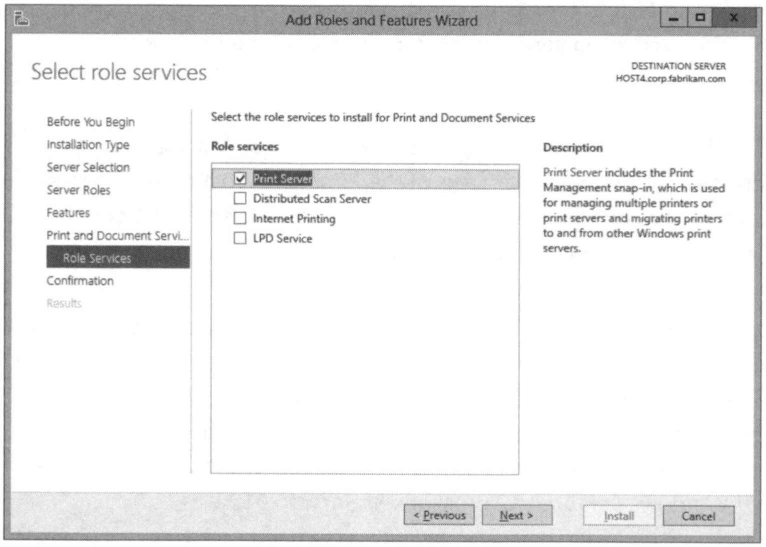

FIGURE 9-1 Configure a server as a print server.

> **REAL WORLD   DEPRECATED FEATURES**
>
> An important aspect of the IT administrator's job is to plan for the future. Because of this, it's important for you to know which features are deprecated in Windows Server 2012 and Windows Server 2012 R2 so that you can find alternate methods for implementing their functionality if it is still required. For a list of changes, see "Features Removed or Deprecated in Windows Server 2012 R2" at *http://technet.microsoft.com/en-us/library /dn303411.aspx*.

Installing the Print And Document Services Tools feature

Print And Document Services Tools is a subfeature of the Role Administration Tools section of the Remote Server Administration Tools feature. You don't need to install the Print And Document Services Tools on the remote servers on which you install the Print Server role. Instead, install the Print And Document Services Tools feature on the computer you will be using to manage all of the print servers in your environment. This computer might be one of the following:

- A server running Windows Server 2012 or Windows Server 2012 R2, in which case you can use the Add Roles And Features Wizard, as shown in Figure 9-2, to install the Print And Document Services Tools feature on the server

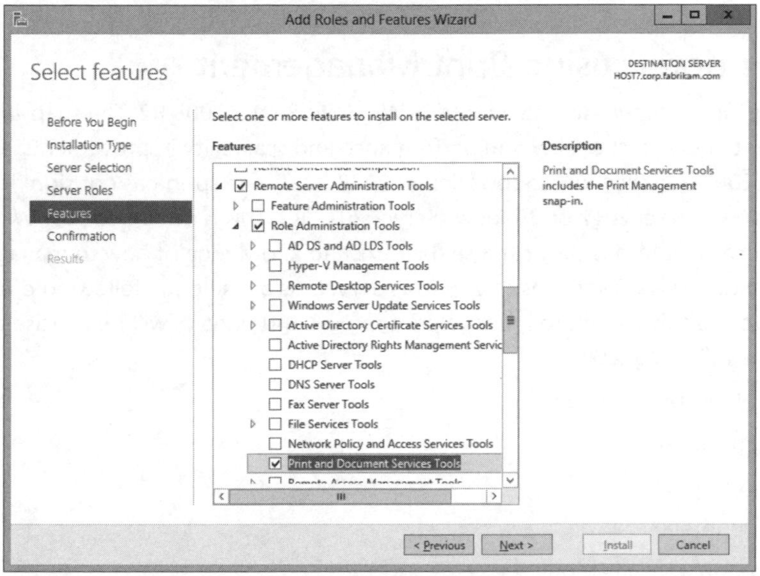

FIGURE 9-2 Install the management tools for print servers.

- A client computer running Windows 8 or Windows 8.1, in which case you can install the Remote Server Administration Tools (RSAT) for Windows 8 or RSAT for Windows 8.1 and enable the Print And Document Services Tools feature on the computer

Installing the Print And Document Services Tools on a computer installs the following tools for managing print servers and printers:

- Print Management Microsoft Management Console (MMC) snap-in
- PrintManagement module for Windows PowerShell

The remainder of this lesson focuses on using the Print Management snap-in to manage the print servers and printers in your environment, and Lesson 2 in this chapter describes how to use the Windows PowerShell cmdlets in the PrintManagement module to do the same.

✔ **Quick check**

- You plan on deploying the LPD role service to allow printing with UNIX clients and servers. Is this a good idea?

> **Quick check answer**
>
> ■ Not really. The LPD role service is deprecated in Windows Server 2012 and Windows Server 2012 R2 and will therefore likely be removed in the next version of Windows Server. So it's best if you find another solution that meets your printing needs.

Managing printers using Print Management

The *Print Management snap-in* was introduced in Windows Server 2003 R2. The snap-in was then enhanced with new functionality and performance and scalability improvements, first in Windows Server 2008 and then in Windows Server 2008 R2. The snap-in has not significantly changed in Windows Server 2012 or Windows Server 2012 R2. This is good news for Windows administrators because it means they can use their existing knowledge of how to manage print servers running previous versions of Windows Server. As a result, the following discussion about how to use this snap-in to manage print servers and printers will be concise and will cover only the following tasks:

■ Launching Print Management

■ Managing print servers

■ Managing printer drivers

■ Managing printers

■ Deploying printer connections

■ Migrating print servers

Launching Print Management

Installing the Print And Document Services role and its role management tools adds a new page called Print Services to Server Manager. (See Figure 9-3.) Using this new page, you can do the following:

■ View printing-related events

■ Restart the Print Spooler service if needed

■ Start performance counters on the print server

■ View a list of installed role services for the Print And Document Services role

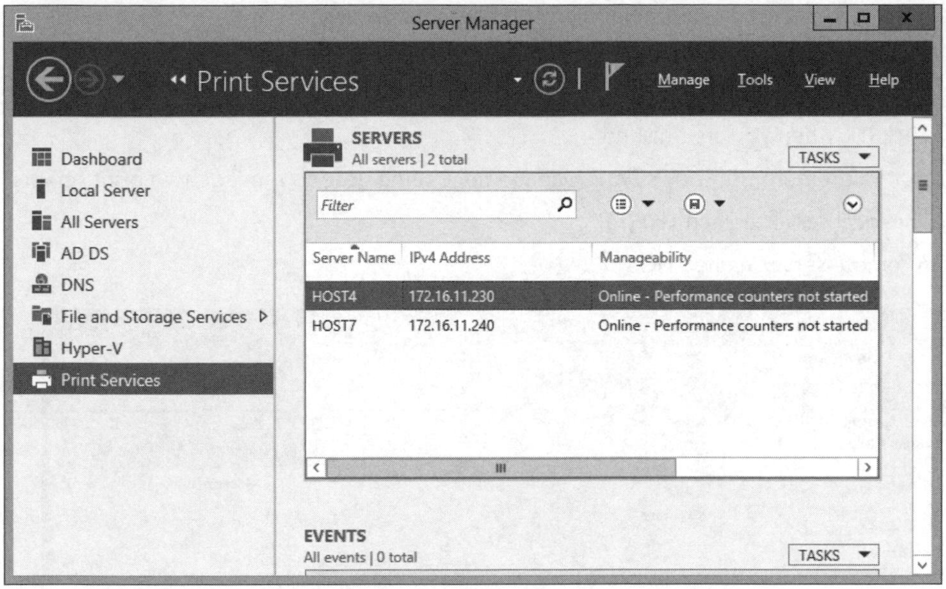

FIGURE 9-3 The Print Services page is added to Server Manager.

You can also launch the Print Management console from the Tools menu in Server Manager. When Print Management is opened on a print server, the local host is visible in the console tree unless it has been removed. You can add other print servers to the console so that you can manage them by doing the following:

1. Right-click the Print Servers node and select Add/Remove Servers to open the Add/Remove Servers dialog box:

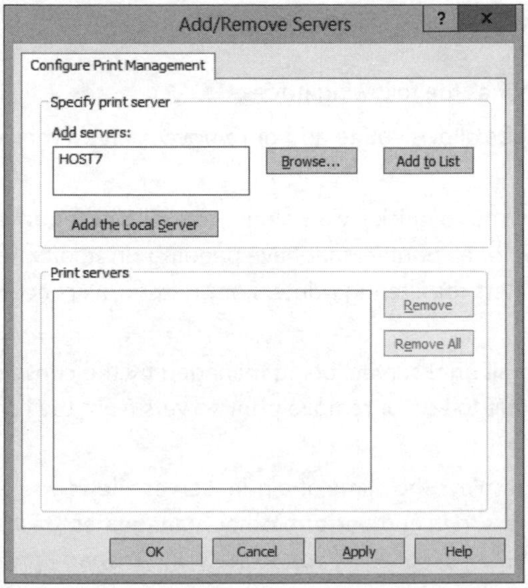

2. If the local server is not visible, click Add The Local Server.

3. In the Add Servers text box, type the name of a remote print server you want to manage and click Add To List. You can also browse for other print servers on the network.

4. Click OK when you are finished.

For example, Figure 9-4 shows Print Management being used to manage two print servers:

- The local server named HOST4
- A remote server named HOST7

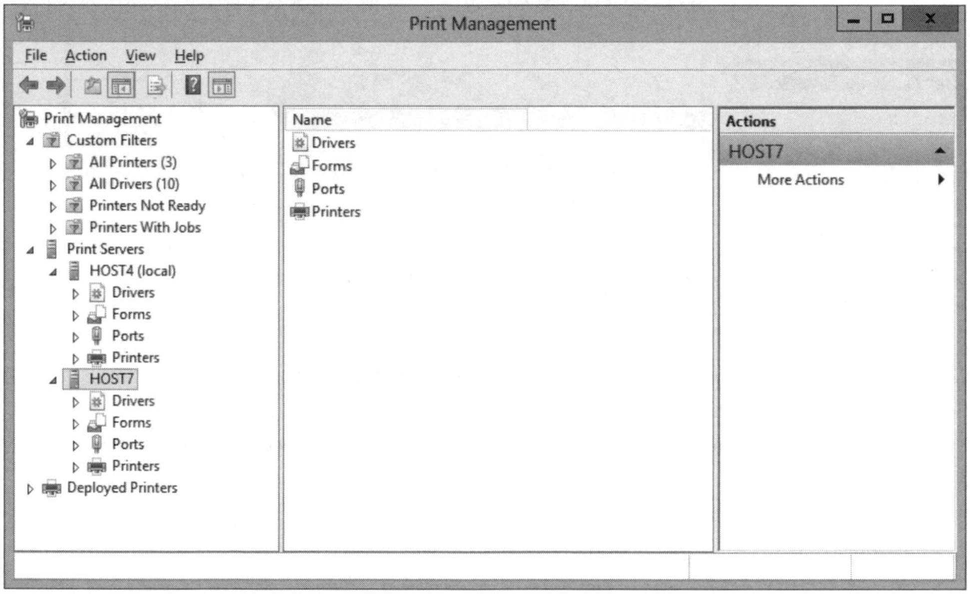

FIGURE 9-4 Manage print servers using the Print Management console.

The console tree of Print Management has the following nodes:

- **Print Management** This root node allows you to add or remove print servers and to migrate printers.

- **Custom Filters** This node allows you to quickly view all printers, all printer drivers, all printers that are not ready to print, or all printers that have pending print jobs. You can also use this node to create new filters for filtering printers or printer drivers according to conditions you specify.

- **Print Servers** This node displays all print servers being managed by the console as subnodes. You can also use this node to add or remove print servers from the console as described previously.

- **<servername>** Each node that displays the name of a print server allows you to manage the print server, add printers to it, and perform other management tasks. Each print server node also has four subnodes that allow you to view and manage printer drivers, printer forms, printer ports, and printers.

- **Deployed Printers** This node allows you to view printers that have been deployed using Group Policy.

The sections that follow provide more details about performing some of these tasks.

Managing print servers

By right-clicking a print server and selecting Properties, you can view or modify the print server's properties. For example, Figure 9-5 shows the Security tab, which you use to configure permissions for different groups and users in your environment to control such things as whether they should be allowed to print to the server. For example, if you wanted to restrict the use of printers on a particular print server to users in a certain department, you could remove the Everyone permissions entry that appears in the Group Or User Names area and add a new entry for a security group to which users in that department belong.

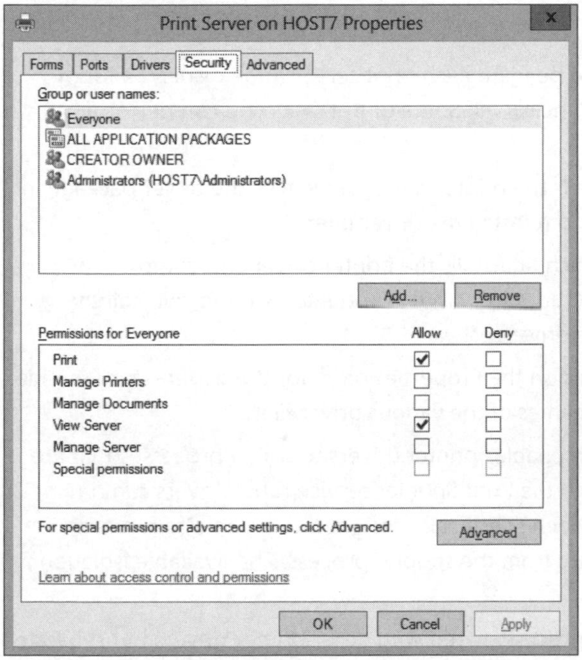

FIGURE 9-5 Configure print permissions for a print server.

Other management tasks you can perform using the Properties page of a print server include:

- Creating new forms for special print requirements—for example, for printing to note-cards or poster paper.
- Adding new printer ports, including local ports and standard TCP/IP ports. For example, before connecting a new network printer you should create a standard TCP/IP port for it.

- Adding new printer drivers to the server—for example, when you will be deploying new printers for which Windows Server 2012 and Windows Server 2012 R2 have no in-box drivers.

- Changing the location of the spooler folder—for example, if the volume the folder currently is on is almost full.

- Displaying or hiding informational notifications for printers.

> **MORE INFO** **CONFIGURING PERMISSIONS**
>
> For detailed information about the different print permissions for a print server and how to configure them, see "Assign Delegated Print Administrator and Printer Permission Settings in Windows Server 2012" at *http://technet.microsoft.com/en-us/library/jj190062*.

Managing printer drivers

As shown in Figure 9-6, the Drivers node beneath each print server node displays a list of the currently installed printer drivers on the server. Some of the tasks you can perform with installed drivers include:

- Deleting the driver, which uninstalls the printer driver but leaves the driver package in the driver store in case you want to reinstall the driver later.

- Removing the driver package, which uninstalls the printer driver and completely removes the driver package from the driver store. If you later want to reinstall the driver you will need to supply the driver software.

- Displaying additional driver details on the Properties page for the driver—for example, the driver type, driver path, and names of the various driver files.

- Configuring *driver isolation*, which enables printer drivers to run in processes that are separate from the process in which the Print Spooler service runs. Drivers can run in isolation mode only if they have been specifically designed to be able to run in an isolated or shared process separate from the spooler process. The available isolation modes include the following:

  - **Shared** The driver runs in a process shared with other printer drivers but separate from the spooler process.

  - **Isolated** The driver runs in a process separate from other printer drivers and from the spooler process.

  - **None** The driver runs in the spooler process.

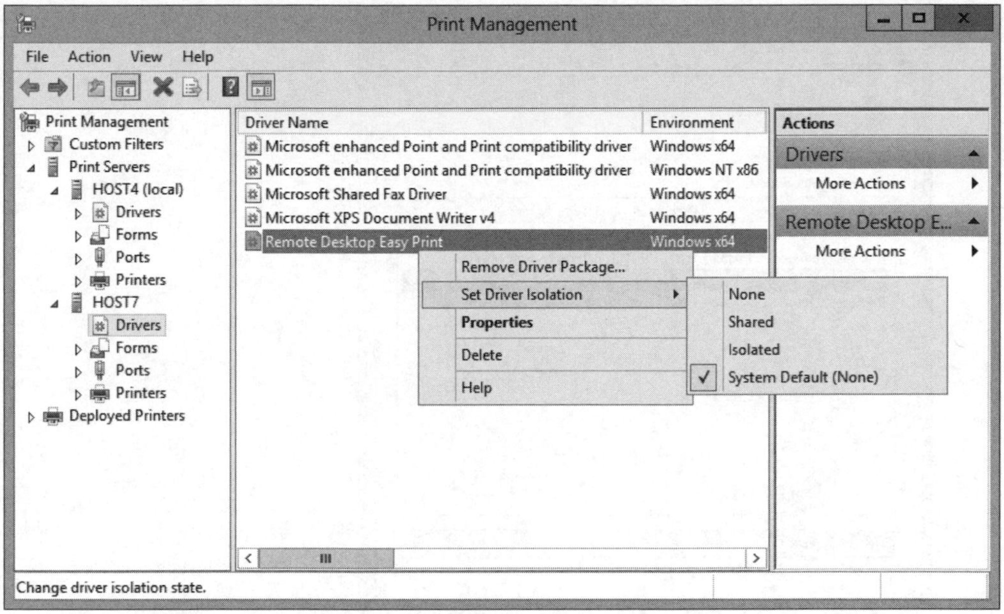

FIGURE 9-6 Configure driver isolation for a printer driver.

You can also right-click the Drivers node for a print server and select one of the following options:

- **Add Driver**   Select this option to launch the Add Printer Driver Wizard, which enables you to install new printer drivers from installation media you provide.
- **Manage Drivers**   Select this option to display the Drivers tab of the print server's Properties page, as shown in Figure 9-7, which you use to display the name, processor, and type for each installed printer driver on the server.

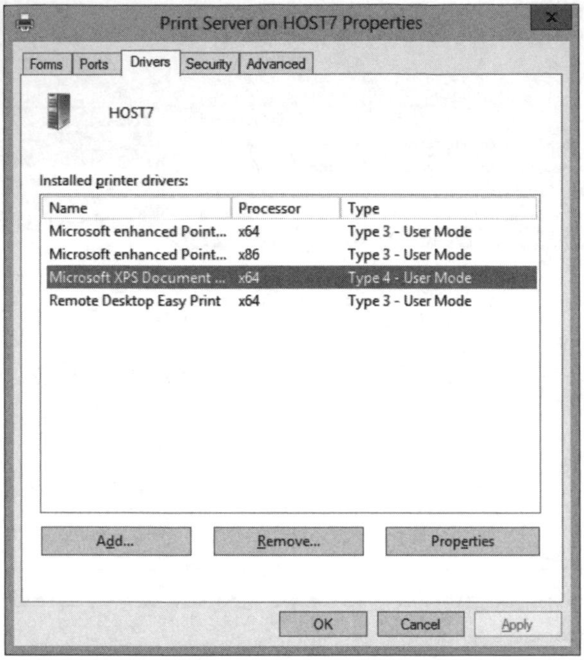

FIGURE 9-7 View the installed drivers on a print server.

> ***NOTE*** **FINDING UPDATED DRIVERS**
>
> **Before you search for updated printer drivers on the vendor's website, try clicking Windows Update on the Printer Driver Selection page of the Add Printer Driver Wizard. Doing this will update the list of printer drivers available for installation from your print server's driver store.**

Windows Server 2012 and Windows Server 2012 R2 print servers support the installation of two types of printer drivers:

- **v4 printer drivers** This type of printer driver was introduced in Windows Server 2012. These drivers have a smaller disk footprint, can support multiple devices, support driver isolation so that they won't crash the application doing the printing if the printer driver fails, and do not require installing drivers that match the client architecture. The v4 printer drivers come in two subtypes:
  - **Print-Class Drivers** These drivers support features for a broad set of devices that use the same printer description language, such as PCL, PS, or XPS.
  - **Model-Specific Drivers** These drivers are designed for specific printer models.
- **v3 printer drivers** This type of driver was introduced in Windows 2000 and was used through Windows Server 2008 R2.

REAL WORLD **DRIVER SPRAWL**

One thing that made managing print servers difficult in previous versions of Windows Server was the v3 printer driver model, which required separate drivers for each client architecture (x64 or x86) and for each model of print device. As a result, administrators of large enterprises often had to manage hundreds—or even thousands—of different printer drivers for the broad range of devices deployed throughout their organization.

Beginning with Windows Server 2012, the v4 printer driver model enables a single printer driver to support multiple models of print devices for any client architecture. This will eventually mean fewer printer drivers to manage across an enterprise, though some vendors might not provide updated v4 drivers for some of their older printer devices. This means you might still need to install some v3 drivers on your Windows Server 2012 or Windows Server 2012 R2 print servers. For more information on v4 printer drivers, see "Print and Document Services Architecture" at *http://technet.microsoft.com/en-us/library/jj134171*.

Managing printers

Right-clicking the Printers node of any print server launches the Network Printer Installation Wizard shown in Figure 9-8. You can use this wizard to search for printers on your network, add a network printer using an existing printer port, or create a new port to add the new printer.

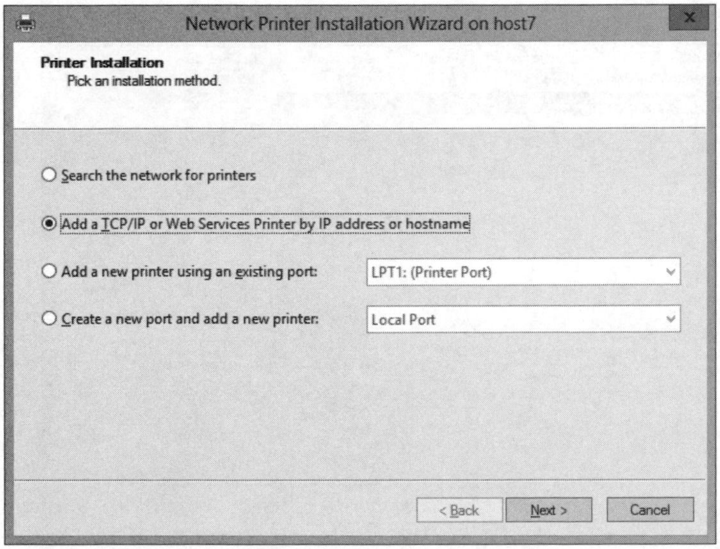

FIGURE 9-8 Install a new TCP/IP network printer.

Selecting the Printers node allows you to view and manage printers that have been installed on the print server. As shown in Figure 9-9, the tasks you can perform on a printer include:

- Opening the print queue to view, pause, resume, restart, or cancel pending print jobs on the printer.
- Listing the printer in Active Directory to make it easier for users to search for printers in the directory.
- Deploying the printer for targeted users or computers using Group Policy.
- Printing a test page to verify the printer is functioning properly.
- Opening the Properties page of the printer to manage the various settings available.
- Enabling *Branch Office Direct Printing*, a feature introduced in Windows Server 2012 and enhanced in Windows Server 2012 R2 that helps branch-office sites reduce their wide area network (WAN) usage by printing directly to a print device instead of spooling print jobs to a print queue on the print server. Branch Office Direct Printing requires print servers to be running Windows Server 2012 or Windows Server 2012 R2 and client computers to be running Windows 8 or Windows 8.1. For more information on this feature, see "Branch Office Direct Printing Overview" at *http://technet.microsoft .com/en-us/library/jj134156* and "Branch Office Direct Printing Technical Details" at *http://technet.microsoft.com/en-us/library/jj134152.aspx.*

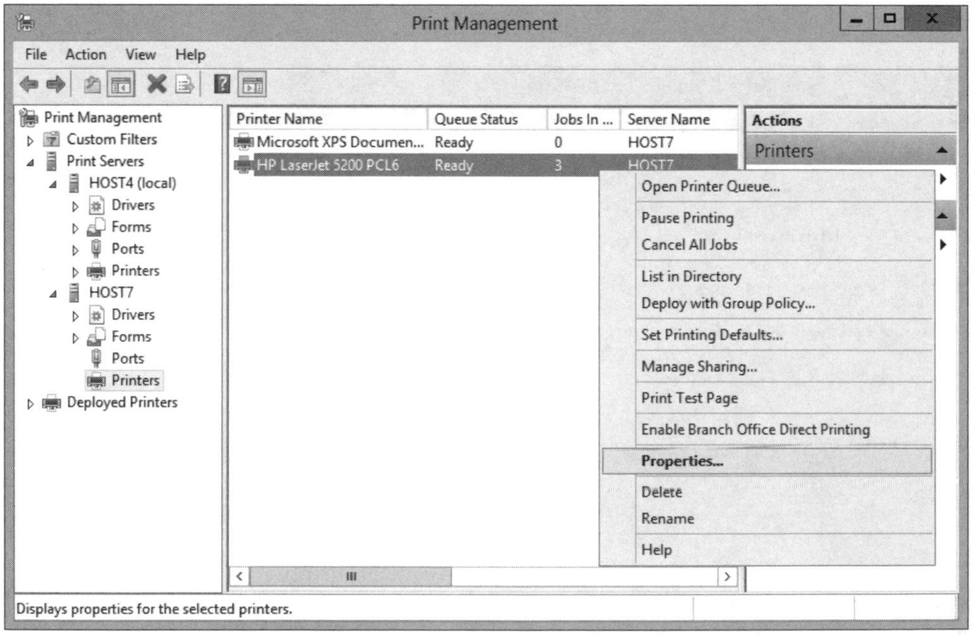

FIGURE 9-9 Manage a printer installed on a print server.

Event Logging for Branch Office Direct Printing

Branch Office Direct Printing has been enhanced in Windows Server 2012 R2 with support for event logging. This means that printing events are written to the print server when Branch Office Direct Printing has been enabled for a print queue. This new functionality makes it easier to identify and fix printing issues at remote office locations. In addition, if connectivity between the branch office (where the user is printing the job) and the main office (where the print server resides) is interrupted, the logged events are automatically cached until connectivity is restored to prevent loss of information.

Event logging is enabled by default for any print queue on which Branch Office Direct Printing has been enabled. For more information on this enhancement, see "Event Logging for Branch Office Direct Printing" at *http://technet.microsoft.com /en-us/library/dn434036.aspx#bkmk_log*.

As Figure 9-10 shows, the Properties page for a printer has various settings grouped onto different tabs as follows:

- **General**   You use this tab to specify the printer's location, configure printing preferences, and print a test page.

- **Sharing**   You use this tab to share or unshare the printer, specify whether to render print jobs on client computers, and specify whether the printer should be listed in the directory.

- **Ports**   You use this tab to select the printer port for the printer, add new ports, and configure or delete existing ports. (See Figure 9-10.) You can also create a printing pool to automatically distribute print jobs to the next available printer when high-volume printing is needed for your environment. A printing pool consists of a single logical printer connected to multiple physical print devices using multiple ports on the print server. With printer pooling, the physical print device that is idle receives the next document sent to the logical printer.

- **Advanced**   You use this tab to specify when the printer is available, the printer's priority, how documents should be spooled, separator pages, and miscellaneous other settings for the printer. By creating multiple logical printers that print to the same physical print device, assigning different priorities to each logical printer, creating different groups for users who should have different levels of priority access to the print device, and configuring permissions for each group using the Security tab, you can allow documents printed by users with high-priority access to bypass a queue of lower-priority documents that are waiting to be printed on the device.

- **Security**   You use this tab to configure permissions that control how different groups or users can use the printer. By default, the built-in Everyone group has the Print permission configured as Allow and the built-in Administrators group on the server has the Print, Manage This Printer, and Manage Documents permissions configured as Allow.

- **Device Settings** You use this tab to specify settings for the print device, such as the form to tray assignment.

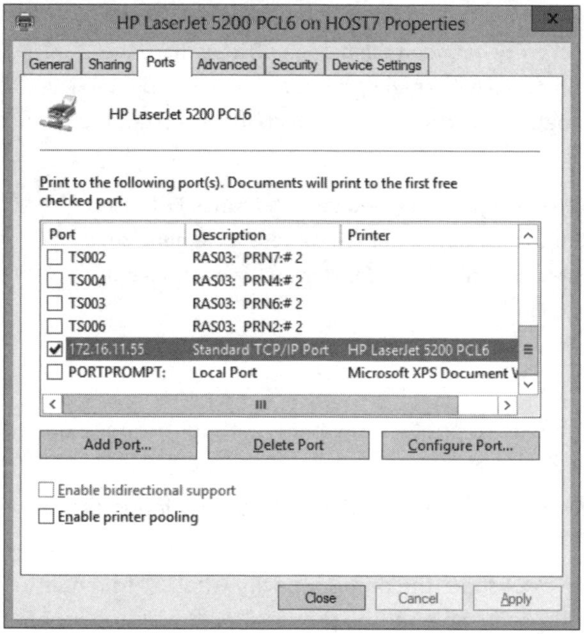

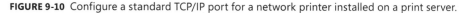

FIGURE 9-10 Configure a standard TCP/IP port for a network printer installed on a print server.

> ***NOTE*** **ADDITIONAL PRINTER PROPERTIES**
>
> Other tabs might be visible on the Properties page of an installed printer. For example, color printers will have a Color Management tab.

Another feature of the Print Management snap-in is Extended View, which you use to view and manage pending print jobs for the selected printer. (See Figure 9-11.) You enable Extended View by right-clicking the Printers node of a print server and selecting Show Extended View from the context menu.

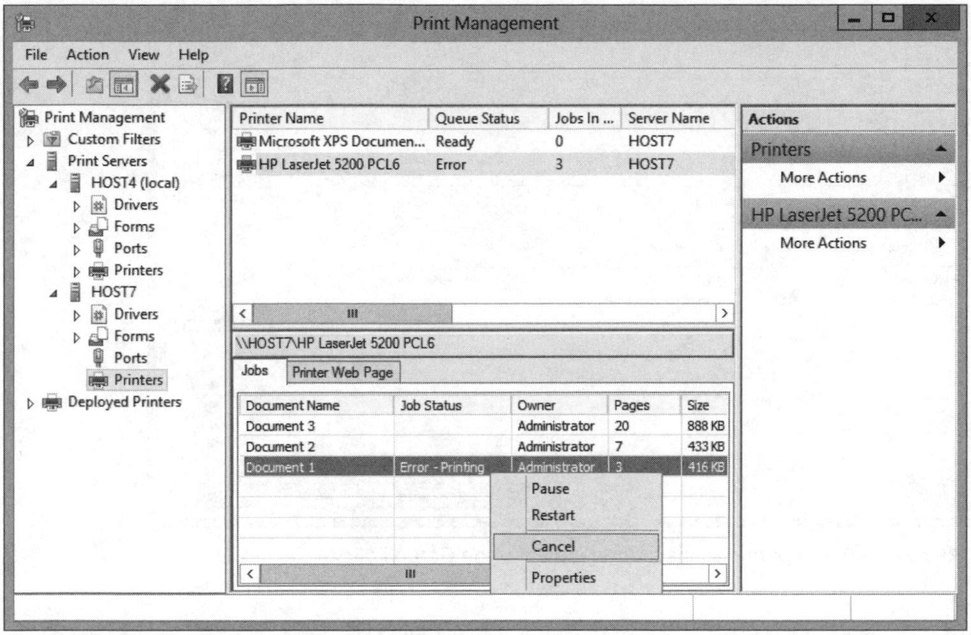

FIGURE 9-11 Cancel a pending print job by using Extended View.

Deploying printer connections

One of the options available in the context menu when you right-click a printer is Deploy With Group Policy. Selecting this option opens the dialog box shown in Figure 9-12, which you use to associate the printer with a specific Group Policy Object (GPO) to enable the printer connection to be deployed automatically to users or computers targeted by the GPO. This method of deploying printers is useful when users of client computers are standard users and not local administrators, because standard users lack sufficient privileges to install printers on their computers.

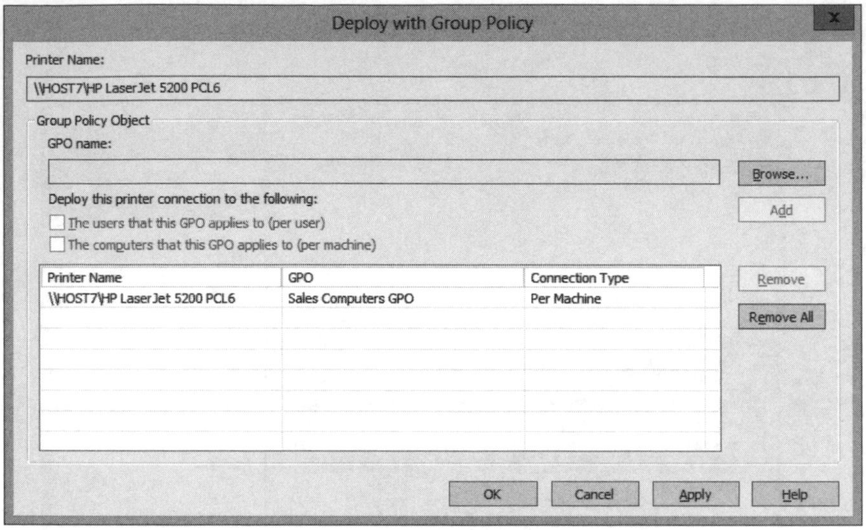

FIGURE 9-12 Deploy a printer connection to a client using Group Policy.

> *NOTE* **PRINTER SHARING**
>
> Windows Server 2012 and Windows Server 2012 R2 support several different ways of enabling the deployment of print shares:
>
> - Enhanced Point and Print, which allows the print server to share a printer with any other supported Windows client without the need for additional drivers. This feature is new in Windows Server 2012 and Windows Server 2012 R2 and is available only when v4 print drivers are being used.
>
> - Package-Aware Point and Print, which allows print servers to distribute signed driver packages to clients. This feature was introduced in Windows Server 2008 to improve security and eliminate the security prompts of the legacy Point and Print method.
>
> - Legacy Point and Print, which was introduced in Windows 2000. With this feature, the server spooler provides the client with just enough information to download the required v3 printer driver files from the server.
>
> - Internet Printing Protocol (IPP), which was also introduced in Windows 2000 and allows clients to install print shares from a webpage if the proper drivers have been staged on the print server.
>
> For more information on printer-sharing technologies supported by Windows Server 2012 and Windows Server 2012 R2, see "Printer Sharing Technical Details" at *http://technet .microsoft.com/en-us/library/jj590748.*

Migrating print servers 5

Administrators who are migrating their organization's infrastructure from earlier versions of Windows Server to Windows Server 2012 or Windows Server 2012 R2 will also want to migrate their print servers to the new platform. Installing the Print And Document Services Tools feature provides you with the following tools for migrating from print servers running Windows Server 2003, Windows Server 2003 R2, Windows Server 2008, or Windows Server 2008 R2:

- The Printer Migration Wizard shown in Figure 9-13, which you can launch from the Print Management console by right-clicking on the root node in the console tree and selecting Migrate Printers

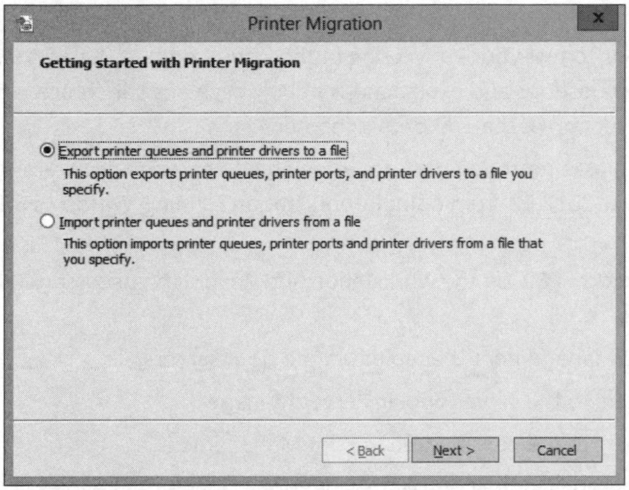

FIGURE 9-13 Use the Printer Migration Wizard.

- The Printbrm.exe command-line tool, which is located in the %windir%\System32\spool\tools folder

> **MORE INFO   MIGRATING PRINT SERVERS**
>
> For detailed guidance on how to migrate print servers to Windows Server 2012 and Windows Server 2012 R2, see "Migrate Print and Document Services to Windows Server 2012" at *http://technet.microsoft.com/en-us/library/jj134150*.

Lesson summary

- You can use Server Manager to install Print And Document Services role services and management tools on the local server or remote servers running Windows Server 2012 or Windows Server 2012 R2.

- You generally should not deploy features that are deprecated in Windows Server 2012 and Windows Server 2012 R2 because they might be removed in future versions of Windows Server.

- You can use the Print Management console to deploy, configure, and manage print servers, printer drivers, and printers.

- You can deploy printer connections to users and client computers using Group Policy.

- Windows Server 2012 and Windows Server 2012 R2 include tools for migrating print queues and printer drivers from print servers running earlier versions of Windows Server.

Lesson review

Answer the following questions to test your knowledge of the information in this lesson. You can find the answers to these questions and explanations of why each answer choice is correct or incorrect in the "Answers" section at the end of this chapter.

1. Which of the following tasks must you perform to be able to manage print servers running Windows Server 2012 R2 from a single workstation running Windows 8.1? (Choose all that apply.)

   A. Install RSAT for Windows 8.1 on the workstation and enable the necessary remote-management tools.

   B. Make sure Remote Management is enabled on the print servers.

   C. Add the print servers to the server pool in Server Manager.

   D. Add the print servers to the console tree in Print Management.

2. Which of the following nodes in the console tree of Print Management allows you to install new printer drivers on a print server? (Choose all that apply.)

   A. The Print Management node

   B. The Print Servers node

   C. A node representing a print server

   D. The Drivers node beneath a node representing a print server

3. You want to improve the reliability of print services in your environment by running the printer driver for each printer installed on your print server in a separate process that is isolated from the Print Spooler service on the server. Which set of requirements will enable you to achieve this goal? (Choose all that apply.)

   A. The printer drivers can be of the v3 type as long as the driver's INF file indicates that the driver supports driver isolation. After the drivers have been installed, you must use Print Management to configure Set Driver Isolation to the value Shared.

   B. The printer drivers can be of the v3 type as long as the driver's INF file indicates that the driver supports driver isolation. After the drivers have been installed, you must use Print Management to configure Set Driver Isolation to the value Isolated.

C. The printer drivers must be of the v4 type. After the drivers have been installed, you must use Print Management to configure Set Driver Isolation to the value Shared.

D. The printer drivers must be of the v4 type. After the drivers have been installed, you must use Print Management to configure Set Driver Isolation to the value Isolated.

Lesson 2: Managing print servers using Windows PowerShell

Although you can use the Print Management snap-in for managing print servers and printers in all sizes of environments, Windows PowerShell provides something more—namely, the ability to automate the management of print servers and printers from the command line or by using scripts. Administrators who need to repeatedly perform certain management tasks on large numbers of printers will find this capability invaluable. This lesson demonstrates some of the ways you can use Windows PowerShell to manage print servers, printers, and printer drivers.

After this lesson, you will be able to:

- Use Windows PowerShell to view information about printers, printer drivers, and print jobs.
- Use Windows PowerShell to manage printers, printer drivers, and print jobs.

Estimated lesson time: 20 minutes

Viewing information about printers, printer drivers, and print jobs

Windows Server 2012 and Windows Server 2012 R2 include a Windows PowerShell module called PrintManagement that contains cmdlets you can use for viewing and managing printers, printer drivers, and print jobs. You can use the Get-Command cmdlet to display a list of PrintManagement cmdlets as follows:

```
PS C:\> Get-Command -Module PrintManagement

CommandType     Name                        ModuleName
-----------     ----                        ----------
Function        Add-Printer                 PrintManagement
Function        Add-PrinterDriver           PrintManagement
Function        Add-PrinterPort             PrintManagement
Function        Get-PrintConfiguration      PrintManagement
Function        Get-Printer                 PrintManagement
Function        Get-PrinterDriver           PrintManagement
```

Function	Get-PrinterPort	PrintManagement
Function	Get-PrinterProperty	PrintManagement
Function	Get-PrintJob	PrintManagement
Function	Remove-Printer	PrintManagement
Function	Remove-PrinterDriver	PrintManagement
Function	Remove-PrinterPort	PrintManagement
Function	Remove-PrintJob	PrintManagement
Function	Rename-Printer	PrintManagement
Function	Restart-PrintJob	PrintManagement
Function	Resume-PrintJob	PrintManagement
Function	Set-PrintConfiguration	PrintManagement
Function	Set-Printer	PrintManagement
Function	Set-PrinterProperty	PrintManagement
Function	Suspend-PrintJob	PrintManagement

The following sections describe how to

- Retrieve a list of printers installed on a print server.
- View information about pending print jobs.
- View information about printers.
- View information about printer drivers and ports.

Retrieving a list of printers installed on a print server

You can use the Get-Printer cmdlet to display a list of the printers installed on a print server. For example, the following command shows that there are four printers installed on a remote print server named HOST7:

```
PS C:\> Get-Printer -ComputerName HOST7 | Format-List Name,DriverName

Name        : Samsung CLP-410 Series PCL6
DriverName  : Samsung CLP-410 Series PCL6

Name        : HP LaserJet 4200L PCL6
DriverName  : HP LaserJet 4200L PCL6 Class Driver

Name        : Microsoft XPS Document Writer
DriverName  : Microsoft XPS Document Writer v4

Name        : HP LaserJet 5200 PCL6
DriverName  : HP LaserJet 5200 PCL6 Class Driver
```

You can pipe the output from the preceding command into the Where-Object cmdlet to determine which of these printers are shared:

```
PS C:\> Get-Printer -ComputerName HOST7 | where Shared -eq $true | fl Name

Name : Samsung CLP-410 Series PCL6
Name : HP LaserJet 4200L PCL6
Name : HP LaserJet 5200 PCL6
```

Viewing information about pending print jobs

Using the Get-Printer cmdlet as follows indicates that one of the printers on HOST7 has Error for its status:

```
PS C:\> Get-Printer -ComputerName HOST7 | where PrinterStatus -eq Error | `
fl Name,JobCount

Name      : HP LaserJet 5200 PCL6
JobCount  : 3
```

To view more information about the cause of this error, you can use the Get-PrintJob cmdlet like this:

```
PS C:\> Get-PrintJob -ComputerName HOST7 -PrinterName "HP LaserJet 5200 PCL6"

Id  ComputerName  PrinterName     DocumentName   SubmittedTime          JobStatus
--  ------------  -----------     ------------   -------------          ---------
3   HOST7         HP LaserJet ... Document 3     8/26/2012 2:08:06 PM   Error, Print...
4   HOST7         HP LaserJet ... Document 2     8/26/2012 2:08:06 PM   Normal
5   HOST7         HP LaserJet ... Document 1     8/26/2012 2:08:06 PM   Normal
```

The first print job in the queue (job #3) is generating the error condition. You can find out more information about this job as follows:

```
PS C:\> Get-PrintJob -ComputerName HOST7 -PrinterName "HP LaserJet 5200 PCL6" | `
where Id -eq 3 | fl JobStatus,UserName

JobStatus : Error, Printing, Retained
UserName  : kberg
```

The fact that the job status includes *Retained* suggests that either the print job is corrupted or the print device is offline or out of paper. Either way, user Karen Berg should probably be informed because the print job belongs to her.

You can also use the Windows PowerShell pipeline with certain combinations of cmdlets in the PrintManagement module. For example, you can pipe the output from the Get-Printer cmdlet into the Get-PrintJob cmdlet to view all pending print jobs on all printers installed on a print server:

```
PS C:\> Get-Printer -ComputerName HOST7 | Get-PrintJob

Id  ComputerName  PrinterName      DocumentName   SubmittedTime          JobStatus
--  ------------  -----------      ------------   -------------          ---------
2   HOST7         Samsung CLP-...  Document 4     8/27/2012 3:54:33 PM   Normal
3   HOST7         HP LaserJet ...  Document 3     8/26/2012 2:08:06 PM   Error, Print...
4   HOST7         HP LaserJet ...  Document 2     8/26/2012 2:08:06 PM   Normal
5   HOST7         HP LaserJet ...  Document 1     8/26/2012 2:08:06 PM   Normal
```

Viewing information about printers

You can use the Get-PrinterConfiguration cmdlet to display the configuration settings for a particular printer:

```
PS C:\> Get-PrintConfiguration -ComputerName HOST7 -PrinterName "HP LaserJet 5200 PCL6"

PrinterName     ComputerName    Collate    Color    DuplexingMode
-----------     ------------    -------    -----    -------------
HP LaserJet ... HOST7           True       False    OneSided
```

Using the pipeline also enables you to display configuration settings for all printers installed on a remote print server:

```
PS C:\> Get-Printer -ComputerName HOST7 | Get-PrintConfiguration

PrinterName     ComputerName    Collate    Color    DuplexingMode
-----------     ------------    -------    -----    -------------
Samsung CLP-... HOST7           False      True     OneSided
Microsoft XP... HOST7           False      True     OneSided
HP LaserJet ... HOST7           True       False    OneSided
HP LaserJet ... HOST7           True       False    OneSided
```

If you want to list all color printers installed on HOST7, you can do it like this:

```
PS C:\> Get-Printer -ComputerName HOST7 | Get-PrintConfiguration | `
where Color -eq $true | fl PrinterName

PrinterName : Microsoft XPS Document Writer
PrinterName : Samsung CLP-410 Series PCL6
```

The Get-PrinterProperty cmdlet enables you to display additional properties for an installed printer like this:

```
PS C:\> Get-PrinterProperty -ComputerName HOST7 `
-PrinterName "Samsung CLP-410 Series PCL6"

ComputerName       PrinterName           PropertyName        Type      Value
------------       -----------           ------------        ----      -----
HOST7              Samsung CLP-410 S...  FormTrayTable       String
HOST7              Samsung CLP-410 S...  Config:DuplexUnit   String    FALSE
HOST7              Samsung CLP-410 S...  Config:OptTray2     String    FALSE
HOST7              Samsung CLP-410 S...  Config:OptTray3     String    FALSE
HOST7              Samsung CLP-410 S...  Config:OptTray4     String    FALSE
HOST7              Samsung CLP-410 S...  Config:OptTray5     String    FALSE
```

Viewing information about printer drivers and ports

Earlier in this lesson, you used the Get-Printer cmdlet to list the printers installed on print server HOST7:

```
PS C:\> Get-Printer -ComputerName HOST7 | Format-List Name,DriverName

Name       : Samsung CLP-410 Series PCL6
DriverName : Samsung CLP-410 Series PCL6
```

```
Name       : HP LaserJet 4200L PCL6
DriverName : HP LaserJet 4200L PCL6 Class Driver

Name       : Microsoft XPS Document Writer
DriverName : Microsoft XPS Document Writer v4

Name       : HP LaserJet 5200 PCL6
DriverName : HP LaserJet 5200 PCL6 Class Driver
```

The drivers for the two HP printers have "Class Driver" in their names, which indicates they are v4 drivers, and the driver for the Microsoft XPS Document Writer printer is clearly a v4 driver as well. But what about the Samsung driver? The driver for this printer has neither "v4" nor "Class Driver" in its driver name, so could it be a v3 driver instead of a v4 driver?

An easy way to determine this is to use the Get-PrinterDriver cmdlet like this:

```
PS C:\> Get-PrinterDriver -ComputerName HOST7 -Name "Samsung*"

Name                      PrinterEnvironment  MajorVersion  Manufacturer
----                      ------------------  ------------  ------------
Samsung CLP-410 Series PCL6  Windows x64       4             Samsung
```

Clearly, the Samsung driver is of the v4 type.

Another useful cmdlet is Get-PrinterPort, which enables you to retrieve a list of printer ports installed on a print server. For example, the following command displays information about all ports on HOST7 of the Standard TCP/IP Port type:

```
PS C:\> Get-PrinterPort -ComputerName HOST7 | where Description -like "*TCP*"

Name           ComputerName   Description          PortMonitor
----           ------------   -----------          -----------
172.16.11.55   HOST7          Standard TCP/IP Port TCPMON.DLL
```

> ✔ **Quick check**
>
> ■ Which Windows PowerShell cmdlet enables you to view the duplexing mode for a printer?
>
> **Quick check answer**
>
> ■ The Get-PrintConfiguration cmdlet

Managing printers, printer drivers, and print jobs

You can use Windows PowerShell not only to view information about printers, printer drivers, and print jobs on remote print servers but also to manage printers, print drivers, and print jobs. The following sections demonstrate two examples of this, specifically:

■ Canceling a print job

■ Installing a network printer

Canceling a print job

Earlier in this lesson, you saw that one of the print jobs for the HP LaserJet 5200 printer had Error for its status. To determine which job it is, you can pipe the output from the Get-PrintJob cmdlet into the Where-Object cmdlet to display all jobs whose JobStatus property has "Error" in its value:

```
PS C:\> Get-PrintJob -ComputerName HOST7 -PrinterName "HP LaserJet 5200 PCL6" | `
where JobStatus -like "Error*"

Id  ComputerName  PrinterName    DocumentName   SubmittedTime          JobStatus
--  ------------  -----------    ------------   -------------          ---------
3   HOST7         HP LaserJet ... Document 3    8/26/2012 2:08:06 PM Error, Print...
```

Having determined that job #3 is the problem, you could use the Remove-PrintJob cmdlet to cancel the problem job:

```
Remove-PrintJob -PrinterName "HP LaserJet 5200 PCL6" -ID 3
```

But instead of doing this, you can just press the Up arrow key to display the previously executed command and pipe its output into Remove-PrintJob as follows:

```
PS C:\> Get-PrintJob -ComputerName HOST7 -PrinterName "HP LaserJet 5200 PCL6" | `
where JobStatus -like "Error*" | Remove-PrintJob
```

Using the Get-PrintJob cmdlet again verifies that the problem has been resolved:

```
PS C:\> Get-PrintJob -ComputerName HOST7 -PrinterName "HP LaserJet 5200 PCL6"
Id  ComputerName  PrinterName    DocumentName   SubmittedTime          JobStatus
--  ------------  -----------    ------------   -------------          ---------
4   HOST7         HP LaserJet ... Document 2    8/26/2012 2:08:06 PM Printing
5   HOST7         HP LaserJet ... Document 1    8/26/2012 2:08:06 PM Normal
```

Installing a network printer

Installing a new network printer using Windows PowerShell generally involves performing the following steps:

1. Installing a printer driver for the new printer

2. Creating a standard TCP/IP port for the printer

3. Installing the printer using the driver and port specified

4. Performing any additional configuration needed for the printer

> **NOTE POSSIBLE ISSUES WHEN INSTALLING NETWORK PRINTERS**
> The procedure outlined in this section generally works when you have a Server With A GUI installation on the remote server. The exception is when you have new printers whose drivers are not included in the default driver store of your Windows Server installation. If this is the case, you might need to update the driver store or even install the full Print Management package on the remote server to successfully install the network printer using Windows PowerShell.

Things get more complicated when the remote server is a Server Core installation because the driver store for this installation option is not as robust as for the Server With A GUI option. For a discussion of the issues involved and some possible workarounds, see "Windows 2012 Server Core Print Server – missing drivers!" at *http://social.technet .microsoft.com/Forums/windowsserver/en-US/c64ee652-ab59-4e71-95ce-944ee0c9cccf /windows-2012-server-core-print-server-missing-drivers.*

As an example, say you want to install a printer that uses the Dell Color Laser PCL6 Class Driver on your print server. You could begin by using the Add-PrinterDriver cmdlet to install the printer driver on the server:

```
PS C:\> Add-PrinterDriver -ComputerName HOST7 -Name "Dell Color Laser PCL6 Class Driver"
```

You could use the Get-PrinterDriver cmdlet to verify the result as follows:

```
PS C:\> Get-PrinterDriver -ComputerName HOST7
```

Name	PrinterEnvironment	MajorVersion	Manufacturer
Dell Color Laser PCL6 Class Driver	Windows x64	4	Dell
Samsung CLP-410 Series PCL6	Windows x64	4	Samsung
HP LaserJet 4200L PCL6 Class Driver	Windows x64	4	HP

...

Next, you could use the Add-PrinterPort cmdlet to add a new port for the printer, like this:

```
PS C:\> Add-PrinterPort -ComputerName HOST7 -Name "172.16.11.63" `
-PrinterHostAddress "172.16.11.63"
```

You could use the Get-PrinterPort cmdlet to verify the result:

```
PS C:\> Get-PrinterPort -ComputerName HOST7
```

Name	ComputerName	Description	PortMonitor
172.16.11.55	HOST7	Standard TCP/IP Port	TCPMON.DLL
172.16.11.63	HOST7	Standard TCP/IP Port	TCPMON.DLL
COM1:	HOST7	Local Port	Local Monitor

...

Next, you could use the Add-Printer cmdlet to install, name, and share the new printer using the driver and port previously specified as follows:

```
PS C:\> Add-Printer -ComputerName HOST7 -Name "Sales Printer" `
-DriverName "Dell Color Laser PCL6 Class Driver" -Shared `
-ShareName "SalesPrint" -PortName "172.16.11.63"
```

Then, you could use the Get-Printer cmdlet to verify the installation of the new network printer:

```
PS C:\> Get-Printer -ComputerName HOST7 | ft Name,DriverName,PortName
```

```
Name                    DriverName              PortName
----                    ----------              --------
Sales Printer           Dell Color Laser PCL6 ... 172.16.11.63
HP LaserJet 5200 PCL6    HP LaserJet 5200 PCL6 ... 172.16.11.55
...
```

Finally, you might want to change the default paper size for the new printer from Letter to Legal, like this:

```
PS C:\> Set-PrintConfiguration -ComputerName HOST7 -PrinterName "Sales Printer" `
-PaperSize Legal
```

You could then use the Get-PrintConfiguration cmdlet to verify the result:

```
PS C:\> Get-PrintConfiguration -ComputerName HOST7 -PrinterName "Sales Printer" | `
fl PaperSize

PaperSize : Legal
```

> **REAL WORLD** **AUTOMATING PRINTER INSTALLATION**
>
> You could also put commands such as the ones just shown in a text file, save the file as New Sales Printer.ps1, and run the script from a Windows PowerShell console on your Windows 8.1 administrative workstation to automate the process of installing and configuring new printers on your print servers. Windows PowerShell is a powerful tool for automating many types of Windows Server management tasks.

Lesson summary

- You can use the Get-Printer cmdlet to retrieve a list of printers installed on a print server.
- You can use the Get-PrintJob cmdlet to view information about pending print jobs.
- You can use the Get-PrintConfiguration and Get-PrinterProperty cmdlets to view information about printers.
- You can use the Get-PrinterDriver and Get-PrinterPort cmdlets to view information about printer drivers and ports.
- You can use the Remove-PrintJob cmdlet to cancel a print job.
- You can use different Windows PowerShell cmdlets to install a printer driver, create a printer port, and install and configure a network printer that uses the new driver and port.

Lesson review

Answer the following questions to test your knowledge of the information in this lesson. You can find the answers to these questions and explanations of why each answer choice is correct or incorrect in the "Answers" section at the end of this chapter.

1. Which Windows PowerShell cmdlet enables you to determine whether any printers installed on a print server are shared?

    A. Get-Printer

    B. Get-PrinterConfiguration

    C. Get-PrinterProperty

    D. Get-PrintServer

2. Which Windows PowerShell cmdlet can you use to unshare a printer that is currently shared?

    A. Set-PrintConfiguration

    B. Set-PrinterProperty

    C. Set-Printer

    D. Get-Printer

3. You want to install a new printer on a print server running Windows Server 2012 R2. The print device uses the HP LaserJet 6L PS Class Driver printer driver and requires a standard TCP/IP printer port. You used Notepad to create a text file named install.ps1 that contains the following Windows PowerShell commands:

```
Add-PrinterPort -Name "TCP66" -PrintHostAddress "172.16.11.66"
Add-Printer -Name "Printer66" -DriverName "HP LaserJet 6L PS Class Driver" `
-ShareName "Printer66" -PortName "TCP66"
```

    You open a Windows PowerShell prompt on the local print server and run the preceding script, but it generates an error. Which of the following could be the cause of the error? (Choose all that apply.)

    A. The required printer driver is not installed on the print server.

    B. There is a syntax error in the first line of the script.

    C. There is a syntax error in the second line of the script.

    D. There is a syntax error in the third line of the script.

4. You modify the install.ps1 script from the previous question so that it no longer generates an error when you run it. After running the script, you use Print Management to verify that the printer driver, printer port, and printer have all been installed successfully and that you can print a test page to the new printer. Unfortunately, your users indicate that they cannot print to the printer. What might be the reason for this?

    A. You haven't yet deployed a printer connection to your users.

    B. The printer has not yet been shared.

    C. The print device has not yet been turned on.

    D. There is a job stuck in the print queue for the printer.

Practice exercises

The goal of this section is to provide you with hands-on practice with the following:

- Managing print servers using Print Management
- Managing print servers using Windows PowerShell

To perform the exercises in this section, you need at least two servers running Windows Server 2012 R2, which for the purposes of these exercises are assumed to be named HOST4 and HOST7. HOST4 should be a domain controller for the fabrikam.com domain, and HOST7 should be a member server in the fabrikam.com domain. Both servers should have no additional roles installed and should have Internet connectivity.

All tasks will be performed from HOST4, and you should log on to this server using an account that belongs to the Domain Admins group of fabrikam.com. To ensure you can remotely manage HOST7 from HOST4, make sure HOST7 has been added to the server pool in Server Manager on HOST4.

Exercise 1: Managing print servers using Print Management

In this exercise, you use Server Manager to install the Print Management console on HOST4 and the Print Server role service on HOST7. You then use the Print Management console on HOST4 to manage print queues and printer drivers on HOST7. Both servers should be running the Server With A GUI installation option of Windows Server.

1. Log on to HOST4 using an account that belongs to the Domain Admins group and open Server Manager.

2. Use the Add Roles And Features Wizard to install the Print And Document Services Tools feature on HOST4. This feature is found under Remote Server Administration Tools\Role Administration Tools in the Add Roles And Features Wizard.

3. Use the Add Roles And Features Wizard to install the Print Server role service of the Print And Document Services role on HOST7.

4. Launch the Print Management console and add HOST7 to the list of print servers managed by the console.

5. Install the HP LaserJet 5200 PCL6 Class Driver on HOST7.

6. View the properties of the driver you just installed and verify that the version is Type 4 User Mode.

7. Add a new port of type Standard TCP/IP Port on HOST7 using an IP address on the local subnet. Give the new port a descriptive name so that you can easily identify it and then configure the port to use Hewlett Packard Jet Direct as its device type.

8. Configure the new port to use TCP port number 9109.

9. Install a new network printer using the port you just created and the driver you just installed on the server. Give the new printer the name "Test Printer" and make sure the printer is shared.

10. Print a test page to your new printer.

11. Open the print queue for your new printer, verify that the status of your print job (printing a test page) is Error, and then close the print queue.

12. Enable Extended View for the Printers node and confirm again that the status of the job is Error. Then cancel the print job.

13. Remove the printer named "Test Printer" from HOST7.

14. Remove the driver package for the HP LaserJet 5200 PCL6 Class Driver printer driver from HOST7.

15. Delete the printer port for the printer you removed and close Print Management.

16. Uninstall the Print Server role service from HOST7.

17. Uninstall the Print And Document Services Tools feature from HOST4.

18. You are now ready to proceed to the next exercise.

Exercise 2: Managing print servers using Windows PowerShell

In this exercise, you use Windows PowerShell to install the Print Management console on HOST4 and the Print Server role service on HOST7. You then run Windows PowerShell commands from HOST4 to manage print queues and printer drivers on HOST7.

1. Log on to HOST4 using an account that belongs to the Domain Admins group and open the Windows PowerShell console.

2. Use the Install-WindowsFeature cmdlet to install the RSAT-Print-Services feature locally on HOST4.

3. Use the Install-WindowsFeature cmdlet to install the Print Server role service remotely on HOST7.

4. Use the Add-PrinterDriver cmdlet to install the HP LaserJet 5200 PCL6 Class Driver on HOST7.

5. Use the Get-PrinterDriver cmdlet to verify the result of the preceding command.

6. Use the Add-PrinterPort cmdlet to add a new port of type Standard TCP/IP Port on HOST7 using an IP address on the local subnet.

7. Use the Get-PrinterPort cmdlet to verify the result of the preceding command.

8. Use the Add-Printer cmdlet to install a new network printer using the port you just created and the driver you just installed on the server. Give the new printer the name "Test Printer" and make sure the printer is shared.

9. Type the command **mkdir C:\data** to create a new directory.

10. Type the command **"Hello World" > C:\data\test.txt** to create a new text file.

11. Type the command **type C:\data\test.txt | Out-Printer –Name "\\HOST7\Test Printer"** to send the text file to the printer.

12. Use the Get-PrintJob cmdlet to view information about pending print jobs in the print queue.

13. Use the Remove-PrintJob cmdlet to delete the print job from the print queue.

14. Use Windows PowerShell to uninstall the printer, uninstall the printer driver, delete the printer port, and remove the Print Server role service from HOST7 and the management tools from HOST4.

Suggested practice exercises

The following additional practice exercises are designed to give you more opportunities to practice what you've learned and to help you successfully master the lessons presented in this chapter.

- **Exercise 1**   Write a Windows PowerShell script that can be used to install the printer described in Exercise 2 by running a single command.

- **Exercise 2**   Modify your script from the Practice 1 exercise so that it installs several printers on several print servers.

Answers

This section contains the answers to the lesson review questions in this chapter.

Lesson 1

1. **Correct answers: A, B, and D**

    A. **Correct:** You must install RSAT for Windows 8.1 on a computer running Windows 8.1 before you can use that computer to remotely manage servers running Windows Server 2012 R2 in your environment.

    B. **Correct:** Managing Windows servers remotely requires that Remote Management be enabled on them.

    C. **Incorrect:** Because you will use the Print Management console and not Server Manager to remotely manage your print servers, you do not need to add the servers to the server pool. However, by adding them to the server pool, you can perform other management tasks on them such as restarting services and viewing alerts raised by event logs on the servers.

    D. **Correct:** Before you can manage a print server using Print Management, you must add the server to the console tree using the Add/Remove Servers dialog box.

2. **Correct answers: C and D**

    A. **Incorrect:** Right-clicking the Print Management node allows you to add or remove print servers in the console and to migrate printers from print servers running earlier versions of Windows Server.

    B. **Incorrect:** Right-clicking the Print Servers node allows you to add or remove print servers in the console.

    C. **Correct:** Right-clicking a node representing a print server allows you to open the Properties page for the print server. You can then use the Drivers tab on this Properties page to install new printer drivers on the server.

    D. **Correct:** Right-clicking the Drivers node beneath a node representing a print server allows you to install and manage printer drivers on the server.

3. **Correct answers: B and D**

    A. **Incorrect:** Printer drivers of the v3 type can run in a separate process that is isolated from the Print Spooler service as long as the setting *DriverIsolation=2* is included in their INF file. If the setting *DriverIsolation=0* is in their INF file, the driver does not support driver isolation. However, using Print Management to configure Set Driver Isolation to the value Shared will cause the driver to run in a process shared with other printer drivers but separate from the spooler process. To configure the driver to run in a process that is separate from other printer drivers and from the spooler process, you must configure Set Driver Isolation to the value Isolated.

B. Correct: Printer drivers of the v3 type can run in a separate process that is isolated from the Print Spooler service as long as the setting *DriverIsolation=2* is included in their INF file. If the setting *DriverIsolation=0* is in their INF file, the driver does not support driver isolation. Using Print Management to configure Set Driver Isolation to the value Isolated will cause the driver to run in a process that is separate from other printer drivers and from the spooler process.

C. Incorrect: Printer drivers of the v4 type have a smaller disk footprint, can support multiple devices, can support driver isolation so that they won't crash the application doing the printing if the printer driver fails, and do not require installing drivers that match the client architecture. However, using Print Management to configure Set Driver Isolation to the value Shared will cause the driver to run in a process shared with other printer drivers but separate from the spooler process. To configure the driver to run in a process that is separate from other printer drivers and from the spooler process, you must configure Set Driver Isolation to the value Isolated.

D. Correct: Printer drivers of the v4 type have a smaller disk footprint, can support multiple devices, can support driver isolation so that they won't crash the application doing the printing if the printer driver fails, and do not require installing drivers that match the client architecture. Using Print Management to configure Set Driver Isolation to the value Isolated will cause the driver to run in a process that is separate from other printer drivers and from the spooler process.

Lesson 2

1. Correct answer: A

   A. Correct: You can use *Get-Printer | where Shared –eq $true* to retrieve the shared printers on a print server.

   B. Incorrect: You use the Get-PrintConfiguration cmdlet to display printer configuration settings such as whether the printer supports collation and the printer's current duplexing mode.

   C. Incorrect: You use the Get-PrinterProperty cmdlet to display printer properties such as the currently selected form and output tray.

   D. Incorrect: Get-PrintServer is not a valid Windows PowerShell cmdlet in Windows Server 2012 R2.

2. Correct answer: C

   A. Incorrect: You use the Set-PrintConfiguration cmdlet to modify printer configuration settings such as whether the printer supports collation and the printer's current duplexing mode.

   B. Incorrect: You use the Set-PrinterProperty cmdlet to modify printer properties such as the currently selected form and output tray.

C. Correct: You can use the Set-Printer cmdlet to update the printer driver, printer port, or permissions of a printer. You can also use Set-Printer to specify whether the printer should be shared.

D. Incorrect: You use the Get-Printer cmdlet to retrieve a list of printers installed on a computer. You can't use the cmdlet for modifying installed printers.

3. **Correct answers: A and B**

A. Correct: The following command should be included at the beginning of the script:

```
Add-PrinterDriver -Name "HP LaserJet 6L PS Class Driver"
```

You need to include this line to install the driver needed by the printer you are installing.

B. Correct: The first line of the script should look like this:

```
Add-PrinterPort -Name "TCP66" -PrinterHostAddress "172.16.11.66"
```

C. Incorrect: The syntax of this line is correct.

D. Incorrect: The syntax of this line is correct.

4. **Correct answer: B**

A. Incorrect: Your organization might be using Point and Print to allow users to install network printers themselves by browsing the network. If this is the case, you might not need to use Group Policy to deploy printer connections to them.

B. Correct: The printer has not yet been shared so that users can access it from the network. To share the printer when installing it using your script, include the *–Shared* parameter in the final line of the script.

C. Incorrect: If you can successfully print a test page, the printer must be turned on.

D. Incorrect: If you can successfully print a test page, there is likely no job stuck in the print queue.

CHAPTER 10

Implementing Group Policy

roup Policy has been the primary method for managing the configuration of Microsoft
Windows client and server systems since Windows 2000. Most administrators are familiar with the basics of Group Policy, but implementing this technology effectively in a large
enterprise environment requires proper planning.

Windows Server 2012 and Windows Server 2012 R2 introduce a number of improvements in how Group Policy is processed and how it can be managed. For example, you can
now perform a remote refresh of Group Policy on targeted computers without logging on
to the computers to run the Gpupdate.exe command. Hundreds of new policies have been
added for managing different features of the Windows 8, Windows 8.1, Windows Server
2012, and Windows Server 2012 R2 operating systems, and you can deploy and enforce
these settings to target computers by configuring Group Policy Objects (GPOs) in the usual
way. New Starter GPOs simplify the tasks of enabling the remote Group Policy refresh capability and collecting Resultant Set of Policy (RSoP) information from computers targeted by
Group Policy. And the NetSecurity module for Windows Firewall with Advanced Security
introduced in Windows Server 2012 enables you to configure firewall profiles and rules in
GPOs. In this chapter, you learn about these new Group Policy capabilities and how to plan,
configure, and manage Group Policy using standard tools, including Windows PowerShell.

Lessons in this chapter:

Before you begin

To complete the practice exercises in this chapter

- You need to know how to perform a clean install of Windows Server 2012 R2 and
  perform initial configuration tasks like configuring the server's TCP/IP settings for
  Internet connectivity.
- You need to know how to promote a server running Windows Server 2012 R2 as a
  domain controller.
- You also should have at least rudimentary knowledge of using Windows PowerShell.

Lesson 1: Planning, implementing, and managing Group Policy

Before you deploy Group Policy in an enterprise environment, you need to design and prepare the infrastructure. This lesson provides guidance in the areas of planning and implementing Group Policy in an Active Directory environment based on Windows Server 2012 or Windows Server 2012 R2.

> **After this lesson, you will be able to:**
>
> - Take Group Policy into consideration when designing a hierarchy of organizational units (OUs) in Active Directory.
> - Configure a central store for Group Policy administrative template files used in a domain.
> - Create new Starter GPOs and use them to create GPOs for a production environment.
> - Perform a remote refresh of Group Policy on computers in an OU.
> - Understand and configure security settings you can configure using Group Policy.
>
> **Estimated lesson time: 30 minutes**

Planning for Group Policy

Planning for an implementation of Group Policy in an enterprise environment involves a number of different tasks and considerations, including the following:

- Understanding policies versus preferences
- Designing an OU structure that supports Group Policy
- Configuring a central store for policy definition files
- Creating and using Starter GPOs
- Understanding how to remotely refresh Group Policy

> *MORE INFO* **DEPLOYMENT GUIDE**
>
> The sections in this lesson cover only a few of the many issues associated with planning for Group Policy deployment. For additional information, see "Group Policy Planning and Deployment Guide" at *http://technet.microsoft.com/en-us/library/cc754948(WS.10).aspx*.

Understanding policies vs. preferences ⌐3

Before you implement Group Policy in your Active Directory environment, you need to understand the difference between policies and preferences. Group Policy allows administrators to deploy two types of settings:

- **Managed settings** These are configuration settings that the organization considers mandatory and that must be strictly enforced. Managed settings are pushed out to targeted user accounts or computers, and they are periodically refreshed to ensure they remain enforced.

  An example of a managed setting might be a corporate-branded desktop background that the company requires on all employees' computers.

  A standard user (a user without administrative rights) cannot modify a managed setting. Although users who are local administrators on their computers might be able to temporarily change a managed setting, the setting will be reapplied the next time the user logs on, the next time the computer restarts, or during a periodic background refresh of Group Policy.

- **Unmanaged settings** These are configuration settings that the organization does not consider mandatory but might consider recommended or advisable. Unmanaged settings are pushed out to targeted user accounts or computers, but unlike managed settings, which are always enforced, unmanaged settings can be modified by users if they want to do so.

  An example of an unmanaged setting is a mapped drive. Because this setting is unmanaged, a user (even a standard user) can delete the mapped drive. The mapped drive might reappear when the user next logs on, depending upon how the administrator has configured the unmanaged setting.

In Group Policy, managed settings are called *policies* and unmanaged settings are called *preferences*. Figure 10-1 shows that a Group Policy Object (GPO) has several types of policies and preferences, some of them per-machine and the others per-user.

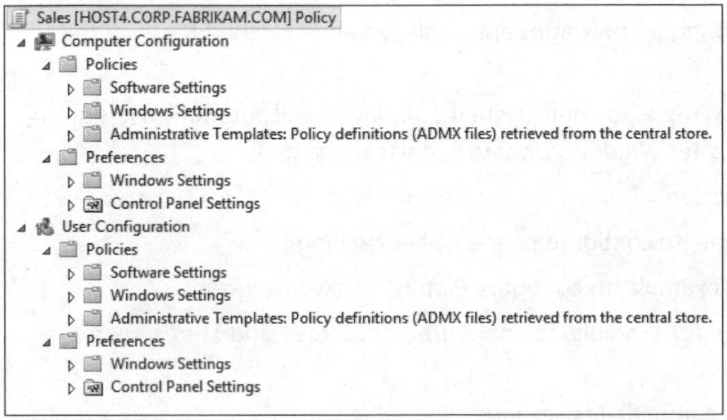

FIGURE 10-1 A Group Policy Object has both managed and unmanaged settings (policies and preferences).

Some of the other differences between policies and preferences include the following:

- A policy disables its associated user interface item on the user's computer; a preference does not.

- A policy is removed when the GPO goes out of scope—that is, when the user or computer is no longer targeted by the GPO. A preference, however, remains configured for the targeted user or computer even when the GPO goes out of scope. Another way of saying this is that preferences *tattoo* the registry on the client computer but policies do not tattoo the registry on the client computer.

- When a policy is applied, the original registry settings on the client computer are not changed. Instead, the policy is stored in a special policy-aware section of the registry on the client. If the policy is later removed, the client's original registry settings are restored. Another way of saying this is that a policy supersedes the corresponding configuration setting in the user interface on the client. With preferences, however, the original registry settings on the client are overwritten and removing the preference does not restore the original setting. In other words, a preference actually modifies the corresponding configuration setting in the user interface on the client. Because of this difference, policies can be effective only for features of Windows operating systems and applications that are Group Policy–aware, but preferences can be effective for any features of Windows operating systems and applications as long as the appropriate preference extension is loaded.

- Policies can be configured in both domain and local GPOs; preferences can be configured only in domain GPOs.

- A preference can be applied only once if desired; policies are always periodically refreshed.

Windows 8, Windows 8.1, Windows Server 2012, and Windows Server 2012 R2 include hundreds of new policies you can use to manage the new features of these platforms. Some of the new types of policies introduced in these platforms include policy settings for managing features such as the following:

- Apps (for example, to configure how apps are displayed and searched for from the Start screen)

- Automatic sign-in (for example, to control whether a device will automatically sign-in the last interactive user after Windows Update restarts the system)

- BitLocker Volume Encryption

- BranchCache (for example, to configure peer-to-peer caching)

- Credential provider (for example, to configure Picture Password sign-in)

- Desktop personalization (for example, to configure Lock screen and Start screen background)

- Device driver setup and compatibility settings

- DNS Client settings (for example, to configure smart protocol reordering and response preferences)
- External boot options for Windows To Go
- File History settings
- Hotspot authentication
- Internet Explorer 10 and Internet Explorer 11 customization (includes over 150 new settings)
- Kerberos armoring
- Logon scripts (for example, to configure the Group Policy client waits after logon before running scripts)
- Managing enterprise installation of Windows 8 apps
- Microsoft accounts (for example, to control whether Microsoft accounts are optional for Windows Store apps that require an account to sign in)
- Multimonitor display (for example, to allow the Start screen to appear on the display the user is using when he or she presses the Windows key)
- Folder Redirection (for example, to configure redirection only on a user's primary computer)
- Remote Desktop Services (for example, to configure RDP 8.0 and RemoteFX)
- Windows Explorer user-interface settings
- Printing (for example, to configure the v4 simplified print-provider architecture)
- Start-screen customization (for example, to configure whether to show Run As Different User on the Start screen)
- Sync Your Settings (for example, to sync to OneDrive)
- TCP/IP (for example, to configure Internet Protocol version 6 [IPv6] stateless autoconfiguration)
- The Trusted Platform Module (TPM) (for example, to configure a backup of TPM to Active Directory)
- User interface customization (for example, to turn off switching between recent apps)
- User profile roaming (for example, to allow roaming only on a user's primary computer)
- VSS Provider Shadow Copies (for the File Server role service)
- Windows OneDrive (for example, to configure the behavior of Windows OneDrive for users)
- Windows PowerShell execution policy
- Windows Runtime apps (for example, to allow an application to revoke access to all content on the device that is protected by a particular enterprise)

- Windows Store (to turn it on or off)
- Windows Update (for example, to configure the behavior Windows Update in your environment)
- Wireless WAN (for example, to configure cost policies for 3G/4G networks)
- Work Folders

See the sidebar titled "A few new policy settings" for examples of some helpful new Group Policy settings introduced in Windows Server 2012 R2.

New policy settings

Windows Server 2012 R2 introduces a number of new Group Policy settings applicable only to computers running Windows Server 2012 R2, Windows 8.1, or Windows RT 8.1. Three policy settings that might be of interest to many administrators are described in this sidebar.

Do not connect to any Windows Update Internet locations

This policy setting is located at

Computer Configuration\Windows Components\Windows Update

Enabling this policy will disable that functionality and may cause connection to public services such as the Windows Store to stop working.

Even when Windows Update is configured to receive updates from an intranet update service, it will periodically retrieve information from the public Windows Update service to enable future connections to Windows Update, and other services like Microsoft Update or the Windows Store. Note that this policy applies only when this PC is configured to connect to an intranet update service using the Specify intranet Microsoft update service location policy.

Configure Logon Script Delay

This policy setting allows you to configure how long the Group Policy client waits after logon before running scripts. It is located at

Computer Configuration\System\Group Policy

By default, the Group Policy client waits five minutes before running logon scripts. This helps create a responsive desktop environment by preventing disk contention.

If you enable this policy setting, Group Policy will wait for the specified amount of time before running logon scripts.

If you disable this policy setting, Group Policy will run scripts immediately after logon.

If you do not configure this policy setting, Group Policy will wait five minutes before running logon scripts.

Enter 0 to disable Logon Script Delay.

Sign-in last interactive user automatically after a system-initiated restart

This policy setting controls whether a device will automatically sign in the last interactive user after Windows Update restarts the system. It is located at

Computer Configuration\Windows Components\Windows Logon Options

If you enable or do not configure this policy setting, the device securely saves the user's credentials (including the user name, domain, and encrypted password) to configure automatic sign-in after a Windows Update restart. After the Windows Update restart, the user is automatically signed in and the session is automatically locked with all the lock screen apps configured for that user.

If you disable this policy setting, the device does not store the user's credentials for automatic sign-in after a Windows Update restart. The user's lock screen apps are not restarted after the system restarts.

MORE INFO **GROUP POLICY SETTINGS REFERENCE**

For more information about new and existing policies in Windows 8, Windows 8.1, Windows Server 2012, and Windows Server 2012 R2, download the appropriate Microsoft Excel workbook from "Group Policy Settings Reference For Windows And Windows Server" at *http://www.microsoft.com/en-us/download/details.aspx?id=25250.*

Group Policy and Active Directory design

Group Policy delivers and enforces policies to targeted objects such as users and computers by creating GPOs and linking them to Active Directory domains, OUs, or sites that contain these objects. The way you design your Active Directory structure can thus have a significant impact on your ability to deploy, manage, and maintain your Group Policy infrastructure.

Most of your Group Policy planning efforts should involve designing the hierarchy of OUs for each of the domains in your forest. You should consider the following issues when designing such an OU structure:

- **Manageability**   Your implementation of Group Policy should be as easy to administer as possible.

- **Delegation**   You might want to delegate administrative control for specific OUs to specific users or groups in your IT department.

- **Inheritance**   When a GPO is linked to a domain, the GPO applies to the users and computers in every OU and child OU in the domain. And when a GPO is linked to an OU, the GPO applies to the users and computers in every child OU of that OU.

- **Precedence**   When multiple GPOs that apply to a user or computer have the same policy configured, the order in which GPOs are applied determines their precedence. By default, GPOs are applied in the following order of precedence:

    1. GPOs linked to the site where the user or computer resides

    2. GPOs linked to the domain where the user or computer resides

    3. GPOs linked to the OU where the user or computer resides

    4. GPOs linked to the child OU where the user or computer resides

    Also, when multiple GPOs are linked to a specific site, domain, or OU, the link order can be modified. Inheritance also can be enforced or blocked on a per-link basis, and GPOs can be selectively targeted to users in specific security groups or computers of specific types by using security filtering or Windows Management Instrumentation (WMI) filtering.

Meeting all of the preceding requirements can be challenging for organizations that have multiple branch offices, special categories of users or devices, or a complex organizational chart. A good place to start when designing an OU structure that supports Group Policy is to do something similar to what is shown in Figure 10-2. The basic elements of this OU structure are as follows:

- Each geographical location, including the head office and any branch offices, is represented by a first-level OU in the domain.

- Second-level OUs are created beneath the head office OU to represent different kinds of users (administrators, ordinary users) and systems (client computers, servers).

- The second-level Computers OU contains two child OUs representing desktop and laptop computers. The Servers OU also contains child OUs for each type of server in the environment.

If different departments in your organization have different requirements, you could modify the OU structure shown in Figure 10-2 by including a new level of departmental OUs (Sales, HR, and so on) in between the first-level and second-level OUs described.

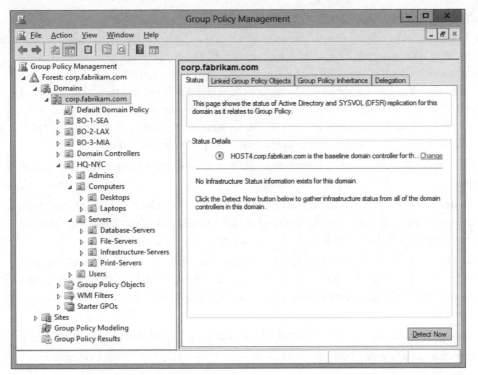

FIGURE 10-2 This is an example of an OU structure designed for Group Policy.

From the perspective of implementing and managing Group Policy, the advantages of the preceding approach to OU design include the following:

- The OU structure is easy to understand and visualize, and your GPO infrastructure will match this simple hierarchy. Keeping things simple is a key to having a manageable environment.

- Delegation of administration is easy to implement. For example, if you delegate the authority to perform Group Policy modeling analyses of objects in the Computers OU by assigning the appropriate permissions to the Support group, the group will automatically be able to perform the same task for objects in the Desktops and Laptops OUs, which are child OUs of the Computers OU.

- GPOs linked to deeply nested OUs can have fewer policies to configure than their parent OUs. For example, the GPO linked to the Computers OU could enforce the policies that apply to all types of computers, including both desktops and laptops. The GPOs linked to the child OUs (Desktops, Laptops) would then only have the few policies configured that apply to those specific types of systems. Group Policy inheritance will then ensure that the settings in the GPO linked to the Computers OU will be processed by computers in both the Desktops and Laptops OUs.

Configuring a central store ⌇

Prior to Windows Vista and Windows Server 2008, all of the default administrative template files (.adm files) were added to the ADM folder of each GPO on a domain controller. Because GPOs are stored in the SYSVOL folder on domain controllers and each GPO typically occupies about 2 MB of disk space, the more GPOs there were in the environment, the greater the size of the SYSVOL folder was. This condition was sometimes referred to as "SYSVOL bloat." Furthermore, because the contents of the SYSVOL folder are automatically replicated to all domain controllers in the domain, this problem was multiplied considerably.

Beginning with Windows Vista and Windows 2008, however, this situation has changed in two ways:

- A new XML-based format for administrative template files called ADMX has replaced the earlier ADM format used for defining registry-based policies in GPOs. An associated format called ADML supports the multilingual display of policies.

- All of the policy definition files (.admx and .adml files) for a domain can be stored in a central store in SYSVOL. This means only one copy of each ADMX template needs to be stored in SYSVOL (instead of a copy of each ADM template for every GPO in the domain).

You can create a central store for a domain by performing the following procedure:

1. Create a folder named PolicyDefinitions in the following UNC path on a domain controller in the domain:

   domain_name\SYSVOL*domain_name*\policies

   For example, for the corp.fabrikam.com domain, you would create the following folder:

   corp.fabrikam.com\SYSVOL*corp.fabrikam.com*\policies\PolicyDefinitions

2. Copy all of the files from the %systemroot%\PolicyDefinitions folder on a Windows 8–based administrative workstation to the PolicyDefinitions folder on a domain controller. Alternatively, you can download the "Administrative Templates (.admx) for Windows 8.1 and Windows Server 2012 R2" at *http://www.microsoft.com/en-us /download/details.aspx?id=41193* and copy them to the PolicyDefinitions folder on a domain controller.

3. Wait for SYSVOL to replicate the changes to all domain controllers in the domain.

Using Starter GPOs

Starter GPOs are basically templates you can use for quickly creating preconfigured GPOs. By creating and configuring a suitable collection of Starter GPOs, you can significantly accelerate the process of implementing Group Policy within a large, distributed environment.

Starter GPOs can be created, edited, imported, exported, backed up, and restored. They can contain only Administrative Template policies, not preferences or other settings such as security settings.

Before you can use Starter GPOs, you must create the Starter GPOs folder for the domain. You can do this by performing the following steps:

1. Select the Starter GPOs node under a domain node in the Group Policy Management Console (GPMC).

2. Click the Create Starter GPOs Folder button in the details pane.

When you perform the preceding steps, a folder named StarterGPOs is created in the SYSVOL share of the domain controllers in the domain. This folder is initially populated with a collection of read-only System Starter GPOs that provide baseline settings for Enterprise Client (EC) and Specialized Security Limited Functionality (SSLF) environments running older versions of Windows client operating systems.

> *NOTE* **GETTING UPDATED SECURITY BASELINES**
>
> For the latest security baselines for Microsoft products, including Windows 8, Windows 8.1, Windows Server 2012, and Windows Server 2012 R2, download the "Microsoft Security Compliance Manager" at *http://www.microsoft.com/en-us/download/details.aspx?id=16776*.

To create a new Starter GPO, perform the following steps:

1. Right-click the Starter GPOs node and select New.

2. Type a descriptive name for your Starter GPO and add an optional comment if desired.

After you have created a new Starter GPO, you need to configure it by following these steps:

1. Right-click the Starter GPO and select Edit to open the Group Policy Starter GPO Editor.

2. Configure the Administrative Template policies as desired.

After you have configured a Starter GPO, you can use it to create new GPOs for the domain. To do this, follow this procedure:

1. Right-click the Starter GPO and select New GPO From Starter GPO:

2. Type a descriptive name for your new GPO:

The new GPO will be created unlinked to any container in Active Directory. By expanding the Group Policy Objects node and selecting the new GPO, you can use the Settings tab to verify that the central store is functioning properly. (See Figure 10-3.) You can link the new GPO to an OU by dragging it onto the node representing the OU.

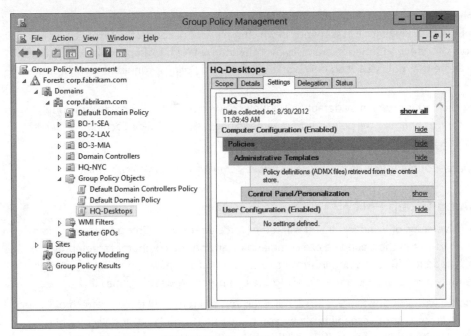

FIGURE 10-3 The HQ-Desktops GPO has been created.

> **NOTE VERIFYING THE CENTRAL STORE**
>
> You can also verify that the central store is functioning properly by using Group Policy Management Editor to open any GPO linked in your domain. If you expand the Policies node beneath either Computer Configuration or User Configuration and you see that the Administrative Templates node has been renamed as Administrative Templates: Policy Definitions (ADMX Files) Retrieved From The Central Store, you know that you have properly configured your central store.

Group Policy caching

Group Policy caching (or policy caching) is a new feature of Group Policy introduced in Windows Server 2012 R2. Policy caching can significantly reduce the amount of time it takes to process Group Policy on a client. Policy caching is only supported for Windows Server 2012 R2, Windows 8, and Windows 8.1, so if your Active Directory environment is still based on Windows Server 2012, then you won't be able to implement this feature.

Policy caching works by having the client download the policy from a domain controller and save a copy of the policy to a local store on the client. Then, when the next Group Policy processing occurs, the client can apply the policy cached in the local store instead of having to download the policy again from the network.

By speeding up Group Policy processing, policy caching can shorten boot times for clients. This can be especially helpful in scenarios in which the network connection experiences latency or is connecting from off-premises over the Internet—for example, in a DirectAccess scenario. Note that policy caching only works when Group Policy is running in synchronous mode.

Policy caching is disabled by default in Windows Server 2012 R2. To enable and configure policy caching, configure the policy setting named Enable Group Policy Caching For Servers, which can be found under

Computer Configuration\Policies\Administrative Templates\System\Group Policy

Refreshing Group Policy

In previous versions of Windows, if you wanted to force a refresh of Group Policy for a computer you had to run the Gpupdate.exe command locally on the computer targeted by the GPO. This made it difficult for administrators to ensure that any new Group Policy settings they configured were applied immediately to the computers targeted by the GPO.

Beginning with Windows Server 2012, however, you can remotely force a refresh of Group Policy. This remote refresh capability allows you to update Group Policy for all computers within an OU with GPOs linked to it. To do this, follow these steps:

1. Right-click the desired OU in the GPMC and select Group Policy Update.

2. Read the confirmation prompt and click Yes if you want Group Policy to be refreshed for computers targeted by the GPOs linked to the OU:

When the progress bar on the Remote Group Policy update Results dialog box indicates Completed, Group Policy update will be forced for all computers in the OU and also for computers in any OUs beneath the OU.

Configuring security settings

As Figure 10-4 shows, Group Policy for Windows 8, Windows 8.1, Windows Server 2012, and Windows Server 2012 R2 includes numerous types of security settings. Most of these policies are per-machine settings found under Computer Configuration\Policies\Windows Settings \Security Settings in the Group Policy Management Editor, but two types of policies are found under User Configuration\Policies\Windows Settings\Security Settings as the figure shows.

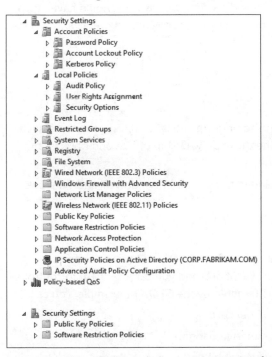

FIGURE 10-4 Group Policy includes numerous types of security settings for computers (above) and users (below).

The following sections briefly discuss some of these categories of security settings, including these:

- User Rights Assignment
- Security Options
- User Account Control
- Audit Policy
- Advanced Audit Policy Configuration
- AppLocker
- Software Restriction Policies
- Windows Firewall with Advanced Security

User Rights Assignment

User Rights Assignment settings are found under Computer Configuration\Policies\Windows Settings\Security Settings\Local Policies\User Rights Assignment, and you can use them to control the user rights assigned to users or security groups for computers targeted by the GPO. You can use these policies to specify users and security groups who should have rights to perform different kinds of tasks affecting the security of your Windows clients and servers. For example, you can control who can

- Access computers from the network.
- Log on locally.
- Shut down the system.

You can also specify who should have rights to perform critical administrative tasks, such as backing up and restoring files and directories, taking ownership of files and objects, and forcing the shutdown from a remote computer.

User Rights Assignment settings are unchanged from those in Windows 7 and Windows Server 2008 R2.

Security Options

Security Options settings are found under Computer Configuration\Policies\Windows Settings\Security Settings\Local Policies\Security Options, and you can use them to control a wide variety of security options for computers targeted by the GPO. For example, you can

- Force users to log off when their logon hours expire.
- Disable Ctrl+Alt+Del for logon to force smartcard logon.
- Force computers to halt when auditing cannot be performed on them.

Windows 8, Windows 8.1, Windows Server 2012, and Windows Server 2012 R2 include four new policies in this category:

- **Accounts: Block Microsoft accounts**   This policy prevents users from adding new Microsoft accounts on this computer.

- **Interactive logon: Machine account threshold** The computer lockout policy is enforced only on computers that have BitLocker enabled for protecting operating system volumes. You should ensure that appropriate recovery password backup policies are enabled.

- **Interactive logon: Machine inactivity limit** Windows notices the inactivity of a logon session, and if the amount of inactive time exceeds the inactivity limit the screen saver will run, locking the session.

- **Microsoft network server: Attempt S4U2Self to obtain claim information** This security setting is used to support clients running a version of Windows prior to Windows 8 that are trying to access a file share that requires user claims. This setting determines whether the local file server will attempt to use Kerberos Service-For-User -To-Self (S4U2Self) functionality to obtain a network client principal's claims from the client's account domain.

User Account Control ⤴

User Account Control (UAC) settings are a subset of the Security Options settings described in the previous section. There are 10 policies that you can use to configure the behavior of UAC on computers targeted by Group Policy, and these policies are the same as those in Windows 7 and Windows Server 2008 R2. For detailed information about each UAC policy, see "UAC Group Policy Settings and Registry Key Settings" at *http://technet.microsoft.com /en-us/library/dd835564(WS.10).aspx*.

One thing that has changed beginning with Windows 8 and Windows Server 2012 is that it is no longer possible to completely disable UAC on the computer. This is because the infrastructure that supports running Windows 8 apps requires UAC. As a result, disabling UAC is no longer supported on Windows 8.

Audit Policy

Policies for basic auditing, which are found under Computer Configuration\Policies\Windows Settings\Security Settings\Local Policies\Audit Policy, allow you to audit account logon events, privilege use, and other user or system activity.

Advanced Audit Policy Configuration

Policies for advanced auditing, which are found under Computer Configuration\Policies \Windows Settings\Security Settings\Advanced Audit Policy Configuration, perform auditing functions similar to those performed by the basic audit policies found under Local Policies \Audit Policy. However, the advanced audit policies allow you to be more selective about the number and types of events you want to audit. For example, basic audit policy provides a single setting for auditing account logons, but advanced audit policy provides four separate settings for this purpose.

One new type of advanced audit policy (Audit Removable Storage) is shown in Figure 10-5. This new policy enables you to track the usage of removable storage devices. If you enable this policy in a GPO that targets users, an audit event is generated each time a user attempts to access a removable storage device. This policy logs two types of audit events:

- Success audits (Event 4663) record successful attempts to write to or read from a removable storage device.
- Failure audits (Event 4656) record unsuccessful attempts to access removable storage device objects.

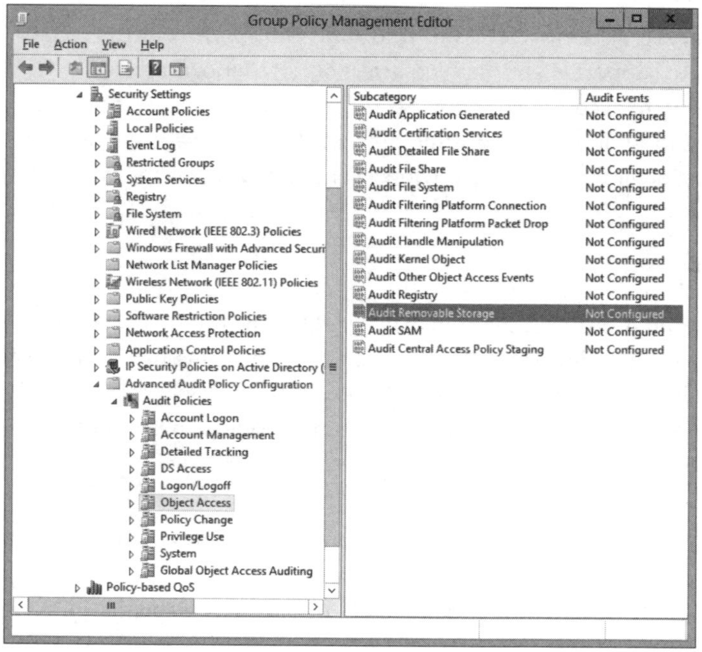

FIGURE 10-5 The new Audit Removable Storage policy enables you to track the usage of removable storage devices.

> **MORE INFO** **AUDITING IMPROVEMENTS**
>
> For more information about auditing improvements introduced in Windows 8 and Windows Server 2012, see "What's New in Security Auditing" at *http://technet.microsoft .com/en-us/library/hh849638*.

AppLocker

You can use AppLocker to control which applications and files users can run on their computers. AppLocker was introduced in Windows 7 and Windows Server 2008 R2, and its policies are found under Computer Configuration\Policies\Windows Settings\Security Settings \Application Control Policies\AppLocker.

Software Restriction Policies 7

The Software Restriction Policies (SRP) feature was introduced in Windows XP and Windows Server 2003 to provide administrators with a policy-driven mechanism to identify programs running on machines in a domain and to control how those programs can execute. SRP settings are found under both Computer Configuration\Policies\Windows Settings\Security Settings and User Configuration\Policies\Windows Settings\Security Settings. SRP is similar to AppLocker but has more limited functionality.

With the introduction of AppLocker in Windows 7 and Windows Server 2008 R2, you should now use AppLocker instead of SRP if all your client computers are running Windows 7 or later. Organizations that include a mix of Windows 8, Windows 7, and older Windows clients can use a combination of AppLocker and SRP to lock down their desktop application environments.

Windows Firewall with Advanced Security

Windows Firewall with Advanced Security provides host-based, two-way network traffic filtering for Windows client and server operating systems. Windows Firewall with Advanced Security was introduced in Windows Vista and Windows Server 2008. Windows Firewall with Advanced Security policies are found under Computer Configuration\Policies\Windows Settings\Security Settings\Windows Firewall with Advanced Security.

Managing Group Policy

Managing Group Policy in an Active Directory environment is a broad topic that has many different aspects. The upcoming sections cover the following basic tasks:

- Viewing infrastructure status
- Creating GPOs
- Managing GPO links
- Configuring security filtering
- Configuring WMI filtering
- Backing up and restoring GPOs

> **MORE INFO** **MANAGING GROUP POLICY**
>
> For more information on Group Policy planning, deployment, operations, and trouble-shooting, see the Group Policy portal at *http://technet.microsoft.com/en-us/windowsserver/bb310732.aspx.*

Viewing infrastructure status

A new feature of the GPMC introduced in Windows Server 2012 is the Status tab shown in Figure 10-6, which provides information about the status of Active Directory and SYSVOL replication. The status information displayed on this tab can be either of the following:

- The status for all GPOs if the node for the domain is selected
- The status for a particular GPO if the node for that GPO is selected

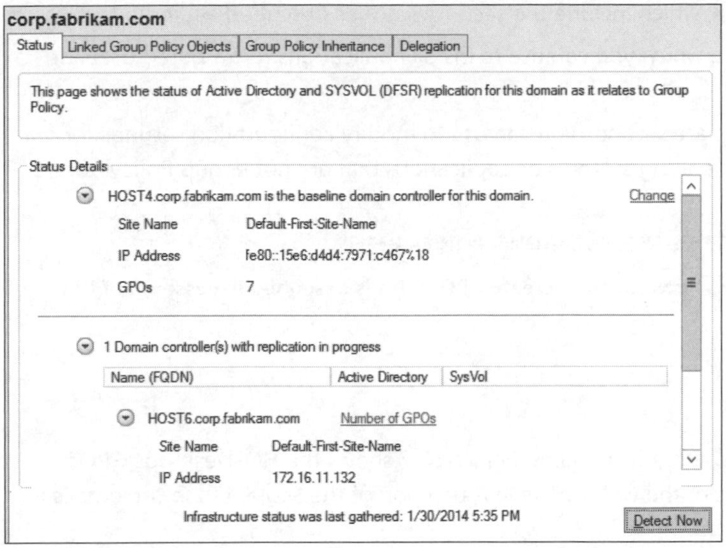

corp.fabrikam.com

| Status | Linked Group Policy Objects | Group Policy Inheritance | Delegation |

This page shows the status of Active Directory and SYSVOL (DFSR) replication for this domain as it relates to Group Policy.

Status Details

⊙ HOST4.corp.fabrikam.com is the baseline domain controller for this domain.　　　Change

    Site Name　　　　Default-First-Site-Name

    IP Address　　　　fe80::15e6:d4d4:7971:c467%18

    GPOs　　　　　　7

⊙ 1 Domain controller(s) with replication in progress

| Name (FQDN) | Active Directory | SysVol |

⊙ HOST6.corp.fabrikam.com　　　Number of GPOs

    Site Name　　　　Default-First-Site-Name

    IP Address　　　　172.16.11.132

Infrastructure status was last gathered: 1/30/2014 5:35 PM　　[Detect Now]

FIGURE 10-6 View the status of SYSVOL replication to monitor Group Policy health.

> ***MORE INFO*** **GROUP POLICY INFRASTRUCTURE STATUS**
>
> For more information on using the new Status tab of the GPMC for monitoring the health of your Group Policy infrastructure, see "Check Group Policy Infrastructure Status" at *http://technet.microsoft.com/en-us/library/jj134176.*

Creating GPOs

By using the GPMC, you can create GPOs either from scratch or from a Starter GPO. You can also create a new GPO so that it is

- Linked to an OU, a site, or the domain by right-clicking the container and selecting New.
- Unlinked to any container in Active Directory by right-clicking the Group Policy Objects node and selecting New.

New GPOs are enabled by default, but after you create a new GPO you can disable

- The GPO's User Configuration settings.
- The GPO's Computer Configuration settings.
- All the GPO's settings.

Once you create a GPO, you can open it in the Group Policy Management Editor and configure the GPO's policies and preferences:

- **Policies** These are settings that Group Policy enforces for users or computers targeted by the GPO. The types of policies include the following:
  - Administrative Templates, which are registry-based settings that are written to a special area of the registry on client computers

- Windows Settings, which include the security settings described earlier in this lesson
- Software Settings, which you can use to install applications for targeted users or computers

- **Preferences**   These are settings you can use to modify configuration settings for features of Windows operating systems or applications that are not Group Policy–aware.

> **NOTE   CREATING GPOS BY USING WINDOWS POWERSHELL**
>
> You can also use Windows PowerShell to create GPOs. This is described in Lesson 2 of this chapter.

Managing GPO links

GPOs can be linked to OUs, sites, or domains. Figure 10-7 shows the HQ-Desktops GPO selected in the console tree of the GPMC. The Links section of the Scope tab in the details pane indicates the following:

- The GPO is linked to the Desktops OU, which is in the Computers OU beneath the HQ-NYC OU of the corp.fabrikam.com domain.

- The link is currently enabled. If you disable the link, the settings in the GPO will not be applied to the users or computers targeted by the GPO.

- The GPO's settings can be blocked by settings inherited from a GPO linked to a parent OU or to the domain. This is indicated by Enforced being set to No.

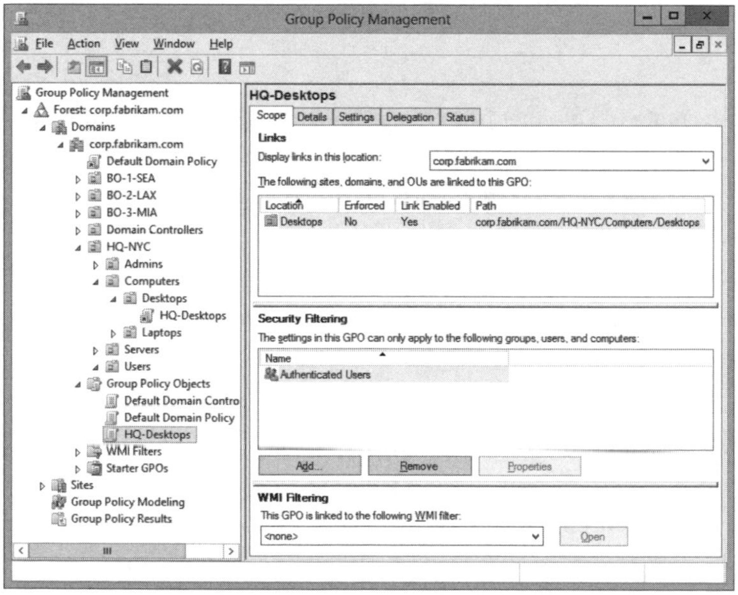

FIGURE 10-7 View information about the links for a GPO.

Configuring security filtering

You can configure security filtering on a GPO to refine which users and computers will receive and apply the settings in the GPO. For example, you can use security filtering to specify that only certain security groups within the OU where the GPO is linked have the GPO applied to them.

To configure security filtering on a GPO, perform the following steps:

1. Select the GPO beneath the Group Policy Objects node in the GPMC.

2. Select the Scope tab in the details pane and click Add in the Security Filtering section of this tab.

3. Browse the directory to select the security group to filter.

4. Once the group you selected is displayed in the Security Filtering section of the Scope tab, select Authenticated Users and click Remove. This ensures that the settings in the GPO will apply only to users and computers that belong to the group you specified.

Configuring WMI filtering

Windows Management Instrumentation (WMI) filtering allows the scope of a GPO to be dynamically determined based on attributes of the target computer. WMI filters are queries written using the WMI Query Language (WQL), a SQL-like language. An example of a WMI filter is the following:

```
select Version from Win32_OperatingSystem where
Version like "6.2%" and ProductType = "1"
```

The preceding query filters based on whether the target computer is running Windows 8. Configuring this query as a WMI filter for a GPO will result in the GPO being applied only to computers running Windows 8. To create and link this filter to a GPO, you do the following:

1. Right-click the WMI Filters node in the GPMC and select New to open the New WMI Filter dialog box.

2. Give the new filter a name and, optionally, a description.

3. Click Add and type your query in the Query field of the WMI Query dialog box. Then click OK to return to the New WMI Filter dialog box:

4. Click Save to save your query. The new filter will be displayed beneath the WMI Filters node.

5. Select the GPO to which you want to link the filter and switch to the Scope tab.

6. In the WMI Filtering section on the Scope tab, select the filter you created from the list of available filters. Click Yes when the confirmation dialog box is displayed.

NOTE **WMI 1.0 NAMESPACE**

The namespace for version 1.0 of WMI was deprecated in Windows Server 2012 and has been removed from Windows Server 2012 R2, so do not configure WMI queries based on this namespace. For an explanation of this change, see "The v2 WMI namespace in Hyper-V on Windows 8" at *http://blogs.msdn.com/b/virtual_pc_guy/archive/2012/05/30/the-v2 -wmi-namespace-in-hyper-v-on-windows-8.aspx*.

IMPORTANT **PERFORMANCE IMPACT OF WMI FILTERS**

Although security filtering is fast, WMI filtering can be slow. Improper use of WMI filtering can therefore have a significant performance impact on how Group Policy is processed and applied. As a result, you should be sure to test the performance of any WMI filter before you deploy it in your production environment. WMI filters that usually evaluate quickly include filters that query for registry keys or environment variables. WMI filters that might evaluate slowly include filters that query the CIM_DataFile namespace or query for installed products using the MSI database.

Backing up and restoring GPOs

You can use the GPMC to back up your GPOs. You can also restore a deleted or previous version of an existing GPO, copy a GPO, import the settings from a GPO, or migrate a GPO to a different domain. By backing up GPOs, you can quickly restore your Group Policy infrastructure in the event of a disaster.

To back up a specific GPO, follow these steps:

1. Right-click the GPO and select Back Up to open the Backup Group Policy Object dialog box.
2. Specify the path to the location where you want to store the backup.

You can also back up all GPOs in a domain as follows:

1. Right-click the Group Policy Objects node and select Back Up.
2. Specify the path to the location where you want to store the backup.

After you back up GPOs, you can manage your backups by right-clicking the Group Policy Objects node and selecting Manage Backups.

Lesson summary

- You need to plan your OU structure to support Group Policy.
- You should configure a central store for storing policy definition files in the domain.
- Creating and using Starter GPOs can simplify the process of deploying new GPOs.
- Windows Server 2012 and Windows Server 2012 R2 allow you to perform a remote refresh of Group Policy on targeted computers.
- Group Policy security settings for Windows Server 2012 and Windows Server 2012 R2 include new policies and capabilities.

Lesson review

Answer the following questions to test your knowledge of the information in this lesson. You can find the answers to these questions and explanations of why each answer choice is correct or incorrect in the "Answers" section at the end of this chapter.

1. You have created a flat OU structure for your domain that has only top-level OUs and no child OUs. Each department's desktops, laptops, and users are contained in different OUs. What is the main reason why this design is a poor choice when it comes to implementing Group Policy for your environment?

   A. It will be difficult to manage Group Policy because of the large number of GPOs you will need.

   B. It will be difficult to delegate Group Policy because of the large number of GPOs you will need.

   C. It will be difficult to manage Group Policy because you won't be able to make effective use of Group Policy inheritance.

   D. It will be difficult to delegate Group Policy because you won't be able to make effective use of Group Policy inheritance.

2. You right-clicked an OU in the GPMC console tree that contains computers and then selected the Group Policy Update menu option from the context menu. The Remote Group Policy Update Results dialog box indicates Completed, and no error message has been displayed. You later discover that at least one of the Computer Configuration policies in the GPO linked to the OU was not refreshed on the computers in the OU. What could be the cause of this failure? (Choose all that apply.)

   A. The necessary firewall ports on the targeted computers have not been opened to enable a remote refresh of Group Policy.

   B. The GPO that should be linked to the OU has become unlinked from the OU.

   C. The Computer Configuration portion of the GPO linked to the OU has been disabled.

   D. The Group Policy Remote Update Firewall Ports Starter GPO has been deleted from the domain.

3. What node should you select in the console tree of the GPMC to view the current status of SYSVOL replication as it relates to Group Policy in a domain?

   A. The root node named Group Policy Management

   B. The node named Forest: <forest_root_domain>

   C. The node named Domains

   D. The node named <domain_name>

Lesson 2: Managing Group Policy using Windows PowerShell

Although you can most easily perform most administrative tasks for Group Policy by using GUI tools such as the GPMC and the Group Policy Management Editor, you can also perform some tasks using Windows PowerShell. This lesson examines some of the ways you can use Windows PowerShell to configure and manage Group Policy in an Active Directory environment based on Windows Server 2012 or Windows Server 2012 R2.

After this lesson, you will be able to:

- Create and link GPOs using Windows PowerShell.
- Configure and perform Group Policy remote refresh using Windows PowerShell.
- Back up and restore GPOs using Windows PowerShell.

Estimated lesson time: 15 minutes

Creating and linking GPOs

To show how you can create and link GPOs using Windows PowerShell, in this lesson you create a new GPO named BO-1-Desktops based on the Starter GPO named Computers-Desktop that you created in Lesson 1 of this chapter. You then link the new GPO to the OU named BO-1-SEA, which represents Branch Office #1 in Seattle in the corp.fabrikam.com domain.

You can start by using the Get-StarterGPO cmdlet to confirm that your Starter GPO exists:

```
PS C:\> Get-GPStarterGPO -Name "Computers-Desktop"

DisplayName        : Computers-Desktop
Id                 : 260220b0-d73e-40f1-b293-9477dd697977
Owner              : BUILTIN\Administrators
CreationTime       : 8/30/2012 11:00:36 AM
ModificationTime   : 8/30/2012 11:05:10 AM
UserVersion        : 0
ComputerVersion    : 1
StarterGpoVersion  :
StarterGpoType     : Custom
Author             :
Description        : This Starter GPO will be used to create GPOs for desktop computers
                     for all locations
```

Next, you can use the New-GPO cmdlet to create the new GPO from your Starter GPO as follows:

```
PS C:\> New-GPO -Name "BO-1-Desktops" -StarterGpoName "Computers-Desktop"

DisplayName        : BO-1-Desktops
DomainName         : corp.fabrikam.com
Owner              : CORP\Domain Admins
```

```
Id              : a2b711b4-ea20-4a42-9cd2-cba11b07b7ea
GpoStatus       : AllSettingsEnabled
Description     :
CreationTime    : 8/30/2012 7:57:35 PM
ModificationTime : 8/30/2012 7:57:36 PM
UserVersion     : AD Version: 1, SysVol Version: 1
ComputerVersion : AD Version: 1, SysVol Version: 1
WmiFilter       :
```

Finally, you can link the new GPO to the targeted OU as follows:

```
PS C:\> New-GPLink -Name "BO-1-Desktops" `
-Target "ou=BO-1-SEA,dc=corp,dc=fabrikam,dc=com"


GpoId       : a2b711b4-ea20-4a42-9cd2-cba11b07b7ea
DisplayName : BO-1-Desktops
Enabled     : True
Enforced    : False
Target      : OU=BO-1-SEA,DC=corp,DC=fabrikam,DC=com
Order       : 1
```

Alternatively, by using the Windows PowerShell pipeline feature, you can create and link the GPO using a single command like this:

```
Get-GPStarterGPO -Name "Computers-Desktop" | New-GPO -Name "BO-1-Desktops" | `
New-GPLink -Target "ou=BO-1-SEA,dc=corp,dc=fabrikam,dc=com"
```

Remotely refreshing Group Policy

You can use the Invoke-GPUpdate cmdlet to refresh Group Policy settings on remote computers. This cmdlet works by scheduling the running of the Gpupdate.exe command on the remote computers. Before you can do this, however, you need to open the necessary firewall ports on the computers you will be targeting, as was explained in the previous lesson in this chapter. You can perform this preliminary step by using Windows PowerShell. For example, the following command creates and links a GPO that will open the necessary firewall ports for all computers in the corp.fabrikam.com domain:

```
New-GPO -Name "EnableRemoteRefresh" `
-StarterGPOName "Group Policy Remote Update Firewall Ports" | `
New-GPLink -Target "dc=corp,dc=fabrikam,dc=com"
```

Once this GPO has been processed, you can perform a remote refresh of Group Policy for computers in a specific OU. For example, the following command remotely refreshes Group Policy for computers in the Desktops OU described earlier in Lesson 1 of this chapter:

```
Get-ADComputer -Filter * `
-SearchBase "ou=Desktops,ou=Computers,ou=HQ-NYC,dc=corp,dc=fabrikam,dc=com" | `
foreach{Invoke-GPUpdate -Computer $_.Name -force -RandomDelayInMinutes 0}
```

The preceding command uses the Get-ADComputer cmdlet to obtain a list of names of computers in the targeted OU. The output from this command is then piped into a *foreach* statement that initiates an immediate refresh of Group Policy on each computer.

Backing up and restoring GPOs

You can use the Backup-GPO and Restore-GPO cmdlets to back up and restore GPOs. For example, the following command backs up the GPO named HQ-Desktops to the local folder named C:\GPOBackups:

```
PS C:\> Get-GPO -Name "BO-1-Desktops" | Backup-GPO -Path "C:\GPOBackups" `
-Comment "Today's backup"

DisplayName     : BO-1-Desktops
GpoId           : aec4900f-f450-4ea6-8187-13cfb014ab2f
Id              : 54937d03-5cb6-49c8-9069-dcdc9aece0d0
BackupDirectory : C:\GPOBackups
CreationTime    : 8/30/2012 8:41:59 PM
DomainName      : corp.fabrikam.com
Comment         : Today's backup
```

You can then use the Get-ChildItem cmdlet to verify the result as follows:

```
PS C:\> Get-ChildItem "C:\GPOBackups" -Recurse

    Directory: C:\GPOBackups

Mode            LastWriteTime      Length Name
----            -------------      ------ ----
d----      8/30/2012    8:41 PM           {54937D03-5CB6-49C8-9069-DCDC9AECE0D0}

    Directory: C:\GPOBackups\{54937D03-5CB6-49C8-9069-DCDC9AECE0D0}

Mode            LastWriteTime      Length Name
----            -------------      ------ ----
d----      8/30/2012    8:41 PM           DomainSysvol
-a---      8/30/2012    8:41 PM     3707  Backup.xml
-a---      8/30/2012    8:42 PM    16700  gpreport.xml

    Directory: C:\GPOBackups\{54937D03-5CB6-49C8-9069-DCDC9AECE0D0}\DomainSysvol

Mode            LastWriteTime      Length Name
----            -------------      ------ ----
d----      8/30/2012    8:41 PM           GPO

    Directory: C:\GPOBackups\{54937D03-5CB6-49C8-9069-DCDC9AECE0D0}\DomainSysvol\GPO

Mode            LastWriteTime      Length Name
----            -------------      ------ ----
d----      8/30/2012    8:41 PM           Machine
d----      8/30/2012    8:41 PM           User

    Directory: C:\GPOBackups\{54937D03-5CB6-49C8-9069-DCDC9AECE0D0}\DomainSysvol\GPO
\Machine

Mode            LastWriteTime      Length Name
----            -------------      ------ ----
-a---      8/30/2012   11:05 AM      558  comment.cmtx
-a---      8/30/2012   11:05 AM      196  registry.pol
```

Lesson summary

- You can use the Get-StarterGPO, New-GPO, and New-GPLink cmdlets to create new GPOs from Starter GPOs and link the new GPOs to OUs.
- You can use the New-GPO cmdlet to create and link a new GPO that will enable Group Policy remote refresh on all computers in your domain.
- You can use the Get-ADComputer GPO and Invoke-GPUpdate cmdlets to perform a remote refresh of Group Policy for computers in a specific OU.
- You can use the Get-GPO and Backup-GPO cmdlets to back up a GPO.

Lesson review

Answer the following questions to test your knowledge of the information in this lesson. You can find the answers to these questions and explanations of why each answer choice is correct or incorrect in the "Answers" section at the end of this chapter.

1. Which two cmdlets can you use together to create a new GPO and link it using a single command?

   A. Get-StarterGPO and New-GPO

   B. New-GPO and New-GPLink

   C. New-GPO and Set-GPLink

   D. Get-GPO and New-GPLink

2. What action does the following command perform?

   Backup-GPO –All –Path \\HOST6\GpoBackups

   A. The command backs up the GPO named All to the C:\GpoBackups folder on HOST6.

   B. The command backs up the GPO named All to the GpoBackups share on HOST6.

   C. The command backs up all GPOs to the C:\GpoBackups folder on HOST6.

   D. The command backs up all GPOs to the GpoBackups share on HOST6.

Lesson 3: Implementing Group Policy preferences

Most administrators are familiar with how to use Group Policy policies for configuring or locking down users' desktop environments, but many are less familiar with the capabilities and benefits of using Group Policy preferences. This lesson provides an overview of how Group Policy preferences work, how to configure them, and the different types of Windows features and settings that you can configure using them.

> **After this lesson, you will be able to:**
>
> - Explain the difference between policies and preferences.
> - Create and configure new preference items.
> - Manage preference items.
> - Understand the different types of preference extensions and what they can be used for.
>
> **Estimated lesson time: 30 minutes**

Understanding preferences ⁊

As explained previously in Lesson 1 of this chapter, Group Policy preferences are unmanaged configuration settings. That is, they are configuration settings that the organization does not consider mandatory but might consider recommended or advisable. Unmanaged settings are pushed out to targeted user accounts or computers, but unlike managed settings, which are always enforced, unmanaged settings can be modified by users if they want to do so.

Group Policy preferences are implemented using client-side extensions (CSEs) and supplement the range of configurable settings available within a GPO. You can use Group Policy preferences to manage the configuration of the following versions of Windows:

- Windows 8.1 and Windows Server 2012 R2
- Windows 8 and Windows Server 2012
- Windows 7 and Windows Server 2008 R2
- Windows Vista and Windows Server 2008
- Windows XP SP2 or later and Windows Server 2003 SP1 or later

> ***NOTE*** **GROUP POLICY PREFERENCES AND EARLIER VERSIONS OF WINDOWS**
>
> To use Group Policy preferences to manage the configuration of Windows XP or Windows Vista, you must download and install the "Group Policy Preferences Client-Side Extension Hotfix Rollup" at *http://support.microsoft.com/kb/974266*.

As Figure 10-8 shows, you can configure Group Policy preferences within a GPO by opening the GPO in the Group Policy Management Editor. You can find preference extensions in both the Computer Configuration and User Configuration sections of the GPO. By right-clicking a preference extension and selecting New from the context menu, you can create a new *preference item* that you can use to distribute the settings configured in the item to users or computer targeted by the GPO.

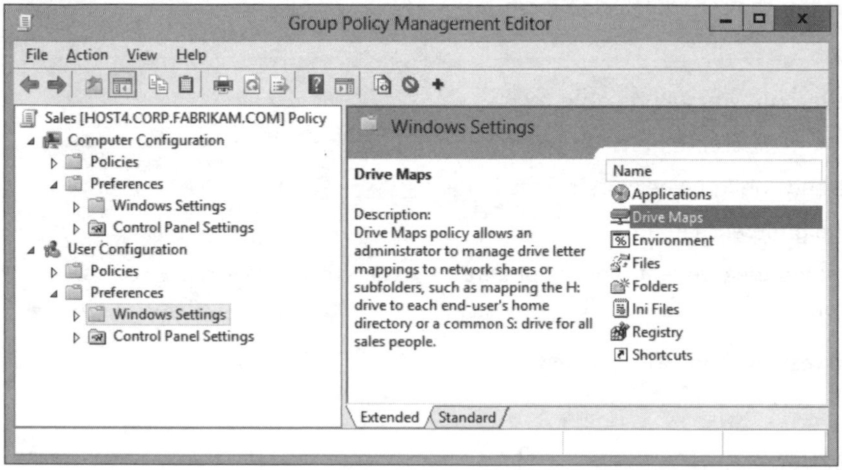

FIGURE 10-8 Configure Group Policy preferences in the Group Policy Management Editor.

> *NOTE* **PREFERENCES AND LOCAL GROUP POLICY**
>
> Unlike policies, which you can configure in both domain and local GPOs, you can configure preferences only in domain GPOs. This means that if you open the Local Computer Policy on a computer by running gpedit.msc, you will not see a Preferences node under Computer Configuration or User Configuration.

Preference categories

As Figure 10-8 shows, preferences can be categorized in two ways:

- **Windows Settings**   These are preferences that you can use to configure different aspects of the Windows environment for targeted users and computers.
- **Control Panel Settings**   These are preferences that you can use to configure Control Panel settings for targeted users and computers.

The different types of Windows Settings and Control Panel Settings preferences are described later in this lesson.

Configuring preferences

Preference options are usually configured using properties sheets. For example, Figure 10-9 shows the General tab on the properties sheet of a New Drive preference item, which you can use to configure new mapped drives for users or computers targeted by a GPO. For most types of preference extensions, when you create a new preference item you have a choice of four actions from which to select:

- **Create** Creates a new preference item for the targeted user or computer—for example, a new mapped drive for users.

- **Delete** Removes a previously created preference item for the targeted user or computer—for example, a previously configured mapped drive for users.

- **Replace** Deletes and re-creates the preference item for the targeted user or computer—for example, deletes a previously mapped drive and creates a new one. The Replace action overwrites all existing settings associated with the previously configured preference item. If the preference item (for example, a drive mapping) does not exist, the Replace action creates a new preference item (for example, a new drive mapping) for the targeted user or computer.

- **Update** Modifies the settings of an existing preference item, such as a mapped drive. Update differs from Replace in that it updates only settings defined within the preference item. If the preference item (for example, a drive mapping) does not exist, the Update action creates a new item (for example, a new drive mapping) for the targeted user or computer.

The remaining configuration options available on the General tab depend on which type of action you selected for the new preference item.

FIGURE 10-9 You can configure preferences on the General tab on the properties sheet of a New Drive preference item.

> **NOTE DEFAULT ACTION**
>
> The default action for a new preference item is Update.

Common options

Several preference options are common to most types of preferences. You can configure these options using the Common tab on the properties sheet of the preference item. For example, Figure 10-10 shows the Common tab displayed when creating a new preference item of the Drive Maps preference type, which you can use to configure new mapped drives for users or computers targeted by a GPO. As you can see, one of the preference options on this tab is unavailable for configuration for this particular type of preference.

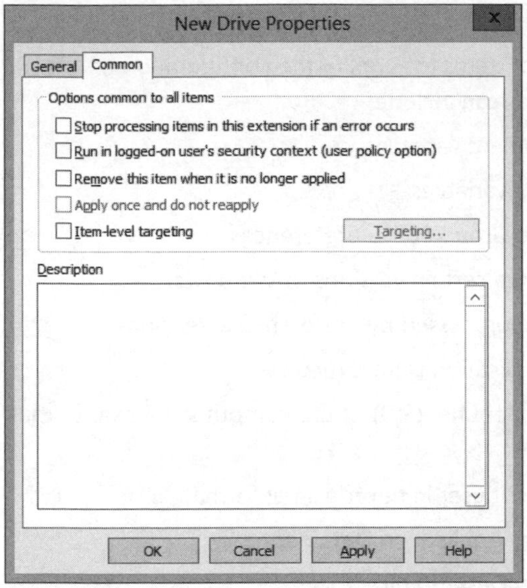

FIGURE 10-10 You can use the Common tab on the properties sheet of a New Drive preference item to configure new mapped drives.

The different options available on the Common tab include the following:

- **Stop Processing Items In This Extension If An Error Occurs** A preference extension can contain one or more preference items. If this option is selected, a preference item that fails to apply will prevent the remaining preference items in the extension from processing.

- **Run In Logged-on User's Security Context (User Policy Option)** By default, preferences are processed using the security context of the SYSTEM account on the client. If this option is selected, the preference will be processed using the security context of the currently logged-on user on the client, which allows user-specific environment variables to be used in file system paths.

- **Remove This Item When It Is No Longer Applied** By default, preference items are not removed from the client when the GPO targeting the user or computer goes out of scope. Selecting this option causes the preference item to be removed from the client when the GPO targeting the user or computer goes out of scope, which is done by deleting and then re-creating the preference item.

- **Apply Once And Do Not Reapply** By default, preference items are rewritten whenever Group Policy is refreshed on the client. Selecting this option causes the preference item to be applied only once to the client.

- **Item-Level Targeting** By default, a preference item configured in a GPO applies to all users and computers targeted by that GPO. Selecting this option allows you to change this behavior as described later in this lesson.

Using environment variables

You can use environment variables in preference items to simplify the configuration of options such as file system paths. These variables can include

- Standard Windows per-machine environment variables.
- Standard Windows per-user environment variables.
- Environment variables that are specific to Group Policy preferences.

In addition, some variables might apply only to certain versions of Windows.

The following is a list of variables that can be processed by preference extensions:

- **%AppDataDir%**   The current user's Application Data directory
- **%BinaryComputerSid%**   The security identifier (SID) of the computer in hexadecimal format
- **%BinaryUserSid%**   The SID of the current user in hexadecimal format
- **%CommonAppdataDir%**   The All Users Application Data directory
- **%CommonDesktopDir%**   The All Users Desktop directory
- **%CommonFavoritesDir%**   The All Users Explorer Favorites directory
- **%CommonProgramsDir%**   The All Users Programs directory
- **%CommonStartMenuDir%**   The All Users Start Menu directory
- **%CommonStartUpDir%**   The All Users Startup directory
- **%ComputerName%**   The NetBIOS name of the computer
- **%CurrentProcessId%**   The numeric identity of the main client process
- **%CurrentThreadId%**   The numeric identity of the main client thread
- **%DateTime%**   The current time (UTC)
- **%DateTimeEx%**   The current time (UTC) with milliseconds
- **%DesktopDir%**   The current user's desktop directory
- **%DomainName%**   The domain name or workgroup of the computer
- **%FavoritesDir%**   The current user's Explorer Favorites directory
- **%LastError%**   The last error code encountered during configuration
- **%LastErrorText%**   The last error code text description
- **%LdapComputerSid%**   The SID of the computer in Lightweight Directory Access Protocol (LDAP) escaped binary format
- **%LdapUserSid%**   The SID of the current user in LDAP escaped binary format
- **%LocalTime%**   The current local time
- **%LocalTimeEx%**   The current local time with milliseconds
- **%LogonDomain%**   The domain of the current user
- **%LogonServer%**   The domain controller that authenticated the current user

- **%LogonUser%**   The user name of the current user

- **%LogonUserSid%**   The SID of the current user

- **%MacAddress%**   The first detected media access control (MAC) address on the computer

- **%NetPlacesDir%**   The current user's My Network Places directory

- **%OsVersion%**   The operating system, which can be a specific Windows operating system or Unknown

- **%ProgramFilesDir%**   The Windows Program Files directory

- **%ProgramsDir%**   The current user's Programs directory

- **%RecentDocumentsDir%**   The current user's Recent Documents directory

- **%ResultCode%**   The client's exit code

- **%ResultText%**   The client's exit code text description

- **%ReversedComputerSid%**   The SID of the computer in reversed-byte-order hexadecimal format

- **%ReversedUserSid%**   The SID of the current user in reversed-byte-order hexadecimal format

- **%SendToDir%**   The current user's Send To directory

- **%StartMenuDir%**   The current user's Start Menu directory

- **%StartUpDir%**   The current user's Startup directory

- **%SystemDir%**   The Windows system directory

- **%SystemDrive%**   The name of the drive from which the operating system is running

- **%TempDir%**   The current user's Temp directory as determined by Windows API

- **%TimeStamp%**   The time stamp of the configurations being implemented

- **%TraceFile%**   The path/name of the trace file

- **%WindowsDir%**   The Windows directory

To select a variable when configuring a preference item, do the following:

1. Open the properties of the preference item and click in any field in which a variable can be used, such as the Location field on the General tab of a Drive Maps item.

2. Press F3 to open the Select A Variable dialog box:

3. Select the variable you want to use in the field used for configuring the preference item.

4. Deselect the Resolve Variable check box if you want the variable instead of the resolved value to appear in the properties of the preference item.

5. Click Select to insert the variable in the preference item properties.

Item-level targeting

The default scope of a preference item is the users or computers targeted by the GPO in which the preference item has been configured. You can modify this default scope by using item-level targeting, which you can use to create one or more targeting items for a preference item. These targeting items can be used to determine whether the preference item should be applied based on various conditions—for example:

- Whether a battery is present in the targeted computer
- Whether the name of the targeted computer matches the name specified in the targeting item
- Whether an environment variable for the targeted user or computer has the value specified

The full list of categories of targeting items is as follows:

- Battery Present
- Computer Name

- CPU Speed
- Date Match
- Disk Space
- Domain
- Environment Variable
- File Match
- IP Address Range
- Language
- LDAP Query
- MAC Address Range
- MSI Query
- Network Connection
- Operating System
- Organizational Unit
- PCMCIA Present
- Portable Computer
- Processing Mode
- RAM
- Registry Match
- Security Group
- Site
- Terminal Session
- Time Range
- User
- WMI Query

Configuring a preference item

As an example of configuring a preference item, in this section you create an item that will map a network drive for a user targeted by a GPO. To do this, follow this procedure:

1. Open the GPO in the Group Policy Management Editor and expand the Windows Settings for the Preferences node under User Configuration to display the Drive Maps preference extension. (See Figure 10-8 earlier in this lesson.)

2. Right-click the Drive Maps preference extension and select New and then select Mapped Drive. This opens the New Drive Properties dialog box with the focus on the General tab, which you configure as follows:

   - **Action** Replace.

- **Location** UNC path to a network share.
- **Reconnect** This option is selected to save the mapped drive in the user's profile and attempt to restore a connection to it at each subsequent logon.
- **Label As** A descriptive label for the new mapped drive.
- **Drive Letter** You can select an available drive letter for the new mapped drive or use the first available drive, starting at the drive letter specified.
- **Connect As** You can use this option to map the drive using different credentials from those of the currently logged-on user.
- **Hide/Show This Drive** You can use this option to configure the visibility of the mapped drive on the client.
- **Hide/Show All Drives** You can use this option to configure the visibility of all mapped drives on the client.

3. Switch to the Common tab and select Remove This Item When It Is No Longer Applied so that the mapped drive will be deleted if the targeted user goes out of scope from the GPO.

After you complete the preceding steps, the new preference item is displayed in the details pane of the Group Policy Management Editor when the Drive Maps extension is selected in the context pane. (See Figure 10-11.)

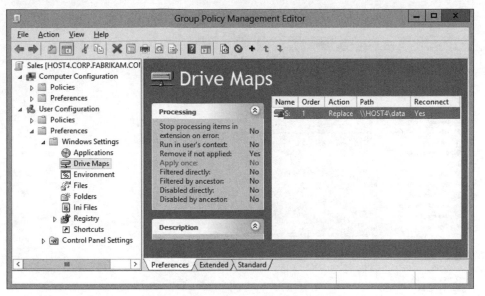

FIGURE 10-11 A new Drive Maps preference item has been created.

As a continuation of the preceding example, you can now use item-level targeting to configure the new Drive Maps item so that it applies only to members of the Sales security group who are targeted by the GPO:

1. With the Drive Maps preference extension selected in the console tree of the Group Policy Management Editor, right-click the new Drive Map item (S drive) and select Properties.

2. Switch to the Common tab and select the Item-Level Targeting option on this tab.

3. Click the Targeting button to open the Targeting Editor.

4. Click the New Item menu option and select Security Group as the item-level target:

5. In the Group field on the Targeting Editor, select the Sales security group as shown here:

6. Click OK to finish configuring item-level targeting for the preference item. As Figure 10-12 shows, the information on the Processing tab will be updated to indicate that the preference item is being filtered using item-level targeting.

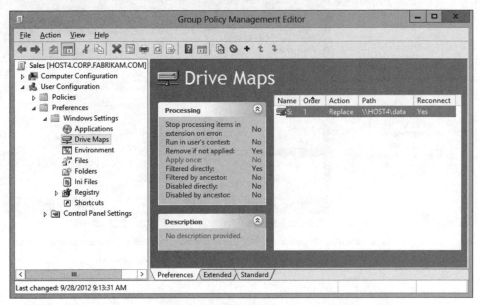

FIGURE 10-12 A preference item is being filtered using item-level targeting.

Managing preference items

Once you have created new preference items in a GPO, you can use the Group Policy Management Editor to manage those items. As Figure 10-13 shows, the management tasks you can perform on preference items include

- Enabling or disabling the item.
- Moving the item up or down in the preference extension item list. Preference items are processed from the bottom of this list to the top.
- Displaying the XML for the item.
- Opening the properties of the item to modify its configuration settings on the General or Common tab.

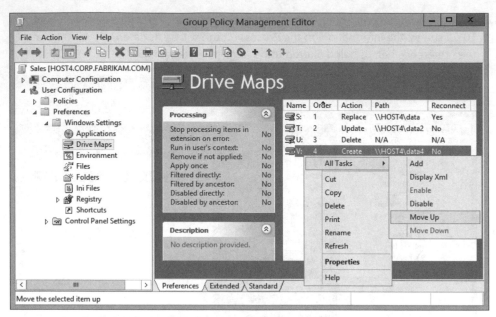

FIGURE 10-13 Manage preference items using the Group Policy Management Editor.

✔ Quick check

- You want to deploy mapped drives only to users who have French configured as their local language. What feature of Group Policy preferences allows you to do this?

Quick check answer

- You can use item-level targeting with Language targeting selected.

IPv6 and Group Policy preferences

New in Windows Server 2012 R2 is support for Internet Protocol version 6 (IPv6) for item-level targeting of Group Policy preferences. Specifically, you can configure the scope of individual preference items so they apply only to computers that have a specific IPv6 address range. For example, here's how you might use this capability to use a GPO to apply a certain power plan to computers running Windows 7 or later whose IPv6 addresses fall within the address range 2001:DB8:3FA9:/48:

1. Open the GPO in the Group Policy Management Editor and expand Computer Configuration, then Preferences, then Control Panel Settings, and then Power Options.

2. Right-click Power Options and select New followed by Power Plan (at least Windows 7 is required).

3. In the New Power Plan Properties dialog box, click the Common tab, select the Item-level Targeting check box, and click Targeting.

4. In the Targeting Editor, click New Item followed by IP Address Range.

5. Select the Use IPv6 check box, as shown below, and specify the IPv6 address and prefix length.

Support for IPv6 has also been introduced into other areas of Group Policy. For example, when you create a new TCP/IP Printer preference item, you can specify an IPv6 address of the network printer, as shown here.

You can find another example of IPv6 support in Group Policy when you create a new VPN Connection preference item, as shown here.

For more information on IPv6 support in Microsoft Windows, see *http://technet .microsoft.com/en-us/network/bb530961.aspx*.

Windows Settings extensions

Figure 10-14 shows the different preference extensions for Windows settings that are available under Computer Configuration and User Configuration. You can use these preference extensions to configure the following types of settings for users or computers targeted by the GPO:

- **Applications**   Use this to configure settings for applications.
- **Drive Maps**   Use this to create, modify, or delete mapped drives and to configure the visibility of all drives.
- **Environment**   Use this to create, modify, or delete environment variables.
- **Files**   Use this to copy, modify the attributes of, replace, or delete files.
- **Folders**   Use this to create, modify, or delete folders.
- **Ini Files**   Use this to add, replace, or delete sections or properties in configuration settings (.ini) or setup information (.inf) files.
- **Network Shares**   Use this to create, modify, or delete (unshare) shares.
- **Registry**   Use this to copy registry settings and apply them to other computers. You can create, replace, or delete registry settings.
- **Shortcuts**   Use this to create, modify, or delete shortcuts.

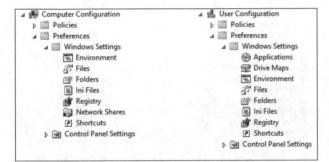

FIGURE 10-14 View the available Windows Settings extensions for Group Policy preferences.

Control Panel Settings extensions

Figure 10-15 shows the different preference extensions for Control Panel settings that are available under Computer Configuration and User Configuration. You can use these preference extensions to configure the following types of settings for users or computers targeted by the GPO:

- **Data Sources**   Use this to create, modify, or delete Open Database Connectivity (ODBC) data source names.
- **Devices**   Use this to enable or disable hardware devices or classes of devices.

- **Folder Options**   Use this to configure folder options; create, modify, or delete Open With associations for file-name extensions; and create, modify, or delete file-name extensions associated with a type of file.

- **Internet Settings**   Use this to modify user-configurable Internet settings.

- **Local Users and Groups**   Use this to create, modify, or delete local users and groups.

- **Network Options**   Use this to create, modify, or delete virtual private networks (VPNs) or dial-up networking connections.

- **Power Options**   Use this to modify power options and create, modify, or delete power schemes.

- **Printers**   Use this to create, modify, or delete TCP/IP, shared, and local printer connections.

- **Regional Options**   Use this to modify regional options.

- **Scheduled Tasks**   Use this to create, modify, or delete scheduled or immediate tasks.

- **Services**   Use this to modify services.

- **Start Menu**   Use this to modify Start menu options.

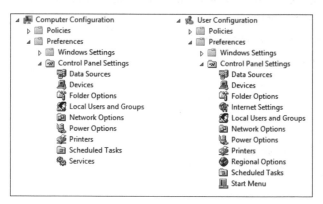

FIGURE 10-15 View the available Control Panel Settings extensions for Group Policy preferences.

Lesson summary

- Preference extensions consist of Windows settings and Control Panel settings.

- You can configure preference items to create, delete, replace, or update a registry-based configuration setting on the client.

- A set of five common configuration options is supported for most preference extensions.

- Environment variables can be used in preference items to simplify the configuration of options such as file system paths.

- You can use item-level targeting to determine whether the preference item should be applied based on various conditions.
- You can manage preference items by right-clicking them in the Group Policy Management Editor.

Lesson review

Answer the following questions to test your knowledge of the information in this lesson. You can find the answers to these questions and explanations of why each answer choice is correct or incorrect in the "Answers" section at the end of this chapter.

1. Which of the following is *not* true concerning Group Policy preferences? (Choose all that apply.)

    A. You cannot configure preferences in local GPOs.

    B. Preferences take precedence over policies when they conflict.

    C. When creating a new preference item, selecting the Create action deletes and re-creates the preference item for the targeted user or computer.

    D. You can press F3 to select a variable when configuring a field of a preference item in which a variable can be used.

2. Which of the following *cannot* be used as a targeting item for preference item-level targeting?

    A. MAC Address Range

    B. Organizational Unit

    C. Registry Match

    D. Desktop Computer

3. You have configured several Drive Maps preference items so that users targeted by the GPO can have mapped drives to make it easier for them to access shared folders on the network. These shared folders are all located on different file servers. Occasionally, one of the file servers is taken down for maintenance, and you want the user to be able to use the remaining mapped drives when this occurs. Which option on the Common tab of the Drive Maps preference item can you configure to allow this?

    A. Stop Processing Items In This Extension If An Error Occurs

    B. Run In Logged-on User's Security Context (User Policy Option)

    C. Remove This Item When It Is No Longer Applied

    D. Apply Once And Do Not Reapply

Practice exercises

The goal of this section is to provide you with hands-on practice with the following:

- Designing and implementing Group Policy
- Creating and managing GPOs using Windows PowerShell

To perform the following exercises, you need at least one clean installation of Windows Server 2012 R2 using the Server With A GUI installation option. The server should be a domain controller in a domain, have Internet connectivity, and have no additional roles or features installed. For the purposes of these exercises, the name of the server is assumed to be HOST4 and the domain is corp.fabrikam.com.

You also need read/write access for Everyone to a shared folder on the network. This shared folder can be on a file server running either Windows Server 2012 R2 or an earlier version of Windows Server.

You should be logged on interactively to HOST4 using a user account that is a member of the local Administrators group.

Exercise 1: Designing and implementing Group Policy

In this exercise, you design an OU structure to support Group Policy, create Starter GPOs, and configure your environment to support a remote refresh of Group Policy.

1. Design and create an OU structure for the corp.fabrikam.com domain that satisfies the following requirements:

   - Fabrikam has its offices located in Chicago and currently has no branch offices.
   - The departments called Executive, HR, IT, and Marketing each have different security requirements for their users and computers.
   - All servers are managed by the IT department.
   - The Remote Desktop Session Host (RDSH) servers have different security requirements than Fabrikam's other servers do.
   - Users in the HR department have only desktops.
   - Users in the Marketing department have only laptops.
   - Users in the Executive and IT departments have both desktops and laptops.

2. Create the following Starter GPOs:

   - **Start-Computers**   You will use this Starter GPO in the next exercise for creating GPOs that will be linked to any OUs containing child OUs for different types of computers.
   - **Start-Users**   You will use this Starter GPO in the next exercise for creating GPOs that will be linked to containers for all types of users except those in the IT department.

- **Start-RDS**   You will use this Starter GPO in the next exercise to configure the security for Fabrikam's RDSH servers.

- **Start-Member**   You will use this Starter GPO in the next exercise to configure the security for Fabrikam's other member servers.

3. Configure a few appropriate policies in each of the new Starter GPOs you just created.

4. Create a new GPO called Refresh that you can use to enable a remote refresh of Group Policy on computers targeted by the GPO. Do not link the new GPO to any container in Active Directory.

Exercise 2: Creating and managing GPOs using Windows PowerShell

In this exercise, you use the Refresh GPO you created in the previous exercise to enable remote refresh of Group Policy for all computers except those used by the IT department. You then create new GPOs from the Starter GPOs you created in the previous exercise and link them to different OUs in your Active Directory infrastructure. Finally, you back up all the GPOs you just created so that you can restore quickly in the event of a disaster, and you test your backup by performing a restore. You perform all tasks in this exercise using Windows PowerShell. Follow these steps:

1. Use the New-GPLink cmdlet to link the Refresh GPO to the OUs that contain computers for different departments except for the IT department.

2. Use the New-StarterGPO, New-GPO, and New-GPLink cmdlets to create and link new GPOs to any OUs containing child OUs for different types of computers.

3. Use the New-StarterGPO, New-GPO, and New-GPLink cmdlets to create and link new GPOs to containers for all types of users except those in the IT department.

4. Use the New-StarterGPO, New-GPO, and New-GPLink cmdlets to create and link new GPOs to configure the security for Fabrikam's RDSH servers.

5. Use the New-StarterGPO, New-GPO, and New-GPLink cmdlets to create and link new GPOs to configure the security for Fabrikam's other member servers.

6. Use the Get-GPO and Backup-GPO cmdlets to back up all GPOs in the corp.fabrikam. com domain to a shared folder on the network.

7. Use the Get-ChildItem cmdlet to verify that the backup was successful.

8. Delete one of the GPOs in your environment.

9. Use the Restore-GPO cmdlet to restore the deleted GPO and its link.

10. Open the restored GPO in the Group Policy Management Editor and verify that the restored GPO contains the policies of the deleted GPO.

Suggested practice exercises

The following additional practice exercises are designed to give you more opportunities to practice what you've learned and to help you successfully master the lessons presented in this chapter.

- **Exercise 1**   Explore using different Group Policy preference extensions to configure different types of settings for Windows clients in your environment.

- **Exercise 2**   Write a Windows PowerShell script that creates a hierarchy of OUs and then creates a new GPO linked to each OU in your hierarchy.

- **Exercise 3**   Learn how to use "AppLocker Cmdlets in Windows PowerShell" at *http://technet.microsoft.com/en-us/library/hh847210*.

Answers

This section contains the answers to the lesson review questions in this chapter.

Lesson 1

1. **Correct answer: D**

   A. **Incorrect:** A flat OU structure like this does not necessarily have more OUs than a hierarchical structure designed for the same purpose. In fact, a hierarchical OU structure often has more OUs and therefore more GPOs.

   B. **Incorrect:** A flat OU structure like this does not necessarily have more OUs than a hierarchical structure designed for the same purpose. In fact, a hierarchical OU structure often has more OUs and therefore more GPOs.

   C. **Incorrect:** Group Policy inheritance can make delegation of authority over GPOs easier to implement. It does not necessarily make a GPO environment more manageable, however.

   D. **Correct:** Group Policy delegation is more difficult to implement in a flat OU structure because Group Policy inheritance cannot be used to pass policies from parent OUs to child OUs.

2. **Correct answers: A, B, and C**

   A. **Correct:** Group Policy remote refresh will not work if the necessary firewall ports on the targeted computers have not been opened.

   B. **Correct:** Group Policy remote refresh will not work if the GPO that should be linked to the OU has become unlinked from the OU.

   C. **Correct:** Group Policy remote refresh will refresh User Configuration policies on the targeted computers only if the Computer Configuration portion of the GPO linked to the OU has been disabled.

   D. **Incorrect:** The Group Policy Remote Update Firewall Ports Starter GPO makes it easier to enable remote refresh of Group Policy on targeted computers. However, you can also enable remote refresh of Group Policy by manually opening the necessary firewall ports on targeted computers or by running a Netsh or Windows PowerShell script to do this.

3. **Correct answer: D**

   A. **Incorrect:** Selecting the root node in the GPMC displays a shortcut to the forest root domain node. Right-clicking this node allows you to add another forest to the console.

   B. **Incorrect:** Selecting the node named Forest: <forest_root_domain_name> displays shortcuts to various nodes in the console. Right-clicking this node allows you to search for GPOs in all domains in the forest.

C. **Incorrect:** Selecting the node named Domain displays a shortcut to the node named <domain_name>. Right-clicking this node allows you to choose which domains to show, manage GPO backups, and open the Migration Table Editor.

D. **Correct:** Selecting the node named <domain_name> allows you to view the current status of SYSVOL replication as it relates to Group Policy in a domain.

Lesson 2

1. **Correct answer: B**

   A. **Incorrect:** You can use Get-StarterGPO and New-GPO to create a new GPO from a Starter GPO but not to link the new GPO.

   B. **Correct:** You can use New-GPO and New-GPLink to create a new GPO and link the GPO using a single command by piping the output of New-GPO into New-GPLink.

   C. **Incorrect:** You can use New-GPO to create a new GPO. You can use Set-GPLink to set the properties of an existing GPO link but not to create a new GPO link.

   D. **Incorrect:** You can use Get-GPO and New-GPLink to link an existing GPO but not to create and link a new GPO.

2. **Correct answer: D**

   A. **Incorrect:** The dash prefixing All indicates that All is a parameter, not the name of a GPO.

   B. **Incorrect:** The dash prefixing All indicates that All is a parameter, not the name of a GPO.

   C. **Incorrect:** \\HOST6\GpoBackups is a network path, not a local path.

   D. **Correct:** The parameter –*All* indicates that all GPOs should be backed up. The parameter –*Path* specifies a UNC path, which means the GPOs will be backed up to a shared folder on the network.

Lesson 3

1. **Correct answers: B and C**

   A. **Incorrect:** Unlike policies, which can be configured in both domain and local GPOs, preferences can be configured only in domain GPOs. This means that if you open the Local Computer Policy on a computer by running gpedit.msc, you will not see a Preferences node under Computer Configuration or User Configuration.

   B. **Correct:** A few policies and preferences overlap and allow you to configure the same setting for targeted users or computers. To resolve such situations, policies always have priority over preferences.

   C. **Correct:** When creating a new preference item, selecting the Create action creates a new preference item for the targeted user or computer. In contrast, selecting the

Replace action deletes and re-creates the preference item for the targeted user or computer.

    D.   **Incorrect:** To select a variable when configuring a preference item, open the properties of the preference item, click in any field in which a variable can be used, and press F3 to open the Select A Variable dialog box.

2.   **Correct answer: D**

    A.   **Incorrect:** A MAC Address Range targeting item allows a preference item to be applied to computers or users only if any of the processing computer's MAC addresses are within the range specified in the targeting item.

    B.   **Incorrect:** An Organizational Unit targeting item allows a preference item to be applied to computers or users only if the user or computer is a member of the organizational unit (OU) specified in the targeting item.

    C.   **Incorrect:** A Registry Match targeting item allows a preference item to be applied to computers or users only if the registry key or value specified in the targeting item exists, if the registry value contains the data specified in the targeting item, or if the version number in the registry value is within the range specified in the targeting item.

    D.   **Correct:** There is no Desktop Computer targeting item available. However, you could use the Portable Computer targeting option for this purpose and select Is Not instead of Is for the targeting condition.

3.   **Correct answer: A**

    A.   **Correct:** A preference extension can contain one or more preference items. If this option is selected, a preference item that fails to apply will not prevent the remaining preference items in the extension from processing.

    B.   **Incorrect:** By default, preferences are processed using the security context of the SYSTEM account on the client. If this option is selected, the preference will be processed using the security context of the currently logged-on user on the client, which allows user-specific environment variables to be used in file system paths.

    C.   **Incorrect:** By default, preference items are not removed from the client when the GPO targeting the user or computer goes out of scope. Selecting this option causes the preference item to be removed from the client when the GPO targeting the user or computer goes out of scope, which is done by deleting and then re-creating the preference item.

    D.   **Incorrect:** By default, a preference item configured in a GPO applies to all users and computers targeted by that GPO. You can select this option to change this behavior.

CHAPTER 11

Configuring Windows Firewall and IPsec

P rotecting an organization's computers is a key role of every IT administrator. Two essential technologies that can help ensure your computers are secure are firewalls and Internet Protocol security (IPsec). Microsoft Windows Server 2012 and Windows Server 2012 R2 include a host-based firewall called Windows Firewall with Advanced Security that helps you protect the servers on your network. Windows Firewall with Advanced Security is also included in the Windows 8 client operating system.

But protecting individual computers on your network is not enough. You must also be able to protect the network traffic that flows between your computers and between your computers and other computers outside the corporate network. You can accomplish this by configuring IPsec on the computers that need to communicate with one another. Windows Firewall with Advanced Security also includes built-in functionality for configuring IPsec on the computer.

This chapter shows how to use Windows Firewall with Advanced Security to configure both firewall and IPsec functionality on computers running Windows Server 2012 or Windows Server 2012 R2.

Lessons in this chapter:

Before you begin

- You need to know how to perform a clean install of Windows Server 2012 or Windows Server 2012 R2 and perform initial configuration tasks such as configuring the server's TCP/IP settings for Internet connectivity.

- You need to know how to deploy Active Directory using Windows Server 2012 or Windows Server 2012 R2 and how to join computers to a domain.

- You also need to have at least rudimentary knowledge of using Windows PowerShell.

Lesson 1: Configuring Windows Firewall with Advanced Security

Firewalls are a key technology for helping ensure the security of an information systems infrastructure. Perimeter firewalls act as gateways to provide a first level of defense against network intrusion, but host-based firewalls are equally important for both client and server systems because they provide an additional layer of protection. This lesson examines how to configure the host firewall functionality of Windows Firewall with Advanced Security on Windows Server 2012 and Windows Server 2012 R2.

After this lesson, you will be able to:

- Describe the architecture and operation of Windows Firewall with Advanced Security.
- Explain how firewall profiles work and how they can be configured.
- Describe the different types of firewall rules supported by Windows Firewall with Advanced Security.
- Explain the order in which Windows Firewall with Advanced Security processes firewall rules.
- Create firewall rules using the Windows Firewall with Advanced Security snap-in and Windows PowerShell.
- Configure firewall rules on target computers using Group Policy.

Estimated lesson time: 30 minutes

Understanding Windows Firewall with Advanced Security

Windows Firewall with Advanced Security is a host-based, stateful firewall included in Windows Server 2012, Windows Server 2012 R2, Windows 8, and Windows 8.1. The feature was first introduced in Windows Vista and Windows Server 2008, and its functionality has been enhanced in several ways in later Windows versions.

 As a *host-based firewall*, Windows Firewall with Advanced Security is designed to protect the local computer—unlike a perimeter firewall, which is designed to protect the network itself. However, to protect a network, you also need to protect each computer on the network because if even a single computer is compromised, it could provide an attacker with a way to compromise the rest of the network.

As a *stateful firewall*, Windows Firewall with Advanced Security can keep track of the state of packets as they travel across the network. Packets that match a specified rule can be either allowed or denied depending on how the rule has been configured. Windows Firewall with

Advanced Security can inspect and filter both inbound and outbound packets, and it supports both Internet Protocol version 4 (IPv4) and Internet Protocol version 6 (IPv6).

Windows Firewall with Advanced Security also includes built-in functionality for creating rules that govern IPsec communications. This means you can use Windows Firewall with Advanced Security to encrypt and secure communications between computers on the network.

Windows Firewall with Advanced Security interoperates with other Windows features to help ensure the security of the computer. To fully understand how Windows Firewall with Advanced Security works, you need to understand these other features:

- Windows Filtering Platform
- Windows service hardening
- Network location awareness

Windows Filtering Platform

Windows Filtering Platform (WFP) is a collection of application programming interfaces (APIs) and system services that allow for the creation of network-filtering applications on Windows Vista or later. By using WFP, third-party developers can create host-based security tools such as these:

- Firewalls
- Intrusion-detection systems
- Network-monitoring tools
- Antivirus programs
- Parental controls

WFP is also the underlying engine used for implementing packet-filtering logic in Windows Firewall with Advanced Security. The components of WFP include the following:

- **Base Filter Engine (BFE)** This component runs in user mode and receives filtering requests from Windows Firewall with Advanced Security. Such requests are then forwarded to the Generic Filter Engine.

- **Generic Filter Engine (GFE)** This component runs in kernel mode and receives filtering requests from the BFE. The GFE then makes such requests available to callout modules that map to different layers of the Transmission Control Protocol/Internet Protocol (TCP/IP) protocol stack. As the TCP/IP protocol stack processes a packet, each callout module calls the GFE to determine whether to accept or reject the packet.

- **Callout modules** These run in kernel mode and are used by the GFE to inspect the different layers of a packet as the packet is passed down the TCP/IP protocol stack. For example, the Transport Layer module is used to inspect the Transport Layer protocol portion of the packet, which is either TCP or User Datagram Protocol (UDP).

When you start a computer running Windows Vista or later, Windows Firewall with Advanced Security initially uses boot-time filters to protect the system during the early stages of the boot process. Once the BFE starts, the boot-time filters are replaced by persistent filters that are stored in the registry and applied whenever the BFE is running. Once the Windows Firewall service starts, the policy rules and settings that have been configured for Windows Firewall with Advanced Security are applied.

Windows service hardening

Windows service hardening is a collection of strategies that helps protect critical Windows services from behaving abnormally. Windows service hardening is thus designed to help reduce the possible damage that could occur if a Windows service is compromised by an attacker.

Windows service hardening is implemented using strategies such as the following:

- Using LocalService or NetworkService instead of LocalSystem as the security context for a service whenever possible

- Assigning services only the minimum Windows privileges they need to perform their function

- Implementing per-service identity using the per-service security identifier (SID), which allows services to apply explicit access control lists (ACLs) to resources used only by the service

- Applying a write-restricted access token to the service process so that attempts by the service to write to resources that do not explicitly grant access to the per-service SID will fail

Windows service hardening also protects Windows services by using service restriction rules, which are not user-configurable. Service restriction rules define the types of network packets that can be transmitted by or received from a Windows service. When a packet is being examined, service restriction rules are applied before Windows Firewall with Advanced Security rules are applied.

Network location awareness

Network location awareness is a feature of Windows Vista and later that allows network-aware applications to change their behavior based on the computer's network connectivity. The three network location types that a computer running Windows can detect are these:

- **Public**   A computer on a public network is considered to be shared with the world. By default, when a Windows computer connects to a new network for the first time, the network location type for that network is configured as public.

- **Private** A computer on a private network is not directly accessible by the world. To configure the network location type of a Windows computer as private, you must be a local administrator on the computer.
- **Domain** A computer that belongs to an Active Directory domain is automatically assigned a network location type of domain.

Windows Firewall with Advanced Security uses network location awareness to determine which firewall profile will be used for protecting each connection on the computer. This is described in more detail in the next section.

> *NOTE* **NETWORK LOCATION AWARENESS ON MULTIHOMED COMPUTERS**
>
> If a computer is multihomed (connected to more than one network), each connection is assigned the appropriate network location type based on the type of network to which it is connected.

Managing firewall profiles 5

Computers today are often connected to different networks at different times, and they might even be connected to several networks at the same time. Each type of network can have a different set of security requirements:

- A computer connected to a public network should consider that network unsafe because of the threat of malware from the Internet. As a result, Windows Firewall with Advanced Security on such a computer should be configured to restrict most forms of traffic.
- A computer connected to a private network, such as a small office/home office (SOHO) with Internet access provided by a network address translation (NAT) router, should have Windows Firewall with Advanced Security configured in a less restrictive way than for a public network. This is necessary to allow the computer to communicate freely with other computers on the same private network.
- A computer that belongs to an Active Directory domain should have Windows Firewall with Advanced Security configured even less restrictively than for a private network. This is because Active Directory environments usually include additional layers of security, such as perimeter firewalls that further isolate the network from the outside world.

A typical day with an enterprise laptop might be as follows:

1. Bob brings his laptop to work, inserts it into the docking station, turns it on, and logs on to Active Directory.

2. Bob takes a lunch break and decides to get more work done, so he uses the Wi-Fi hotspot at the coffee shop to establish a connection to the Internet and browses the news for a while. Because his company has implemented DirectAccess, Bob can safely connect to resources on his company's network even while he's connected to the public Internet.

3. When Bob returns to the office, he is informed that he has to visit a small customer site to help the customers troubleshoot a problem on their workgroup network. When Bob arrives at the customer site, he connects his laptop to their network so that he can help them resolve their problem.

4. While connected to the customer's network, Bob realizes he needs to access a resource on his own company's network. Unfortunately, the NAT router on the customer's network has not been configured to allow DirectAccess traffic, so Bob has to establish a virtual private network (VPN) connection to his company's network.

Examining the day just described for Bob, you can see that the following scenarios came into play:

1. In the morning, Bob connects to one network (his company's network). This network has a network location type of domain.

2. At lunch, Bob connects to two networks:

   - A Wi-Fi network, which has a network location type of public

   - His company's network (via DirectAccess), which has a network location type of domain

3. At the customer site, Bob initially connects to one network (the customer's network). Because this network is a workgroup and not a domain, the network location type is private.

4. Later at the customer site, Bob needs to remain connected to the customer's network while also connecting to his own company's network. To do this, Bob establishes a VPN connection to his company's network. At this point, Bob is connected to two networks:

   - The customer's network, which has a network location type of private

   - His own company's network, which has a network location type of domain

Although the preceding example uses client systems, it's common for servers to be multihomed and connected to multiple networks in certain scenarios. For example, a clustered Hyper-V host in a production environment might be simultaneously connected to the following networks:

- **Production network**   This is the network that client systems are able to access and from which they can consume services.

- **Management network**   This network is used only for managing the servers using a systems-management platform such as Microsoft System Center Configuration Manager.

- **Failover clustering network**   This network is used for failover cluster communications, such as heartbeat communications, and for connecting to a cluster shared volume (CSV).

- **Live migration network**   This network is used to support the live migration of virtual machines.

Multihomed servers are also common in edge scenarios in which the server is connected to both the corporate intranet and the public Internet.

Windows Firewall with Advanced Security makes securing the preceding scenarios possible by implementing a separate firewall profile for each network connection on the computer. A *firewall profile* is a grouping of firewall rules and other configuration settings that are applied to a network connection that has a specific network location type. Windows Firewall with Advanced Security applies firewall profiles to all types of network connections on the computer, including network adapters and tunnel interfaces.

Windows Firewall with Advanced Security has three firewall profiles, which correspond to the three network location types on the Windows platform:

- **Domain profile** This profile is automatically applied to any network connection that Windows identifies as having a network location type of domain.
- **Private profile** This profile is automatically applied to any network connection that Windows identifies as having a network location type of private.
- **Public profile** This profile is automatically applied to any network connection that Windows identifies as having a network location type of public.

All three profiles can be active at the same time on a computer if Windows detects that there are network connections of each type present. You can view the status of each firewall profile on a computer by opening the Windows Firewall with Advanced Security Microsoft Management Console (MMC) snap-in. One way of doing this on Windows Server 2012 or Windows Server 2012 R2 is by selecting Windows Firewall with Advanced Security from the Tools menu of Server Manager. Once the snap-in is open, select the root node in the console tree and examine the Overview section in the details pane.

Figure 11-1 shows an example of this for a computer that has only one network connection of the domain type. Note that all three profiles have Windows Firewall turned on for them, but only the domain profile is active. The other profiles are turned on so that if a connection to a private or public network is established on the computer, firewall protection will immediately be implemented for such a connection.

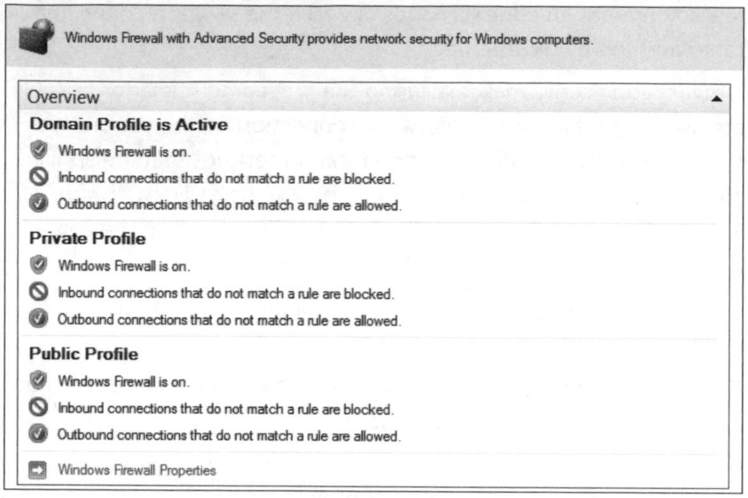

FIGURE 11-1 View the status of firewall profiles.

Configuring profiles

By default, all three firewall profiles are enabled on Windows computers. You can change the state of any profile or configure its properties by right-clicking the root node in the Windows Firewall with Advanced Security snap-in and selecting Properties. Doing this opens the Windows Firewall with Advanced Security properties shown in Figure 11-2.

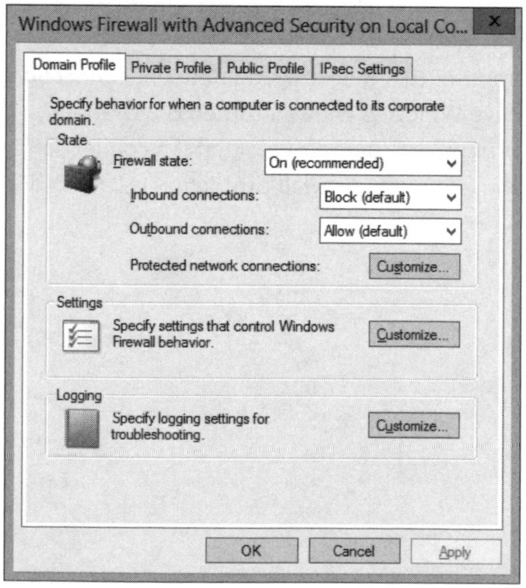

FIGURE 11-2 Configure the firewall profile settings.

You can use this properties dialog box to configure the following properties for the selected profile:

- **Firewall State** You use this setting to enable or disable Windows Firewall with Advanced Security for the selected profile. Microsoft recommends that you always leave this set to On.

- **Inbound Connections** You use this setting to configure how Windows Firewall with Advanced Security handles incoming traffic. These are the three available options:

  - **Block** Blocks all connections that do not have firewall rules that explicitly allow the connection

  - **Block All Connections** Blocks all connections, regardless of any firewall rules that explicitly allow the connection

  - **Allow** Allows the connection unless there is a firewall rule that explicitly blocks the connection

  The default value for the inbound connections property is Block. This means that if an inbound rule for the profile explicitly allows a certain type of incoming traffic, the host will accept any traffic matching that rule. But if a certain type of incoming traffic does not match any of the inbound rules for the profile, the host will not accept that type of traffic.

- **Outbound Connections** You use this setting to configure how Windows Firewall with Advanced Security handles outgoing traffic. The only two options available here are Block and Allow. The default setting for the Outbound Connections property is Allow, which means that all traffic leaving the host is allowed to pass through the firewall unless an explicit outbound rule prohibits this for a certain type of outgoing traffic.

- **Protected Network Connections** This setting opens a dialog box you can use to specify which network connections should be protected by the rules associated with the selected profile. For example, on a multihomed computer with two network connections to different networks of type private, the dialog box for the private profile would display two check boxes. By default, both private networks would be protected, but by clearing the check boxes you can disable this protection for either or both networks.

The Settings and Logging options are described in the next two sections.

Configuring profile settings

Clicking Customize in the Settings section of a profile's properties opens the dialog box shown in Figure 11-3, which you can use to specify other settings that control the behavior of Windows Firewall with Advanced Security. For example, you can do the following:

- Specify whether Windows Firewall with Advanced Security should display a notification to the user when a program on the user's computer is blocked from receiving inbound connections. When such a notification is displayed, the user can select an option that unblocks the program as long as the user has sufficient privileges (belongs to the local Administrators or Network Configuration Operators security group). When the user chooses to unblock a program, an inbound program rule for the program is automatically created on the user's computer.

- Allow unicast responses to multicast or broadcast requests to allow Windows Firewall with Advanced Security to wait several seconds for unicast responses from other computers to which the local computer has sent multicast or broadcast messages.

- Rule merging allows users who are members of the local Administrators or Network Configuration Operators security group on the computer to create and apply local rules that are merged with any rules being applied to the computer by Group Policy.

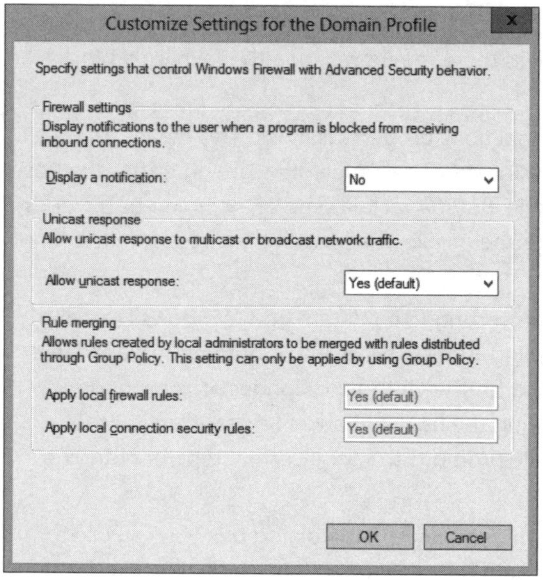

FIGURE 11-3 Configure other settings for a firewall profile.

Configuring logging

Clicking Customize in the Logging section of a profile's properties opens the dialog box shown in Figure 11-4, which you can use to specify how Windows Firewall with Advanced Security logging operations will behave for the selected profile. For example, you can do the following:

- Specify a location for the firewall log file to be saved.

- Specify the maximum size in kilobytes (KBs) to which the log file can grow. Once the log file reaches this size, the file has .old appended to its file name and a second file is created. When the second file reaches the maximum size, the existing *.old file is deleted and the second file becomes the new *.old file.

- Specify whether a log entry should be created when Windows Firewall with Advanced Security disallows a connection for any reason. These entries can be identified by the word DROP in the Action field.

- Specify whether a log entry should be created when Windows Firewall with Advanced Security allows an inbound connection for any reason. These entries can be identified by the word ALLOW in the Action field.

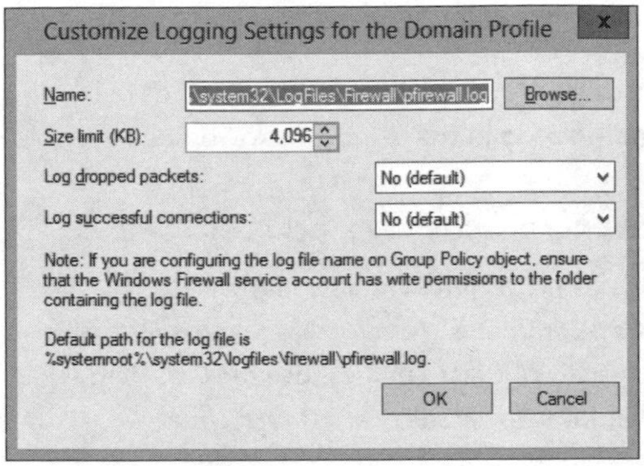

FIGURE 11-4 Configure logging for a firewall profile.

> **NOTE FIREWALL OPERATIONAL LOGS**
>
> Another useful source for viewing information about firewall policy changes for Windows Firewall with Advanced Security is the operational log found here in Event Viewer:
>
> ```
> Applications and Services Logs/Microsoft/Windows/Windows Firewall with
> Advanced Security/Firewall
> ```
>
> You can also enable the FirewallVerbose operational log if you need more detailed information about firewall policy events.

Configuring profiles using Windows PowerShell

You can also use Windows PowerShell to view and configure settings for firewall profiles. For example, you can use the Get-NetFirewallProfile cmdlet to display the currently active settings for the domain profile on the local computer like this:

```
PS C:\> Get-NetFirewallProfile -Name Domain -PolicyStore ActiveStore

Name                       : Domain
Enabled                    : True
DefaultInboundAction       : Block
DefaultOutboundAction      : Allow
AllowInboundRules          : True
AllowLocalFirewallRules    : True
AllowLocalIPsecRules       : True
AllowUserApps              : True
```

```
AllowUserPorts                   : True
AllowUnicastResponseToMulticast  : True
NotifyOnListen                   : False
EnableStealthModeForIPsec        : True
LogFileName                      : %systemroot%\system32\LogFiles\Firewall\pfirewall.log
LogMaxSizeKilobytes              : 4096
LogAllowed                       : False
LogBlocked                       : False
LogIgnored                       : True
DisabledInterfaceAliases         :
```

To modify any of these profile settings, use the Set-NetFirewallProfile cmdlet. For help using this cmdlet, type **Get-Help Set-NetFirewallProfile** in the Windows PowerShell console.

> ***MORE INFO*** **WINDOWS FIREWALL WITH ADVANCED SECURITY CMDLETS**
>
> To display a list of all Windows Firewall with Advanced Security cmdlets in the NetSecurity module for Windows PowerShell, type **Get-Command –Module NetSecurity** in the Windows PowerShell console. To get help for any of these cmdlets, use the Get-Help cmdlet or see "Network Security Cmdlets in Windows PowerShell" at *http://technet .microsoft.com/en-us/library/jj554906.aspx*.

Configuring firewall rules

The core functionality of Windows Firewall with Advanced Security is expressed by rules. A *rule* is a set of criteria that determines whether a network packet should be handled. The two basic types of rules you can configure in Windows Firewall with Advanced Security are

- **Firewall rule**   A set of criteria that specifies whether a particular type of traffic passing between the local computer and other computers on the network should be accepted (passed) or rejected (blocked).
- **Connection security rule**   A set of criteria that specifies how traffic passing between the local computer and other computers on the network should be protected using IPsec.

The remainder of this lesson deals with firewall rules. Connection security rules are covered in Lesson 2 later in this chapter.

Types of firewall rules

As Figure 11-5 shows, you can use Windows Firewall with Advanced Security to configure two types of firewall rules:

- **Inbound rule**   A rule that specifies how incoming network traffic should be handled—that is, traffic originating from other computers and having the local computer as its destination

- **Outbound rule** A rule that specifies how outgoing network traffic should be handled—that is, traffic originating from the local computer and having other computers or network devices as its destination

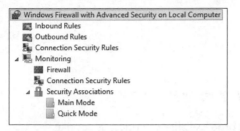

FIGURE 11-5 Firewall rules can be either inbound or outbound.

You can configure both inbound and outbound rules to either allow (permit) or deny (block) traffic based on the criteria contained in the rule. Because many types of network traffic are possible, Windows Firewall with Advanced Security also has special rules called *default rules* that determine how traffic should be handled when it doesn't match any of the criteria contained in any of the inbound and outbound rules. Unless otherwise configured by the system's administrator, the default rules for all three firewall profiles are as follows:

- **Inbound default rule** Block all traffic originating from other computers and having the local computer as its destination
- **Outbound default rule** Allow all traffic originating from the local computer and having other computers or network devices as its destination

You can configure the inbound and outbound default rules for each firewall profile on the corresponding tab of the properties sheet of the root node in the Windows Firewall with Advanced Security snap-in. To see how to do this, refer to Figure 11-2 earlier in this chapter.

Rules processing

When Windows Firewall with Advanced Security processes a packet of network traffic, one or more rules might apply to that particular packet. Figure 11-6 shows the order in which rules are applied to both inbound and outbound traffic, which is as follows:

1. Any rules that allow traffic that would otherwise be blocked are applied first. These rules have the Override Block Rules option selected, and they are discussed in Lesson 2 later in this chapter. If the packet matches such a rule, the rule is applied and rules processing stops at this point.

2. Rules that explicitly block traffic are applied second. If the packet matches such a rule, the rule is applied and rules processing stops at this point.

3. Rules that explicitly allow traffic are applied third. If the packet matches such a rule, the rule is applied and rules processing stops at this point.

4. The default rule is applied last.

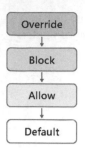

FIGURE 11-6 Windows Firewall with Advanced Security processes rules in this order.

When Windows Firewall with Advanced Security processes firewall rules, as soon as a packet matches a rule the rule is applied and rules processing stops at that point. For example, if a block rule (described in step 2) blocks a particular type of packet, an allow rule (described in step 3) for the same type of packet would not be applied because allow rules have a lower priority than block rules. So the net result is to block that particular type of packet.

Rule groups

Windows Firewall with Advanced Security includes a number of predefined inbound and outbound rules. These rules are used for filtering the different types of traffic associated with different Windows features and services. As Figure 11-7 shows, these predefined rules are grouped into *rule groups*. Each rule group contains one or more rules used to control traffic for a particular Windows feature or service. For example, the Windows Remote Management (HTTP-In) rule group contains two rules: one that applies to only the public profile and another that applies to both the domain and private profiles.

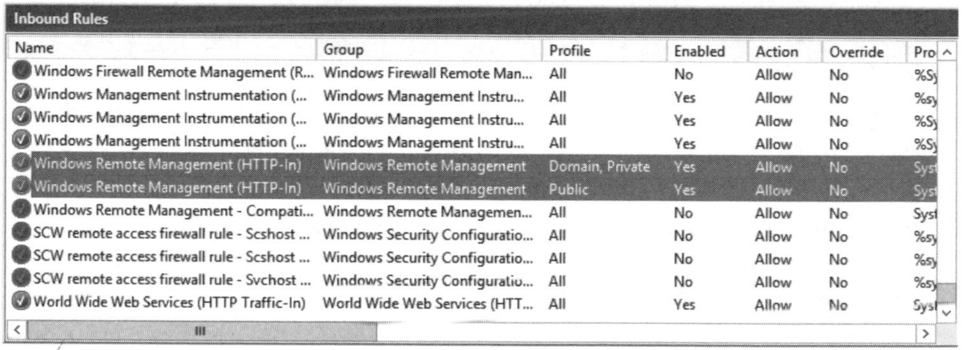

Inbound Rules

Name	Group	Profile	Enabled	Action	Override	Pro
Windows Firewall Remote Management (R...	Windows Firewall Remote Man...	All	No	Allow	No	%Sy
Windows Management Instrumentation (...	Windows Management Instru...	All	Yes	Allow	No	%sy
Windows Management Instrumentation (...	Windows Management Instru...	All	Yes	Allow	No	%Sy
Windows Management Instrumentation (...	Windows Management Instru...	All	Yes	Allow	No	%Sy
Windows Remote Management (HTTP-In)	Windows Remote Management	Domain, Private	Yes	Allow	No	Sys
Windows Remote Management (HTTP-In)	Windows Remote Management	Public	Yes	Allow	No	Sys
Windows Remote Management - Compati...	Windows Remote Managemen...	All	No	Allow	No	Syst
SCW remote access firewall rule - Scshost ...	Windows Security Configuratio...	All	No	Allow	No	%sy
SCW remote access firewall rule - Scshost ...	Windows Security Configuratio...	All	No	Allow	No	%sy
SCW remote access firewall rule - Svchost ...	Windows Security Configuratio...	All	No	Allow	No	%sy
World Wide Web Services (HTTP Traffic-In)	World Wide Web Services (HTT...	All	Yes	Allow	No	Syst

FIGURE 11-7 This is an example of a rule group.

Creating firewall rules

You can manually create new firewall rules (either inbound or outbound) using either Windows Firewall with Advanced Security or Windows PowerShell. As Figure 11-8 shows, there are four types of firewall rules you can create:

- **Program rule**   This is a rule that specifies how traffic associated with a specific program (executable) running on the local computer should be handled.

- **Port rule**   This is a rule that specifies how traffic associated with a specific TCP or UDP port or port range on the local computer should be handled.

- **Predefined rule**   This is a rule that specifies how traffic associated with a specific Windows feature or service running on the local computer should be handled.

- **Custom rule**   This is a rule that specifies how traffic should be handled based on any of the traffic-filtering criteria supported by Windows Firewall with Advanced Security.

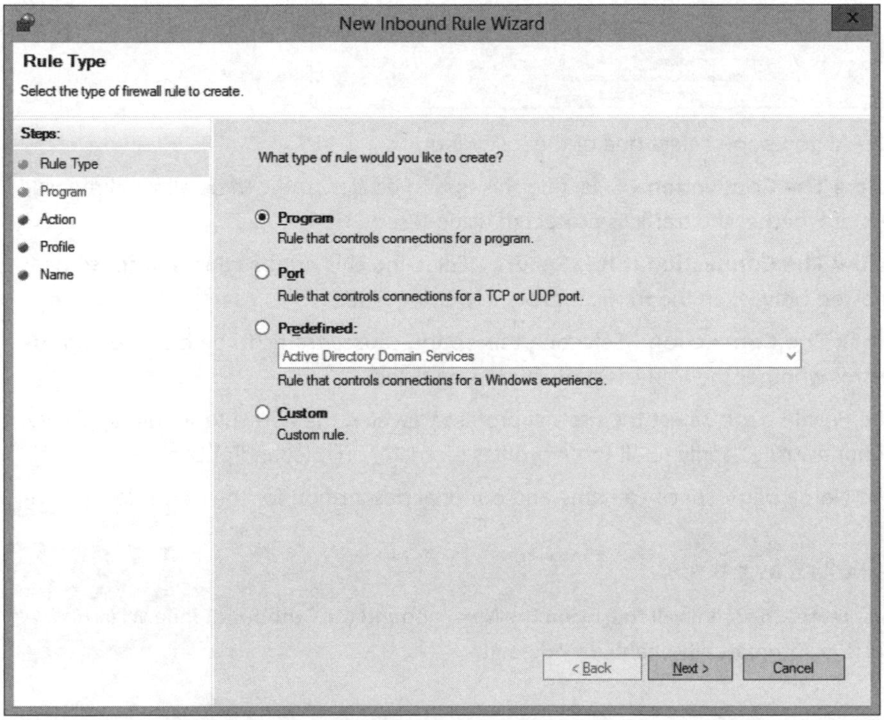

FIGURE 11-8   You can create these types of firewall rules using Windows Firewall with Advanced Security.

To create new firewall rules using the New Inbound (or Outbound) Rule Wizard, right-click the Inbound (or Outbound) node in the Windows Firewall with Advanced Security snap-in, select New Rule, and follow the steps of the wizard. The sections that follow explain more about the steps involved in creating each of these different types of firewall rules.

Creating a program rule

You can take the following steps to create a new program rule using the Windows Firewall with Advanced Security snap-in:

1. Launch the New Inbound (or Outbound) Rule Wizard and select Program on the Rule Type page.

2. On the Program page, specify the full program path and executable name of the program on the local computer to which you want the new rule to apply. Alternatively, you can select All Programs to have the new rule apply to all traffic that matches the criteria specified in the rule:

> Does this rule apply to all programs or a specific program?
>
> ● **All programs**
>   Rule applies to all connections on the computer that match other rule properties.
>
> ○ **This program path:**
>
>   [   ] [Browse...]
>
>   Example: c:\path\program.exe
>   %ProgramFiles%\browser\browser.exe

3. On the Action page, select one of the following:

   - **Allow The Connection**   Selecting this option causes traffic to be allowed regardless of whether the traffic is protected using IPsec.

   - **Allow The Connection If It Is Secure**   Selecting this option causes traffic to be allowed only when the traffic is protected using IPsec.

   - **Block The Connection**   Selecting this option causes traffic to be blocked regardless of whether the traffic is protected using IPsec.

4. On the Profile page, select the firewall profiles to which the new rule should apply. By default, new rules apply to all three profiles (domain, private, and public).

5. On the Name page, specify a name and optional description for the new rule.

> *NOTE* **ENABLED BY DEFAULT**
>
> When you create a new firewall rule using the New Inbound (or Outbound) Rule Wizard, the new rule is automatically enabled by default.

> *MORE INFO*   **THE ALLOW THE CONNECTION IF IT IS SECURE OPTION**
>
> The Allow The Connection If It Is Secure option will be discussed in more detail in Lesson 2, which covers connection security rules.

Creating a port rule

You can take the following steps to create a new port rule using the Windows Firewall with Advanced Security snap-in:

1. Launch the New Inbound (or Outbound) Rule Wizard and select Port on the Rule Type page.

2. On the Protocols And Ports page, begin by specifying whether the new rule should apply to TCP or UDP ports. Then specify whether the rule should apply to all local ports or to only specific ports:

Does this rule apply to TCP or UDP?

- ◉ **TCP**
- ○ **UDP**

Does this rule apply to all local ports or specific local ports?

- ○ **All local ports**
- ◉ **Specific local ports:** [   ]

  Example: 80, 443, 5000-5010

3. The options on the Action, Profile, and Name pages are the same as those described in the previous section.

Creating a predefined rule

You can take the following steps to create a new predefined rule using the Windows Firewall with Advanced Security snap-in:

1. Launch the New Inbound (or Outbound) Rule Wizard and select Predefined on the Rule Type page.

2. Click the list control shown in Figure 11-8 earlier and select the Windows feature or service that you will use the new rule to control.

3. On the Predefined Rules page, select one or more predefined rules to be created.

4. The options on the Action page are the same as those described earlier.

Once you have created a predefined rule, you can open its properties by double-clicking the rule in either the Inbound Rules or Outbound Rules sections of the Windows Firewall with Advanced Security snap-in. As Figure 11-9 shows, predefined rules are called out with a special informational message bar, and the administrator can configure only a subset of the criteria in the rule. This is true regardless of whether the predefined rule was created automatically when you installed its associated Windows feature or you manually created the rule.

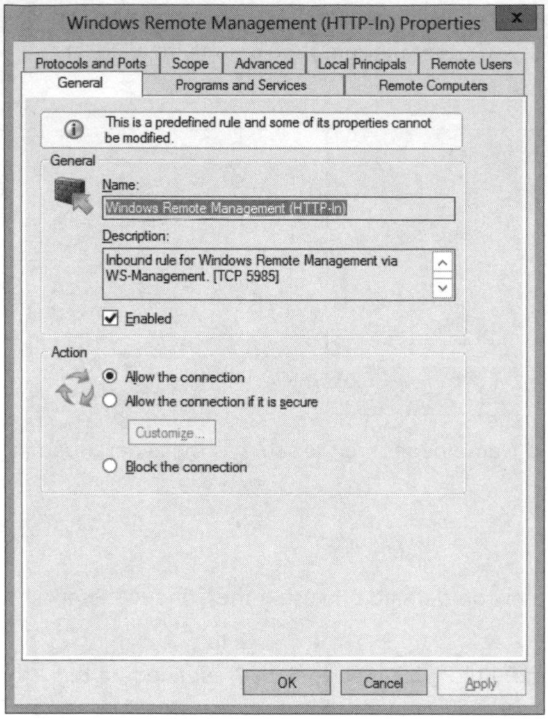

FIGURE 11-9 Predefined rules have limited options you can configure.

Creating a custom rule

You can take the following steps to create a new program rule using the Windows Firewall with Advanced Security snap-in:

1. Launch the New Inbound (or Outbound) Rule Wizard and select Custom on the Rule Type page.

2. On the Program page, specify the full program path and executable name of the program on the local computer to which you want the new rule to apply. Alternatively, you can select All Programs to have the new rule apply to all traffic that matches the criteria specified in the rule:

Does this rule apply to all programs or a specific program?

◉ **All programs**
Rule applies to all connections on the computer that match other rule properties.

○ **This program path:**

[   ] Browse...

Example: c:\path\program.exe
             %ProgramFiles%\browser\browser.exe

Services   Customize...
Specify which services this rule applies to.

You can also click Customize to specify the Windows services to which the new rule should apply. Doing this opens the Customize Service Settings dialog box, which you use to configure the rule so that it applies to one of the following:

- All programs and services running on the local computer
- All services running on the local computer
- A particular service running on the local computer
- A particular service that has a specified short name running on the local computer

Customize Service Settings   ✕

Apply this rule as follows:

◉ Apply to all programs and services
○ Apply to services only
○ Apply to this service:

Name	Short Name
Active Directory Domain Services	NTDS
Active Directory Web Services	ADWS
Application Experience	AeLookupSvc
Application Host Helper Service	AppHostSvc
Application Identity	AppIDSvc
Application Information	Appinfo
Application Layer Gateway Service	ALG
Application Management	AppMgmt
Background Intelligent Transfer Service	BITS

○ Apply to service with this service short name (example: eventlog):

[   ]

                                    OK   Cancel

3. On the Protocols And Ports page, begin by specifying the type of protocol to which the rule should apply. Supported protocol types include TCP, UDP, ICMPv4, IGMP, IPv6, ICMPv6, L2TP, and others. If you select either ICMPv4 or ICMPv6, you can click Customize to specify whether the rule should apply to all types or to specific types of ICMP messages. You can also select Any to have the rule apply to all types of protocols or select Custom to have the rule apply to a protocol number you specify.

Then specify whether the rule should apply to all local ports or only to specific ports for both local and remote ports:

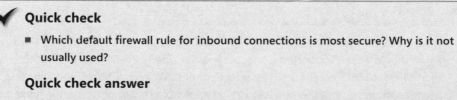

4. On the Scope page, specify the local and remote IP addresses to which the new rule should apply:

5. The options on the Action, Profile, and Name pages are the same as those described earlier.

> ✔ **Quick check**
>
> ■ Which default firewall rule for inbound connections is most secure? Why is it not usually used?
>
> **Quick check answer**
>
> ■ Block All Connections is the most secure because it blocks all inbound traffic to the local computer. This setting is usually not used, however, because it prevents the user from downloading webpages, receiving email, or otherwise communicating over the network.

Creating firewall rules using Windows PowerShell

You can also use Windows PowerShell cmdlets from the NetSecurity module to view, create, modify, and remove firewall rules on both the local and remote computers. For example, to display a list of inbound rules in the Network Discovery rule group on the local computer, you can use the Get-NetFirewallRule cmdlet like this:

```
PS C:\> Get-NetFirewallRule -PolicyStore ActiveStore `
-DisplayGroup "Network Discovery" -Direction Inbound | `
ft Name,DisplayName,Enabled,Action -AutoSize


Name                        DisplayName                            Enabled Action
----                        -----------                            ------- ------
NETDIS-UPnPHost-In-TCP      Network Discovery (UPnP-In)             False   Allow
NETDIS-NB_Name-In-UDP       Network Discovery (NB-Name-In)          False   Allow
NETDIS-NB_Datagram-In-UDP   Network Discovery (NB-Datagram-In)      False   Allow
NETDIS-WSDEVNTS-In-TCP      Network Discovery (WSD EventsSecure-In) False   Allow
NETDIS-WSDEVNT-In-TCP       Network Discovery (WSD Events-In)       False   Allow
NETDIS-SSDPSrv-In-UDP       Network Discovery (SSDP-In)             False   Allow
NETDIS-FDPHOST-In-UDP       Network Discovery (WSD-In)              False   Allow
NETDIS-LLMNR-In-UDP         Network Discovery (LLMNR-UDP-In)        False   Allow
NETDIS-FDRESPUB-WSD-In-UDP  Network Discovery (Pub-WSD-In)          False   Allow
```

As a second example, you can create a new rule to block outgoing traffic over TCP port 80 on the local computer by using the New-NetFirewallRule cmdlet as follows:

```
PS C:\> New-NetFirewallRule -DisplayName "Block Outbound Port 80" `
-Direction Outbound -LocalPort 80 -Protocol TCP -Action Block


Name                  : {19e3a3b5-ec0d-4e17-b98d-a0005e96bf20}
DisplayName           : Block Outbound Port 80
Description           :
DisplayGroup          :
Group                 :
Enabled               : True
Profile               : Any
Platform              : {}
Direction             : Outbound
Action                : Block
EdgeTraversalPolicy   : Block
LooseSourceMapping    : False
LocalOnlyMapping      : False
Owner                 :
PrimaryStatus         : OK
Status                : The rule was parsed successfully from the store. (65536)
EnforcementStatus     : NotApplicable
PolicyStoreSource     : PersistentStore
PolicyStoreSourceType : Local
```

The *PolicyStoreSource* property for the new rule is *PersistentStore*. This means the new rule is a static rule that is configured in the local policy store on the computer instead of through Group Policy. By default, the new rule is enabled and is configured for all three firewall profiles.

Creating rules for refreshing Group Policy

As indicated in Lesson 1 of Chapter 10, "Implementing Group Policy," beginning with Windows Server 2012 you can remotely force a refresh of Group Policy on computers belonging to an Active Directory domain. For this to work, certain firewall ports on the remote computer must be opened. Instead of manually creating the necessary rules in Windows Firewall with Advanced Security on the remote computer, you can use two new built-in Starter GPOs included in Windows Server 2012 and Windows Server 2012 R2 to create Group Policy Objects (GPOs) that have firewall rules designed for special purposes. These new Starter GPOs are shown in Figure 11-10 and are as follows:

- **Group Policy Remote Update Firewall Ports**   The Group Policy remote-refresh capability described in Chapter 10 requires that certain firewall ports be opened on the computers targeted by a refresh action. You can use the Group Policy Remote Update Firewall Ports Starter GPO as a template for creating a GPO that automatically opens the firewall ports required for this purpose on computers targeted by the GPO. The required inbound firewall rules that must be enabled are as follows:

  - Remote Scheduled Tasks Management (RPC-EPMAP)

  - Remote Scheduled Tasks Management (RPC)

  - Windows Management Instrumentation (WMI-in)

- **Group Policy Reporting Firewall Ports**   The capability of the Group Policy Management Console (GPMC) to collect Resultant Set of Policy (RSoP) information from a remote computer requires that certain firewall ports be opened on the remote computer. You can use the Group Policy Reporting Firewall Ports Starter GPO as a template for creating a GPO that automatically opens the firewall ports required for this purpose on computers targeted by the GPO. The required inbound firewall rules that must be enabled are as follows:

  - Remote Event Log Management (RPC-EPMAP)

  - Remote Event Log Management (RPC)

  - Remote Event Log Management (NP-in)

  - Windows Management Instrumentation (WMI-in)

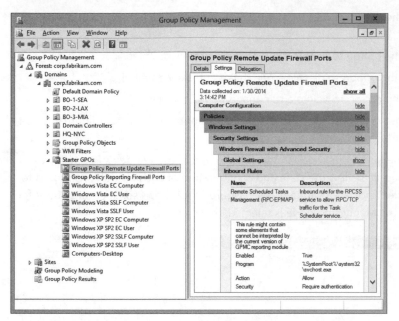

FIGURE 11-10 Firewall rules are defined in Starter GPOs for enabling a remote refresh of Group Policy.

Viewing and managing rules

You can view and manage firewall rules using either the Windows Firewall with Advanced Security snap-in or Windows PowerShell. As Figure 11-11 shows, you can use the Windows Firewall with Advanced Security snap-in to filter inbound or outbound rules in several ways:

- **Filter By Profile**   Use this option to display all rules associated with a specific firewall profile.

- **Filter By State**   Use this option to display either all enabled rules or all disabled rules.

- **Filter By Group**   Use this option to display all the rules associated with a specific rule group.

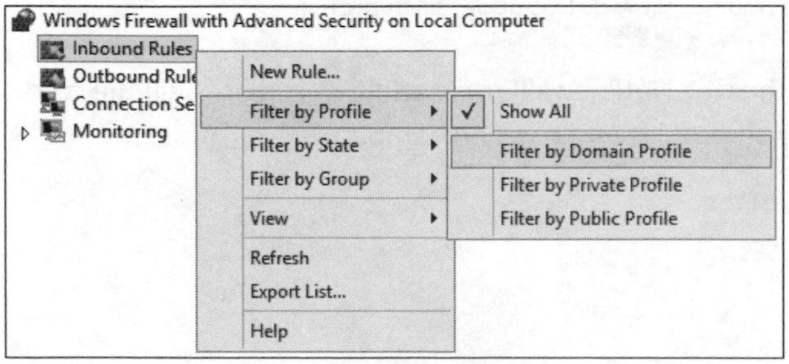

FIGURE 11-11 Filtering rules can make them easier to manage.

After you display the rules you want to manage, you can right-click them and select any of the following options:

- **Enable**   Use this option to enable a rule that is currently disabled.
- **Disable**   Use this option to disable a rule that is currently enabled.
- **Delete**   Use this option to delete a rule that is no longer needed.
- **Properties**   Use this option to open the properties of the rule and configure any editable criteria for the rule.

You can also use the Monitoring node in the console tree of the Windows Firewall with Advanced Security snap-in to view the state and configuration of each firewall profile and to view active firewall rules associated with a firewall. Figure 11-12 shows some details about the Domain Profile when the Monitoring node is selected on a computer.

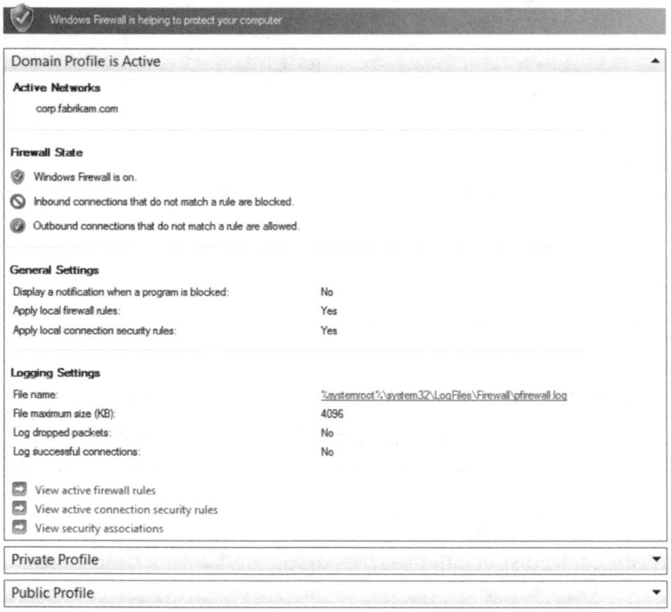

FIGURE 11-12 You can use the Monitoring node to view details about each profile.

As shown previously, you can use the Get-NetFirewallProfile and Get-NetFirewallRule cmdlets to display information about firewall profiles and rules on computers.

Configuring rules using Group Policy

Although Windows Firewall with Advanced Security is useful for configuring firewall rules and settings on the local computer, in managed environments you will want to use Group Policy to deploy firewall rules and settings on targeted computers. To do this, you can follow these steps:

1. Use the Group Policy Management Editor to either create a new GPO or open a GPO that targets the computers on which you want to deploy the firewall policy. You typically do this using the Group Policy Management Console.

2. Expand the console tree to display the following policy node (as shown in Figure 11-13):

```
Computer Configuration\Policies\Windows Settings\Security Settings
\Windows Firewall with Advanced Security\Windows Firewall with Advanced Security
```

FIGURE 11-13 Configure firewall rules and settings on targeted computers using Group Policy.

3. In the details pane, click Windows Firewall Properties if you want to deploy settings for firewall profiles to the targeted computers.

4. To deploy inbound rules to the targeted computers, right-click Inbound Rules and select New Rule. Then complete the steps in the New Inbound Rule Wizard to configure the new inbound rule.

5. To deploy outbound rules to the targeted computers, right-click Outbound Rules and select New Rule. Then complete the steps in the New Outbound Rule Wizard to configure the new outbound rule.

NOTE **CONNECTION SECURITY RULES**

Configuring connection security rules is discussed in the next lesson of this chapter.

You can also use Windows PowerShell to configure firewall rules and settings in a GPO and then use the GPO to deploy the firewall policy to targeted computers. For example, you can start by using the Get-NetFirewallProfile cmdlet to view the value of the NotifyOnListen policy setting for the domain firewall profile in the Sales GPO of the corp.fabrikam.com domain:

```
PS C:\> Get-NetFirewallProfile -Name Domain -PolicyStore corp.fabrikam.com\Sales | `
fl NotifyOnListen

NotifyOnListen : NotConfigured
```

The command output indicates that this firewall policy setting is not configured in the Sales GPO. To enable this setting, you can pipe the output of the preceding command into the Set-NetFirewallProfile command like this:

```
C:\> Get-NetFirewallProfile -Name Domain -PolicyStore corp.fabrikam.com\Sales | `
Set-NetFirewallProfile -NotifyOnListen True
```

You can use Get-NetFirewallProfile again to verify the result:

```
PS C:\> Get-NetFirewallProfile -Name Domain -PolicyStore corp.fabrikam.com\Sales | `
fl NotifyOnListen

NotifyOnListen : True
```

Now you can create a new rule to block outgoing traffic over TCP port 80 on computers targeted by the Sales GPO. To begin, using the Get-NetFirewallRule cmdlet to target the Sales GPO indicates that there are currently no firewall rules configured in this GPO:

```
PS C:\> Get-NetFirewallRule -PolicyStore corp.fabrikam.com\Sales
```

You can use the New-NetFirewallRule cmdlet to create the new rule in the GPO as follows:

```
PS C:\> New-NetFirewallRule -PolicyStore corp.fabrikam.com\Sales `
-DisplayName "Block Outbound Port 80" -Direction Outbound -LocalPort 80 `
-Protocol TCP -Action Block

Name                 : {0c7a9c6c-af48-4acf-bcdd-adcf8d9790b2}
DisplayName          : Block Outbound Port 80
Description          :
DisplayGroup         :
Group                :
Enabled              : True
Profile              : Any
Platform             : {}
Direction            : Outbound
Action               : Block
EdgeTraversalPolicy  : Block
LooseSourceMapping   : False
LocalOnlyMapping     : False
Owner                :
```

```
PrimaryStatus          : OK
Status                 : The rule was parsed successfully from the store. (65536)
EnforcementStatus      : NotApplicable
PolicyStoreSource      :
PolicyStoreSourceType  : GroupPolicy
```

Opening the Sales GPO in the Windows Firewall with Advanced Security snap-in will verify that the new rule has been configured as expected in the firewall policy for the GPO.

Lesson summary

- Windows Firewall with Advanced Security interoperates with other Windows features—such as Windows Filtering Platform, Windows service hardening, and network location awareness—to help ensure the security of the computer.

- A *firewall profile* is a grouping of firewall rules and other configuration settings that are applied to a network connection that has a specific network location type.

- Windows Firewall with Advanced Security has three firewall profiles (domain, private, and public) that correspond to the three network location types.

- All three firewall profiles can be active at the same time on a computer if Windows detects that there are network connections of each type present.

- Firewall rules can be either inbound rules or outbound rules. Types of firewall rules include program, port, predefined, and custom.

- The default firewall rule for inbound connections can be configured as Block, Block All Connections, or Allow. By default, it is set to Block.

- The default firewall rule for outbound connections can be configured as Block or Allow. By default, it is set to Allow.

- Windows Firewall with Advanced Security processes firewall rules in the following order of priority: override, block, allow, default. As soon as a packet matches a rule, the rule is applied and rules processing stops at that point.

- You can configure and manage firewall policy and rules by using Windows Firewall with Advanced Security, the cmdlets in the NetSecurity module of Windows PowerShell, or the Windows Firewall with Advanced Security node in a Group Policy Object.

Lesson review

Answer the following questions to test your knowledge of the information in this lesson. You can find the answers to these questions and explanations of why each answer choice is correct or incorrect in the "Answers" section at the end of this chapter.

1. Which of the following statements is *not* true regarding firewall profiles in Windows Firewall with Advanced Security? (Choose all that apply.)

    A. The domain profile is automatically applied to any network connection that Windows identifies as having a network location type of domain.

B. Only one firewall profile can be active at any given time.

C. The default behavior of the domain profile is to block inbound connections unless those connections are explicitly allowed by firewall rules.

D. To display the currently active settings for the domain profile on the local computer, you can use the Get-NetFirewallProfile cmdlet with the *–PolicyStore PersistentStore* parameter.

2. You have two firewall rules configured on the computer as follows:

- Rule A explicitly blocks outbound traffic from the svchost.exe process running on the computer.

- Rule B explicitly allows outbound traffic from the svchost.exe process running on the computer.

In addition, the outbound default rule is set to Block.

The svchost.exe process running on the computer attempts to send a packet to another computer on the network. Which answer best describes what will happen?

A. The packet will be allowed because rule B has a higher priority than rule A.

B. The packet will be blocked because rule B has a higher priority than rule A.

C. The packet will be blocked because rule A has a higher priority than rule B.

D. The packet will be blocked because the outbound default rule is set to Block.

3. You want to create a firewall rule that blocks inbound traffic to %windir%regedit.exe on the computer. Which type of rule can you use to do this? (Choose all that apply.)

A. Program rule

B. Port rule

C. Predefined rule

D. Custom rule

Lesson 2: Configuring IPsec

Internet Protocol security (IPsec) is a set of extensions that bring network-level peer authentication, data-origin authentication, data integrity, data confidentiality (encryption), and replay protection to the TCP/IP protocol suite. IPsec enables administrators to protect network traffic against eavesdropping, interception, and modification. This lesson examines how to implement IPsec in different scenarios using Windows Firewall with Advanced Security on Windows Server 2012 and Windows Server 2012 R2.

Understanding connection security

You can implement IPsec using Windows Firewall with Advanced Security by creating and configuring connection security rules. A *connection security rule* is a set of criteria configured in Windows Firewall with Advanced Security that specifies how IPsec will be used to secure traffic between the local computer and other computers on the network. You can use connection security rules to specify whether a network connection between two computers must be authenticated before data can be exchanged between them. You can also use connection security rules to make sure any data exchanged between the computers is encrypted to protect against eavesdropping or modification.

To understand how you can implement connection security using IPsec, you first need to understand the following IPsec concepts:

- Encapsulation

- IPsec protocols

- Security associations

- Key-exchange algorithms

- Authentication methods

- Data-integrity algorithms

- Data-encryption algorithms

The sections that follow go into more detail about these concepts as they apply to Windows Server 2012, Windows Server 2012 R2, Windows 8, and Windows 8.1.

Encapsulation

IPsec protects data sent over an unsecure network by encapsulating a payload of network packets. This can be done in two ways:

- **Transport mode**   The payload is encapsulated with an IPsec header.
- **Tunnel mode**   The payload is encapsulated with an additional IP header.

IPsec protocols

IPsec supports two protocols for encrypting the payload of packets, encapsulating the payload of packets, or both:

- **Authentication Header (AH)**   This mechanism provides data-origin authentication, data integrity, and anti-replay protection for the entire packet (both the IP header and the data payload carried in the packet) except for the fields in the IP header that are allowed to change in transit. It does not provide data confidentiality, which means that it does not encrypt the data. The data is readable but protected from modification.

- **Encapsulating Security Protocol (ESP)**   This mechanism provides data-origin authentication, data integrity, anti-replay protection, and the option of confidentiality for the IP payload only. ESP in transport mode does not protect the entire packet with a cryptographic checksum, and the IP header is not protected.

Security associations

A *security association* (SA) is a mutually agreed-upon collection of cryptographic keys and policies that one IPsec-enabled computer uses for secure unicast communications with another IPsec-enabled computer. You can think of an SA as a kind of contract that specifies how the computers will use IPsec to securely exchange information with each other.

To establish an SA between them, the computers can use one of the following IPsec protocols:

- **Internet Key Exchange (IKE)**   This mechanism is defined in RFC 2409 and combines the Internet Security Association and Key Management Protocol (ISAKMP) of RFC 2408 with the Oakley Key Determination Protocol (Oakley) of RFC 2412. IKE is supported on computers that are running Windows 2000 or later.

- **Authenticated IP (AuthIP)**   This mechanism is a Microsoft proprietary extension of IKE that provides improved negotiation of authentication methods and supports additional authentication methods not included in IKE. AuthIP is supported on computers running Windows Vista, Windows Server 2008, or later.

When two computers negotiate to establish IPsec communications between them, key exchange is performed during two phases:

- **Main mode**   This phase of IPsec negotiation is performed first and is used to generate a shared master key that the computers can use to securely exchange keying information.

- **Quick mode**   This phase of IPsec negotiation uses the master key from main mode to generate one or more session keys that the computers can use to ensure data integrity and encryption.

Because each SA defines only one-way communications, an IPsec session requires two SAs.

> *REAL WORLD*   **MAKING VPN CONNECTIONS MORE RELIABLE**
>
> Support for Internet Key Exchange version 2 (IKEv2), a virtual private network (VPN) tunneling protocol described in RFC 4306, was first introduced in Windows 7 and Windows Server 2008 R2. Beginning with Windows Server 2012, IKEv2 supports additional scenarios, including IPsec end-to-end, transport-mode connections, and support for Suite B (RFC 4869) requirements. From a practical standpoint, this improvement means that a Windows Server 2012 or Windows Server 2012 R2 VPN server allows a security association to remain unchanged despite changes in the underlying connection.

Key-exchange algorithms

In cryptographic systems, keys are used to encrypt and decrypt communications between different entities. To send and receive encrypted traffic over a network, IPsec-enabled computers must have access to the same shared session key. The key must first be securely exchanged between the computers. This sharing of keys is accomplished through a process called *key exchange*.

The key-exchange algorithms supported for IPsec communications in Windows 8, Windows 8.1, Windows Server 2012, and Windows Server 2012 R2 are as follows:

- **Diffie–Hellman Group 1 (DH Group 1)**   This algorithm is not recommended and is provided for backward compatibility only.

- **DH Group 2**   This algorithm is stronger than DH Group 1.

- **DH Group 14**   This algorithm is stronger than DH Group 2.

- **DH Group 24**   This algorithm was introduced in Windows Server 2012 and is stronger than DH Group 14.

- **Elliptic Curve Diffie–Hellman P-256**   This algorithm is stronger than DH Group 2. It has medium resource usage and is compatible only with Windows Vista and later.

- **Elliptic Curve Diffie–Hellman P-384**   This algorithm has the strongest security but also the highest resource usage. It is compatible only with Windows Vista and later.

Authentication methods

In reference to IPsec, an *authentication method* is a process by which IPsec-enabled computers verify their identity with each other before secure communications can begin. A number of authentication methods are supported for IPsec communications in Windows 8, Windows 8.1, Windows Server 2012, and Windows Server 2012 R2. The authentication methods available depend on whether they are being used for first or second authentication.

The authentication methods available for first authentication are as follows:

- **Computer (Kerberos V5)**   This authentication method is compatible with Windows 2000 or later.

- **Computer (NTLMv2)**   This authentication method can be used on networks that include systems running an earlier version of the Windows operating system and on stand-alone systems.

- **Computer certificate**   The default signing algorithm for this authentication method is RSA, but Elliptic Curve Digital Signature Algorithm (ECDSA)–P256 and ECDSA-P384 are also supported signing algorithms. You can also use an intermediate certificate authority (CA) as a certificate store in addition to using a root CA, and certificate-to-account mapping is also supported. Note that you can also configure first authentication to accept only health certificates when using a network access protection (NAP) infrastructure.

- **Preshared key**   This authentication method is not recommended except for test environments.

The authentication methods available for second authentication are as follows:

- **User (Kerberos V5)**   This authentication method is compatible with Windows 2000 or later.

- **User (NTLMv2)**   This authentication method can be used on networks that include systems running an earlier version of the Windows operating system and on stand-alone systems.

- **User certificate**   The default signing algorithm for this authentication method is RSA, but ECDSA-P256 and ECDSA-P384 are also supported signing algorithms. You can also use an intermediate CA as a certificate store in addition to using a root CA, and certificate-to-account mapping is also supported.

- **Computer health certificate**   The default signing algorithm for this authentication method is RSA, but ECDSA-P256 and ECDSA P384 are also supported signing algorithms. You can also use an intermediate CA as a certificate store in addition to using a root CA, and certificate-to-account mapping is also supported.

Data-integrity algorithms

Data integrity ensures that the data exchanged between IPsec-enabled computers has not been modified in transit between them. Data integrity is accomplished by the use of message hashes, which are used to digitally sign packets so that the computer receiving them can be sure that the packets haven't been tampered with.

The data-integrity algorithms supported for IPsec communications in Windows 8, Windows 8.1, Windows Server 2012, and Windows Server 2012 R2 are as follows:

- **Message-Digest Algorithm 5 (MD5)**   This algorithm is not recommended and is provided for backward compatibility only.

- **Secure Hash Algorithm 1 (SHA-1)**   This algorithm is stronger than MD5 but uses more resources.

- **SHA 256-bit (SHA-256)**   This algorithm can be used for main mode only and is supported on Windows Vista SP1 and later.

- **SHA-384**   This algorithm can be used for main mode only and is supported on Windows Vista SP1 and later.

- **Advanced Encryption Standard-Galois Message Authentication Code 128-bit (AES-GMAC 128)**   This algorithm can be used for quick mode only and is supported on Windows Vista SP1 and later. It is equivalent to AES-GCM 128 for integrity.

- **AES-GMAC 192**   This algorithm can be used for quick mode only and is supported on Windows Vista SP1 and later. It is equivalent to AES-GCM 192 for integrity.

- **AES-GMAC 256**   This algorithm can be used for quick mode only and is supported on Windows Vista SP1 and later. It is equivalent to AES-GCM 256 for integrity.

- **AES-GCM 128**   This algorithm can be used for quick mode only and is supported on Windows Vista SP1 and later. It is equivalent to AES-GMAC 128 for integrity.

- **AES-GCM 192**   This algorithm can be used for quick mode only and is supported on Windows Vista SP1 and later. It is equivalent to AES-GMAC 192 for integrity.

- **AES-GCM 256**   This algorithm can be used for quick mode only and is supported on Windows Vista SP1 and later. It is equivalent to AES-GMAC 256 for integrity.

Data-encryption algorithms

Data encryption ensures that data exchanged between IPsec-enabled computers is protected from viewing. IPsec can regenerate encryption keys so that if one key is exposed, all the data is not compromised.

The data-encryption algorithms supported for IPsec communications in Windows 8, Windows 8.1, Windows Server 2012, and Windows Server 2012 R2 are as follows:

- **Data Encryption Standard (DES)**   This algorithm is not recommended and is provided for backward compatibility only.

- **Triple-DES (3DES)**   This algorithm is more secure than DES but has higher resource usage.

- **Advanced Encryption Standard-Cipher Block Chaining 128-bit (AES-CBC 128)** This algorithm is faster and stronger than DES. It is supported on Windows Vista and later.

- **AES-CBC 192** This algorithm is stronger than AES-CBC 128 and has medium resource usage. It is supported on Windows Vista and later.

- **AES-CBC 256** This algorithm has the strongest security but also the highest resource usage. It is supported on Windows Vista and later.

- **AES-GCM 128** This algorithm can be used for quick mode only. It is faster and stronger than DES and is supported on Windows Vista and later. Note that AES-GCM 128 must be specified for both data integrity and encryption if this algorithm is used.

- **AES-GCM 192** This algorithm can be used for quick mode only. It has medium resource usage and is supported on Windows Vista and later. Note that AES-GCM 192 must be specified for both data integrity and encryption if this algorithm is used.

- **AES-GCM 256** This algorithm can be used for quick mode only and is faster and stronger than DES. It is supported on Windows Vista and later. Note that AES-GCM 256 must be specified for both data integrity and encryption if this algorithm is used.

Configuring IPsec settings

In contrast to firewall settings, which are configured for each firewall profile separately, IPsec settings are systemwide settings that define defaults for IPsec communications between the local computer and other computers on the network. You can configure these systemwide IPsec settings using the Windows Firewall with Advanced Security snap-in (using the Windows Firewall with Advanced Security policy node under Computer Configuration\Policies\Windows Settings\Security Settings in a GPO) or Windows PowerShell.

To configure IPsec settings using the Windows Firewall with Advanced Security snap-in on the local computer, right-click the root node in the console tree, select Properties, and switch to the IPsec Settings tab as shown in Figure 11-14. These are the settings you can configure here:

- **IPsec Defaults** Use this option to configure the default IPsec settings that the local computer will use when attempting to establish secure connections with other IPsec-enabled computers. To configure these settings, click the Customize button to open the Customize IPsec Defaults dialog box shown in Figure 11-15 in the next section.

- **IPsec Exemptions** Use this option to configure how IPsec handles Internet Control Message Protocol (ICMP) traffic. By default, ICMP traffic is not exempted from using IPsec, but you can change this by selecting Yes from the list control.

- **IPsec Tunnel Authorization** Use this option to configure the users and computers that you want to be authorized to establish IPsec communications with the local computer. To configure these settings, select Advanced and click the Customize button to open the Customize IPsec Tunnel Authorizations dialog box shown in Figure 11-19 later in this lesson.

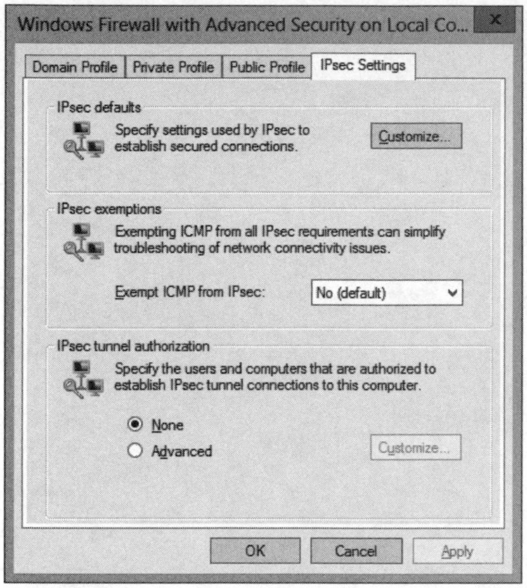

FIGURE 11-14 Configure systemwide IPsec settings on the computer.

Customizing IPsec defaults

As described in the previous section, the Customize IPsec Defaults dialog box shown in Figure 11-15 is used to configure the default IPsec settings that the local computer will use when attempting to establish secure connections with other IPsec-enabled computers. The types of default settings you can configure include settings for the following:

- Key exchange (main mode)
- Data protection (quick mode)
- Authentication method

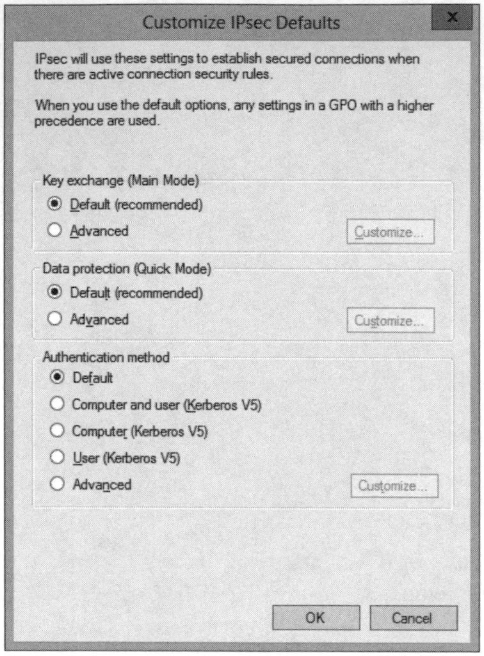

FIGURE 11-15 This is the dialog box for customizing IPsec defaults.

Figure 11-16 shows the default IPsec settings for key exchange. The process for applying them is as follows:

1. Start by attempting to use the Diffie–Hellman Group 2 key-exchange algorithm to negotiate using SHA-1 for data integrity and AES-CBC 128 for data encryption.

2. If that fails, attempt to use DH Group 2 to negotiate using SHA-1 for data integrity and 3DES for data encryption.

You can add other security methods to the list of methods the computer should attempt to use. You can also configure key lifetimes and other key-exchange options using this dialog box.

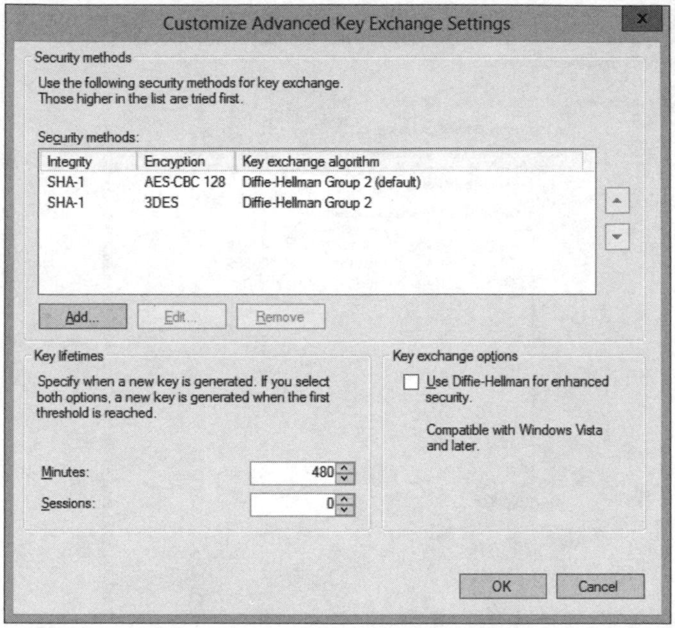

FIGURE 11-16 Configure advanced key-exchange settings.

Figure 11-17 shows the default IPsec settings for data protection. The process for applying them is as follows:

- If data integrity is required but data encryption is not, then do the following:

    1. Start by attempting to use ESP to negotiate using SHA-1 for data integrity.

    2. If that fails, attempt to use AH to negotiate using SHA-1 for data integrity.

- If both data integrity and encryption are required, then do the following:

    1. Start by attempting to use ESP to negotiate using SHA-1 for data integrity and AES-CBC 218 for data encryption.

    2. If that fails, attempt to use AH to negotiate using SHA-1 for data integrity and 3DES for data encryption.

You can use this dialog box to add other data-integrity and encryption algorithms to the list of algorithms the computer should attempt to use. You can also use it to require encryption for all IPsec communications on the computer.

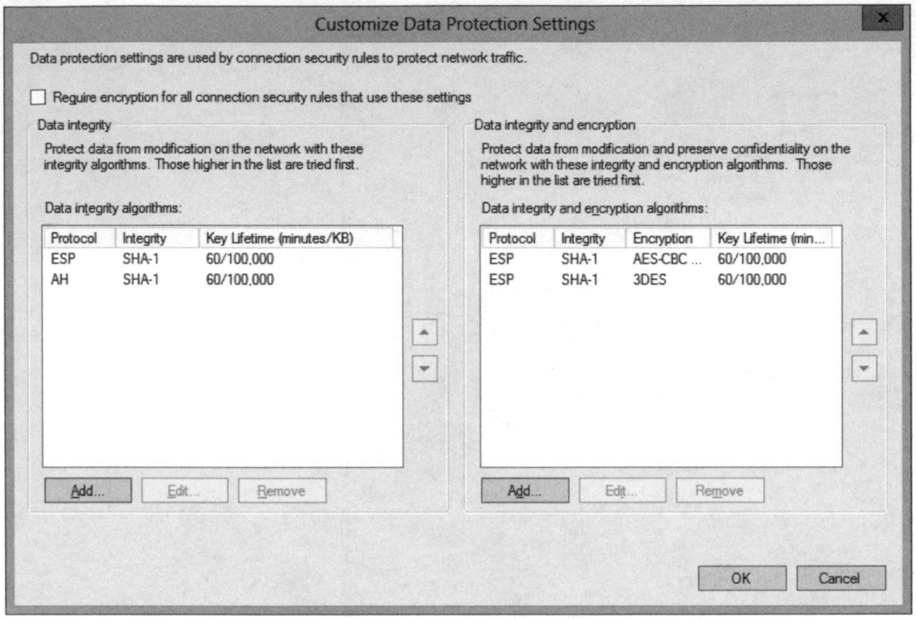

FIGURE 11-17 Configure data-integrity and encryption settings.

As Figure 11-18 shows, the default authentication methods that IPsec uses for first and second authentication are as follows:

- For first authentication, the only authentication method attempted is Computer (Kerberos V5). If desired, you can add authentication methods and prioritize how they are used.

- For second authentication, no authentication is attempted. If desired, you can add authentication methods and prioritize how they are used.

You can also use this dialog box to specify whether first or second authentication should be considered optional.

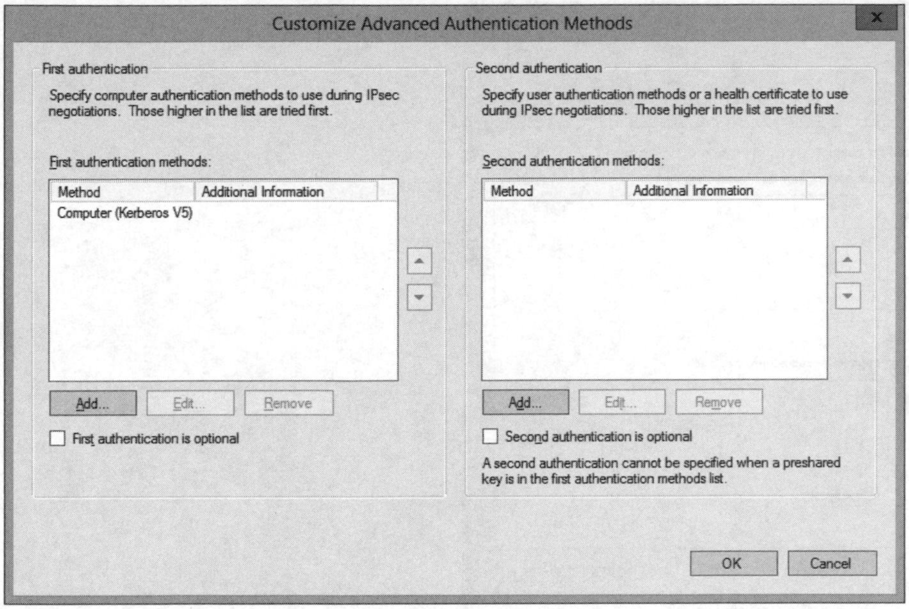

FIGURE 11-18 Configure authentication methods.

Customizing IPsec tunnel authorizations

If IPsec tunnel connections will be allowed with the computer, you can use the Customize IPsec Tunnel Authorizations dialog box shown in Figure 11-19 to configure this. Using this dialog box, you can specify

- Which computers are authorized to establish tunnel connections with the local computer.
- Which users are authorized to establish tunnel connections with the local computer.

You can also specify exceptions for each of the preceding settings.

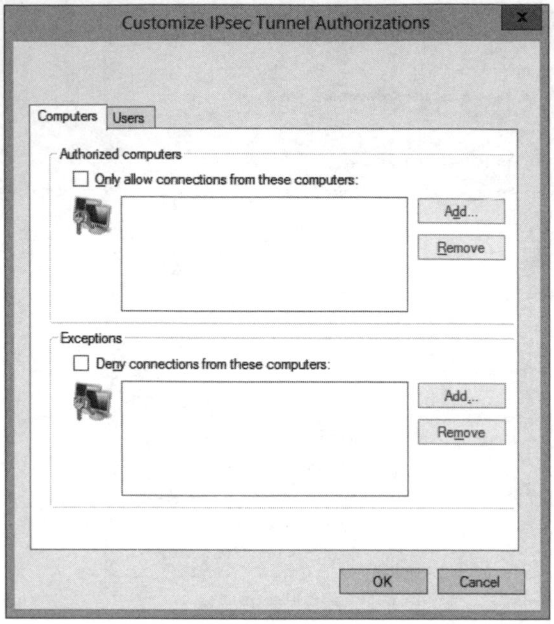

FIGURE 11-19 Configure IPsec tunnel authorizations.

Configuring IPsec settings using Windows PowerShell

You can also use Windows PowerShell to configure IPsec settings in the policy store on the local computer, a remote computer, or a GPO. You can do this using the cmdlets from the NetSecurity module of Windows PowerShell.

For example, you can use the Get-NetIPsecMainModeCryptoSet cmdlet to display the main mode cryptographic sets on a computer:

```
PS C:\> Get-NetIPsecMainModeCryptoSet -PolicyStore ActiveStore

Name              : {E5A5D32A-4BCE-4e4d-B07F-4AB1BA7E5FE1}
DisplayName       : Service Hardcoded Default Phase1 CryptoSet
Description       : Service Hardcoded Default Phase1 CryptoSet
DisplayGroup      :
Group             :
Proposal          : {
                      0 : Encryption: AES128
                        : Hash: SHA1
                        : KeyExchange: DH2
                      1 : Encryption: DES3
                        : Hash: SHA1
                        : KeyExchange: DH2
                    }

MaxMinutes        : 480
MaxSessions       : 0
ForceDiffieHellman : False
```

```
PrimaryStatus           : OK
Status                  : The rule was parsed successfully from the store. (65536)
EnforcementStatus       :
PolicyStoreSource       : No Policy Store (Hardcoded)
PolicyStoreSourceType   : Hardcoded
```

Compare the preceding command output to Figure 11-16 earlier in this lesson. To configure the main mode cryptographic sets on the computer, you can use the Set-NetIPsecMainModeCryptoSet cmdlet.

As a second example, you can use the Get-NetIPsecPhase1AuthSet cmdlet to display how first authentication is configured on the computer:

```
PS C:\> Get-NetIPsecPhase1AuthSet -PolicyStore ActiveStore

Name                    : {E5A5D32A-4BCE-4e4d-B07F-4AB1BA7E5FE3}
DisplayName             : Service Hardcoded Default Phase1 AuthSet
Description             : Service Hardcoded Default Phase1 AuthSet
DisplayGroup            :
Group                   :
Proposal                : {
                            0 : MachineKerb
                          }

PrimaryStatus           : OK
Status                  : The rule was parsed successfully from the store. (65536)
EnforcementStatus       :
PolicyStoreSource       : No Policy Store (Hardcoded)
PolicyStoreSourceType   : Hardcoded
```

Compare the preceding command output to Figure 11-18 earlier in this lesson. To configure first authentication on the computer, you can use the Set-NetIPsecPhase1AuthSet cmdlet.

✔ Quick check

- A local computer running Windows Server 2012 R2 is using the 3DES algorithm for data encryption when using IPsec to communicate with a remote computer running an unknown operating system. Why is the local computer not using the more secure AES-CBC 128 algorithm instead?

Quick check answer

- This is probably because the operating system on the remote computer does not support data encryption using the AES-CBC 128 algorithm. By default, Windows Server 2012 R2 starts by attempting to use the Diffie–Hellman Group 2 key-exchange algorithm to negotiate using SHA-1 for data integrity and AES-CBC 128 for data encryption. If that fails, it attempts to use DH Group 2 to negotiate using SHA-1 for data integrity and 3DES for data encryption.

Configuring connection security rules

After you configure the IPsec defaults for the computer, you can create connection security rules. As explained at the start of this lesson, a connection security rule is a set of criteria that specifies how IPsec will be used to secure traffic between the local computer and other computers on the network. You can use connection security rules to specify whether a network connection between two computers must be authenticated before data can be exchanged between them and to make sure any data exchanged between the computers is encrypted to protect against eavesdropping or modification.

Types of connection security rules

You can create connection security rules by using the New Connection Security Rule Wizard. As Figure 11-20 shows, Windows Firewall with Advanced Security supports five types of connection security rules:

- **Isolation**   You can use this type of connection security rule to isolate computers from other computers. For example, you can use isolation rules to protect computers that are joined to your domain from computers that are outside your domain.

- **Authentication Exemption**   You can use this type of connection security rule to specify computers that should be exempted from being required to authenticate, regardless of any other connection security rules that have been configured. For example, you can use authentication exemption rules to allow access to domain controllers and other infrastructure servers with which the computer needs to communicate before authentication can be performed.

- **Server-To-Server**   You can use this type of connection security rule to protect communications between two computers, two groups of computers, two subnets, or some combination of these, such as between a computer and a subnet. For example, you can use server-to-server rules to protect communications between a database server and a front-end web server.

- **Tunnel**   You can use this type of connection security rule to protect communications between two computers using IPsec tunnel mode instead of IPsec transport mode. For example, you can use tunnel rules to specify a gateway computer that routes traffic to a private network.

- **Custom**   You can use this type of connection security rule to configure custom rules using criteria from other rule types except tunnel rules.

To create new connection security rules using the New Connection Security Rule Wizard, right-click the Connection Security Rules node in the Windows Firewall with Advanced Security snap-in, select New Rule, and follow the steps of the wizard. The sections that follow explain in more detail the steps involved in creating each of these different types of connection security rules.

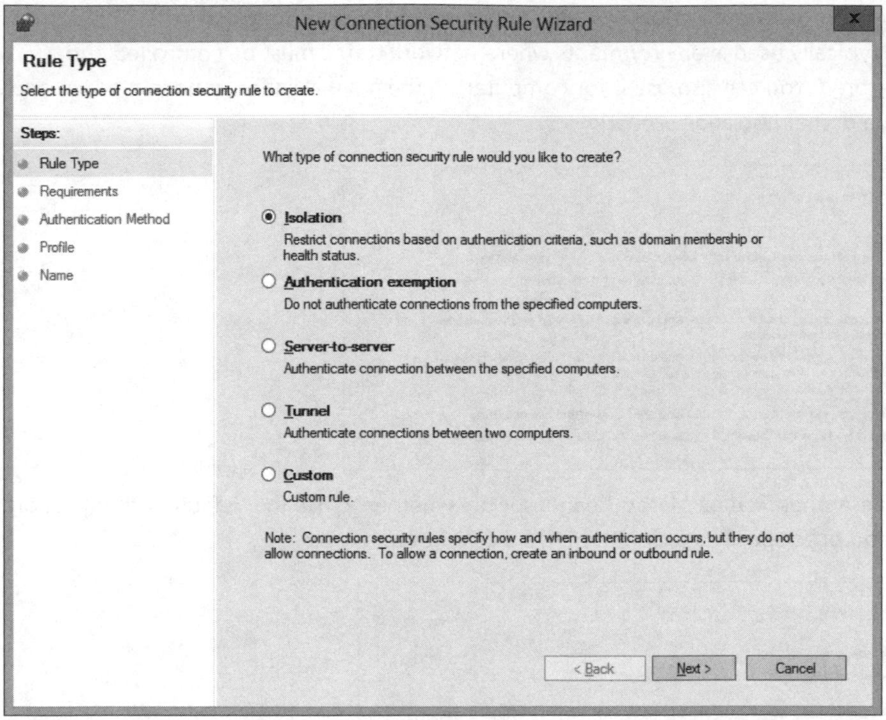

FIGURE 11-20 Windows Firewall with Advanced Security supports five types of connection security rules.

Creating an isolation rule

You can take the following steps to create a new isolation rule using the Windows Firewall with Advanced Security snap-in:

1. Launch the New Connection Security Rule Wizard and choose Isolation on the Rule Type page.

2. On the Requirements page, specify whether to request or require authentication for inbound connections, outbound connections, or both by selecting one of the following options:

   - **Request Authentication For Inbound And Outbound Connections** This option is typically used in low-security environments or those in which computers are unable to use the IPsec authentication methods available with Windows Firewall with Advanced Security. You can also use it for computers in the boundary zone in a server and in a domain isolation scenario.

   - **Require Authentication For Inbound Connections And Request Authentication For Outbound Connections** This option is typically used in environments where computers are able to use the IPsec authentication methods available with Windows Firewall with Advanced Security. You can also use it for computers in the main isolation zone in a server and in a domain isolation scenario.

- **Require Authentication For Inbound And Outbound Connections** This option is typically used in environments where network traffic must be controlled and secured. You can also use it for computers in the main isolation zone in a server and in a domain isolation scenario.

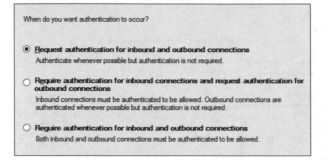

3. On the Authentication Method page, specify whether to use the default authentication method or to specify a different method or list of methods:

4. On the Profile page, select the firewall profiles to which the new rule should apply. By default, new connection security rules apply to all three profiles (domain, private, and public).

5. On the Name page, specify a name and optional description for the new rule.

> **NOTE   ENABLED BY DEFAULT**
>
> When you create a new connection security rule using the New Connection Security Rule Wizard, the new rule is automatically enabled by default.

Creating an authentication exemption rule

You can take the following steps to create a new authentication exemption rule using the Windows Firewall with Advanced Security snap-in:

1. Launch the New Connection Security Rule Wizard and select Authentication Exemption on the Rule Type page.

2. On the Exempt Computers page, specify the computers to which the exemption should apply:

> Which remote computers are exempt from authentication requirements?
>
> | Add... | Edit... | Remove |

By clicking Add on this page, you can specify exempted computers by the following characteristics:

- An IP address (IPv4 or IPv6)
- An IP subnet (IPv4 or IPv6)
- A range of IP addresses (IPv4 or IPv6)
- A predefined set of computers such as DHCP servers, DNS servers, computers on the local subnet, and so on

3. The options on the Profile and Name pages are the same as those described in the previous section.

Creating a server-to-server rule

You can take the following steps to create a new server-to-server rule using the Windows Firewall with Advanced Security snap-in:

1. Launch the New Connection Security Rule Wizard and select Server-To-Server on the Rule Type page.

2. On the Endpoints page, specify an IP address or range of addresses for each of the two endpoints in the secured connection:

Create a secured connection between computers in Endpoint 1 and Endpoint 2.

Which computers are in Endpoint 1?

◉ Any IP address

○ These IP addresses:

	Add...
	Edit...
	Remove

Customize the interface types to which this rule applies: [Customize...]

Which computers are in Endpoint 2?

◉ Any IP address

○ These IP addresses:

	Add...
	Edit...
	Remove

3. On the Requirements page, specify whether to request or require authentication for inbound connections, outbound connections, or both by selecting one of the same three options described earlier for isolation rules.

4. On the Authentication Method page, specify whether to use a computer certificate as the authentication method or specify a custom list of first and second authentication methods. If you choose to use a computer certificate as the authentication method, there are some additional settings you can configure.

5. The options on the Profile and Name pages are the same as those described in the previous section.

Creating a tunnel rule

You can take the following steps to create a new tunnel rule using the Windows Firewall with Advanced Security snap-in:

1. Launch the New Connection Security Rule Wizard and select Tunnel on the Rule Type page.

2. On the Tunnel Type page, specify the type of tunnel you want to create as indicated by the options shown here:

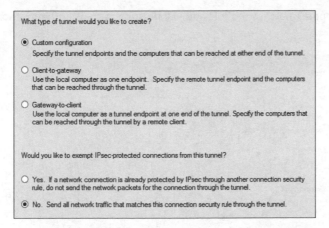

What type of tunnel would you like to create?

⦿ Custom configuration
Specify the tunnel endpoints and the computers that can be reached at either end of the tunnel.

◯ Client-to-gateway
Use the local computer as one endpoint. Specify the remote tunnel endpoint and the computers that can be reached through the tunnel.

◯ Gateway-to-client
Use the local computer as a tunnel endpoint at one end of the tunnel. Specify the computers that can be reached through the tunnel by a remote client.

Would you like to exempt IPsec-protected connections from this tunnel?

◯ Yes. If a network connection is already protected by IPsec through another connection security rule, do not send the network packets for the connection through the tunnel.

⦿ No. Send all network traffic that matches this connection security rule through the tunnel.

3. On the Requirements page, choose one of the available authentication options. Depending on which tunnel type you specified on the previous wizard page, these options might include the following:

   - **Require Authentication For Inbound And Outbound Connections** This option is typically used in environments where network traffic must be controlled and secured.

   - **Request Authentication For Inbound And Outbound Connections** This option is typically used in low-security environments or those in which computers are unable to use the IPsec authentication methods available with Windows Firewall with Advanced Security.

   - **Require Authentication For Inbound Connections. Do Not Establish Tunnels For Outbound Connections** This option is typically used on a computer that serves as a tunnel endpoint for remote clients. The rule is used to indicate that the tunnel applies only to inbound network traffic from the clients.

   - **Do Not Authenticate** This option is typically used to create an authentication exemption for connections to computers that do not require IPsec protection.

4. On the Tunnel Endpoints page, specify the IP addresses of the endpoints for the tunnel connection. The options available on this page will depend on which option you selected on the Tunnel Type page.

5. The options on the Authentication Method, Profile, and Name pages are the same as those described in the previous section.

Creating a custom rule

Creating a custom rule involves configuring options on the Endpoints, Requirements, Authentication Method, Protocols And Ports, Profile, and Name pages. The only new page here is the Protocol And Ports page shown in Figure 11-21. You can use this page to specify which protocol and which port or ports specified in a network packet match this connection security rule. Once you have done this, only network traffic that matches the criteria on this page and the Endpoints page matches the rule and will be subject to its authentication requirements.

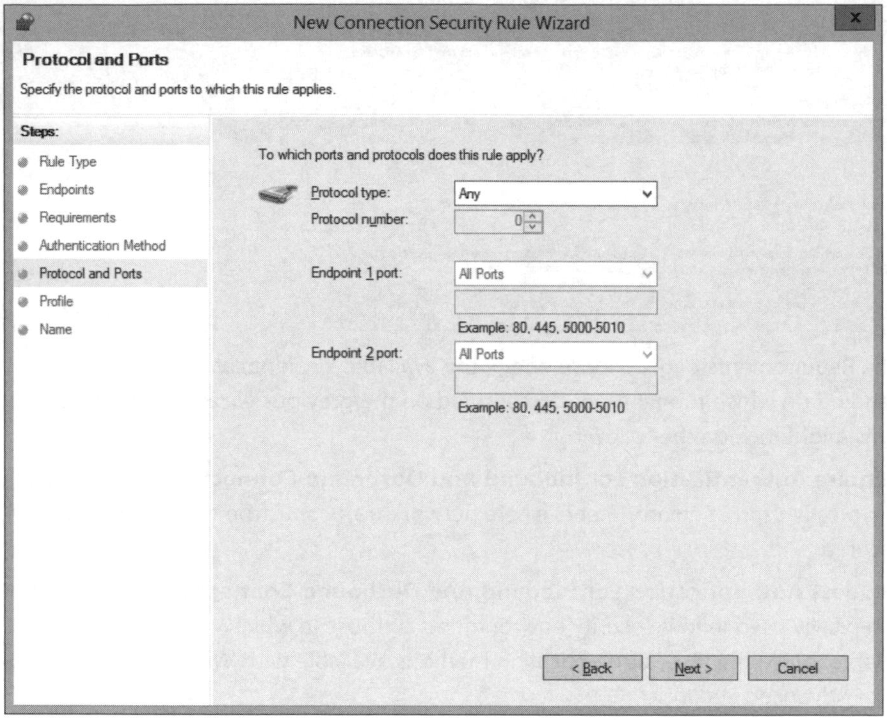

FIGURE 11-21 Configure protocols and ports for a custom connection security rule.

Creating connection security rules using Windows PowerShell

You can also use Windows PowerShell to view, create, configure, and remove connection security rules in the policy store on the local computer, a remote computer, or a GPO. You can do this using the cmdlets from the NetSecurity module of Windows PowerShell.

For example, you can use the New-NetIPsecRule cmdlet to create a new server isolation rule in the persistent store on the local machine that requires both inbound and outbound authentication:

```
PS C:\> New-NetIPsecRule -DisplayName "Server Isolation Rule" `
-InboundSecurity Require -OutboundSecurity Require

IPsecRuleName         : {8215b76f-e6f2-42da-a8b9-1f8416b9a358}
DisplayName           : Server Isolation Rule
Description           :
DisplayGroup          :
Group                 :
Enabled               : True
Profile               : Any
Platform              : {}
```

```
Mode                    : Transport
InboundSecurity         : Require
OutboundSecurity        : Require
QuickModeCryptoSet      : Default
Phase1AuthSet           : Default
Phase2AuthSet           : Default
KeyModule               : Default
AllowWatchKey           : False
AllowSetKey             : False
LocalTunnelEndpoint     :
RemoteTunnelEndpoint    :
RemoteTunnelHostname    :
ForwardPathLifetime     : 0
EncryptedTunnelBypass   : False
RequireAuthorization    : False
User                    : Any
Machine                 : Any
PrimaryStatus           : OK
Status                  : The rule was parsed successfully from the store. (65536)
EnforcementStatus       : NotApplicable
PolicyStoreSource       : PersistentStore
PolicyStoreSourceType   : Local
```

If you open the Windows Firewall with Advanced Security snap-in at this point and select the Connection Security Rules node, you will see the new rule that you created.

You can also use the Get-NetIPsecRule cmdlet to view connection security rules, Set-NetIPsecRule to modify them, or Remove-NetIPsecRule to delete them. For more help concerning any of these cmdlets, use the Get-Help cmdlet.

Configuring authenticated bypass

In Lesson 2 of this chapter, you learned how to create firewall rules using the New Inbound (or Outbound) Rule Wizard, which you can launch from the Windows Firewall with Advanced Security snap-in. One of the configuration options in that wizard was deferred until later because it has to do with how firewall rules interact with IPsec. That setting is the Allow The Connection If It Is Secure option on the Action page. (See Figure 11-22.)

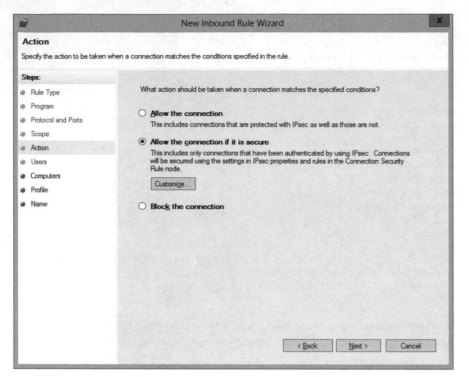

FIGURE 11-22 Configure a new firewall rule to allow only connections that are protected by IPsec.

Selecting this option specifies that only connections protected by IPsec will be allowed by the new firewall rule. Such IPsec protection is implemented separately using connection security rules.

As Figure 11-22 shows, selecting the Allow The Connection If It Is Secure option also adds two new wizard pages named Users and Computers to the New Inbound (or Outbound) Rule Wizard. You can use these two new pages to specify trusted users, computers, or both that are allowed to connect to the local computer.

The default behavior of a firewall rule that has the Allow The Connection If It Is Secure option selected is for network traffic matching the firewall rule to be allowed if the traffic is both authenticated and integrity-protected by IPsec. This default option is supported on computers running Windows Vista, Windows Server 2008, or later.

By clicking Customize on the Action page, you can change this behavior by selecting a different option on the Customize Allow If Secure Settings dialog box shown in Figure 11-23. Specifically, you can select from the following options:

- **Require The Connections To Be Encrypted**   Choosing this option adds the requirement of data encryption to the default requirements of authentication and data integrity. If you are creating an inbound rule, you can also select Allow The Computers To Dynamically Negotiate Encryption to allow the network connection to send and receive unencrypted traffic while an IPsec encryption algorithm is being negotiated after IPsec authentication has been achieved.

- **Allow The Connection To Use Null Encapsulation** Choosing this option requires that matching network traffic use IPsec authentication, but it does not require either integrity or encryption protection. You should select this option only if you have network equipment or software that is not compatible with either the ESP or AH integrity protocols.

- **Override Block Rules** Choosing this option allows matching network traffic to override any firewall rules that would block such traffic. In general, firewall rules that explicitly block a connection take priority over firewall rules that explicitly allow the connection. But if you select the Override Block Rules option, the connection will be allowed even if a different rule is configured to block it.

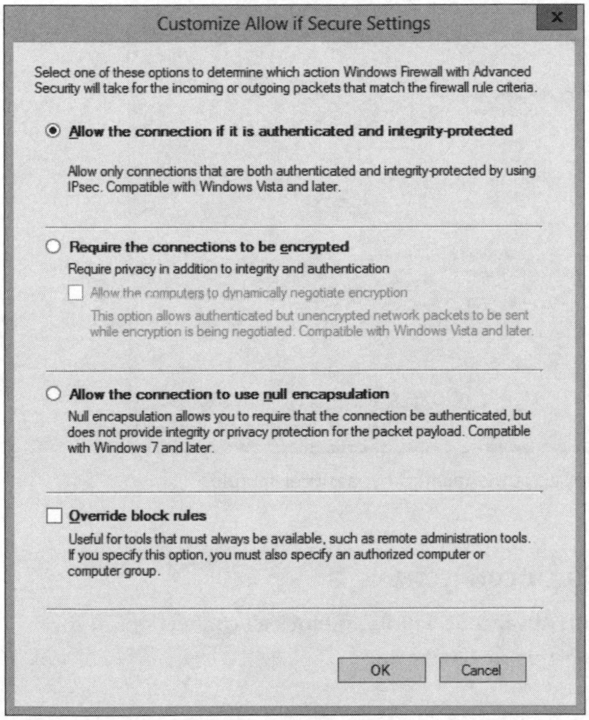

FIGURE 11-23 Configure the behavior of a firewall rule that has the Allow The Connection If It Is Secure option selected.

IMPORTANT **SECURITY WARNING**

If you select the Allow The Computers To Dynamically Negotiate Encryption check box shown in Figure 11-23, network traffic will be sent in clear text while an encryption algorithm is being negotiated.

Selecting the Override Block Rules option when creating a new firewall rule is called *authenticated bypass* because it means that matching network traffic is allowed because it has been authenticated as coming from an authorized and trusted user or computer. As Figure 11-24 shows, you must specify at least one trusted computer when configuring authenticated bypass for a firewall rule.

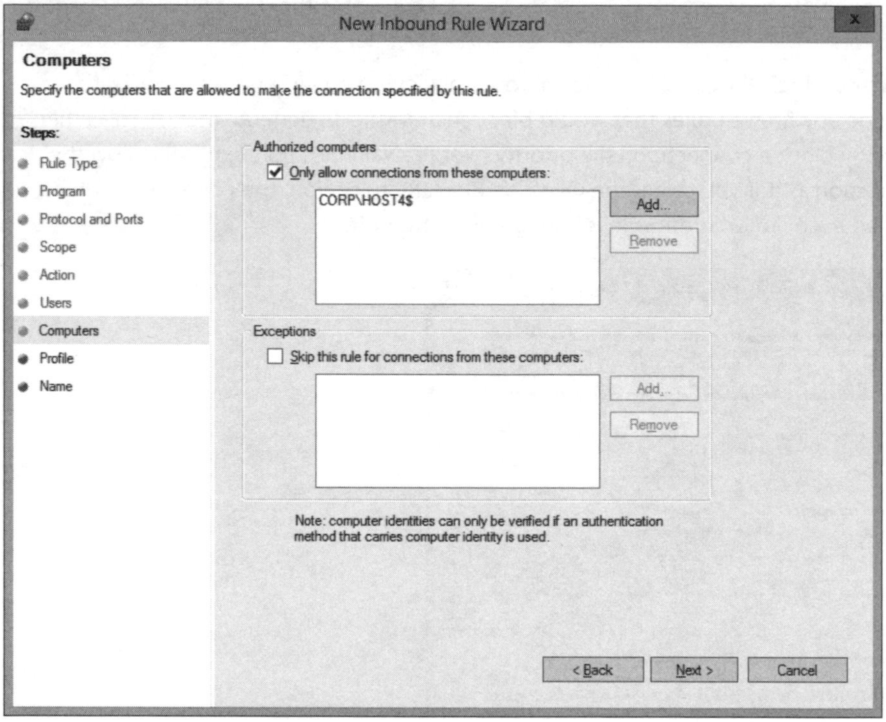

FIGURE 11-24 Configure trusted computers for an authenticated bypass firewall rule.

> **NOTE CANNOT OVERRIDE BLOCKING ALL CONNECTIONS**
>
> If you configured Windows Firewall with Advanced Security to block all connections, the Override Block Rules option will not override such behavior.

Monitoring IPsec

After you create and configure connection security rules, you can use both the Windows Firewall with Advanced Security snap-in and Windows PowerShell to monitor IPsec communications between the local computer and other computers on the network.

As Figure 11-25 shows, you can select the Connection Security Rules node under the Monitoring node to view all active connection security rules configured on the computer. This includes rules created manually on the computer and rules configured by Group Policy targeting the computer. To view more information about any rule, right-click the rule and select Properties.

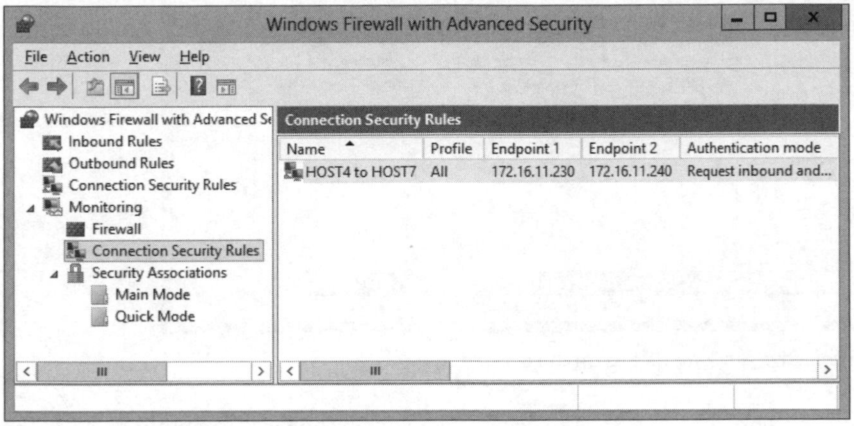

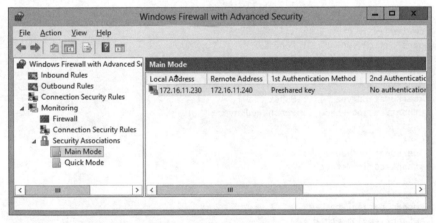

FIGURE 11-25 View active connection security rules on the computer.

As Figure 11-26 shows, you can select the Main Mode node under the Connection Security Rules node to view all active main mode SAs and their endpoints, authentication methods, and other properties.

FIGURE 11-26 View active main mode SAs on the computer.

As Figure 11-27 shows, you can select the Quick Mode node under the Connection Security Rules node to view all active quick mode SAs and their endpoints, ports, protocols, and other properties.

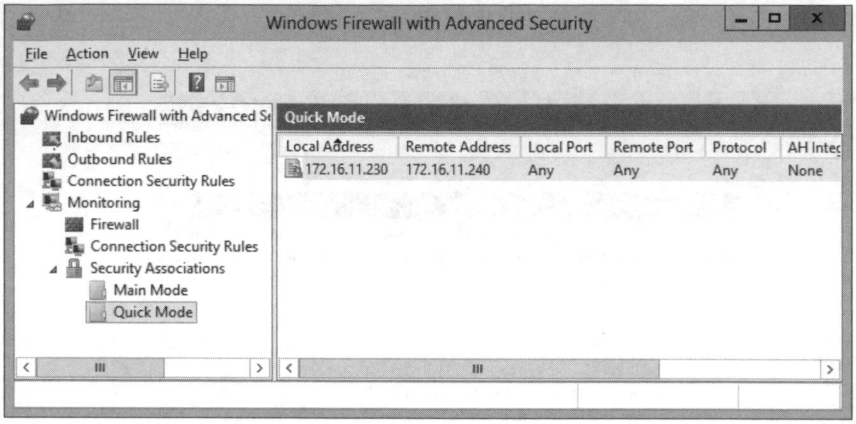

FIGURE 11-27 View active quick mode SAs on the computer.

You can also use Windows PowerShell to view active SAs on the local computer or a remote computer. For example, you can use the Get-NetIPsecMainModeSA cmdlet to view a list of active main mode SAs for the local computer as follows:

```
PS C:\> Get-NetIPsecMainModeSA

Name                                : 246
LocalEndpoint                       : 172.16.11.230
RemoteEndpoint                      : 172.16.11.240
LocalFirstId.Identity               :
LocalFirstId.ImpersonationType      : None
LocalFirstId.AuthenticationMethod   : PresharedKey
LocalFirstId.Flags                  : None
RemoteFirstId.Identity              :
RemoteFirstId.ImpersonationType     : None
RemoteFirstId.AuthenticationMethod  : PresharedKey
RemoteFirstId.Flags                 : None
LocalSecondId.Identity              :
LocalSecondId.ImpersonationType     :
LocalSecondId.AuthenticationMethod  :
LocalSecondId.Flags                 :
RemoteSecondId.Identity             :
RemoteSecondId.ImpersonationType    :
RemoteSecondId.AuthenticationMethod :
RemoteSecondId.Flags                :
CipherAlgorithm                     : AES128
HashAlgorithm                       : SHA1
GroupId                             : DH2
KeyModule                           : IkeV1
MaxQMSAs                            : 0
LifetimeSeconds                     : 28800
LocalUdpEncapsulationPort           :
RemoteUdpEncapsulationPort          :
ExtendedFilterId                    : 0
```

As a second example, you can use the Get-NetIPsecQuickModeSA cmdlet to view a list of active quick mode SAs for the local computer like this:

```
PS C:\> Get-NetIPsecQuickModeSA

Name                          : 1
LocalEndpoint                 : 172.16.11.230
RemoteEndpoint                : 172.16.11.240
TransportLayerFilterName      : HOST4 to HOST7
EncapsulationMode             : Transport
Direction                     : Inbound
LocalPort                     : 0
RemotePort                    : 0
IpProtocol                    : 0
InterfaceAlias                : vEthernet (CONTOSO Virtual Switch)
RealIfProfileId               : 3
LocalUdpEncapsulationPort     :
RemoteUdpEncapsulationPort    :
SPI                           : 1339644182
FirstTransformType            : EspAuth
FirstIntegrityAlgorithm       : SHA1
FirstCipherAlgorithm          : None
SecondSpi                     :
SecondTransformType           : None
SecondIntegrityAlgorithm      : None
SecondCipherAlgorithm         : None
Flags                         : NdBoundary, NoExplicitCredMatch, AllowNullTargetNameMatch,
                                NdPeerBoundary, PeerSupportsGuaranteeEncryption
MmSaId                        : 246
PfsGroupId                    : None
PeerV4PrivateAddress          : 0.0.0.0
QuickModeFilterid             : 76478
LifetimeSeconds               : 3600
LifetimeKilobytes             : 100000
LifetimePackets               : 2147483647
IdleDurationSeconds           : 300
NdAllowClearTimeoutSeconds    : 10
NapContext                    : 0
QmSaId                        : 2592036190
VirtualIfTunnelId             : 0
TrafficSelectorId             : 0
MmTargetName                  :
EmTargetName                  :
ExplicitCredentials           :

Name                          : 1
LocalEndpoint                 : 172.16.11.230
RemoteEndpoint                : 172.16.11.240
TransportLayerFilterName      : HOST4 to HOST7
EncapsulationMode             : Transport
Direction                     : Outbound
LocalPort                     : 0
RemotePort                    : 0
IpProtocol                    : 0
InterfaceAlias                : vEthernet (CONTOSO Virtual Switch)
```

```
RealIfProfileId              : 3
LocalUdpEncapsulationPort    :
RemoteUdpEncapsulationPort   :
SPI                          : 928181826
FirstTransformType           : EspAuth
FirstIntegrityAlgorithm      : SHA1
FirstCipherAlgorithm         : None
SecondSpi                    :
SecondTransformType          : None
SecondIntegrityAlgorithm     : None
SecondCipherAlgorithm        : None
Flags                        : NdBoundary, NoExplicitCredMatch, AllowNullTargetNameMatch,
                               NdPeerBoundary, PeerSupportsGuaranteeEncryption
MmSaId                       : 246
PfsGroupId                   : None
PeerV4PrivateAddress         : 0.0.0.0
QuickModeFilterid            : 76478
LifetimeSeconds              : 3600
LifetimeKilobytes            : 100000
LifetimePackets              : 2147483647
IdleDurationSeconds          : 300
NdAllowClearTimeoutSeconds   : 10
NapContext                   : 0
QmSaId                       : 2592036190
VirtualIfTunnelId            : 0
TrafficSelectorId            : 0
MmTargetName                 :
EmTargetName                 :
ExplicitCredentials          :
```

> **REAL WORLD** **CONNECTION SECURITY OPERATIONAL LOGS**
>
> Another useful source for viewing information about IPsec policy changes for Windows
> Firewall with Advanced Security is the operational log found in Event Viewer:
>
> ```
> Applications and Services Logs/Microsoft/Windows/Windows Firewall with
> Advanced Security/ConnectionSecurity
> ```
>
> You can also enable the ConnectionSecurityVerbose operational log if you need more
> detailed information about IPsec policy events.

Lesson summary

- IPsec involves a number of different concepts, mechanisms, and technologies that
  you should understand before you attempt to implement it in your production
  environment.

- IPsec can provide authentication, data integrity, data encryption, or any combination
  of the three to protect network traffic.

- You can configure IPsec settings on a computer by using the Windows Firewall with
  Advanced Security snap-in, Group Policy, or Windows PowerShell.

- Connection security rules can be of the isolation, authentication exemption, server-to-server, tunnel, or custom type.

- You can create and manage connection security rules using the Windows Firewall with Advanced Security snap-in, Group Policy, or Windows PowerShell.

- Authenticated bypass allows matching network traffic that has been authenticated as coming from an authorized and trusted user or computer.

- You can monitor main mode and quick mode security associations by using the Windows Firewall with Advanced Security snap-in or Windows PowerShell.

Lesson review

Answer the following questions to test your knowledge of the information in this lesson. You can find the answers to these questions and explanations of why each answer choice is correct or incorrect in the "Answers" section at the end of this chapter.

1. Diffie–Hellman Group 14 is an example of what?

    A. An IPsec authentication method

    B. An IPsec data-integrity algorithm

    C. An IPsec data-encryption algorithm

    D. An IPsec key-exchange algorithm

2. You want to use IPsec to protect communications between a server and computers on a specific subnet of your network. Which type of connection security rule can you create to do this? (Choose all that apply.)

    A. Isolation rule

    B. Authentication exemption rule

    C. Server-to-server rule

    D. Custom rule

3. When creating connection security rules, which authentication option would you typically use in an environment that includes computers unable to use the IPsec authentication methods available with Windows Firewall with Advanced Security?

    A. Request Authentication For Inbound And Outbound Connections

    B. Require Authentication For Inbound Connections And Request Authentication For Outbound Connections

    C. Require Authentication For Inbound And Outbound Connections

    D. Do Not Authenticate

Practice exercises

The goal of this section is to provide you with hands-on practice with the following:

- Configuring firewall rules
- Implementing IPsec

To perform the following exercises, you need at least two domain-joined installations of Windows Server 2012 R2 using the Server With A GUI installation option. For example, one of the servers could be a domain controller in the corp.fabrikam.com domain and the other server could be a member server in the same domain. The servers can be either physical servers or virtual machines. You should be logged on to each server using a user account that is a member of the Domain Admins group. For the purposes of these exercises, the names of the servers are assumed to be HOST4 and HOST7 and their IP addresses are, respectively, 172.16.11.230 and 172.16.11.240. If your servers have different names or IP addresses, you should modify the steps in these exercises accordingly.

Exercise 1: Configuring firewall rules

In this exercise, you create and configure firewall rules and examine what happens when firewall rules conflict with one another.

1. Log on to HOST4 and use Server Manager to install the Web Server (IIS) role on the computer.

2. Use the Local Server page of Server Manager to turn off the IE Enhanced Security Configuration for Administrators.

3. Launch Internet Explorer and verify that you can open the default IIS8 home page of the Default Web Site on the local computer by typing **http://localhost** into the address bar.

4. Log on to HOST7 and use the Local Server page of Server Manager to turn off the IE Enhanced Security Configuration for Administrators.

5. Launch Internet Explorer and verify that you can open the default IIS8 home page of the Default Web Site on HOST4 by typing **http://** followed by the host's IP address (for example **http://172.16.11.230**) into the address bar.

6. Open the Windows Firewall with Advanced Security snap-in from the Tools menu of Server Manager, right-click the root node, and select Properties.

7. Configure the settings on the Domain Profile tab so that the default firewall rule for outbound connections is to block traffic. Then click Apply.

8. Delete the browsing history in Internet Explorer, making sure to deselect the Preserve Favorites Website Data option, and then press F5 to attempt to open the site http://172.16.11.230 again.

   Question: Why can't the site be displayed?

Answer: The default rule is applied last when firewall rules are processed. Because the default outbound rule is Block, access to the site is blocked.

9. Change the settings on the Domain Profile tab so that the default firewall rule for outbound connections is to allow traffic. Then click OK.

10. Press F5 in Internet Explorer to verify that you can open the Default Web Site on HOST4.

11. Right-click the Outbound Rules node in the Windows Firewall with Advanced Security snap-in and select New Rule to launch the New Outbound Rule Wizard.

12. On the Rule Type page, select Port.

13. On the Protocols And Ports page, select TCP, select Specific Remote Ports, and type **80** in the text box.

14. On the Action page, leave Block The Connection selected.

15. Accept the default settings on the Profile page.

16. Type **Block TCP port 80** on the Name page and click Finish to create the new firewall rule.

17. Delete the browsing history in Internet Explorer, making sure to deselect the Preserve Favorites Website Data option, and then press F5 to attempt to open the Default Web Site on HOST4 again.

    Question: Why can't the site be displayed?

    Answer: An explicit outbound port rule blocks the HTTP request from accessing the site on TCP port 80.

18. Select the Inbound Rules node, right-click the rule named Block TCP port 80, and select Disable Rule.

19. Press F5 in Internet Explorer to verify that you can open the Default Web Site on HOST4.

    Question: Why is the site now displayed?

    Answer: The outbound port rule to block TCP port 80 has been disabled, and the default outbound rule is to allow outgoing traffic.

20. Right-click the Outbound Rules node in the Windows Firewall with Advanced Security snap-in and select New Rule to launch the New Outbound Rule Wizard again.

21. On the Rule Type page, select Program.

22. On the Program page, select TCP, select This Program Path, and browse to select the following executable:

    C:\ProgramFiles (x86)\Internet Explorer\iexplore.exe

23. On the Action page, leave Block The Connection selected.

24. Accept the default settings on the Profile page.

25. Type **Block Internet Explorer** on the Name page and click Finish to create the new firewall rule.

26. Delete the browsing history in Internet Explorer, making sure to deselect the Preserve Favorites Website Data option, and then press F5 to attempt to open the Default Web Site on HOST4.

    Question: Why can't the site be displayed?

    Answer: An explicit outbound program rule blocks the HTTP request from accessing the site on TCP port 80.

27. Select the Inbound Rules node, right-click the rule named Block Internet Explorer, and select Disable Rule.

28. Right-click the rule named Block TCP port 80 and select Enable Rule.

29. Delete the browsing history in Internet Explorer, making sure to deselect the Preserve Favorites Website Data option, and then press F5 to attempt to open the Default Web Site on HOST4 again. You should not be able to access the site because of the outbound rule that blocks access to TCP port 80.

30. At this point, you should continue directly to practice exercise 2.

Exercise 2: Implementing IPsec

In this exercise, you create connection security rules to implement IPsec communications between HOST4 and HOST7.

1. Switch to HOST4 and open the Windows Firewall with Advanced Security snap-in.

2. Right-click the Connection Security Rules node beneath the root node and select New Rule to open the New Connection Security Rule Wizard.

3. On the Rule Type page, select Server-To-Server.

4. On the Endpoints page, in the Which Computers Are In Endpoint 1? section, select These IP Addresses. Then click Add, type the IIP address for HOST4, and click OK.

5. On the same page, in the Which Computers Are In Endpoint 2? section, select These IP Addresses. Then click Add, type the IP address for HOST7, and click OK.

6. On the Requirements page, leave Request Authentication For Inbound And Outbound Connections selected.

7. On the Authentication Method page, select Advanced and click Customized to open the Customize Advanced Authentication Methods dialog box.

8. In the First Authentication Methods section, click Add, select Preshared Key (Not Recommended), type **mytestkey**, and click OK twice. Click Next.

9. Accept the default settings on the Profile page and click Next.

10. Type **HOST4 to HOST7** on the Name page and click Finish to create the new connection security rule.

11. Select the Connection Security Rules node under the Monitoring node, and verify that the new connection security rule is active (listed).

12. Open a Windows PowerShell prompt and **ping HOST7** to attempt to establish IPsec communications between HOST4 and HOST7.

13. Switch to the Windows Firewall with Advanced Security snap-in and select the Main Mode node under the Connection Security Rules node.

    Question: Why hasn't a main mode SA been established yet between HOST4 and HOST7?

    Answer: Connection security rules must be configured on both computers before IPsec communications can be established between them.

14. Switch to HOST7 and open the Windows Firewall with Advanced Security snap-in.

15. Right-click the Connection Security Rules node beneath the root node and select New Rule to open the New Connection Security Rule Wizard.

16. On the Rule Type page, select Server-To-Server.

17. On the Endpoints page, in the Which Computers Are In Endpoint 1? section, select These IP Addresses. Then click Add, type the IP address for HOST7, and click OK.

18. On the same page, in the Which Computers Are In Endpoint 2? section, select These IP Addresses. Then click Add, type the IP address for HOST4, and click OK.

19. On the Requirements page, leave Request Authentication For Inbound And Outbound Connections selected.

20. On the Authentication Method page, select Advanced and click Customized to open the Customize Advanced Authentication Methods dialog box.

21. In the First Authentication Methods section, click Add, select Preshared Key (Not Recommended), type **mytestkey**, and click OK twice. Click Next.

22. Accept the default settings on the Profile page and then click Next.

23. Type **HOST7 to HOST4** on the Name page and click Finish to create the new connection security rule.

24. Select the Connection Security Rules node under the Monitoring node and verify that the new connection security rule is active (listed).

25. Open a Windows PowerShell prompt and **ping HOST4** to attempt to establish IPsec communications between HOST7 and HOST4.

26. Switch to the Windows Firewall with Advanced Security snap-in and select the Main Mode node under the Connection Security Rules node. You should see a main mode SA with HOST7's IP address as the local address and HOST4's IP address as the remote address.

27. Right-click the main mode SA and select Properties. Click OK after viewing the properties of the SA.

28. Select the Quick Mode node under the Connection Security Rules node. You should see a quick mode SA with 172.16.11.240 as the local address and 172.16.11.230 as the remote address.

29. Right-click the quick mode SA and select Properties. Click OK after viewing the properties of the SA.

30. Launch Internet Explorer and attempt to open the Default Web Site on HOST4. You should see a message saying that the page can't be displayed. This is because the outbound firewall rule you created earlier to block TCP port 80 is still in effect on HOST7.

31. Select the Outbound Rules node in the Windows Firewall with Advanced Security snap-in.

32. Right-click the rule named Block TCP Port 80 and select Properties to open the properties for the firewall rule.

33. On the General tab, select Allow The Connection If It Is Secure and then click OK.

34. Press F5 in Internet Explorer to verify that you can open the Default Web Site on HOST4.

Suggested practice exercises

The following additional practice exercises are designed to give you more opportunities to practice what you've learned and to help you successfully master the lessons presented in this chapter.

- **Exercise 1** Redo practice exercise 1 using Windows PowerShell commands instead of using the Windows Firewall with Advanced Security snap-in.

- **Exercise 2** Redo practice exercise 2 using Windows PowerShell commands instead of using the Windows Firewall with Advanced Security snap-in.

Answers

This section contains the answers to the lesson review questions in this chapter.

Lesson 1

1. **Correct answers: B and D**

   A. **Incorrect:** Windows Firewall with Advanced Security has three firewall profiles, which correspond to the three network location types on the Windows platform. The domain profile is automatically applied to any network connection that Windows identifies as having a network location type of domain. The private profile is automatically applied to any network connection that Windows identifies as having a network location type of private. The public profile is automatically applied to any network connection that Windows identifies as having a network location type of public.

   B. **Correct:** All three profiles can be active at the same time on a computer if Windows detects that there are network connections of each type present.

   C. **Incorrect:** The Inbound Connections setting lets you configure how Windows Firewall with Advanced Security handles incoming traffic. The default option is Block, which blocks all connections that do not have firewall rules that explicitly allow the connection. The other two options are Block All Connections, which blocks all connections regardless of any firewall rules that explicitly allow the connection, and Allow, which allows the connection unless there is a firewall rule that explicitly blocks the connection.

   D. **Correct:** To display the currently active settings for the domain profile on the local computer, you can use the Get-NetFirewallProfile cmdlet with the *–PolicyStore ActiveStore* parameter. The active store is policy store that contains the currently active policy, which is the sum of all policy stores that apply to the computer. The persistent store is the policy store that contains the persistent policy for the local computer. This policy is not from GPOs and has been created manually or programmatically (during application installation) on the computer.

2. **Correct answer: C**

   A. **Incorrect:** Rules that explicitly allow some form of traffic have lower, not higher, priority than rules that explicitly block the same form of traffic. Because rule A is a block rule and rule B is an allow rule, rule A has higher priority than rule B.

   B. **Incorrect:** Rules that explicitly allow some form of traffic have lower, not higher, priority than rules that explicitly block the same form of traffic. Because rule A is a block rule and rule B is an allow rule, rule A has higher priority than rule B.

   C. **Correct:** Rules that explicitly block some form of traffic are applied before rules that explicitly allow the same form of traffic. Because rule A is a block rule and rule

B is an allow rule, rule A has higher priority and is applied first. The result is that outbound traffic from the svchost.exe process running on the computer is blocked.

    D. **Incorrect:** When firewall rules are processed by Windows Firewall with Advanced Security, as soon as a packet matches a rule the rule is applied and rules processing stops at that point. Because outbound traffic from the svchost.exe process running on the computer matches rule A, rules processing stops at that point and the outbound default rule is not applied to the traffic.

3. **Correct answers: A and D**

    A. **Correct:** A program rule specifies how traffic associated with a specific program (executable) running on the local computer should be handled.

    B. **Incorrect:** A port rule specifies how traffic associated with a specific TCP or UDP port or port range on the local computer should be handled.

    C. **Incorrect:** A predefined rule specifies how traffic associated with a specific Windows feature or service running on the local computer should be handled.

    D. **Correct:** A custom rule specifies how traffic should be handled based on any of the traffic-filtering criteria supported by Windows Firewall with Advanced Security. These criteria include being able to specify a program (executable) running on the local computer.

Lesson 2

1. **Correct answer: D**

    A. **Incorrect:** IPsec authentication methods include computer or user (Kerberos V5), computer or user (NTLMv2), computer or user certificate, computer health certificate, and preshared key.

    B. **Incorrect:** IPsec data-integrity algorithms include MD5, SHA-1, SHA-256, SHA-384, AES-GMAC 128, AES-GMAC 192, AES-GMAC 256, AES-GCM 128, AES-GCM 192, and AES-GCM 256.

    C. **Incorrect:** IPsec data-encryption algorithms include DES, 3DES, AES-CBC 128, AES-CBC 192, AES-CBC 256, AES-GCM 128, AES-GCM 192, and AES-GCM 256.

    D. **Correct:** IPsec key-exchange algorithms include, Diffie–Hellman Group 1, Diffie–Hellman Group 2, Diffie–Hellman Group 14, Diffie–Hellman Group 24, Elliptic Curve Diffie–Hellman P-256, and Elliptic Curve Diffie–Hellman P-384.

2. **Correct answers: C and D**

    A. **Incorrect:** You can use isolation rules to isolate computers from other computers. For example, you can use isolation rules to protect computers that are joined to your domain from computers that are outside your domain.

    B. **Incorrect:** You can use authentication exemption rules to specify computers that should be exempted from being required to authenticate, regardless of any other connection security rules that have been configured. For example, you can use authentication exemption rules to allow access to domain controllers and other infrastructure servers with which the computer needs to communicate before authentication can be performed.

C. **Correct:** You can use server-to-server rules to protect communications between two computers, two groups of computers, two subnets, or some combination of these, such as between a computer and a subnet. For example, you can use server-to-server rules to protect communications between a database server and a front-end web server.

D. **Correct:** You can configure custom rules using criteria from other rule types except tunnel rules. This means you can create a custom rule that has the same effect as a server-to-server rule.

3. **Correct answer: A**

A. **Correct:** The Request Authentication For Inbound And Outbound Connections option is typically used in low-security environments or those in which computers are unable to use the IPsec authentication methods available with Windows Firewall with Advanced Security. You can also use it for computers in the boundary zone in a server and in a domain isolation scenario.

B. **Incorrect:** The Require Authentication For Inbound Connections And Request Authentication For Outbound Connections option is typically used in environments where computers are able use the IPsec authentication methods available with Windows Firewall with Advanced Security. You can also use it for computers in the main isolation zone in a server and in a domain isolation scenario.

C. **Incorrect:** The Require Authentication For Inbound And Outbound Connections option is typically used in environments where network traffic must be controlled and secured. You can also use it for computers in the main isolation zone in a server and in a domain isolation scenario.

D. **Incorrect:** The Do Not Authenticate option is typically used to create an authentication exemption for connections to computers that do not require IPsec protection.

Index

Numbers

A

C

D

E

M

S

W

About the author

 MITCH TULLOCH is a well-known expert on Windows Server administration and virtualization. He has published hundreds of articles on a wide variety of technology sites and has written or contributed to over two dozen books from Microsoft Press, including the *Windows 7 Resource Kit*, for which he was lead author; *Understanding Microsoft Virtualization Solutions: From the Desktop to the Datacenter*; the free ebooks *Introducing Windows Server 2012* and *Introducing Windows Server 2012 R2*, which together have been downloaded almost a million times; the free ebook *Introducing System Center 2012 R2 Technical Overview*; and the free ebook *Introducing Windows Azure for IT Professionals*. You can download these titles in PDF, MOBI and EPUB format from the ebook landing page of the Microsoft Virtual Academy at *http://www.microsoftvirtualacademy.com/ebooks*. In addition, Mitch is also Series Editor for an expanding series of free ebooks published by Microsoft Press on the Microsoft System Center platform. You can also find download links for these titles on the same ebook landing page.

Mitch has been repeatedly awarded Most Valuable Professional (MVP) status by Microsoft for his outstanding contributions to supporting the global IT community. He is a nine-time MVP in the technology area of Windows Server Software Packaging, Deployment & Servicing. You can find his MVP Profile page at *http://mvp.microsoft.com/en-us/mvp /Mitch%20Tulloch-21182*.

Mitch is also Senior Editor of WServerNews (*http://www.wservernews.com*), a weekly newsletter focused on system administration and security issues for the Windows Server platform. With more than 100,000 IT pro subscribers worldwide, WServerNews is the largest Windows Server–focused newsletter in the world.

Mitch runs an IT content development business based in Winnipeg, Canada, that produces white papers and other collateral for the business decision maker (BDM) and technical decision maker (TDM) audiences. His published content ranges from white papers about Microsoft cloud technologies to reviews of third-party products designed for the Windows Server platform. Before starting his own business in 1998, Mitch worked as a Microsoft Certified Trainer (MCT) for Productivity Point.

For more information about Mitch, visit his website at *http://www.mtit.com*.

You can also follow Mitch on Twitter at *http://twitter.com/mitchtulloch* or like him on Facebook at *http://www.facebook.com/mitchtulloch*.

Now that you've read the book...

Tell us what you think!

Was it useful?
Did it teach you what you wanted to learn?
Was there room for improvement?

Let us know at http://aka.ms/tellpress

Your feedback goes directly to the staff at Microsoft Press,
and we read every one of your responses. Thanks in advance!

 Microsoft

Training Guide: Installing and Configuring Windows Server 2012 R2 and Exam 70-410

This book is designed to help build and advance your job-role expertise. In addition, it covers some of the topics and skills related to Microsoft Certification Exam 70-410, and may be useful as a complementary study resource. Note: This book is not designed to cover all exam topics; see chart below. If you are preparing for the exam, use additional materials to help bolster your readiness, in conjunction with real-world experience.

EXAM OBJECTIVES/SKILLS	SEE TOPIC-RELATED COVERAGE HERE
Install and Configure Servers	
Install servers	Chapters 1 and 2
Configure servers	Chapters 2 and 3
Configure local storage	Chapter 8
Configure Server Roles and Features	
Configure file and share access	Chapter 8
Configure print and document services	Chapter 9
Configure servers for remote management	Chapters 2, 3, and 11
Configure Hyper-V	
Create and configure virtual machine settings	Chapter 7
Create and configure virtual machine storage	Chapter 7
Create and configure virtual networks	Chapter 7
Deploy and Configure Core Network Services	
Configure IPv4 and IPv6 addressing	Chapter 6
Deploy and configure the Dynamic Host Configuration Protocol (DHCP) service	Chapter 6
Deploy and configure the DNS service	Chapter 6
Install and Administer Active Directory	
Install domain controllers	Chapter 4
Create and manage Active Directory users and computers	Chapter 5
Create and manage Active Directory groups and organizational units (OUs)	Chapter 5

Create and Manage Group Policy	
Create Group Policy objects (GPOs)	Chapter 10
Configure security policies	Chapter 10
Configure application restriction policies	Not covered
Configure Windows Firewall	Chapter 11

For complete information on Exam 70-410, go to *http://www.microsoft.com/learning/en/us /exam.aspx?ID=70-410*. And for more information on Microsoft certifications, go to *http://www .microsoft.com/learning*.